Theories of Personality

Theories of Personality

Understanding Persons

 SUSAN C. CLONINGER, Russell Sage College

 Prentice Hall, Englewood Cliffs, New Jersey 07632

Library of Congress Cataloging-in-Publication Data

Cloninger, Susan C.
Theories of personality : understanding persons / by Susan C. Cloninger.
p. cm.
Includes bibliographical references and index.
ISBN 0-13-915307-1
1. Personality. 2. Personality—Philosophy. I. Title.
BF698.C543 1993
155.2—dc20

92-1768
CIP
AC

Editorial/production supervision: Joan E. Foley
Acquisitions editor: Susan Finnemore Brennan
Editorial assistant: Jennie Katsaros
Interior designer: David Levy
Cover designer: Bruce Kenselaar
Photo researcher: Anita Dickhuth
Copy editor: James Tully
Supplements editor: Sharon Chambliss
Prepress buyer: Kelly Behr
Manufacturing buyer: Mary Ann Gloriande

Additional acknowledgments appear on page 531 and constitute a continuation of the copyright page.

Printed in the United States of America
10 9 8 7 6 5 4 3 2 1

ISBN 0-13-915307-1

Prentice-Hall International (UK) Limited, *London*
Prentice-Hall of Australia Pty. Limited, *Sydney*
Prentice-Hall Canada Inc., *Toronto*
Prentice-Hall Hispanoamericana, S.A., *Mexico*
Prentice-Hall of India Private Limited, *New Delhi*
Prentice-Hall of Japan, Inc., *Tokyo*
Simon & Schuster Asia Pte. Ltd., *Singapore*
Editora Prentice-Hall do Brasil, Ltda., *Rio de Janeiro*

FOR MOM AND DAD,
WHO TAUGHT ME MY FIRST LESSONS
ABOUT PEOPLE. THANKS!

BRIEF CONTENTS

Contents

PART I
THE PSYCHOANALYTIC PERSPECTIVE 25

CHAPTER 2
FREUD: CLASSICAL PSYCHOANALYSIS 28

CHAPTER 3
JUNG: ANALYTICAL PSYCHOLOGY 61

PART III
THE TRAIT PERSPECTIVE 179

CHAPTER 7
ALLPORT: PERSONOLOGICAL TRAIT THEORY 183

CHAPTER 8
CATTELL: FACTOR ANALYTIC TRAIT THEORY 214

CHAPTER 10
MASLOW: HUMANISTIC PSYCHOLOGY AND THE HIERARCHY OF NEEDS 276

PART V
THE LEARNING PERSPECTIVE 303

CHAPTER 11
B.F. SKINNER: RADICAL BEHAVIORISM 305

PART VI
THE COGNITIVE LEARNING PERSPECTIVE 369

CHAPTER 13
MISCHEL AND BANDURA: COGNITIVE SOCIAL LEARNING THEORY 372

CHAPTER 14
GEORGE KELLY: THE PSYCHOLOGY OF PERSONAL CONSTRUCTS 409

Preface

The scientific study of personality builds on philosophical discussions of human nature. As a field within modern psychology, the study of personality has roots in both the clinical tradition of psychotherapy and the scientific tradition of empirical research. This text draws on both roots, representing the belief that each can enrich the other. Yet the two traditions do not merge easily. Are human behavior and thought determined, so that they can be objectively studied within the scientific paradigms of our day? Or is human consciousness "free"; can psychologists in the treatment room offer psychological freedom to their clients? Should personality theorists emphasize broad concepts that seem readily applicable to the lives that people lead, or more focused, precise concepts that lend themselves to controlled experimental research? Each position has merit. The field has not achieved consensus on a common paradigm.

This book begins with personality theories that originated in the clinical practice of psychoanalysis. Freud and theorists who modified his psychoanalytic approach—Jung, Adler, Horney, and Erikson—proposed theories that enabled them to understand, and help, patients in therapy. These personality theories had implications for nonpatients as well, suggesting how people develop in healthy as well as unhealthy directions. These theories have inspired empirical research in both clinical and nonclinical settings.

The psychoanalytic clinical legacy provided diagnostic-like labels for individual differences and various conceptions of mental health and maladaptation. The next two approaches can be thought of as extending these individual differences, labels, and concepts of health from a clinical population to a normal population. Allport and Cattell developed the concept of personality traits and considered many issues that continue to concern researchers, such as the impact of both personality and situations on behavior. A major impact of their work has been the development of assessment tools, primarily self-report questionnaires, for describing individual differences. Next, the humanistic psychologists are considered. Rogers and Maslow built upon clinical concerns about health and adaptation by extending this concern beyond clinical populations, to everyday people and to those who have attained the highest levels of mental health, or self-actualization.

The book concludes with a consideration of theorists in the behavioral tradition. Skinner's theory represents the challenge of strict laboratory-controlled experimentation, which claimed to have discovered causes of behavior outside the person. Dollard and Miller attempted to develop an integrated theory of personality that synthesizes the behavioral challenge with the clinical phenomena reported by psychoanalysis. Modern cognitive behavioral theorists, Bandura and Mischel, further extended behaviorism by detailed consideration of the implications of human thought for a behavioral theory. Kelly's personal construct approach, which was one source for cognitive behavioral ideas, presents an elaborate model of thought processes that influence personality, with particular relevance for therapy. And so the clinical and academic approaches are intertwined throughout the history of the search for a better personality theory.

Throughout the book, research is reviewed that tests propositions from the various theories, and clinical applications of theories are described. Major contributions of each theory are summarized in table format at the end of each chapter, and the final chapter discusses these contributions across theorists.

The study of particular individuals, through psychobiography, is experiencing a new resurgence of interest among personality psychologists. Psychobiographical analyses are presented to illustrate the theories covered in this text. Such attention to particular individuals is not only interesting in its own right. It also grounds theoretical considerations in the subject matter of our discipline, which is the study of individual persons. This grounding helps clarify theoretical concepts and fosters their further development.

I am grateful to the many undergraduate and graduate students at Russell Sage College who have studied with me in recent years, reading earlier drafts of this manuscript and improving it with their questions and comments. Their interest has sustained me through the writing process. I also wish to thank Nancy Spiak and her staff for cheerful and efficient duplication of many versions of the manuscript. Jane Ainslie, Lynne King, Jane Neale, and other librarians at Russell Sage College have helped in many ways, leading me to truly appreciate the skills of professional librarians. Several reviewers offered advice that has considerably improved the manuscript: Georgia Babladelis, California State University—Hayward; Mark Friedman, Western International University; Charles W. Johnson, University of Evansville (Indiana); Michele Y. Martel, Northeast Missouri State University; Robert A. Neimeyer, Memphis State University; Elizabeth L. Paul, Henry A. Murray Research Center of Radcliffe College and Wellesley College;

Diane Pfahler, Crafton Hills College; and Teddy D. Warner, Iowa State University. Prentice Hall has provided expertise throughout the many months that it has taken to convert a rough manuscript to a final product. Though it is not possible to thank all who deserve it, two editors deserve particular thanks: Susan Finnemore Brennan, the psychology editor, and Joan Foley, the production editor. Never again will I think of writing as a task for one person alone. Finally, my family, John and Jim, have been encouraging and patient, for which I thank them enormously.

CHAPTER

Introduction to Personality Theory

Writers and philosophers have been informing us about personality for centuries. They tell us about the basic motivations and emotions of human nature.

> We would all be idle if we could. (Samuel Johnson, quoted in Boswell's *Life of Johnson*)
>
> Anger is a short madness. (Horace, *Epistles*, line 62)
>
> Unlimited power is apt to corrupt the minds of those who possess it. (William Pitt, Speech, House of Lords, January 9, 1770)

They tell us about various types of people.

> The true artist will let his wife starve, his children go barefoot, his mother drudge for his living at seventy, sooner than work at anything but his art. (George Bernard Shaw, *Major Barbara*, act 1)
>
> A fool uttereth all his mind. (Prov. 29:11)

Some of these observations about personality seem contradictory.

> Virtue is bold, and goodness never fearful. (Shakespeare, *Measure for Measure*, act 3, line 215)

> Boldness is a child of ignorance and baseness. (Francis Bacon, *Essays*, line 12)

Such sayings do not always agree about what *causes* people to be as they are.

> To be good is to be happy. (Nicholas Rowe, *The Fair Penitent*, act 2, line 1)
>
> Goodness does not more certainly make men happy than happiness makes them good. (Walter Savage Landor, *Imaginary Conversations, Lord Brooke and Sir Philip Sidney*)

We will perhaps agree with George Bernard Shaw that insights into our own nature may be flawed.

> An Englishman thinks he is moral when he is only uncomfortable. (George Bernard Shaw, *Major Barbara*, act 3)

Charming as such sayings are, they are not conducive to the development of a thorough, systematic understanding of human nature. For that, we turn to psychology.

Personality: The Study of Individuals

Psychology in the past century has used the methods of science to come to some clearer and less ambiguous (if, alas, less literary) understandings of human nature.

Personality is the field within psychology that studies individuals. How is one person different from another, and why? Or are people fundamentally similar rather than different? How can we understand the functioning of a whole person?

Definition of Personality

Personality may be defined as *the underlying causes within the person of individual behavior and experience.* Many opinions exist about what these underlying causes are, as the many theories in this text suggest.

There are three types of questions that personality theory addresses. First, how can personality be described? Personality **description** asks what are the ways in which one person differs from another? Second, how can we understand personality **dynamics**? What are the processes by which a person adapts to the world? Third, what can be said about personality **development**? How does personality change over the life of an individual?

Description of Personality

The most fundamental theoretical question is this: What are the units of personality? What constructs are useful for describing personality, especially the differences between people?

Types, Traits, and Factors

Many ways of describing **individual differences** have been suggested. In traditional, prescientific approaches to personality, broad categories of personality **types** were proposed. Hippocrates described four types of temperament: sanguine (optimistic, hopeful), melancholic (sad, depressed), choleric (irascible), and phlegmatic (apathetic) (Merenda, 1987). Types are *categories of people with similar characteristics.* A small number of types suffice to describe all people. Some personality theorists have proposed broad typologies. Jung (1971), for example, distinguished between introverts and extroverts. (His full typology, described in Chapter 3, lists eight types.) More recently, Type A and Type B personalities have been proposed as cardiovascular risk groups (Friedman & Rosenman, 1974; Strube, 1989).

However, scientists generally think quantitatively rather than qualitatively. That is, they prefer to give each person a score on a dimension, which may range all the way from very low to very high or anything in between, rather than simply saying, in a categorical all-or-none way, that the person belongs to the type or does not (Gangestad & Snyder, 1985). For this reason, personality researchers generally avoid classifying people into types, preferring more quantitative measures: traits and factors (see Table 1.1).

In contrast to types, traits cover a narrower scope of behavior. Traits are widely used in common sense descriptions of personality, and many psychologists find them useful as well (e.g., Allport, 1937b; A. H. Buss, 1989). A personality **trait** is a characteristic that distinguishes one person from another and that causes a person to behave consistently. One person might be "outgoing," "confident," and "athletic," while another person has different traits.

Traits permit a more precise description of personality than types, because each trait refers to a more focused set of characteristics. More traits than types are necessary to describe a personality. In fact, the number of traits can be astonishing. To eliminate unnecessary redundancy (for example, between "shy" and "withdrawn," which hardly seem to be two separate traits), some researchers have statistically examined which trait scores tend to be correlated and on that basis have proposed broader **factors** of personality. These differ from traits by being broader, and from types by being quantitative; people receive a score, rather than simply being placed into one type category or another. Cattell (1957) proposed a well-known set of 16 basic personality factors (see Chapter 8).

Researchers are not always consistent in differentiating types as categorical and factors as quantitative constructs. Oftentimes broad dispositions are called "types" but are measured by quantitative scales. Jung, for example,

TABLE 1.1 Examples of Types, Traits, and Factors

Types	introverts, extroverts (Jung and others)
	psychotics, neurotics, and normals (clinical diagnosis)
Traits	internal vs. external locus of control (Rotter, 1966)
	16 Personality Factors (Cattell, 1979)
Factors	4 factors, with various names (Lester, 1990a; Merenda, 1987)
	emotionality, activity, sociability, and impulsivity (Buss & Plomin, 1975)
	the "Big Five" factors: surgency, agreeableness, conscientiousness, emotional stability, and culture

(Digman, J. M., & Inouye, J. (1986). Further specification of the five robust factors of personality. *Journal of Personality and Social Psychology,* 50, 116-123. Copyright 1986 by the American Psychological Association. Adapted by permission.)

spoke of introverts and extroverts as different types of people, seeing the world so differently that they often misunderstood one another. Yet research instruments measuring these constructs do not simply categorize people, but give them quantitative scores. These scores are distributed throughout the range of possible scores, rather than being clumped at the extremes, evidence that the dispositions are traits or factors, not types (which would be bimodal).

Idiographic and Nomothetic Approaches

Idiographic approaches study individuals one at a time, without making comparisons with other people. Totally idiographic approaches preclude the kinds of generalizations across people that are necessary for a general theory of personality. In practice, strictly idiographic approaches may even be impossible, since any description of a person (for example, saying "Mary is outgoing") implies comparison with other people. Although implicit comparisons with other people are unavoidable, we call research idiographic if it focuses on the particularities of an individual case. Case histories and psychobiographical analyses, which will be discussed later, are idiographic approaches.

In a **nomothetic** approach, groups of individuals are studied, and each person is described using the same concepts. The nomothetic approach explicitly makes comparisons among people. Most often, groups of subjects are given a personality test and their scores are compared. Each person is assigned a score to indicate "how much" of the trait (or other construct being measured) he or she possesses. Mary might be given a "10" for extroversion to indicate that she is outgoing, whereas quiet David is scored only "3" to indicate that he is less extroverted.

Ever since Allport (1937b) first proposed the terms "idiographic" and "nomothetic," personality psychologists have debated the value of the two approaches. Some have advocated idiographic approaches and have suggested how they could be implemented in research (e.g., I.E. Alexander, 1990; D.J. Bem, 1983; Bem & Funder, 1978). However, most personality research is nomothetic. Critics of the idiographic approach argue that only nomothetic research is science; idiographic research lacks the necessary replications and controls of science (Corsini, 1986; Dreger, 1986; Eysenck, 1954, 1986; Robinson, 1984; Skaggs, 1945; Stroud, 1984).

Despite its scientific advantages, the nomothetic method has drawbacks. It requires studying many people using comparable measures, which makes it difficult to obtain a very complete understanding of any one person. In a classic criticism, R. Carlson (1971) criticized personality research for focusing on only one or a small number of variables in each study, which was not enough to provide an understanding of any individual. Carlson concluded that "not a single published study [out of the 226 studies she reviewed] attempted even minimal inquiry into the organization of personality variables within the individual" (Carlson, 1971, p. 209). Carlson also criticized personality research for investigating only a limited range of people (71 percent investigated only college students), a shortcoming that has continued in subsequent years (Sears, 1986). Nomothetic research, the predominant type of personality research, tends to focus on variables rather than on understanding whole persons.

The relationships among variables found in nomothetic research may not be replicated in idiographic research, and vice versa. It is an error to assume that one kind of relationship can be generalized to the other. An individual in a temporary state of anxiety, for example, may not behave like those with a trait of chronic anxiety. Particular research designs have been devised to determine whether research relationships reflect differences between persons, or variations within persons (S. Epstein, 1983a; J.V. Wood, Saltzberg, Neale, Stone, & Rachmiel, 1990).

Both nomothetic and idiographic approaches have something to contribute to personality psychology (Hermans, 1988). Studies of individuals may make possible a more complete description of personality (Lamiell, 1981), providing constructs that can be causal, not only predictive (cf. Manicas & Secord, 1983, 1984). Yet studies of groups are also necessary. Runyan (1988b) reminded personality psychologists of Kluckhohn and Murray's (1953) classic assertion: "Every man is in certain respects (a) like all other men, (b) like some other men, (c) like no other man" (p. 53). Today we would broaden this assertion to include women as well as men, but the fundamental point remains valid. Personality psychology has three goals: to discover what is true of all people; what is true of groups of people (varying by sex, race, culture, and so forth); and what is true of particular individuals (Runyan, 1988b). (See Figure 1.1.)

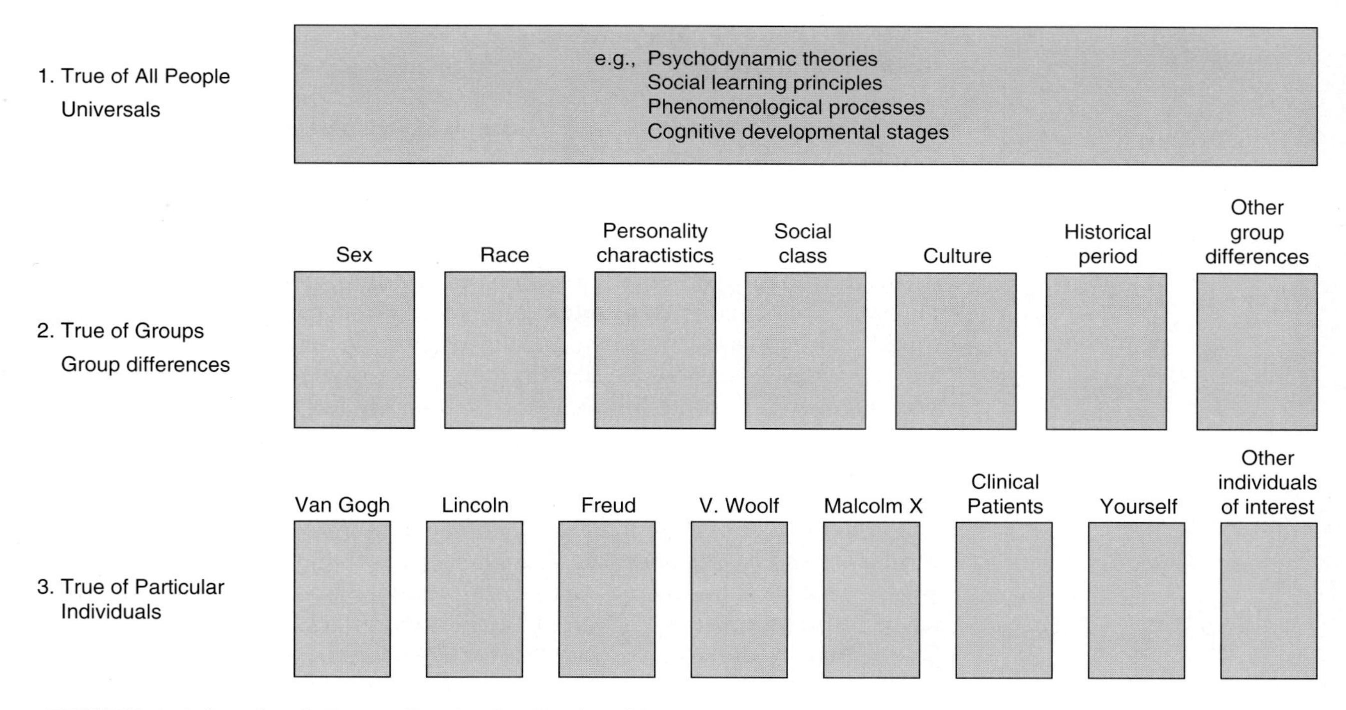

FIGURE 1.1 Levels of Generality in the Study of Lives

(Runyan, W.M. "Idiographic goals and methods in the study of lives," *Journal of Personality*, vol. 51. Copyright 1983, Duke University Press, Durham, NC. Reprinted by permission.)

Consistency of Personality

Personality, as the underlying cause of an individual's behavior, would be expected to produce consistent behavior across changing situations. W. Mischel (1968b) argued that research evidence failed to support this assumption of **consistency.** Instead, he found that situations are more powerful than personality as determinants of behavior. Much research and controversy has focused on this issue of the relative importance of personality traits and situations in determining behavior (Funder, 1983; Kenrick & Funder, 1988; Mischel, 1984a; Mischel & Peake, 1982, 1983). To some extent, the trait versus situation controversy is artificial. Depending upon the specific situations and traits investigated, either may appear more powerful.

After much research, what can be said about cross-situational behavioral consistency? Houts, Cook and Shadish (1986) caution that the available evidence does not permit a clear statement. Sechrest (1986) criticized researchers for inadequate conceptualization, saying "the trait vs. situation controversy would likely never have occurred had the issues been addressed with greater methodological, and logical, rigor" (p. 318). The controversy has, however, stimulated personality theorists to specify more precisely what they mean by traits, and how personality influences behavior (Hyland, 1985).

Description Is Not Enough

Traits (and types and factors) may be useful summary labels to describe a person's behavior, but they do not necessarily explain it. To say that a person talks a lot because of a trait of talkativeness, while knowing that the person has the trait of talkativeness only because of the observed behavior of talking a lot, is blatantly circular reasoning. Traits must be embedded in a broader theory. Unfortunately, even traits that originate in broad theory can, through misuse, lose their full meaning (Rotter, 1990). Personality theory must go beyond description and provide concepts about personality dynamics and development (cf. Pervin, 1985).

Personality Dynamics

Personality is the underlying cause of behavior, but the relationship between personality and observable behavior is often subtle and nonobvious. The term "personality **dynamics**" refers to the mechanisms by which personality is expressed, focusing on the motivational aspect of personality. Most theorists acknowledge that biological factors, such as physical needs and heredity, have some influence on personality, but theorists vary in how much attention they pay to such factors. Social motivations, based on interactions with other people in the family and beyond, are generally given greater emphasis.

Some theorists assume that the fundamental motivations of all people are similar. Freud suggested that sexual motivation underlies personality; Rogers proposed a universal actualizing tendency; learning theorists describe reinforcement as a key to personality dynamics. Other theorists suggest that motivational forces vary from one person to another. For example, H. Murray (1938) listed dozens of motives that are of varying importance to different people. One person might be motivated by achievement, another by power.

Several recent researchers have suggested new ways for understanding individual dynamics. Rosenzweig (1958, 1986a, 1986b, 1988) has offered a model for considering personality dynamics from an idiographic point of view. Rosenzweig's concept of "idiodynamics" implies that more attention should be paid to the experiential and biographical details of a person's life. Cantor (1990; Cantor & Kihlstrom, 1987; Zirkel & Cantor, 1990) suggests focusing on people's *life tasks*, which direct their striving. A related conceptualization focuses on goals (Read, Jones, & Miller, 1990). These new models go beyond the descriptive limitations of trait perspectives, complementing them with a dynamic model.

Adaptation and Adjustment

Personality encompasses an individual's way of coping with the world, of adapting to demands and opportunities in the environment (**adaptation**). This emphasis reflects the strong historical association between personality theory and clinical psychology. Many theories of personality have roots in the clinical treatment of patients. Observations of their maladjustment (and of increasing adjustment with treatment) suggested more general ideas about personality that were applied broadly to nonclinical populations. Personality measures, which have been considerably developed since early theory-building, can now predict coping (Bolger, 1990).

Multiple Influences

Personality dynamics involve multiple influences, both from the environment (situations that influence behavior, triggering adaptation), and from within the person. Several aspects of personality may combine to influence behavior. For example, both achievement needs (or traits) and affiliation needs (or traits) influence the behavior of "studying with a friend."

The concept of multiple causation (or, as it is sometimes called, multiple determinism) is not controversial. Putting it into a precise theoretical statement, however, is formidably difficult. Statistical analyses of multiple causes are complicated, and there is no clear agreement among researchers about how multiple causes should be combined (Carver, 1989; M.G. Evans, 1991). Many researchers have attempted to assess the relative contributions of situations and personality to behavior (S. Epstein & O'Brien, 1985). Interactional psychology (Emmons, Diener, & Larsen, 1986; Endler & Magnusson, 1976; Magnusson & Endler, 1977) has gone beyond the controversy described earlier over the relative importance of personality and situations as determinants of behavior. Interactional psychology has tackled the issue of how personality and situations *combine* to influence behavior, but it has not produced a definitive model.

Personality Development

Another major issue in personality theory concerns the formation and change of personality. To what extent is personality influenced by biological factors, such as heredity? To what extent can personality be changed by learning? How critical is childhood for personality development, and how much change can occur in adulthood?

Biological Influences

Some children seem to have been quiet, or energetic, or whatever, from birth. Could it be that personality is genetically determined? Experts have various opinions.

The term **temperament** refers to consistent styles of behavior that are present from infancy onward, presumably due to biological influences. Some theorists stress the inheritance of personality (e.g., Baker & Daniels, 1990; Heath & Martin, 1990; Plomin, 1986), even arguing that personality theory could be integrated with biology (D.M. Buss, 1984). Eysenck (1982) postulated a physiological basis for major personality variables, and this line of research continues (e.g., Gray, 1987; Lester, 1989b). One recent review (Rowe, 1987) concludes that much of personality is genetic. These themes were anticipated in biosocial approaches of early psychologists, such as McDougall and Murphy (Cheek, 1985).

Cattell (Chapter 8) investigated the role of heredity as a determinant of personality and found that some aspects of personality are strongly influenced by heredity, while others are not. Sex differences are attributed primarily to biological influences by some theorists (e.g., Freud and Jung) but to learning by others (e.g., Horney). For the most part, though, the theories covered in this text stress that experience plays a far larger role than heredity in shaping the complex organism that we call human.

Experience in Childhood and Adulthood

Personality develops over time. Experience, especially in childhood, influences the way each person develops toward his or her unique personality. Many of the major personality theories described in this text make statements about the development of personality. Freud, for example, emphasized the experience of the preschool years in forming personality. Many other theorists, especially in the psychoanalytic tradition, agree that the early years are important (e.g., Horney and Adler). Erikson extended the consideration of development throughout adulthood, to old age.

How much do individuals change? Conley (1984a) and McCrae and Costa (1984) argue that personality is stable across time. Current personality research does not focus on development as much as some think it should (see Kagan, 1988), although several theorists are making advances in this direction (Caspi, 1987; Kenny & Campbell, 1989; Lerner & Tubman, 1989; Schachter & Stone, 1985).

These three major issues—description, dynamics, and development—are interpreted differently in various personality theories. How are individual differences explained (description)? What motivates a person, and what concepts are offered to understand adaptation and mental health (dynamics)? What biological and social forces produce personality in childhood and adulthood (development)? Browsing through the summary tables presented at the end of each chapter of this text will provide an overview of the diverse ideas offered by these theorists.

The Scientific Approach

Personality theories, like psychology more generally, test their assertions about people through the **scientific method**. The scientific method requires systematic observation and a willingness to modify understanding based on these observations. The assumption of **determinism** is central to the scientific method. Determinism refers to the assumption that the phenomena being studied have causes, and that these causes can be discovered

THEORETICAL LEVEL (theoretical constructs)	high self-esteem →	social responsibility
OBSERVABLE LEVEL (operational definitions)	liking oneself talking about one's successes dressing nicely smiling high score on Self-Esteem Test	obeying the law joining political groups recycling high score on Social Responsibility Scale

FIGURE 1.2 Levels of Thinking in Theory

by empirical research. Even personality theorists of otherwise different persuasions agree on this point (Kimble, 1984).

In the scientific method, two different levels of abstraction are important (see Figure 1.2).

In Figure 1.2, two abstract concepts are proposed at the *theoretical level*, "high self-esteem" and "social responsibility." They are said to be causally related in a theoretical proposition that reads, "High self-esteem causes social responsibility." Abstract concepts cannot be directly observed. They do, however, correspond to observable phenomena, indicated at the *observable level* in Figure 1.2. Notice, in Figure 1.3, that the constructs and observations can be phrased in reverse, without changing the meaning.

However phrased, Figure 1.2 suggests that at the level of observables, people who score high on a self-esteem test should like themselves, talk about their successes, smile, and dress nicely, and that the opposite behaviors (Figure 1.3) will be observable among people who score low on a self-esteem test. Furthermore, the high self-esteem people should also be

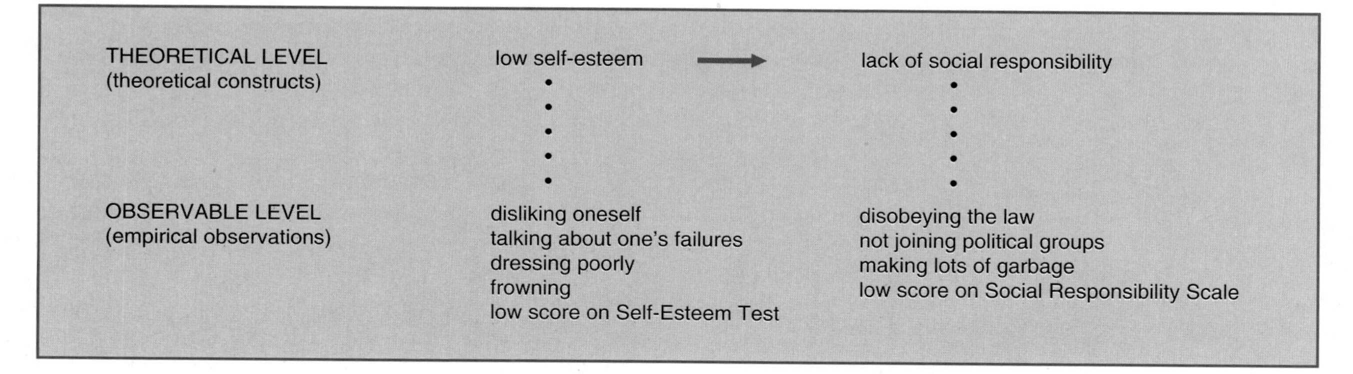

FIGURE 1.3 Levels of Thinking in Theory: Another View

observed engaging in behaviors that are observable evidences of the abstract concept "social responsibility." They should obey the law, join political groups, recycle, and score high on a test of Social Responsibility. The opposite behaviors should occur for those low in self-esteem.

Theory A **theory** is a conceptual tool for understanding certain specified phenomena. It includes concepts (theoretical constructs) and statements about how they are related (theoretical propositions).

The concepts of a theory are called theoretical **constructs**. One kind of theoretical construct that has already been mentioned above is a personality trait. Traits are often considered to be the underlying units of personality. Because traits are assumed to remain constant and determine behavior, people are expected to behave consistently at different times and in different situations. Examples of traits include "shy," "intelligent," "athletic," and so on.

Traits, like all theoretical constructs, are not themselves directly observable. They are related to observable behaviors through **operational definitions**, statements about what observable phenomena are evidence of a particular trait. In Figures 1.2 and 1.3, the trait "self-esteem" is operationally defined to correspond to various observable behaviors: talking about successes (rather than failures), dressing nicely (rather than poorly), and scoring high on a self-esteem test (rather than scoring low). Each trait or other theoretical construct can have many different operational definitions. Because they all correspond to the same trait, we would expect these observations to be positively correlated with one another.

A theory contains many **theoretical propositions**, which describe how the constructs are related. For example, in Figure 1.4, the theoretical proposition that is diagrammed hypothesizes that "self-esteem causes social responsibility." Both "self-esteem" and "social responsibility" are theoretical constructs, and as such they are abstract conceptual tools that cannot be directly observed. Theoretical propositions are also abstract statements, and are not themselves directly observable (cf. Clark & Paivio, 1989).

To test a theory, predictions about observable phenomena are logically derived from the theoretical propositions. Consider the example of a classic theoretical proposition in psychology that states that "frustration leads to aggression." When this proposition is stated in terms of observable phenomena (that is, in terms of the constructs as operationally defined), we have a **hypothesis**, which can be tested by **empirical** observation (see Figure 1.4).

Research testing the relationship between frustration and aggression will be considered in Chapter 12, in the context of Dollard and Miller's original proposal of the "frustration-aggression hypothesis." Research tests whether hypotheses derived from theory are consistent with empirical observations. The more hypotheses derived from a theory are tested and confirmed by empirical research, the more confidence we have in the theory. When observations differ from prediction, the theory is disconfirmed. If this happens often, the theory will be revised or abandoned.

THEORETICAL CONSTRUCTS:	Frustration Aggression
THEORETICAL PROPOSITION:	Frustration leads to aggression.
OPERATIONAL DEFINITIONS:	
Frustration	Losing 75 cents in a soda machine. Failing an exam. Losing one's job.
Aggression	Kicking the soda machine. Rating the instructor as "poor". Beating one's spouse.

HYPOTHESES:

1. Subjects who lose 75 cents in a soda machine (which is rigged by the experimenter) will kick the soda machine more often than a control group, which does not lose money.
2. Students who are told that they have failed an exam will rate their instructor lower than students who are told that they have passed the exam.
3. When unemployment rises, the number of reported spouse beatings will increase.

FIGURE 1.4 Hypotheses Derived From a Theoretical Proposition

Criteria of a Good Theory

Several criteria are generally accepted for evaluating scientific theories.

PRECISION

The constructs of a theory should be described with **precision** so that it is clear what is meant by the construct. Consider the "frustration-aggression" example in Figure 1.4. Is "kicking a soda machine" really aggression? Is "rating a teacher as poor" an example of aggression? Vaguely defined constructs are of little use in a scientific theory. Psychoanalytic theory is often criticized for having many concepts (e.g., "ego" and "libido") that are not clearly defined. Humanistic theory is similarly criticized for vague concepts such as "self-actualization."

VERIFIABILITY

The propositions of a theory should be **verifiable**—that is, testable through empirical methods. This requires, first, that the operational definitions of the theoretical constructs must be clear and reliably measurable. Operational definitions may include written tests, clinical judgments, interpersonal ratings, observations of behavior, and other well-specified ways of making observations. Second, the theory must predict relationships among these measurements so clearly, in the form of hypotheses, that observations can be made to support or refute the prediction. It is always possible to find supportive evidence for a vaguely formulated theory. This criterion requires that it be possible to describe potential evidence that would refute the theory.

Comprehensiveness

A good theory is characterized by **comprehensiveness**. That is, it explains a broad range of behavior. Most traditional personality theories are broad, comprehensive theories dealing with many phenomena: developmental processes in childhood, adaptation or mental health, self-image, social interactions with other people, and so forth. Most of these theories, however, are almost exclusively "psychological." They are not broad enough to encompass physiological influences, such as those suggested by physiological studies of emotions and brain physiology (e.g., Davidson, Ekman, Saron, Senulis, & Friesen, 1990; Ekman, Davison & Friesen 1990; Tomarken, Davidson, & Henriques, 1990).

All else being equal, the wider range of phenomena that can be explained, the better the theory. In practice, however, if a theory attempts to explain too much, its concepts tend to become fuzzy and ill-defined, so that the theory cannot be tested adequately. While comprehensiveness is a desirable characteristic in a theory, it is regarded by researchers as less important than empirical verifiability. In recent years, as theories in personality have been subjected to increasing research validation, they have become less comprehensive, but more precise.

Parsimony

A good theory should be **parsimonious**. That is, it should not propose an excessive number of narrow constructs or propositions, if a smaller number of broad constructs could explain the phenomena under consideration. To do so makes the theory unnecessarily complicated. On the other hand, humans are complex creatures, so a theory with too few constructs or propositions may be too simplistic to permit detailed prediction.

Applied Value

A theory that has **applied value**, offering practical strategies for improving human life, has an edge over theories that are simply intellectually satisfying. For example, personality theories may have applied value in suggesting therapeutic interventions or in guiding child care. Traditionally, personality research has been predominantly **basic research**, conducted for the purpose of advancing theory and scientific knowledge, rather than **applied research**, which is conducted to solve practical problems. Nonetheless, applications are a desirable bonus.

Studies of the effectiveness of psychotherapy do not clearly identify one approach as superior to another, despite their very different strategies. Stiles, Shapiro, and Elliott (1986) argue that improvements in theory, making more precise and specific theoretical statements, would contribute to better comparisons of therapies, and hence to better therapies.

Heuristic Value

Scientific understanding is not static. Scientists build on the work of earlier scientists, moving toward an improved understanding. Does a theory foster this progress, or tend to bring it to a halt? The ability of a theory to suggest new ideas for further theory and research is called its **heuristic value**. Another term for heuristic value is "fertility" (e.g., G.S. Howard, 1985).

Relationship Between Theory and Research

Research and theory-building in personality, ideally, go hand in hand. At the level of theory, constructs and theoretical propositions are proposed. By a process of deductive reasoning, hypotheses are derived and, through research, tested. Data analysis is the link between observable events and theoretical concepts, a link that has been strengthened by the availability of sophisticated computer analyses (I.B. Weiner, 1991). Theoretical developments often require new measuring instruments tailored to fit the new conceptualizations (cf. Fiske, 1973).

Theory may lead to research, but the opposite is also true (Gigerenzer, 1991). Unexplained observations lead scientists to think inductively. They then suggest new or revised theoretical constructs and propositions. Sometimes theoretical work is neglected, replaced by a flood of facts accumulating from research studies. Some researchers have recently emphasized the importance of theoretical concerns (e.g., Hogan & Nicholson, 1988; Kagan, 1988; Kukla, 1989; Landy, 1986). Theory without adequate research becomes stagnant. Research without adequate theory wanders aimlessly.

Methods in Personality Research

Throughout its history, personality research has used certain favorite research methods: personality scales and questionnaires, projective techniques, observer judgments, and laboratory methods (Craik, 1986). Some methods, used in early research and then neglected for several decades, are now returning, among them the biographical approach (Craik, 1986). Although some researchers naturally prefer certain methods over others, personality can best be studied using a variety of research methods (Duke, 1986).

Personality Measurement

Measurement of personality involves operationally defining theoretical constructs by specifying how they will be assessed. The most common type of measurement is a self-report personality test in which a person answers many questions, often in multiple-choice format, under a standard set of instructions. Inadequate measurement can seriously compromise research, yet many tests used in research are at best minimally adequate (West, 1986). What makes for sound measurement? Some qualities are described below.

Reliability

Measurement should be **reliable**, yielding consistent scores from one time to another. Reliability is determined in several ways. *Test-retest reliability* is determined by testing the same subjects on two occasions and calculating the extent to which scores agree. Do the same people who score high on the first occasion also score high the second time? They will if the test is reliable. Could it be, though, that they simply remember how they answered the first time (even if they were guessing), and that is why the scores don't change? The method of *alternate forms reliability* gets around this problem by giving different versions of the questionnaire on each occasion.

If subjects are tested only once, reliability can be estimated by calculating subscores based on two halves of the questionnaire. Generally, all the odd-numbered items are added together for one score, and all the even-numbered items for the other score. The correlation between these two subscores is computed; this correlation is called *split-half reliability*.

Unreliability can result from several factors. Short tests are generally less reliable than are longer tests. Tests combining unrelated items are less reliable than those composed of closely correlated items; the latter are called *homogeneous* items. Other factors that reduce reliability are ambiguous test items and situational factors influencing responses. In addition, real changes can occur over time in the psychological characteristic being measured, although perhaps in this last case it would be better to speak of personality change, rather than unreliability of measurement. In general, the longer the time that passes between two administrations of a test, the lower the reliability of the test (Schuerger, Zarrella, & Hotz, 1989).

VALIDITY

Someone could claim to assess your intelligence by measuring the circumference of your head, or your morality by examining your skull for bumps in particular locations, as phrenologists once did. Undoubtedly, except in very unusual cases, these would be quite reliable measures. Yet we would not accept them. Such measures might be reliable, but they are not valid.

Validity is present if a test measures what it claims to measure. While reliability can be assessed straightforwardly, determining validity requires careful specification of the theoretical construct. *Predictive validity* is established if a test predicts a behavior that the researcher accepts as a criterion for the construct being measured (for example, if a test of assertiveness predicts the number of times a person initiates conversations). In the "known groups method," a test is given to different groups of people who are known to differ in what the test measures. For example, a test of mental well-being should produce higher scores among college students than among psychiatric patients (Hattie & Cooksey, 1984).

Lack of validity can result from several factors, including respondents' intentional distortion of responses (Furnham, 1990b), their misunderstanding of test items, and their lack of knowledge or insight about the material being asked.

Predictive validity focuses primarily on the validity of a particular test. What about the validity of the theoretical construct? This question goes beyond measurement. If a theoretical construct is valid, it will be possible to define it operationally in a variety of ways and to conduct a whole series of studies relating it to other variables as the theory predicts. When several research studies have been conducted, presenting converging lines of evidence for the usefulness of a theoretical construct, **construct validity** has been established (Cronbach & Meehl, 1955).

Measurement Techniques

Various measurement techniques have been used in personality research. *Direct self-report measures*, including questionnaires (which measure one trait or construct) and inventories (which measure several traits or constructs), are widely used (e.g., the Self-Monitoring Scale, the California Personality Inventory, and the Minnesota Multiphasic Personality Inventory). Self-report measures are often reliable, but they have disadvantages, including inaccuracies attributable to limitations in subjects' self-knowledge, falsification of responses, and the development of response sets, such as the tendency to agree with items regardless of content (Vane & Guarnaccia, 1989; P. White, 1980). Personality research depends heavily on self-report questionnaires, generally without a theory to say what self-report means (Ericsson & Simon, 1980). Although it would be a mistake to blindly assume that questionnaires based on self-report can be taken at face value, they do provide valuable data.

Alternatively, personality can be measured through *indirect methods*. For example, *projective tests* present subjects with ambiguous stimuli (such as inkblots) to which they respond. This approach can avoid some of the shortcomings of verbal reports. It accesses material of which the person is unaware, and thus avoids intentional deception and the limitations of conscious experience. Projective tests include the famous Rorschach inkblot test and the Thematic Apperception Test (TAT), which asks subjects to make up stories based on pictures.

Test scores can be misleading. Testing may be biased because of content, interpersonal testing situations, and differences among populations, leading to scores that do not mean what they might under other conditions (Cole, 1981). It is a mistake to generalize to populations (other races, ages, or socioeconomic groups, for example) without evidence that the test is valid for them. Failure to recognize this can lead to racial and ethnic bias in psychological tests (Schmidt & Hunter, 1974).

Behavioral measures are sometimes included in personality research. Observers may watch people in real life or in a laboratory setting. Or subjects can be asked to provide information about their real-life experiences. This type of measurement helps to develop understandings of personality in its real-world context. Such self-reports, though, are not always accurate (Sanitioso, Kunda, & Fong, 1990; Strauman, 1990).

Correlational Studies

Much personality research is correlational. **Correlational research** measures two or more variables so as to study how they are related. Correlational research is vital to refining descriptions of personality. If a theoretical construct is measured in two or more ways, these measures should be correlated. Theoretical propositions describing causes and effects can be tested by correlating the cause (operationally defined) with the effect (also operationally defined).

Factor analysis is a statistical technique that systematically examines the relationships among many measures. It is helpful for determining whether there are one or several underlying dimensions in a questionnaire consisting of several items. (Factor analysis is described more fully in Chapter 8.)

A weakness of correlational research, however, is that it cannot provide strong proof of causation. Results can always be given alternative causal interpretations. Two observations can be correlated because one causes another (either one may be the cause), or because both are caused by a third variable. For example, suppose a correlational research study finds that two variables are associated in a study of elementary school children: number of hours of television watched (Variable A) and children's aggressiveness, determined by observing behavior on the playground (Variable B). What can we conclude based on this correlational research? It is possible that *A* causes *B*—that is, watching television increases the children's aggressive behavior. Or, it is possible that *B* causes *A*. Aggressive children may be rejected by friends after school and, having no one to play with, they watch television instead. Third, it is possible that another variable, *C*, causes both *A* and *B*, leading to their correlation without either causing the other. What might such a *third variable* be? Perhaps having neglectful parents causes children to watch more television (since they are not encouraged to do other activities that would place more demands on their parents), and also causes them to be aggressive on the playground (since they have not been taught more mature social skills). The point is that correlational research is always ambiguous about the *causes* underlying the associations observed. From such a study it is not clear that aggressiveness could be reduced by limiting television, or by increasing parental attention, or by changing any of the other potential causes that could account for the relationship.

Sophisticated statistical models based on structural equation modeling can test causal hypotheses (Judd, Jessor, & Donovan, 1986; West, 1986), but such techniques require more extensive data collection, using multiple measures over time, than most correlational studies provide. Causal ambiguities can be resolved through another research strategy—experimentation.

Experimentation

In **true experimental research**, hypothesized "cause-effect relationships" are put to a direct test. An **independent variable**, which the researcher suspects is the "cause," is manipulated by the researcher. An **experimental group** is exposed to the independent variable. A **control group** is not exposed to the independent variable. These two groups are then compared to see whether they have different scores on the **dependent variable**, which is the hypothesized "effect."

An experiment could be conducted for the example above to test whether watching a lot of television causes an increase in aggressive behavior. An experimental group would be assigned to watch a great deal of television. A control group would watch little television. Then their aggressive behavior on the playground would be observed. If watching television (the independent variable) is the cause, there will be differences between the two groups in their level of aggression (the dependent variable). If some other **variable** is the cause, the two groups will not differ in aggression.

Logically, it is easier to imagine "situations" as independent variables in an experiment than "personality." It is fairly easy to manipulate television viewing. In contrast, how could we manipulate "aggressiveness," a personality trait, if we believe that the trait of aggressiveness is the cause of aggressive behavior? If personality is a characteristic of people, how can it be manipulated by an experimenter? One strategy is to *change* personality for an experimental group through some kind of situational manipulation or therapy program. Mischel and Bandura (whose theories are presented in Chapter 13) have conducted much experimental research in which situations or training interventions are manipulated to change aspects of personality, and then effects on behavior are observed. Similarly, a program of research by McClelland and Winter (1969) changed businessmen's trait of "need for achievement" through a training program and found that this brought about changes in their business activities. Experimental techniques have occasionally been used by psychoanalytically oriented researchers who have experimentally aroused unconscious material to investigate psychodynamics (e.g., Shulman & Ferguson, 1988; Silverman, 1976, 1983). Nonetheless, experimental research in personality is less common than correlational research, in which personality is measured rather than manipulated.

Experimental research has also been conducted that combines a manipulated situational variable with a measured personality variable, a "hybrid" form of experimental personality research (West, 1986). Such a design permits stringent controls of the manipulated variables, which can be interpreted as causes. Yet the measured personality variables still must be interpreted with all the cautions of a correlational study; that is, they are not necessarily "causes" of the dependent variables with which they are associated.

Constructs derived from experimental research are not necessarily interchangeable with those derived from correlational research (Brogden, 1972; West, 1986). For example, a generally anxious person (with a "trait" of anxiety) may not be comparable to a generally calm person who is temporarily anxious because of a crisis (with a temporary "state" of anxiety). Though they can't be taken for granted, convergences across correlational and experimental research can sometimes be demonstrated (Feldman & Hass, 1970; Mischel, 1984a).

Experimental research does not always involve groups of people. There are experimental research designs that can be used with individual subjects (Dukes, 1965; Hersen & Barlow, 1976; Kratochwill, 1978). Other approaches—case studies and psychobiography—investigate individuals without the stringent controls of experimental research.

Case Studies and Psychobiography

A **case study** is an intensive investigation of a single individual. For example, a clinician may describe an individual client, or an educational psychologist may describe an individual child. When the focus is on theoretical considerations, case studies are called **psychobiography**. In psychobiography, the researcher often works from archival data, such as letters, books, and interviews, rather than directly interacting with the person being described.

Sometimes the analysis of individuals is prompted by practical, even political, considerations. For example, in 1943 U.S. government officials requested a psychological analysis of Adolf Hitler (Runyan, 1982c), an analysis that was later published (Langer, 1972). In the early 1960s, a similar request was made for an analysis of the Soviet leader Nikita Khrushchev (Mack, 1971). In these cases, the analyses were prompted by practical, rather than theoretical, significance, making them special cases of applied research.

Psychobiographical studies need not be limited to one person. They can investigate several individuals representing a particular group, such as women (H.M. Buss, 1990) or homosexuals (G. Sullivan, 1990).

Studies of individuals using nonexperimental methods lack both the statistical advantages of large correlational studies and the advantages stemming from control of independent variables in the experimental method. Without these controls, many interpretations of the same material are possible (Runyan, 1981), making definitive analyses elusive. Methodological flaws have often exceeded what could be excused as a shortcoming of the method, leading to considerable distrust of psychobiographical and case-history approaches (Runyan, 1982a, 1982c; Stannard, 1980). Greater attention should be paid to the reporting of case studies to enhance their scientific value (Edelson, 1985).

Runyan defines psychobiography as "the explicit use of formal or systematic psychology in biography" (1982c, p. 233). Though various theories can be utilized, much psychobiography in the past has been based on psychoanalytic theory. The first psychobiography was written by the founder of psychoanalysis, Sigmund Freud (1910/1957): a study of Leonardo da Vinci. This study has been criticized for not following the standards of sound psychobiography that Freud set out in the same work (Elms, 1988a). Psychoanalytic theory has been the predominant theory guiding psychobiographical analyses ever since Freud's initial effort (e.g., Baron & Pletsch, 1985; Ciardiello, 1985; Erikson, 1958b; Freud & Bullitt, 1966). This theory stresses the importance of childhood. Psychoanalysis warns that subjective factors ("transference") can be a source of error in psychobiography (Schepeler, 1990).

Psychoanalytic theory has some shortcomings as a guiding model for psychobiography. For one thing, evidence about childhood experience, which is so important in psychoanalytic formulations, is often poor (Runyan, 1982c). The theory often leads to overemphasis on a particular period, the "critical period fallacy," or specific life events, "eventism" (Mack, 1971). The theory also does not call attention to historical and cultural factors that influence personality (L. Stone, 1981).

Currently there is a resurgence of interest in psychobiography (Runyan, 1982b, 1987, 1988b, 1988c), with increasing use of nonpsychoanalytic approaches and more careful consideration of methodological issues (De Waele & Harré, 1979; Elms, 1988b; McAdams, 1988; Munter, 1975b; Runyan, 1988a, 1988b, 1990). Some researchers apply existing theories to biographical analysis. For example, W.J. Wright (1985) applied Cattell's theory to an analysis of Martin Luther and other Reformation leaders. Winter and Carlson (1988) applied a motivational theory derived from Murray's personality theory to a psychobiographical study of Richard Nixon.

New theoretical developments are emerging. R. Carlson (1981, 1988) advocates using Tomkins's script theory as a sophisticated alternative to psychoanalytic psychobiography. Abelson (1981) considers the script concept to be a theoretical construct that can help integrate personality theory with understandings from other areas of psychology, including learning, developmental, clinical, social, and cognitive psychology. Unlike psychoanalytic theory, script theory does not need to trace adult life back to infantile experience. It focuses on affect and cognition, thus connecting with some major themes in current psychological research. Other researchers have used similar methods (e.g., I.E. Alexander, 1988, 1990; McAdams, 1990; Ochberg, 1988). Researchers who use existing materials (personal documents, diaries, letters, dream records) have developed new ways for systematically analyzing them (Gruber, 1989; Stewart, Franz, & Layton, 1988).

R. Carlson claims that psychobiography is especially useful at the stage of "clarifying . . . the theory," rather than at the prior stage of developing it or the later stage of testing it (1988, p. 106). It forces researchers to clarify constructs and theoretical propositions by considering how they apply in a particular instance (e.g., Howe, 1982), and can prompt revisions of hypotheses when predictions of the individual are not confirmed (Elms, 1988b). Furthermore, a particular individual can only be understood by taking into account the situational and cultural influences that impact that life. Although psychobiography is an idiographic technique, it can contribute broader understandings; it may direct attention to influences overlooked in nomothetic research that may not be sufficiently considered in existing theory (cf. Lomranz, 1986). R. Carlson claims "the development of psychobiographical work might rescue contemporary personality psychology from its method-bound stasis" (1988, p. 105).

Nonscientific (Implicit) Personality Theories

Making distinctions among individuals is second nature to people in their everyday lives (cf. Lupfer, Clark, & Hutcherson, 1990). Everyday unscientific beliefs about personality are sometimes called **implicit theories of personality**. We assume that certain phenomena that we have seen are accompanied by other personality characteristics, even though we may not have had an opportunity to observe them. Attractive people, for example, are assumed to be warm and good.

Early studies of implicit personality theory focused on identifying the relationships people perceive among various personality traits (Schneider, 1973) and comparing the accuracy of implicit personality theories with empirical studies of the relationships among personality traits (e.g., D.N. Jackson, Chan, and Stricker, 1979; Mirels, 1976, 1982). In recent years, interest in the accuracy of implicit personality theory has continued (e.g., Borkenau & Ostendorf, 1987; Krzystofiak, Cardy, & Newman, 1988; Semin & Krahe, 1987). In addition, implicit personality theory has been interpreted in terms of cognitive processes, which are increasingly of interest in psychological theory (e.g., Chaplin, John, & Goldberg, 1988; deSoto, Hamilton, & Taylor, 1985; Hampson, John, & Goldberg, 1986; Van der Kloot, Kroonenberg, & Bakker, 1985).

While most studies in this area involve asking research subjects to complete questionnaires, other approaches are possible. Rosenberg and Jones (1972) have presented a different method, based on content coding, to investigate the implicit personality theory expressed in the fictional works of a well-known author, Theodore Dreiser. This method, which could be made less time-consuming through computerization of the content analysis, makes it possible to discover the implicit personality theory of anyone who has written enough about people, even without getting the person to participate as a subject in a formal research study.

The concept of implicit personality theory implies that we bring preconceptions to the formal study of personality. These beliefs may bias us in favor of theories that match our own implicit theories. Kalliopuska (1985) reports that students' implicit personality theories more closely match those of some theorists (Murray, Allport, Erikson, Freud, and Kelly) than others. Theorists themselves are likely to develop theories that formalize their own preconceptions. Well-planned research studies, though, should correct many errors emanating from implicit theories.

One Theory or Many? Eclecticism

Most personality psychologists prefer an **eclectic** approach, one that combines insights from many different theories. No theoretical perspective is so convincingly validated by empirical research that others are made obsolete. In the language of Thomas Kuhn (1970), there is no single **paradigm** in personality theory. There are, instead, competing paradigms, including psychoanalysis, learning theory, trait approaches, and humanistic psychology.

Some attempts have been made to integrate theories (e.g., Messer, 1986; Messer & Winokur, 1980). For the most part, though, theories simply coexist, each developing its own theoretical and research literature. Why?

First, some of this fragmentation is due to larger divisions in psychology between what have traditionally been called the "two disciplines" (Cronbach, 1957, 1975) or "two cultures" (Kimble, 1984) of psychology. One side emphasizes experimentation and studies groups of people. The other side is more interested in individuals and is content to compromise experimental rigor to focus on aspects of the person that cannot be studied experimentally. Kimble (1984) is pessimistic about the chances for achieving an integration of the two orientations (see Table 1.2).

Second, theories may have different areas of usefulness. For example, one theory may be useful for understanding people's subjective experience of life, and another for predicting how people will behave in a given situation. Some theories may help us understand the mentally ill or individuals distraught by overwhelming stress; other theories may be more useful in understanding the creative heights of those without disturbance. Some theories may seem only to apply to males, or to those with enough food to be concerned with less mundane issues than mere survival.

TABLE 1.2 Kimble's Analysis of "Scientific" vs. "Humanistic" Psychology

	Scientific Culture	*Humanistic Culture*
Research Setting	laboratory	field study and case study
Generality of Laws	nomothetic	idiographic
Level of Analysis	elementism	holism
Scholarly Values	scientific	humanistic
Source of Knowledge	observation	intuition

(Kimble, G. A.(1984). Psychology's two cultures. *American Psychologist,* 39, 883-839. Copyright 1984 by the American Psychological Association. Adapted by permission.)

By keeping several theories, we have tools for understanding a greater variety of personality issues. Together they encompass a more comprehensive domain of phenomena than any single theory can explain. However, eclecticism is not very satisfying as a final state of personality theory.

The Future of Personality Theory

Some argue that a new paradigm is emerging, based on cognitive perspectives (e.g., Mischel, 1977a), including more of a sense of human agency (Rychlak, 1984b, 1986), and less bound to the model of neutral, value-free science (G.S. Howard, 1985; G.S. Howard & Conway, 1986; Sampson, 1981; Sperry, 1988). As new theories develop, we may hope that they will be more comprehensive. They should take into account more of the diversity of human experience, including the perspectives of women and minorities, and they should more fully recognize the impact of situational and sociocultural events on personality (Enns, 1989; Franz & White, 1985; Helson & Picano, 1990; Lerman, 1986b; Lott, 1985; Lykes, 1985; Naffin, 1985; Torrey, 1987; Veroff, 1983; Winbush, 1977).

Past and current personality theories both help and hinder progress toward such new theory. They help, to the extent that they provide useful and heuristic concepts. They hinder, to the extent that theoretical preconceptions, like implicit personality theories, blind us to new directions. How can we remove such blinders? One suggestion, to borrow advice from the British statesman Benjamin Disraeli, is to

> Read . . . biography, for that is life without theory. (*Contarini Fleming*, pt. i, chap. 23)

Summary

Personality is defined as the underlying causes within the person of individual behavior and experience. Psychologists in the field of personality study individuals. They seek to understand how the general laws of personality apply to individuals, and to develop their own concepts for understanding individual people. Three areas are addressed by personality theory: *description*, *dynamics*, and *development*. Personality has been *described* in terms of broad *types* or more numerous, and narrower, *traits*. Using statistical techniques, traits can be combined into personality *factors*. Personality is usually described by making comparisons with other people, the *nomothetic* approach. In contrast, studies of single individuals use the *idiographic* approach. Some researchers have questioned the assumption of personality *consistency*, suggesting that personality traits, conceived as stable characteristics of individuals, may not be the best way to describe personality. Personality *dynamics* refers to the motivational aspect of personality. Various dynamics have been proposed, including biological and social motivations. Some theorists emphasize common motivations, which influence all people, while others focus on individual differences in personality dynamics. Personality dynamics permit *adaptation* to the world and may be studied in terms of adjustment or mental health. Multiple influences affect personality dynamics. Personality *development* in childhood and adulthood is also described by the various theories, recognizing biological and social influences on development.

The scientific approach to personality assumes *determinism* and makes systematic observations to test and revise theories. Theoretical *constructs* and *propositions* are made testable through operational definitions and hypotheses. Theories can be evaluated according to six criteria: precision, verifiability, comprehensiveness, parsimony, applied value, and heuristic value. Theory and research mutually influence one another. Personality measurement should be reliable and valid. Various measurement techniques are used, including self-report measures, projective measures, measures of life experiences, and behavioral measures. Research techniques include *correlational* research, in which associations are examined among various measures, and *experimental* research, in which cause-effect relationships are tested by manipulating an *independent variable* to examine its effect on a *dependent variable.* In addition, *case studies* and *psychobiography* study one individual intensively. Psychobiography, in which theory is systematically used to understand one individual, can offer suggestions for theory development.

People have informal *implicit theories* of personality with which they try to understand others. Personality psychologists use many *paradigms* for understanding personality. Many adopt an *eclectic* approach. Others seek to integrate competing theories, and some anticipate the development of a new, more inclusive paradigm.

GLOSSARY

adaptation coping with the external world

applied research research intended to have practical uses

applied value the ability of a theory to guide practical uses

basic research research intended to develop theory

case study an intensive investigation of a single individual

comprehensiveness the ability of a theory to explain a broad variety of observations

consistency repeatable, predictable (as personality is traditionally assumed to be)

construct a concept used in a theory

construct validity the usefulness of a theoretical term, evidenced by an accumulation of research findings

control group in an experiment, the group not exposed to the experimental treatment

correlational research research method that examines the relationships among measurements

dependent variable the "effect" in an experimental study

description theoretical task of identifying the units of personality, with particular emphasis on the differences between people

determinism the assumption that phenomena have causes that can be discovered by empirical research

development formation or change (of personality) over time

dynamics the motivational aspect of personality

eclectic combining ideas from a variety of theories

empirical based on scientific observations

experimental group in an experiment, the group exposed to the experimental treatment

factor a statistically derived, quantitative dimension of personality that is broader than a trait

heuristic value the ability of a theory to suggest new questions or ideas

hypothesis a prediction to be tested by research

idiographic focusing on one individual

implicit theories of personality ideas about personality that are held by ordinary people (not based on formal theory)

independent variable in an experiment, the "cause" that is manipulated by the researcher

individual differences qualities that make one person different from another

nomothetic involving comparisons with other individuals; research based on groups of people

operational definition procedure for measuring a theoretical construct

paradigm a basic theoretical model, shared by various theorists and researchers

parsimonious describing the quality of a theory that uses concepts efficiently, avoiding unnecessarily complicated explanations

personality the underlying causes within the person of individual behavior and experience

precision clear and unambiguous specification of theoretical constructs

psychobiography the application of a personality theory to the study of an individual's life; contrasted with a "case study" by its theoretical emphasis

reliable repeatable, as when a measurement is repeated at another time or by another observer, with similar results

scientific method the method of knowing based on systematic observation

temperament consistent behavioral styles present throughout life, presumably caused by biological factors

theoretical proposition theoretical statement about relationships among theoretical constructs

theory a conceptual tool, consisting of systematically organized constructs and propositions, for understanding certain specified phenomena

trait personality characteristic that makes one person different from another and/or that describes an individual's personality

true experimental research research strategy that manipulates a "cause" in order to determine its effect

type a category of people with similar characteristics

variable in research, a measurement of something across various people (or times, or situations), which takes on different values

verifiable the ability of a theory to be tested by empirical procedures, resulting in confirmation or disconfirmation

STUDY QUESTIONS

1. Define personality.
2. List and explain the three issues that personality theory studies.
3. Contrast types, traits, and factors as units of description in personality.
4. Explain the difference between "idiographic" and "nomothetic" approaches.
5. Explain why personality consistency is important for personality theory.
6. Explain what is meant by "personality dynamics."
7. What are some important influences on personality development?
8. Describe the scientific approach to personality. Include in your answer theoretical constructs, propositions, operational definitions, and hypotheses.
9. List and explain the criteria of a good theory.
10. Describe some ways in which personality can be measured.
11. Explain reliability and validity of measurement.
12. Explain the difference between correlational studies and experimental studies.
13. What is psychobiography? Discuss the strengths and weaknesses of this approach to understanding personality.
14. What is an "implicit theory of personality"? How is it different from a formal personality theory?
15. What is "eclecticism"? Why might someone prefer to have more than one theory?

PART 

The Psychoanalytic Perspective

The psychoanalytic perspective on personality has become one of the most widely known approaches outside of psychology. Within psychology, it has steadfast adherents and forceful critics.

The central idea of the psychoanalytic perspective is the *unconscious.* Simply put, this concept says that people are not aware of the most important determinants of their behavior. Self-understandings are quite limited and often incorrect.

All psychoanalytic approaches maintain the concept of a *dynamic* unconscious, that is, one that has motivations or energies. Various psychoanalytic theories describe the unconscious differently. Freud (see Chapter 2) proposed that the unconscious consists of sexual and aggressive wishes that are unacceptable to the conscious personality. For Jung (see Chapter 3), the unconscious is not primarily sexual; it consists of more general motivations, which may have spiritual content. Other theorists, including Melanie Klein (1946) and Harry Stack Sullivan (1953), have described the unconscious as consisting of primitive concepts about the self and other people, especially the mother, as the first "other" the infant encounters.

Despite these variations, psychoanalysts share characteristic assumptions: (1) Personality is strongly influenced by unconscious determinants; (2) the unconscious is dynamic, or motivational, and is in conflict with other aspects of the unconscious and with consciousness; and (3) the unconscious originates in early experience.

Psychoanalysis originated and has continued to be developed in the context of psychotherapy. Its primary data consist of reports by patients in therapy. In therapy, patients are encouraged to express thoughts that would otherwise be dismissed. Psychoanalysts infer the content of a patient's unconscious from what the patient says. Psychoanalysts generally doubt that the complexities of personality, especially unconscious processes, can be measured by objective instruments (cf. Sugarman, 1991). When formal measurement is used, psychoanalysts most often use *projective techniques*. Projective techniques present ambiguous stimuli, such as inkblots in the well-known Rorschach test, and ask the patients (or research subjects) to say what they see in them. Such techniques are generally less reliable than questionnaires, but their advocates claim that they access deeper levels of motivation not available to conscious awareness.

Psychoanalytic personality theory assumes that these reports provide information that is broadly applicable, not only to those who seek therapeutic assistance, but also to the general population. This assumption is, however, challenged by those outside the psychoanalytic framework. They question the validity of psychoanalytic clinical evidence and insist that external validation is required for any theory claiming to be scientific.

Several objections have been offered concerning clinical evidence. Patients' reports may be inaccurate because of the influence of the analyst, who may bias the kinds of information reported, subtly encouraging reports that are consistent with psychoanalytic assumptions and discouraging others. Also, therapists' reports of what they have heard may be distorted; they may forget evidence that is contrary to their theoretical expectations.

Another objection is that psychoanalytic theorists have not clearly specified the types of evidence that would refute psychoanalytic theory. Often, personality is described as consisting of one kind of conscious motivation (e.g., self-control) and an opposite unconscious motivation (e.g., sexual freedom). In such a case, any observed behavior is consistent with the theory. If a person behaves with self-control, the conscious is presumed to be the cause; if promiscuity is observed, the unconscious is said to have determined this behavior. Scientifically, a theory cannot be tested if no observation is inconsistent with it. It is not *verifiable*, as explained in Chapter 1. In potentially explaining every observation, psychoanalysis has weakened its scientific status. In terms of the model of theory presented in Chapter 1, this objection can be identified in this way: Psychoanalytic theory has not clearly specified the operational definitions of its theoretical constructs. Because these operational definitions are vague, empirical observations are not linked to theoretical constructs in a way that can be clearly specified in advance. Instead, intuition ("clinical insight") makes these links. Metaphorical thinking occurs where the hard-nosed scientist would prefer concrete, rigorous thinking.

Because of weak operational definitions, psychoanalytic theoretical concepts are isolated from empirical observations. These disjointed, abstract theoretical statements are a *metapsychology*, a set of metaphors and assumptions upon which actual psychology (which must be closely tied to empirical observations) is based. Psychoanalytic metapsychology has been the object of much criticism (e.g., Holt, 1981; Kline, 1972). Psychoanalytic metapsychology is based on outdated, nineteenth-century anatomy and physics. Rather than directing observation or providing a tentative theory that can be modified on the basis of observation, psychoanalytic metapsychology seems immune to change, and it serves as a theoretical justification for beliefs not empirically derived.

Those who reject psychoanalytic theory have proposed alternative explanations, more easily researched, for the phenomena that psychoanalytic theory attempts to explain. For example, Dollard and Miller (1950) interpret clinical phenomena in terms of learning theory. More recently, cognitive models have been proposed for phenomena traditionally explained in psychoanalytic terms, such as dreams (e.g., Martinetti, 1985).

A few researchers have used experimental techniques to test psychoanalytic hypotheses (Shulman & Ferguson, 1988; Silverman, 1983). Their strategy is to present experimentally stimuli intended to activate particular unconscious dynamics, and to see whether subjects under this condition will behave as psychoanalytic theory predicts. (This method is discussed further in Chapter 2.) Not only does this research method allow experimental investigation of the psychoanalytic notion of the unconscious but it also permits tests of competing psychoanalytic postulates. For example, is narcissistic conflict best understood as due to a fragmented self, as Kohut (Kohut & Wolf, 1978) theorizes, or to oral aggressive needs, as Kernberg (1975) suggests? (See also Shulman & Ferguson, 1988.)

Another way of evaluating psychoanalytic theory is to test its effectiveness as a therapy (Wallerstein, 1989). While benefits have been found, psychoanalysis does not seem to be any more, or any less, effective than other therapies based on other theoretical models (Stiles, Shapiro, & Elliott, 1986).

Outside of psychology, psychoanalytic theory has become popular. Its influence is reflected in art and literature, in film and popular culture. With the decline of traditional religion and of mystical thinking, psychoanalysis has, for many, become a way of contacting the irrational forces within the human personality, which is sufficiently "scientific" to be permissible in the twentieth century. Whether this is a legitimate function, and whether psychoanalysis fulfills it adequately, are matters of debate.

CHAPTER 

Freud: Classical Psychoanalysis

BIOGRAPHY OF SIGMUND FREUD

Sigmund Freud

Sigmund Freud was born in 1856 into a Jewish family in predominantly Catholic Freiberg, Moravia (then part of the Austro-Hungarian Empire, but now part of Czechoslovakia). By the time he was 4 years old, Sigmund's family moved to Vienna, which remained Freud's home until near his death.

Freud was one of eight children, including two older half-brothers by his father's first marriage. Freud's father remarried at age 40, and his young wife bore six children. Sigmund was the oldest, and by all accounts was a favorite of his mother. She expected him to be great, gave him the only oil lamp in the house, and did not permit his sister to disturb him by practicing piano when he was studying. His father, a not particularly successful wool merchant, was a strict authority figure within the family.

Freud studied medicine at the University of Vienna, specializing in neurology. He intended to become an academician, and had five research publications by the age of 26. In the light of his later theory, known for its emphasis on sex, it is an interesting historical footnote that one of his neurological research papers reported the discovery of the testes in an eel. He studied the anesthetic properties of cocaine, and narrowly missed fame when a colleague published in this area before he did. Realistically, though, academic medicine did not pay well, and discrimination against Jews made it unlikely that he would achieve as high a position as he wished. Thus, Freud took the advice of a professor, turned to private practice as a clinical neurologist, and soon was able to marry his fiancée of four years, Martha Bernays. The union produced five children, including a daughter Anna, who followed her father's footsteps as a psychoanalyst.

In his practice, Freud saw a variety of psychiatric patients, including many diagnosed as suffering from hysteria. Over a long career, he developed new ways of thinking about these disorders, formulating the theory of psychoanalysis. His reputation grew beyond Vienna. He was well received in the United States, especially after his lecture series in 1909 at Clark University in Massachusetts. His theory was controversial because of its emphasis on childhood sexuality. It was also criticized as a Jewish science, dealing with psychiatric disturbances, then thought to affect Jews particularly. The Nazis burned the works of Freud and others in 1933, part of their attacks against Jewish intellectuals (including Einstein), and they raided his house in Vienna frequently in the years prior to World War II. Freud's personal health was failing at this time; he had cancer of the mouth, aggravated by his addiction to cigars. He finally fled Vienna in 1938, at the age of 82, and went to London, where he died in 1939.

ILLUSTRATIVE BIOGRAPHIES

Psychoanalytic interpretation of biography began with Freud's own studies of Leonardo da Vinci (S. Freud, 1910/1957), Woodrow Wilson (S. Freud & Bullitt, 1966), and Moses (S. Freud, 1939/1955), though the last is less psychobiographical and more mythic (Elms, 1988b). Psychoanalytic psychobiography has remained popular (Baron & Pletsch, 1985; Bergmann, 1973; B.C. Meyer, 1987). One of the reasons that psychoanalytic theory has been so attractive to psychobiographers is that it considers in detail the particulars of an individual's life. Two otherwise very different people who can be understood from this perspective are the artist Georgia O'Keeffe and the dictator Adolf Hitler.

CLASSICAL PSYCHOANALYSIS

Probably no theory of personality is as widely known or as controversial as that proposed by Sigmund Freud. Freud compared his theory to those of Copernicus, who claimed that humans do not live at the center of the universe, and of Darwin, who discredited the idea that humans were a separately created species. Humanity was further humbled by Freud's assertion that reason does not rule behavior (S. Freud, 1925/1958, p. 5). Freud pro-

Georgia O'Keeffe

Georgia O'Keeffe is perhaps the best-known twentieth-century female artist. She is widely acclaimed for her "feminine" oil paintings of gigantic flowers and sun-bleached animal bones. Many have interpreted her paintings as Freudian symbols for male and female genitals (Robinson, 1989). Is this an insightful interpretation, or psychoanalysis gone wild?

Georgia O'Keeffe was born in 1887 to Hungarian and Irish immigrants in Sun Prairie, Wisconsin, where she grew up on a large dairy farm with an older brother and five younger siblings (Lisle, 1980). She declared her ambition to be an artist at the age of 12. Already an individualist in early life, she usually dressed in somber and simple black, ignoring popular fashion. She studied at the Art Institute of Chicago, the Art Students League in New York, and the University of Virginia. Although she worked for a while as a commercial artist and an art teacher, for most of her adult life O'Keeffe lived out her early dream, supporting herself as an artist by selling her paintings, and commanding high prices for them.

Her work was first displayed at a New York gallery by Alfred Stieglitz, a photographer who befriended promising American artists. Though 23 years older than Georgia and married, he became her lover and, after his divorce, her husband. The marriage fostered the careers of both parties. Stieglitz encouraged Georgia's career and managed the business aspects. She, in turn, posed for some of his best-known photographs. Despite her undisputed love for Stieglitz, O'Keeffe kept her maiden name and, beginning in her forties, left Stieglitz for several months each year to paint in New Mexico, where she felt more at home than in New York. When her husband died, she moved there year-round.

How did this woman come to be an artist with such individuality and creativity? Does her choice of subjects (New Mexico hills, flowers, and skulls) have any psychological significance? In more general terms, what is the relationship between personality and art? These are some of the questions that we may ask of psychoanalytic theory.

posed that unconscious psychological forces powerfully affect human thought and behavior. These forces originate in the emotions of childhood and continue their influence throughout life. Freud portrayed humans as driven by instincts that "in themselves are neither good nor evil" (S. Freud, 1925/1958, p. 213) but that have both kinds of effects. These forces fuel the positive achievements of culture, but also lead to war, crime, mental illness, and other human woes.

Psychoanalytic theory has transformed our understanding of sex and aggression and has led people in the post-Freudian era to never quite trust their

Adolf Hitler

Adolf Hitler is probably the most infamous tyrant of the twentieth century, perhaps of all time. This charismatic dictator was responsible for the deaths of millions of Jews and others in the extermination camps of Nazi Germany during World War II.

Hitler's origins did not promise greatness. Adolf was born in 1889 in Austria, near the German border, the son of a customs officer and his second wife. Adolf's father, who was an illegitimate child, had been able to marry Adolf's mother only after receiving a dispensation from the Pope; this was necessary because Adolf's parents were second cousins (through adoption, not by blood). His mother was over-protective, in part because her other children had died of illness in childhood.

Hitler resisted his father's efforts to have him follow his footsteps as a government official. He aspired to be an artist but was not talented. Though his family needed money, Hitler did not go to work, even after his father died. Instead, he deceived family and friends into thinking that he was attending art school in Vienna, not confessing that he had failed the entrance exam. He read independently and played the role of a student, fantasizing massive architectural renovations of many German cities. When his money ran out, he became a homeless street person, and then earned a meager existence as an "artist," selling postcards and small paintings.

Adolf Hitler moved to Germany, avoiding the Austrian military draft and adopting Germany as his homeland. He served in the Bavarian army in World War I. He became active in politics in the period of discontent following Germany's defeat in the war and dreamed of a restoration of German glory. He even served time in prison for anti-government activities. His election as Chancellor of Germany in 1933 led quickly to invasion of neighboring countries in Europe; the hostilities escalated to become World War II. Far from restoring Germany glory, the result of Hitler's ambitions was the destruction of cities throughout Europe and the extermination of millions of Jews and other prisoners in concentration camps. Ultimately, Hitler, his lover Eva Braun, and some close associates committed suicide in the face of defeat in May 1945.

How did Hitler become the despotic leader of a murderous empire? Did his genocide against the Jews reflect personal psychopathology, or was this simply a matter of political strategy? Does his rise to power reflect any general principles of the relationship between personality and political leadership? These are some of the questions his biography suggests for psychoanalytic theory.

conscious experience. Freud's theory has to a great extent achieved the revolution he claimed, convincing most twentieth-century people that much human motivation is determined by unconscious, irrational forces. Freudian symbolism is even used to sell products (Ruth, Mosatche, & Kramer, 1989).

The Unconscious

Psychic Determinism

At first Freud, like psychiatrists of his day, looked for physical causes of psychiatric disorders. As a neurologist, he knew that damage to the brain and neurons could cause people to behave in strange ways, including physical symptoms such as paralysis and anesthesia and emotional symptoms such as anxiety and depression. For some patients, though, physical causes could not be found. Freud's colleagues thought such patients were "shamming" or faking their symptoms. Forces outside of mainstream medicine were already preparing the way for another, psychodynamic, approach (Ellenberger, 1970). Popular healers treated physical and psychological disorders by laying on of hands and by "animal magnetism." A few French psychiatrists treated patients with hypnosis, although the medical mainstream regarded hypnosis as quackery. At Salpêtrière, a hospital in Paris where Freud studied for four months during 1885 and 1886, Freud saw Jean Martin Charcot demonstrate that psychiatric symptoms could be induced through hypnosis. Later, he was impressed by Josef Breuer's discovery that a patient who recalled earlier memories while in a hypnotic trance was relieved of her symptoms when the trance was ended.

These evidences of hypnosis converted Freud from the purely physical model of psychiatric disorder to "dynamic" (psychological) psychiatry (Ellenberger, 1970). Freud became convinced that unconscious forces have the power to influence behavior, an assumption called *psychic determinism.* The term "determinism" refers to the fundamental scientific assumption of lawful cause and effect. The concept of psychic determinism allows psychological factors to be causes.

At first, Freud tried to understand how psychic factors, such as traumatic events, produced physical changes in the nervous system (S. Freud, 1895/1966b). For example, he postulated that the anxiety of a traumatic sexual encounter could, by modifying connections in the nervous system, produce anxiety symptoms in later life. Freud realized that the microscope would not be an appropriate investigative tool for his theory. Neurologists would not know where to look; after all, these changes were far more subtle than the gross lesions with which they generally dealt. So Freud turned to less direct investigative methods, through the analysis of clinical material. The clinical method is well accepted within neurology, where nerve damage is often diagnosed on the basis of behavioral symptoms such as paralysis and pain, rather than by physical examination of the neurons.

As his theory developed, Freud turned away from neurology, which rests upon a physical model of human behavior, and founded a new science, which he called **psychoanalysis**, based on psychic causes. Psychoanalysis pays close attention to the content of thought, rather than the neurons that make thought possible. If a physiologically oriented neurologist can be thought of as tracking neural pathways, then the psychoanalytic practitioner can be thought of as tracking pathways of ideas. As Freud discovered, much thought is hidden, even from the thinker.

Levels of Consciousness

Some of our thought is easily known, and it may seem that is all there is to our mind. This was especially so in Freud's time, when the new view of humankind devised by the Enlightenment emphasized human rationality and its promises of a better world (cf. Ellenberger, 1970). Freud saw the limits of this view. "What is in your mind is not identical with what you are conscious of; whether something is going on in your mind and whether you hear of it, are two different things" (S. Freud, 1925/1958, p. 8).

Freud postulated three levels of consciousness and compared the mind to an iceberg floating in the water. Like an iceberg, only a small part of the mind is readily seen: the **conscious** mind. Just at the water's surface, sometimes visible and sometimes submerged, is the **preconscious** mind. Like an iceberg, great dangers lurk in what is not seen. Finally, there is a great mass, which is most of the mind, that is hidden, like the bulk of an iceberg that is under water: the **unconscious** mind.

THE CONSCIOUS

The **conscious** level refers to experiences of which a person is aware, including memories and intentional actions. Consciousness functions in realistic ways, according to the rules of space and time. We are aware of consciousness and accept it as us; we "identify with" it.

THE PRECONSCIOUS

Some material that is not in awareness at a particular time can be brought to awareness readily; this material is called **preconscious**. It includes information that is not at the moment being thought about but that can be easily remembered if needed—for example, your mother's middle name. The content of the preconscious is not fundamentally different from that of consciousness. Thoughts move readily from one to the other.

THE UNCONSCIOUS

The third level of consciousness is different. Its contents do not readily move into consciousness. The *unconscious* refers to mental processes of which a person is not aware. Such material remains in the unconscious because making it conscious would produce too much anxiety. This material is said to be "repressed," that is, it resists becoming conscious.

Among the contents of the unconscious are forgotten traumatic memories and denied wishes. A child who has been sexually abused, for example, will often repress this memory, having amnesia for the terrifying event. This forgetting protects the victim from the anxiety that would accompany recall of traumatic experiences. Desires also may cause anxiety if we are ashamed of what we wish. For example, a child may wish that a younger sibling were dead, so that there would be no competition for the love of the parents. This wish is rejected by consciousness as horrid and evil, so it is repressed. Freudians call such wishes "denied wishes," because we deny that we have them. The unconscious becomes, in effect, the garbage pile of what consciousness throws away. It is emotionally upsetting and is less civilized than consciousness.

Effects of Unconscious Motivation

Behavior is determined by a combination of conscious and unconscious forces. These may act together smoothly so that a person's actions appear comprehensible and rational, as though consciousness alone determined behavior. Alternatively, unconscious forces may interfere with conscious intentions. This conflict produces irrational thoughts and behavior. Freud's particular interest, as a clinician, was in cases where the forces of the conscious and the unconscious mind conflict.

Physical Symptoms, Including Hysteria

Many of Freud's patients had physical symptoms for which no organic cause could be found. Influenced by his study of hypnosis under Charcot, Freud argued that cases of **conversion hysteria** represent the impact of unconscious forces on the body to produce physical symptoms of paralysis, mutism, deafness, blindness, tics, or other maladies that resemble physical diseases but that occur in physically normal, undamaged bodies (Breuer & Freud, 1925/1955), although the diagnosis is less often made today (M.M. Jones, 1980).

One particularly striking example of such a conversion hysteria is *glove anesthesia.* In this disorder, a patient has no physical sensation of touch or pain on the hand in the area that a glove would cover. Sensation on the arm above the wrist is normal. There is no pattern of neurons that, if damaged, could produce this disorder, since those nerve cells responsible for sensation in the thumb also influence feeling in part of the forearm above the wrist, while those neurons that influence the fingers also serve other parts of the forearm. Glove anesthesia is impossible, physically. So why does it occur in some patients? Freud argued that glove anesthesia is produced by psychological forces. A patient thinks of the hand as a unit, and the arm as another unit; they are psychological units (though not neurological ones). A person who is very anxious about what the hand might feel or do could be driven by this psychological reason to have glove anesthesia as a symptom.

Hypnosis

In hypnosis, an individual (the "subject") experiences a highly suggestible state, dissociated from normal experience (Hilgard, 1976), in which the suggestions of a hypnotist strongly influence what is experienced or recalled. People vary in their hypnotizability (Hilgard, 1965). In *age regression,* hypnotic subjects appear to return to an earlier age. Research indicates that no actual memories are retrieved, but rather subjects are filling in what they imagine (Nash, 1987, 1988). In the phenomenon of *posthypnotic suggestion,* the hypnotist suggests that a particular action or experience (sensation) will occur when the hypnotic trance is ended. For example, a hypnotist may suggest that a subject will feel a choking sensation when puffing a cigarette; after the trance is ended, the subject will experience the choking sensation, making hypnosis an effective way to quit smoking.

Psychosis

An extreme form of mental disorder is termed a *psychosis.* In the extreme, psychotics lose touch with reality and experience the unconscious in raw form, through *hallucinations,* seeing and hearing things that are not actually present. The irrationality of psychotic behavior reflects the underlying irrationality of the unconscious.

Dreams

Freud praised dreams as "the royal road to the unconscious." In waking life, conscious forces powerfully restrain the unacceptable forces of the unconscious. During sleep, the restraining forces of consciousness are relaxed, and the unconscious threatens to break into awareness. This triggers anxiety, which threatens to waken the dreamer. Sleep is protected by disguising the unconscious into less threatening symbolic form in a dream.

Usually a dream disguises the fulfillment of a repressed wish (Freud, 1900/1953). Consider the following dream of a young man:

> I was on a beach with my girl and other friends. We had been swimming and were sitting on the beach. My girl was afraid that she would lose her pocketbook and kept saying that she felt certain she would lose it on the beach. (Hall, 1966, pp. 57–58)

The recalled dream (here, the story of the beach and the pocketbook) is termed the **manifest content** of the dream. *Dream interpretation* is the process of inferring the unconscious wishes disguised in the dream. Its hidden meaning, revealed by interpreting the dream symbols, is termed the **latent content** of the dream. A pocketbook is a Freudian symbol for female genitals, so the dream symbolizes the dreamer's wish that his girlfriend would lose her virginity on the beach. Dream interpretation is like "decoding." The "coding" process, which has produced the dream, is called *dream-work.* Ideas are expressed by symbols. Material is condensed to much briefer form. Troublesome ideas are displaced from their original objects to disguise ideas that would produce conflict (S. Freud, 1935/1963a, pp. 86–87).

Alternative psychoanalytic models of dream interpretation have been developed, such as that proposed by Carl Jung (see Chapter 3). Psychologists have proposed models for understanding dreams drawing on modern cognitive theory and an enhanced understanding of neurology (Antrobus, 1991; Cicogna, Cavallero, & Bosinelli, 1991), yet Freud is generally acknowledged as the theorist who brought dreams into the domain of scientific investigation.

The characteristics of dream-work that Freud described (condensation, displacement, symbolism, and so forth) represent the functioning of the unconscious more generally. Freud understood not only dreams and psychosis, but even aspects of everyday normal behavior, as results of unconscious motivation.

The Psychopathology of Everyday Life

Freud described the impact of the unconscious in a wide variety of behaviors of normal people. He termed such phenomena, in German, *Fehlleistungen,* which could be translated, according to Strachey (S. Freud, 1933/1966a, p. 25), as "faulty acts" or "faulty functions." The unfortunate English translation for this concept is an invented word, **parapraxes**. More commonly, people refer to them as Freudian slips, or "the psychopathology of everyday life."

One of the most common of these **Freudian slips** is a misstatement, or "slip of the tongue." For example, in parting from a boring party, one might say, "I'm so glad I have to leave now," intending to say, "I'm so sorry I have to leave now." The unconscious tells the truth, lacking the tact of consciousness. "Errors of memory" are another kind of Freudian slip—for example, forgetting the birthday of a disliked relative. Other Freudian slips include errors of hearing, losing or misplacing objects, and errors of action. Alfred Stieglitz, in 1935, wrote letters to his wife, Georgia O'Keeffe, and to his lover, Dorothy Norman, but placed each letter into the wrong envelope, so that his wife received the letter intended for his lover (Lisle, 1980, p. 227). Was this merely an error, or did Stieglitz unconsciously wish to confront his wife with his other relationship? Such "accidents," to a Freudian, are not random, but are motivated by unconscious wishes. Psychic determinism holds us strictly accountable for all our actions.

HUMOR

We laugh at jokes if they express issues or conflicts that are unconsciously important, but consciously unacceptable (but see Ruch & Hehl, 1988, for contrary evidence). A bigot, for example, will find racial jokes particularly amusing. Freud gave many examples of jokes in his writing. One that survives translation from the German is the following:

> Two Jews met in the neighbourhood of the bath-house. "Have you taken a bath?" asked one of them. "What?" asked the other in return, "is there one missing?" (S. Freud, 1916/1963b, p. 49)

Like a dream, the joke is terse, using the technique of **condensation**. Its humor, achieved by the double meaning of the word "taken," depends on the anti-Semitic attitude that Jews are thieves, rather than clean.

A master of humor, Charlie Chaplin agreed that the irrational is the key to humor. He wrote, "Through humor, we see in what seems rational, the irrational; in what seems important, the unimportant. It . . . preserves our sanity. Because of humor we are less overwhelmed by the vicissitudes of life. It activates our sense of proportion and reveals to us that in an overstatement of seriousness lurks the absurd" (Chaplin, 1964, pp. 211–212). On that note, let us be glad that the unconscious, the irrational, is part of the experience of all of us, and not only of psychiatric patients.

Origin and Nature of the Unconscious

Where does this powerful, pervasive unconscious come from?

PHYLOGENETIC INHERITANCE

According to Freud, some of the unconscious is inherited as "primal fantasies," based on phylogenetic (that is, species, not individual) experience. Freud referred to a "primal horde" in which a group of sons rebelled against their father who, according to prehistoric practice, dominated all the other males and kept all the women for himself. The "primal father" was killed and his women were taken by the sons. As a result, they felt remorse and guilt. This distant phylogenetic memory, according to Freud, is the basis of every man's Oedipus complex (which is described later in this chapter) and guilt. Other theorists, especially Carl Jung, have emphasized an inherited unconscious even more than Freud. The phylogenetic hypothesis is generally disbelieved today, however, because it depends upon the possibility of inheriting memories of ancestral experience, which is inconsistent with modern biological theory.

REPRESSION

Freud's primary interest was in understanding how *personal* experience creates the unconscious. This happens through the all-important mechanism of **repression**. No one likes to focus on unpleasant thoughts if they can be avoided. According to Freud's *hedonic hypothesis*, people seek pleasure and avoid pain. Repression is a mechanism for removing unpleasant thoughts from consciousness. Thoughts and memories are repressed (that is, made unconscious) if they are painful or if they are associated with something painful.

Structures of the Personality

To describe more clearly the tension between the unconscious, which "seeks expression," and consciousness, which tries to hold unconscious forces back, Freud described three structures of personality. The **id** is primitive and the source of biological drives. It is unconscious. The **ego** is the rational and coping part of personality. It is the most conscious structure of personality (though not entirely conscious). The third structure, the **superego**, consists of the rules and ideals of society that have become internalized by the individual. Some of the superego is conscious but much of it remains unconscious.

Although they have become among the best known of his concepts, Freud introduced the terms "id," "ego," and "superego" (his structural hypothesis) rather late in the development of his theory. His book *The Ego and the Id*, which describes these structures, was not published until 1923, when he was already in his late sixties.

Each structure serves a different function. For example, consider the various aspects of eating. A person feels hungry and wants to eat. That motivational function belongs to the id. Before hunger can be satisfied, it is necessary to cook or go to a restaurant, perhaps even to plant a crop and harvest it. These planning and coping functions belong to the ego. In addition, there are "oughts" to be considered: advice about what is nutritious and standards of gourmet cuisine. These ideal and moral standards belong to the superego.

Considering the metaphor of driving, the id corresponds to the motor of a car; the ego corresponds to the steering wheel; and the superego represents the rules of the road. In the metaphor of Freud's day, the ego

> is like a man on horseback, who has to hold in check the superior strength of the horse. . . . Often a rider, if he is not to be parted from his horse, is obliged to guide it where it wants to go; so in the same way the ego is in the habit of transforming the id's will into action as if it were its own. (S. Freud, 1923/1962b, p. 15)

Like Freud's horseback rider, the ego may seem to be steering more than it truly is.

The Id The *id*, which contains biological drives, is the only structure of personality present at birth. The id functions according to the **pleasure principle**. It is hedonistic; it aims to satisfy its urges, which reduces tension and thus brings pleasure.

LIBIDO

Freud proposed that the id is the source of psychic energy, called **libido**, which is sexual. Motivation for all aspects of personality is derived from this energy, which can be transformed from its original instinctive form through socialization. All energy for cultural achievements—for works of art, for politics, for education—is sexual energy, transformed. Conversely, repression ties up energy, making it unavailable for higher achievements.

EROS AND THANATOS

Psychic energy is of two kinds. **Eros**, the "life instinct," motivates life-maintaining behaviors and love. At first, Freud felt that all libido was of this kind, and it is the usual energy described in his theory. Later he postulated a second form of psychic energy, also innate. **Thanatos**, the "death instinct," is a destructive force directing us inevitably toward death, the ultimate release from the tension of living. It motivates all kinds of aggression, including war and suicide.

CHARACTERISTICS OF INSTINCTS

Because Freud understood all personality functioning as derived from instinctive energy, knowing the fundamental principles regulating instincts provides a basic framework for understanding personality. These can be summarized as four basic aspects of instincts: source, pressure, aim, and object.

1. Source. All psychic energy is derived from biological processes in some part or organ of the body. There is no separate, exclusively mental energy. The amount of energy a person has does not change throughout life, although it is transformed so that it is "invested" differently.

2. Pressure. The pressure of an instinct refers to its force or motivational quality. It corresponds to the strength of the instinctual drive; it is high when the drive is not satisfied, and falls when the need is met. For example, a hungry infant has high pressure of the hunger drive; one just fed has hunger at low pressure. When pressure is low, the instinct may not have noticeable effects, but when pressure is high, it may break through, interrupting other activities. A hungry baby wakes up, for example.

3. Aim. Instincts function according to a principle of homeostasis, or steady state, a principle borrowed from biology. Instincts aim to preserve the ideal steady state for the organism. Changes away from this steady state are experienced as tension. The aim of all instincts is reduce tension, which is pleasurable. (Think of the good feeling of eating when you are hungry.) Instincts operate according to what Freud called the *pleasure principle*;

they aim simply to produce pleasure by reducing tension, immediately and without regard to reality constraints.

Tension reduction occurs when the original biological instinct is directly satisfied—for example, when a hungry infant is fed, or when a sexually aroused adult achieves orgasm. It would be a mistake, however, to conclude that only direct biological drive satisfaction can reduce tension. Some transformations of libido also allow tension reduction. An artist may experience tension reduction when a creative problem is solved. Charlie Chaplin described when, in his film making, "the solution [to a creative problem] would suddenly reveal itself, as if a layer of dust had been swept off a marble floor—there it was, the beautiful mosaic I had been looking for. *Tension was gone*" (Chaplin, 1964, p. 188; emphasis added). Such healthy, socially acceptable ways of reducing tension are termed "sublimation." However, indirect expressions of libido do not always reduce the pressure of the instinct. Thus a chronic deviation from a restful, homeostatic state occurs in people who have not found ways to reduce tension, for example, in neurotics.

4. Object. The object of an instinct is the person or thing in the world that is desired so that the instinct can be satisfied. For example, the object of the hunger drive of an infant is the mother's breast: It brings satisfaction. The object of a sexually aroused adult is a sexual partner. Investment of psychic energy in a particular object is called **cathexis**.

What kind of partner? It is with respect to the object of an instinct that there is the most variation, the most influence of experience on the fundamental motivations of people. Some sexually aroused men look for a woman just like Mother; others look for a very different kind of woman, or for a man, or even a picture or underwear or a child or any of a vast assortment of sexual objects. Women, of course, also vary widely in their choice of sexual objects.

The fact that libido is capable of being directed toward so many diverse objects, not fixed biologically, is termed the *plasticity* of the instinct. This plasticity is much greater in humans than in lower animals, who seem to come with instincts "pre-wired" to very specific objects. Learning from experience—selecting objects from the possibilities in the environment and learning to adapt to reality—occurs in the ego. The id, in contrast, functions according to a very primitive mechanism, called primary process.

Primary Process

The id functions according to the purely instinctive and unsocialized **primary process**. Primary process is as blind and inflexible as the instinctive impulses that draw a moth to a candle flame, and its consequences can be as deadly. Primary process ignores time, recognizing no past and no future, only the present moment. It demands immediate gratification; it cannot wait or plan. If reality does not satisfy its urges, it may resort to hallucinatory wish fulfillment, that is, simply imagine that its needs are met. As a sexually aroused dreamer conjures up a lover, a psychotic person might hallucinate a boat in a stormy sea. This, of course, is not adaptive in the real world.

Simple organisms in natural environments may be able to function quite well with only their biological drives (or id) operating according to the primary process. Humans, though, must adapt to a complex social environment, and the id, functioning according to primary process and blind instinct, cannot adapt or learn. It is the ego that can profit from experience.

The Ego

The **ego** is the structure of personality that brings about the unity of personality and that is in touch with the real world. It operates according to the **reality principle**. It can accurately understand reality and can adapt itself to the constraints of the real world. The ego can delay gratification and plan. These abilities are termed **secondary process**.

Mental health requires a strong ego, one that can defend against anxiety while still allowing the individual to thrive in the real external world with enjoyment. A weak ego may not adequately defend against anxiety, or it may require a person to behave in rigid ways so as to avoid anxiety. If the ego breaks down altogether, a psychotic episode will occur.

The Superego

The third structure of personality, the *superego,* is the internal representative of the rules and restrictions of family and society. It generates feelings of guilt when we act contrary to its rules. In addition, the superego presents us with an *ego ideal,* which is an image of what we would like to be, our internal standards. Because the superego develops at a young age, it represents an immature and rigid form of morality. In psychoanalytic jargon, the superego is "archaic" and largely unconscious. Freud argued that our sense of guilt is often out of touch with current reality, representing the immature understandings of a young child.

Anna Freud gives examples that illustrate the archaic nature of the superego. One case is a man who, as a child, stole sweets. He was taught not to do so, and internalized the prohibition in his superego. As an adolescent, he blushed with guilt every time he ate sweets, even though they were no longer forbidden (A. Freud, 1935, p. 97). In another case, a woman could not select "an occupation which would necessitate sharing a room with companions" (p. 99) because of early punishment for nakedness. In both these cases, the superego was based on parental restrictions in childhood and failed to adapt to the adult situation.

Freud dismissed much religion as similarly immature. For Freud, mature ethics are not achieved through the superego, but rather through the ego, the only structure of personality that adapts to current reality.

Intrapsychic Conflict

The id, ego, and superego do not always peacefully coexist. The id demands immediate satisfaction of drives, while the superego threatens guilt if any pleasurable satisfaction of immoral impulses is attempted. Thus there is **intrapsychic conflict**.

The ego tries to repress unacceptable desires, but it does not always succeed. The repressed materials have energy, and this energy tries to return the repressed material to consciousness. It is like an iceberg or ice cube that is pushed completely under the surface of the water: it keeps bobbing up again. Like a forgotten bill or dentist appointment, repressed material threatens to come back to us. Because pain is associated with repressed material, we keep trying to repress it—like a hand pushing the ice back under the water.

The ego tries to reconcile the conflicting demands of the id and superego while at the same time taking into account external reality, with its limited opportunities for drive satisfaction.

Energy Hypothesis

Freud understood these phenomena in terms of his *energy hypothesis.* Repression of unacceptable thoughts or impulses requires psychic energy. The force of the impulse that "seeks expression" must not exceed the repressive force or repression will fail and the repressed material will become conscious. The more energy that is tied up in such intrapsychic conflict, the less is available for dealing with current reality.

Anxiety

Anxiety signals that the ego may fail in its task of adapting to reality and maintaining an integrated personality. *Neurotic anxiety* signals that id impulses may break through (overcome repression) and be expressed. *Moral anxiety* indicates fear that one's own superego will respond with guilt. *Reality anxiety* indicates that the external world threatens real danger.

Defense Mechanisms

The ego uses various strategies to resolve intrapsychic conflict. These **defense mechanisms** are adopted if direct expression of the id impulse is unacceptable to the superego or dangerous in the real world.

REPRESSION

All defense mechanisms begin with repression of unacceptable impulses, that is, forcing them to be unconscious. However repression ties up energy. To conserve energy, the ego uses a variety of defense mechanisms that disguise the unacceptable impulse. By distorting the source, aim, and/or object of the impulse, they avoid the retaliation of the superego, allowing the impulse, in effect, to sneak past the censor. In this way, total repression of the impulse is not necessary. This reduces the energy requirements for repression, analogous to the way that letting steam out of a pressure cooker reduces the force required to hold on the lid.

Denial is a primitive defense mechanism in which the person does not acknowledge some painful or anxiety-provoking aspect of reality or of the self. For example, a person may deny that smoking is contributing to health problems despite clear statements to that effect by a competent physician. Denial involves a major distortion of reality, and thus is primitive and maladaptive.

In **reaction formation**, an unacceptable impulse is repressed and its opposite is developed in exaggerated form. For example, a child who hates a younger sister may repress this, and instead feel love for the sister. The defense may be diagrammed thus:

"I hate sister" → "I love sister"

When only love is acknowledged, but not its opposite, a psychoanalyst suspects that hatred is also present, but denied. Similarly, highly modest persons may be suspected of defending against exhibitionism.

In **projection**, the person's own unacceptable impulse is instead thought to belong to someone else. A man who is tempted to steal but whose strong ethical sense (superego) will not allow him to even think of stealing may project his unacceptable impulse onto another person:

"I want to steal" → "That person is stealing"

Cultural scapegoats often become projective targets. In this way, individual intrapsychic conflict contributes to prejudice.

The defense mechanism of **displacement** distorts the object of the drive. Displacement is less primitive than projection, because the impulse is correctly seen as belonging to the individual; only the object is distorted. For example, a child who is angry with the father may not consciously be able to acknowledge the anger because of fear of retaliation and guilt. The aggressive impulse may be disguised by directing it toward a brother:

"I want to hurt Dad" → "I want to hurt my brother"

We suspect that the feelings are due to displacement, rather than caused by the brother's actual behavior, if they are disproportionately strong, compared to what the current situation would warrant, or if a person is frequently ready to experience aggressive impulses in a wide variety of situations. Displacement of other emotions, such as dependency and sexuality, can also occur.

Identification is a process of borrowing or merging one's identity with that of someone else. It is part of normal development; boys identify with their fathers, girls with their mothers, and all of us with cultural heroes. It can also be a defense mechanism, avoiding the recognition of one's own inadequacies, and wishfully adopting someone else's identity instead. An example of identification as a pervasive defense mechanism is Grey Owl, an Englishman who identified so strongly with stories of Indians in the West that he moved to Canada, lived with the native people, and eventually became so like them in manner and appearance that he passed as an Indian (Dickson, 1973). Identification sometimes functions to overcome feelings of powerlessness. Adopting the identity of someone who has power over us, even if that power is not used for our benefit, is termed *identification with the aggressor.*

In the defense mechanism of **isolation**, thoughts related to some unpleasant occurrence are disassociated from other thinking and thus do not come to mind. In addition, emotions that would ordinarily be connected with the thoughts are gone. For example, a person who has lost a loved one through death may isolate this experience, not thinking of the loved one because of the grief it might bring.

The defense mechanism of **rationalization** involves giving plausible, but false, reasons for an action in order to disguise the true motives. For example, a parent might rationalize spanking a child, saying this will teach the child to be more obedient, though the true motivation may be that the parent resents the child. Rationalization involves relatively little distortion, so it is considered a relatively mature defense mechanism.

The defense mechanism of **intellectualization** prevents clear, undistorted recognition of an impulse through excessive or distorted explanation. A person who overeats may give many reasons: "I need extra vitamins to deal with stress"; "I always gain weight in the winter"; and so on. Sometimes intellectualization works like a "sour grapes" attitude; we intellectually convince ourselves that we didn't want what we can't have. Margaret Sanger described the loss of her newly built home to fire: "I was neither disappointed nor regretful. . . . In that instant I learned the lesson of the futility of material substances. Of what great importance were they spiritually if they could go so quickly? . . . I could . . . be happy without them" (Sanger, 1938/1971, p. 64). This defense mechanism is adaptive, although defensive in that it distorts the grief of the tragedy.

Sublimation

Sublimation is the most desirable and healthy way of dealing with unacceptable impulses. It occurs when the individual finds a socially acceptable aim and object for the expression of an unacceptable impulse. This allows indirect discharge of the impulse, so that its pressure is reduced. Sublimation occurs when artists transform primitive urges into works of art. Aggressive impulses may be sublimated into athletic competitiveness. A Freudian would even interpret Mother Teresa's acts of love, bathing and feeding the "poorest of the poor" (Gonzalez-Balado & Playfoot, 1985), as sublimation of sexual motivation. Within Freudian theory, this is the most laudatory interpretation that can be made about anyone.

Creative individuals are particularly interesting models of sublimation, and they have been of interest to psychoanalysts, beginning with Freud (1910/1957). They retain the ability, lost by most of us, to access the fantasy world of the id. Unlike psychotics, they do not get caught irretrievably in the id, and unlike children, they can function with a mature ego. They are capable of what psychoanalysis describes as "regression in the service of the ego" (Kris, 1952/1964). Research confirms the psychoanalytic hypothesis that creative artists can shift more readily from controlled thinking (an ego function) to unregulated thought (the unconscious) than can psychotics, who have difficulty with ego functions, or "normals," who are less able to access the unconscious (Wild, 1965). Surrealistic artists, such as Salvador Dali, explicitly portray the less controlled aspects of this process in their work, though Freud only came to respect Dali after he became convinced of his capacity for control, as well as expression (Romm & Slap, 1983; Rose, 1983).

Measuring Defenses

Most descriptions of defense mechanisms are based on clinical case histories. Several empirical studies have been conducted, however. Defense mechanisms have been scored from the Thematic Apperception Test (P. Cramer, 1987) and from the Rorschach test (Cooper, Perry, & Arnow, 1988; Cooper, Perry & O'Connell, 1991; Exner, 1986; Meloy & Singer, 1991; Schafer, 1954; Viglione, Brager, & Haller, 1991). Nazi war criminals were tested in 1946, while awaiting trial, with the Rorschach test. These protocols have been studied various times over the years. One study, which included methodological precautions against biased scoring, concluded that the Nazi prisoners were not very introspective and were cognitively rigid, probably character disordered (a psychiatric term for an unhealthy but not neurotic or psychotic personality). Nonetheless, overall they were not very different from average German citizens or from nonpsychiatric samples in the United States (Resnick & Nunno, 1991).

Self-report inventories have also been developed to assess people's preferred defense mechanisms (Banks & Juni, 1991; Juni, 1982). Some studies indicate that experimental manipulations influence defensiveness (P. Cramer, 1991). It has not been demonstrated, however, that these various measures are valid indicators of people's use of defense mechanisms in their everyday lives. Psychoanalytic understanding of the specific defense mechanism of projection has also been criticized on the basis of empirical studies (Holmes, 1978; Tennen & Affleck, 1990).

Personality Development

Personality development involves a series of conflicts between the individual, who wants to satisfy instinctual impulses, and the social world (especially the family), which constrains this. Through development, the individual finds ways to obtain as much hedonic gratification as possible, given the constraints of society. These adaptational strategies constitute the personality.

Freud proposed that the mucous membranes of the body could be the physical source of id impulses, the *erogenous zones* where libido is focused. These zones are highly responsive to sensation and can be associated with increased tension and reduction of tension, as the libido model requires. Different zones are central at different ages, because of maturational changes (that is, physical changes associated with age). For the adult, the erogenous zone is the genitals. In early life, though, other zones give more pleasure: in infancy, the mouth; in toddlerhood, the anus.

Driven by maturational factors, all people develop through the same *psychosexual stages* (see Table 2.1).

The infant, under the tyranny of the pleasure principle, wants to be fed immediately whenever it experiences hunger. In reality, feeding is sometimes delayed, and ultimately the child will be weaned. This is the conflict of the first psychosexual stage, the **oral stage**. In the second or **anal stage**, the toddler enjoys controlling the bowels, retaining and expelling feces according to his or her own will; but conflict with the restrictive forces of society arises, as the family demands toilet training. Conflict over drive satis-

TABLE 2.1 Stages of Psychosexual Development

Stage	*Age*	*Conflict*	*Outcomes*
Oral Stage	birth to 12 months	weaning	optimism or pessimism addictions to tobacco, alcohol
Anal Stage	1 to 3 years	toilet training	stubbornness miserliness
Phallic Stage	3 to 5 years	masturbation & Oedipus/Electra conflict	sex role identification morality (superego) vanity
Latency	5 years to puberty		
Genital Stage	puberty to adulthood		

faction in the third psychosexual stage, the **phallic stage**, focuses on punishment for masturbation and the child's complex fantasy of a sexual union with the opposite sex parent—a wish that is frustrated because it conflicts with the universal taboo of incest.

Personality development occurs as the ego finds new strategies to cope with the frustrations imposed by socialization. If socialization is too severe or too sudden, the young ego cannot cope, and personality development is impaired. Sudden, severe shocks that are beyond the child's capacity to cope, called *psychic trauma*, include sexual abuse and early witnessing of adults' sexual intercourse (the "primal scene"). Such events produce **fixation**, in which impulses are repressed, rather than outgrown.

The Five Psychosexual Stages

There are five universal stages of development. Freud believed that personality was essentially formed by the end of the third stage, at about age 5. By then, basic strategies for expressing impulses, which constitute the core of personality, have been developed.

THE ORAL PERIOD

The oral period of development occurs from birth to about age 1. During this period, the erogenous zone is the mouth, and pleasurable activities center around feeding (sucking). At first, in the *oral erotic* phase, the infant passively receives reality, swallowing what is good or (less passively) spitting out what is distasteful. Later in the oral period, a second phase, termed *oral sadism*, involves the development of a more active role, epitomized by biting.

Because the infant's needs are met without effort, he or she is said to feel "omnipotent." This feeling passes in normal development, but is retained in some psychoses. The feeling of infantile omnipotence normally gives way to realization that needs are satisfied through loved objects in the world, not magically. As the infant learns to associate the mother's presence with satisfaction of the hunger drive, the mother becomes a separate "object," and the first differentiation of self from others occurs. Fixation in the first psychosexual stage results in development of an **oral character** personality type, whose traits typically include *optimism*, *passivity*, and *dependency*. People with evidence of fixation at this stage (oral imagery on the Rorschach test) conform more to others' judgments on an Asch-type judgment task, particularly in the presence of a high-status authority figure (Masling, Weiss, & Rothschild, 1968; Tribich & Messer, 1974) and they are more likely to indicate needing help on personality tests (O'Neill & Bornstein, 1990).

THE ANAL PERIOD

During the second and third years, the toddler's pleasure is experienced in a different part of the body: the anus. The toddler's desire to control his or her own bowel movements conflicts with the social demand for toilet training. Pleasure is experienced at first through the newly formed ability to retain feces, the *anal retentive* phase, and then in the experience of willful defecation, the *anal expulsive* phase. Lifelong conflicts over issues of control, of holding on and letting go, may result if there is fixation at this stage. The **anal character** is characterized by three traits, *orderliness, parsimony,* and *obstinacy,* which are correlated in many empirical studies (Greenberg & Fisher, 1978, but see a contrary opinion by A.B. Hill, 1976).

The Phallic Period

From age 3 to 5 (or a bit later), the primary erogenous area of the body is the genital zone. Freud called this stage of development the *phallic period,* reflecting his conviction that the phallus (penis) is the most important organ for the development of both males and females. (Critics chastise Freud for being "phallo-centric.") The child's desire for sexual pleasure is expressed through masturbation (often called "autoeroticism" by psychoanalysts), which is accompanied by important (and, to critics, incredible) fantasies. At this stage, males and females follow different developmental paths.

Male Development: The Oedipus Conflict. According to Freud, the young boy wants to kill his father and to replace him as his mother's sexual partner. This universal male **Oedipus conflict** is derived from Sophocles' play *Oedipus Rex,* in which Oedipus unwittingly murders his father and takes his own mother as his wife. The young boy fears that if his father knew what he desired, he would punish him with the most appropriate punishment for the crime: castration. **Castration anxiety**, the fear that his penis will be cut off, is the motivating anxiety of the young boy at this stage. While such castration anxiety may seem an incredible idea, threats of castration do occur in some bizarre circumstances. We are told, for example, that Adolf Hitler ordered artists to be castrated if they used the wrong colors for skies and meadows (Waite, 1977, p. 30).

In normal development, castration anxiety is repressed. Unconscious castration anxiety may be displaced, experienced as fear of tonsillectomy (Blum, 1953, p. 87) or as fear of disease. Freud regarded "syphilidophobia," fear of being infected with syphilis, as derived from castration anxiety (S. Freud, 1933/1966a, p. 552). Presumably he would regard exaggerated fear of AIDS as evidence of a similar displacement today.

In a healthy resolution of the Oedipal conflict, the boy gives up his fantasy of replacing his father and instead decides to become *like* his father. By this *identification* the boy achieves two important developments: (1) the internalization of conscience, called *superego,* and (2) appropriate male sex-typing. Conscience is fueled by castration anxiety: The stronger the castration fear, the stronger the superego. Or, as Freud so memorably phrased it, "The superego . . . is the heir of the Oedipus complex" (S. Freud, 1923/1962b, p. 38).

Female Development: The Electra Conflict. Girls develop differently. Seeing that they lack a penis, girls believe that they have been castrated. According to Freud, girls interpret their clitoris as inferior to a penis and wish that they had one (*penis envy*). Like boys, girls in the phallic period fantasize sexual union with the opposite-sex parent. Unlike boys, girls must shift their erotic attachment from the mother (the first, pre-Oedipal love object for both sexes) to the father. This change of object is facilitated by the girl's anger toward her mother for not being powerful enough to protect her from castration.

Freud lists three possible outcomes of the girl's castration complex: sexual inhibition or neurosis; a masculinity complex; or normal femininity (S. Freud, 1933/1966a, p. 590). By *masculinity complex*, Freud meant that the woman strives for achievements inappropriate for females, such as career advances to the exclusion of traditional feminine family commitments. Normal feminine development, according to Freud, results in acceptance of the role of wife and mother and development of the "normal" feminine traits of passivity and masochism. Without castration anxiety to motivate their development, girls are less psychologically developed than males, with a weaker superego.

Many aspects of Freud's theory of women are disconfirmed by the empirical evidence. For example, women do not generally regard their bodies more negatively than do men (Greenberg & Fisher, 1983). Understandably, Freud has been much criticized for his claim that females are doomed biologically to be less developed psychologically. His theory does not recognize the impact of culture on sex roles (e.g., Lerman, 1986a, 1986b; Rudnytsky, 1987). Freud's theory is often criticized as overly conservative. That is, it aims to adapt people to the status quo rather than constituting a force for social change. Feminists assert that the *biology is destiny* assumption of Freud locks women into traditional sex roles unfairly. Others, though, have regarded the feminist protest as excessive (e.g., Lampl-de Groot, 1982).

Incest: Freud's Abandonment of the Seduction Hypothesis. Freud developed and revised his theory over many decades. The theory that has been presented above is his final view. In it, the girl's fantasy of a sexual relationship with her father is just that: fantasy. Earlier, Freud had believed that actual, rather than imagined, incest was important in the histories of his female patients. His *seduction hypothesis*, which he later abandoned, held that the father's seduction (or, more appropriately translated, rape) of his daughter was responsible for her development of psychiatric problems, specifically, hysteria (Freud, 1896/1962a; McGrath, 1986). Why did Freud change his mind?

Freud's abandonment of the seduction hypothesis is accepted by orthodox Freudians as the correction of an earlier error. A critic, Jeffry Masson, accused Freud of a "loss of courage" (Masson, 1984, p. 134). Masson characterized the orthodox view as a comfortable one for the psychiatric profession, since it allies the therapist with the powerful father and avoids dealing with the troublesome reality of the widespread sexual abuse of children. Others have defended Freud (e.g., Lawrence, 1988; R. Paul, 1985; Rosenman, 1989). They argue that Freud did recognize that incest really occurs (though less frequently than he earlier thought) and is an issue of concern, although his focus was more on thoughts than on actual events. The issue about which Freud changed his mind was, more narrowly, the cause of hysteria. The controversy has been bitter and personal (Masters, 1988), leading to professional ostracism of those who argue that sexual abuse is widespread and a central problem (DeMause, 1988; Masson, 1984). It is not a new issue in psychoanalysis; as early as 1932, Ferenczi argued for Freud's seduction theory, which Freud had already abandoned (A.W. Rachman, 1989). Theoretical issues aside, analysts have not paid sufficient attention to the actual facts of their patients' lives (Mack, 1980).

Empiricists are now studying the incidence of incest, though it is particularly difficult to get accurate data in this sensitive area (Alter-Reid, Gibbs, Lachenmeyer, Sigal, & Massoth, 1986; Vander Mey & Neff, 1982). Although these studies are not methodologically perfect, they have convinced many that incest is more frequent than most people realize, and that Freud may have been closer to a painful truth when he wrote of actual incest rather than fantasies of seduction. The issue is more complex than simply the prevalence of incest. The relationship between incest and adverse mental health outcomes also must be examined. Many studies find that incest has serious adverse emotional effects on its victims, including depression and suicide, anxiety, drug and alcohol abuse, sexual victimization, difficulty in relationships, and poor self-esteem (Alter-Reid and others, 1986; Browne & Finkelhor, 1986; deChesnay, 1985; Kiser, Heston, Millsap, & Pruitt, 1991; Leifer, Shapiro, Martone, & Kassem, 1991; Shapiro, Leifer, Martone, & Kassem, 1990). For some, the issue of incest is inextricably related to men's power in society (Herman & Hirschman, 1977). The controversy is far from over, with continuing debate on the prevalence of incest, its effects, and Freud's motivations for abandoning the seduction hypothesis. The broader issue of the role of the Oedipus complex in development is also being reconsidered (Simon, 1991).

Effects of Fixation. Psychoanalytic theory says that fixation at the phallic period results in difficulties of superego formation, sex role identity, and sexuality, including sexual inhibition, sexual promiscuity, and homosexuality. Problems with sex role identification (accepting cultural standards for male or female behavior) may stem from difficulties at this period. This classic formula assumes that cultural sex norms will be accepted by healthy individuals; it does not allow for the possibility that sex role norms are themselves in need of change.

Freud's theory asserts that love objects are selected based on developmental experiences. All types of love, from the mother onward, are learned. It is not surprising, then, that many people learn to select someone of the same sex as a sexual partner. Although no consensus exists among researchers about the causes of homosexuality, Fisher and Greenberg (1977) concluded, on the basis of their review of available studies, that Freud's description of the typical parents of homosexual sons was accurate: a father who is unfriendly, threatening, or difficult to associate with, and a mother who is close and seductive to her son. Freud suggested that homosexual men have high castration anxiety, and Fisher and Greenberg's review of research confirmed that homosexual men are especially concerned about getting hurt and preoccupied with physical frailty. While lesbianism is less researched, Fisher and Greenberg reported that the fathers of homosexual women are, like those of homosexual men, also unfriendly and unpleasant. Nonetheless, critics charge that Freud's explanation of homosexuality did not take into account the very powerful social forces that vary from one culture to another and that influence the development of sexual preferences (Godbill, 1983). Freud believed that a tendency toward homosexuality might be inherited, an assertion that has not been confirmed by research.

Freud asserted that personality is largely formed during these first three psychosexual stages, when the basic ego mechanisms for dealing with libidinal impulses are established. If fixation has occurred, the specific neurosis will depend upon the stage at which development was impaired. Freud suggested that schizophrenia, paranoia or obsessional neurosis, and hysteria result from serious fixation at the first three stages, respectively (Sulloway, 1979). These correlations of personality or defensive style are based upon reconstructions from the psychoanalysis of adults. More direct evidence from observations of children has been undertaken (Bowlby, 1988; S. Brody, 1982; Schibuk, Bond, & Bouffard, 1989).

The Latency Period

Middle childhood is a period of relative calm for the sexual instincts, so Freud's model of libidinal tension says little about this stage. (It is, however, an important period of development according to other theories.)

The Genital Period

The **genital stage** begins at puberty. In contrast to the autoerotic and fantasy sexual objects of the phallic child, the genital adult develops the capacity to experience sexual satisfaction with an opposite-sex object. The **genital character** is Freud's ideal of full development. It develops if fixations have been avoided or if they have been resolved through psychoanalysis. Such a person has no significant pre-Oedipal conflicts, enjoys a satisfying sexuality, and cares about the satisfaction of the love partner, avoiding selfish narcissism.

Freud regarded neurosis as essentially a sexual dysfunction. Because of the inherent conflict between biological demands and the requirements of civilization, some degree of neurotic conflict is inevitable, but it could be minimized through enlightened acceptance of sexual needs. In the post-Freudian era, sexual performance and enjoyment are widely accepted as standards to be attained.

Psychoanalytic Treatment

In the healthy adult, both direct sexual satisfaction and indirect sublimation of sexual instincts occur, leading to Freud's famous criterion of mental health, *Lieben und Arbeiten*, that is, "love and work." Such an outcome occurs if there are no major fixations in development, or if fixations are resolved through psychoanalytic treatment. Freud described psychoanalysis with the metaphor of archaeology. The analytic process tries to "dig up" primitive material long "buried" by repression, and to bring it to the surface, to consciousness, so that it can be considered with the skills of the more developed ego. Freud's formula for achieving health is "Where id was, there shall ego be" (1933/1966a, p. 544).

The psychoanalyst uses the principle of psychic determinism to discover the unconscious ideas and conflicts of the patient. The basic technique of psychoanalysis is **free association**, which requires the patient "to say whatever came into his head, while ceasing to give any conscious direction to his thoughts" (S. Freud, 1935/1963a, p. 75). Suspension of conscious control allows the forces of the unconscious, which are usually obscured by the consciousness, to be observed directing thoughts and memories.

The emergence of buried feelings from the unconscious is called **catharsis**. These feelings, including fear and grief, often accompany the recall of forgotten memories. Like the removal of infectious material when a wound is lanced, catharsis frees the unconscious of troublesome repressions.

Psychoanalytic treatment produces **insight**, that is, understanding of true motives. To be therapeutic, insight must be accompanied by emotional awareness. While the insight into unconscious motivations, even if accompanied by emotional catharsis, is a major step toward overcoming the symptoms produced by the unconscious, it does not provide a magical, once-and-for-all cure. In addition to this dramatic recall, modern psychoanalysis recognizes that unconscious conflicts must be confronted again and again in a psychoanalytic treatment. The patient must "work through" the conflict, discovering the many circumstances that have been influenced by the conflict and essentially reconstructing personality to replace these unconscious irrational determinants with more reasonable and mature motivations.

A major phenomenon in psychoanalytic treatment is **transference**. During the course of psychoanalytic treatment, the patient develops a relationship to the therapist based on unconscious projections from earlier life. The patient perceives the therapist erroneously and experiences emotions that were repressed when felt toward earlier significant others. It is common, for example, for a female patient to "fall in love with" her male analyst based on transference into the analytic session of the love she felt for her father during childhood. Negative as well as positive emotions occur. Transference is, strangely enough, desirable. It permits the earlier unresolved issues to be present in the analytic session where they can be resolved. More problematic are the analyst's emotional reactions to the patient, termed **countertransference**, which may interfere with treatment because they represent the analyst's unresolved complexes. Some modern analysts, though, have become more receptive to countertransference as potentially providing useful information about the patient (Chessick, 1986; Jennings, 1986).

Psychoanalytic treatment is considerably more time-consuming and expensive than alternative modes of treatment. A typical analysis may take three to seven years, three sessions each week.

In his day, Freud's theory was a force for the humane treatment of the mentally ill because it interpreted their disorders as matters of disease (the "medical model"), rather than as moral failures. Critics argue that the medical model has adverse effects as well. It treats people as passive victims of pathological forces, undermining their active effort and responsibility for their own psychological well-being. The medical model tends to place the wisdom of the physician over the experience of the patient and is insensitive to the role of social factors in causing psychopathology (cf. Boyers, 1971; Steiner and others, 1975; Szasz, 1965). How ironic that Freud, whose theory began with the premise that the experience of patients must be taken seriously, should be criticized for such a shortcoming.

Empirical Verification

Freud's theory is frequently criticized as difficult to verify with scientific methods. Freudian concepts such as id, ego, libido, and repression cannot be seen physically, and it is difficult to measure them even indirectly. Self-report measures are problematic, since the theory itself is based on the premise that people have little insight into their own psychodynamics. Projective tests such as the Rorschach inkblot test (Pichot, 1984), which are commonly used to measure unconscious motivations, have low reliability, which impedes research.

For Freud, the psychoanalytic method provided the data to verify his theory, though others have frequently called for separate empirical verification (e.g., Rapaport, 1959b). The psychoanalytic tradition has generally been disinterested in subjecting psychoanalytic theory to verification outside the consulting room, and some still defend this source of evidence, recognizing its difficulties (e.g., Arlow, 1977; Jaffe, 1990; Meissner, 1990; Rubinstein, 1980; E.R. Wallace, 1989). Disinterest in research, however, has been seriously challenged, even from within psychoanalysis (e.g., Grünbaum, 1984, 1990; Holzman, 1985).

Is psychoanalysis any more effective than alternate therapies? There has been much scepticism even about Freud's own therapeutic effectiveness (e.g., Ellenberger, 1972; Mahony, 1986). For many psychological disorders, alternative therapies are as effective as psychoanalytic treatment (Wallerstein, 1989). For some problems (for example, phobias), psychoanalysis is less effective than alternative therapies (in this case, behavior therapy). For psychosomatic disorders, it seems to be more effective (Fisher & Greenberg, 1977).

Besides outcome studies, researchers study the process of psychoanalytic therapy, using clinicians' notes and even recordings of sessions in order to understand what particular therapy techniques work (e.g., E.E. Jones & Windholz, 1990; Wallerstein & Sampson, 1971; Weiss, 1988). These techniques provide data that are more reliable than the biased reporting of cases, which has occurred since the outset of psychoanalysis (Wolpe & Rachman, 1960). Insight seems less important to successful treatment than psychoanalytic theory predicts (Wallerstein, 1989).

Research has tested psychoanalytic hypotheses outside of therapy as well. According to the reviewers of this huge literature, some aspects of the theory fare well under such scrutiny, while others must be discarded (Greenberg & Fisher, 1978). (See Table 2.2.)

Fisher and Greenberg (1977), in reviewing research testing psychoanalytic propositions, found support for the concept of an oral character. Dependency, passivity, and pessimism, the oral personality traits, were significantly intercorrelated in several studies. Furthermore, oral imagery on the Rorschach inkblot test predicted obesity, alcoholism, and conformity. Fisher and Greenberg also concluded that the concept of an anal character is supported by research.

Silverman (1976, 1983) has conducted a series of evaluations that, unlike the above correlational studies, offer experimental tests of the unconscious. Calling his method *subliminal psychodynamic activation*, Silverman presented stimuli using a tachistoscope, which is essentially a slide projector beamed through a camera shutter. This device allows very brief presenta-

TABLE 2.2 Empirical Evidence Testing Psychoanalytic Theory

Freudian Concept	*Supports or Refutes Freud*	*Evidence*
Treatment	supports	Psychoanalytic patients do better than untreated controls.
	refutes	Psychoanalytic patients do no better than other therapies.
	supports	Psychoanalytic patients improve physically (ulcers, colitis, etc.)
Dreams	supports	Dreams vent tensions.
	supports	Dreams are more intense in neurotics, psychotics, and people under stress.
	refutes	Manifest content may be as revealing as latent content.
Homosexuality	insufficient evidence	Homosexuality may have a biological basis.
	supports	Fathers of homosexual men and women are unfriendly and threatening.
	supports	Male homosexuals are concerned about physical frailty ("castration").
Oedipus complex	supports	Children have erotic feelings toward the opposite-sex parent.
	supports	Children have hostile feelings toward the same-sex parent.
	supports	Sexually aroused men fear bodily harm ("castration").
	supports	Women are afraid of loss of love.
	refutes	Females do not regard their bodies as inferior.
	refutes	Sexually mature women do not prefer vaginal to clitoral stimulation.
Orality	supports	The oral traits—dependency, passivity and pessimism—are correlated.
	supports	Orals on the Rorschach crave approval and praise.
	supports	Orals are likely to overeat, smoke, and drink much alcohol.
Anality	supports	The anal traits—orderliness, parsimony and obstinacy—are correlated.
	supports	Anals are motivated by money.

(Adapted from Greenberg & Fisher, 1978.)

tions (4 milliseconds) of stimuli. Subjects reported that they could see only brief flickers of light. Though they could not consciously identify the subliminal messages, they were influenced by them. Schizophrenics exposed to a conflict-arousing stimulus, "I am losing Mommy," increased their psychotic symptoms. This is predicted by Freud's theory because a schizophrenic uses hallucination, a primitive ego defense mechanism of infancy, to deal with conflicts about losing the mother, the object just developing in the oral period. When Silverman's tachistoscope conveyed the unconscious message, "Mommy and I are one," psychotic symptoms were reduced, presumably because the conflict was unconsciously reduced.

Using other cues with other patient populations, Silverman claimed that unconscious arousal of the specific conflict identified by psychoanalytic theory to be associated with each diagnosis (e.g., oral conflict for schizophrenics, anal conflict for stutterers) could produce an increase or decrease of symptoms (Silverman, Bronstein, & Mendelsohn, 1976). An appropriate stimulus ("Beating Dad is OK") was even reported to improve dart-throwing performance in college males (Silverman, Ross, Adler, & Lustig, 1978). Silverman's later work tested the cue "Mommy and I are one" in a variety of populations. He reported that it had a variety of beneficial effects in reducing phobias (Silverman, Frank, & Dachinger, 1974), reducing homosexual threat (Silverman, Kwawer, Wolitzky, & Coron, 1973), and facilitating weight loss in obese women (Silverman, Martin, Ungaro, & Mendelsohn, 1978). If the stimuli were presented at longer exposures, so that they could be consciously recognized, then there was no effect on symptoms; only unconscious dynamics produced changes in symptoms. Silverman's work has been criticized for failures of replication and for methodological problems (Balay & Shevrin, 1988). One systematic statistical review of research using the subliminal activation technique concluded that it is effective in reducing pathology, and that replications by other researchers not associated with Silverman's laboratory also confirm the effect (Hardaway, 1990).

Silverman's work represents the most elaborate, but not the only, attempt to verify hypotheses derived from psychoanalytic theory through experimental research. Many experimental studies of repression have been conducted, though they often do not correspond precisely to Freud's conceptualization (Geisler, 1985). Other approaches, reviewed by Shulman (1990), include hypnotic induction of unconscious ideas to test their behavioral effects (e.g., Reyher, 1962) and examination of situational effects on Freudian slips (e.g., Motley, Baars, & Camden, 1983). Though others have criticized psychoanalytic concepts for being too vague to verify empirically, Shulman expressed optimism that psychoanalytic theory can be tested with well-controlled experimental studies.

Psychoanalysis and Neurology

Although Freud abandoned his early attempt to describe the neurological basis of psychic forces, those efforts have been revived. Researchers have sought to describe brain areas that correspond to psychodynamic structures (A.W. Epstein, 1987; Frick, 1982; L. Miller, 1989; Reiser, 1985; Stillman & Walker, 1989; Tinnin, 1989a, 1989b). Similarly, though Freud achieved a psychological transformation of biological instincts (Sulloway, 1979), some modern theorists have suggested that psychoanalysis can be merged with psychobiology (Leak & Christopher, 1982). Such neurological and sociobiological approaches, however, risk reductionism (Parisi, 1987), distracting attention from the psychic focus that Freud advocated.

Summary

Freud's psychoanalytic theory proposes that behavior is caused by psychological forces, according to the assumption of *psychic determinism.* Unconscious forces often overpower consciousness, producing symptoms of neurosis, dreams, and mistakes in everyday life. Dreams can be interpreted by seeking their symbolic meanings (*latent content*). The *unconscious* develops when unacceptable thoughts are repressed. Personality can be described in terms of three structures. The *id* functions according to primary process and the pleasure principle, unconsciously seeking immediate satisfaction of biologically based drives, and is the source of psychic energy (*libido*). The *ego* functions according to secondary process and the reality principle; it adapts to reality using defense mechanisms to cope with intrapsychic conflict. The *superego* represents society's restrictions, and produces guilt and an ego ideal. (See Table 2.3 for a summary of Freud's contributions.)

Personality develops through five psychosexual stages. It is largely formed during the *oral, anal,* and *phallic* stages, which occur from birth to age 5. The *latency* stage provides a lull before the final, *genital,* stage of adulthood. Fixation, especially at the first three stages, impedes development and may produce symptoms treatable by *psychoanalysis.* The basic technique of psychoanalysis is *free association*, which permits discovery of unconscious material. Other key elements of treatment are dream interpretation, catharsis, and insight.

Though most psychoanalysts, like Freud, believe that the observations of psychoanalytic treatment provide sufficient evidence for the theory, others have attempted empirical verification through research, with mixed results. Some modern theorists are trying to find neurological bases of psychoanalytic phenomena, bringing Freud's model full circle to its historical origins.

TABLE 2.3 Contributions of Freud's Theory to Various Topics

Biological	Sexual motivation is the basis of personality. Hereditary differences may influence level of libido and phenomena such as homosexuality.
Child Development	Experience in the first five years is critical for personality formation. The oral, anal, and phallic (Oedipal) psychosexual conflicts are central.
Adult Development	Adult personality changes very little.
Mental Health	Health involves the ability to love and to work. Psychoanalysis provides a method for overcoming early fixations, through insight and catharsis.
Society	All societies deal with universal human conflicts. Traditional religion is challenged.
Cognitive Processes	Conscious experience cannot be trusted because of defense mechanisms.
Individual Differences	People differ in their ego defense mechanisms, which control expression of primitive forces in personality.

ILLUSTRATIVE BIOGRAPHIES: CONCLUDING REMARKS

Georgia O'Keeffe believed that her paintings were studies in form, with no symbolic meaning. Adolf Hitler aspired to rule a restored German nation, and he justified atrocities beyond description to purify the race. Freudian theory challenges the conscious self-perceptions of the creative genius as well as the psychopathic demagogue, finding core human motivations buried deep in the unconscious mind.

Georgia O'Keeffe

How can psychoanalysis help us understand the creativity of an artist such as Georgia O'Keeffe? While the good fortune of her genetic giftedness is beyond the scope of the theory, psychoanalysis does describe the dynamics that allow the blossoming of creative potential and interprets the particular directions in which it is expressed.

Childhood is the critical time for personality development, according to Freudian theory. The available evidence suggests that O'Keeffe's childhood was free of obvious trauma. She said of herself, "I seem to be one of the few people I know of to have no complaints against my first twelve years" (Lisle, 1980, p. 23). She was not overprotected, but was given room to develop her individuality. Indeed, her mother was cool and aloof and seemed to favor Georgia's older brother and a younger sister. Consequently, she became closer to her father. Close identification with the father, in fact, is a common pattern among creative women.

There is no indication that O'Keeffe was sexually inhibited in the coarsest sense (although she did not show much interest in males while in school, focusing on her painting instead). She lived openly with Alfred Stieglitz as his lover even while he was married to his first wife, and she posed for his many photographs of her, including sensuous nude photos. Stieglitz, old enough to be her father, could have been a father substitute whom she seduced away from his first wife, as Freud would say she had unconsciously wished to seduce her father away from her mother.

The major psychoanalytic concept for understanding artists is the concept of *sublimation*. Sublimation occurs when libidinal drives are transformed into socially desirable outlets, including painting. In art, unfulfilled sexual motivation may be expressed symbolically.

To many observers, O'Keeffe's paintings of flowers, with their emphasis on concave spaces and openings, look like female genitals, and the hills of her New Mexico landscapes also resemble the female body. One flower painting was similar enough to human anatomy that a father used it to illustrate a sex education lesson for his young daughter! Her paintings of Jack-in-the-pulpit flowers show exaggerated phallic-like "jacks." In addition, her first individual show contained a single sculpture, an object much resembling a phallus. Could these be artistic expressions of sexual longing and penis envy?

Georgia O'Keeffe described an early childhood episode in which she was trying to paint a male figure. She couldn't get it right; the knees were at the wrong angle. When she turned the man on his back, it looked right! Could this symbolize an unconscious desire to overturn men? As an adult, Georgia took pride in attaining recognition in a predominantly male field. Such competition toward men, according to psychoanalytic theory, comes from unresolved penis envy.

Freud regarded having children as the normal, healthy resolution of feminine conflicts over penis envy. However, Stieglitz discouraged Georgia from having children, fearing that it would interfere with her artistic development. O'Keeffe recognized that an artist could not paint if subjected to a child's interruptions. Freudian theory would add to these practical considerations the concept of psychic economy; libidinal energy would have been expressed in motherhood, and so would be unavailable for sublimated symbolic expression through painting.

O'Keeffe discounted Freudian interpretation of her work, saying that the forms themselves interested her. Flowers were simply flowers, not symbols of genitals; skulls were simply beautiful forms, not symbols of death; and a sun-bleached pelvic bone did not symbolize her own empty birth canal. From a psychoanalytic perspective, however, consciousness is limited, so that conscious denial does not disprove unconscious symbolism. Perhaps O'Keeffe would have protested less vigorously had she appreciated that the most positive interpretation Freudian theory can make about any personality is to say that sexual energy is sublimated.

Adolf Hitler

Can psychoanalysis help us understand Hitler and his mass destructiveness? Freud's concept of *Thanatos*, the "death instinct," is of obvious relevance. (In fact, Freud developed this theoretical concept late in his life; one could argue that Hitler's role in history influenced this concept in Freud's theory.) According to the concept of Thanatos, aggression and violence are inherent to human nature, whether expressed against others (as in the "final solution" of the extermination camps) or against oneself (as in Hitler's suicide).

Hitler's biography provides ample evidence of psychopathology. As a general description of mental health, Freud said that a healthy person loves and works. In late adolescence and early adulthood, Hitler was a loafer. Despite the fact that his father was dead (having died when Hitler was 14), his mother was fatally ill, and the family needed money, Hitler refused to work. In terms of love, reports of his sexual encounters with women are replete with tales of perversity (Waite, 1977). He did not marry until shortly before his suicide, when, in his Berlin bunker, he married his longtime lover, Eva Braun.

There are many "symptoms" evidenced in Hitler's life. At various times he is reported to have suffered from hysterical blindness, insomnia, and sexual perversions. More serious were his delusions (false beliefs). Hitler is reported to have thrown a tantrum when the lottery ticket he had purchased did not win, contrary to his firm belief that it would. Late in the war, he suffered delusions about the movements of fantasy troops. These false beliefs are typical of psychotics. It is likely, however, that some of his later symptoms were due to drugs prescribed by his doctor; these drugs were reportedly made more powerful through tampering by spies.

As one might expect of a severely disturbed personality, difficulties can be related to the various developmental stages, but especially the oral period (because of maternal overprotectiveness) and the phallic period (because of trauma and an abusive father). Oral fixation is evidenced by Hitler's cravings for sweets, his vegetarianism, and his habit of sucking his fingers.

Hitler's lack of a moral sense would be expected because of difficulties in the Oedipal period, interfering with superego development. When Hitler was 3 years old, he thought he saw his drunk father rape his mother. This incident constitutes psychic trauma, and would impede development at this period. Hitler's father was often away from home, at work or at the local pub. Because of his job, the father lived apart from the family for a year when Adolf was 5. When he was at home the father was a severe disciplinarian and frequently beat Adolf. Adolf felt fear and hatred toward his father and lacked the positive role model essential for normal development of the superego and a masculine identity.

Problems with sexuality are readily apparent in Hitler's biography. He was a late maturer, and was missing a left testicle. He buoyed up his sense of self-worth by injecting himself with bull testicles and by projecting onto women his fear of sexuality. Even the Nazi salute, a stiff raised hand, has been described as a symbolic erect penis. Once Hitler boasted to a female visitor, "I can hold my arm like that for two solid hours. I never feel tired. . . . I never move. My arm is like granite—rigid and unbending. . . . That is four times as long as Goering. . . . I marvel at my own power" (Waite, 1977, p. 49). He was, symbolically, claiming sexual potency.

The defense mechanism of "projection" occurred on a massive scale in Hitler's life. Hitler echoed and amplified the anti-Semitic feelings of his era, and the Jewish people became projective targets for repressed characteristics. Some biographers have argued that Hitler's own grandfather was Jewish, and that denial of this ancestry intensified his persecution of the Jewish people. Loewenberg (1988) suggests that Hitler was aware that "the real enemy lay within" (p. 143); perhaps Hitler's projection of evil onto Jews was not entirely unconscious, but rather a political strategy.

Anti-Semitism was not unique to Hitler, but rather contributed to his popularity as a charismatic leader. Indeed, whenever the citizenry of a country feel frustrated (as the German people did because of the oppressive political conditions imposed on Germany after World War I), they are likely to elevate a leader who gives expression to their unresolved conflicts. Thus we may understand Hitler's psychopathology from the perspective of personality theory; but the magnification of these pathologies on the pages of history requires an historical understanding.

How does it come to be that one person's psychodynamics lead to atrocities beyond description, while for another the unconscious produces beautiful and creative works of art? Both creative and destructive potentials exist in all of us. It is noteworthy that Hitler tried, but failed, as an artist. Yet not every failed artist becomes a demagogue.

For Freud, the conditions of drive satisfaction in early life determine character structure. A strong ego, capable of umpiring the forces of the unconscious, must develop gradually, protected from psychic trauma and supported by nurturant and guiding parents in areas it cannot yet master. From a Freudian perspective, then, the parents, especially the mother, are credited or (more often) blamed for the child's personality. Hitler's mother was overprotective, and his father was abusive. Georgia O'Keeffe's childhood was more favorable. Thus, Hitler's ego never was strong enough to contain his destructive id impulses, whereas O'Keeffe, the creative artist, could explore her libidinal forces symbolically, secure in the ego strength that her development provided. The ego, for Freud, is the source of mental health and the hope of civilization.

GLOSSARY

anal character personality type resulting from fixation at age 1 to 3, characterized by orderliness, parsimony, and obstinacy

anal stage the second psychosexual stage of development, from age 1 to 3

castration anxiety fear that motivates male development at age 3 to 5

catharsis therapeutic effect of a release of emotion when previously repressed material is made conscious

cathexis investment of psychic energy in an object

condensation combining of two or more images; characteristic of primary processes (e.g., in dreams)

conscious aware; cognizant; mental processes of which a person is unaware

conversion hysteria form of neurosis in which psychological conflicts are expressed in physical symptoms (without actual physical damage)

countertransference the analyst's reaction to the patient, as distorted by unresolved conflicts

defense mechanisms ego strategies for coping with unconscious conflict

denial primitive defense mechanism in which material that produces conflict is simply repressed

displacement defense mechanism in which energy is transferred from one object or activity to another

ego the most mature structure of personality; mediates intrapsychic conflict and copes with the external world

Eros the life instinct

fixation failure to develop normally through a particular developmental stage

free association psychoanalytic technique in which the patient says whatever comes to mind, permitting unconscious connections to be discovered

Freudian slip a psychologically motivated error in speech, hearing, behavior, and so forth (for example, forgetting the birthday of a disliked relative)

genital character healthy personality type

genital stage the adult psychosexual stage

id the most primitive structure of personality; the source of psychic energy

identification defense mechanism in which a person fuses or models after another person

insight conscious recognition of one's motivation

intellectualization defense mechanism in which a person focuses on thinking and avoids feeling

intrapsychic conflict conflict within the personality, as between id desires and superego restrictions

isolation defense mechanism in which conflictful material is kept disconnected from other thoughts

latent content the hidden, unconscious meaning of a dream

libido psychic energy, derived from sexuality

manifest content the surface meaning of a dream

Oedipus conflict conflict that males experience from age 3 to 5 involving sexual love for the mother and aggressive rivalry with the father

oral character personality type resulting from fixation in the first psychosexual stage; characterized by optimism, passivity, and dependency

oral stage the first psychosexual stage of development, from birth to age 1

parapraxis (plural: *-es*) a psychologically motivated error, more commonly called a "Freudian slip"

phallic stage the third psychosexual stage of development, from age 3 to 5

pleasure principle the id's motivation to seek pleasure and to avoid pain

preconscious mental content of which a person is currently unaware, but which can readily be made conscious

primary process unconscious mental functioning in which the id predominates; characterized by illogical, symbolic thought

psychoanalysis Freud's theory, and its application in therapy

projection defense mechanism in which a person's own unacceptable impulse is incorrectly thought to belong to someone else

rationalization defense mechanism in which reasonable, conscious explanations are offered rather than true unconscious motivations

reaction formation defense mechanism in which a person thinks or behaves in a manner opposite to the unacceptable unconscious impulse

reality principle the ego's mode of functioning in which there is appropriate contact with the external world

repression defense mechanism in which unacceptable impulses are made unconscious

secondary process conscious mental functioning in which the ego predominates; characterized by logical thought

sublimation defense mechanism in which impulses are expressed in socially acceptable ways

superego structure of personality that is the internal voice of parental and societal restrictions

Thanatos the death instinct

transference in therapy, the patient's displacement onto the therapist of feelings based on earlier experiences (e.g., with the patient's own parents)

unconscious mental processes of which a person is unaware

STUDY QUESTIONS

1. Describe what Freud claimed was revolutionary about his theory of personality.
2. Explain the concept of *psychic determinism.*
3. Briefly describe what is found in the conscious, preconscious, and unconscious levels of the mind. How are these levels like an iceberg?
4. How does *conversion hysteria* illustrate psychic determinism?
5. Describe a Freudian approach to dream interpretation. Explain, in your answer, the terms *manifest content* and *latent content.*
6. Describe how repression produces the unconscious.
7. List the three structures of personality. Describe each one.
8. List and explain the four characteristics of instincts.
9. Distinguish between primary process and secondary process.
10. What is *intrapsychic conflict?* Describe the roles of the id, ego, and superego in this conflict.

11. Explain the *energy hypothesis.* How does this hypothesis interpret the benefits of psychoanalytic therapy?
12. List and explain the three types of anxiety.
13. What is the purpose of defense mechanisms? List several defense mechanisms and give examples of them.
14. Explain *sublimation.* Give an example.
15. Describe development through the five psychosexual stages.
16. Discuss the controversy over Freud's *seduction hypothesis.*
17. Describe psychoanalytic treatment. What is its basic technique?
18. Discuss empirical evidence testing psychoanalytic theory.

CHAPTER 

Jung: Analytical Psychology

BIOGRAPHY OF CARL JUNG

Carl Jung

Carl Gustav Jung was born in Switzerland in 1875, the son of a Protestant minister. Jung had one sister, who was nine years his junior. His father and several uncles were Protestant clergymen. Jung suspected, even as a child, that his father did not genuinely believe the Church's teachings but was afraid to face his doubts honestly. Jung's mother was emotionally unstable and, according to Jung, psychic.

As a young psychiatrist, Jung lectured at the University of Zurich, developed a word-association technique for uncovering the emotional complexes of his patients, and had a private practice. He greeted Freud's work on psychoanalysis enthusiastically and supported it in his own professional writing, even though it was controversial. After a period of mutually admiring correspondence, the two met at Freud's office in Vienna. This first meeting lasted 13 hours, attesting to the breadth of their mutual interest and respect. They continued an active correspondence, which has been published (McGuire, 1974). They traveled together to the United States in 1909 to present psychoanalysis at the G. Stanley Hall Conference at Clark University, and both were well received (Jung, 1910/1987).

Jung presided over a psychoanalytic association in Zurich, and Freud intended to have Jung succeed him as president of the International Psychoanalytic Association, thinking it would be advantageous to broaden psychoanalysis beyond its Jewish circle. He conveyed this intent to Jung in a letter in which he referred to Jung as a "crown prince," and Jung responded with gratitude, referring to Freud as a father figure.

Before this could be achieved, however, the personal relationship between Freud and Jung was disrupted. There were intellectual disagreements, to be sure; Jung felt that Freud overemphasized the role of sexuality in his theory and underestimated the potential of the unconscious to contribute positively to psychological growth. It was a personal conflict as well as an intellectual one (Goldwert, 1986; Marcovitz, 1982; Stern, 1976), part of a mid-life crisis in which Jung withdrew from his academic pursuits and devoted himself to introspection. His own personal conflicts, explored in this period, have been interpreted in terms of fragmentation of the self, which in his case did not lead to the pathology that such splits sometimes produce (Ticho, 1982). Jung believed that Freud's emphasis on maintaining his authority prevented him (Freud) from dealing fully with his own unconscious conflicts, while Freud feared that Jung had abandoned science for mysticism.

Jung had long been interested in mystical phenomena. His medical dissertation had reported experiments on his cousin, a spiritualistic "medium." In later life he continued subjective explorations of the unconscious, read esoteric texts on mysticism and alchemy, and built a primitive retreat at Bollingen, on Lake Zurich. He reported several personal experiences of psychic phenomena, which he understood as manifestations of a broad, transpersonal "collective unconscious." For example, Jung is said to have dreamt of Winston Churchill whenever the English politician came near Switzerland, even though Jung had no conscious awareness of his coming (G. Wehr, 1988, p. 357). Understanding this collective unconscious was Jung's major life task. Indeed, legend has it that many of Jung's students had nightmares before learning of his death in 1961.

ILLUSTRATIVE BIOGRAPHIES

In addition to case histories (e.g., C.N. Lewis, 1990), Jungian theory has much potential for psychobiographical analysis. Greene (1976), for example, has used Jungian concepts to understand American politicians, including Richard Nixon and Lyndon Johnson. Jungian theory describes personality differences in introversion and extroversion and in cognitive and emotional functions that are basic dimensions of individual differences. These dimensions offer a basic typology for classifying people. Furthermore, Jungian theory attempts to understand phenomena that even Freud avoided. It recognizes a level of human experience that transcends the personal. This collective experience may be experienced in many ways. Some, like Martin Luther King, Jr., devote themselves to collective tasks of social justice. Others, like Shirley MacLaine, report paranormal experiences of the irrational.

Shirley MacLaine

Shirley MacLaine is a gifted dancer and Oscar-winning movie actress. She has published a series of autobiographical books since 1970 (MacLaine, 1970, 1975, 1983, 1985, 1987) that describe her childhood in Virginia and her ongoing relationship with both parents, her marriage and its dissolution, her child, and an assortment of love affairs, as we have come to expect of Hollywood personalities. What has caught the attention of the media and of the public is Shirley MacLaine's vivid descriptions of paranormal experiences, including ESP and control of the weather.

She claims to have experienced out-of-body experiences ("astral projections") and to recall a diversity of previous incarnations, including life as a nomadic woman in the Gobi Desert, as a young Inca male training for mystical experience, and as a blind Japanese singer. In many of these former lives, she claims, she interacted with people now reincarnated in her present life, and their current interactions are shaped by the karma of unfulfilled issues from past lives.

What are we to make of these astounding tales? Has Ms. MacLaine gone off the deep end, experiencing psychotic-like delusions? Has she simply found a clever angle for selling books? Does personality theory have anything to say about reports of such paranormal experiences, or is this entirely outside the bounds of psychology as science? The theory of Carl Jung treats such reports with respect, and offers a framework for a psychological understanding of accounts of psychic phenomena. (Most other theories, to be sure, avoid such topics entirely or label such experiences as abnormal.)

ANALYTICAL PSYCHOLOGY

Like Freud, Carl Jung proposed a theory of personality that gives a prominent role to the unconscious. For Jung, however, the libido was not primarily sexual, but was a broad psychic energy with spiritual dimensions. Jung described the most interesting personality developments as occurring in adulthood, not in childhood. Like Freud, Jung allowed himself to experience the unconscious firsthand through dreams and fantasies, comparing his role to that of an explorer. He considered himself strong enough to make

Martin Luther King, Jr.

Martin Luther King, Jr., was a world-famous black American whose leadership role in the nonviolent civil rights movement was honored with a Nobel Peace Prize in 1964 (Garrow, 1986). He was still, then, a young man, a Baptist minister in a segregated congregation, and the father of four young children, the oldest only 8 years old. Within less than four years, at the age of 39, King was assassinated, leaving his widow, Coretta Scott King, to raise their family (C.S. King, 1969), and his fellow civil rights activists to continue the struggle for racial equality in America.

What insights can Jungian theory give into the personality of this world-famous American? What made him decide, despite early reservations, to become a minister like his father and grandfather, and then to assume a national leadership role, although it required neglecting the more personal demands of his congregation, his family, and his own health?

this dangerous voyage and to come back to tell others what he found there. Unlike Freud, who tried to understand the unconscious from the objective perspective of a scientist, Jung felt that science was an inadequate tool for knowing the psyche.

Jung preferred to describe the psyche in the language of mythology, rather than science. He rejected "rational, scientific language" in favor of

> a dramatic, mythological way of thinking and speaking, because this is not only more expressive but also more exact than an abstract scientific terminology, which is wont to toy with the notion that its theoretical formulations may one fine day be resolved into algebraic equations. (Jung, 1959, p. 13)

Needless to say, this anti-scientific attitude places Jung outside mainstream psychology. Even Freud was vehemently opposed to Jung's mysticism. Nonetheless, many people have found that his sensitive description of symbols offers therapeutic guidance through personal experience of the unconscious. Jung's work strengthens the bridge Freud had begun between psychology and symbolic expressions in literature, art, and religion.

Psychological Types

Jung's description of personality types is one of the more straightforward aspects of his theory. People vary along three dimensions: introversion-extroversion; thinking-feeling; and sensation-intuition. To describe a person's psychological type, it is first necessary to determine the fundamental attitude of the individual, whether oriented toward the inner world (introversion) or toward external reality (extroversion). Next, one assesses which of four psychological functions (thinking, feeling, sensation, or intuition) the person prefers. This is labeled the **dominant function**. The dominant function is directed toward external reality if the person is an extrovert, or toward the inner world if the person is an introvert (O'Roark, 1990). Finally, which of the other functions is preferred for dealing with the other direction (internal reality for an extrovert, external reality for an introvert)? This is labeled the **auxiliary function** (see Figure 3.1).

The fundamental attitudes (introversion and extroversion) can be combined with the four functions (thinking, feeling, sensation, and intuition) in eight different ways, constituting eight *psychetypes* (see Table 3.1).

Jung described the four psychic functions as constituting two pairs of functions. The two "rational functions," thinking and feeling, enable us to make judgments or decisions. The two "irrational functions," sensation and intuition, provide us with information upon which to base these judgments. If the dominant function is a rational (decision) function, then the auxiliary function will be an irrational (information-gathering) function, and vice versa (McCaulley, 1990).

Altogether, considering both the psychetype and the auxiliary function, 16 different patterns are possible, which are listed in Table 3.2.

Introversion and Extroversion

Even people with no psychological training use the terms "introverts" and "extroverts" to indicate whether people are shy or sociable. Introverts withdraw from company, whereas extroverts mix easily with other people.

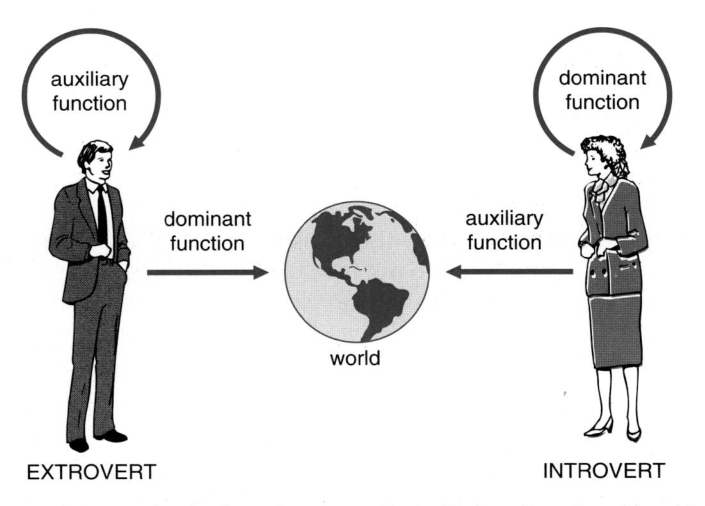

An extroverted type uses the dominant function to deal with the external world and the auxiliary function to deal with inner reality. An introverted type uses the dominant function to deal with inner reality and the auxiliary function to deal with the external world.

FIGURE 3.1 The Dominant and Auxiliary Functions in Extroverts and Introverts

TABLE 3.1 Personality Psychetypes

Introverted Thinking	Interested in ideas (rather than facts); interested in inner reality; pays little attention to other people
Introverted Feeling	Superficially reserved, but sympathetic and understanding of close friends or of others in need; loving, but not demonstrative
Introverted Sensation	emphasizes the experience that events trigger rather than the events themselves (ex: musicians and artists)
Introverted Intuition	concerned with possibilities rather than what is currently present; in touch with the unconscious
Extroverted Thinking	interested in facts about objects external to the self; logical; represses emotions and feelings; neglects friends and relationships
Extroverted Feeling	concerned with human relationships; adjusted to the environment (especially frequent among women, according to Jung)
Extroverted Sensation	emphasizes the objects that trigger experience; attentive to facts and details, and sometimes pleasure-seeking
Extroverted Intuition	concerned with possibilities for change in the external world rather than with the familiar; an adventurer

(Adapted from Fordham, 1966.)

Jung described the subjective experience of these types. Introverts turn their attention and their libido inward, to their own thoughts and inner states, while extroverts direct their energy and attention outward, to people and experiences in the world. The orientations of these two types are so fundamentally different that they often do not understand one another. The extrovert, unaware of his or her own inner dynamics, thinks the introvert is "egotistical and dull." The introvert, minimally concerned with other people, regards the extrovert as "superficial and insincere" (Fordham, 1966, p. 33).

Jung believed that introverts and extroverts were so fundamentally different in orientation that they could not be close friends in the long run. He understood his own personal conflict with Freud as an example of such a clash of types. Jung's introversion was always suspect to the extrovert, Freud. Knowing the basis for such interpersonal conflicts cannot eliminate conflict, but it can at least provide a counterforce against the tendency to devalue the other type of person.

Jung believed that a person remains an introvert or an extrovert, without change, for a lifetime. Heredity determines whether the libido is directed to "flow inward" to the inner world or to "flow outward" to external reality. This stability of the introversion-extroversion trait, incidentally, is consistent with empirical research using non-Jungian measures of introversion and extroversion.

TABLE 3.2 Personality Psychetypes with Auxiliary Functions

Attitude and Dominant Function	*Auxiliary Function*	*MBTI Type*
Introverted Thinking	Sensation	ISTP
Introverted Thinking	Intuition	INTP
Introverted Feeling	Sensation	ISFP
Introverted Feeling	Intuition	INFP
Introverted Sensation	Thinking	ISTJ
Introverted Sensation	Feeling	ISFJ
Introverted Intuition	Thinking	INTJ
Introverted Intuition	Feeling	INFJ
Extroverted Thinking	Sensation	ESTJ
Extroverted Thinking	Intuition	ENTJ
Extroverted Feeling	Sensation	ESFJ
Extroverted Feeling	Intuition	ENFJ
Extroverted Sensation	Thinking	ESTP
Extroverted Sensation	Feeling	ESFP
Extroverted Intuition	Thinking	ENTP
Extroverted Intuition	Feeling	ENFP

Note: The last column describes the personality type as scored from the Myers-Briggs Type Indicator. In order, the letters correspond to Introversion (I) or Extroversion (E), Sensation (S) or Intuition (N), Thinking (T) or Feeling (F), and Perception (P) or Judging (J).

The Four Functions

THINKING AND FEELING

Thinking and **feeling** are alternative ways of making value judgments. Some people decide what is worthwhile by how they feel emotionally, whether positive or negative. They "go for it" if emotions are positive, such as excitement, pleasure, or joy. They avoid doing what brings negative emotions, such as anxiety, pain, or sorrow. As examples of "feeling types" Malone (1977) lists Emily Dickinson, Albert Schweitzer, Norman Mailer, Gerald Ford, and Vincent van Gogh.

Other people think things through logically, considering reasons and principles. Benjamin Franklin, who led a carefully organized life and kept systematic records of his efforts toward his goals, was a thinking type. Malone (1977) lists Sigmund Freud, Jimmy Carter, Aristotle, Albert Einstein, and John F. Kennedy among his examples of "thinking types."

Ultimately, if development continues toward a healthy maturity, an adult must develop a balance between thinking and feeling. A person who, in youth, makes decisions emotionally must ultimately learn to think things through logically as well, and a coldly logical person must learn to pay attention to feelings.

SENSATION AND INTUITION

Sensation and **intuition** are complementary ways of getting information about the world. The sensation type knows what comes through the five senses: what is seen, heard, touched, tasted, or smelled. The sensation type is unlikely to take hints, for to do so requires making an inference beyond the concrete details. President Harry Truman, famous for his "I'm from Missouri, show me!" attitude, exemplifies the sensation type's concern with concrete details. This type risks becoming so focused on the particularities of a situation that he or she may miss the big picture. Among "sensation types" Malone (1977) includes Ernest Hemingway, Mohandas Gandhi, Joe Namath, Burt Reynolds, and Richard Nixon.

The intuitive type person is very good at grasping the big picture, although often unable to say exactly why he or she understands it. Jung suggested that intuitive types are skilled at knowing what other people experience, almost seeming like mind readers in their ability to get on the same wavelength as others. That's because the other person gives off cues unconsciously and unintentionally, and the intuitive-type person picks those up, often with uncanny accuracy. Given their ability to "read between the lines," they often recognize potential developments in situations that the detail-oriented sensation type misses. Intuition is higher among creative and artistic people (Sundberg, 1965). Among "intuitive types" Malone (1977) includes Richard Wagner, General George Patton, Walt Disney, Carl Jung, and Marilyn Monroe.

Like the thinking-feeling dimension, the sensation-intuition dimension develops through adulthood. Eventually an adult should develop both skills, however one-sided he or she may have been when younger.

Malone (1977) offers dozens of examples of each type. Obviously, great diversity exists within each type because of the influence of the other functions and individual life experiences, among other factors. People with similar career choices are often not placed in the same category by Malone, which is somewhat surprising given the correlations between personality and occupational choice reported in many empirical studies. Of course, his categorization is based on his own impressions of the personalities, since these famous persons did not take standard personality tests.

Measurement and Research

Although other tests have been devised (Keirsey & Bates, 1978; Ware, Yokomoto, & Morris, 1985; Wheelwright, Wheelwright, & Buehler, 1964), the most commonly used psychological test for measuring the Jungian functions is the **Myers-Briggs Type Indicator** (Briggs & Myers, 1976; McCaulley, 1990; Myers & McCaulley, 1985), which gives scores for introversion-extroversion, and the four paired functions (thinking-feeling and sensation-intuition). An additional dimension indicates how the external world is approached (judging-perceiving). This fourth dimension indicates the dominant function of extroverts as either a judging function (thinking or feeling, whichever was higher) or a perceiving function (sensation or intuition, whichever was higher); for introverts, it identifies the auxiliary function (McCaulley, 1990). Because the Myers-Briggs Type Indicator specifies the auxiliary function in addition to the basic psychetype, it produces 16 types, rather than only 8 (see Table 3.2). A comparable Type Indicator for children has more recently been developed (Meisgeier & Murphy, 1987). Seegmiller and Epperson (1987) have demonstrated that the thinking-feeling dimension can be coded from samples of spoken verbal material.

Research using the Myers-Briggs Type Indicator confirms that it is a reliable and valid measure (J.G. Carlson, 1985; J.B. Murray, 1990; Thompson & Borrello, 1986) that correlates with other psychological tests as one would expect (e.g., J.B. Campbell & Heller, 1987). The four scales have been confirmed by the statistical technique of factor analysis, which will be described in a later chapter (Johnson & Saunders, 1990; Thompson & Borrello, 1986; Tzeng, Ware, & Chen, 1989), although the dimensions are not entirely independent. In particular, the sensing-intuition and judging-perception dimensions have often been found to be correlated. Some questions have been raised about specific scales. Perhaps the extroversion dimension is simply sociability, rather than the more general "turning energy outward," which Jung proposed. The judgment-perception scale seems to tap impulsivity (Sipps & Alexander, 1987; Sipps & DiCaudo, 1988). It has also been suggested that an alternative measurement procedure, which did not pair the scales but measured them separately, would be better able to measure the differentiation of each function within people, as Jung proposed should occur with development (Cowan, 1989; but see the rebuttal by O'Roark, 1990). Despite these concerns, the scales of the Myers-Briggs instrument have stood up well to empirical testing.

Research supports the idea that people behave differently depending upon their psychological type. The Myers-Briggs Type Indicator has been used extensively in research, guidance, and especially in business (Bubenzer, Zimpfer, & Mahrle, 1990). It is said by one reviewer to be "the most widely used personality instrument for nonpsychiatric populations" (J.B. Murray, 1990, p. 1187). Although Jung's theory refers to "types" rather than "traits" (as distinguished in Chapter 1), evidence is more consistent with an interpretation of the four bipolar scales as continuous, thus trait-like, rather than discontinuous, yielding discrete personality types (J.B. Murray, 1990).

Correlates of the Myers-Briggs scales support the meanings given to these measures. Extroversion is correlated with other psychological measures of that trait (Apostal & Marks, 1990; Sipps & Alexander, 1987). Extroverts are higher in Self-Monitoring than are introverts (Hicks, 1985; Mill, 1984) and are more likely to work in sales (Sundberg, 1965). Introversion, measured by the Keirsey-Bates Temperament Sorter, is correlated with subclinical depression in a college student sample (Lester, 1989a).

Higher scores on Intuition are correlated with more frequent recall of archetypal dreams (Cann & Donderi, 1986), greater creativity (Myers & McCaulley, 1985), and greater accuracy interpreting facial expression of emotion (Carlson & Levy, 1973). Intuition is reported to be related to higher scores on Type T, a measure of thrill-seeking (Morehouse, Farley, & Youngquist, 1990); this surprising finding may be clarified by further research distinguishing various types of Type T (mental, physical, and so forth). Sensation types are overrepresented among people with coronary heart disease (Thorne, Fyfe, & Carskadon, 1987). Professional psychodramatists are most frequently extroverted-intuitive types with feeling as an auxiliary function (Type ENFP) (Buchanan & Taylor, 1986).

Besides the four usual dimensions, the Myers-Briggs instrument can also be scored for creativity. Intuitive-perceptive types are more creative (Myers & McCaulley, 1985; Tegano, 1990).

In business and other organizations, training advocates propose that decision making can be improved through awareness that people's decision-making style varies with psychological type (Olson, 1990; Rideout & Richardson, 1989). Sensation types have been found to perform better than Intuitive types on computer-simulated business decisions (Davis, Grove, & Knowles, 1990). The Myers-Briggs instrument has been used successfully in stress-reduction interventions, based on the assumption that people of different psychological types do not experience stress the same way (Goodspeed & DeLucia, 1990).

Depending on psychological type, students approach their work differently. Whether students approach academic advisement with an emphasis on detail (Sensation types) or breadth of information (Intuitive types) varies with psychological type (J.B. Crockett & Crawford, 1989). Psychological type has been studied in relation to a variety of academic issues, including course selection (E.S. Martin, 1989), learning styles and strategies (Ehrman & Oxford, 1989; Fourqurean, Meisgeier, & Swank, 1990), and teacher certification exam scores (Schurr, Ruble, Henriksen, & Alcorn, 1989). Some researchers have recommended tailoring educational activities to students of different psychological types, although this is probably a premature application of the research. At any rate, it can be concluded that the theory of Jungian types helps to understand the diversity of ways in which students experience the educational environment. The applicability of the type measure to education supports the construct validity of the measure.

The psychological functions have been described as cognitive differences (e.g., R. Carlson, 1980; Davis, Grove, & Knowles, 1990; Ruble & Cosier, 1990), and it is sensible that the above studies would find them useful in understanding problem solving (Hunter & Levy, 1982) in work and school settings. These cognitive differences also have implications for phenomena that have been studied by social psychologists. One such area is research on eyewitness testimony. Ward and Loftus (1985) reported that when eyewitnesses were questioned about what they had seen, Introverted and Intuitive types (measured by the Myers-Briggs Type Indicator) were particularly influenced by the wording of questions. If questions were misleading (for example, referring to a stop sign that really wasn't there), Introverted and Intuitive subjects made more errors of recollection. On the other hand, if questions were consistent with what was seen, these types gave more accurate testimony than did their opposite (Extraverted and Sensation) types. The reason for this effect is unclear, although the researchers suggest that Intuitive Introverts are particularly unlikely to trust their own senses, and hence are influenced by immediate information from questions (see Figure 3.2).

Another experiment also demonstrates the differential impact of environmental manipulations on people depending on psychological type. A robust finding in social psychology is the "fundamental attribution error" (Ross, 1977), a finding of particular interest to personality psychologists. What is the fundamental attribution error? Most people attribute too much importance to personality and too little importance to situations when they give reasons for other people's behavior. For example, when reading essays said to have been written by other students that take a position on a social issue (anti-abortion, pro-abortion, anti-nuclear arms, pro-nuclear arms, and so

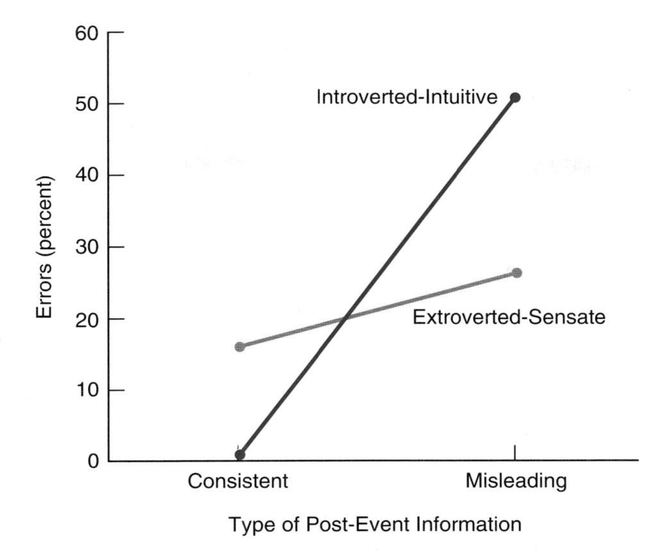

FIGURE 3.2 Errors in Eyewitness Testimony for Two Psychetypes

(*Journal of General Psychology*, 112 (2), 191-200 (1985). Reprinted with permission of the Helen Dwight Reid Educational Foundation. Published by Heldref Publications, 1319 Eighteenth St., N.W., Washington, D.C. 20036-1802. Copyright © 1985.

forth), subjects typically judge that the essay writer's attitude is accurately reflected in the essay, *even if subjects are told that the position expressed in the essay was assigned by the instructor* (Jones & Nisbett, 1972). Hicks (1985) found that there is one personality type relatively resistant to this error: the Intuitive Thinking type. In a setting in which most students hold anti-nuclear positions, Intuitive Thinking types judge that an essay writer probably does too, even if the essay was pro-nuclear, since they have been told that the essay position was assigned. Other types minimize the constraint of the situation (the essay assignment) and judge that the person who wrote a pro-nuclear essay must have a pro-nuclear attitude (see Figure 3.3). Hicks notes that Intuitive Thinking types are especially likely to enter scientific careers, which is consistent with their more objective judgments.

Beyond the descriptive level, there has been little research on the determinants of psychological type. Sex differences are minimal, except that females tend to score higher on the Feeling scale and males on the Thinking scale (Myers & McCaulley, 1985). Shiflett (1989) reports that the Sensation-Intuition and Judging-Perceiving scales are related to hemispheric dominance, as measured by another self-report instrument, the Human Information Processing Survey. It is tempting to conclude that physiological differences, such as the dominance of the left or right cerebral hemisphere, correspond to Jungian functions, but it would be premature to conclude a physiological basis for psychological types without further research. Such an interpretation has, however, been proposed in a psychobiographical analysis in which Beethoven was said to have a dominant right hemisphere (Ehrenwald, 1979).

Overall, the Myers-Briggs Type Indicator is a useful instrument for personality research and has promise in applied settings, although it would be

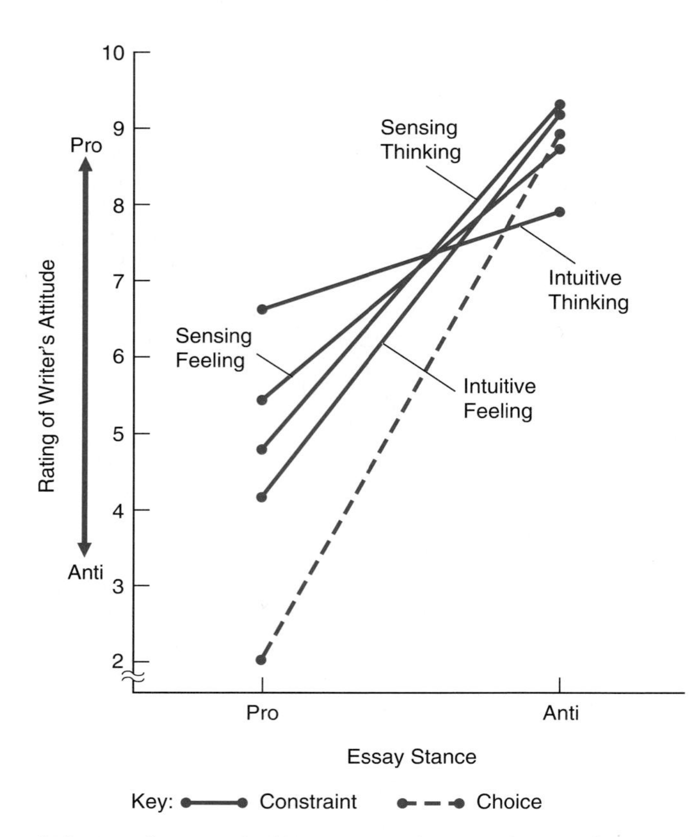

Judgment of essay writer's attitude as a function of essay stance for Choice group and Constraint subgroups based on Myers-Briggs Type Indicator scores

Note: The more a line deviates from the dotted line, collected under the Choice condition, the greater the attributional error.

FIGURE 3.3 Attributional Differences by Psychetype

(From Hicks, 1985, p. 444.)

premature to consider it a proven instrument for individual assessment (J.G. Carlson, 1989a, 1989b; Healy, 1989a, 1989b).

Some adaptation of usual psychometric methods, which presume traits, is necessary to deal appropriately with this type model (cf. Chambers, 1985; Hicks, 1985a). Much research using the Myers-Briggs Type Indicator, however, uses continuous and univariate measurement methods, thus missing the nuances of Jung's theory.

Despite the enthusiasm with which researchers have adopted the Myers-Briggs Type instrument and the Jungian concept of psychological types, Hillman (1980) cautions that Jung never intended his types to be applied to differentiate among people. Rather, the types present descriptions of psychic functions existing in everyone and that need to be recognized and developed in each person if the task of becoming a fully developed human being is to be achieved.

The Structure of Personality

The Psyche and the Self: The Personality as a Whole

Jung generally did not refer to "personality," but rather to the "psyche," a Latin word that originally meant "spirit" or "soul" (Hall & Nordby, 1973, p. 32). This term avoids the connotation of a scientific dissection of personality into unrelated functions, suggesting instead the integration of all aspects of personality.

Jung referred to the total, integrated personality as "the Self." In Jungian writing, "Self" is usually capitalized, which helps to distinguish it from the more conscious and social "self" of other theorists. The Self includes all of a person's qualities and potentials, whether or not they have become apparent or conscious at a particular stage of life. Discovering all the potentials of this Self is the goal of personality development, although some of it will always remain unconscious.

Throughout life, we sometimes emphasize conscious growth (for example, in developing a career identity), while at other times we are more focused on inner development. Jung compared this flow of libido outward (adapting consciously to the world) and then inward (to serve inner needs) to the ebb and flow of the tides. In contrast to the aim of Freud, Jung did not believe it was possible or desirable to live entirely consciously; that would be like trying to dike the ocean. It isn't healthy to give all energy to the unconscious either; that would be like a flood. Learning from the tides, people should expect sometimes to deal consciously with the external world, and other times to turn to the inner world for psychic rejuvenation.

Consciousness and the unconscious coexist in people. Jung described this relationship as one of **compensation**. The unconscious compensates for the onesidedness of consciousness by emphasizing those aspects of psychic totality that have been neglected by consciousness. For example, a person who is consciously a "thinking type" will have the feeling function predominate in the unconscious. A person who is a concrete sensation type consciously will have an intuitive unconscious. Because of this compensation, the unconscious has much to offer. It has the "missing pieces" to allow the development of the Self toward psychic wholeness.

Individuation

The psyche begins as a unified whole, although unconscious. During the course of development, various aspects of the psyche come into consciousness and are further developed, while other areas remain unconscious and undeveloped. In childhood and adolescence, the person develops and becomes aware of a social identity (the "persona," discussed below), but tends to ignore personal shortcomings and failures (the "shadow," described below). As parts of the personality are developed in consciousness, an imbalance in the original wholeness is inevitable.

This imbalance is restored during adult development in mid-life. Unconscious potentials are explored and reintegrated with the total Self in a process Jung called **individuation**. The goal of individuation is to develop latent potentials of the unconscious to achieve full development of the Self or, in Jung's metaphor, to move the center of personality from the ego to some midpoint between the ego and the unconscious. The **transcendent function** is the aspect of personality that integrates the diverse aspects into a unified whole in the latter phases of the individuation process.

The unconscious plays an active role in directing this process by selectively offering material to consciousness and by reintegrating developments into the whole Self. If new experiences are not allowed into consciousness, owing to factors such as anxiety or personality type, then individuation is impeded. If the unconscious is consistently ignored, it may act in extreme ways to block consciousness, creating symptoms (including psychogenic illness and neurosis) that force attention to neglected issues. Lester's (1989c) research failed to support his hypothesis that the thinking-feeling dimension of personality is related to symptoms of the underdeveloped pole, but this may be because his subjects were young (mean age 20.7), and the activation of the unconscious is described by Jung as a development of a later stage of life.

Only through the adult development of individuation can the person become truly an "individual," and not simply a carrier of unconscious images and other people's projections. When this developmental process does not proceed, tragic consequences can result. For example, Marilyn Monroe's inability to individuate herself left her trapped in her cultural image as a sex goddess, without a genuinely individual identity.

Ego

Jung, like Freud, described the ego as the aspect of personality that is most conscious (Jung, 1959). Nothing can become conscious without going through the ego, which serves as "the gatekeeper to consciousness." The ego is essential for a feeling of personal identity, without which we would be overwhelmed by the perceptions, thoughts, feelings, and memories of day-to-day life. In the midst of his own intense explorations into the unconscious, Jung stabilized his identity by reminding himself of the bases of his ego identity, that is, his role as a therapist and family member.

The ego is also the center of our will. It enables us to strive for conscious goals. There are, however, limits to will power because of limitations to consciousness itself. To use Jung's metaphor, the ego is part of personality, but it is not the *center* of personality. Many people identify too closely with their consciousness, in effect putting it at the center of personality. Probably the most common way of being out of balance, especially in the first half of life, is to identify too closely with conscious experience and intentions. Jung called this **ego inflation**. To be "inflated" is to make too much of oneself, to believe one's ego is more important than, in fact, it is. Many mid-life crises occur when people finally realize the limitations of their consciousness, often because of adverse circumstances such as a career setback or a failed marriage.

Alternatively, but less often, psychic inflation can result from overvaluation of the unconscious. Mystics and spiritualistic mediums, as well as psychotics, suffer from this kind of psychic imbalance. The remedy for either type of psychic inflation is individuation, which involves finding a proper balance between consciousness and the unconscious.

Persona

The **persona** is the aspect of personality that adapts to the world. The term originally meant the mask that actors wore in the theater, and it still reflects the roles that we play, not in the theater but in society. The persona is shaped by the reactions we elicit in other people. To the extent that people respond to us as good-looking, or bright, or athletically skilled, that becomes our self-image, or persona. We strive to behave in ways that will earn for us a positive social image, emphasizing aspects of our selves that are valued by others and trying to ignore or deny the rest. Franz Fanon, an African political activist, described the attempts of black Africans to adopt the speech and social mannerisms of white colonialists so as to earn a positive persona; but that effort was doomed to failure because of racism (Fanon, 1967).

When social roles change, we may experience great discontinuity in personality. For example, when a person retires, the persona based on the work role, which has been the basis of identity and social interaction for decades, is no longer relevant. Other ways of relating to people must be found, and this requires a change in the persona.

Changes in persona are celebrated throughout life with publicly visible symbols of the new status. Rites of initiation among primitive societies were occasions in which members were given a symbol of their entry into adulthood. Marriage ceremonies celebrate a change of persona, marked often by a change of name for the bride or, in modern times, sometimes both parties. New clothes or costumes, as at a wedding or graduation, underscore the change in persona. Because clothing often symbolizes the persona, an inadequate persona may be symbolized by the common dream of being naked in a public place—embarrassed.

The persona is generally well established by young adulthood. Two other psychic elements, the shadow and the anima (in men) or animus (in women), are more problematic. Bringing these elements to awareness and integrating them with consciousness are major tasks of adult development.

Shadow

While consciousness has been occupied with creating a socially acceptable persona, other potentials in personality have been neglected or actively repressed. The term **shadow** refers to those aspects of the psyche that are rejected from consciousness by the ego because they are inconsistent with one's self-concept. Unacceptable sexual and aggressive impulses are especially characteristic of the shadow.

A classic literary portrayal of the shadow is Robert Lewis Stevenson's tale of Dr. Jekyll and Mr. Hyde. The respectable gentleman, Dr. Jekyll, represents the socially desirable persona, whereas the evil Mr. Hyde represents the shadow. Another literary portrayal of the shadow appears in Oscar Wilde's story, *The Picture of Dorian Gray.* Dorian Gray maintained the outward appearance of a fine and upstanding citizen. Dorian's hidden portrait of himself, meanwhile, took on the hideous look of his secret crimes. His picture represented his shadow—hidden and evil. Like Dorian Gray, we show our persona to the world and hide the shadow. As we do so the shadow gets more and more ugly, and the split between persona and shadow, which for a time disrupts our wholeness, widens. If we were instead to deal more consciously with shadow issues, the shadow would not become so ugly.

The shadow mediates between consciousness and unconsciousness and can be regarded as "the gatekeeper to the unconscious." Our shadow is experienced as frightening or evil when we fear our unconscious. Emergence of the shadow from the unconscious produces the experience of moral conflict. When a person comes to terms with the unconscious, the experience changes. The shadow then is less repulsive and more playful, and it brings zest and liveliness to experience. The shadow, when integrated with consciousness, is a source of creativity and pleasure.

According to Jung, there are some rare exceptions to the general rule that the shadow is negative. A few people have an identity that is consciously evil and have repressed their own positive qualities into a *positive shadow* (Jung, 1959, p. 8). For example, powerful tyrants may pride themselves on brutality and reject humane qualities as "weak."

PROJECTION OF THE SHADOW

The shadow is symbolized in literature and in dreams by various images of evil, disturbed, and repulsive people: criminals, psychotics, and others whom we despise or pity, including racial groups. Jung asserted that in dreams, the shadow is symbolized by a figure who is the same sex as the dreamer. The specific repulsive qualities of a shadow figure give clues to the material that the person has repressed in forming a conscious self-concept. Thus a man who is proud of his intelligence may represent his shadow in a dream as a mentally retarded man; a sexually controlled woman may symbolize her shadow in a dream of a prostitute.

The tendency to project shadow elements onto persons of other races in waking life, as well as in dreams, obviously contributes to racial prejudice. Fanon suggested that people project their instinctive, animal characteristics onto blacks, and their threatening intellectual qualities onto Jews (1967, p. 165), an interpretation that Jung would probably have accepted.

Anima and animus

People consciously reject not only qualities that are evil or inconsistent with their persona (the shadow), but also qualities incompatible with their sex-role identity. These sex-inappropriate qualities, traditionally exemplified by traits such as emotionality for males and power for females, constitute the **anima** (a man's repressed feminine-typed qualities) and the **animus** (a woman's repressed masculine-typed qualities). Jung referred to the anima as "a man's inner woman." The animus is a woman's "inner man."

A person usually enters adulthood with an ego and a persona that are conscious; the rest of the psychic apparatus, the shadow and anima or animus, are not yet differentiated and are still unconscious.

Sometimes a person becomes "possessed" by his anima or her animus, which is Jung's way of describing a condition in which unconscious qualities control behavior without being integrated into consciousness. Jung felt that the anima represents Eros, the principle of relatedness. Men possessed by their anima act moody and emotional, and they project the anima onto women, especially their mothers and the women with whom they fall in love. Jung referred to the animus as "the paternal Logos," claiming that logic and reason (Logos) are masculine qualities. Jung described women as possessed by the animus if they were opinionated and preoccupied with power.

Women project the animus onto men, both fathers and the men with whom they fall in love.

Jung's focus on masculinity and femininity seems, to some researchers, consistent with key dimensions of individual differences measured by self-report inventories (Coan, 1989). Others, though, are offended by Jung's emphasis on sex differences. Although Jung stressed the importance for each sex to develop psychological androgyny, he is accused of describing women's animus development more harshly than men's explorations of the anima (Torrey, 1987). He seemed to accept cultural realities rather than moving toward an improved, less sexist, society. At issue is whether sex differences are culturally determined, as the critics assume, or biologically given, as Jung assumed.

PROJECTION OF THE ANIMA OR ANIMUS

The unconscious anima or animus is projected onto people of the opposite sex, who trigger various emotions (such as fear, rejection, or longing) depending on one's attitude toward one's own unconscious anima or animus. A man may project negative or positive qualities onto women, depending on whether he is still at the early stage of rejecting his "inner femininity," or at a more developed stage of acceptance. A man who belittles a woman for her sentimentality is, by projection, rejecting his own sentimentality. When he is ready to integrate it, he will stop criticizing women in whom he sees that quality. Similarly, women who speak against men, who energetically attack or fear qualities such as independence in men, may be projecting their own rejected animus. These projections, too, will become more positive as the animus is integrated into consciousness.

One of the most common, and potentially healthy, instances of projection of the anima or animus is the experience of falling in love (Jung, 1931/1954). What a romantic image! Falling in love promises to restore the missing piece of the psyche that was left behind in the unconscious when the conscious personality was developed. This experience is, of course, quite irrational, outside the realistic, willful planning of the ego. That is the essence of romance, whether it progresses positively, as in the fairy tale of *Cinderella*, or tragically, as in Shakespeare's *Romeo and Juliet.* Each lover feels psychologically whole when with the beloved, because the anima or animus, both of which are not yet consciously developed, is felt to be present with the loved one. Gradually, through this love relationship, the woman develops her own masculine potentials and the man becomes more conscious of his own repressed feminine qualities.

In the process of such a psychologically healthy love relationship, the shadow is also accepted into consciousness. The lover accepts the other in his or her entirety, even rejected aspects of the shadow. Thus love facilitates psychological development. It helps transcend the limits of the conscious ego and fosters the development of the anima (for a man) or animus (for a woman), and the shadow (for both sexes), so that these potentials can be differentiated and then integrated into consciousness.

Does research confirm the Jungian model of romantic relationships? Carlson and Williams (1984) reported that husbands and wives tended to be similar in type on the Sensation-Intuition and Thinking-Feeling scales. Dissimilar couples were rarer, and less happy. Carlson and Williams suggested that projection of dissimilarity may be more characteristic of disturbed relationships and of the Introversion-Extroversion dimension, rather than the psychological functions. This finding does not confirm the most straightforward prediction from Jung's theory, which would anticipate dissimilarity between spouses.

Personal Unconscious

The anima or animus and the shadow together constitute what Jung called the **personal unconscious**. This is the unconscious of each individual that is developed because of the person's unique experiences. The shadow is somewhat closer to consciousness than is the anima (or animus), and it can and should be assimilated to consciousness. During this process, the person becomes more aware of personal shortcomings and more accepting of them in himself or herself and in others on whom they may have been projected. The anima or animus is somewhat deeper in the personal unconscious, but much of it, too, can be differentiated and made conscious. As this happens, the individual develops more androgynous qualities.

In describing the personal unconscious, Jung and Freud used different language, but both agreed that the content of this unconscious is determined by the experience of a person in the world. There are differences, however: Freud assumed consciousness as the starting point and explained how some material is repressed into the unconscious because of emotional conflict; Jung presumed at the outset an unconscious totality, from which consciousness emerges.

Collective Unconscious

Jung also described a deeper layer to the unconscious. This **collective unconscious** is the core of Jung's mysticism and is the concept least accepted by mainstream psychology.

The collective unconscious is inherited. It is contained in human brain structure and does not depend on any experience to develop. It can be described as "pre-wired circuits" in our brain, to use an electrical metaphor, or ROM ("read-only memory") chips, to use a computer metaphor: content that is built into the machine at the factory, and not changed by the user.

The collective unconscious can also be illustrated with imagery from science fiction. Human beings, no matter how far they might travel to distant galaxies, bear the imprint of ancestors who originated on a planet with seasons and with 24-hour days. These intergalactic travelers would long for what their ancestors experienced, even if they had been born in a spaceship somewhere in space and had never personally experienced life on Earth. They would bear its imprint in their genes.

The collective unconscious is shaped by the remote experiences of the human species and transmitted to each individual through genetic inheritance. This is a particularly strange concept for modern psychology, which has been profoundly influenced by behaviorism and its emphasis on environmental determinism. Biological determination of mental imagery sounds far-fetched.

We know from physiological psychology that there are basic neural units of sensation and perception. Certain neurons respond only to particular colors, shapes, or angles. We know from animal psychology that some rather complex behaviors occur instinctively, without individual experience; for example, a bird, raised entirely in isolation, nonetheless at maturity will build a species-appropriate nest, though it has never seen one. If an instinct can tell an animal how to behave, why can't it tell a human how to think?

Jung suggested that it can. He claimed that the collective unconscious contains "primordial images," called **archetypes**, which are similar in all people. These archetypes are the basic units of the collective unconscious, and they function as "psychic instincts" that predispose us to experience the world in certain universally human ways. According to Jung, we have images that tell us what a mother is, what a spiritual leader is, even what God is. These images are part of our very nature; without them we would not be human. All personal experience is interpreted through these archetypal patterns.

Genetics and the Collective Unconscious

One of Jung's controversial ideas was that the collective unconscious follows the laws of genetic inheritance. It is different in humans from animal species, of course. Jung suggested that various races and families inherit somewhat different variations of the collective unconscious, just as they inherit different physical characteristics.

This notion of a "racial unconscious" was exploited in the Nazi era as a scientific rationalization for the racially motivated extermination of non-Aryan people, especially Jews. Psychologists in the post–World War II era, horrified by the concentration camps, naturally avoided Jung's unfortunate genetic hypotheses, and some have blamed Jung for racial bias or at least stupidity for developing genetic theories in a racist era (Dalal, 1988; Odajnyk, 1976; Sherry, 1986).

The Shadow and the Anima or Animus as Archetypes

As described earlier, the *content* of the shadow and the anima or animus, with associated emotional conflicts or complexes, is part of the personal unconscious. The content of the shadow would be different if a person were raised with different messages about what is right and wrong. (For a vegetarian Hindu, such as Mahatma Gandhi, eating meat is a shadow characteristic; for an American or an English person, it is not.) The content of the anima or animus varies depending upon the sex roles taught in a culture.

Though personal experience shapes the particular content of the shadow and the anima or animus of an individual, the predisposition to develop these images is collective, independent of personal experience. There are, in the collective unconscious, archetypes corresponding to the shadow and to the anima or animus, and much more.

Other Archetypes

Because the shadow and the anima or animus are closest to consciousness, they are the archetypes with the most noticeable effects on experience. The other archetypes discussed below are said to be "deeper" in the collective unconscious. They less often influence conscious experience. When they do, they feel more foreign.

The Great Mother. The archetype of the Great Mother reflects the ancestral experience of being raised by mothers. Humans are not, for example, hatched from an egg on a lonely shore, like a turtle or a Dali vision. The Great Mother is widely represented in mythology and art, from the carved fertility symbols of ancient cultures to paintings of the Virgin Mary and modern sculptures by Henry Moore. Even the rock star Madonna borrows from this archetype of the Great Mother, and in so doing illustrates the diversity of particular forms that can be inspired by an archetype.

All archetypes have an ambivalent quality, with both positive and negative aspects. Sentimentality about "motherhood and apple pie" does not recognize the negative aspects of the Great Mother. This archetypal feminine principle encompasses not only the fertile womb but also death and the grave. The Hindu goddess Kali symbolizes the archetype with both positive and negative aspects. Not only does she nurse infants but she also drinks blood (Neumann, 1963, p. 152). Many primitive myths relate fertility of harvest and human reproduction with death, thus expressing both aspects of the archetype. For example, the myth of Demeter and Persephone celebrates the coming of spring only after a woman's journey to the underworld.

The Spiritual Father. In his descriptions of the father archetype, Jung contrasted instinctive qualities, which he claimed were more feminine, with the spiritual qualities of the archetypal father. By asserting that spiritual qualities, Logos, are archetypal aspects of the father, Jung suggested that humans are predisposed to associate spirituality with father images, however unspiritual their own fathers may have been. The association of spirituality with masculinity did not originate with Jung; it has a long history in the Judeo-Christian tradition (Daly, 1978; Lacks, 1980; Patai, 1967).

The Hero. The hero of mythology and folklore conquers great enemies and wins mighty battles. He is often, like Daniel in the lion's den or Parsifal of the Grail myth, a relatively weak individual, but seems in touch with special forces that allow him to conquer great opponents. Jung describes this archetype as associated with the internal psychic struggle to become an individual, separate from regressive ties to the mother. It also relates to external battles with threatening forces in the world. Many varieties of the hero myth are described by a Jungian scholar, Joseph Campbell (1949).

The Trickster. The Trickster appears in various cultures as a simple-minded prankster who seems to be outwitted, but who ultimately brings good results—for example, in Grimms' fairy tale of "Stupid Hans." Trickster figures are less common in our culture than in some others (for example, in American Indian mythology), but can be seen in the revelries of Mardi Gras and in circus clowns. Jung referred to the trickster as "a collective shadow figure, a summation of all the inferior traits of character in individuals" (Jung, 1969, p. 150). Because they provide a symbolic expression of this shadow, trickster myths may be helpful in assisting individuals to incorporate the shadow, to find creative energies for growth in previously repressed material.

Mandala. A **mandala** is an archetype of order, usually symbolized by a circle or a square, or often a square within a circle. Examples range from the World Wheel of Hinduism to modern flying saucers (see Figure 3.4). Dreams of mandalas often occur when people are experiencing great conflict, and they are interpreted to mean that the unconscious has developed more of a solution to the conflict than the person yet consciously recognizes. Thus the symbol anticipates the development of a more "well-rounded," balanced Self (Coward, 1989). Mandalas may be understood as related to the symbolism of numbers. We number or count when we try to bring order to things. The number "4" in particular suggests order or completion, and a circle is a more perfect, more developed phase of this quaternity. Many religions include mandalas as symbols facilitating spiritual development (Coward, 1989). Because the mandala represents emerging psychic wholeness, the goal of the development of the Self, we can also speak of the archetype of the Self (Edinger, 1968).

Transformation. **Transformation** is symbolized by many mythic and individual symbols. Alchemists struggled to find the secret that would transform base metal into gold: the quest for the philosophers' stone. Myths of great journeys, such as Odysseus's wanderings in ancient Greece, are classic par-

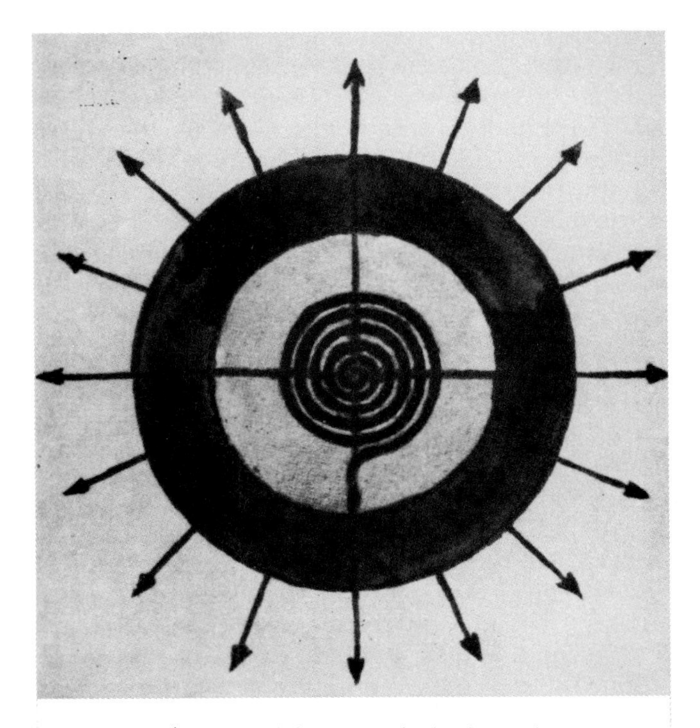

FIGURE 3.4 A Mandala, a Symbol of Psychic Wholeness

(From Jung, 1950b, *Concerning Mandala Symbolism*, Princeton University Press.)

allels to more mundane images of crossing bridges or crossing streets. Such crossings symbolize psychological transformation, the changes that occur with continued development (Jung, 1944/1968b).

Besides the archetypes described by Jung, it has been suggested that the near-death experience may also be archetypal. People who have been nearly dead or even clinically dead and then revived frequently report similar phenomena, often including a tunnel of light and a sense of calm (Groth-Marnat & Schumaker, 1989; Quimby, 1989).

Symbolism and the Collective Unconscious

Like Freud, Jung believed that the unconscious manifests itself in symbols. These symbols reach deep into the psyche, beyond the effects of personal experience, into the collective unconscious. A symbol is formed at the meeting point between the unconscious and consciousness. It is shaped by both conscious experience and unconscious material, including archetypes.

Because the collective unconscious is determined by heredity rather than personal experience, its contents are similar from person to person, although they may live in different environments, even different centuries. Symbols tap this shared archetypal substratum, and thus have some more or less universal meanings (cf. Chetwynd, 1982; Cirlot, 1971), despite the modification of symbolic expression that occurs because of each individual's unique experience.

Jung took great delight in finding similarities between the experiences of psychotic patients and the symbols of ancient art and mythology. For him, this similarity confirmed the existence of the collective unconscious. For example, he reported parallels between drawings made by a psychiatric patient and symbols on a newly discovered Greek papyrus. Jung said the modern drawing couldn't have come from any knowledge based on experience, so it must have come from the collective unconscious.

Symbols that tap the collective unconscious are felt as ego-alien. The collective unconscious has a feeling that Jung called **numinous**, meaning spiritual or "awesome." It can never be totally assimilated into individual consciousness, but it can be approached through symbols, which give access to the energy of the unconscious. This is, for Jung, the function of religion, mythology, and the arts. Such symbols are often culturally given, but they may also be individually created.

When unconscious contents are symbolized, they can become known to the conscious mind. Without symbolism there can be no conscious experience of unconscious contents; in that case, if they break through into behavior, they are not tempered by the civilizing influence of ego controls, and therefore can be highly destructive. Bettelheim (1976) found when he exposed young boys to only "safe" versions of traditional fairy stories, with all monsters, witches, and frightening episodes removed, the boys were much more disruptive than were children exposed to traditional, frightening Grimms' stories. Symbolic representation of fearsome emotions through fairy tales brings these issues to consciousness, where they can be dealt with by ego strengths. If these negative forces are not symbolized, then they remain unchanged in the primitive unconscious, from which they emerge untransformed and uncivilized. This produces psychological difficulties such as the antisocial "acting out" behaviors of these disturbed boys.

Myths and Religion

Myths express the collective unconscious. This, for Jung, is the reason why myths are often similar across diverse cultures. (An alternative explanation is the *diffusion hypothesis*, which assumes that communication of the myths was made by travelers from one culture to another in the distant past.) Myths provide people with a means of tapping the deeper, creative levels of human potential, without being destroyed by it (as in psychosis).

In our scientific era, we sometimes misinterpret myth as merely primitive science. A myth of the sun rising, for example, is dismissed as the outdated statement of people before it was known that the earth revolved around the sun. Fertility rites are, from this view, outdated by our increased understanding of natural science. For Jung, however, myths are far more than primitive science because they deal with human *experience* of the events of nature. A myth of the sun "setting" not only describes the sun going deep into the earth but also expresses the grief of people to see the departing of the sun and their fear of the dangers that come with the night. Science, which is intentionally neutral in the emotional sphere, cannot replace this emotional function of myth. Perhaps a sense of this loss has contributed to anti-science tendencies in our modern era.

Religious myths are probably the most important myths, providing valuable guidance for living and for development. Some people take offense at the labeling of religion as "myth" and try to defend religious assertions by scientific standards. The debate over creationism versus evolution is an example. To judge religion by scientific criteria is to misunderstand, and underestimate, the nature of myth, and is really no more sensible than sending a dishwasher to the repair shop because it cannot bake a cake.

Modern Myths

Old myths, therefore, are not made obsolete by scientific advances. They, and the collective unconscious which they tap, contain "the wisdom of the ages lying dormant in the brain," and so offer valuable guidance for human life. Influenced by Jungian theory, many scholars are investigating old myths for wisdom. There is particular interest in myths of the feminine, to balance what is perceived as an overemphasis on masculine values in Western culture (e.g., Bolen, 1984; Goldenberg, 1979; Lauter & Rupprecht, 1985; Stone, 1976; D.S. Wehr, 1987; Whitmont, 1982). We also need new myths to guide us through the new challenges of our age (Atkinson, 1991; May, 1991). At its best, mythmaking is an active and vital process in human culture. According to Jung, when humans lose the capacity for mythmaking, they lose touch with the creative forces of their being.

Modern myths are described by various Jungian scholars, especially the mythologist Joseph Campbell (1972). Examples include the *Star Wars* films (Ryback, 1983) and other science-fiction works. One of Campbell's students, George Lucas, has produced several well-known movies that are modern myths—*Raiders of the Lost Ark*, *Indiana Jones and the Temple of Doom*, and *Indiana Jones and the Last Crusade*—which extends the medieval imagery of the Holy Grail legend. The television character "Doctor Who" has been interpreted as a modern version of a mythic hero (Stannard, 1988). These creative new myths, in the Jungian tradition, may be our guide to the development of new ways of relating to the collective human unconscious. Technological and social change have made old myths obsolete, even dangerous. Contrasting forces at the archetypal and mythic level have been described as contributing to the threat of a nuclear holocaust (Kull, 1983; Perlman, 1983).

Nondeterministic Assumptions

Jung's collective unconscious constitutes a transpersonal level of experience. It forms the basis for "paranormal" phenomena that have no causal explanation in a deterministic science. Scientists dismiss phenomena such as extrasensory perception (ESP), spiritualism, and mental telepathy as superstitious or fraudulent phenomena. In contrast, Jung was fascinated by them. He studied spiritualistic seances; he wrote in laudatory terms about J.B. Rhine's experiments into ESP; and he wrote about flying saucers (Jung, 1964). Had he abandoned science and common sense altogether, as Freud feared?

Writers sympathetic to Jung argue that he was not really a "believer" in these phenomena (e.g., Hall & Nordby, 1973). Rather, he felt that prescientific explanations offered a target onto which people projected their preexisting concepts and ideas, especially their archetypal images. For example, when the medieval alchemists described their search for the process of transforming base metal into gold, they inadvertently used symbols that provided clues to their archetypal patterns of thought (Jung, 1944/1968b; 1959; 1968a; 1970).

This view of Jung, though it is accurate, is incomplete. It tends to present Jung as more of an objective observer than, by his own account, he was. Jung experienced a world in which events sometimes had no deterministic explanation. Jung's autobiography (1961) is full of incidents of paranormal experiences. For example, he reported waking from sleep with a pain in his head at the time when, unknown to him, a patient shot himself in the head. He dreamt bloody forebodings of war. He discovered that a story he made up about fictitious criminal activity was actually the real life story of a man he had just met. These are only a few of Jung's self-reported paranormal experiences.

Synchronicity

Jung (1960b) proposed the term **synchronicity** to describe experiences that logically can only be coincidental but that in a feeling sense have meaning. In short, these are "meaningful coincidences." In addition to the above examples, Jung reported the following incident. When he was a therapist, a woman patient reported a dream of a scarab, a sacred beetle in Egyptian lore. At that instant an insect banged on his window. He let it in. It was the closest insect relative in Switzerland to the Egyptian scarab (Jung, 1960b, p. 22). Another "meaningful coincidence" occurred when he was talking to Freud. They both heard a loud, startling sound emanating from the bookcase and wondered what it was. Jung said it was the forces of their contact, and to prove it he predicted it would happen again. It did (Jung, 1961). For Jung, such synchronistic events are based on the collective unconscious. They occur when this level of experience is activated by circumstances such as the meeting of these two analysts. To most people, though, it is simply a coincidence that the bookcase settled or perhaps cracked at that moment.

Paranormal phenomena, such as extrasensory perception (ESP), are examples of synchronistic events. People who believe that such events really occur differ in psychological type from those who do not accept them. Belief in paranormal phenomena is associated with higher scores on Perceiving and Intuition (Huot, Makarec, & Persinger, 1989; Lester, Thinschmidt, & Trautman, 1987) and Feeling (Lester, Thinschmidt, & Trautman, 1987). Personality factors outside Jungian theory that are associated with belief in paranormal phenomena include high Private Self-Consciousness and low Social Anxiety (M.F. Davies, 1985). People who report having experienced paranormal phenomena have been described as showing signs of unusual activity in the temporal lobe of the brain (Huot, Makarec, & Persinger, 1989; Persinger & Valliant, 1985), suggesting (to a determinist) that abnormal neuronal firing may produce the experiences. A more Jungian interpretation analyzes one paranormal phenomenon, channeling, as a result of unconscious repressions (Corey, 1988).

Jung was interested in the **I Ching**, a traditional Chinese method of "consulting an oracle," or, more bluntly, of fortune-telling (Wilhelm, 1960). The I Ching is based upon a number system, with 64 hexagrams corresponding to various phases in the ever-changing conditions of human experience (K.L. Phillips, 1980). Traditionally, the Chinese draw straws to select the relevant answer to their question. Alternatively, Jung used a method of flipping coins. He carried a bag of special coins for this purpose. It was his way of transcending the limitations of ego consciousness when life seemed to pose difficulties irresolvable through reason. Even if an oracle provides random advice (though Jung was not so rationally cynical), there probably is something to be said for having a way out of the ever-deepening ruts of imperfect conscious decision-making strategies.

Jung's mystical side is at odds with the deterministic assumptions of science. Some have argued that most personality theory is based on a model of reality derived from outmoded physics. Developments in relativity theory and in quantum physics, it is argued, provide a better model for psychology, one that allows indeterminism and free will, and which is more compatible with subjective, even mystical, approaches (Herbert, 1988; Keutzer, 1984; Slife, 1981; von Franz, 1964).

Another way to interpret Jung's mysticism derives from his theory of types. Traditional science is based on thought, which is more logical and concrete (the sensation and thinking functions). Jung's theory holds that any approach which does not use all four functions is incomplete. His mystical side can be viewed as an exploration of the implications of the underrepresented functions (intuition and feeling). The issue, then, is whether personality theory should encompass this material, or whether its commitment to science (and therefore sensation and thinking) necessarily must exclude Jung's mysticism and the work of others who write of human potential in nonempirical ways (e.g., Washburn, 1990; Wilber, 1990). This issue addresses unresolved questions in the philosophy of science, which are further discussed in Chapter 15.

Therapy

Jungian analysis, like Freudian analysis, focuses largely on dreams and symbolic material. The aim of analysis is to help the patient resolve emotional complexes and learn to live a symbolic life. Symbolic living allows access to unconscious creative forces that foster growth. The unconscious is an ally, rather than the enemy. Its energies, properly communicating with consciousness, are creative, rather than destructive.

The direction of growth, in therapy and outside, is toward greater wholeness. Parts of the psyche that have been broken off from the whole must be retrieved and integrated with the rest of the personality. Often these isolated pieces take the form of **complexes**. These are networks of emotional and ideational materials that are conflictful and unconscious. They center around a common theme, which is archetypal (Edinger, 1968). Complexes may appear in symptoms or dreams. They also can be elicited through the Word Association Test, which Jung (1973) devised. This technique has been elaborated in subsequent research (Zivkovic, 1982).

In the Word Association Test, the patient listens to a word and is instructed to say whatever comes to mind. Unusual associations and delays in responding are indicators that a psychological complex has been activated. Jung's Word Association Test was, incidentally, an influence on Hermann Rorschach, Jung's colleague at the Burghölzli hospital, in his development of the famous Rorschach inkblot test (Pichot, 1984). In one research study, undergraduate subjects served as judges. They were instructed to decide which of several word-association protocols was produced by a "suspect" who had role-played a thief. The results suggested that people who approached the task in a playful, heuristic manner, rather than more logically, were most successful (Dollinger, Levin, & Robinson, 1991). Clinical interpretation, too, requires intuition.

Jung dispensed with Freud's couch. He preferred a face-to-face encounter between the therapist and the patient. This reflected his conviction that the therapist should not hide behind authority and a guise of scientific objectivity.

Dreams

Jung, like Freud, regarded dreams as products of the unconscious. Because the Jungian unconscious contains multiple levels, personal and collective, various kinds of dreams can be distinguished. Many dreams reveal the individual's unresolved emotional complexes. These dreams, which tap the personal unconscious, are comparable to Freudian dreams, although Jung did not interpret them sexually (Jung, 1974). Often patients have dreams early in analysis that, in effect, are statements by the unconscious of the therapeutic task. Dreams can also reflect physical disease (R.A. Lockhart, 1977).

Other dreams reach into the collective unconscious and incorporate archetypal imagery. Research suggests that neurotics (as measured by the Eysenck Personality Inventory) have fewer archetypal dreams, while Intuitive types (as measured by the Myers-Briggs Type Inventory) have more (Cann & Donderi, 1986). Occasionally, according to Jung, dreams are not personal at all, but are like the "big dreams" of American Indians: messages to humanity at large, with the individual only a receiving medium.

Interpretation of dreams involves three stages. First the dreamer *recalls* the dream, retelling it in detail. Secondly, in the **amplification** of the dream, the dreamer elaborates on the dream images, describing associations to the people and symbols contained in the dream (Mattoon, 1978). Jungians also often add a third stage, **active imagination**, in which the dreamer continues with the dream imagery in waking imagination, adding new episodes or otherwise continuing the symbolic work begun in the dream.

Jung interpreted all persons and symbols of a dream as aspects of the dreamer's psyche. The way they interact in the dream describes efforts and obstacles in the developmental task of individuation. For example, dreaming of exploring a long-forgotten basement and being frightened at the monsters that live there may reflect the a person's fear of exploring the unconscious.

Many dreams can be interpreted according to the principle of *compensation* (Jung, 1974; Mahoney, 1966). That is, the dream presents ideas or emotions that supplement the limitations of consciousness. Such dreams, if understood, prompt the dreamer to have a more balanced approach to current life issues. Jung (1961) described one of his own dreams in which he looked across a valley and, straining to look up, saw one of his female patients. He interpreted this dream, according to the principle of compensation, to mean that in real life he had been "looking down on" the patient with a condescending attitude. That interpretation, which he shared with the patient, prompted a change in his attitude, which facilitated therapeutic progress.

For dreams that primarily reflect personal complexes, this level of dream interpretation is all that is necessary or appropriate. For dreams that reach into the collective unconscious, familiarity with archetypal symbolic language is essential to amplify the dream images.

Psychosis

Jung's theory provides a framework for understanding psychotic symptoms (Jung, 1960a). He interpreted psychotic hallucinations and delusions as direct expressions of the collective unconscious. Drugs can trigger psychosis by chemically inducing an encounter with images of the archetypal unconscious. Without the conscious ego to act as a mediator, this powerful (Jung would use the term "numinous") collective unconscious overwhelms the individuality of the person and makes manifest what is latent in the rest of us.

The Symbolic Life

Human beings nonetheless struggle to be in touch with these archetypes. We need mediators between our individual personalities and the collective unconscious to make the contact safe. How can we tap collective energies without being destroyed by them? That is the function of mythology, religion, and cultural ritual. Jung encouraged people to participate in the religious traditions in which they had been raised. He discouraged Westerners from switching to Eastern religions.

Unfortunately, cultural rituals can stagnate. More individualized exploration, through psychoanalysis or through structured workshops (e.g., Progoff, 1975), may be useful. At its most desirable conclusion, Jungian therapy prepares individuals to create new symbolic forms. They actively participate in the ongoing human task of tapping the creative energies of the unconscious, thus contributing to an evolving human destiny. One who has successfully completed a Jungian analysis must lead a "symbolic life."

Summary

Jung proposed a theory of personality in which the unconscious contains broad psychic energy, rather than simply sexual energy as Freud postulated. He described eight *psychetypes*, based on the dimension of introversion-extroversion and the functions of thinking-feeling and sensing-intuition. These dimensions can be measured by the widely used Myers-Briggs Type Indicator. Research in business, education, and laboratory settings has confirmed that the types vary in their experience and behavior (see Table 3.3).

Jung emphasized the development of all aspects of the Self. Consciousness and the unconscious exist in a relationship of compensation. During the *individuation* process of adulthood, unconscious aspects of personality are developed and integrated with those of consciousness. In this process, the center of personality is shifted away from the ego. The *persona* is challenged by the emergence of the *shadow* and the *anima* or *animus* from the unconscious. Projection of the shadow contributes to racism. Projection of the anima or animus occurs in romantic love. Jung has been criticized for both racism and sexism.

The *personal unconscious* contains material repressed during individual experience. The *collective unconscious* contains transpersonal, inherited material, including several *archetypes* that serve as patterns for experience. Jung encouraged people to encounter the unconscious through symbols in dreams, myths, religion, and cultural rituals. Modern myths, as well as ancient ones, are valuable and should continue to be developed by people

TABLE 3.3 Contributions of Jung's Theory to Various Topics

BIOLOGICAL	Inheritance includes mental contents (a "collective unconscious") as well as physical characteristics.
CHILD DEVELOPMENT	Early experience is of little interest to Jung.
ADULT DEVELOPMENT	Mid-life change (individuation) involves exploration of the creative potentials of the unconscious.
MENTAL HEALTH	The unconscious has an important role in healthy maturity and should be explored through symbolism.
SOCIETY	Cultural myths and rituals provide ways of dealing with the unconscious. Important differences exist among cultures and should be preserved.
COGNITIVE PROCESSES	Individual differences in thought and intuition influence social interactions and the course of development.
INDIVIDUAL DIFFERENCES	Individuals differ in level of introversion-extroversion, which is stable throughout life, and in the extent to which they have developed the four functions (thinking, feeling, sensation, and intuition). They also differ in their access to the personal and collective unconscious.

leading a creative symbolic life. Jung discussed mystical, paranormal phenomena in his concept of *synchronicity,* or meaningful coincidence. He developed a *Word Association Test.* He interpreted dreams as compensatory to conscious awareness.

ILLUSTRATIVE BIOGRAPHIES: Concluding Remarks

Though Shirley MacLaine and Martin Luther King, Jr., are quite different in many ways, both lives can only be understood when the symbolism of their experience is appreciated. For both, powerful symbols tapped deep unconscious energies, which they expressed in public statements—one, as a mystical heroine, witnessing unreal worlds, the other as a hero in the struggle against injustice in our so very real world. Such public figures serve as conduits through which the archetypal energies described by Jung are brought into our cultural experience. Indeed, it is only because we resonate to these images that we have made their bearers famous.

Martin Luther King, Jr. and Shirley MacLaine experienced the unconscious in quite different ways, which Jung would understand as a consequence of their different personality types.

Shirley MacLaine

Shirley MacLaine can be classified as an extroverted feeling type with sensation as an auxiliary function. Her descriptions of life experiences are full of the concrete details characteristic of the sensation function. For example, she described her daughter before birth as "only a big stomach, something that moved and kicked intermittently," but after birth she rejoiced that "I had *seen* her move, *heard* her cry, and soon I would *hold* the small, hopeful, demanding person" (MacLaine, 1970, p. 80). As Jung's theory (1954) predicts (though R. Carlson & Williams, 1984, disagree) for a sensation-type woman, MacLaine fell in love with an opposite type but was troubled when she realized that "he never once mentioned what he ate, what he touched, what he saw, what he smelled, how he felt" (MacLaine, 1983, p. 41). Shirley MacLaine claimed that in a past life she was blind, and so she developed her other senses more, in ways that still affect her current incarnation (MacLaine 1985, p. 394).

Shirley MacLaine's descriptions of astral projection and past lives can be explained as outward projections of inner experiences. An extroverted feeling type reports as real external events what an introverted thinking type (such as Martin Luther King, Jr.) would describe as personal inward experiences (cf. Jung, 1971, pp. 353–354). MacLaine described floating or flying above the earth as "an experience and not a dream, even though it happened when I was asleep, because it felt more real than a dream" (1983, p. 3). This choice of reifying language is a reflection of the extrovert's tendency to minimize the reality of inner experiences.

Shirley MacLaine underscored the concept of androgyny by claiming to have actually lived as both male and female in past lives. She described her life as a quest for "a missing dimension in myself" (1985, p. 305), and she went so far as to proclaim "that everything that happened in my life was occurring because *I* was creating it in order to learn about myself" (1987, p. 5). This parallels Jung's concept of individuation, the development of a more complete Self.

While Shirley MacLaine's autobiographies are readily understandable from a Jungian perspective, we should bear in mind that she had read Jungian works and may well have been influenced by his theory. Indeed, in her later books she used Jungian language, such as "synchronicity."

Martin Luther King, Jr.

Martin Luther King, Jr. would have been sympathetic to the effort to make a psychological analysis of his life. He did so himself in graduate school, at which time he was favorable toward both psychoanalytic and behavioral approaches (Oates, 1982, p. 36). Had he studied Jungian theory, he might have found there the psychological analysis of the religious symbols and racial conflicts central to his life's work.

Even at the outset, it is apparent that a typological analysis will not be simple. The fundamental question, was he an introvert or an extrovert, was answered by King, who called himself an "ambivert" (Oates, 1982, p. 40). Within the types listed by Jung, King could best be classified as an intuitive introvert. As an introvert, he was in touch with his own inner life. He drew richly from this symbolic realm in his sermons. He turned prayerfully inward at critical moments—for example, when deciding whether to take a leading role in the Southern Christian Leadership Conference, despite the conflicting demands of his congregation and his young family. Jung said (1971, p. 400) that introverted intuitive types are often prophets, and many, including King himself, applied this term to his ministry.

His auxiliary function was probably thinking rather than feeling, given his intense motivation for education, which prompted him to complete a doctorate degree, despite the early disadvantage of an inferior education in segregated schools.

Throughout his ministry, Dr. King spoke to his congregation and to the world in symbols that mobilized the energies of the unconscious. Both Jung and King were undoubtedly influenced by their family traditions of Christian ministers, largely sharing a symbolic language. King's most famous speech, delivered in August 1963, described his **dream** from the **mountaintop**, his vision of racial equality. King worked to make his dreams real in the world, but described that as a future potential (with which intuitive types are typically concerned) rather than a current reality.

Jung recommended that people stay within the symbols and mythology of their own heritage, and King did so. He borrowed the ideas of nonviolence from Gandhi's teachings in India and South Africa, but presented them within the Christian framework of his own Baptist heritage.

Jungian theory also helps us to understand the public's response to King. Jung described the archetype of "The Hero." This concept suggests that people would have a readiness to project onto certain leaders, such as Dr. King, the combination of several characteristics: a promise of a better life, the expectation that the hero will fight difficult battles on behalf of others, and, in many myths, the tragic finale in which the hero, once crowned as king, must die.

From prophecy to assassination, Martin Luther King, Jr.'s life story reads as hauntingly archetypal. It was Jung's life work to explore the archetypes so that they could coexist with rational consciousness, rather than blindly driving human experience. As long as masses of people are unconscious of the archetypal realm, we will continue to act out these various tragic scripts.

Jung's typological approach provides a framework for understanding how people, including Martin Luther King, Jr., and Shirley MacLaine, can have such widely different experiences of life, each embodying only part of the entire human potential. Finally, it is from other people that we can learn much about our own potential for a fully developed humanity.

GLOSSARY

active imagination technique for exploring the unconscious by encouraging waking fantasies

amplification elaboration of dream images as a step toward dream interpretation

anima the femininity that is part of the unconscious of every man

animus the masculinity that is part of the unconscious of every woman

archetypes contents of the collective unconscious; innate patterns of experience

auxiliary function the second most developed function of a personality

collective unconscious the inherited unconscious

compensation principle of the relationship between the unconscious and consciousness, by which the unconscious provides what is missing from consciousness to make a complete whole

complexes emotionally charged networks of ideas (such as those resulting from unresolved conflicts)

dominant function a person's predominant psychological function

ego inflation overvaluation of ego consciousness, without recognizing its limited role in the psyche

feeling psychological function in which decisions are made based on the emotions they arouse

I Ching ancient Chinese method of fortune-telling

individuation the process of becoming a fully developed person, with all psychic functions developed

intuition psychological function in which material is perceived with a broad perspective, emphasizing future possibilities rather than current details

mandala symbolic representation of the whole psyche, emphasizing circles and/or squares

Myers-Briggs Type Indicator psychological test for measuring the psychic functions in an individual

numinous experience of spiritual or transpersonal energies

persona a person's social identity

personal unconscious that part of the unconscious derived from an individual's experience

sensation psychological function in which material is perceived concretely, in detail

shadow the unconscious complement to a person's conscious identity, often experienced as dangerous and evil

synchronicity the acausal principle, in which events are determined by transpersonal forces

thinking psychological function in which decisions are made based on logic

transformation modification of psychic energy to higher purposes, for example, through ritual

transcendent function the process of integrating all opposing aspects of personality into a unified whole

STUDY QUESTIONS

1. Contrast Jung's description of the unconscious with that of Freud.
2. List the three dimensions Jung used to determine a person's psychological type (psychetype). Describe them.
3. Describe the Myers-Briggs Type Indicator. Describe a few research results using this instrument.
4. Explain Jung's concept of the *Self.* What is the relationship between consciousness and the unconscious in the Self?
5. Describe the process of *individuation.*
6. What is *ego inflation?*
7. Explain the term *persona.*
8. Describe the *shadow.* How can it contribute to racial prejudice? What can it contribute, in a positive way, to personality?
9. Describe the *anima* and the *animus.* Discuss Jung's understanding of sex differences, androgyny, and falling in love.
10. Explain the term *collective unconscious.* List several *archetypes* of the collective unconscious.
11. Why are symbolism and mythology important for personality?
12. Discuss Jung's mystical concepts, including *synchronicity.*
13. Contrast Jungian therapy with Freudian psychoanalysis.
14. Describe the *Word Association Test.*
15. Explain Jung's approach to dream interpretation.

PART 

The Psychoanalytic-Social Perspective

Freud's psychoanalytic theory inspired many clinicians and theorists to consider personality in dynamic terms. Their extensions of Freud's theory led to new developments in psychoanalytic theory. In particular, many theorists emphasized *ego functions* to a greater extent than did Freud (Hartmann, 1939/1958). They stressed the capacity of the individual to delay gratification, not simply to be driven by unconscious id impulses. Freud had developed the description of the ego in the later years of his theorizing, from the 1923 publication of *The Ego and the Id* onward (Rapaport, 1959a), so these developments follow reasonably from his theory.

The boundary between "psychoanalytic" and "psychoanalytic-social" perspectives is fuzzy. It includes many who regarded themselves as orthodox Freudians. Freud's daughter, Anna Freud, elaborated his concept of ego defenses in her classic book, *The Ego and the Mechanisms of Defense* (A. Freud, 1936/1966). Heinz Hartmann (1939/1958) stressed the role of the ego in organizing or integrating personality. While Freud's theory emphasized the role of the ego in moderating conflict among id, superego, and reality, Hartmann described ego functions that were relatively autonomous from the drives. Alfred Adler, a member of Freud's inner circle, emphasized the striving aspects of personality and the social context of development, which are characteristic of the psychoanalytic-social perspective.

The ego's role includes adapting to relationships with other people. Infancy is reinterpreted to emphasize the development of a relationship with the mother (E.H. Erikson, 1950; H.S. Sullivan, 1953). An infant nursing at the mother's breast, for example, is viewed by Freud as satisfying libidinal drives. In contrast, Adler and the ego psychologists, influenced by Adler's departure from Freud, emphasized the infant's relationship of cooperation with the mother, each needing the other (T. Davis, 1986).

Theorists presented in the next three chapters—Alfred Adler, Erik Erikson, and Karen Horney—discussed interpersonal aspects of the ego's functioning beginning in the family and extending to society generally. Culture, not simply biology, determines sex differences, according to Adler and Horney. Erikson remained traditionally psychoanalytic in his biological explanation of sex differences, although he stressed cultural influences in other respects. Besides reinterpreting sex roles as cultural products, the social emphasis has encouraged the development of typologies of interpersonal behavioral styles. Adler ("getting," "ruling," and "avoiding" types) and Horney ("moving toward," "moving against," and "moving away" types) each offered such typologies. More detailed typologies have subsequently been developed (Kiesler, 1983; Wheeler, 1989). Thus, in addition to emphasis on the *ego* within personality, these theorists gave more attention to *society,* the context in which personality develops.

Erik Erikson has presented the most complete developmental theory of ego functions. He described eight stages of ego development that extend throughout the life span. Furthermore, like other theorists in this tradition, he stressed the role of society in shaping ego development.

The psychoanalytic-social theorists agree with theorists in the psychoanalytic perspective on two important points. The unconscious is a useful concept for understanding personality, and childhood experience is important in determining personality. In addition, theorists in the psychoanalytic-social-perspective have distinctive assumptions. (1) The *ego,* the adaptational force in personality, is more important than in Freud's theory; (2) the development of a sense of *self* is described; (3) *interpersonal relationships,* beyond the relationships with the parents, are important aspects of personality; and (4) *social and cultural factors* influence personality.

Most psychoanalytic-social theorists, like Freudian and Jungian psychoanalysts, have based their theories on clinical data. However, a research tradition in ego development has also emerged. Many studies of Erikson's theory have been conducted using self-report data, as we shall see in that chapter. In addition, Jane Loevinger (1966, 1976, 1979; Loevinger and others, 1985) has developed an extensive theoretical and research program that measures ego development using questionnaires, thus enabling researchers to investigate ego development in nonclinical populations.

Theorists in the psychoanalytic-social tradition have presented an approach that is not so narrowly biological as classical psychoanalysis. They stress the adaptational and interpersonal aspects of personality and have provided concepts for understanding the ways society shapes human development.

CHAPTER 4

Adler: Individual Psychology

BIOGRAPHY OF ALFRED ADLER

Alfred Adler

Alfred Adler was born in a suburb of Vienna (Penzing) in 1870, the second son in a family of four boys and two girls. His father was a grain merchant. His family was financially comfortable, and was one of the few Jewish families in his village. In protest against the isolation of orthodox Judaism, Alfred converted to Christianity.

As a young child, Alfred was unhealthy. He suffered from rickets. His earliest reported memory is as a 2-year-old, bandaged so that he could barely move, while his older brother moved freely about. His childhood, he said, was often made unhappy by the greater achievements of his older brother, with whom Alfred unsuccessfully competed. At the age of 5, Alfred heard a doctor tell his father that Alfred's pneumonia was so serious that he would die; treatment was useless. This must have seemed credible, since Alfred's younger brother, with whom he shared a room, had died in bed two years earlier. On the advice of a second physician, however, treatment was given, and Alfred recovered. He decided to become a doctor himself "in order to overcome death and the fear of death" (Ansbacher & Ansbacher, 1956, p. 199). In addition to all this, he was run over twice when he was 4 or 5!

Eventually, with the courage which he later was to urge on his patients, Adler overcame his physical difficulties. He was active in sports and became popular with his classmates (but not with his older brother). He also compensated for early shortcomings in the academic area. He began as a mediocre student with special weakness in mathematics. He finally improved, even becoming, as Bottome (1947) said, a "mathematical prodigy, solving problems as fast as they could be put to him" (p. 28). Throughout life, Adler loved music, attending various performances and singing in a wonderful tenor voice that, some thought, should have made him an opera singer.

Adler married a Russian émigré, a member of the intelligentsia whose ideas were far more liberal than those typical in Austria at the time. She undoubtedly influenced Adler to deplore the restrictions of traditional attitudes toward women. For example, he reported one study he conducted which found that successful girls often had mothers with careers. Alfred and his wife, Raissa, had four children.

Adler received his medical degree from Vienna University in 1895. He worked at Vienna General Hospital and Polyclinic for two years and began practice as an ophthalmologist, later becoming a general practitioner. He was interested in the contribution of psychological factors to illness and its cure, but he did not limit his practice to psychiatry until 1910, after his break with Freud. As a general practitioner, his life-long concern with the social context of illness is exemplified by his pamphlet, "The Health of Tailors," in which he exposed the working conditions leading to high rates of disease in this occupational group. During World War I, Adler served as a physician in the Austrian army, treating war neuroses (later to be called "shell shock").

Adler (like Jung) was impressed by Freud's book on dreams and defended it in print against critics, although at the time he did not know Freud personally. Freud responded with gratitude. In 1902 Freud invited Adler to join his weekly discussion group, later known as the Vienna Psychoanalytic Society. Though Adler was not psychoanalyzed by Freud or anyone else, he did participate in these discussions. He became Freud's successor as president of the group in 1910 and co-edited its journal (the *Zentralblatt für Psychoanalyse*). He took over many of Freud's cases and was Freud's personal physician.

In 1911, though, Freud broke with Adler, unable to reconcile Adler's theoretical contributions with his own. Freud questioned Adler's intellectual ability and criticized him as a paranoiac. One biographer sympathetic to Adler describes Freud as motivated by jealousy over Adler's brilliance (Bottome, 1947). Freud accused Adler of failing to recognize the importance of the unconscious, thereby fundamentally missing the point of psychoanalysis. Adler, from his side, regarded Freud as a pampered child who had never overcome the self-indulgence of childhood and who clung to authority out of defensiveness.

Adler had many supporters. When he left Freud's circle, resigning the presidency of the Psychoanalytic Society in 1911, 9 of the 35 other members left with him. Adler never returned to Freud's group. In 1912 he established an independent psychoanalytic association, the Society for Individual Psychology, and in 1914 he founded his own journal.

Adler was particularly interested in problems with children, including the prevention of delinquency. He set up nearly 50 child-guidance clinics in Vienna and elsewhere in Europe. He is reported to have established rapport with astonishing success, even in difficult cases. Surgeons summoned him to calm their child patients, and he was especially effective with depressive patients. However, he directed his message more to the public than to medical experts and did not like empirical research studies. This popular orientation impeded his recognition among academicians, though it is echoed by those who urge psychologists to "give psychology away" (G. Miller, 1969) to the public. Nonetheless, those inspired by his theory have been conducting considerable empirical research in recent decades. (Overviews are presented by Watkins, 1982a, 1983, 1986.)

Adler wrote extensively, publishing over 300 articles and books (Dinkmeyer & Dinkmeyer, 1989). His reputation spread internationally, and he lectured both in the United States and throughout Europe. Like many Europeans during the politically troubled times prior to World War II, Adler moved to the United States in 1935. He taught at the Long Island College of Medicine. In 1937, at the age of 67, he died of cardiac problems, with little forewarning and after a healthy adulthood, while on a lecture tour in Scotland.

Adler acknowledged that his theory drew on his own life experience. It is easy to see how a boy who was ill, diagnosed as a terminal case, would aspire to become a physician and would write a theory describing the overcoming of physical defects as a major motivating force.

ILLUSTRATIVE BIOGRAPHIES

Adler's "Individual Psychology" offers perspectives on psychohistory and psychobiography that, more than psychoanalysis, recognize the mutual influence of the individual and society (Pozzuto, 1982). Lewis's (1983) analysis of Gordon Liddy focuses on the theme of power from childhood to the national political arena. Hellinga's (1975) biography of Sir Henry Morton Stanley, the explorer who discovered Dr. Livingstone in Africa and uttered the well-known lines, "Dr. Livingstone, I presume?" focuses on Stanley's insecurity and his goal of acceptance and fame.

Adler's theory, in contrast to those of Freud and Jung, emphasizes people's conscious striving to improve their lives. It offers concepts for understanding people who, through hard work, become successful. What about those who do not try? Rather than accepting their lack of effort as a consequence of forces beyond their conscious control, Adler's theory holds these individuals responsible for their faulty choices.

Two modern personalities who illustrate Adler's concepts are Donald Trump, who built on his father's success to become a billionaire real estate tycoon, and Tina Turner, who overcame the adversities of poverty, a broken home, and physical abuse to achieve success as a popular singer.

Donald Trump

Donald Trump became a billionaire through aggressive real-estate development, primarily in New York City. Besides his real-estate dealings, Trump acquired a football team, the New Jersey Generals. Trump married but later divorced a former fashion model, Ivana, with whom he had three children.

Born in 1946, Donald was the fourth of five children. He was the second son of a contractor who was accumulating wealth by building government-subsidized housing on the outskirts of New York City. His father, although his office was unimpressive and in a humble neighborhood, drove a limousine and owned a multimillion dollar business that he had started himself. Few sons could expect to surpass such a father.

Trump's striving throughout his career was directed toward building ambitious projects, more elegant than his father's residential developments. He built office buildings, apartments, a casino, and more. He demanded excellence: high-quality workmanship, completed on time and within budget.

Trump often featured his name prominently on his buildings: Trump Tower, Trump Plaza, Trump Parc, and so on. During one rehabilitation project, he had a banner with the Trump name over Grand Central Terminal; it was visible throughout the Midtown Manhattan area, causing speculation that Trump was redoing the train station itself.

Trump extended his construction expertise to a New York City project, much to the embarrassment of city officials. New York City had a conspicuous record of delays, shoddy work, and cost overruns in trying to repair an outdoor ice skating facility, Wollman Rink, in Central Park. Trump volunteered to take over the project. He completed the renovation quickly and under budget.

Trump credited his success in part to "total focus," which he described as "almost . . . a controlled neurosis, which is a quality I've noticed in many highly successful entrepreneurs" (Trump, 1987, p. 47). He said he did not gamble, but took measured risks, and did not smoke or drink. He reported relying heavily on his intuition, his gut reaction to a possible undertaking. He claimed not to be motivated by money per se, "except as a way to keep score" (Trump, 1987, p. 63). By this count, his intelligence and hard work, when combined with a favorable economic climate, made him a winner. When the real-estate market tumbled, however, the score turned against him.

INDIVIDUAL PSYCHOLOGY

Alfred Adler was one of the earliest and most influential dissenters from Freud's inner circle of early psychoanalysts. Unlike Freud, who emphasized the universal conflicts that all people experience, Adler focused attention

Tina Turner

Tina Turner, a successful rhythm and blues singer, recorded hits such as "A Fool in Love," "Honky Tonk Women," and "Nutbush City Limits." Like many superstars, her personal life included humble and painful times before she became famous.

Tina was born Anna Mae Bullock in 1939. She grew up in the small town of Nut Bush, Tennessee, officially segregated from the whites because of her black and American Indian ancestry. Her parents fought, both verbally and physically. Anna Mae was raised by relatives intermittently, beginning at age 3, when her parents separated.

Anna Mae bore an illegitimate son just after her high school graduation, and a second son when she was 20. The father of the second son was Ike Turner, a successful rock musician who had taken Anna Mae into his performing group and then included her among his many lovers. As her singing career became increasingly successful, Ike recorded and toured with her (to the disapproval of his common-law wife), renamed her "Tina Turner," and later married her.

The marriage of Ike and Tina Turner was troubled by Ike's infidelity and abuse. He beat her frequently, leaving visible bruises and cuts. She attempted suicide once, overdosing on Valium. Finally, she left Ike, but with no money, dependent on the goodwill of friends and welfare until her independent career soared.

How could a poor, mixed-race, insecure girl from a broken family achieve superstardom? Why did she marry Ike Turner over her own doubts, and stay with him through repeated beatings? Though Adler's theory recognizes the ultimate role of choice and free will in determining life's course, he offers concepts that help us understand Tina Turner's success story.

on the uniqueness of each person. He named his theory "Individual Psychology." His ideas have so influenced other psychoanalysts, including Karen Horney, Erich Fromm, and Harry Stack Sullivan, that they should perhaps be called "neo-Adlerians" rather than "neo-Freudians" (Wittels, 1939). Even Freud was influenced. He borrowed many Adlerian ideas, although often calling them by a new name: defense mechanisms (from Adler's "safeguarding tendencies"); ego-ideal (from Adler's "self-ideal"); and superego (from Adler's "counter-fiction") (Ansbacher & Ansbacher, 1956, pp. 21–22). Adler's discussions of masculine protest contributed to Freud's postulate of the Oedipus complex. In fact, considerable mutual influence took place in the Freud–Adler relationship.

Adler argued that people must be understood from a social perspective, not a biological one. He opposed Freud's exclusive emphasis on sex as a source of energy, and he asserted that any deterministic approach that does not consider the individual's goals is incomplete and cannot provide an effective therapy. His views present a challenge to develop a theory consistent with determinism (Christopher & Leak, 1982). Adler's emphasis on the innate tendency toward social interest and on a holistic approach to personality is an historical precursor to the humanistic psychologists' concept of self-actualization (Runyon, 1984). His emphasis on growth and free will is an important counterforce to the deterministic attitude of Freud. We may say that Adler defended the role of the "soul" or the "self" in psychological theory (cf. Ansbacher & Ansbacher, 1956, p. 62; Weiss-Rosmarin, 1958/1990).

Adler gave credit to Freud for his contributions, referring to him as a "giant." Yet Freud could not tolerate Adler's dissenting ideas. Freud labeled Adler's teachings as "incorrect and dangerous for the development of psychoanalysis" (Ansbacher & Ansbacher, 1956, p. 72). Freud said that Adler's neuroses impeded his insight. Adler rebutted that to have been psychoanalyzed would have been a mistake because "the rigorous acceptance of his [Freud's] doctrine destroys scientific impartiality" (Adler, 1936/1964, p. 254).

Throughout the subsequent history of personality theory, Adler's influence is clear. His emphasis upon the whole person is reflected in the work of Allport, Maslow, and Rogers. His attention to the social context is echoed in the work of Horney and modern social psychologists. Even Freud himself adopted some of Adler's ideas (for example, "confluence of drives"), though often without acknowledgment. Some Adlerian concepts have become so popular that they seem more like common sense than psychological theory (for example, the "inferiority complex").

Striving from Inferiority Toward Superiority

Inferiority

Almost everyone has heard the term "inferiority complex," which describes being overcome by a feeling of lack of worth. This concept was developed and popularized by Alfred Adler, although he may not have originated the particular term (Ansbacher & Ansbacher, 1956, p. 256).

For Adler, the basic human motivation is to strive "from a felt minus situation towards a plus situation, from a feeling of inferiority towards superiority, perfection, totality" (Ansbacher & Ansbacher, 1956, p. 1). This is a process triggered by the dissatisfaction of the "felt minus."

What is this "felt minus"? All people begin life as infants. They feel inferior and helpless because their survival depends on others. With development, each person's sense of what is negative and what would be more positive emerges in a unique and personal way. Adler's terminology changed as he developed his theory over the years, grappling to understand this process.

Organ Inferiority. At first, influenced by his medical practice, Adler referred to "organ inferiority" as the source of the felt minus. Inherited inferiorities intensify "the normal feeling of weakness and helplessness" all young children experience (Adler, 1923/1929, p. 18). A person with weak limbs (like Adler himself, having suffered from rickets) considers his legs to be inferior. A child with hearing problems would feel inferior in auditory capacity. Delayed puberty can also be a source of this sense of organ inferiority, leading to the notion that one will always remain a child (Adler, 1921/1927, p. 72).

It is subjective experience that is important in determining the sense of inferiority. The child makes comparisons with other children and the demands of the social world. Severe socialization and environmental demands can produce a sense of inferiority that would be avoided, given the same physical condition, in a more benign environment.

The weak organ may become the basis of a neurotic maladjustment, in which the person exploits the physical deficiency as an excuse for avoiding life's tasks. Physically handicapped children face this psychological danger. It takes a particularly skilled parent or teacher, like Anne Sullivan (Helen Keller's inspired teacher) to help such a child live more courageously.

On the other hand, in a healthy adjustment the child strives to *compensate for* the organ inferiority. Adler did so as a youngster. He worked very hard to overcome his physical weakness so as to perform adequately as an athlete with his age-mates. Adler suggested that children with defective ears may compensate by developing a musical capacity. He cited Beethoven, who became totally deaf in adulthood, as an example (1926/1988b). Early research suggested that people with deficient color vision or hearing compensate for these organ inferiorities, confirming Adler's theory (Overton, 1958).

Not everyone with an organ inferiority, of course, is able successfully to compensate for it. Nonetheless, the attempt to do so directs motivation. If compensation fails, the individual may instead develop an incapacitating sense that the inferiority cannot be overcome; hence, an *inferiority complex.*

Aggressive Drive. The second term Adler used for this process, as his theory evolved, was **aggressive drive**. The struggle toward the "felt plus" may take the form of fighting and cruelty. Or it may be expressed in a more socialized form as athletic competition or other striving for dominance, including politics. It is in this sense that we speak of "aggressive sports" or an "aggressive campaign," or even an "aggressive business deal." Consciously, the aggressive drive may be experienced as anger.

Masculine Protest. In a third stage of his thinking, Adler referred instead to **masculine protest**, an assertion of manliness that implies greater competence, superiority, and control. Such traits as aggressiveness and activity are seen as masculine, whereas submissiveness and obedience are feminine. Adler noted that traditional sex roles in culture, which give females a subordinate position, contribute to the experience of "masculine protest." He did not accept the sex roles of his culture as ideal, since they have adverse effects on both sexes (Adler, 1917/1988a). He wrote critically of "the arch evil of our culture, the excessive pre-eminence of manliness" (Ansbacher & Ansbacher, 1956, p. 55). Unequal valuation of the sexes, he reasoned, is a fundamental premise of the social fact of prostitution (Adler, 1923/1929).

Females, as well as males, are motivated by masculine protest as they struggle against the constraints of the less socially valued female role. Physical problems may result, including menstrual difficulties, difficulties with pregnancy and childbirth, and sexual disorders. Or masculine protest may lead women to become career-oriented, marry late or not at all, have fewer children, turn lesbian, or become nuns as a rejection of their feminine role. Despite the value judgments implicit in these "symptoms," Adler warned the therapist to "not bring his own value judgments about masculine and feminine traits to the analysis" (1978, p. 35).

Superiority Striving. In yet another stage of thought, Adler spoke of **superiority striving.** He did not mean eminence, so much as self improvement. He meant striving to achieve one's own "personal best," rather than striving to be better than others.

Perfection Striving. The final term Adler used for the process was "perfection striving." Perhaps more than any of his previous words, this connotes an inherent growth process within the individual. Other theorists, Rogers and Maslow (see Chapters 9 and 10), described a process that sounds quite similar to Adler's basic motivation. They called it "self-actualization."

Inferiority feelings are central to Adler's theory, yet explicit research on this topic has been hampered by lack of a suitable research instrument (Dixon & Strano, 1989). A Comparative Feeling of Inferiority Index has been proposed (Strano & Dixon, 1990).

INFERIORITY AND SUPERIORITY COMPLEX

Inferiority Complex. When the growth process stagnates, a person may fall victim to an **inferiority complex**. In this case, the "felt minus" situation is too powerful to be overcome and the person accepts an exaggerated sense of inferiority as an accurate self-description. All neurotics have an inferiority complex, according to Adler. Even non-neurotic people have *inferiority feelings*; but only in their exaggerated form, when they overwhelm attempts to move to the "felt plus" and stagnate growth, are they called a "complex."

Superiority Complex. Some neurotics repress their feelings of inferiority and believe themselves better than others. This outcome is termed a **superiority complex**. Because it masks an unconscious sense of inferiority, it is not a healthy outcome. People with a superiority complex often behave arrogantly; they exaggerate their achievements, which may be intellectual, athletic, or emotional, depending upon the unique strengths of the individual. They may adopt idiosyncratic behavior that sets them apart from others. Adler suggests that claims of telepathic powers may spring from a superiority complex. An exaggerated sense of one's superiority over other races and nationalities is another form of superiority complex.

Fictional Finalism

As described in Chapter 2, Freud was committed to the scientific assumption of determinism in even the psychological realm. This assumption led to a theory that treated humans as passive products of various forces, primarily biological. In contrast, Adler viewed individuals as causes, rather than effects. He argued that personality is *creative*. People make choices and determine their own outcomes in life. External factors present challenges and choices but do not wholly determine the outcomes. Or, to use an Adlerian phrase that captures this point of view, the person is a **creative self** who is trying to discover or create experiences that lead to fulfillment. For Adler, each person is "the artist of his own personality" (Ansbacher & Ansbacher, 1956, p. 177).

In his or her life situation, each person imagines a better situation than the present. This ideal situation is different for each person. It is an image of the fulfillment of what is lacking at the present time: a strong healthy body, if the person is ill; a fortune, if the person feels held back by lack of money; admiration, if the person feels unappreciated; and so forth. Horatio Alger sought a fortune, but that is not everyone's goal. Doctors, according to Adler, are often compensating for some early experience with death, trying to overcome it through their careers. Others are directed by a "redeemer complex," trying (not necessarily consciously) to save someone, perhaps through entering medicine or the ministry.

This imagined goal, the desirable future state, Adler called the **fictional finalism** of the individual. (Adler credited this term to the philosopher Hans Vaihinger). The "fictional finalism" is the individual's image of the goal. It is a subjective experience, rather than an objective reality. It gives direction to the individual's striving.

People do not ordinarily have a clear and complete idea of the fictionally final goal that directs them. This goal is "dimly envisaged," partly known and partly not known. The unknown part of the goal constitutes the *unconscious.* (Obviously this is a far different "unconscious" from Freud's, which emphasized the past, rather than the future.) Throughout life, the fictionally final goal may be modified. The general direction of striving remains, but the specific understanding of the goal may change. While a healthy person modifies the goal, a neurotic may have such an inflexible "fictional finalism" that behavior is not adaptive.

Since an individual's fundamental motivation is to move toward this fictionally final goal, a person cannot be understood without knowing the unique goal. Once it is understood, it explains the consistency of a person's striving.

Adler's assertion that individuals may interpret the same event as either threatening or challenging has been echoed by other psychologists (Folkman, 1984). Researchers have studied "hardiness," a trait that enables some people to experience stress without adverse health effects while others become ill under such stress; this concept is also consistent with Adler's concept (Kobasa, 1979; Kobasa, Maddi, & Kahn, 1982; Wiebe, 1991).

The Unity of Personality

Adler emphasized the unity of personality (1932/1988c, 1937/1982b). Before separating from Freud, he explained this unity as resulting from a "confluence of drives." As his theory evolved he abandoned the drive model and described personality as held together by the fictionally final goal and unique style of life.

This emphasis on unity contrasts sharply with Freud's description of conflict within personality. Freud thought that Adler was missing the point. According to Freud, unity is a façade created by the defense mechanism of overcompensation; it masks deeper conflicts within the personality. According to Freud, Adler did not understand the importance of repression and the unconscious. He, to be blunt, missed the point of the psychoanalytic revolution. Adler rejected the idea of conflict between the conscious and the unconscious as "an artificial division . . . that has its origin merely in psycho-analytic fanaticism" (Adler, 1936/1964, p. 93). Adler believed that the conscious and the unconscious worked together more often than they conflicted (Ansbacher, 1982).

Style of Life

A person's goal directs a unique **style of life**. The style of life begins as a compensatory process, making up for a particular inferiority. It leads to consistency of personality as the person compensates, even overcompensates, for this inferiority. Besides the goal, the style of life includes the individual's concepts about the self and the world and his or her unique way of striving toward the personal goal in that world.

First Memories

A person's style of life, according to Adler, is established by the age of 4 or 5. In this, he agreed with Freud about the importance of early experience in determining personality. A key to identifying the style of life is a person's *first memory.* The first memory sticks out because a person has thought about it repeatedly over the years, and it captures what has been subjectively important for the person.

The key to the importance of this early memory is not the objective facts recalled, but rather the psychological importance of the early memory for the individual. The first reported memory may not be factually accurate, but even erroneous memories are useful clues to personality. Adler himself reported an erroneous early memory. He recalled, as a child, running back and forth across a cemetery to overcome his fear of death. The memory must have been inaccurate, since there was no cemetery in the place he described. Nonetheless, the false memory is an important clue to Adler's own consistent efforts to overcome death (Monte, 1980). Adler regarded patients' reports of incredibly early events, such as memories of their own birth or maternal care in early infancy, as factually suspect but psychologically revealing.

Adler said that a person's "memories represent his 'Story of My Life'; a story he repeats to himself to warn him or comfort him, to keep him concentrated on his goal, and to prepare him by means of past experiences, so that he will meet the future with an already tested style of action" (Ansbacher & Ansbacher, 1956, p. 351). Memories are thus consistent with, and a key to, the style of life. Memories of accidents may suggest a lifestyle based on avoiding danger. Memories of the mother may suggest issues concerned with her care or lack of it. Memories of the first day at school may suggest "the great impression produced by new situations" (Ansbacher & Ansbacher, 1956, p. 354). (More examples of common early memories are interpreted there and in Adler, 1936/1964, chap. 12.)

Adler said he would always include questions about first memories in a personality analysis. People are willing to report them because they don't realize how much they disclose to a psychologist. Any early memories, even if they are not the very first memories, are still valuable clues to a person's unique style of life.

Early memories are routinely assessed in Adlerian counseling and are useful with clients of all ages, including the elderly (Sweeny & Myers, 1986). They can also be measured by the Early Recollections (ER) Questionnaire (Altman & Rule, 1980). When collected in a relaxed state of hypnogogic reverie (a self-hypnosis procedure), more detailed memories are produced (C. Warren, 1990). Validity studies have been conducted for several decades relating early memories to other measures (Taylor, 1975). Early memories are significantly related to vocational interest and vocational choice (Elliott, Amerikaner, & Swank, 1987), to delinquency (Davidow & Bruhn, 1990) and criminality (Hankoff, 1987), and to depression (Acklin, Sauer, Alexander, & Dugoni, 1989; Allers, White, & Hornbuckle, 1990). Correlations with various clinical scales (including the Minnesota Multiphasic Personality Inventory [MMPI] and the Symptom Checklist 90–Revised) confirms the hypothesis that early memories express "relationship paradigms," and thus can reflect adjustment or maladjustment (Acklin, Bibb, Boyer, & Jain, 1991). Borderline patients report more negative early memories, whereas neurotics report more happy early memories (Arnow & Harrison, 1991). Some researchers and theorists have investigated early memory from a cognitive perspective (e.g., Bruhn, 1990; Strauman, 1990).

Mistaken and Healthy Styles of Life

Adler did not like the practice of presenting typologies because they ignore the uniqueness of each individual. For teaching purposes, however, he conceded to describe four different types (Adler, 1935/1982a). His intent was not to classify people, but to make it easier to grasp his concept of styles of life.

Mistaken Styles of Life

Not all styles of life are equally desirable. Sometimes, early in life, people develop strategies for improving their situations that are, in the long run, maladaptive. For example, a child may become overly dependent upon doting parents, or overly rebellious. Adler referred to these as "mistaken styles of life." He listed several types, which we shall examine here.

Ruling Type. People adopting this mistaken lifestyle seek to dominate others. They may actively confront life's problems in a selfish way, becoming "delinquents, tyrants, sadists" (Ansbacher & Ansbacher, 1956, p. 168). Or, if less active, they may attack others indirectly through suicide, drug addiction, or alcoholism. Not all people of this type are despicable. Some, with talent and hard work, are high achievers, but they are vain and overly competitive. They may express their sense of superiority over others by belittling them, a tendency which Adler called the **deprecation complex** (Adler, 1921/1927, p. 161).

Getting Type. People adopting this mistaken lifestyle lean on others. They are dependent. They adopt a passive, rather than active, attitude toward life, and they may become depressed. Adler said that pampered children and females are subject to environmental pressures that encourage this neurotic style, but it is always the choice of the individual, rather than external circumstances, that determines the style of life.

Avoiding Type. Persons adopting this lifestyle try to avoid dealing with problems, thereby avoiding the possibility of defeat. Agoraphobia, an irrational fear that confines people to their homes, is one form of this maladaptive style of life. The avoiding type tends to be isolated and may strike others as cold. This outward appearance hides an underlying, but fragile, superiority belief. Whole classes, religious groups, and nations may adopt this style, which hinders the progress of civilization (Adler, 1921/1927, p. 186).

The Healthy Style of Life: The Socially Useful Type

If the lifestyle is, however, adaptive, Adler referred to it as a **socially useful type**. To be so characterized, a person must act in ways beneficial to others. This does not necessarily imply economic productivity or acts generally considered altruistic. Adler included artists and poets as people who "serve a social function more than anyone else. They have taught us how to see, how to think, and how to feel" (Ansbacher & Ansbacher, 1956, p. 153). These people have a well-developed sense of "social interest," which is described in a later section of this chapter. In addition, they feel a sense of internal control (Minton, 1968), an attitude that is especially important in the cognitive social learning theories of Rotter, Mischel and Bandura.

Although the concept of style of life is central to Adlerian theory, it has received little explicit research attention. A few self-report instruments have been developed to assess style of life, and they include other lifestyles besides the four suggested by Adler (Kern & White, 1989; Langenfeld & Main, 1983; Mullis, Kern, & Curlette, 1987; Watkins, 1982b). Data for the validity of these instruments are sparse, but they seem to contain the kinds of content that Adler's theory suggests, and they are offered as adjuncts to Adlerian counseling. Identification of style of life in childhood is particularly important, because intervention may prevent undesirable patterns from becoming resistant to change (Ansbacher, 1988).

The Development of Personality

Although Adler said that each person was fully responsible for his or her own choices in life, he did recognize that circumstances could incline people toward either undesirable or desirable styles of life. He was critical of restrictive sex roles (especially for women), of warlike orientations in government, of poverty and adverse living conditions. These societal factors impede the development of a psychologically healthy lifestyle.

Because style of life is developed early, the family is of particular importance. Adler, like Freud, described relationships with parents. In addition, he considered the impact of siblings on personality development.

Parental Behavior

A child begins life in a helpless state. Parents can help or hinder the development of a healthy lifestyle to compensate for this fundamental "felt minus." They can help prevent neurosis by protecting the child from tasks too difficult to be successfully completed and by ensuring that appropriate tasks are available. Parents err if they try to make their children always superior to everyone else, more symbols of parental worth than individuals in their own right.

The mother, in particular, influences the development of social feeling, the cooperative attitude that distinguishes healthy from unhealthy styles of life. The father, traditionally the authority in the family, teaches the child about power and its selfish or socially responsible expression. (Adler, like Freud, developed his theory in the context of the traditional two-parent nuclear family.)

Dreikurs and Soltz (1964) have summarized Adler's advice for raising healthy children (see Table 4.1).

The Pampered Child

Some of Adler's most critical remarks were directed toward parental **pampering** of children. Youngsters who are treated with overindulgence come to expect that others will cater to their needs. They are, in a word, spoiled. Ultimately, because the real world is far less indulgent than they have come to demand, they will not be loved.

Adler criticized Freudian theory as the construction of a pampered child. Who but a spoiled child, he asked, would propose a universal "Oedipus complex" in which the child wanted complete possession of the mother?

The Neglected Child

Parental **neglect** also contributes to maladaptive development. Children who have been neglected, including orphans and unwanted or illegitimate children, are likely to believe that others will not support them. The tasks of life seem overwhelmingly difficult.

Strangely, parental neglect can lead a child to adopt a pampered style of life. It is the desire to be pampered, the fictional goal of being cared for, rather than the fact of having been pampered, that characterizes the pampered style of life. Thus, neglected children, as well as overindulged chil-

TABLE 4.1 Advice for Raising Healthy Children, Derived from Adler's Approach

Encourage the child, rather than simply punishing.
Be firm, but not dominating.
Show respect for the child.
Maintain routine.
Emphasize cooperation.
Do not give the child too much attention.
Do not become engaged in power struggles with the child.
Show by your actions, not by your words.
Do not offer excessive sympathy.
Be consistent.

(Adapted from Dreikurs & Soltz, 1964.)

dren, can become overly dependent upon others for recognition and for nurturance.

Parental Training Programs

Parenting training programs have been developed based on Adlerian principles. Two types of such programs are Parent Study Groups (based on Dreikurs & Soltz, 1964) and the STEP or Systematic Training for Effective Parenting (Dinkmeyer & McKay, 1976). A major goal of these programs is to teach parents to understand the reasons for their children's misbehavior, so that they can more effectively influence it. Dreikurs (1950) identified four goals of children's behavior: "attention-getting, struggle for power or superiority, desire to retaliate or get even, and a display of inadequacy or assumed disability" (Dinkmeyer & Dinkmeyer, 1989, p. 28). Overall, these programs do improve parents' attitudes (Burnett, 1988; Dembo, Sweitzer, & Lauritzen, 1985). Some researchers report that they also lead to measurable improvement in the behavior of both parents and children and produce improvements in children's self-concept (Burnett, 1988), but others (Dembo, Sweitzer, and Lauritzen, 1985) are more skeptical.

Family Constellation

Interactions among sisters and brothers in childhood have important influences on the development of personality. Since other psychoanalysts have largely limited their descriptions of family influence to parent-child interactions, this emphasis on **family constellation** (the number, age, and sex of siblings) was an important and distinct contribution of Adler.

Firstborn Child

The firstborn child begins life with the full attention of the parents, and this child is often pampered or spoiled. Then, when other children arrive, the eldest must share the parents' attention with the new baby. Only the oldest child has had the full attention of the parents, and so only the firstborn feels so acutely the loss of parental, especially maternal, love. Adler described the eldest child as "dethroned" by the arrival of later children and noted, with some derision toward his former colleague, that even Freud had adopted his phrasing (Adler, 1936/1964, p. 231).

To compensate for having to share the mother with a new baby, the oldest child may turn to the father. Or he or she may take on a somewhat "parental" protective (and, not incidentally, powerful) role in relationship to the younger siblings. Eldest children may long for the past (that is, the time before competition), and they tend to overvalue authority and hold conservative values. Often, according to Adler, oldest children do not cope well with dethronement. They are likely to become "problem children, neurotics, criminals, drunkards, and perverts" (Ansbacher & Ansbacher, 1956, p. 377). Most problem children, he claimed, are firstborns.

Second-Born Child

The second-born, seeing the headstart that the older sibling has on life, may feel envious, experiencing "a dominant note of being slighted, neglected" (Adler, 1921/1927, p. 127). This often makes him or her rebellious, even revolutionary. This experience presents a challenge that can usually be successfully overcome.

The older sibling serves as a "pacemaker," Adler's analogy with a racer. Thus, the second-born child is stimulated to higher achievement. Observing the pace set by the older sibling, the second-born does not waste energy by trying an impossible pace. (In contrast, the firstborn may become exhausted by trying too hard, like a long-distance runner without a pacer.) Unlike the oldest child, the second child always has had to share parental love, and therefore is unlikely to have been spoiled. Adler regarded the second child as having the most favorable position.

Youngest Child

Often youngest children, said Adler, become problem children. The youngest child, as the baby of the family, is likely to grow up in a warmer atmosphere than the older youngsters (Adler, 1921/1927, p. 123). This poses the risk of being pampered and, as a spoiled child, lacking the incentive to develop independence. With too many pacemakers, the youngest child may compete in many directions, leading to a diffuseness and sense of inferiority. Success may be attainable if an area of effort not already claimed by other family members can be found. This is less true of female children, owing (at the time of Adler's writing) to the fewer opportunities available to women (Adler, 1936/1964, p. 239).

Only Child

The only child never competes with siblings for parental attention. This child is likely to be pampered and overly attached to the mother, who is often overprotective, so that the only child develops a "mother complex" (Ansbacher & Ansbacher, 1956, p. 381). Constant parental attention gives the only child an unrealistic sense of personal worth.

Other Aspects of the Family Environment

In addition to sibling position, many particular aspects of the family environment may modify these outcomes. Children whose talents are quite different from those of their siblings are in a far different situation from those who compete more directly. The spacing between children is significant. If many years pass between the birth of various children, they will all have some characteristics of an only child. The number of boys and girls also influences the encouragement of masculinity or femininity in each child.

Research on Birth Order

Research often reports significant effects of birth order on personality, but not always in the direction hypothesized by Adler. Research does not generally support Adler's claim that second-born children are the highest achievers; firstborns generally achieve highest (Forer, 1976; Goertzel, Goertzel, & Goertzel, 1978; S. Schachter, 1963) and are overrepresented among world political leaders (Hudson, 1990). Firstborns are more often Type A (time-pressured, coronary-prone) persons (Ivancevich, Matteson, & Gamble, 1987; Strube & Ota, 1982), especially if they are female (Phillips, Long, &

Bedeian, 1990). Firstborn males experience more anxiety than other positions (Fullerton, Ursano, Wetzler, & Slusarcick, 1989). Some evidence suggests that later-born males have better psychological well-being than do males in other positions (Fullerton and others, 1989), which is inconsistent with Adler's portrayal of a pampered child. Inconsistent findings are reported relating birth order to nightmares (Brink & Matlock, 1982; McCann, Stewin, & Short, 1990). In a study of early memories, later-borns were more likely than firstborns to include family members in their recollections, whereas firstborns were more likely to recall people outside the family, and to recall traumatic events such as injury; otherwise, the memories were similar (Fakouri & Hafner, 1984).

Several studies show that parents treat children in the various sibling positions differently. Parents generally have higher expectations for the firstborn child, to whom they give more responsibility (Hoffman, 1991). Lasko (1954), in a longitudinal study observing families at their homes, found that mothers' attention varies over time and is influenced by the number of siblings. Firstborns received a great deal of attention until a sibling was born, at which point the firstborn received very little attention. A study exploring the relationship between sibling position and the perception that one is the mother's or father's favorite child (Kiracofe & Kiracofe, 1990) found that sibling position was not very important; instead, children perceived favoritism by the parent of the opposite sex.

There is evidence that the effect of birth order may be different for females and males (Fullerton and others, 1989; Phillips, Long, & Bedeian, 1990), though more research is needed before we can clearly identify these differences. Additional studies are also needed to clarify the processes by which birth order has its sometimes powerful but not always consistent effects. Several studies fail to control for family size, making results ambiguous (Weinstein & Sackhoff, 1987). In addition, self-report measures may overestimate differences between siblings (Hoffman, 1991).

Although Adler described birth-order effects quite clearly, his theory emphasized that external conditions do not determine outcomes. Ultimately, individuals create their own styles of life.

Psychological Health

Adler's description of psychological health was phrased in more social, less purely individual, terms than Freud's intrapsychic model.

Social Interest

Humans are inherently social. A sense of community is essential for human survival. Adler considered the individual as "socially embedded." The more **social interest** the person has, the more that person's efforts are channeled into shared social tasks, rather than selfish goals, and the more psychologically healthy the person is.

In German, Adler used the term *Gemeinschaftsgefühl,* which has been translated as "social interest," "social feeling," "community feeling," and so forth. It should not be confused with extroversion. Nor is it simply the need for affection, although Adler did use that concept earlier in the development of his theory (Ansbacher & Ansbacher, 1956, p. 40).

Social interest is an innate potentiality to live cooperatively with other people. It enables the person to value the common good above personal welfare. Although social interest is an inborn potential, it must be fostered. In early life the mother serves as the "first bridge to social life" (Ansbacher & Ansbacher, 1956, p. 372) by being trustworthy and loving, but not possessing, and by fostering cooperative interactions with others.

Social interest is a core concept for Adler. All neurosis stems from inadequate social feeling. An extreme lack of social feeling occurs in schizophrenia. Criminals, too, lack sufficient social interest, as do those who commit suicide (Adler, 1937/1958). Baumeister lists "feelings of responsibility and fear that others will disapprove" (1990, p. 107) as one of several deterrents to suicide. Such feelings seem to correspond closely to Adler's concept of social interest, although Baumeister's theory is considerably broader.

Groups, as well as individuals, can be described by social interest or the lack thereof. Lack of social interest leads "groups and nations toward the abyss of self-extermination" (Ansbacher & Ansbacher, 1956, p. 449). Societies impede the development of social interest through the glorification of war, the death penalty, physical punishment and abuse, and failure to provide humane conditions for all classes and categories of people (Adler, 1936/1964, pp. 280–281). Healthy social institutions, including religion, teach "Love thy neighbor" (Ansbacher & Ansbacher, 1956, p. 449), thus fostering social interest.

Adler assessed social interest through an interview and history (see Table 4.2).

Several self-report scales have been developed to measure social interest. The most commonly used are the Social Interest Scale (Crandall, 1975) and the Social Interest Index (Greever, Tseng, & Friedland, 1973). Social interest can also be coded from questionnaires and rating scales measuring early recollections (Baruth & Eckstein, 1981). A Tasks of Life Survey also purports to measure social interest in four areas: work, friendship, intimacy, and self-significance (Zarski, Bubenzer, & West, 1986). The diversity of measures is troublesome. They do not seem to be all measuring the same thing (Leak, Millard, Perry, & Williams, 1985; Mozdzierz, Greenblatt, & Murphy, 1988), leaving ambiguity about what precisely is meant by social interest, or which scale best measures it. Furthermore, self-report measures of social interest cannot be taken at face value, since social desirability influences at least some scores (Leak, 1982).

TABLE 4.2 Examples of Questions Suggested by Adler to Measure Psychological Health in Children

1. Did the child make friends easily, or was he unsociable, and did he torment people and animals?
2. Is the child inclined to take the lead? Or does he stand aside?
3. Does the child have rivalries with siblings?
4. Does the child interrupt other children's games?
5. In what respect is the child discouraged? Does he feel himself slighted? Does he react favorably to appreciation and praise?
6. Does the child speak openly of his lack of ability, of his "not being gifted enough" for school, for work, for life? Has he thoughts of suicide?

(Adapted from Adler, 1936/1964, pp. 299–307.)

Although not all measures of social interest yield the same results, several studies confirm theoretical predictions. People who score high on social interest score low on narcissism (Miller, Smith, Wilkinson, & Tobacyk, 1987), low on alienation (Leak & Williams, 1989), and low on MMPI scales that indicate maladjustment (Mozdzierz, Greenblatt, & Murphy, 1988). They score high on the Affiliation, Nurturance, and Aggression scales of the Personality Research Form and on scales of the Life Styles Inventory thought to be associated with self-actualization (Leak and others, 1985). Some studies report that measures of social interest correlate with prosocial behaviors: volunteering in legal advocacy (but not other kinds of) agencies (Hettman & Jenkins, 1990) and having more friends (Watkins & Hector, 1990).

High scorers are also more satisfied with their jobs (Amerikaner, Elliot, & Swank, 1988), suggesting that they have dealt better with this life task than have those low in social interest. They are also healthier. Perhaps they can resist the effects of negative life experiences and hassles on health. In a correlational study, though, it is also possible that causality is reversed, that is, that health leads to social interest (Zarski, Bubenzer, & West, 1986).

Overall, researchers in the area of social interest are convinced that this construct is useful and that Adler's conceptualization was sound, although they have some unresolved questions about its measurement.

The Three Tasks of Life

Life in society requires cooperation, and therefore social interest. This is readily seen by considering the three fundamental tasks of life: work, love, and social interaction. Success in all three areas is evidence of mental health.

Work

Work refers to the task of having an occupation, earning a living by some socially useful job. Division of labor is a means for organizing cooperation among people in providing for the necessities and wants of everyone. Any occupation that contributes to the community is desirable. When children describe their occupational aspirations, they provide insight into their whole style of life. Occupational aspirations may change as the child learns more about reality. This, said Adler, is a healthy sign (Ansbacher & Ansbacher, 1956, pp. 430–431). Criminals fail in the work task (as also in the other two tasks), and this failure can usually be observed from early in their life histories (Ansbacher & Ansbacher, 1956, p. 412).

Love

The love task refers to sexual relationships and marriage between men and women, including the decision to have children (Ansbacher & Ansbacher, 1956, p. 432). Adler recommended monogamy as the best solution to the love task (Ansbacher & Ansbacher, 1956, p. 132) and remonstrated against premarital sex, saying it detracts from "the intimate devotion of love and marriage" (Ansbacher & Ansbacher, 1956, p. 434). Someone who falls in love with two people simultaneously is, by doing so, avoiding the full love task (Ansbacher & Ansbacher, 1956, p. 437).

Adler thought that many sexual dysfunctions and perversions, and even disinterest in the partner, stem from lack of social interest rather than from purely physical causes. Equality between men and women is essential for success in the task of love, according to Adler. Successful love affirms the worth of both partners. In other ways his attitudes sound less modern. Although he did suggest that birth control and abortion should be a woman's choice (Ansbacher & Ansbacher, 1956, p. 434), Adler criticized the decision by some women not to have children. It is interesting to speculate how he would resolve this issue now, as we approach the end of the twentieth century on an overpopulated planet. Is there a conflict between his recommendation of parenthood as the norm of healthy individual choice and the need for humankind to maintain a habitable planet?

Social Interaction

This task refers to "the problems of communal life" (Adler, 1936/1964, p. 42), that is, social relationships with others, including friendship. Unlike the two preceding tasks, social interaction is not one that Freud listed when he described a healthy person as someone who can "love and work." People perform this life task better if they are high in social interest. All social relationships should be based upon a strong sense of social interest, which prevents a self-centered, narcissistic attitude.

All three tasks are interrelated. None can be solved in isolation. None can be solved adequately unless there is sufficient social interest. If there is a fourth life task, Adler suggested, it is art (Bottome, 1947, p. 81).

Adler described children's different levels of confidence about meeting life's tasks. The optimistic child believes the tasks are attainable, whereas the pessimistic child timidly and distrustfully does not expect to succeed (Adler, 1921/1927, pp. 332–333). In this observation, Adler anticipated the modern concept of "self-efficacy," which has been a fruitful theoretical and therapeutic idea (cf. Bandura, 1977, and this text, Chapter 13).

Therapy and Other Interventions

Like all psychoanalysts, Adler discussed the role of formal psychotherapy in overcoming psychological distress. Some specific intervention is often needed to overcome developmental errors from childhood. We do not learn readily from life itself because we interpret life experience according to the often erroneous directions of our style of life (Adler, 1921/1927, p. 222).

Besides formal psychotherapy, the principles of individual psychology can be applied in other interventions as well, such as schools.

School

Adler thought that schools have great potential for personality growth, but only if traditional authoritarian methods are replaced by practices designed to foster social interest. Teachers should encourage cooperation among students. When problems arise, even problems traditionally handled by teachers, such as laziness, they should be discussed by the students. The problem child should not be personally identified, but will learn from the group (Ansbacher & Ansbacher, 1956, p. 402).

Adler recommended having classmates help teach slower learners. He favored clubs. He thought it was a good idea for a teacher to have the same students for several years to permit more effective intervention in personality development.

Adler taught his concepts of Individual Psychology in over 30 Child Guidance Clinics that he established in Vienna during the 1920s. In these clinics he interviewed a problem child in front of an audience of teachers, using this demonstration to instruct them in the principles of his psychology. These clinics were well attended and successful, but in the early 1930s, political changes in Europe forced them to close. During the years the clinics operated, court cases of juvenile delinquency and neuroses in Vienna were substantially decreased (Bottome, 1947, p. 51).

The city of Vienna also established a public Individual Psychology Experimental School as a place for Adlerian ideas to be applied. The original school operated only from 1931 to 1934 when, along with the child-guidance clinics, it was closed. Demonstration schools were reopened after World War II (Ansbacher & Ansbacher, 1956, p. 404).

Adlerians continue to develop new intervention programs in schools (Corsini, 1989; Dinkmeyer, McKay, & Dinkmeyer, 1982; Morse, Bockoven, & Bettesworth, 1988).

Therapy

Because Individual Psychology regards all personality failures as resulting from a lack of social interest, Adlerian therapy aims to foster the person's social interest, that is, to take over a maternal function (Ansbacher & Ansbacher, 1956, p. 119). In stressing the social nature of the human, Adlerians also have been highly involved in family therapy (Dinkmeyer & Dinkmeyer, 1989; Sherman & Dinkmeyer, 1987).

The client's style of life is assessed at the beginning of therapy, often in the first consultation. It provides a context for understanding the patient's specific problem. By asking a patient, "What would you do if you had not got this trouble?" Adler was able to determine what the patient was trying to avoid (Bottome, 1947, p. 148). The style of life provides a general strategy for avoiding life's tasks, and the specific problem that the patient presents in therapy is often intertwined with the style of life. The symptom, therefore, cannot be removed without modifying the style of life.

Changing to a healthier style of life necessarily involves increases in social interest. Benefits are expected not only for the client but also for others. Tinling (1990) suggested that the mother of a female incest victim unwittingly contributed to the family problem by an unhealthy, victimized style of life; an increase in her social feeling would make incest less likely in the family. (Obviously, this is only one perspective on a complex issue; the mother is not the only one to blame or to change.)

Adler gave the example of a man unrealistically distrustful that his fiancée would break their engagement. The man's first memory (always an important clue to the style of life) was of being picked up by his mother in a crowd, but then put down again so that his younger brother could be picked up. This memory suggests a lifestyle based on a sense of not being the favorite one, which of course would contribute to later doubts about the earnestness of his intended spouse (Adler, 1921/1927, pp. 30–31).

Dreams are interpreted as indicators of the individual's unique style of life. The key to understanding dreams, for Adler, is the emotion they create.

These emotions are the ones needed by the dreamer to solve life's current problems. Adler cited the example of a man who dreamt that his wife had failed to take care of their third child, so that the child became lost. He woke feeling critical of his wife. This emotion, although triggered by a dream that was not accurate in terms of facts, was the emotion the man needed to deal with his own dissatisfaction with his marriage (Ansbacher & Ansbacher, 1956, p. 361).

Like Freud, Adler considered it important to understand childhood experiences. Unlike Freud, he tried to avoid the development of a transference relationship, which he thought unnecessarily complicates and prolongs psychotherapy. Adler thought that treatment should show some success within the first three months. Adlerian therapy is typically brief (Ansbacher, 1989). As in schools, Adler recommended avoiding an authoritarian approach in analysis. The therapist can coach and advise, but it is the effort and courage of the client that determine whether there will be a favorable outcome (cf. Sizemore & Huber, 1988). Adler explicitly encouraged his patients to accept this responsibility. He did not intimidate patients with his scholarly expertise, preferring to talk to them "like an old grandmother," according to a close friend (Bottome, 1947, p. 41).

Adlerian therapy aims to enhance the self-esteem of the client. A sense of inferiority is the basis of all unhealthy styles of life. Adler said, "I believe that by changing our opinion of ourselves we can also change ourselves" (Bottome, 1947, p. 83). He, of course, challenged the false self-presentations of his patients, but he did his "unmasking . . . with love" (Bottome, 1947, p. 42). The atmosphere in Adler's sessions was supportive, with minimal tension. Adler used humor frequently. He told his biographer that a chapter should be titled "Therapeutic Jokes" (Bottome, 1947, p. 119). Perhaps surprisingly, a formal therapeutic intervention using humor has been devised (Prerost, 1989), although not within a specifically Adlerian context.

Adler respected the religious commitments of his patients. He regarded the idea of God as reflection of the basic human striving for a better condition. The patient's religious commitments could facilitate this growth process. (Freud, in contrast, emphasized the defensive function of religion.)

Physical as well as psychological improvement can result from therapy. Adler reported relief from "nervous headaches, migraine, trigeminal neuralgia, and epileptiform attacks" (Adler, 1936/1964, p. 78) in cases not caused by organic problems. He claimed that even thyroid problems can respond to psychological treatment (1936/1964, p. 181). He recognized genuine physical components to disease and insisted that psychotherapists be supervised by a physician if they were not medically trained themselves. Yet psychological factors are almost incredibly involved in some physical conditions. Adler described a patient who had a rash identical to her mother's, supposedly due to hereditary factors. The mother's testimony that the girl had been adopted in infancy supported Adler's belief that many apparent hereditary and physical diseases are largely psychologically determined (Bottome, 1947, p. 68).

Adler's claims of the importance of psychological factors in physical disease are more persuasive because of his many years as a general practitioner preceding his specialization in psychiatry. He had a reputation for competence as a medical doctor (Bottome, 1947). We may regard Adler as a pioneer in the field of psychosomatic medicine, which recognizes psychogenic components in many physical illnesses. Even cancer has been proposed to have some psychological etiology, a postulate far from proven but which is compatible with Adlerian thought (O'Connor, 1987). Longitudinal research shows that pessimistic explanatory style predicts poor health decades later (Peterson, Seligman, & Vaillant, 1988); it seems reasonable to interpret the health-producing optimistic explanatory style as an indicator of Adlerian creative striving. Style of life has also been related to physical well-being. Research shows that wellness orientation—that is, a person's orientation to take care of his or her physical health—is associated with style of life. People with "Achieving" styles of life are high in wellness orientation, and those with "Detaching" and "Avoiding" lifestyles are low (Britzman & Main, 1990).

Adler was innovative in his therapeutic techniques. He once got a patient whose speech was extremely slow, the result of depression, to speak more quickly simply by continuing to ask questions at a normal pace, whether the patient had finished responding yet or not (Dreikurs, 1940/1982). A behaviorist might say that he succeeded by withholding reinforcement (attention) for slow speech. Indeed, Pratt (1985) argued that Adlerian therapy is a primitive statement of operant conditioning principles. Adlerian therapists continue to explore new techniques, including hypnosis as a means of producing lifestyle change (Fairfield, 1990). W. O'Connell (1990) claims that his "natural high" approach encompasses Adlerian principles of holism and transcendence.

Summary

Adler emphasized conscious striving and the creative self, in contrast to Freud's unconscious determinism. He described the fundamental motivation to strive from a "felt minus" to a "felt plus." A person with an *inferiority complex* feels overcome by a lack of worth and ceases striving. In this striving, a person is guided by *fictional finalism,* the image of the goal. Adler viewed personality as a unity. A person's unique *style of life* is evidenced by early memories. Although he thought of each person as unique, Adler listed types of mistaken styles of life: the ruling type, getting type, and avoiding type of person. In contrast, a healthy style of life is socially useful (see Table 4.3).

Parents contribute to unhealthy styles of life by *pampering* or *neglecting* their children. Adler's theory has inspired training programs for parents. *Family constellation,* particularly birth order, influences personality development. Adler regarded the second-born as in the most desirable position, although research does not confirm his prediction of higher achievement for this sibling position.

Social interest is the key factor in psychological health. A healthy person succeeds in three tasks of life: work, love, and social interaction. Adler intervened in schools to deal with problem children. Adlerian therapy supports self-esteem and aims to change the style of life to a *socially useful* one. Adler described physical as well as psychological benefits of therapy.

TABLE 4.3 Contributions of Adler's Theory to Various Topics

Biological	Organ inferiority provides the direction of personality development through compensation.
Child Development	Extensive guidelines for childrearing are provided, especially the caution to avoid pampering. Birth order affects personality.
Adult Development	Throughout life, people create their own personalities through goal-setting.
Mental Health	Health involves love, work, and social interaction, and is the responsibility of each individual.
Society	Society influences people through social roles, including sex roles. Schools are especially influential.
Cognitive Processes	Conscious experience and thought are important and generally trustworthy.
Individual Differences	Individuals differ in their goals and in how they try to achieve them, their "style of life."

ILLUSTRATIVE BIOGRAPHIES: Concluding Remarks

Adler's theory emphasizes the purposive striving of the individual and the early selection of a goal, a *fictional finalism,* which directs later striving. Both Tina Turner and Donald Trump attained great success, and much in their life stories fits Adler's theory.

Donald Trump

Donald Trump described his philosophy as "think big." He aspired to surpass his father and another real-estate developer, William Zeckendorf. This aspiration illustrates Adler's concept of masculine protest, which "intensifies the desires of the child, who then seeks to surpass the father in every respect" (Ansbacher & Ansbacher, 1956, p. 48).

This striving is reflected in early childhood memories. Trump recalled, as a youngster, begging his father to take him to see the Empire State Building, then the tallest structure in the world (Trump, 1987, p. 337). One of his childhood constructions was such a tall building that it used all his blocks and several of his brother's. To keep his brother from taking back his blocks, Donald glued them all together (Trump, 1987, p. 72)! Already, his lifestyle included clever and extraordinary means to claim "the tallest" for himself, although it would be years before he planned to build in New York the world's tallest building.

Trump recalled that he was always assertive, even aggressive. In the second grade he punched his music teacher, giving him a black eye (Trump, 1987, p. 71). (One wonders how Adler would have intervened in a school clinic.) This early experience, combined with the aggressiveness of his business dealings, makes Trump fit Adler's description of a "ruling type."

Trump's trademark emphasis on the conspicuous display of his name can also be traced to a childhood memory. He observed that the designer of a major Hudson River bridge was not named in an otherwise elaborate bridge opening ceremony (Tuccille, 1985). Trump seems to have vowed never to let that happen to him. In addition, he must have been sensitive in childhood that his older brother had the privilege of being his father's namesake. His conspicuous public display of his own name may vindicate a particular sense of inferiority on this point.

Trump's father, Fred Trump, had intended for his eldest son, Fred Jr., to follow in his footsteps as a real-estate developer. However, this son showed no interest in the business. He later became alcoholic, resulting in an early death. Donald, however, was interested in his father's work ever since childhood. In this case, Adler's prediction that the second child will be the most successful is confirmed if we agree for this construction business to disregard the female children.

There is no clear evidence that the adult Donald Trump would so readily confine women to traditional roles. Though Trump's mother was a housewife, he reported "I've hired a lot of women for top jobs, and they've been among my best people" (Trump, 1987, p. 173). His wife, Ivana, before their divorce, also participated actively in some aspects of his business.

Adler suggested that the mark of mental health is social interest. How does Trump measure up by this criterion? The aim to build exceptional projects and, thereby, to amass a fortune surely seems selfish rather than other-oriented. His service to New York City in renovating the Wollman Rink may reflect social interest; but the publicity was a boost to his career, so his motivation is debatable. Even his offer to house the homeless in one of his apartments was, despite his disclaimers, motivated selfishly. At the time he was attempting to evict residents of the apartments, who were protected by rent controls, in order to renovate the building.

Perhaps the development of social interest is a mid-life task for Donald Trump. In his autobiography, Trump said, "The biggest challenge I see over the next twenty years is to figure out some creative ways to give back some of what I've gotten" (Trump, 1987, pp. 366–367). In his early forties at the time of that statement, several decades still remain to meet the Adlerian criterion of social interest.

Tina Turner

Tina Turner's childhood (as Anna Mae Bullock) epitomizes the plight of the neglected child, a situation Adler described as often leading to a faulty lifestyle. She was abandoned by her parents at age 3, and again later after a temporary return. She sensed that her sister was her mother's favorite. Consistent with Adler's description of second-born children, Tina responded with a rebellious attitude, but she was unable to overcome the feeling of being unloved. She said bluntly, "I had no love from my mother or my father from the beginning, from birth" (T. Turner, 1986, p. 10).

Turner described herself as a "brazen tomboy" (1986, p. 11). Adler would surely call this "masculine protest." The "felt minus" situation she was trying to overcome stemmed from her dissatisfaction with the impoverished and cold atmosphere of her family and the town where she lived. The town was poor and had unpaved streets and outdoor plumbing. Although her family was less impoverished than many other blacks, she was aware that white folks had finer homes and more loving families.

According to Adler, feeling unloved and being exposed to poverty and racial segregation contribute to a sense of inferiority. Tina Turner's negative self-image contributed to the acceptance of physical abuse from Ike Turner. Although her stage image was successful, as a real person Tina said, "I was like a shadow. I almost didn't exist. . . . I used to hate myself back then. . . ." (T. Turner, 1986, pp. 130–131).

An early memory, though, provides a clue to a positive element in her self-image, an aspect of her unique style of life that was eventually to lead Tina Turner to a more positive future. When shopping with her mother, the child Anna Mae, as she was then still called, would sing, and the sales clerks and customers would give her praise, and also money. "I got a big glass bank, and I started filling it up. . . . I can still see that bank in my mind, filled with those shiny coins. Just for singing" (T. Turner, 1986, p. 16).

Her goal, which gave enduring direction to her striving, was to achieve a life with more glamour. She enjoyed shopping and used it as an escape. Tina Turner pursued this goal with a "getting" style of life, an unhealthy style that contributed to the suffering of her early adult years. She leaned particularly on her husband for meeting her financial and professional needs.

Her mother said Anna Mae usually played alone as a child, behavior that Adler interprets as characteristic of people with low social interest. Her suicide attempt at age 28 is also evidence of low social interest. There is no evidence in her autobiography of success at the "love" task, and few close friendships are reported. The "work" task, at least, has been accomplished with considerable success.

After leaving Ike, Tina Turner made significant changes in her style of life. She became more assertive and prepared for a "socially useful" stage of life. She probably had not completed the transition at the time her autobiography was written, although she was freer to give to others than in her earlier years. She participated in the widely publicized benefit for African famine relief, singing "We Are the World" with dozens of other celebrities in a communal endeavor with obvious positive social value. She remarked, "I'm not ripe enough to teach anybody." She was referring to the spiritual lessons she herself was still learning (T. Turner, 1986, p. 252). She displayed courage, an attribute Adler described as essential for the development of a healthy style of life.

These two people, Tina Turner and Donald Trump, clearly worked hard for their success. Adler's theory would credit them both for their success, but would also demand that social interest be added to material success.

GLOSSARY

aggressive drive one of Adler's terms for positive striving, emphasizing anger and competitiveness

creative self the person who acts to determine his or her own life

deprecation complex unhealthy way of seeking superiority by belittling others

family constellation the configuration of family members, including the number and birth order of siblings

fictional finalism a person's image of the goal of his or her striving

inferiority complex stagnation of growth in which difficulties seem too immense to be overcome

masculine protest one of Adler's terms for positive striving, emphasizing manliness

neglect parental behavior in which a child's needs are not adequately met

pampering parental behavior in which a child is overindulged or spoiled

social interest innate potential to live cooperatively with other people
socially useful type a personality that is well-adjusted
style of life a person's consist way of striving
superiority complex a neurotic belief that one is better than others
superiority striving effort to achieve improvement in oneself

STUDY QUESTIONS

1. How does Adler's approach to personality differ from that of Freud?
2. Describe a person's fundamental motivation, according to Adler. List five terms he used in the development of this idea.
3. Distinguish between a feeling of inferiority and an inferiority complex.
4. Explain the term *fictional finalism.* Give an example.
5. Explain how early memories are a key to personality.
6. What is a *style of life*? List three mistaken styles of life. What did Adler call a healthy style of life?
7. How do parents contribute to their children's development of unhealthy styles of life?
8. Discuss Adler's theory of the relationship between birth order and personality. What does research show?
9. Explain what is meant by *social interest.*
10. List and explain the three tasks of life.
11. Describe Adler's interventions in schools.
12. Describe Adlerian therapy.

CHAPTER

Erikson: Psychosocial Development

BIOGRAPHY OF ERIK ERIKSON

Erik Erikson

Erik Homberger Erikson (as we now call him) was born in Germany in 1902. Erik was raised by his mother, who was Jewish and of Danish ancestry, and his stepfather, a Jewish pediatrician. Erik believed that his stepfather was his biological father and was given his last name, Homberger. His biological father, a Danish Protestant, had left Erik's mother before Erik was born. Erik was not accepted as fully Jewish because of the physical appearance that was the legacy of his Danish parents: tall, blonde, and blue-eyed. Yet he hadn't been raised to think of himself as Danish. This somewhat confused background contributed to his own keen interest in "identity," as he later said.

Erikson studied art and wandered through Europe in his youth, trying to become an artist (Wurgaft, 1976). In a job found at the suggestion of a friend, Erikson taught art to children of Freud's entourage. His future wife, Joan Serson, was studying to be a psychoanalyst, and she introduced him to psychoanalysis. (Interestingly, in later years he became the psychoanalyst and she the artist.) Erikson was analyzed by Freud's daughter, Anna, and was recruited as an analyst, a "lay analyst" because of his nonmedical training. In 1933, he and his wife, Joan, left Germany, where anti-Semitism was becoming increasingly overt. They went briefly to Denmark, his ancestral home, and then to the United States. To mark the identity change in his own life, he took "Erikson" as a last name at this time.

Although he had no college degree, Erikson became a child analyst and taught at Harvard. There he was affiliated with the Harvard Psychological Clinic, under Henry Murray (Erikson, 1963). He also was affiliated, at various stages in his career, with the Yale Institute of Human Relations; the Guidance Study in the Institute of Human Development at the University of California at Berkeley; and the Austen Riggs Center in the Berkshires. Besides his clinical and developmental studies, his association with anthropologists permitted him to observe development among two American Indian cultures, the Sioux at Pine Ridge, South Dakota, and the Yurok, a California fishing tribe.

At the time that Erikson was a Professor of Psychology and a Lecturer in Psychiatry at the University of California at Berkeley, the United States was undergoing a wave of concern about Communist infiltration in schools. Faculty members were required to sign an additional loyalty oath, besides the oath in which they had already routinely pledged to uphold the national and state constitutions. Erikson and several others refused, resulting in dismissal, although this was overturned in court. In explaining his action, Erikson argued that the anticommunist hysteria that had prompted the requirement of a loyalty oath was dangerous to the university's historical role as a place where truth and reason can be freely sought, and where students learn critical thinking (Erikson, 1951b). Undoubtedly his experience with German nationalism under the Nazis figured in his position.

Although he considered himself a Freudian, Erikson proposed many theoretical innovations that emphasized the ego and social factors. Most notably, he theorized that ego development continues throughout life. In his eighties, he and his wife were still active, interviewing a group of elderly Californians to learn more about this last stage of life (Erikson, Erikson, & Kivnick, 1986).

Erikson's most important contribution was to provide a model of personality development that extends throughout the life span. His description of adolescent identity development has been highly influential, and his contribution to the understanding of aging has influenced thinking in the field of gerontology. The concept of ego development, though by no means exclusively Erikson's contribution (cf. Hartmann, 1958; Loevinger, 1966), has been made much more popular as a consequence of his work. His impact on the interdisciplinary fields of psychohistory and psychobiography has also been immense.

ILLUSTRATIVE BIOGRAPHIES

Erikson has been a major influence in the fields of psychohistory (Pois, 1990) and psychobiography. He described the psychobiographer's task as one involving "disciplined subjectivity" (1975, p. 25). It requires undistorted self-knowledge, which can be achieved through psychoanalysis. His 1958 book, *Young Man Luther*, triggered renewed interest in applying psychological theory to historical figures and became a model for psychohistorians (Coles, 1970; Hutton, 1983; Schnell, 1980). It helped move psychohistory beyond a stage in which it documented the impact of great people on history, and toward a stage that recognizes the mutual influences of psychological and historical forces (Fitzpatrick, 1976). Erikson (1958b, 1975) proposed that the conflicts of the people studied in psychobiography were not simply individual conflicts, but that they represent the conflicts of the society in which the person lived. Thus the study of individuals can enlighten historical understanding.

Erikson's psychobiographical approach has been praised as valuable to the study of aging (Weiland, 1989). Some critics (Fitzpatrick, 1976; Hutton, 1983; Manuel, 1971) question whether Erikson's theory should perhaps be applied only to biographies of people living in the twentieth century, since the experience of childhood and adolescence, and even the concept of midlife change, is a recent historical phenomenon.

Besides Luther, Erikson wrote brief analyses of George Bernard Shaw (1968b), of Hitler and Gorky (1963) and of Gandhi (1969). His analysis of Gandhi, *Gandhi's Truth: On the Origins of Militant Nonviolence* (1969), won the Pulitzer Prize and the National Book Award.

Mahatma Gandhi

Mohandas Gandhi (later called "Mahatma," or "Great Soul," to honor his spiritual leadership) was born in 1869 in Porbandar, India, to the young fourth wife of a government administrator. His father's family had, for several generations, served in government offices under British rule. According to the custom of his large Hindu family, Gandhi was married at age 13. This was a real marriage, not simply an engagement. Mohandas and his bride, Kasturba, lived together and conceived a child, who died shortly after birth. This occurred not long after the death of Gandhi's father, when Gandhi was 16. Later, he and Kasturba had other children, four sons.

Gandhi went to England for his law degree. Members of his caste refused approval of this voyage. In leaving, he became an outcast, and he was socially ostracized upon his return. His mother's consent was given only after he had vowed to abstain from meat, wine, and women. Gandhi promised, not confessing that he had already eaten meat with a friend. He honored this vow to his mother in England and thereafter. He refused meat, meat broth, eggs, and milk, even when doctors advised them to treat illness. There was one exception when he took goat's milk, legalistically reasoning that he had only promised his mother to refrain from the milk of cows and buffalo; but he regretted this action. In fact, his dietary restrictions expanded, so that for the most part his diet consisted of fruit and nuts.

After earning his law degree, and because it was difficult to become established as a lawyer in India, Gandhi worked as a lawyer for an Indian company in South Africa. There he was the victim of racial prejudice. Indians were resented for their economic threat and different living habits. Despite his British education, he was refused hotel accommodation and first-class train travel. Once he was beaten simply for being in the wrong neighborhood. Gandhi embarked on a larger career of public service and political activism on behalf of Indians in South Africa, and, later, in India. He was influential in ending the practice of indentured labor. In India he founded an *ashram* (a traditional communal living arrangement), and boldly admitted an Untouchable family to membership, violating traditional Indian caste practices. He organized Indian fabric workers against exploitation by their employers, and he organized a civil disobedience movement to protest the British salt tax. He went to prison for his political activities. Throughout, he was guided by the principle of *ahimsa,* or nonviolence, which seeks to do no harm to others (Gandhi, 1957, p. 349; Teixeira, 1987). He fasted as a political strategy.

Much in the life of this world-renowned leader invites psychoanalytic analysis. His focus on concerns of eating and of sexual restraint match two of the areas of libidinal focus named by Freud. The other, anality, is also well represented in his autobiography, with frequent concern about unsanitary conditions, which were prevalent in India because of lack of indoor plumbing. To explain how his personal psychology relates to the public and political arenas, however, it is necessary to theorize beyond the psychosexual level, as Erikson's psychosocial theory does.

Eleanor Roosevelt

Eleanor Roosevelt was born in October 1884, the oldest child of a New York City society family related to Theodore Roosevelt (Eleanor's uncle). Her childhood was disrupted by the deaths of all her family except one brother. Her mother died when Eleanor was 8 and her father (who had been away from the family for several years, in treatment for alcoholism) when she was 9. One of her two younger brothers died of diphtheria shortly before her father's death. After her mother's passing, Eleanor was raised by her grandmother.

In her teens, Eleanor spent three years at a boarding school in England. The headmistress, Mlle. Souvestre, inspired her not only to learn the social skills expected for her role in "Society," but also to think intelligently about the larger world.

At 19, Eleanor Roosevelt married Franklin D. Roosevelt, a distant cousin who shared her last name. Her uncle, President Theodore Roosevelt, attended the ceremony. Eleanor and Franklin later had four sons and a daughter. A sixth child died in the first few weeks of life. A close relationship with Franklin's mother aroused conflicting feelings of affection and resentment in Eleanor. Early in the marriage, Eleanor's sense of self was defined primarily by her role as mother and wife. She presided over the large household, staffed by servants (for they were affluent), and supported her husband as he rose politically from assistant secretary of the Navy, to governor of New York, to ultimately become the thirty-second President of the United States (1933–1945).

The marriage between these two strong personalities was threatened by her husband's affair with Lucy Mercer. Eleanor offered him a divorce. He refused, she thought, out of concern for his political career. In her autobiography, Eleanor Roosevelt described this crisis as a turning point in her life. Thereafter, she involved herself in interests outside the home, writing for magazines and speaking on the radio and in lectures. She continued these activities as First Lady and thereafter. Yet her activities were closely intertwined with those of Franklin. She became a sounding board and an informal access route to the presidency during the White House years. Though she had not attended college, she spoke many languages and was acquainted with European cultures, so she could facilitate personal relationships between the President and the heads of state of several European nations. As the President's wife, she was an important partner, not simply a source of emotional support. In fact, her political influence seems to have diminished her capacity for purely emotional support. She would not permit Franklin to rest, any more than she herself would place personal enjoyment ahead of duty. Franklin is said to have prayed, "O Lord, make Eleanor tired" (Lash, 1972, p. 162).

When her husband died in office, only months before the end of World War II, many expected that Eleanor Roosevelt's public life would subside. It did not. Besides continuing her newspaper column, she served as a delegate to the United Nations. She chaired the committee that prepared a statement on human rights, negotiating vigorously with the Russians who objected to the emphasis on individual rights over economic issues. Eleanor won the respect of those who had questioned her appointment and ultimately saw the adoption of a statement on human rights by the United Nations General Assembly, which recognized her contribution with a standing ovation.

PSYCHOSOCIAL DEVELOPMENT

Each person develops within a particular society that, through its culturally specific patterns of child rearing and social institutions, profoundly influences the way the person resolves conflicts. The ego is concerned not only with biological (psychosexual) issues, but also with interpersonal concerns, which Erikson termed **psychosocial.** His emphasis on culture was Erikson's fundamental contribution to psychoanalysis. To be born in a Sioux tribe, or in Germany of the 1930s, or in a particular racial, ethic, and socioeconomic group at the present time in the United States, profoundly influences the formation of personality.

In contrast to Freud's emphasis on sexuality, Erikson proposed that the prime motivation for development is social:

> Personality . . . can be said to develop according to steps determined in the human organism's readiness to be driven toward, to be aware of, and to interact with a widening radius of significant individuals and institutions. (1968b, p. 93)

The Epigenetic Principle

Erikson based his understanding of development on the **epigenetic principle**: "that anything that grows has a *ground plan*, and that out of this ground plan the *parts* arise, each part having its *time* of special ascendancy, until all parts have arisen to form a *functioning whole*" (1959, p. 52). This principle applies to the physical development of fetuses before birth (where it is easy to visualize the gradual emergence of increasingly differentiated parts) and to the psychological development of people throughout their lives. For a whole, healthy ego to develop, several parts must develop sequentially. These parts are the ego strengths Erikson identified, and they develop in eight stages. At each stage, there is a particular focus on one aspect of ego development: trust in infancy, autonomy in toddlerhood, and so on.

The Eight Psychosocial Stages

Erikson (1959) reinterpreted Freud's psychosexual stages, emphasizing the social aspects of each stage. Further, he extended the stage concept throughout life, giving what is now popularly called a "life span approach" to development. Erikson's first four stages correspond to Freud's oral, anal, phallic, and latency stages. Freud's genital stage encompasses Erikson's last four stages (see Table 5.1).

Each stage involves a crisis; conflict centers on a distinctive issue. A crisis can be thought of as a developmental turning point (Erikson, 1964). Just as, biologically, heart, arms, and teeth develop most rapidly at different times, so it is with ego strengths of hope, will, purpose, and so on. Out of each cri-

TABLE 5.1 Stages of Psychosocial Development Compared with Psychosexual Development

Psychosocial Stage	*Psychosexual Stage and Mode*	*Comparable Freudian Stage*	*Age*
1. Trust vs. Mistrust	Oral-Respiratory, Sensory-Kinesthetic (Incorporative Mode)	Oral	Infancy
2. Autonomy vs. Shame, Doubt	Anal-Urethral, Muscular (Retentive-Eliminative Mode)	Anal	Early childhood
3. Initiative vs. Guilt	Infantile-Genital Locomotor (Intrusive, Inclusive Mode)	Phallic	Play age
4. Industry vs. Inferiority	"Latency"	Latency	School age
5. Identity vs. Identity Diffusion	Puberty	Genital	Adolescence
6. Intimacy vs. Isolation	Genitality	Genital	Young adulthood
7. Generativity vs. Self-absorption	Procreativity	Genital	Adulthood
8. Integrity vs. Despair	Generalization of Sensual Modes	Genital	Old age

sis emerges an ego strength, or "virtue," which corresponds specifically to that stage (Erikson, 1961). The strength then becomes part of the repertoire of ego skills for the individual throughout life. Each strength develops in relation to an opposite, or negative, pole. The strength of trust develops in relation to mistrust, the strength of autonomy in relation to shame, and so forth. In healthy development, there is a larger ratio of the strength than of the weakness. Furthermore, these strengths develop in relationships with significant people, beginning with the mother and expanding more broadly throughout life (see Table 5.2).

Though each ego skill has its period of crisis, of greatest growth, at a distinct period in life, earlier developments pave the way for that strength, and later development can to some extent modify an earlier resolution (see Figure 5.1). For example, being a grandparent offers many elderly people a second chance at developing the ego strength (generativity) that had its primary focus of development in the previous stage (Erikson, Erikson, & Kivnick, 1986).

In Erikson's theory, each of these stages must be considered not simply from the individual's point of view but also from a social point of view. An adolescent's identity develops in relationship to the older generation's ideals and values. Significant others, as members of society, are inextricably involved at each stage. Infant development implies not only the infant's needs but also the complementary needs of the mother to nurture (Erikson, 1968b; Erikson, Erikson, & Kivnick, 1986). To some, Erikson's theory offers a rationale for enhancing programs that increase intergenerational contact (ReVille, 1989).

TABLE 5.2 Strengths Developed at Each Stage of Psychosocial Development and Their Social Context

Psychosocial Stage	*Strength*	*Significant People*	*Related Elements in Society*
1. Trust vs. Mistrust	Hope	Maternal person	Cosmic order (e.g., religion)
2. Autonomy vs. Shame, Doubt	Will	Parental persons	Law and order
3. Initiative vs. Guilt	Purpose	Basic family	Ideal prototypes (e.g., male, female, socioeconomic status)
4. Industry vs. Inferiority	Competence	Neighborhood, school	Technological order
5. Identity vs. Identity Diffusion	Fidelity	Peer groups and outgroups Models of leadership	Ideological worldview
6. Intimacy vs. Isolation	Love	Partners in friendship, sex, competition, cooperation	Patterns of cooperation and competition
7. Generativity vs. Self-absorption	Care	Divided labor and shared household	Currents of education and tradition
8. Integrity vs. Despair	Wisdom	"Mankind" and "My kind"	Wisdom

(Adapted from THE LIFE CYCLE COMPLETED, A Review, by Erik H. Erikson, by permission of W. W. Norton & Company, Inc. Copyright © 1982 by Rikan Enterprises Ltd.)

		1	2	3	4	5	6	7	8
Old Age	VIII								INTEGRITY vs. DESPAIR
Adulthood	VII							GENERATIVITY vs. STAGNATION	
Young Adulthood	VI						INTIMACY vs. ISOLATION		
Adolescence	V	Temporal Perspective vs. Time Confusion	Self-Certainty vs. Self-Consciousness	Role Experimentation vs. Role Fixation	Apprenticeship vs. Work Paralysis	IDENTITY vs. IDENTITY CONFUSION	Sexual Polarization vs. Bisexual Confusion	Leader- and Followership vs. Authority Confusion	Ideological Commitment vs. Confusion of Values
School Age	IV				INDUSTRY vs. INFERIORITY	Task Identification vs. Sense of Futility			
Play Age	III			INITIATIVE vs. GUILT		Anticipation of Roles vs. Role Inhibition			
Early Childhood	II		AUTONOMY vs. SHAME, DOUBT			Will to be Oneself vs. Self-Doubt			
Infancy	I	TRUST vs. MISTRUST				Mutual Recognition vs. Autistic Isolation			

Each ego development has a particular period of ascendancy, yet development concerning each issue occurs throughout the life span (the vertical columns), and at any age, developments may revise earlier stage resolutions and prepare for latter crises (the horizontal rows).

FIGURE 5.1 The Epigenetic Chart

(Adapted from IDENTITY, YOUTH AND CRISIS by Erik H. Erikson, by permission of W. W. Norton & Company, Inc. Copyright © 1968 by W. W. Norton & Company, Inc.)

Stage 1: Trust versus Mistrust

During the first year of life, the infant develops *basic* **trust** and *basic* **mistrust.** Basic trust is the sense that others are dependable and will provide what is needed, as well as the sense that one is trustworthy oneself (Erikson, 1968b, p. 96). It is based on good parenting (traditionally, Erikson emphasized good mothering), with adequate provision of food, of caretaking, and of stimulation. The infant approaches the world with an *incorporative* mode, taking in not only milk and food but also sensory stimulation, looking, touching, and so on. This begins relatively passively at first, but becomes increasingly active in later infancy. This stage is one of mutuality, not simply of receiving; the infant seeks the mother's care, and seeks to explore the environment tactilely, visually, and so on.

To the extent that the infant does not find the world responsive to his or her needs at this stage, *basic mistrust* develops. Some mistrust is inevitable, since no parental nurturing can be as reliable as the umbilical connection. Some amount of basic mistrust is not only inevitable but even necessary for later adaptation. The world the individual will confront after infancy will not always be trustworthy, and the capacity to mistrust will be required for realistic adaptation. In a healthy resolution of the crisis between basic trust and basic mistrust, trust will predominate, providing strength for continued ego development in later stages.

Stage 2: Autonomy versus Shame and Doubt

During the second year of life, the toddler develops a sense of **autonomy**. This period includes the issue of toilet training, which Freud emphasized, but also broader issues of control of the musculature in general (becoming able to walk well) and control in interpersonal relationships. The toddler experiments with the world through the modes of *holding on* and *letting go.* He or she requires the support of adults in order to develop, gradually, a sense of autonomy. If the toddler's vulnerability is not supported, a sense of **shame** (of premature exposure) and *doubt* develop. As in the first stage, a higher ratio of the positive pole (autonomy) should prevail, but some degree of shame and doubt are necessary for health, and for the good of society.

Stage 3: Initiative versus Guilt

Four- and 5-year-old children face the third psychosocial crisis: **initiative** versus **guilt**. The child can make choices about what kind of person to be, based in part on identifications with the parents. Erikson agreed with Freud that the child at this age is interested in sexuality and in sex differences and is developing a conscience (superego). The young child acts in an *intrusive mode,* physically and verbally intruding into others' space. The child approaches the unknown with curiosity. For the boy, this intrusion is congruent with early awareness of sexuality, described by Freud's "phallic stage." For the girl, awareness of her different physical sexual apparatus is significant at this stage, according to Erikson, who claimed that children reflect these different sexualities in their play (as will be described in a later section). If the stage is resolved well, the child develops more initiative than guilt.

Stage 4: Industry versus Inferiority

The remainder of childhood, until puberty, is devoted to the school-age task of Stage 4: the development of a sense of **industry**. The negative pole, in contrast, is **inferiority**. The child at this stage "learns to win recognition by *producing things*" (Erikson, 1959, p. 86). A child who works at tasks until completion achieves satisfaction and develops perseverance. The quality of the product matters. If the child cannot produce an acceptable product, or fails to obtain recognition for it, a sense of inferiority prevails. Teachers are especially important at this stage, since much of this development occurs at school.

Stage 5: Identity versus Identity Confusion

Erikson's best-known concept is the *identity crisis,* the customary, if not easy, developmental stage of adolescence. In this time of transition toward adult roles, the adolescent struggles against **identity confusion** to attain a sense of **identity**. Erikson defined the sense of ego identity as "the awareness of the fact that there is a self-sameness and continuity to the ego's synthesizing methods, the *style of one's individuality,* and that this style coincides with the sameness and continuity of one's *meaning for significant others* in the immediate community" (1968b, p. 50). To somewhat oversimplify, the task is to find an answer to the question "Who am I?" that is mutually agreeable to the individual and to others. Earlier identifications with parents and other role models have influence, but the adolescent must develop a personal identity that goes beyond these identifications. An occupational identity is often an important core of identity development, and exploring different career possibilities is an important part of the process of achieving an identity. Sex, race, and ethnic identification are also often important. Black Americans have particular difficulties with identity because of the society's unresponsiveness to them (Erikson, 1968b, pp. 295–320).

Identity confusion occurs if a coherent identity cannot be achieved. In earlier works (e.g., 1968a), Erikson used the term "diffusion" instead of "confusion." No one identity prevails as the core. Another undesirable resolution of the identity crisis is the development of a **negative identity**, that is, an identity based on undesirable roles in society, such as the identity as a juvenile delinquent. Culture provides clear images of such negative identities, making them appealing as solutions to the identity crisis for people who find that a positively valued identity seems unattainable (Erikson, 1968b).

Erikson remarked that identity first became noticeable to him in his psychiatric practice when he immigrated to the United States. People here, coming from diverse backgrounds (especially in large urban centers), must define themselves anew, as did Erikson himself when he changed his name.

Society assists the resolution of this stage by providing a *moratorium,* a period when the adolescent is free to explore various possible adult roles without having the obligations that will come with real adulthood. At a simple level, having the opportunity to study various fields, even to change majors, in college before settling down to a career commitment provides a moratorium. Erikson stressed the importance of exploration, fearing that too early a commitment to a particular identity would risk a poor choice. Further, it would not provide an opportunity to develop the ego strength of this stage: *fidelity,* which he defined as "the ability to sustain loyalties freely pledged in spite of the inevitable contradictions of value systems" (Erikson, 1964, p. 125).

Stage 6: Intimacy versus Isolation

The first of three stages of adulthood is Stage 6: the crisis of **Intimacy** versus **Isolation**. Psychological *intimacy* with another person cannot occur, according to Erikson, until individual identity is established. Intimacy involves a capacity for psychological fusion with another person, whether a friend or lover, secure that individual identity will not be destroyed by the merging. This intimacy is selective. Erikson referred to *distantiation* as the counterpart of intimacy, defining it as "the readiness to repudiate, to isolate, and, if necessary, to destroy those forces and people whose essence seems dangerous to one's own" (1959, pp. 95–96). The adult who does not satisfactorily resolve this crisis remains self-absorbed and isolated. For many young adults, this crisis is experienced through the social role of marriage, although marriage is no guarantee that the crisis will be successfully resolved. Furthermore, psychological intimacy is not the same as sexual intimacy, and a spouse is not the only significant other who may play a role in resolving this stage. Erikson's descriptions of intimacy have been criticized as heterosexist, ignoring the potential of homosexual relationships to also foster the development of intimate mutuality (Sohier, 1985–1986).

Stage 7: Generativity versus Stagnation

The seventh task is to develop the ego strength of **generativity**, "the interest in establishing and guiding the next generation" (Erikson, 1959, p. 97), often but not necessarily through the role of parenting. To be a teacher or a mentor may substitute. Failure to develop optimally in this stage leaves a person with a sense of **stagnation**, not being able to be fully involved in caring for others in a nurturing way.

Stage 8: Integrity versus Despair

The task of old age is to resolve the crisis of Integrity versus Despair. The sense of **integrity** means being able to look back upon one's own life and decide that it is meaningful as it has been lived, without wishing that things had been different. In its absence, **despair** occurs instead, and unwillingness to accept death, which will prevent the accomplishment of what would be necessary to make life meaningful.

The Role of Culture in Relation to the Eight Stages

The stages themselves, Erikson said, are universal, but each culture organizes the experience of its members. The way people experience and resolve each stage internalizes the culture's particular characteristics.

Culture not only provides the setting in which psychosocial crises are encountered and mastered; culture also provides continuing support for the ego developments that have occurred, supporting ego strengths when they are threatened in later life. Each stage has its own cultural institution to support its development. Erikson listed these relationships, and observed that

> just as there is a basic affinity of the problem of basic trust to the institution of religion, the problem of autonomy is reflected in basic political and legal organization and that of initiative in the economic order. Similarly, industry is related to technology; identity to social stratification; intimacy to relationship patterns; generativity to education, art, and science; and integrity, finally, to philosophy. (Erikson, 1963, pp. 278–279)

Influence goes both ways. The individual is supported by the social institutions. In addition, "each generation can and must revitalize each institution even as it grows into it" (Erikson, 1963, p. 279).

The First Stage: Religion

Positive developments in the first psychosocial stage leave the person with the capacity for **hope**. For many people, religious faith provides social confirmation of the capacity to hope. Erikson observed that "religion through the centuries has served to restore a sense of trust at regular intervals in the form of faith while giving tangible form to a sense of evil which it promises to ban" (1959, p. 65). In this way, it supports the ego developments of the first stage of psychosocial development: basic trust and basic mistrust. Other cultural supports for these ego strengths may substitute for religion. Erikson listed "fellowship, productive work, social action, scientific pursuit, and artistic creation" as sources of faith for some people (1959, p. 64).

The Second Stage: Law

Positive developments in the second psychosocial stage leave the person with the capacity for **will**, or will power, which develops out of the toddler's struggle for autonomy. Institutional support for will is found in law, which legitimizes and provides boundaries for an individual's autonomy.

The Third Stage: Ideal Prototypes

The third stage of psychosocial development leaves the child with the basic virtue of **purpose**. The corresponding element of the social order for this stage consists of the "ideal prototypes" of society. Erikson said that primitive cultures provide a small number of unchanging prototypes, which are close to the economy of the tribe—for example, the buffalo hunter of the Sioux Indians. This provides straightforward models for children to channel their initiative in play (for example, playing at buffalo hunting with a toy bow and arrow), and for adults to channel and support their initiative in the serious versions of these roles. In contrast, in civilized cultures, prototypes are numerous, fragmented, and changing. What roles shall children play that will continue to be significant in their adulthood? American culture, according to Erikson, supports a "deliberate tentativeness" about identity (1959, p. 42), requiring people to continue to believe that they can change.

Americans value socioeconomic status, and they respond with guilt when it is threatened, according to Erikson, as third-stage development would predict (cf. Erikson, 1959, p. 28). Such socioeconomic status is abstract and fragmented, however, compared with the whole person of the buffalo hunter prototype. Another ideal prototype that Erikson discussed is the military prototype (1959, p. 27), which channels the aggressive ideals important at this stage (1968b, p. 122). Sex roles are important ideal prototypes that, ideally, continue to support the ego strength of initiative developed in the third stage. Erikson's conceptualization invites detailed consideration of the specific roles offered as ideal prototypes for various members of society (white men, white women, black men, black women, and so on).

The Fourth Stage: Technological Elements

The sense of **competence** that develops in the fourth stage is supported by technological elements in culture, particularly the way that labor is divided among people. Opportunities unfairly limited by discrimination are particularly harmful to the developments of this stage, as is an overemphasis on work as a basis of identity (cf. Erikson, 1968b, pp. 122–128).

The Fifth Stage: Ideological Perspectives

The virtue of **fidelity**, which emerges from the fifth psychosocial stage, enables the individual to be faithful to an ideology. Thus the "ideological perspectives" of a society support, sometimes even exploit, this ego strength. The cause may be political, social, or occupational, or it may take another form. Erikson outlined a complex relationship between developmental stages and cultural change:

> It is through their ideology that social systems enter into the fiber of the next generation and attempt to absorb into their lifeblood the rejuvenative power of youth. Adolescence is thus a vital regenerator in the process of social evolution, for youth can offer its loyalties and energies both to the conservation of that which continues to feel true and to the revolutionary correction of that which has lost its regenerative significance. (Erikson, 1968b, p. 134)

One major issue now being faced, according to Erikson, is reassessing the role of technology and the challenge of finding its appropriate limits (cf. Erikson, 1968b, p. 259; Côté & Levine, 1988c). Another issue is the creation of a more inclusive identity that can encompass both the racial identity and the American identity of black Americans (Erikson, 1968b, p. 314). Because of the interrelatedness of the individual and society, this problem cannot be solved wholly at an individual level. However, the personal identity developments of especially developed people, such as Gandhi, may help point the way in which society should be directed.

The Sixth Stage: Patterns of Cooperation and Competition

Successful resolution of the sixth stage brings the ego strength that Erikson called a capacity to **love**. This strength is supported and channeled through what Erikson termed "patterns of cooperation and competition." For many, marriage serves this role. Cultures may provide other forms besides the nuclear family for shaping the sense of community.

The Seventh Stage: Currents of Education and Tradition

The strength of **care** develops in the seventh stage of development. Erikson described this as the stage in which a person plays the nurturing role of the older generation toward the younger generation—for example, as parents, teachers, and mentors. Societal involvement is clearly evident in such institutionalized forms as school systems. Erikson suggested that the psychosexual procreative urge (which he felt was not sufficiently emphasized by Freud) can be channeled into career paths such as teaching if, by choice or for other reasons, an individual does not become a parent. Besides looking at the relationship between the individual and society by asking what society provides for the individual, we can turn the issue around. What must the individual bring to society to be a good parent or teacher? Erikson's concept of "generativity" provides at least a sketch of an answer.

The Eighth Stage: Wisdom

Given demographic changes, culture is becoming more aware of its oldest members. What does society offer them for their continuing psychological development, and what do they have to offer society? The ego strength developed during old age is **wisdom**, described by Erikson as "informed and detached concern with life itself in the face of death itself" (1982, p. 61). The individual, ideally, becomes connected with the "wisdom of the ages," which seeks to understand the meaning of individual and collective human life. This interest is expressed in religious and/or philosophical interests.

Elderly Californians interviewed by Erikson and his wife and a younger collaborator generally expressed this development by saying, in essence, "There are no regrets that I know of for things that have happened or that I've done" (Erikson, Erikson, & Kivnick, 1986, p. 70).

These relationships, which Erikson proposed between individual ego development and cultural supports (religion, law, and so on), have been neglected in empirical research. His suggestion that personality and culture are intertwined is widely applauded, but it should be explored in more detail in research as well.

Any theory that attempts to discuss cultural factors risks bias owing to the experience and values of the theorist. Erikson's list of ego strengths, emphasizing "industry" and "initiative," has been criticized as reflecting middle-class Western ideology (Henry, 1967). Erikson has also been criticized for his interpretation of sex roles, as will be discussed below.

Rituals and Ritualisms

Rituals, both cultural and individual, sustain the ego strengths. Prayer and atonement—for example, in the ritual Sun Dance of the Dakota Sioux—support "the paradise of orality," the trust of the first stage (Erikson, 1963, p. 147). Different societies practice different rituals, each supporting the ego strengths of its members in a unique way. Cultural rituals tend to enhance the ego strengths necessary for the specific needs of the culture. For example, the Yurok Indians, who depend on catching abundant salmon during the brief period in the year when they can be netted in the river, practice rituals that develop oral character traits, including strict eating rituals. These prepare them for the unpredictability of each salmon catch. Such cultural rituals are adaptive.

Individuals may also develop their own rituals for maintaining certain ego strengths (for example, obsessive hand-washing). When such rituals stagnate, defending the ego rather than strengthening it, Erikson (1977) called them **ritualisms**.

Research on Development Through the Psychosocial Stages

Erikson based his theory on clinical evidence (Erikson, 1958a). Perhaps because of this, like other psychoanalytic approaches, Erikson's theory has been criticized as elusive and therefore difficult to verify (Chess, 1986; Fitzpatrick, 1976; Wurgaft, 1976). This criticism is probably more justified as applied to his psychohistorical work than his developmental stages, which have stimulated substantial empirical research, particularly concerning adolescent identity development. Some suggest that this research has reached the point where interventions to enhance identity resolution should be attempted (Waterman, 1988). The identity status paradigm has, however, developed along its own path, becoming more separate from Erikson's theory than is generally acknowledged (Côté & Levine, 1988b; Waterman, 1988).

Measurement of Stage Level

Several measures have been devised to assess subjects' status in the psychosocial stages (e.g., Constantinople, 1969; Ochse & Plug, 1986; Rosenthal, Gurney, & Moore, 1981; Wessman & Ricks, 1966). Most of these scales do not cover the last two stages, Generativity and Integrity. Many measures test only a single stage, usually Identity (Bronson, 1959; Côté, 1986;

Grotevant & Adams, 1984; Mallory, 1989; Marcia, 1966; Rasmussen, 1964; Simmons, 1970; Tan, Kendis, Fine, & Porac, 1977). A self-report measure of Stage 4, Industry, has been developed for elementary-school children (Kowaz & Marcia, 1991). Snyder and others (1991) have presented a measure of "hope," which may correspond to some people's hope, as it is supported through work and social action (cf. Erikson, 1959, p. 64), though the emphasis in this measure on goal-seeking makes it seem inconsistent with less active forms of hope.

Though identity is usually studied in college students, it has been measured among early adolescents from sixth grade (Archer, 1982) or age 12 (R.M. Jones & Streitmatter, 1987). The many measures of identity do not all intercorrelate highly (e.g., Craig-Bray & Adams, 1986); they may be tapping various aspects of identity, or perhaps some are not valid measures. Given the diversity of methods, ranging from self-report to depth interviews, and the fact that some try to assess identity as a global construct while others consider identity in various areas (e.g., occupation, friendship, religion, politics, sex roles, and dating), it is not surprising that the measures do not correlate highly. Better theoretical development, to help select measures optimally appropriate for particular research purposes, would help bring order to this area.

The most frequently used measure of identity is assessed from an interview. Questions probe crisis and commitment in the areas of occupation and ideology (Marcia, 1966). Marcia reasoned that complete identity development occurs if an individual has experienced crisis and has come through it with a reasonably firm commitment to an occupation and/or ideology. This mature outcome Marcia calls **identity achievement**. Three less mature outcomes are also possible: **identity diffusion**, in which neither crisis nor commitment has been experienced (the least mature outcome); **moratorium**, in which crisis is being currently experienced but no commitment has yet been made; and **identity foreclosure**, in which a commitment has been made without crisis and without much exploration of alternatives, often by simply accepting parental choices. (Marcia used the term "identity diffusion" rather than "identity confusion," because that was Erikson's earlier term, which he was still using when the scale was developed.) Marcia reasoned that people enter this stage in a state of identity diffusion, and must pass through moratorium to identity achievement in order to develop optimally. Foreclosure is an undesirable outcome; it can be a permanent dead end or can be temporary if exploration (moratorium) is later chosen, on the way to identity achievement. This original developmental sequence has been challenged on the basis of research findings (Côté & Levine, 1988a, 1988c).

When researchers who have published in this field responded to a survey asking them to describe the prototypical person in each identity status (Mallory, 1989), these were among the most descriptive characteristics they chose:

Identity Achiever: clear, consistent personality; productive

Moratorium: philosophically concerned; rebellious, nonconforming

Identity Diffusion: unpredictable; reluctant to act

Foreclosure: conventional; moralistic

Domino and Affonso (1990) developed a self-report questionnaire assessing positive and negative aspects of all eight stages of development. This Inventory of Psychosocial Balance seems reliable and valid, based on preliminary data. Subjects respond by rating the extent to which they agree with each of 120 items on a 5-point Likert-type scale from "strongly agree" to "strongly disagree." Sample items are:

I can usually depend on others. (Trust scale)
I genuinely enjoy work. (Industry scale)
Sometimes I wonder who I really am. (Identity scale)
Life has been good to me. (Ego Integrity scale)
(Domino & Affonso, 1990)

Age Changes

As expected, scores on the Inventory of Psychosocial Balance generally increased in older groups of subjects, although there were several exceptions to this pattern. Further research may determine whether some of the apparent exceptions are due to effects of current social factors in subjects' lives. For example, elderly people who have lost a spouse may score lower on Intimacy as a result of the loss, if the scale taps not only a psychological development but also a current state.

Other researchers, using various measures, have also found that assessed stage increases with age (Adams & Fitch, 1982; Archer, 1982; Ciaccio, 1971; Constantinople, 1969; Dignan, 1965; Marcia, 1966; Meilman, 1979; Ochse & Plug, 1986; Waterman, Geary, & Waterman, 1974). Longitudinal studies sometimes show anomalies, changes in the opposite direction than postulated developmentally, which may be due to methodological difficulties in scoring (Waterman, 1988). Or, more seriously, these reversals call into question the generally accepted direction of development, which proceeds from diffusion to moratorium to identity achievement, with a possible detour into foreclosure (Côté & Levine, 1988a).

Correlates of Stage Measures

Higher scores on measures of the psychosocial stages are associated with better functioning in several studies. Protinsky (1988) reported that problem adolescents scored lower on three of the first five psychosocial stages (trust, initiative, and identity) compared with normal adolescents. Though more work needs to be done identifying specific behavioral implications of the various stages (Hamachek, 1988), much research has already been conducted, particularly with the fifth stage.

Identity is the most frequently studied of Erikson's stages. Many studies report that subjects who score high on various measures of ego identity function better. They perform better under stress on a concept-attainment task (Marcia, 1966), get better grades (Cross & Allen, 1970), have higher self-concepts (Lobel & Winch, 1988), and score higher on a measure of moral judgment (Podd, 1972). They have greater recall of personal memories (G.J. Neimeyer & Rareshide, 1991), and their early memories reflect themes that are more mature, when scored for psychodynamic imagery (Orlofsky & Frank, 1986).

Moratorium subjects experience higher anxiety, which can slow their performance (Marcia, 1967; Podd, Marcia, & Rubin, 1970). They score higher on a measure of Death Anxiety (Sterling & Van Horn, 1989), and are less satisfied with college (Waterman & Waterman, 1970). They are less committed to an occupational choice, although they are exploring occupations, as have identity-achieved undergraduates (Blustein, Devenis, & Kidney, 1989). Foreclosed subjects are more authoritarian (Marcia, 1967) and impulsive (Cella, DeWolfe, & Fitzgibbon, 1987).

Undergraduates with lower identity scores seem less prepared for intimacy tasks. They score high on a measure of "desperate love" (Sperling, 1987), and report less social support from others, perhaps because they do not recognize support that may be available (Caldwell, Bogat, & Cruise, 1989). This relationship between identity and intimacy is stronger among males than among females (Levitz-Jones & Orlofsky, 1985). Lower ego identity status has been reported to be associated with less maternal identification among college women (Dignan, 1965). A longitudinal study by Kroger and Haslett (1988) suggests that changes in identity over a two-year interval in college students are predictive of changes in interpersonal attachment style, consistent with Erikson's claim that identity is a prior stage to the intimacy developments of his sixth stage.

Intimacy resolution is correlated with self-reported interpersonal behaviors. College males who score low on resolution of the Intimacy stage ("Isolates") report having had fewer friends when growing up (Orlofsky, 1978b).

Generativity can be measured by various scales that do not all correlate with one another, but that correlate with a measure of the personality trait of nurturance in a broad sample of adults of varying ages (Van De Water & McAdams, 1989). Erikson's proposal that generativity involves a "belief in the species" is supported in these data, but the expectation that generativity would be related to age (in a sample ranging from age 22 to 72) was not confirmed. The researchers suggested that clearer conceptualization of the multiple dimensions of generativity, associated with appropriate measurements, was needed (Van De Water & McAdams, 1989). McAdams, Ruetzel, and Foley (1986) found that generativity, as scored from mid-life adults' descriptions of their plans for the future, was positively correlated with a measure obtained by summing together scores on power and intimacy motivation, as coded from TAT (Thematic Apperception Test) stories. The researchers reasoned that generativity involves two steps, creating a product and offering it to others, corresponding, respectively, to power and intimacy.

Because parenting is a major role for generativity, we would expect to find different child-rearing outcomes for parents who differ in ego development. There are effects, but they are not straightforward. Longitudinal observations of parents and their children from before birth to age 5 revealed that the relationship of autonomy and affiliation to marital and child-rearing outcomes was not uniform. Complicated sex differences and socioeconomic status effects were found (Grossman, Pollack, Golding, & Fedele, 1987).

Ego Integrity (Stage 8), as assessed by a written measure, was investigated among elderly males and females living in a nursing home and in a residential apartment complex. Those with higher Integrity scores reported less fear of death (Goebel & Boeck, 1987). Domino and Hannah (1989) studied Elderhostel participants. High scores on the Generativity scale of the Inventory of Psychosocial Balance (Domino & Affonso, 1990) predicted Self-Realization, measured by the California Personality Inventory. However, virtually all of the other seven developmental stages were also predictive, even when their positive intercorrelations were taken into account. It is not clear how to interpret this finding. Perhaps it should be interpreted as support for Erikson's epigenetic principle, which would predict that the strengths and weaknesses of each stage continue to influence functioning throughout life. On the other hand, it may be that the scales measuring the eight stages lack discriminant validity (that is, are more highly correlated than they should be).

Relationships Among the Stages

Erikson's theory would predict positive associations among measures of the various stages that a person has experienced, since earlier strengths help bring about a positive resolution of each later stage. Measures scored for several stages have reported such positive correlations (Domino & Affonso, 1990; Domino & Hannah, 1989). Aside from theoretical prediction, such positive correlations could also occur if the scores measuring the various stages inadvertently and inappropriately included some general factor such as social desirability.

Studies of infants and toddlers confirm the importance of a positive mother–child interaction in early life, which Erikson described as an interaction producing basic trust. For example, infants who at 12 months are judged to be "securely attached" to their mothers on a standard developmental measure (Ainsworth, Blehar, Waters, & Wall, 1978) are more cooperative and compliant with suggestions from mothers and an adult female experimenter in a laboratory play situation at 21 months (Londerville & Main, 1981). Securely attached infants are also less dependent on teachers in preschool (Sroufe, Fox, & Pancake, 1983) and more curious and likely to explore their environments as preschoolers (Arend, Gove, & Sroufe, 1979; Jacobson & Wille, 1986). These findings suggest that they bring more ego skills to the next developmental stages described by Erikson, namely autonomy and initiative. They also have more positive interactions with playmates at age 3 (Jacobson & Wille, 1986; Lieberman, 1977; Waters, Wippman, & Sroufe, 1979). Thus what developmental psychologists call "secure attachment," interpreted here as an indicator of Erikson's concept of "basic trust," predicts a variety of later positive developments.

Satisfactory resolution of the stage of identity predicts a better outcome in later stages, including intimacy (Orlofsky, Marcia, & Lesser, 1973). Intimacy status in college males, assessed from an interview, was associated with higher levels on the first six of Erikson's stages as assessed by the Marcia scale (Orlofsky, 1978b). This suggests that males who succeed in earlier psychosocial stages are better able to resolve the stage of intimacy by the junior and senior years of college.

Therapeutic Implications

Hamachek (1988) suggests that different therapies may be particularly effective for clients with ego weaknesses at different psychosocial stages. Rogerian therapy, with its emphasis on unconditional positive regard, may be especially helpful for clients with difficulties in basic trust (Stage 1). Cognitive-behavioral therapies, which focus on specific problems and behaviors, seem suited for clients with difficulties concerning autonomy (Stage 2) and initiative (Stage 3). Adlerian therapy, focusing on inferiority issues, seems suited to Stage 4 problems. These suggestions are, at the moment, speculative, but they are an interesting application of Erikson's theory to the more general issue of identifying ways of matching clients to therapies.

Other practical implications follow from conceptualizing personality as ego skills. Mitchell (1989) suggests that therapy for co-dependents (family members of substance abusers) can be improved by awareness of their Eriksonian ego deficiencies. Mitchell lists specific therapeutic activities for each stage, activities that seem, on their face, applicable to other populations as well. No research evidence is presented to verify that these activities do, in fact, increase functioning at the stages for which they are identified, but the availability of measures such as those described earlier suggests that this would be a feasible research question.

Differences Between Groups

Cross-Cultural Studies

Erikson's studies of the Sioux and Yurok Indian cultures (1963) portray individual development as intertwined with social, economic, and cultural factors, as described above. This relationship is much more complicated in complex societies, however. An individual's ego cannot be integrated with all aspects of a complex culture, but only with a fragment of it (Erikson, 1963; Fitzpatrick, 1976).

As history progresses, the relationship between character and its social manifestations may change dramatically, and what seemed positive and admirable may become reprehensible. In his earlier writing, Erikson wrote of the adaptability and individuality of the American character. These same character traits were held responsible for the racism and imperialism of later American history (Fitzpatrick, 1976).

Cross-cultural studies report differences among national and ethnic groups on some psychosocial stages (McClain, 1975; Ochse & Plug, 1986). For example, a diverse sample of black adults in South Africa scored lower on identity, compared to whites (Ochse & Plug, 1986). Mexican-Americans have been reported more often identity-foreclosed than Anglo-Americans on ideological, but not interpersonal, identity (Abraham, 1986). Erikson's theory attributes such differences to cultural factors, such as racism. Other studies, though, find similarity in identity development processes across ethnic groups (Lamke & Peyton, 1988).

Gender

Despite Erikson's awareness of the social context of development, he nonetheless agreed with the psychoanalytic proposition that biological differences between males and females are fundamental determinants of their personality differences. Erikson (1951a, 1968b, 1975) observed 300 children, ages 10 to 12, equal numbers of boys and girls, over a period of two years. He asked each to construct an exciting scene, like one from a movie, with a variety of toys, including human figures and blocks. Erikson reported differences in the types of constructions produced by the two sexes. Girls, he reported, emphasized interior, peaceful scenes with elaborate doorways. Boys built high towers and portrayed more movement and activity, and sometimes collapse of the structures. These sex differences were interpreted by Erikson as projections in play of the children's own genital apparatus: enclosures symbolizing the womb, and towers the penis. Womanhood, from childhood on, emphasizes the "inner space," leaving the "out world space" to males, for good or ill (see Figure 5.2).

Though it may be stretching the metaphor of "inner space," research on the sense of self in adolescence does find that females score higher on the Private Self than do males (Blasi & Milton, 1991). Female adolescents also use more psychoanalytic ego defenses categorized as "internalization" (turning against the self), whereas males use more "externalization" defenses (projection and "aggression-outward") (Levit, 1991).

Erikson's play configuration study has been replicated by P. Cramer and Hogan (1975), who found similar sex differences in tower-building in a group of children aged 11½ but not in younger children, aged 5½. They found no sex differences in building enclosures at either age. Caplan (1979), reanalyzing Erikson's data, concluded that the data do not support Erikson's broad claims of sex differences. Those of his claims that were statistically significant accounted for under 2 percent of the variance, and, in any event, boys built three to four times as many enclosures as towers. Furthermore, Erikson's subjects were ages 11 to 13, yet he made general interpretations for all ages. He assumed, for example, that these differences existed in the preschool years as well.

Another interpretation of the data, suggested by Caplan, is that sex-role

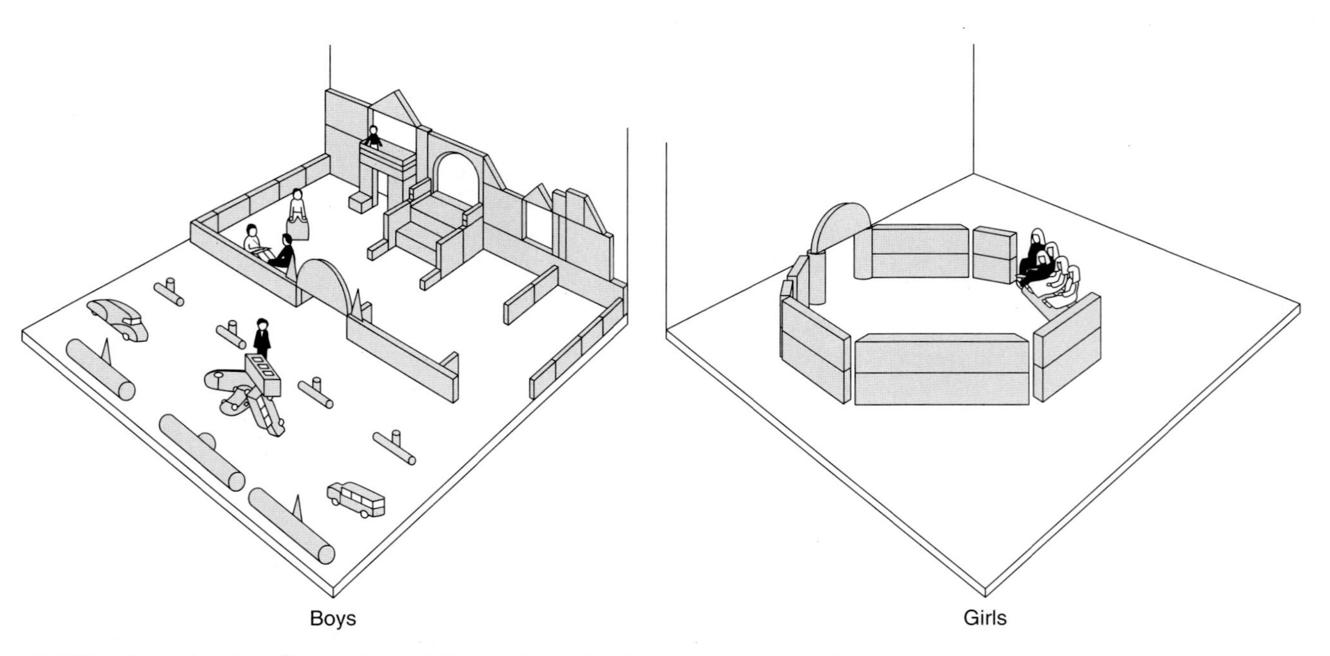

FIGURE 5.2 Play Configurations Erikson Described for Boys and Girls

(Reproduced from CHILDHOOD AND SOCIETY, Second Edition, by Erik H. Erikson, by permission of W. W. Norton & Company, Inc., and Faber and Faber Ltd. Copyright 1950, © 1963 by W. W. Norton & Company, Inc. Copyright renewed 1978, 1991 by Erik H. Erikson.)

socialization was responsible for the differences. Boys felt more comfortable playing with blocks and girls with furniture and figures of people, because these correspond to the sex-typed toys they had been given for years. Caplan investigated the effect of type of toy by having subjects construct play structures with (1) blocks only, (2) toys only, and (3) a combination of blocks and toys. Using preschool children (who would be less exposed to socialization than older subjects), Caplan reported no significant sex differences in building towers, structures, or enclosures. Budd, Clance, and Simerly (1985) also reported that the specific play materials are significant. In fact, they found that females, rather than males, built more structures if only blocks were used. It does seem that Erikson's findings are less robust than he claimed, which casts doubt on his anatomical interpretation.

Erikson consistently asserted that males and females are, and should remain, distinct. Even in his futuristic vision of a world community not divided by conflicting group identities, he described men's contribution as changing technology from destructive to nurturing applications, and women's role as developing "the powerful potential of protective mothering" (Erikson, 1985). Though he parenthetically included both sexes in both the technological and parenting roles, his message clearly differentiated the sexes into traditional roles.

Though much of his theory was different from Freudian psychoanalysis in emphasizing social rather than sexual determinants of personality, Erikson accepted an anatomical basis for sex differences. This biological interpretation contrasts with the more social emphasis of feminist and social-role theorists (e.g., Eagly, 1987b; Eagly & Wood, 1991; Gilligan, 1982). Critics of his theory focus on sex differences as an area in which he did not go far enough in replacing Freudian biological determinism with a recognition of the impact of culture (Lerman, 1986a, 1986b). Perhaps it is the biological metaphor of the epigenetic principle itself that prevents Erikson's theory from being fully cultural. P.H. Wolff (1986) has criticized the epigenetic model even within neurobiology. This model tends too simply to point to a "species-typical end point" (P.H. Wolff, 1986, p. 160), without adequate explanation of the mechanisms by which this end point is achieved; it erroneously sees continuity in development where a more refined analysis shows discontinuity and changing mechanisms.

Sex differences in development through the psychosocial stages have been reported by several researchers. Constantinople (1969) reported that male students made more developmental advances over the four years of college than did females. She suggested that the difference might occur because vocational development, more culturally important for males, is more directly fostered by the college environment than are predominant female concerns: preparation for marriage and parenthood and resolution of role conflict between career and family. Of course, this study was conducted some years ago, and roles have to some extent changed.

Erikson (1965) suggested that women's identity is not completely resolved at the adolescent stage. A.N. O'Connell (1976), based on adult women's retrospective reports, agreed with Erikson's claim that women's identity significantly changes after adolescence. Women with traditional or neotraditional patterns (that is, who stayed home with young children, returning later to work in the neotraditional pattern) showed major increases in the resolution of identity issues when their children began school. Nontraditional women (who worked even when their children were small) showed a more gradual resolution of identity throughout the adult years. (Of course, these data are retrospective, so they may be distorted by recollection errors.) O'Connell also distinguished between identity that is personally achieved, and that which is based on reflected identity (based on the achievements of others); these bases for identity change with life stage, particularly among traditional and neotraditional women, whose identity is primarily reflected once they have children. Nontraditional women, in this study, had a predominantly personal identity through the time period studied, from adolescence through having children of school age.

Many researchers suggest that women resolve identity issues differently from men. The sequence of development from identity to intimacy may describe the development of men but not women (Lobel & Winch, 1988; Ochse & Plug, 1986). Women's identity may involve interpersonal issues, in contrast to men's occupational and ideological issues (Josselson, 1973, 1987; Levitz-Jones & Orlofsky, 1985). Women may defer resolution of identity until intimacy issues have been more fully developed, compared to men (Douvan & Adelson, 1966; Hodgson & Fischer, 1979), and they may experience identity crises when relationships, rather than occupations, are in crisis (Josselson, 1987). Several researchers have noted that the moratorium status is more consistently related to positive functioning in males than in females. Female subjects in the foreclosure status seem to function more positively than do males (Orlofsky & Frank, 1986; Waterman, 1982). Probably the psychosocial moratorium provided by college (which is where most research subjects have been found) functions differently for the two sexes.

Lobel and Gilat (1987) suggest that the degree of compatibility between a person's personality and the sex-role stereotype influences the ease with which the identity crisis is resolved. This interpretation explains their finding that Type B (relaxed, non-time-pressured) females are less identity diffused than are Type A females or Type B males. However, research on sex typing and identity does not confirm the implied hypothesis that masculine males and feminine females would be more advanced in identity resolution. In contrast, masculinity is usually associated with identity resolution and well-being for both sexes (Della Selva & Dusek, 1984; Lamke & Peyton, 1988; Markstrom-Adams, 1989; Orlofsky, 1977; Schiedel & Marcia, 1985). One obstacle to career-oriented college women's identity resolution is the relative absence of female models of achievement, especially among their mothers (Cella, DeWolfe, & Fitzgibbon, 1987).

Kroger (1986) suggests that identity measurement would be improved if researchers focused on the content area (e.g., occupation, religion, politics, and so forth) identified by each individual as the basis for his or her identity. Such a strategy would recognize individual differences in the content of identity as well as its level. Such a focus on areas would also clarify differences in identity development among youth of different social classes (Munro & Adams, 1977). Some studies report females to be more advanced in resolving identity issues in the areas of family roles (Archer, 1989) and sexuality (Orlofsky, 1978a; C.K. Waterman & Nevid, 1977). Males and females are generally similar in occupational identity development (Archer,

1989; Kroger, 1986; Waterman, 1982). A review of the literature finds that the sexes do not differ in level of identity and other measures of individualism (self-actualization, internal locus of control, and principled moral reasoning); furthermore, these measures predict positive psychological functioning equally well for women and men, supporting an interpretation that the sexes are really quite similar in the processes of identity resolution and psychological individualism (Archer & Waterman, 1988). In general, males and females seem quite similar in the process of identity development (e.g., Archer, 1982, 1989; Mallory, 1989; Waterman, 1982).

Identity research has been dominated by studies focusing on identity statuses, that is, levels of development, rather than on investigation of the processes by which identity is sought, with a few exceptions (Berzonsky & Neimeyer, 1988; Mandrosz-Wroblewska, 1989; Von Broembsen, 1989). More attention to processes (Côté & Levine, 1988c) and to longitudinal research (Waterman, 1982) would be desirable. Côté and Levine (1988a, 1988b, 1988c) urge that a social psychological perspective be considered more thoroughly. This would ground the discussion of gender differences in the current (and changing) cultural context; it would also provide a better framework for discussing cultural and ethnic differences. Such influences affected Erikson's original development of the concept of identity but they have been neglected by researchers. The social-psychological perspective they recommend (Côté & Levine, 1988a, 1988c) would interpret a "moratorium" as a period for exploration provided by society, rather than as a developmental stage. This interpretation would be closer to Erikson's theory, and would help account for anomalous findings regarding the moratorium status in the literature. Côté and Levine suggest that an institutionalized moratorium is provided for college students in the humanities rather than in technological fields, which suggests that research with college students should investigate more precisely the relationship between career choice and identity resolution. A more explicitly social perspective would enable investigation of the ways in which "culture, social structure, social class, interaction networks, and so forth may function to aid or hinder certain forms of development" (Côté & Levine, 1988b, p. 216). It would fulfill Erikson's intent when he wrote: "We are in need, then, of concepts which throw light on the *mutual complementation* of ego synthesis and social organization, the cultivation of which on ever higher levels is the aim of all therapeutic endeavor, social and individual" (Erikson, 1968b, p. 53).

Measures other than, or in addition to, global assessments of identity resolution can help understand the processes of identity formation. Researchers outside the Eriksonian model have investigated "life tasks," such as the task among college students of "being on my own (without family)" (Zirkel & Cantor, 1990, p. 175). College students vary in the degree to which they are invested in such tasks, and these variations are related to satisfaction in college and to plans after college in a longitudinal sample (Zirkel & Cantor, 1990). Though these researchers did not measure Eriksonian "identity" per se, their life task model taps some of the same change processes within individuals that the identity model describes. Its precise focus on the behaviors and experiences of real life could lead to theoretical insights for the identity model.

Pseudospeciation

Like many theorists, Erikson believed that his theoretical concepts had implications for improving the human condition, as well as understanding it (Wurgaft, 1976). A clear statement of his ethical judgments is given in his discussion of **pseudospeciation** (Erikson, 1968b, 1985). This term refers to the exaggerated sense that many groups have, especially national and ethnic groups, that they are different from others, as though they were a separate species. In times of primitive cultures, where intergroup contact was less than it is today, that was not such a dangerous belief. In the nuclear age, though, Erikson warned that such beliefs increase tensions and the threat of nuclear war. As a solution, he suggested the development of a broader, more inclusive sense of identity that would include all of the human species with its diverse members, overcoming tendencies toward "pseudospeciation."

Summary

Erikson proposed a theory of *psychosocial development* that described eight stages in the life span. According to the *epigenetic principle,* these stages build on one another and occur in invariant sequence across cultures. In each stage, the individual experiences a crisis, which is resolved in the context of society. These stages are: Trust versus Mistrust, Autonomy versus Shame and Doubt, Initiative versus Guilt, Industry versus Inferiority, Identity versus Identity Confusion, Intimacy versus Isolation, Generativity versus Stagnation, and Integrity versus Despair. In each stage, culture influences development. Conversely, individuals also influence culture through the way they develop at each stage, but particularly through their identity development (see Table 5.3).

Considerable research has been conducted on the psychosocial stages. Predicted age changes have been found, and measures of identity formation show predicted positive correlates of higher identity status.

Erikson's cross-cultural studies of the Sioux and Yurok Indians explored the relationship between individual ego development and the culture. He said that biological factors strongly influence sex differences, and supported his point with observations of children's play structures. These conclusions have been criticized for neglecting social influences. Erikson warned that conflict among groups is increased because of *pseudospeciation,* and urged the development of more inclusive identities to help reduce political and social conflict in the world.

ILLUSTRATIVE BIOGRAPHIES: Concluding Remarks

Erikson's approach to psychobiography emphasizes the immediacy of the person's experience, rather than reducing the person to an object to be studied with distancing and judgmental categories (Schnell, 1980). His theory calls attention to the cultural context in which an individual develops, and it acknowledges the potential of an individual, through a highly developed ego, to have an impact on culture (Nichtern, 1985).

TABLE 5.3 Contributions of Erikson's Theory to Various Topics

Biological	Biological factors are important determinants of personality. Sex differences in personality are strongly influenced by differences in the "genital apparatus."
Child Development	Children develop through four psychosocial stages, each of which presents a crisis in which a particular ego strength is developed.
Adult Development	Adolescents and adults develop through four additional psychosocial stages. Again, each involves a crisis and develops a particular ego strength.
Mental Health	A strong ego is the key to mental health. It comes from good resolution of the eight stages of ego development, in which the positive ego strength predominates over the negative pole (trust over mistrust, etc.).
Society	Society shapes the way in which people develop. (Thus the term "psycho*social*" development.) Cultural institutions continue to support ego strengths (religion supports trust or hope, and so forth).
Cognitive Processes	The unconscious is an important force in personality. Experience is influenced by biological modes, which are expressed in symbols and in play.
Individual Differences	Individuals differ in their ego strengths. Males and females differ in personality owing to biological differences.

Mahatma Gandhi

Erikson's respect for Gandhi and openness to learn from him is clear in his book (Erikson, 1969). He even addressed a long section to Gandhi in conversational terms, as "I" to "you" (1969, pp. 229–254). Erikson described his task in his analysis of Gandhi: "to confront the spiritual truth as you [Gandhi] have formulated and lived it with the psychological truth which I [Erikson] have learned and practiced" (1969, p. 231). Erikson suggested that psychoanalysis is the counterpart of Gandhi's philosophy of Satyagraha (roughly meaning "passive resistance," or "militant nonviolence") "because it confronts the *inner* enemy nonviolently" (1969, p. 244). Lorimer (1976) suggested that Erikson's objectivity was compromised in this analysis. Erikson, though, did not claim objectivity, instead characterizing his method as "disciplined subjectivity" (1975, p. 25).

The concept of *identity* is the central concept by which Erikson attempted to understand Gandhi. Erikson interpreted Gandhi's period of study in England as a psychosocial moratorium, a period in which he could explore his identity. Gandhi's connection with his personal mother and with his Indian motherland was strengthened by his dietary vows, which continued to remind him of that maternal connection in a strange land. (How ironic that Gandhi's return to India brought him the news of his mother's death.) Even deciding to study law, however, provoked identity issues. His caste was opposed. They feared the corrupt practices of the British (eating meat, drinking wine, and so on), and they banned him as an "outcast" when he left. His minority position in London made him more conscious of his identity as an Indian, which he explored by reading about vegetarianism and Hinduism. The greatest identity "crisis," however, Erikson (1969, p. 47) suggested, occurred when Gandhi was first in South Africa. Gandhi was thrown off a train and denied the right to travel first class, despite having purchased a ticket, because of his race. His reaction was to devote himself to the political and religious cause of improving the life of poor Indians, solidifying his identity.

Erikson honored Gandhi immensely for his work toward a more inclusive identity for humankind. In Erikson's terms, Gandhi worked to rise above the divisions that mark "pseudospeciation" by envisioning a more inclusive identity. Pseudospeciation is inherent in colonialism, causing individuals to experience "guilt and rage which prevent true development" (Erikson, 1969, p. 433). At this particular historical moment, then, Gandhi's solution to the problem of identity moved history forward toward greater peace and mutual acceptance. There were strongly proud and egoistic aspects to this identity, too. Gandhi repeatedly evidenced that he felt himself the only one who could achieve what needed to be done (e.g., Erikson, 1969, p. 166), a belief which had its origins in his position as a favored youngest child in his family, one who, unlike his older brothers, largely escaped his father's punitiveness.

Although Erikson admired Gandhi, he also criticized him. Erikson suggested that Gandhi did not resolve the crises of Intimacy and Generativity adequately. Gandhi gave no evidence of psychological intimacy with his wife, Kasturba. According to Erikson, "one thing is devastatingly certain: nowhere is there any suggestion of joyful intimacy" (1969, p. 121). On the contrary, Gandhi deplored his sexuality and treated Kasturba and other women as temptresses who aroused regrettable desires. His decision to give up a sexual relationship with her so as to devote himself to "higher" purposes (and, incidentally, to prevent conceiving another child) was made without consulting her. Erikson says that Gandhi retained "some vindictiveness, especially toward woman as the temptress" (1969, p. 122), and even sadism (p. 234). Erikson interpreted one incident on Gandhi's commune as an example of this attitude against women. Gandhi directed young boys and girls to bathe together, which to his naive surprise led to difficulties, with some boys making fun of the girls. (The details are not given in Gandhi's autobiography.) Gandhi's solution was to cut the girls' beautiful long hair, thus making them less tempting to the boys, a solution Erikson criticizes (1969, pp. 237-242). Had Gandhi been able to confront his own sexuality more honestly, rather than denying it, he would not have in essence punished the girls for their sexual attractiveness.

Gandhi sought throughout his life for a relationship to take the place of the disrupted relationships with his mother and father (cf. Muslin & Desai, 1984, who interpret this in terms of Kohut's psychoanalytic theory). Erikson noted that Gandhi, in relationship to his mother, did not acknowledge the extent of his dependency on her (e.g., 1969, p. 110), even refusing to cry openly when he learned of her death. His dietary restrictions served as a ritual to preserve hope, the legacy of the first psychosocial conflict, Trust versus Mistrust (Erikson, 1969, p. 154). The extremity of his dietary control suggests unacknowledged Mistrust. His dietary restrictions can be considered obsessive (Erikson, 1969, p. 152), though "it is always difficult to say where, exactly, obsessive symptomatology ends and creative ritualization begins" (Erikson, 1969, p. 157). Surely the physicians who unsuccessfully urged Gandhi to take milk or meat for his health would have agreed with the more negative clinical label.

Erikson expressed disappointment that Gandhi's sexual renunciation would be unacceptable to the West, limiting the extent to which we could learn from his nonviolent political activism (Erikson, 1969, p. 251). Yet we must ask whether Erikson's eight stages can be used, without modification, as universal developmental standards against which to evaluate someone from such a different culture. To fault Gandhi for failing to develop all the strengths that Erikson outlined presumes that the strengths described in this Western theory apply even in the quite different cultures of the East. Is intimacy, as described in the context of a tradition of Western love and marriage, to be expected in a culture where child marriage, arranged by parents, is accepted? Or would such a psychological interpretation be parallel to the economic colonialism against which Gandhi and other leaders of his country struggled so courageously?

Eleanor Roosevelt

Published psychological analyses of Eleanor Roosevelt have been admiring. In the language of Maslow's humanistic theory, she has been labeled "self-actualized," which indicates a high level of ego development (Maslow, 1976; Piechowski & Tyska, 1982). Eleanor Roosevelt was the subject of a brief analysis by Joan Erikson (1967; see also E. Erikson, 1969, pp. 126–127). Erik Erikson characterized Eleanor's life as marked by "the overweening theme of owing maternal care to all of mankind, as well as to special groups and individuals" including, of course, her husband, Franklin (Erikson, 1969, p. 126). Joan Erikson suggested that Eleanor Roosevelt was able to emerge from earlier shy indecisiveness when Franklin's polio elicited this maternalism.

Both the biographical evidence of Eleanor's first two years and the adult personality that she developed later suggest that the first two stages were resolved well, with greater proportions of trust and autonomy than of distrust and shame or doubt. The third stage, Initiative versus Guilt, was more problematic. At this age, her father was sent away from the family because of his alcoholism, though Eleanor was not then fully aware of the reasons. Erikson's theory suggests that nonoptimal ego development at this age will produce a preponderance of guilt, rather than initiative. Much in the biographical and autobiographical record supports this hypothesis. Eleanor, by her own interpretation and that of others, was straight-laced and Puritanical, a teetotaler who supported Prohibition. It is also apparent, though, that she reworked the issues of initiative and guilt later. Positive social actions were stimulated by her sense of social responsibility, a more mature version of childhood guilt. Her actions on behalf of the poor and the black suggest that, with a more mature ego, she found ways to act with initiative that also expressed the guilt (or responsibility, to better label this adult expression) that had developed early. Without the impetus of early development of the "negative pole" of guilt, Eleanor would not have developed these social concerns. Yet equally, without the positive pole of initiative, positive actions would have been impossible. This interpretation emphasizes Erikson's recognition that both poles of each "crisis" are important for healthy ego development.

At the age of the Industry versus Inferiority crisis, both her parents and one of her two brothers died. There is ample evidence that Eleanor Roosevelt experienced inferiority about her physical appearance. She had been called "Gramma" by her mother, who was sorry that her daughter was not beautiful, as she herself had been, and who encouraged Eleanor to develop her intelligence and personality to compensate for her deficit of physical beauty. In schoolwork and in likeableness, Eleanor did achieve excellence and social recognition.

The stage of Identity is particularly interesting theoretically for women because of its interrelationships with the next stage, Intimacy versus Isolation. Erikson suggested that females may express their identity in the man to whom they are attracted, recognizing the close relationships between his Stages 5 and 6 for women. This dynamic is clearly evidenced in Eleanor Roosevelt's case. The political and social reform aspirations of her husband helped give expression to her own identity. From the perspective of ego development, it is important to distinguish between an intimate relationship that permits a woman's identity to be expressed and an intimate relationship that defines the woman's identity by simply giving her a role in relationship to another's identity. Theoretically, only the first of these represents the healthy ego development described by Erikson. Biographical evidence can help distinguish the two in a given case, particularly at times when the intimate relationship is disrupted. The more identity is simply "borrowed," the more that threats to the relationship will be disruptive of identity. Eleanor Roosevelt experienced disruptions in her relationship with Franklin, particularly when she discovered her husband's long-term affair. This was clearly a painful and difficult experience for her, and she claimed that it ended her love for her husband (Lash, 1971, p. 723). Yet her identity, not a separate identity but the merged identity that the marriage made possible, continued strong. Throughout Franklin's political career, until his death early in the fourth term of his presidency, Eleanor enacted her identity as a writer, political activist, and humanitarian. His death, like his affair, did not end this identity. Thus, for Eleanor Roosevelt, while ego developments in the area of Intimacy were integrated with her Identity developments, Identity was not hostage to Intimacy.

Generativity issues focus within the family on the role of parent. Eleanor raised five children, yet the biological fact of parenthood does not alone ensure ego development. She expressed some regret that she had not made more decisions personally about the raising of her children, relying instead on nurses and governesses (Roosevelt, 1958). While this statement can be interpreted in various ways, it may be that she was expressing recognition that, by delegating aspects of the parental role, she was missing this opportunity to develop her own ego strength of "care" as described by Erikson for the seventh stage of development. Later she expressed, and developed, generativity more broadly to the needy outside her family: the unemployed, the poor, the black, the war refugees, the wounded and despondent soldiers of World War II. She preferred a personal touch, perhaps because it provided the contact she needed to fulfill her own generativity needs. As characterized by Henry Kissinger, "She brought warmth rather than abstract principles" (E.D. Sherman, 1983). The generations, in Erikson's theory, have interacting needs.

The last stage of ego development is evidenced both by the external evidence of a meaningful life and by Eleanor Roosevelt's own statement on her seventy-fifth birthday. "I knew that I had long since become aware of my overall objective in life," which was to help people in need (Roosevelt, 1958, p. 412).

Both Eleanor Roosevelt and Mahatma Gandhi found that personal meanings were intrinsically connected with larger social issues.

GLOSSARY

autonomy the positive pole of the second psychosocial stage

care ability to nurture the development of the next generation; the basic virtue developed during the seventh psychosocial stage

competence sense of workmanship, of perfecting skills; the basic virtue developed during the fourth psychosocial stage

despair the negative pole of the eighth psychosocial stage

epigenetic principle the principle for psychosocial development, based on a biological model, in which parts emerge in order of increasing differentiation

fidelity ability to sustain loyalties freely pledged; the basic virtue developed during the fifth psychosocial stage

generativity the positive pole of the seventh psychosocial stage

guilt the negative pole of the third psychosocial stage

hope fundamental conviction in the trustworthiness of the world; the basic virtue developed during the first psychosocial stage

identity sense of sameness between one's meaning for oneself and one's meaning for others in the social world; the positive pole of the fifth psychosocial stage

identity achievement status representing optimal development during the fifth (adolescent) psychosocial stage

identity confusion the negative pole of the fifth psychosocial stage

identity diffusion the negative pole of the fifth psychosocial stage (earlier terminology)

identity foreclosure inadequate resolution of the fifth psychosocial stage, in which an identity is accepted without adequate exploration

industry the positive pole of the fourth psychosocial stage

inferiority the negative pole of the fourth psychosocial stage

initiative the positive pole of the third psychosocial stage

integrity the positive pole of the eighth psychosocial stage

intimacy the positive pole of the sixth psychosocial stage

isolation the negative pole of the sixth psychosocial stage

love ability to form an intimate mutual relationship with another person; the basic virtue developed during the sixth psychosocial stage

mistrust the negative pole of the first psychosocial stage

moratorium period when an adolescent is sufficiently free of commitments to be able to explore identity

negative identity identity based on socially devalued roles

pseudospeciation the exaggerated sense that many groups have, especially national and ethnic groups, that they are different from others, leading to conflict among groups

psychosocial Erikson's approach to development, offered as an alternative to Freud's "psychosexual" approach

purpose orientation to attain goals through striving; the basic virtue developed during the third psychosocial stage

ritual cultural practice or tradition that supports ego strengths

ritualism an individual's maladaptive, repetitive actions intended to make up for weak aspects of ego development

shame the negative pole of the second psychosocial stage

stagnation the negative pole of the seventh psychosocial stage

trust the positive pole of the first psychosocial stage

will conviction that what one wants to happen can happen; the basic virtue developed during the second psychosocial stage

wisdom mature sense of the meaningfulness and wholeness of experience; the basic virtue developed during the eighth psychosocial stage

STUDY QUESTIONS

1. Contrast Erikson's view of motivation with Freud's psychosexual model.
2. Explain Erikson's "epigenetic principle."
3. List Erikson's eight psychosocial stages. Describe the crisis of each stage. Describe the consequences of each stage for ego development.

4. List and explain various outcomes of the identity crisis. What is the healthiest outcome?
5. What is a psychosocial moratorium? Give an example.
6. Discuss the importance of the negative pole of the crisis at various Eriksonian stages. How does the negative pole contribute to healthy ego development?
7. Discuss the way culture, as you know it, contributes to ego development at various stages. Do you think culture fails to provide adequate supports at any particular stage? Explain.
8. Explain Erikson's ideas about the relationship between identity and race.
9. What is the difference between *ritual* and *ritualism*?
10. Describe research on Erikson's eight stages of development. Include a description of Marcia's measure of identity.
11. How did Erikson understand sex differences? Describe his report of sex differences in play constructions. Summarize research that challenged his conclusions.
12. Describe research on sex differences in identity development.
13. Explain Erikson's concept of *pseudospeciation.*

CHAPTER

Horney: Interpersonal Psychoanalysis

BIOGRAPHY OF KAREN HORNEY

Karen Horney

Karen Danielson, who upon marriage assumed the name Horney, was born near Hamburg, Germany, on September 15, 1885. She was the second child in an unhappy marriage of an often absent Norwegian sea captain and his beautiful, somewhat higher-class wife. Karen and her older brother, Berndt (who later became a lawyer), were disciplined strictly by their tyrannical Lutheran father when he was home from his long sea voyages around Cape Horn to the Pacific coast of South and Central America. She retained a strongly independent character, regarding her father's outspoken religious attitudes as hypocritical and questioning the fundamentalist teachings of her Church. She participated enthusiastically in some of the new opportunities for women.

The secondary education traditionally available to German girls would have precluded a university education. This was, however, a time of social change in Germany. Young Karen prevailed upon her father to allow her to attend a newly opened nontraditional school that offered girls the course work necessary to prepare for the university entrance exams. Her father agreed, and Karen entered the University of Freiburg in 1906, in a class of 58 women and 2,292 men. There she studied medicine. She was popular and was included in the partying and study sessions with her male classmates. She married one frequent companion, Oskar Horney, in 1909. They moved to Berlin, where she continued her medical studies and he began a business career.

Karen Horney was a psychoanalytic patient of the famous Freudian analyst Karl Abraham. This was an avant-garde interest at that time. It was characteristic of her to explore new ideas, but she sought relief from personal problems as well. Horney was experiencing depression, fatigue, and dissatisfaction with her marriage, which she expressed by having an affair with her husband's friend. Her father died about this time, and she had ambivalent feelings toward him to sort out: anger because of the unhappiness of her parents' marriage, which had culminated in separation a few years before, but also more fondness for him than she admitted. The demands of combining a medical education with family life, without much encouragement from her husband, also required coping. Her analyst thought highly of her, as she later told Freud (A.N. O'Connell, 1980). Besides the analytic sessions, she kept a personal diary at this time, as she had in past years.

Though psychoanalysis was held in low esteem by the medical and psychiatric establishment, Karen decided to make it her professional specialty. While she was a student, this interest was kept discreetly quiet. After receiving her traditional psychiatric degree in 1915, she dared to lecture on the controversial Freudian theory and to defend it against critics including, interestingly, Adler and Jung (Quinn, 1988, p. 151). Her own challenges to the theory were still brewing. Unlike many psychoanalysts of this time, however, she did not visit Freud in Vienna, and so did not know him personally (Quinn, 1988). Freud did, however, chair a session in which Karen Horney in 1922 presented a paper on "The Genesis of the Castration Complex in Women" (A.N. O'Connell, 1980).

Karen and Oskar Horney had three daughters. (One, Marianne Horney Eckardt, became a Horneyan analyst.) But the couple continued to have a troubled marriage and finally separated. Karen Horney poured increasing energy into her career. She became one of the founding members of the Berlin Psychoanalytic Institute in 1920 and published several papers on male and female development, relationships, and marriage. Her 14 papers between 1922 and 1935 outlined a theory of female psychology that was clearly critical of Freud's theory. Horney's first suggestions were presented in a spirit of intellectual debate within classic Freudian theory, the sort of challenge that fosters the development of any science. The psychoanalytic community, however, dismissed her points and attacked her motivations. Freud is reported to have said of her, "She is able but malicious—mean" (Quinn, 1988, p. 237). He accused her of an inadequate analysis, saying that she did not accept her own "penis envy" (Symonds, 1991).

Given this hostile professional environment in Germany, it is no wonder that Dr. Horney accepted an invitation to become associate director of a new Institute for Psychoanalysis in Chicago, under Franz Alexander, in 1932. The invitation came with Freud's approval (Berger,

1991; Clemmens, 1984). Horney became dissatisfied with her position at the institute, and in 1934 she moved to New York. Ironically, the same sort of professional debates over theoretical orthodoxy that had impelled her to leave Germany divided the New York Psychoanalytic Institute. She had begun writing books in which she explicitly referred to her ideas as a new theory, different from that of Freud. Finally, the orthodox Freudians could no longer tolerate Horney's dissenting views. In 1941 the New York Psychoanalytic Society voted to remove Horney from her role as a teacher and clinical supervisor, demoting her to "instructor."

Horney and her followers quickly formed a new organization, the Association for the Advancement of Psychoanalysis, and founded the *American Journal of Psychoanalysis.* The announcement of the new training institute contained a statement of commitment to nonauthoritarian teaching: "Students are acknowledged to be intelligent and responsible adults. . . . It is the hope of the Institute that it will continue to avoid conceptual rigidities, and to respond to ideas, whatever the source, in a spirit of scientific and academic democracy" (cited in Quinn, 1988, p. 353).

It was not only the orthodox Freudians who were suspicious of her. The FBI kept a file on her because of her alleged communist sympathies, and because of this she was for a while denied a passport to travel to Japan (Quinn, 1988). The basis for this accusation seems to have been her affiliation with the liberal New School for Social Research in New York. She was ultimately granted the passport, and in Japan she stayed at several Zen monasteries (A.N. O'Connell, 1980). In December 1952, within months of her return from Japan, she died of abdominal cancer, which had not been previously diagnosed.

As a person, Karen Horney seems to have had a capacity for enjoying life, despite the seriousness of her career and the disappointments of her marriage. She liked to eat in the best restaurants and to attend concerts and parties. During Prohibition, she at least once spiked the punch by writing her own prescription for "medicinal" alcohol (Quinn, 1988). She enjoyed relationships with men and had several affairs. Her lovers included the famous psychoanalyst Erich Fromm and, it was rumored, a trainee at the Chicago Institute for Psychoanalysis, who was also her patient (Quinn, 1988).

Horney challenged Freud's claim that he had discovered universal developmental conflicts. Instead, she argued that personality and its development are greatly influenced by culture, and therefore vary from one society to another. This energetic and nontraditional woman proposed new understandings of women, and of men, which today are more widely accepted than the classical Freudian theory she challenged. For women in psychology, she is praised as an important role model (A.N. O'Connell & Russo, 1980). She is not only considered a neo-Freudian and a social psychoanalytic theorist, but also "a humanist for her holistic view and emphasis on self-realization; and a feminist for her development of a feminine psychology" (A.N. O'Connell, 1980, p. 81). Yet from her early interest in feminine psychology, Karen Horney turned later to the development of a general systematic theory of neurosis in which sex differences were not inevitable, but rather developments that occur only in particular cultural contexts (Eckardt, 1991; Symonds, 1991).

ILLUSTRATIVE BIOGRAPHIES

Several psychobiographical analyses have been published based on Horney's theory (Paris, 1989), including analyses of the Kennedys (Clinch, 1973), Jimmy Carter (Glad, 1980), Lyndon Johnson (Huffman, 1989), Robespierre (Shulim, 1977), and Stalin (Tucker, 1973, 1985). Paris predicts that the "immense biographical potential [of Horney's theory] has just begun to be explored" (1989, p. 182).

Society presents different demands and stereotypes to men and women. Horney's theory deals with these messages as social pressures, not simply as the biologically inherited sex differences that Freud acknowledged. Those who live out the culture's stereotypes of "masculine" and "feminine" serve as symbols of these messages to all of us. Mike Tyson, the heavyweight boxer, and Marilyn Monroe, the movie star, have surely epitomized these sex roles in American culture.

Marilyn Monroe

Although she has been dead since 1962, Marilyn Monroe is a timeless embodiment of an image of femininity. Marilyn epitomizes sexual beauty; her picture on a nude calendar was admired by many men and envied by many women. She also had a tragic side, arousing sympathy for the helpless victim.

Marilyn Monroe had many lovers and three, possibly four, husbands. Much as she sought love, her longest marriage lasted only 4½ years. She loved children, but never raised her own. Many were conceived; reportedly she had over a dozen abortions. (She reported that she bore an illegitimate child as a teenager, but it is unclear whether this is fact or imagination.) When motherhood was acceptable, as Arthur Miller's wife, she miscarried. Throughout adulthood, Marilyn took very high doses of barbiturates and attempted suicide on several occasions. It is likely that her death was either an intentional suicide or an accidental overdose. Theories of murder are favored by some, who argue that the FBI, the Kennedys, and the

Mafia all had reasons to be involved in her death. Whatever the circumstances, her death occurred on the fifth anniversary of her much-mourned miscarriage.

Is it simply coincidental that the sex goddess of her age was also a drug abuser and unsuccessful in love, or is there some causal connection between the social image and the tragic side? Does Marilyn Monroe paint, in bold strokes, themes that typify feminine personality of her time, in her culture, as Gloria Steinem (1986) suggested? Horney's theory, which offers particular contributions to the understanding of women and of culture, promises insights into this mysterious woman.

Mike Tyson

Michael Tyson became, at the age of 20, the youngest world champion heavyweight boxer in history, earning millions of dollars defending and then losing the title. In the ring, he defeated many opponents by knockouts. Out of the ring, he captured the attention of the media by his well-publicized marriage to actress Robin Givens, but this story ended unhappily with accusations of abuse and a bitter divorce. In 1992 he was sentenced to prison for the rape of a beauty pageant contestant.

As a child, Tyson was raised in the Bedford-Stuyvesant section of New York, an impoverished and crime-ridden inner-city neighborhood. Through his boxing success, Mike Tyson became wealthy and famous. Yet his story is not simply one of triumphant success. It is also a tragedy, with fame and glory masking deeper conflicts.

Karen Horney's theory, which is sensitive to interpersonal dynamics and claims awareness of the impact of culture and society, offers promise for understanding Mike Tyson.

INTERPERSONAL PSYCHOANALYSIS

Like traditional Freudian psychoanalysts, Karen Horney firmly believed that the unconscious is a powerful determinant of personality. (In this way she was far more "orthodox" than Alfred Adler.) However, she questioned

Freud's premise that the unconscious consists of conflicts over the expression of libido. It is not sexual conflict, according to Horney, that drives personality. In fact, Horney reported that some of her neurotic patients experienced fully satisfying, orgasmic sex lives, a phenomenon that is impossible according to classical Freudian theory. According to Horney, the most important conflicts are based on unresolved interpersonal issues, not libidinal fixations. Horney agreed with Freud that the fundamental conflicts that hobble personality originate early in childhood, and that these conflicts focus on parent–child interactions. She argued that cultural forces strongly affect these developments and that the personality differences between men and women are influenced more by social forces than by anatomy.

Basic Anxiety and Basic Hostility

Infants and young children are highly dependent upon their parents, not only for physical survival but also for a sense of psychological security. In the ideal case, the infant senses that he or she is loved and protected by the parents, and therefore is safe. Under less than ideal circumstances, the child feels intensely vulnerable. This helplessness in childhood, in the absence of adequate parenting, produces a feeling of **basic anxiety**, which Horney described as "the feeling a child has of being isolated and helpless in a potentially hostile world" (Horney, 1945, p. 41).

Parental neglect and rejection make the child angry, a condition Horney called **basic hostility**. However, the young child is not able to express the hostility, since it would result in punishment or loss of love. This repressed hostility increases the anxiety. The neurotic, then, develops a basic conflict between "fundamentally contradictory attitudes he has acquired toward other persons" (Horney, 1945, pp. 40–41). The child needs the parents and wants to approach them but, on the other hand, hates them and wants to punish them. This is the basic conflict, the driving force behind neurosis. It is an interpersonal conflict, in contrast to Freud's libidinal conflict between sexual desire and the restricting forces of society (see Figure 6.1).

Three Interpersonal Orientations

What then is the child to do? Three choices are available: accentuate dependency and *move toward* the parents; accentuate hostility and *move against* them; or give up on the relationship and *move away* from them. The young child resolves the conflict with the parents using whichever of these strategies seems to best fit his or her particular family environment. This choice becomes the person's characteristic interpersonal orientation.

Ideally, a healthy person should be able to move toward people, against them, or away from them, flexibly choosing the strategy that best fits the particular circumstances. In contrast, neurotics are imbalanced in their interpersonal behavior. Some choices of interpersonal activity have been so fraught with anxiety that they simply are not options. The young child who was never permitted to express any criticism of the parents, for example, is unlikely to be able to compete wholeheartedly against others in adulthood. The rejected child will continue to have difficulty moving toward people.

For the most part, neurotics emphasize one interpersonal trend. Horney offered a three-type categorization of neurotics: those who **move toward** people, those who **move against** people, and those who **move away** from

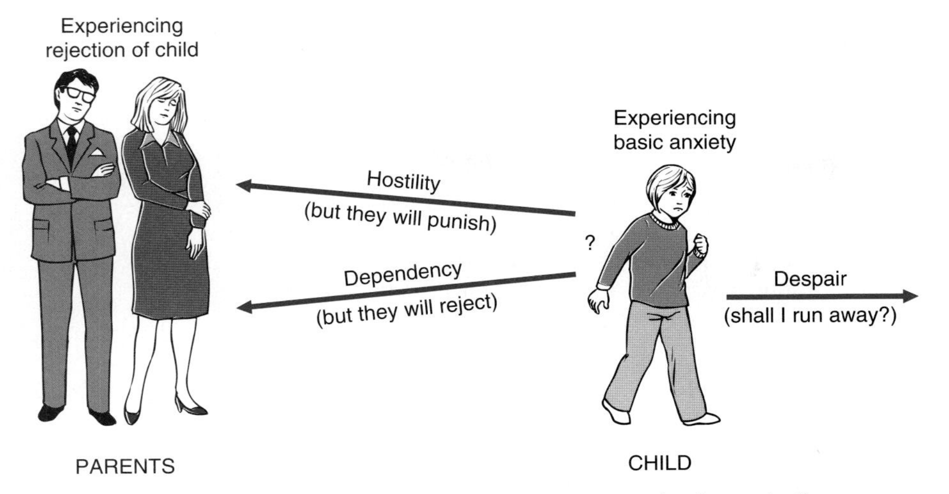

The child, needing to be loved, wants to move towards the parents, but fears rejection. The child also feels hostility and wants to retaliate by moving against the parents, but fears punishment. The child may give up and move away from the parents.

FIGURE 6.1 Horney's Model of Neurotic Conflict

people. Paris (1989) observed that these three orientations correspond to "the basic mechanisms of defense in the animal kingdom—fight, flight, and submission" (p. 186).

Horney said that neurotics who emphasize moving toward people were adopting the **self-effacing solution** to neurotic conflict, seeking *love,* and minimizing any apparently selfish needs that could interfere with being loved. She said that neurotics who emphasize moving against people were adopting the **expansive solution** to neurotic conflict, seeking *mastery,* even if it impeded close relationships with others. Finally, neurotics who emphasize moving away from people were adopting the **resignation solution**, seeking *freedom,* even at the expense of relationships and achievement. Each of these basic trends could be expressed in a variety of ways (see Table 6.1).

Moving Toward People: The Self-Effacing Solution

Some people turn to others for the love and protection lacking in their early life. Because of this dependency, they must be careful to do nothing to alienate others. Horney referred to these as "compliant" types (Horney, 1945). Some of them may be dominated by a need for affection, living as though their motto were "If you love me you will not hurt me" (Horney, 1937, p. 96). Others are better characterized as dominated by a submissive attitude, as though they felt, "If I give in, I shall not be hurt" (Horney, 1937, p. 97).

In order to be lovable, a person will do things to endear others: becoming sensitive to their needs, seeking their approval, and acting in unselfish ways, generous to a fault. The need for love may be expressed in an exaggerated need to be "in love," or involved in sexual relationships where the part-

TABLE 6.1 Horney's Three Neurotic Solutions

1. Self-Effacing Solution: The Appeal of Love
The Compliant Personality
"Moving toward" people
Morbid dependency: the need for a partner (friend, lover, or spouse)
"Poor little me": feeling of being weak and helpless
Self-subordination: assumption that others are superior
Martyrdom: sacrifice and suffering for others
Need for love: desire to find self-worth in a relationship
2. Expansive Solution: The Appeal of Mastery
The Aggressive Personality
"Moving against" people
Narcissistic: in love with idealized self-image
Perfectionistic: high standards
Arrogant-vindictive: pride and strength
Need to be right: to win a fight or competition
Need for recognition: to be admired
3. Resignation Solution: The Appeal of Freedom
The Detached Personality
"Moving away from" people
Persistent resignation and lack of striving: the aversion to effort and change
Rebellious against constraints or influences: the desire for freedom
Shallow living: an onlooker at self and life, detached from emotional experiences and wishes
Self-sufficient and independent: uninvolved with people
Need for privacy: keeps others outside the magic circle of the self

(Adapted from Horney, 1945, 1950.)

ner takes control. Women, especially, are subjected to cultural pressures toward this need for love.

The compliant type of person makes few demands on others, instead acting subordinate to others, playing a "poor me" role that emphasizes the feeling of helplessness. This is reflected in a low self-esteem. Such a person "takes it for granted that everyone is superior to him, that they are more attractive, more intelligent, better educated, more worthwhile than he" (Horney, 1945, pp. 53–54). The repression of hostility may result in physical symptoms, such as headaches and stomach problems (Horney, 1945, p. 58).

Moving Against People: The Expansive Solution

Other people try to solve the problem of conflict over unresolved early needs by mastery and by asserting their power over others. Horney refers to these as "aggressive" types (Horney, 1945). They seem to live by the motto, "If I have power, no one can hurt me" (Horney, 1937, p. 98).

Power and mastery seem to offer protection from the vulnerability of being helpless. This type of person may exert obvious interpersonal power, domineering over others. Or power may be sought through competitive mastery. Prestige protects against humiliation; others are humiliated instead, while the individual seeks recognition and admiration.

The aggressive type has some advantages in our competitive world, if aggression does not become overt hostility. The competitiveness of many careers taps this trend. Horney noted that males are more likely than females to adopt this strategy, which is consistent with the difficulty experienced by many women in "climbing the corporate ladder." There may be disadvantages for society, though, in the competitiveness and aggressiveness endemic in many career fields. We think first of the callousness of the corporate world, but it exists elsewhere as well. Suzuki (1988), for example, criticized the machismo grantsmanship attitude that prevails in scientific research, arguing that this competitive attitude does not bring about optimal use of scientific talent.

Aggressive types need not behave in ways that would endear them to others. Did Attila the Hun try to be liked? or Hitler? or Jack the Ripper? Power makes love seem an unnecessary weakness. From her clinical experience, Horney noted that patients of this type seem to have particular difficulty when they do, in the course of therapy, begin to come close to other people in love or friendship.

Moving Away from People: The Registration Solution

Other people adopt a strategy similar to that of the fox, in Aesop's fable, who could not reach grapes hanging over his head. After all attempts to reach them failed, the fox finally gave up, avoiding disappointment by telling himself that the grapes were probably sour anyway. In Horney's theory, some people try to do without other people, having given up on solving the problem of basic anxiety through love or power. Horney refers to these as "detached personality" types (Horney, 1945). They seem to live by the motto, "If I withdraw, nothing can hurt me" (Horney, 1937, p. 99).

Detached types try to be self-sufficient. They may develop considerable resourcefulness and independence; Horney cites the example of Robinson Crusoe. Or they may restrict their needs. They protect their privacy and prefer to be alone. Creative people are often detached types. They may express their feelings with a safe, but creative, detachment, facilitated by the isolation that reduces distractions.

Healthy versus Neurotic Use of Interpersonal Orientations

A neurotic person favors one interpersonal orientation over others. In contrast, the healthy person adopts, when appropriate, all of these three orientations toward people, since each is adaptive in certain situations. For example, while it is pathological to be aggressive toward everyone, the healthy person must be capable of "adequate aggressiveness," involving "taking initiative; making efforts; carrying things through to completion; attaining success; insisting upon one's rights; defending oneself when attacked; forming and expressing autonomous views; recognizing one's goals and being able to plan one's life according to them" (Horney, 1935/1967e, p. 228). The current term would be "assertiveness" rather than "aggressiveness," but the list of behaviors is strikingly modern. People who lack such adequate aggressiveness have difficulties with achievement (Bernay, 1982). Similarly, while excessive dependency ("moving toward") is neurotic, the inability to ask for appropriate help (a deficit in the "moving toward" orientation) is also maladaptive.

Measurement of Interpersonal Orientations

This typology of interpersonal styles can be measured by a self-report instrument, the Cohen CAD Scale, which gives scores for compliance ("moving toward"), aggression ("moving against") and detachment ("moving away") (J.B. Cohen, 1967). The instrument asks respondents to rate the desirability, on a 6-point scale from "extremely undesirable" to "extremely desirable," of 35 items, for example:

1. "To have something good to say about everyone seems . . ." [scored "Compliance"]
2. "For me to have enough money or power to impress self-styled "big shots" would be . . ." [scored "Aggression"]
3. "Being free of social obligations is . . ." [scored "Detachment"]

(Munson & Spivey, 1982, pp. 894–895)

While the instrument has been criticized (Noreager, 1979), research with female subjects has confirmed its factor structure; that is, evidence supports the claim that it does measure three different dimensions (Munson & Spivey, 1982). Differences on the scale have been reported for various occupational groups (J.B. Cohen, 1967; Rendon, 1987). Rendon (1987) reported that a sample of registered nurses studying to complete their baccalaureate degrees scored higher on the Compliant ("moving toward") scale and on the Detachment ("moving away") scale than did three norm groups (students in social welfare, business administration, and geology programs). (See Figure 6.2.) In another study, the student role (among a group of registered nurses returning to school) was more satisfying for those who scored high on the "Compliance" scale (Rendon, 1987), which invites speculation that student passivity may be a reaction to the structure of the student role.

Except for the CAD, mentioned above, which is not well known among psychologists, there does not seem to be an instrument devised specifically for the measurement of these interpersonal tendencies. Instead, researchers have used instruments devised for other purposes, interpreting them from the perspective of Horney's theory. For example, Roemer (1986) and Wheeler (1989) have suggested that Horney's types can be understood within the framework of a more extensive interpersonal model offered by Leary (1957). Leary's model proposed eight types of personality, which can be schematically arranged in a circle. The primary dimensions differentiating the types are *affect* (ranging from hostility to affiliation) and *power* (ranging from dominance to submission). The Leary model has implications for psychotherapy (Andrews, 1989), as it should if it corresponds to Horney's theory. In addition, Jabin (1987) reported that Horney's interpersonal modes predict various types of prejudicial attitudes toward disabled persons.

Raskin, Novacek, and Hogan (1991) described two interpersonal styles, "warriors" and "worriers," which seem to correspond to Horney's "moving

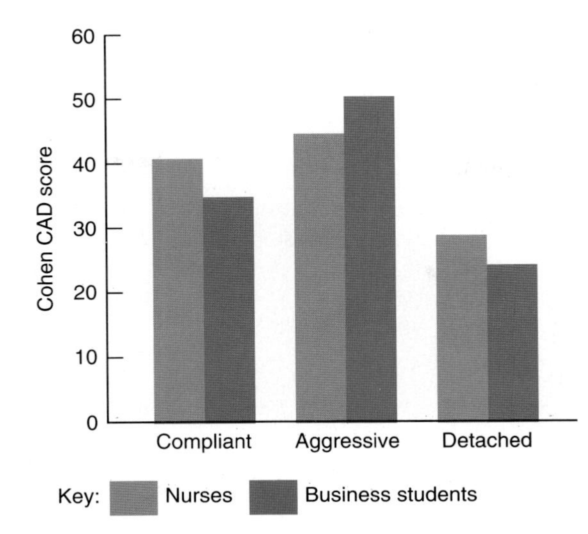

FIGURE 6.2 Different Interpersonal Orientations of Nurses and Students in Three Other Norm Groups
(From Rendon, 1987, p. 137.)

against" and "moving toward" orientations (though the researchers did not cite Horney's theory). They described data, including a Narcissistic Personality Inventory, supporting a clinical pattern of interrelated hostility, grandiosity, dominance, narcissism, and self-esteem. This portrait is similar to that described by Freud, Kernberg, Kohut, and other clinical theorists. It bears marked resemblance to Horney's conceptualization of a grandiose ideal self, fueled by hostility, leading to a "moving against others" interpersonal orientation.

Roemer (1986, 1987) and Hamon (1987) have suggested that the literature on personality and coronary risk makes sense within Horney's model. Type A persons, the time-pressured, competitive, hostile personality types who suffer an elevated risk of heart disease (Friedman & Rosenman, 1974; Jenkins, Rosenman, & Zyzanski, 1974), correspond to Horney's "expansive personality" type (and Leary's power and aggressiveness dimension). Low-risk Type B's correspond to Horney's "self-effacing" pattern (Roemer, 1987). (See Table 6.2.) Horney's theory enlightens the Type A literature by suggesting the concept of an "idealized self," which Type A's pursue aggressively, often through their work. The psychological dimensions of other diseases may also be understood from Horney's model—for example, the experience of diabetic patients (Bergman, Akin, & Felig, 1990).

Research would be facilitated by the development and use of a measure explicitly designed to measure Horney's interpersonal orientations. Perhaps the Cohen CAD Scale (J.B. Cohen, 1967), described above, would suffice, but it has been neglected by researchers who cite Horney's theory.

Major Adjustments to Basic Anxiety

To solve conflicts over basic anxiety, the person adopts defense mechanisms. Horney continued to recognize many of the defense mechanisms that previous analysts had described, such as repression. In addition, she greatly expanded the list of defensive maneuvers.

TABLE 6.2 Type A and Type B Subjects' Typical Responses on Two Personality Tests, Understood in Terms of Horney's Theory

	Self-Perception (ACL)		*Role Behavior (MMPI)*	
A–B Group	***Emphasize***	***Avoid***	***Emphasize***	***Avoid***
Type A	Power Aggressiveness	Affiliation Helplessness	Power Affiliation Aggressiveness	Helplessness
Type B	Affiliation Helplessness	Power Aggressiveness	Helplessness Affiliation Aggressiveness	Power

Note: The personality tests are the Adjective Check List (ACL) and the Minnesota Multiphasic Personality Inventory (MMPI).

(From Roemer, 1987, p. 121.)

All neurotics use some mixture of four major strategies for resolving the basic conflict between helplessness and hostility. These strategies do not solve the conflict or lead to growth, but they may allow the person to adapt sufficiently to cope with daily life.

Eclipsing the Conflict: Moving Toward or Against Others

First, the neurotic may "eclipse part of the conflict and raise its opposite to predominance" (Horney, 1945, p. 16). Since the conflict is between helplessness and hostility, a person who "eclipses" hostility will emphasize helplessness and to turn dependently toward others. On the other hand, a person who "eclipses" helplessness will emphasize hostility and turn angrily against other people. These constitute two of the basic interpersonal orientations: *moving toward* and *moving against* people.

Detachment: Moving Away from Others

Instead, neurotic individuals may detach themselves from others. Because the conflicts are inherently interpersonal, simply moving away from people reduces the experience of conflict. If this tendency is much stronger than eclipsing, it leads to Horney's third interpersonal orientation, *moving away* from people.

The Idealized Self: Moving Away from the Real Self

The third major adjustment strategy of the neurotic is to turn away from the real self toward some seemingly better (less helpless, less angry) **idealized self**. The **real self** is "the alive, unique, personal center of ourselves" (Horney, 1950, p. 155). It is involved in healthy psychological growth (which many humanists call "self-actualization"). The real self is abandoned in neurosis. For the sake of clarity, Horney offered a different term to describe everything that we really are at a given time, neurotic as well as healthy; this she called the **actual self** (1950, p. 158). What the neurotic turns away from is growth potential (the real self), not reality (the actual self).

Alienation from the Real Self

As a result of basic anxiety, the person comes to believe, often unconsciously, that he or she is inadequate. While a healthy adult who is neglected or rejected can turn to other relationships, confident in his or her own self-worth, the young child does not have the resources to do so. Consequently, the sense of self, which is just in the process of developing, emerges already wounded. The child comes to have a low self-esteem, feeling that his or her *real self* is unworthy. This alienation produces neurosis.

The neurotic turns to an imagined *idealized self,* which would not be despised. The idealized self fits the interpersonal orientation of the individual. "Perhaps if I am very, very good and kind, I will be lovable," thinks one child. "Or," imagines another, "if I impress people with my achievements and power, they will not be able to hurt me, and may even admire me." "Or," muses a third, "maybe I don't need people after all; I can manage alone."

The real self is repressed, and the person tries to become the idealized self. The idealized self may become the basis for intense striving; for example, Lyndon Johnson's idealized self channeled his political career, ultimately leading to the presidency (Huffman, 1989).

Sometimes this repression of the real self seems to work, and the person's conscious self image is like the idealized self, at least while environmental conditions are favorable. It is always a struggle to maintain the pretense that one is like the idealized self, rather than like the rejected real self. When the effort fails, a person must confront the underlying conflict. Anxiety or even panic may result.

The profoundly disturbing consequences of this turning from the real to the idealized self are suggested by the comparison Horney makes. The process corresponds to "the devil's pact, . . . the selling of one's soul" (Horney, 1950, p. 155). The neurotic is like Faust, who sold his soul to the Devil for a bit of fleeting pleasure and power.

The Tyranny of the Shoulds

Each person develops ways for strengthening the idealized self and avoiding painful confrontation with the repressed real self. "I *should* act kind to everyone," or "I *should* be able to do the work better than anyone else," or "I *should* not have to depend on other people." These are the sorts of demands, often not fully conscious, that people make upon themselves.

Horney called these demands the **tyranny of the shoulds**. They urge us ever closer to the idealized self, but at the expense of increased alienation from the real self. Thus, they get in the way of optimal health. Horney even referred to the idealized image as "a bit of psychosis woven into the texture of neurosis" (1945, p. 97). (In this way, Horney clearly disagreed with the judgment of Alfred Adler, whose similar "fictional finalisms" are conducive to growth, rather than stagnation.)

Externalization: Projection of Inner Conflict

A fourth major adjustment strategy has the neurotic projecting inner conflicts onto the outside world, a process Horney called **externalization.** This does not heal the original conflict between the individual and the outside world, but rather increases it. Though it does not produce growth, it does reduce anxiety, at least for a while.

Externalization refers to "the tendency to experience internal processes as if they occurred outside oneself and, as a rule, to hold these external factors responsible for one's difficulties" (Horney, 1945, p. 115). It includes the defense mechanism of projection, as traditional psychoanalysis understands it, in which our own unacceptable tendencies (such as anger or sometimes ambitiousness) are perceived as characteristic of other people, but not ourselves. Externalization can also include, besides impulses, our unrecognized feelings. Horney cited the example of a man unaware of his own feeling of oppression, who, by externalization, was "profoundly disturbed by the oppression of small countries" (1945, p. 116).

Horney described some of the things that neurotics often externalize. Self-contempt may be externalized, either by thinking that others despise us (projection of the impulse) or by despising others (displacement of the object of contempt). Compliant types (those who "move toward" others) are likely to externalize in the first way, and aggressive types (those who "move against" others) in the second way. In either case, the neurotic is protected from becoming aware of deep self-contempt. Horney suggested that the therapist should not challenge these neurotic tendencies prematurely because of the hopelessness that may result. (Insight, if premature, is not therapeutic.)

Rage is also externalized in various ways: by irritation against other people, by fear that others will be irritated with us, and by converting the rage into bodily disorders.

These four attempts at solution occur in all neuroses, though not with equal strength. For example, some people withdraw very much from others, so that it becomes a major characteristic of their personality. Other people are involved with others in many interdependent activities, but guard certain aspects of their private selves from others. These neurotic attempts only "create an artificial harmony" (Horney, 1945, p. 16), rather than actually resolving the problem.

Secondary Adjustment Techniques

In addition to the major defensive strategies (eclipsing, detachment, the idealized self, and externalization), there are also many "auxiliary" strategies for reducing anxiety. Horney believed these secondary adjustment techniques, like the major adjustment techniques, do not really solve the neurotic problem in any lasting way, as she made clear in the title by which she introduced the concepts: "Auxiliary Approaches to Artificial Harmony" (1945, p. 131). Let us examine how these strategies reduce the experience of conflict.

Blind Spots

People are often unaware of aspects of their behavior that are blatantly incompatible with their idealized self-image. Horney cited the example of a patient who "had all the characteristics of the compliant type and thought of himself as Christlike," but who blindly failed to recognize the aggression expressed by his symbolic murders of co-workers. "At staff meetings he would often shoot one colleague after another with a little flick of his thumb" (Horney, 1945, p. 132). Such **blind spots** prevent conscious awareness of the conflict between the behavior and our self-image.

Another way to prevent the recognition of conflict is by **compartmentalization**, allowing the incompatible behaviors to be consciously recognized, but not at the same time. Each is allowed to be experienced in a separate "compartment" of life: family or outsiders, friends or enemies, work or personal life, and so forth. For example, a person may be loving within the family, but a ruthless business competitor outside the family.

Compartmentalizing

Horney called **rationalization** "self-deception by reasoning" (1945, p. 135). Using rationalization, we explain our behaviors so that they seem consistent with what is socially acceptable, and with the desirable qualities that we have accepted as part of our personality. Horney provided these examples: If a person is helpful, a compliant type will rationalize this as due to feelings of sympathy (ignoring a tendency to dominate, which may also be present); an aggressive type will explain the helpfulness as an expedient behavior. In both cases, rationalization bolsters the idealized self-image.

Rationalization

Excessive self-control prevents people from being overwhelmed by a variety of emotions, including "enthusiasm, sexual excitement, self-pity, or rage" (Horney, 1945, p. 136). Rage is particularly dangerous, and is most actively controlled. People using this defense mechanism typically avoid alcohol because it would be disinhibiting. They have particular difficulty with free association in psychotherapy. When emotions threaten to break through, these people may fear that they are going crazy.

Excessive Self-Control

Arbitrary rightness "constitutes an attempt to settle conflicts once and for all by declaring arbitrarily and dogmatically that one is invariably right" (Horney, 1945, p. 138). Inner doubts are denied, and external challenges are discredited. The rigidity of these people makes them avoid psychoanalysis, which challenges a person's core defensive beliefs.

Arbitrary Rightness

Elusiveness is quite the opposite of arbitrary rightness. These people do not commit themselves to any opinion or action because they "have established no definite idealized image" (Horney, 1945, p. 139) to avoid the experience of conflict. Though conflict is experienced, the person who is elusive does not stick with a conflict long enough to really work at resolution. "You can never pin them down to any statement; they deny having said it or assure you they did not mean it that way. They have a bewildering capacity to becloud issues" (Horney, 1945, p. 138).

Elusiveness

They are reminiscent of the joke about the neighbor who, asked to return a borrowed bucket, says he didn't borrow it, and besides it was leaking when he borrowed it, and besides, he already returned it.

Cynicism avoids conflict by "denying and deriding . . . moral values" (Horney, 1945, p. 139). A Machiavellian-type person is consciously cynical, seeking to achieve his or her goals without moral qualms. Others use cynicism unconsciously; they consciously accept society's values, but do not live by them.

Cynicism

Cultural Determinants of Development

Horney stressed social and cultural determinants of personality, in addition to orthodox Freudian biological forces. She acknowledged more biological determinism than some feminist critics would wish (Garrison, 1981; Lerman, 1986b), and she did not become an activist for social change (Garrison, 1981).

Horney thought that it was necessary to know something about the culture and specific family environment in which a person was raised in order to understand the development of neurosis. She stated that "there is no such thing as a normal psychology that holds for all mankind" (Horney, 1937, p. 19). Specific family experiences, such as having domineering or self-sacrificing mothers, only occur under particular cultural conditions (Horney, 1937, p. viii). This view contrasts with Freud's description of universal family psychodynamics. For Horney, even the Oedipal complex occurs because of rivalry within the family that is only characteristic of certain cultural conditions, not universal.

Cultural factors are even involved in the labeling of certain behavior patterns as abnormal. Unlike medical disorders, such as broken bones, Horney argued that behaviors such as seeing visions or shame about sexuality are neurotic in some cultures but quite normal in others. Similarly, a woman who sacrifices her own career for her husband's career is considered "normal" in our culture, even if the wife is more gifted (Horney, 1939, p. 181).

Horney argued that sex was becoming less important as a source of anxiety at the time she wrote than in Freud's somewhat earlier era (1937, p. 62). Instead, she regarded the conflict between competitiveness and love to be more important. "In our culture," she wrote, "the most important neurotic conflict is between a compulsive and inconsiderate desire to be the first under all circumstances and the simultaneous need to be loved by everybody" (Horney, 1937/1967d, p. 258).

Parental Behavior and Early Childhood Experience

Within the family the "basic evil is invariably a lack of genuine warmth and affection" (Horney, 1937, p. 80). If the environment is loving, the sorts of traumas identified by Freud, such as premature weaning or toilet training, or witnessing the primal scene, could be tolerated. Parental behavior that undermines a feeling of safety will lead to neurotic development. This includes parental neglect, indifference, and even active rejection of the child.

The ideal family atmosphere provides warmth, goodwill, and "healthy friction with the wishes and wills of others" (Horney, 1950, p. 18). Such an environment allows the child to develop a secure feeling of belonging, instead of basic anxiety. Healthy parenting requires that the parents themselves be capable of genuinely loving the child, and that is not possible if they themselves have emotional problems. Many parents fall short of this ideal. One of the goals Horney described for psychoanalysis was to gain more understanding of the optimal way of treating children, so that parents could be advised how to raise healthy youngsters. What might come naturally for emotionally healthy parents could then, perhaps, be approximated by others with the guidance of psychoanalysts, thus breaking the repeating cycle of neurosis through each generation.

Because Horney developed her theory by working with adult clients, her ideas about parental behavior were speculative. It is possible now to compare her ideas with research evidence collected by developmental psychologists (Feiring, 1984). Studies of parenting styles have been conducted, based on Baumrind's (1967, 1971) descriptions of various types of parenting. As Horney expected, neglectful parents have children with greater difficulties. "Authoritative" parents, who provide both direction and acceptance, rear children who are better adjusted (Lamborn, Mounts, Steinberg, & Dornbusch, 1991).

Ainsworth (1972; Ainsworth, Blehar, Waters, & Wall, 1978) has studied *infant attachment* to the mother (as the primary caretaker) by observing infants' responses to strangers. These theorists were primarily concerned with the development of a secure attachment between infant and parent as a basis for emotional health and coping in later life. They observed how infants behaved when in the presence of a stranger. Some infants are frightened; others seem comforted by their mothers' presence. The various attachment patterns they described can be interpreted as evidence confirming Horney's patterns of moving toward or away from people (Feiring, 1984). Some infants resist being comforted (Ainsworth's "Type A"), analogous to Horney's "moving away" types. Others show anger toward a stranger (Ainsworth's "Type C"), early evidence perhaps of Horney's "moving against" mode of relationship. Type B infants are considered securely attached and are likely to show positive indices of interpersonal relationships and development later in life. This group can be subdivided, however; those who are most likely to cling to the mother (Ainsworth's "Type B_4") may be interpreted (according to Feiring, 1984) as showing Horney's pattern of "moving toward," while those who explore a new environment rather than clinging to the mother (Type B_1) have the balanced interpersonal mode that Horney regarded as most healthy (see Table 6.3). Feiring (1984) further suggested that the parental behaviors found in developmental research to be associated with these types confirm Horney's statements. However, Chess (1986) cautioned that the Ainsworth experimental situation is quite unusual for the infant, and so may result in misleading observations. She further noted that "there is no simple and direct correlation between early life

TABLE 6.3 Ainsworth's Description of Infant Temperament Types Compared with Horney's Model of Interpersonal Orientations

Infant Type	*Infant Behavior*	*Horney's Interpersonal Orientation*
Type A	resists being comforted	Moving Away
Type B	securely attached comforted by mother	
Type B_1	explores new environment	Balance of the three interpersonal orientations
Type B_4	stays near mother for comfort	Moving Toward
Type C	ambivalent toward mother shows anger toward stranger	Moving Against

(Adapted from Feiring, 1984.)

experiences and later development" (1986, p. 142); humans are remarkably adaptable, and sometimes they overcome severe environmental deficits.

Having an alcoholic parent has adverse consequences for development, which Lyon and Greenberg (1991) interpret within the framework of Horney's theory. Adult children of alcoholics may, maladaptively, seek relationships with alcoholics in which they play the role of a "co-dependent" who is pathologically dependent and inadvertently supports alcoholism. Lyon and Greenberg argue that this pattern corresponds to Horney's description of "morbid dependency," an extreme form of "moving toward" others. They found, in an experimental study, that college women who had an alcoholic parent were willing to volunteer more time to help an experimenter who was portrayed as exploitative than one who was portrayed as nurturant. Subjects without an alcoholic parent did the reverse. Thus patterns of interactions that originate with parents continue into later life, even when the patterns may be dysfunctional.

Social Roles and Gender

Cultures define what is masculine and what is feminine (Eagly, 1987b; Eagly & Wood, 1991). Horney argued that female masochism, which traditional psychoanalysis says is a result of anatomy, is instead due to cultural factors. Culture produces low self-esteem in many women. As Horney put it, "in our culture it is hard to see how any woman can escape becoming masochistic to some degree" (1935/1967e, p. 231). Sex roles in our culture have traditionally prescribed nurturance for females and power for males, to such an extent that the short form of the Bem Sex-Role Inventory "masculine" scale is virtually identical to a scale derived by factor analysis called "Interpersonal Potency," and the Bem "feminine" scale is virtually identical to an "Interpersonal Sensitivity" scale (Brems & Johnson, 1990).

Rather than accepting the Freudian view of female masochism as the enjoyment of pain, Horney suggested "that masochistic phenomena represent the attempt to gain safety and satisfaction in life through inconspicuousness and dependency" (1939, p. 113). Horney's emphasis on the importance of culture in defining men's and women's psychodynamics is echoed by others (Chodorow, 1978; Dinnerstein, 1976; Lerman, 1986b). Because of the pervasive influence of sex roles, the "self" develops as specifically feminine (Buss, 1990; Menaker, 1990) or masculine for each individual.

An empirical study of couples found that the strategies people use to influence their intimate partners vary with the person's structural strength or weakness in the relationship, as indicated by income, education, and age. The more powerful member of a couple (usually the male in a heterosexual relationship) was more likely to use bullying and autocratic tactics to influence the partner, whereas the weaker partner was more likely to use supplication and manipulation (Howard, Blumstein, & Schwartz, 1986). This association held for both heterosexual and gay and lesbian couples. The structural strength of the role position was a better predictor of behavior than personality measures of sex role orientation. This study supports Horney's claim that social roles, rather than purely intrapsychic factors such as masochism, must be considered to understand why people behave as they do.

Although the prevailing view among psychologists used to be that women who work and have professions suffer personality disturbances (labeled "penis envy" or otherwise), and that traditionally feminine women were psychologically healthier than less traditional women, recent studies do not support this view (Helson & Picano, 1990; Yogev, 1983). A review of the research relating sex roles to mental health indicated that psychological masculinity (as measured on sex-typing instruments such as the Bem Sex Role Inventory) was associated with better mental health, in both men and women, while femininity was not consistently related to mental health (Bassoff & Glass, 1982). This finding, impressive because it was based on a meta-analysis (that is, a statistically sophisticated literature review) of 26 studies, confirmed Horney's general idea that sex roles may help or hinder mental health. However, it is not the presence of "feminine" characteristics, such as empathy and nurturance, but rather the absence of "masculine" qualities, such as assertiveness, that interferes with healthy adaptation for women and, equally, for men. Furthermore, the results reported by Bassoff and Glass challenge literature that suggests "androgyny" is conducive to mental health (e.g., S.L. Bem, 1974, 1976; Spence, Helmreich, & Stapp, 1975; Worell, 1978). Only the masculinity component of the androgyny measure was associated with mental health in the studies reviewed. Further investigation of the relationship between ego development and sex typing seems warranted, perhaps focusing on the specifically interpersonal aspects of sex roles, and on the "agency" or activity component (Schwarz & Robins, 1987).

Horney argued that culture, rather than anatomy, was the important force behind the "penis envy" Freud had postulated. Women envy the power and privilege that humans with penises have, rather than the organ itself. For Horney, penis envy represented an avoidance of the feminine role (Horney, 1923/1967c, 1926/1967a; Siegel, 1982). Furthermore, men experience an equally important **womb envy**, in which they feel inferior to women's reproductive capacity.

Horney described sex roles concerning achievement in ways that anticipated later psychological research. Women, she claimed, are especially likely to become "compliant" types who do not risk achievement. She suggested that "our cultural situation . . . stamps success a man's sphere" (1937, p. 204). Because of this, men are encouraged to become competitive, while women are discouraged, and may even develop a "fear of success" (Horney, 1937, pp. 210–214). Research confirms that males are more likely to perceive situations as competitive than are females, and that for females, but not for males, competition reduces liking of others (Deberry, 1989).

Many people do not realize that the term "fear of success" was originally used by Karen Horney, who suggested that fear of success may come from a conflict between competition and the need for affection. For example, a woman motivated by fear of success may feel that, if she succeeds, she will lose her friends. Fear of success was first measured by a projective test (Horner, 1972). Horner conceptualized the fear of success as a motive to *avoid* achievement. While the concept generally refers to the achievement domain, a fear of success in the social domain has also been investigated, and it is reported to function for females but not for males (Senchak & Wheeler, 1988).

Horner's work on fear of success has been criticized on methodological and conceptual grounds (Paludi, 1984; Tresemer, 1974, 1977; Zuckerman & Wheeler, 1975). Theoretically and politically, it has been criticized because, treated as a trait, fear of success seems to locate the cause of women's lower achievement within their personalities, rather than in cultural factors (Lott, 1985; Wallston, 1987). Furthermore, those interested in fear of success (as in other areas, such as moral development, cf. Greeno & Maccoby, 1986) have often been overly ready to accept evidence for sex differences (Mednick, 1989). The popularity of the "Fear of Success" concept has been immense, considering its shaky empirical basis.

Most personality theory emphasizes individuality and striving, rather than connectedness and serving others, thus neglecting central themes in the lives of most women (Torrey, 1987). Writers on the psychology of women have often challenged male bias in culture and in psychological theory by proposing that feminine values, especially relationship-oriented values like nurturance and empathy, should be more highly valued by the culture as a whole (Gilligan, 1982; J.B. Miller, 1976; Symonds, 1991). Westkott (1989), however, has challenged this very popular orientation from the perspective of Horney's theory. She contends that women's valuing of relationships often takes the form of an idealized self, which in Horney's theory is neurotic. Thus, feminist theory and feminist therapy, by affirming relationship values, unwittingly support women's neurotic idealized self. This makes it more difficult for women to become the well-balanced ideal Horney envisaged for healthy people, and perpetuates a cultural expectation that women should take care of men (Westkott, 1986a, 1986b, 1989).

Therapy

Therapy must analyze the entire personality. No quick interventions, focused only on specific presenting symptoms, are possible in any psychoanalytic therapy. Horney acknowledged that briefer psychotherapies may have some promise, but not for neurosis (1945, p. 240).

The therapist must uncover the unconscious strategies the patient has been using to deal with neurotic conflict. These have implications for interpersonal relationships, self-image, and perception of the world. Then the detailed implications of these strategies for living are explored with the patient. These insights provide guidance for the building of new, less neurotic, ways of resolving the conflict. The idealized self must be given up, replaced by the real self with its sense of "felt aliveness" (J.A. Lerner, 1986).

Though orthodox in her acceptance of the importance of childhood experience in developing personality, Horney did not believe that all psychoanalytic treatment required delving into childhood recollections. Horney criticized Freudian overemphasis on the exploration of childhood origins of neurosis. She believed that the important insight for therapy was to understand unconscious tendencies and their functions. Except to the extent that exploring childhood enlightens this understanding, it is not useful. Sometimes focus on the present is more effective in producing change. Patients may try to avoid confronting their neurotic conflicts through an exaggerated interest in past origins in childhood. Horney advised the therapist to keep bringing the patient back to the present, seeing how neurotic trends influence current life. This is more painful for the patient, but more pertinent to the task of therapy, which is personality change.

Inevitably, the patient's idealized image must be challenged; but this must be done carefully and slowly, since it is the basis for the personality, wounded but not destroyed, that the patient brings to analysis. Eventually, though, the idealized image must be replaced by a more realistic self-concept. The term "shrink," applied to the analyst, seems particularly fitting for this function.

Psychotherapy's ultimate goal is to make fundamental changes in personality. This involves many aims: to increase patients' responsibility for themselves; to become more genuinely independent of others; to experience feelings more spontaneously; and to become "wholehearted," unpretentious, and fully and sincerely involved in life (Horney, 1945, pp. 241–242).

Self-Analysis

Although Horney recommended professional analysis for neurosis, she did think that some progress toward greater health could be achieved by a person working alone. One time when this would be particularly practical, she suggested, was in intervals between the end of one analysis and the beginning of another. The momentum of growth begun in psychotherapy could be continued by the individual working alone.

Self-analysis can be undertaken occasionally to deal with a particular problem that presents itself. Horney cited the example of a woman who analyzed her own foolish behavior in one incident, when she persisted climbing a mountain path under dangerous circumstances. Through self-analysis she traced it to an adolescent experience (Horney, 1950, pp. 101–102). Or self-analysis can be done systematically, with a commitment to regular individual work. For example, some people analyze all their dreams; others systematically note their emotional reactions and observe how they deal with life. Horney practiced this advice herself by systematically keeping a diary of self-exploration.

Sometimes the function of a symptom can be analyzed rather simply. Horney offered the example of a patient whose self-analysis revealed that his headaches were always due to anger (1942, pp. 157–158). He cured his headaches by this self-analysis, but he did not achieve the deeper insights and more fundamental personality reconstructions that a professional analysis would have allowed.

There are limits to what can be achieved through self-analysis. The blind spots accompanying neurotic defenses are particularly resistant, even in professional psychotherapy, and they are unlikely to yield to an individual working alone. It is difficult for a person to overcome a feeling of "resignation," that certain difficulties are insurmountable. The secondary gains achieved through neurotic tendencies may be too satisfying to yield readily to analysis.

Though self-analysis cannot hope to substitute for professional analysis, it can be an important supplement. Still, all therapy, professional as well as self-analysis, leaves some problems unsolved. According to Horney, "There is no such thing as a complete analysis" (1942, p. 303).

Horney has influenced modern psychoanalysis, which has expanded upon the concept of "the self" (Ingram, 1985; Kernberg, 1975; Kohut, 1971; H.A. Paul, 1985; Van den Daele, 1981). Many of Horney's ideas are early statements of ideas further developed within psychology by the humanistic psychologists. For example, she described a neurotic as having lost "all inner sense of direction" (1942, p. 291), an idea that anticipates Carl Rogers' concept of the "organismic valuing process." Her discussion of the "self" anticipates a key idea in Rogers' theory.

Horney's theory, clearly formulated without the abstruse metapsychology of Freudian theory, is readily researchable (Van den Daele, 1987). Horney frequently described issues to be determined by later empirical research. She identified specific questions that should be investigated, not only by analysts but also by gynecologists, anthropologists, sociologists, and others (e.g., 1935/1967e, pp. 224–233). It seems evident that she would have been pleased to test her theory through empirical research and to revise it as the evidence suggested, since she repeatedly encouraged psychoanalysis to be scientific rather than dogmatic. As closely related as a theorist's personality is to her or his theory, the theory must be considered impersonally if the theory of personality and the science of personality research are to be integrated. Much research supports concepts in Horney's theory; much research remains to be conducted.

Summary

Karen Horney revised psychoanalytic theory to emphasize interpersonal factors. The child experiences *basic anxiety* as a result of parental rejection or neglect. This anxiety is accompanied by *basic hostility,* which cannot be expressed because of the child's dependence on the parents. The child attempts to resolve the conflict by adopting one of three interpersonal orientations: *moving toward* people (the self-effacing solution), *moving against* them (the expansive solution), or *moving away* from them (the resignation solution). The neurotic cannot flexibly use all three orientations, as can the healthy person (see Table 6.4).

TABLE 6.4 Contributions of Horney's Theory to Various Topics

Biological	Biology is far less important than orthodox psychoanalysis claims.
Child Development	Basic anxiety and hostility are the fundamental emotions of childhood, caused by inadequate parental love.
Adult Development	Few major changes in personality occur after childhood.
Mental Health	Health involves balanced interpersonal modes, moving toward, against, and away from people. Horney provides full descriptions of neurotic trends. Psychoanalysis is the preferred therapy, but self-analysis can be an important supplement.
Society	Culture is very important in shaping personality, especially through sex roles.
Cognitive Processes	Blind spots and other defense mechanisms limit insight, but courageous self-examination can lead to growth.
Individual Differences	Individuals differ in the balance among the three interpersonal orientations: moving toward, moving against, and moving away (from people).

Little empirical research has resulted explicitly from Horney's theory, although some studies support the usefulness of the interpersonal orientations concept.

Horney described four basic strategies for resolving neurotic conflict: *eclipsing* the conflict, *detachment,* the *idealized self,* and *externalization.* The neurotic individual turns away from the *real self,* which has the potential for healthy growth, to an *idealized self.* The *tyranny of the shoulds* supports the idealized self. In addition, Horney described several *secondary adjustment mechanisms:* blind spots, compartmentalization, rationalization, excessive self-control, arbitrary rightness, elusiveness, and cynicism.

Horney emphasized the cultural determinants of development. Parenting patterns vary from society to society; even the Oedipus complex is not a universal human experience in her theory. Horney discussed sex roles as developments shaped by particular cultures, and which can change if cultures change.

Horneyan therapy seeks to uncover unconscious conflicts originating in childhood, but emphasizes their implications for present life. The patient's idealized self-image is challenged. Self-analysis can be a useful supplement to psychoanalysis.

ILLUSTRATIVE BIOGRAPHIES: CONCLUDING REMARKS

Karen Horney's theory described people as turning away from their real selves for some idealized version of the self that seems safer or more lovable. Cultural pressures defining masculinity and femininity have shaped the development of both Marilyn Monroe and Mike Tyson, encouraging in each a culturally influenced idealized self.

Marilyn Monroe

Marilyn Monroe felt unloved. Gloria Steinem quoted Marilyn as saying: "I never dreamed of anyone loving me as I saw other children loved. . . . That was too big a stretch for my imagination. I compromised by dreaming of my attracting someone's attention (besides God), of having people look at me and say my name" (Steinem, 1986, pp. 181–182). Marilyn herself offered insights into her "idealized self," one that would be noticed, perhaps even with affection. Even the attainment of stardom, though, brought a loss of self, for the name she had when she fantasized being called by name was not Marilyn Monroe, but rather her given name, Norma Jeane.

This lack of love had its origins in childhood. Norma Jeane (Marilyn) was raised at first by her mother alone, unsure who her father was. Her mother suffered serious depression and was institutionalized when Norma Jeane (Marilyn) was 7, and for most of her life thereafter. Marilyn then grew up in foster homes and an orphanage. As an actress, she continued to describe the sense of abandonment she felt as a child, enjoying what Horney called "neurotic suffering." The "poor me" identity became her self-image, as is characteristic of people with a neurotic need for affection. Marilyn even claimed to remember her grandmother's attempt to suffocate her when she was a year old (Steinem, 1986, pp. 182–183). While it is difficult to know whether this is an accurate memory, it does clearly portray the sort of "hostile world" described by Horney.

Some of Marilyn Monroe's exaggerated concern for the suffering of animals and even plants can be interpreted as an "externalization" of her own sense of "helplessness in a hostile world." For example, when she found boys trapping pigeons to sell in New York City, she bought the birds from the boys every week to set the birds free. Another rather bizarre externalization occurred when she saw nasturtiums cut by a lawn mower. As her husband, Arthur Miller, tells it, "crying as if she were wounded," Marilyn demanded that they stop the car as they drove past. "Then she rushed about picking up the fallen flowers, sticking the stalks back into the ground, to see if they might recover" (Summers, 1985, p. 200; cf. Horney, 1945, p. 116).

Physical beauty can be a way of ensuring love; it therefore takes on great value for those with a neurotic need for affection (Horney, 1950, p. 138). Marilyn's exhibitionist tendencies trace back to childhood (Steinem, 1986). Horney suggested (1937/1967d, pp. 256–257) that a neurotic need for love can also be expressed as a series of sexual relationships, surely characteristic of Marilyn, whose promiscuity was legendary.

Marilyn was treated by a Freudian analyst, a psychiatrist known internationally for his scholarly publications and a former close friend of the Freud family. Rather than challenging her need for love as neurotic, apparently her Freudian psychiatrist played along. At times, Marilyn was even taken into his home. Gloria Steinem reported that the psychiatrist "advised Miller that his wife needed unconditional love and devotion, that anything less was unbearable to her" (Steinem, 1986, p. 155). Of course, it is impossible to judge analysis from a distance; but if the therapy did not get beneath the neurotic need for affection, then it was not addressing the core neurosis and could not hope to achieve a personality reconstruction. One suspects that Horney would even fault the therapist for allowing "morbid dependency" in the doctor–patient relationship (cf. Horney, 1950, p. 243).

In people who have adopted this pattern of a neurotic, compulsive need for love, hostility is particularly repressed. If expressed, it would interfere with being loved. Thus, feeling hostility leads to anxiety. In the case of Marilyn Monroe, the frustrations of life, which must have led to hostility (including the extraordinary pressures of her stardom and the complications of her entanglements with the Kennedys), undoubtedly led to anxiety, which she tried to drown out with drugs. Drug use stems from the underlying problem of self-contempt (cf. Horney, 1950, p. 152).

One anecdote strongly suggests how much suppressed hostility must have pervaded her lovemaking. At a party, where a game required disclosure of personal fantasies, "she said she imagined disguising herself in a black wig, meeting her father, seducing him, and then asking vindictively, 'How do you feel now to have a daughter that you've made love to?'" (Steinem, 1986, p. 144).

Even Marilyn's Monroe's physical difficulties are consistent with Horney's theory. Monroe suffered extreme menstrual pain. She was reportedly frigid, compulsively seeking intercourse but not experiencing orgasm. If Horney's paper had not originally been published in 1926, we might have thought Horney had Marilyn Monroe in mind when she observed "that frigid women can be even erotically responsive and sexually demanding, an observation that warns us against equating frigidity with the rejection of sex" (1926/1967b, p. 74). Horney reported (1926/1967b) that frigid women may convert their sexual functioning into a variety of menstrual disorders, including pain and miscarriage. (Though most of Marilyn's numerous pregnancies were terminated by abortion, the desired pregnancy with Arthur Miller resulted in miscarriage.) Hollywood studios discouraged their stars from becoming pregnant, and conflicts about motherhood lead to premenstrual tension in Horney's theory (1926/1967b).

What of Marilyn Monroe's suicide attempts? She said she made two attempts while still a teenager, and numerous other attempts occurred throughout adulthood. According to Horney, suicide threats are manipulative techniques characteristic of masochistic persons (1939, p. 262).

Horney emphasized the importance of culture on the development of personality. This theme is the dominant note in Steinem's (1986) biography of Marilyn. Understanding culture helps us understand Marilyn, but the opposite is also true: Understanding Marilyn Monroe enlightens us about our culture.

Mike Tyson

If there is such a thing as a prototypical "moving against" type, it surely must be a champion boxer such as Mike Tyson. Ever since childhood, his life was dominated by the theme of aggression. On the streets of Brooklyn's Bedford-Stuyvesant, weakness was dangerous, and Tyson learned that attacking others first and hardest was a strategy that earned respect. So he fought, smoked, drank, stole, and, at the age of 12, having been arrested over 40 times, was finally sentenced to a term in a reformatory. Of course, we cannot hold Tyson's ghetto background entirely responsible for this aggressive pattern. Nonetheless, for a large, muscular young man, this cultural setting clearly was a significant determining factor. Horney emphasized the importance of cultural factors in shaping solutions to neurotic conflicts.

The *idealized self* that Mike Tyson developed was one aptly described by Horney's suggested motto for this type, "If I have power, no one can hurt me" (Horney, 1937, p. 98). However, neurotic pride based on the idealized image of such power requires the support of others' praise and deference. Thus, Tyson's sense of his own worth, his belief that he was in fact the ideal powerful self of his fantasy, could be secure only as long as others treated him accordingly. As a child, he found neighborhood youths respected his fighting ability; they didn't even dare steal from his mother, because Mike would retaliate. As a winning boxer, his success in the ring surely supported this idealized self-image, especially since many of his wins were by knockouts. Once he worried about a threat to his glorified self-image, experiencing an anxiety attack before a fight and sobbing, "No one will like me if I lose" (Torres, 1989, p. 58). He did lose, later.

Mike Tyson's sexual history, as reported by Joe Torres (1989), who was himself a champion boxer, also can be read as a saga of conquest. Apparently women, including many prostitutes, were readily available to be conquered. Sex and love, however, are different, as Horney reminded us. "Love . . . always implies surrender" (1937, p. 171). Aggressive types have particular difficulty with love because it threatens their idealized self-image of power and independence. An intimate relationship threatens to expose a real self, which is not so powerful, and it therefore loosens fragile defenses against basic anxiety. This threat can be, ironically, more frightening than the fear of the boxing ring, because there the fighter may hope to be powerful enough to maintain his glorified self. In intimacy, power fails to work, and there is no way within the relationship to maintain the neurotic solution based on the powerful glorified self. One may try. Tyson confessed to his biographer, "I like to hurt women when I make love to them. . . . I like to hear them scream with pain, to see them bleed. . . . It gives me pleasure" (Torres, 1989, p. 107).

When asked to describe "the best punch he'd ever thrown in his life," Tyson described throwing his wife Robin Givens against "every . . . wall in the apartment" (Torres, 1989, p. 132). Attempts to intimidate the partner through threats, even escalating to physical attacks, may be understood as efforts to gain support for the idealized image of the powerful self.

Horney traced the onset of neurotic trends back to early childhood. Tyson's biological father was distant, and the father figure present in Mike's home had frequent and bloody fights with Tyson's mother. Surely these conditions did not foster the sense of loving security necessary for healthy development. Horney pointed out that family dynamics are fostered by culture. Tyson's family depended on a welfare check for food and could not make it to the end of the month without some very sparse meals (consisting only of flour-water biscuits). This cultural context polarizes people into helpless victims and powerful exploiters.

With Mike Tyson, as with Marilyn Monroe, we see that the early family experience that led to a neurotic adaptation to life has origins in a culture shared by many Americans. Horney's theory, then, has implications beyond an understanding of this ultrafeminine woman and this extraordinarily macho man.

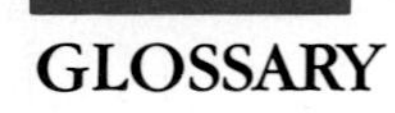

GLOSSARY

actual self what a person really is at a given time, seen objectively

arbitrary rightness secondary adjustment technique in which a person rigidly declares that his or her own view is correct

basic anxiety feeling of isolation and helplessness resulting from inadequate parenting in infancy

basic hostility feeling of anger by the young child toward the parents, which must be repressed

blind spots secondary adjustment technique in which a person is unaware of behavior inconsistent with the idealized self-image

compartmentalization secondary adjustment technique in which incompatible behaviors are not simultaneously recognized

cynicism secondary adjustment technique in which the moral values of society are rejected

elusiveness secondary adjustment technique in which a person avoids commitment to any opinion or action

excessive self-control secondary adjustment technique in which emotions are avoided

expansive solution attempting to solve neurotic conflict by seeking mastery; moving against people

externalization defense mechanism in which conflicts are projected outside

idealized self an image of what a person wishes to be

moving against interpersonal orientation emphasizing hostility

moving away interpersonal orientation emphasizing separateness from others

moving toward interpersonal orientation emphasizing dependency

rationalization secondary adjustment technique in which a person explains behaviors in socially acceptable ways

real self the vital, unique center of the self, which has growth potential

resignation solution attempting to solve neurotic conflict by seeking freedom; moving away from people

self-effacing solution attempting to solve neurotic conflict by seeking love; moving toward people

tyranny of the shoulds inner demands to live up to the idealized self

womb envy men's envy of women's reproductive capacity (the complement of Freud's "penis envy")

STUDY QUESTIONS

1. Contrast Horney's understanding of the unconscious with that of Freud.
2. Describe the emotional conflicts of early life. Include an explanation of *basic anxiety* and *basic hostility*.
3. List and describe the three interpersonal orientations.
4. Explain the terms *self-effacing solution, expansive solution,* and *resignation solution* in relation to the three interpersonal orientations.
5. Explain the difference between healthy and neurotic use of the interpersonal orientations.
6. Discuss research on Horney's interpersonal orientations.
7. List and explain the four major adjustments to basic anxiety.
8. Describe the neurotic's attitude toward the *real self*.
9. Explain the *tyranny of the shoulds*.
10. List and explain the seven secondary adjustment techniques.
11. Discuss the role of culture in determining development. What did Horney say was the most important conflict of our time?
12. Discuss research on infant attachment from the perspective of Horney's theory.
13. How did Horney explain female masochism?
14. Explain what is meant by *womb envy*.
15. Discuss *fear of success* research. How did Horney's theory contribute to this research?
16. Describe Horneyan therapy. Explain the role and limitations of *self-analysis*.

PART 

The Trait Perspective

People have been talking about one another, labeling one another, since before history was recorded. Raymond Cattell (1943a) remarked that "all aspects of human personality which are or have been of importance, interest, or utility have already become recorded in the substance of language" (p. 483, quoted by Borkenau, 1990). The "lexical approach" attempts to derive a description of personality by systematically examining language, usually beginning with words in the dictionary (John, Angleitner, & Ostendorf, 1988). Both theorists covered in this perspective conducted lexical studies (Allport & Odbert, 1936; Cattell, 1943b). Everyday language is, however, full of subtleties that make it less straightforward than scientific constructs should be. Besides describing people, language conveys evaluation (Borkenau, 1990) and causality (C. Hoffman & Tchir, 1990).

A *trait* is a theoretical construct describing a basic dimension of personality. Psychologists generally agree that traits should not be evaluative. Should traits simply describe? Or should they refer to causes of behavior? Here, there is no consensus. The two theorists considered in Part III had different opinions. Cattell's theory deals with *descriptive traits,* whereas Gordon Allport's theory proposes *dynamic traits.*

Cattell focused on the descriptive issue of individual differences. He refined the gross descriptions of people, which language provides, using sophisticated statistical procedures to determine the fundamental ways in which people differ from one another, and he developed psychological tests to measure these differences. In contrast, Allport regarded a trait as a motivational force residing within an individual. Henry Murray (1938) also emphasized a motivational approach to traits. The dynamic emphasis is involved in current work that emphasizes personal strivings (Emmons, 1986) and goal-seeking (Read, Jones, & Miller, 1990). This dynamic emphasis has been less popular and less well understood than the descriptive emphasis. Borkenau (1990) suggests that dynamic, motivational terms should not even be considered as traits. It is no wonder that, although Allport and Cattell for a time had offices next door to one another at Harvard University, their students had difficulty reconciling the two different emphases.

Both of these trait approaches to personality share certain distinctive elements. First, they emphasize *individual differences*. For dynamic traits, individual differences are assumed to be pervasive, cross-situational consistencies in behavior (Wright & Mischel, 1987; Zuroff, 1986). For descriptive traits, people may be less consistent in different situations, but aggregating several behaviors will yield differences from one person to another (Wright & Mischel, 1987). Second, trait approaches emphasize the *measurement* of these traits through tests, often self-report questionnaires.

Single traits are often proposed based on observations of behaviors, and they then undergo a process of theoretical refinement and research before they are accepted into the field of personality (Furnham, 1990a). Modern empirical approaches refine the personality dimensions by using the statistical technique of factor analysis. This procedure is central to Cattell's approach and will be described in Chapter 8. The method can be used to determine whether a personality test measures only one dimension (as it generally should), or whether it combines two or more aspects of personality that would be better kept apart (cf. R. Lennox, 1988). S.R. Briggs and Cheek (1986) recommend that all personality tests be analyzed with factor analysis as they are developed so as to keep them unidimensional, that is, to avoid combining items that are really measuring different characteristics.

Hundreds of traits have been proposed and measured. The sheer number makes it difficult to form a cohesive theory of personality. An alternative approach would be to turn away from traits in favor of *types*, which are broad categories of people (see Chapter 1). Galen's ancient set of four types (Melancholic, Sanguine, Phlegmatic, and Choleric) has even been reported to predict people's moods (Howarth & Zumbo, 1989). For the most part, though, less global "traits" are preferred by researchers because they can be defined more precisely.

Still, the attempt to find the "basic" dimensions of personality has motivated many researchers. Considerable interest has been generated in recent years in the "Big Five" dimensions of personality: Extraversion, Agreeableness, Neuroticism, Conscientiousness, and Openness (Boyle, 1989; Brand & Egan, 1989; Digman, 1989, 1990; Digman & Inouye, 1986; Dollinger & Orf, 1991; McCrae & Costa, 1985, 1987, 1991; Noller, Law, & Comrey, 1987; Norman, 1963; Peabody, 1984; Piedmont, McCrae, & Costa, 1991; Strack & Lorr, 1990; Trapnell & Wiggins, 1990). These dimensions (sometimes named differently) emerge from analyses of different personality tests, supporting the interpretation that they represent robust dimensions of individual differences.

Cattell's approach (Chapter 8) identifies 16 dimensions, rather than 5. The apparent discrepancy can be resolved by considering a hierarchical model, in which a larger number of more specific factors, which are not entirely uncorrelated with one another, correspond to a smaller number of more general factors (Boyle, 1989). By way of analogy, a person who claims that there are only two things to study in college, liberal arts or professional training, does not really disagree with a person who says that there are several dozen things to study, and then lists all the departments in the college. They are simply speaking at different levels of generality. In the study of personality, the number of "basic dimensions" uncovered depends on how general or specific are the dimensions sought (Marshall, 1991a). Theorists have not agreed, however, on what are the fundamental dimensions of personality (e.g., Eysenck, 1991).

Considerable heated discussion has occurred in recent decades over the issue of the consistency of behavior, a central assumption of the trait approach. Mischel (1968a, 1968b, 1984a) has spearheaded the attack on the "trait paradigm." Mischel argues that behavior is too inconsistent across time and across situations to warrant the assumption of stable traits. The "person-situation debate" in the literature has considered whether individual differences (such as personality traits) or situational variation is the primary determinant of behavior (Bem, 1983; S. Epstein, 1983b; Funder, 1983; Jackson & Paunonen, 1985; Mischel & Peake, 1982, 1983). The debate has instigated much research and renewed concern with methodological issues, such as the adequate sampling of personality variables and of situations (Funder & Colvin, 1991; Houts, Cook, & Shadish, 1986).

Evidence suggests that the weak relationship that Mischel described between traits and behavior is increased if several behavior observations are aggregated (S. Epstein, 1980b). Some behaviors, such as those involving the ego or sense of self, may be stable enough without aggregation. Funder and Colvin (1991) report that when behaviors are coded in terms of more general psychological meanings, rather than simply specific behaviors, quite high cross-situational consistency can result, more so with some behaviors than with others. Nonetheless, based on their review of the controversy, Houts, Cook, and Shadish conclude that "it is still premature to reach any conclusion about the cross-situational magnitude of behavioral consistency" (1986, p. 99).

The prediction of behavior from personality can be improved by including additional variables in the prediction. Moderator variables, which suggest when a trait will predict behavior and when it will not, increase the trait–behavior relationship (Zuckerman, Koestner, DeBoy, Garcia, Maresca, & Sartoris, 1988). Some traits are simply more important for particular persons; not all nomothetic traits apply equally to everyone (e.g., Bem & Allen, 1974; Bem & Funder, 1978). If subjects or others who know them well are asked to indicate which traits apply particularly to them, behavior can be predicted better by focusing on these traits, rather than averaging in all the traits that do not apply (Kenrick & Braver, 1982; Kenrick & Stringfield, 1980). These are idiographic approaches (cf. Chapter 1). Other researchers, however, defend traditional nomothetic assessment (Rushton, Jackson, & Paunonen, 1981).

The trait versus situation controversy has resulted in more careful attention to the nature of the trait–behavior relationship. Traits and situations influence one another and combine to influence behavior (Kenrick & Funder, 1988). Besides the *descriptive* and *dynamic* traits discussed above, a third type can be construed: a *conditional* trait (Wright & Mischel, 1987). (Wright and Mischel's terminology is somewhat different from that used here. They use the terms "summary" rather than descriptive traits and "causal" rather than dynamic traits.) Conditional traits recognize that the relationship between traits and behavior often depends upon the situation. For example, Jane may be quiet when in class, but not at other times. Both Allport and Cattell mentioned such conditionality in their theories. Perhaps if they had emphasized it more, their divergences on the descriptive versus dynamic issue would not have seemed so contradictory. Cattell included situational factors in his theory in the form of situational indices in the specification equation by which he predicted behavior. (This is explained in Chapter 8.) Allport recognized that behavior is often inconsistent because of the effects of situations, although he failed to develop an explicit theoretical description of the ways that situations interact with personality (Zuroff, 1986).

Current researchers and theorists are actively debating theoretical points concerning traits. It seems fair to say that a more coherent paradigm is emerging. It has even been argued that a trait approach provides the basis for a coherent paradigm of personality theory in the natural science tradition, since "in any science, taxonomy precedes causal analysis" (Eysenck, 1991, p. 774).

CHAPTER 7

Allport: Personological Trait Theory

BIOGRAPHY OF GORDON ALLPORT

Gordon Allport

Gordon Allport was born in 1897 in Montezuma, Indiana, the fourth son of a businessman who was changing careers to become a country doctor. The family moved several times when Gordon was very young. They finally settled in Cleveland, Ohio, where Gordon grew up in a hard-working, midwestern Protestant environment. His mother, who had been a school teacher, encouraged the educational and religious interests of her four sons, and his father expected them to help out in the office.

Gordon graduated second in his high school class of 100. He then followed his second brother, Floyd, who was seven years older, to Harvard University, where Floyd was a graduate student in psychology. Gordon Allport was a subject in his brother's research on social influence. After a shockingly poor set of first exam grades, Gordon began working to the higher standards expected at Harvard and earned A's. He studied psychology and social ethics. He did volunteer work at a Boston boys' club throughout college. After graduation he taught English and sociology briefly overseas, in Constantinople; later he was awarded a fellowship for graduate study in psychology back at Harvard.

On his return trip to the United States, Allport stopped in Vienna to visit his brother, Fayette. While there he requested a meeting with Sigmund Freud. Freud was accustomed to receiving visitors from throughout the world, and he granted an appointment. Allport was only 22 at the time. Looking back upon the visit later, Allport said he was motivated to meet with Freud by "rude curiosity and youthful ambition" (Allport, 1967, p. 8). In his naiveté, he had not thought to prepare an introductory statement to Freud explaining the reason for the meeting. Freud sat in silence, probably expecting that this was a therapeutic consultation, since his reputation drew many patients from distant places. As Allport tells it:

> I was not prepared for silence and had to think fast to find a suitable conversational gambit. I told him of an episode on the tram car on my way to his office. A small boy about four years of age had displayed a conspicuous dirt phobia. He kept saying to his mother, "I don't want to sit there . . . don't let that dirty man sit beside me." To him everything was *schmutz*. His mother was a well-starched *Hausfrau,* so dominant and purposive looking that I thought the cause and effect apparent.
>
> When I finished my story Freud fixed his kindly therapeutic eyes upon me and said, "And was that little boy you?" Flabbergasted and feeling a bit guilty, I contrived to change the subject. . . . Freud's misunderstanding of my motivation was amusing. . . . This experience taught me that depth psychology . . . may plunge too deep, and that psychologists would do well to give full recognition to manifest motives before probing the unconscious. (Allport, 1967, p. 8)

Freud's clinical intuition suggested to him that Allport feared being "dirtied" by this contact with psychoanalysis. Allport argued that it was not a therapeutic meeting, and the "manifest" (conscious) level of his experience, which was simply a desire to impress Freud with his powers of observation, was the appropriate level at which to interpret his anecdote about the little boy. This theme, that psychology should pay more attention to conscious self-reports, was a major element of Allport's theory as it developed over the next several decades.

For his doctoral dissertation, Gordon Allport investigated personality traits. This was then a new topic, and one criticized by more traditional, experimentally minded psychologists. His first publication on personality traits was jointly authored with his brother, Floyd (Allport & Allport, 1921). Gordon received his doctorate in 1922, at the age of 24. He then did postdoctoral study in Europe. There he learned more about Gestalt psychology and the German doctrine of types, themes reflected in his later consideration of holism and his development of a type inventory. He accepted a teaching position at Harvard in social ethics in 1924. In 1925, Allport married Ada Lufin Gould, a clinical psychologist. They had one son, Robert, who became a pediatrician.

Allport taught at Harvard, his alma mater, for most of his professional life, with the exception of four years at Dartmouth College beginning in 1926. He developed a new course called *Personality: Its Psychological and Social Aspects,* which he reported was probably the first personality course taught in the United States. He did much writing and research on social psychology as well as personality. For a time he chaired Harvard's Department of Psychology. He joined the University's Department of Social Relations when, in 1946, it separated from the psychology department. It was there that he pursued interdisciplinary work with sociology and anthropology.

Allport rose to prominence in national circles. He edited the major journal in the field, the *Journal of Abnormal and Social Psychology* (1937–1948), and was president of the American Psychological Association (1939). Allport was one of the founders, in 1936, of the Society for the Psychological Study of Social Issues, an organization that applies psychological insights to practical social issues, and he became its president in 1944. Allport was one of several American psychologists who assisted intellectuals in Europe to find work in the United States so they could flee Nazi Germany. Another contribution at the time of the war was his effort to help control wartime rumors, reflected in his daily newspaper column and his later book on rumors (Allport & Postman, 1947). He was awarded many professional honors. Gordon Allport died of lung cancer on October 9, 1967, at age 69.

ILLUSTRATIVE BIOGRAPHIES

Allport's theory has not been popular among psychobiographers, although his emphasis on unique individuals and his own interest in case histories (Allport, 1929, 1965; Allport, Bruner, & Jandorf, 1941) suggest that it could be (T.T. Lewis, 1985).

Allport urged psychologists to take people's statements about themselves more or less at face value. Thus it is appropriate to seek our case studies in autobiography. Both Jerry Falwell, the conservative Baptist minister, and Beverly Sills, the opera star, have written about their lives, their adaptation to social reality, and their values. Though Allport eschews depth interpretation, his theory offers useful concepts for understanding these two people.

PERSONOLOGICAL TRAIT THEORY

As an early personality theorist in an academic (as opposed to clinical) setting, Gordon Allport taught the first personality course in the United States and wrote a text for it. In the preface to his 1937 text, *Personality,* Allport wrote that the study of personality was then a new and increasingly popular area in colleges. "The result of this rising tide of interest is an insistent demand for a guide book that will *define* the new field of study—one that will articulate its objectives, formulate its standards, and test the progress made thus far" (Allport, 1937b, p. vii). Thus he formulated some of the issues that the field of personality has continued to debate.

Allport's early outline of the field of personality has had broad impact. Personality traits have become a major concern of personality research.

Jerry Falwell

Jerry Falwell is best known as the Baptist preacher who spearheaded the Moral Majority, a conservative political movement that opposed abortion and that was credited by some pollsters with bringing about Ronald Reagan's victory in the 1980 presidential election.

Falwell and his fraternal twin, Gene, were born in 1933 in Lynchburg, Virginia, at a time when racial segregation was a way of life. Their father was a hard-drinking businessman who finally died of cirrhosis of the liver. Their mother was the churchgoer of the family, though she was quiet about her faith, since her husband rejected religion.

Jerry was a mischievous child, leading friends in pranks. Once they retaliated against a disliked gym teacher by overpowering him, pulling off his pants and leaving him in a school storage area. At the age of 18, he experienced a religious conversion, and from then on he considered himself a "born again" Christian. Throughout his autobiography (Falwell, 1987), he expressed his religious beliefs (the reality of sin, the infallibility of the Bible), apparently finding it impossible to tell his own life story without preaching. When scandal broke over another television preacher, Jim Bakker, Jerry Falwell was asked to take over leadership of that ministry to salvage it from infamy as well as financial disaster.

What would Gordon Allport make of this life story? Can his theory of personality help us to identify and understand continuities in Falwell's life? How would Allport understand Falwell's religious convictions? Would Allport have characterized Falwell as a psychologically healthy adult?

Allport's ideas about personality traits have provided a focus for the ongoing debate about whether personality theory should emphasize the identification of individual differences or focus on personality processes. Allport identified the "self" as a major issue in personality. He urged personality theorists to use concepts that took into account the unique capacities of humans (as opposed to animals), and that emphasized healthy functioning. His emphasis on the whole person, the "self," has continued in the humanistic movement (Maddi & Costa, 1972). Finally, Allport was concerned about the implications of personality for society, and he contributed both to social psychology and to personality theory.

His approach was eclectic, including contributions from various schools of psychology. "Better to expand and refashion one's theories until they do some measure of justice to the richness and dignity of human personality, than to clip and compress personality until it fits one closed system of

Beverly Sills

A prima donna of opera, Beverly Sills has been one of America's most renowned opera sopranos. Born in 1929 in Brooklyn, the third child and only girl in a Jewish family, she was bright in school and astonishingly talented in music throughout childhood. Her mother made sure that she had excellent musical training. Beverly won talent contests as a child and sang on the radio for several years, beginning at the age of 4. At 17 she was given her first opera role.

Sills's operatic career was phenomenally successful. She starred throughout the United States and Europe, even at the famed La Scala opera house in Milan. Her home company, the New York City Opera, was less prestigious than the Metropolitan Opera, which did not invite her to perform until after her European successes. In 1979 Beverly retired as a singer. She then undertook the exhausting role of general director of her beloved New York City Opera. The company was on the brink of financial collapse. Her financially astute husband recommended that she declare the company bankrupt. Instead, with tremendous work at management and fund-raising, she brought the company out of debt by 1986.

Besides her professional life, Beverly Sills was a wife, a stepmother to three children, and the mother of a son and a daughter. Both of her natural children suffered from birth defects; her daughter was deaf and her son was autistic, requiring institutional care. Beverly Sills herself had ovarian cancer and skin cancer, but recovered.

Can Allport's theory help us understand this energetic woman so that we know the person behind the glamorous success?

thought" (Allport, 1937b, p. vii). Though he taught both psychoanalysis and learning theory, he viewed these approaches as limited. Psychoanalysis overemphasized the unconscious and did not pay enough attention to conscious motivation, while learning theory missed uniquely human qualities that cannot be understood through an animal model. Allport challenged the emphasis on scientific methodology of the behaviorist school, represented by John Watson and by B. F. Skinner, his colleague at Harvard.

Allport argued that it was a mistake for methodology to overshadow the content of a field. In its early years, he said, personality was better served by paying attention to common sense and to philosophy and the liberal arts. Despite his own attitude against methodology, he correctly predicted that methodological issues would dominate the future of personality.

Major Themes in Allport's Work

Allport had a major influence on the selection of issues that would concern the field of personality as it developed during the decades which followed. Here are some of the issues identified by Allport, and which personality theorists have grappled with ever since.

Personality Consistency

The concept of personality consistency across time and across situations is central to the field of personality. Allport argued strongly that humans are consistent. He said that people are remarkably recognizable, even though they vary from situation to situation and across time. The consistency begins early: "*from early infancy there is consistency in the development of personality*" (1937b, p. 125; italics in original). Consistency is not perfect, yet even when people seem to behave inconsistently, Allport suggested that an underlying consistency is often present. There has been considerable controversy ever since Allport proposed his theory concerning the extent to which personality is consistent (e.g., Bem & Allen, 1974; S. Epstein, 1979, 1980b; Mischel, 1984a; Mischel & Peake, 1982; Moskowitz, 1982). Allport's views have sometimes been misrepresented to imply broader consistency, ignoring situational variation, than he intended (Zuroff, 1986).

Social Influence

Allport was quite aware that people live in a social environment that exerts a significant influence. He considered specific social issues. For example, he wrote a major work on prejudice that has become a classic text (Allport, 1954). He studied rumor transmission (Allport & Postman, 1947). The two fields of social psychology and personality were, in the past, much more closely related than they have become in recent decades.

The Concept of Self

In an age when many other psychological approaches were reductionistic, Allport argued for the notion of "self" as a major focus of personality growth. The "self" is now a major theoretical concept in personality and social psychology, widely used in areas as diverse as humanistic clinical psychology and cognitive social psychology.

Interaction of Personality with Social Influence

It is no surprise that a psychologist who was both a personality psychologist and a social psychologist would not think of personality and situations as "either–or" causes, but would rather consider how they work together as joint influences. Situations influence people, but they influence individuals in different ways, as the interactionist approach to personality recognizes (Endler & Magnusson, 1976). In Allport's words, "The same heat that melts the butter hardens the egg" (Allport, 1937b, pp. 102, 325). He did not, however, develop the notion of the interaction between personality and environment beyond this brief sketch. He acknowledged that in his emphasis on personality traits, he had "neglect[ed] the variability induced by ecological, social, and situational factors" (1966b, p. 9). Allport recognized that further theoretical advances were needed to develop this concept of interactionism (Zuroff, 1986).

In summary, Allport anticipated many of the themes that would concern personality psychology in the more than half century which has passed since his classic personality text was first published. Current approaches are more sophisticated in their analysis of empirical data, certainly. Nonetheless, the basic themes of consistency, social influence, the self, and the interaction of personality with the environment have remained important foci.

Allport's Definition of Personality

After a review of 49 other definitions of personality in psychology, theology, philosophy, law, sociology, and common usage, Allport proposed what has become a classic definition of **personality**: "*Personality is the dynamic organization within the individual of those psychophysical systems that determine his unique adjustments to the environment*" (Allport, 1937b, p. 48; italics in original).

Although the definition is much quoted, it is not universally accepted because it contains assumptions that not all personality theorists accept. Let us look in detail at Allport's explanation of the five major concepts in his definition of personality, since it provides us with a broad outline of his theory.

Dynamic Organization

Allport referred to "the dynamic organization" of personality in order "to stress active organization" (Allport, 1937b, p. 48). The issue of people getting integrated, "getting it all together," is central to Allport's notion of personality. He suggested that abnormal personalities are less integrated than healthy ones. Dynamic organization evolves as a developmental process, and a failure of integration is a mark of psychopathology.

This theme of organization, or unity, is not shared by all theories. Traditional learning theories deal, instead, with isolated behavioral units, or stimulus-response associations. Psychoanalysis tends to fragment people into conflicting parts. Allport believed that psychoanalysis has a restricted view of personality because it is based on clinical populations and studies people who have not become wholly integrated, whose symptoms don't seem to fit with the rest of their personality. In contrast, for healthy individuals personality becomes an organized and self-regulating whole.

Psychophysical Systems

Personality is subject to biological as well as psychological influences. Mind and body are inextricably united. Allport accepted empirical research then available that indicated inherited differences in **temperament** constitute a biological foundation for personality. Inherited *physique* and *intelligence,* together with temperament, are "the three principal raw materials of personality" (1937b, p. 107).

Allport did not try to assign heredity some percentage responsibility for personality, and experience the remaining percentage. Rather, both are always important. "*No feature of personality is devoid of hereditary influences*" (1937b, p. 105; italics in original). Allport offered a mathematical expression of this pervasive influence of heredity through a multiplicative equation:

$$\text{Personality} = f\ (\text{Heredity}) \times (\text{Environment})$$

"The two causal factors are not added together, but are interrelated as multiplier and multiplicand. If either were zero there could be no personality," he stated (1937b, p. 106). The mathematical properties of an alternative, *additive* model, would be different, since then heredity and environment could have independent effects, and either could be zero without negating the effect of the other.

This was a broadly theoretical statement. Allport did not conduct research on hereditary influences. He did not develop a detailed theory or typology of temperament, physique, or intelligence. This work was left to others (e.g., Sheldon, Cattell, Eysenck). Advances in biological and medical research are obviously relevant to understanding biological contributions to personality. Allport commented, "I believe . . . we'll never have a complete psychology of personality until we have a much better knowledge of genetic factors" (R.I. Evans, 1981a, p. 49).

Determinative

For some theorists, personality concepts are useful predictors, but not themselves real. Allport disagreed, using "determine" to emphasize that personality is a *cause* of behavior. Allport said that the term "determine" "is a natural consequence of the biophysical view. Personality *is* something and *does* something" (1937b, p. 48). Traits are real, in a physical sense. "Traits are not creations in the mind of the observer, nor are they verbal fictions; they are here accepted as biophysical facts, actual psychophysical dispositions related—though no one yet knows how—to persistent neural systems of stress and determination" (1937b, p. 339).

This assertion of traits as determinative distinguishes Allport's view of personality from two alternatives. The first alternative is the view that personality traits are simply conceptual abstractions, that is, useful conceptual tools for predicting behavior. This argument recognizes that the concepts of personality are useful, since they summarize many observations. Nonetheless, it denies that personality is real and determinative; it simply is convenient to speak "as if" it were real.

The second alternative is the more pessimistic objection that using personality traits to explain behavior is a meaningless circular argument. For example, you see a man talking to a lot of people, so you say that he is outgoing. Then, asked why he talks to a lot of people, you say it is because he is outgoing. This is circular reasoning (see Figure 7.1). If the same behavior that prompts inferring the trait is predicted to result from it, the trait cannot fail. Without the possibility of disconfirmation, a theoretical construct is not

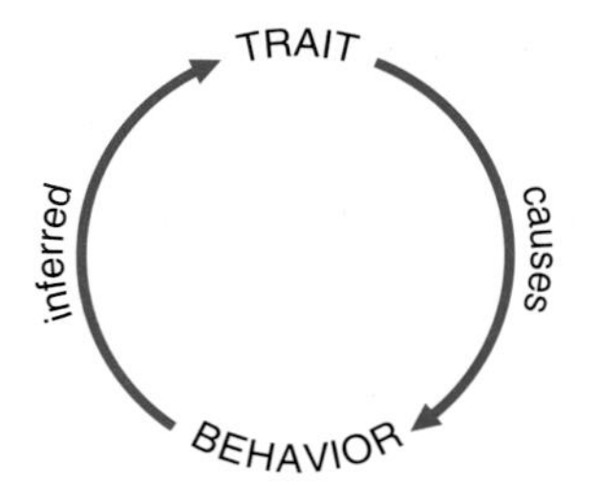

Critics of *trait* concepts argue that it is circular reasoning to say a trait *causes* the same behavior that is the basis for inferring the trait exists.

FIGURE 7.1 Circular Reasoning

useful. Allport was not ignorant of the potential problem of circular reasoning, that labeling is not really an answer. He discussed this issue in relationship to the question of whether the concept of a "self" is necessary in psychology (Allport, 1955, pp. 54–55), but he did not feel the circular reasoning argument invalidated the usefulness of his personality concepts.

Unique

For Allport, traits are highly individualized, or unique. Allport explicitly disagreed with theorists who asserted that one or a few motives, or instincts, are determinative for all people. People, rather, are motivated by diverse traits reflecting the differences in their learning.

> But are not the purposes of different people far too diverse and too numerous to be traced to a few primal motives shared by all the species? Are the directions of striving after all innately determined? Is it not necessary to allow for the learning of *new* motives and for the acquisition of *novel* interests as personality matures? (Allport, 1937b, p. 113)

Adjustments to the Environment

Allport emphasized the adaptive, coping functions of personality. "Personality results from the attempts of the central nervous system to establish security and comfort for the individual torn between his own affective cravings and the harsh demands of his environment" (1937b, p. 118). Allport was far more interested in these, which would be called ego functions by psychoanalysis, than in the internal conflicts preventing adaptation that occur in the mentally unhealthy. These adaptations are unique to each individual because of differences in heredity and environment.

Personality Traits

Allport's Definition of "Trait"

The primary unit of personality is the **trait** (Allport, 1931, 1937b). Allport defined a trait as

> ***a generalized and focalized neuropsychic system (peculiar to the individual), with the capacity to render many stimuli functionally equivalent, and to initiate and guide consistent (equivalent) forms of adaptive and expressive behavior.*** (1937b, p. 295; italics in original)

In this definition, he reiterated themes from his definition of personality: the psychophysical emphasis, the uniqueness of the individual, the focus on adaptation, and the concept of the trait as a determinative entity. Traits develop over time, with experience. They may change as the person learns new ways of adapting to the world (Allport, 1937b, p. 146).

Allport identified various kinds of traits, thus outlining for later theorists and researchers the different perspectives from which personality can be studied.

Individual Traits and Common Traits: Idiographic versus Nomothetic Approaches

Based on the work of the German philosophers Windelband and Stern (Hermans, 1988), Allport distinguished **individual traits**, which are possessed by only one person, from **common traits**, which are possessed by many people, each to a varying extent. The distinction may appear simple at first, but its implications are enormous.

In everyday speech, we often describe people using common traits comparing "how much" of a trait each person has. For example, we may describe Lee Iacocca as "more entrepreneurial" than others, or Einstein as "more intelligent" than the rest of us.

Psychologists, too, recognize that various people seem to have traits similar enough to be called by the same name and considered together. Thus a psychologist may investigate how aggressive or submissive various people are in a competitive society. Allport regarded such inquiry as legitimate (cf. Allport, 1937b, p. 298).

However such "common traits" are not the ultimate real unit of personality in Allport's theory. The real units of personality are **unique traits**, which exist within an individual and which have status as psychophysical realities. Thus the psychologist comparing people on ascendance-submission, or any other common trait,

> does not measure directly the full-bodied individual trait that alone exists as a neuro-psychic disposition and as the one irreducible unit of personality. What he does is to measure a common *aspect* of this trait, such a portion thereof as takes common cultural forms of expression and signifies essentially the same manner of adjusting within the social group. (Allport, 1937b, p. 298)

Allport asserted that "In the strict sense of the definition of traits . . . the common (continuum) trait is not a true trait at all, but is merely a measurable aspect of complex individual traits" (1937b, p. 299).

Traits are individualized adaptive entities, unique to each person. Allport argued that, "Strictly speaking, no two persons ever have precisely the same trait" (1937b, p. 297). Thus in principle all traits are unique to the individual. According to his argument, it is not possible to fully describe differences between people by simply scoring them on a set of universally applied traits. He thus rejected the *nomothetic approach* to personality description as inadequate. Though he accepted nomothetic research as a rough approximation for research purposes, it would never result in identifying the fundamental drives of all people (Allport, 1940). To understand an individual fully, it would be necessary to have a list of traits specifically chosen for that person. That is, only an *idiographic approach* can adequately describe an individual.

To most theorists, Allport's assertion of the "realness" of traits has been unconvincing. His description of unique traits seems unnecessarily to defend a "hypothetical construct" (a physical reality) when a more abstract "intervening variable" is the appropriate conceptualization. His view would require that traits be identified that are actually causal at the individual level, and not merely useful predictors of individual differences. Allport did not differentiate between idiographic methods (single-subject research) and idiography as a theoretical position (that each person is unique), which has led to confusion (Marceil, 1977).

The idiographic view has been given theoretical and methodological elaboration since Allport (e.g., Lamiell, 1981; Rosenzweig, 1958, 1986a, 1986b; Runyan, 1983). Runyan argued that personality psychology seeks understanding at three levels: that which is true of all people, that which is true of particular groups (e.g., men, women, whites, blacks), and that which is true of particular individuals. He asserted that "the goal of understanding individual persons is one of the most important objectives of personality psychology" (1983, p. 417), a perspective with which Allport would, no doubt, have agreed. Nonetheless, a long tradition questions whether any wholly idiographic study can be considered truly scientific (Eysenck, 1954; Skaggs, 1945), although such studies may be a source of hypotheses for science (Falk, 1956). The idiographic approach is said to be useful only for generating, but not testing, hypotheses, to be logically impossible (since implicit comparisons with others are always present), and to be unlikely to produce knowledge generalizable to other people (Emmerich, 1968; Holt, 1962). Most psychologists since Allport have adopted a nomothetic approach.

Allport emphasized the need to individualize trait conceptions. In one study (Conrad, 1932), which Allport described, teachers rated students on various traits. Reliability of these ratings wasn't particularly high overall. However, if teachers indicated with a star (*) which traits particularly described the child, those starred ratings had a much higher agreement (Allport, 1937b, p. 301). Thus the same set of traits is not useful for describing every person, but the central traits of a person can be rated reliably. Other researchers since Allport have essentially replicated this finding (Cheek, 1982; Markus, 1977). However, Paunonen (1988) contended on the basis of statistical considerations that the moderating effect of trait importance is spuriously overestimated. A recent theoretical proposal by Baumeister and Tice (1988; Baumeister, 1991) seems to offer a quasi-idiographic approach to normative data analysis. They suggest that each trait can be thought of as having an associated "metatrait," which is simply whether or not the individual has the trait (at any level, low, medium, or high). They offer statistical ways of dealing with Allport's general belief that not everyone possesses the same traits.

Inferring Traits

Allport described several methods for inferring a person's traits.

Inferring Traits from Language: The Dictionary Study. Allport and Odbert (1936) did a study in which they listed all of the trait words in the 1925 edition of Webster's *New International Dictionary* used to describe individuals. This turning to everyday language is characteristic of Allport's belief that psychologists should begin with the wisdom of common experience. He commented, "As inadequate as common speech may be in representing the complex structure of personality, it is several grades more adequate than the mathematical symbols and neologisms that psychologists sometimes employ" (1937b, p. 310).

Excluding obsolete terms, Allport and Odbert identified 17,953 trait names, which was 4.5 percent of the total words in the dictionary. Allport and Odbert then classified these trait names into four categories:

1. Neutral Terms Designating Personal Traits (e.g., "artistic," "assertive")
2. Terms Primarily Descriptive of Temporary Moods or Activities (e.g., "alarmed," "ashamed")
3. Weighted Terms Conveying Social or Characterial Judgments of Personal Conduct, or Designating Influence on Others (e.g., "adorable," "asinine")

4. Miscellaneous: Designations of Physique, Capacities, and Developmental Conditions; Metaphorical and Doubtful Terms (e.g., "alone," "Anglican")

They believed that the first, purely descriptive category would be most useful to personality psychologists as a compilation of nonevaluative terms for enduring traits.

Inferring Traits from Behavior. Traits may also be inferred from behavior. People who talk a lot are judged to be "outgoing"; people who exercise regularly are called "athletic." Allport suggested that *interests* are a good clue to personality. Behavioral inferences can be made in natural circumstances. For example, children can be observed in their everyday lives, using a time-sampling procedure (Allport, 1937b, pp. 315–316). Or observations can be made in an experimental setting if subjects are given a diverse set of tasks.

Allport and Vernon (1933) conducted such an experimental study to determine whether **expressive traits** could be inferred. These traits are concerned with the *style* of behavior. Allport and Vernon intensively studied 25 male subjects. They obtained exhaustive measures of handwriting, walking, tapping, reading, and so on, and had raters code these behaviors (e.g., measuring the length of check marks). Allport and Vernon concluded that there are consistent expressive traits. This work is not regarded highly today within academic psychology. One source of embarrassment is that Allport and Vernon provided personality sketches of people based upon handwriting ("graphology"), which academic psychology banishes to the realm of pseudoscience.

Inferring Traits from Documents: Letters from Jenny. We can infer traits from many documents or records of people's lives including diaries, letters, public statements, and so forth. Sometimes "existing documents," those not produced specifically for research purposes, may be unusually rich. Allport was given a collection of 301 letters written by a woman, Jenny Grove Masterson, to friends (her son's former college roommate and his wife). The letters covered a period of 11 years, beginning in 1926, until her death at the age of 70. The letters disclose an interesting but sad tale of a woman who found life difficult, worried about money, and complained frequently about her son's neglect. Allport and his students read these letters and interpreted them from assorted theoretical perspectives, including various psychoanalytic approaches (Freudian, Jungian, Adlerian, and ego approaches) and learning theory.

Allport's own approach, which he called *structural-dynamic,* was in essence a *content analysis* of the letters. (Content analysis is a research strategy in which material is coded to summarize what it contains, with minimal interpretation.) He and research assistants and students read the letters and listed adjectives describing the personality traits they inferred from the letters. Combining analyses by 36 raters, Allport concluded that Jenny's personality could be summarized by eight traits:

quarrelsome-suspicious
self-centered

independent-autonomous
dramatic-intense
aesthetic-artistic
aggressive
cynical-morbid
sentimental (Allport, 1965, pp. 193–194).

One of Allport's students, Jeffrey Paige, used a computer procedure called the General Inquirer to analyze Jenny's letters. He examined frequencies with which certain themes appeared together in the various letters and, using factor analysis, described eight recurring themes: acceptance, possessiveness, need for affiliation, need for autonomy, need for familial acceptance, sexuality, sentience, and martyrdom (Allport, 1965, pp. 200–201). Allport noted that this list of factors was remarkably similar to the categories he had earlier derived "from common-sense interpretation" (1965, p. 201), though not identical to it. Allport remarked that both types of content analysis—that aided by computer and that done "longhand"—focus the researcher's attention on the data, namely Jenny's letters, and thus prevent unwarranted theoretical flights of fantasy. He preferred to remain close to the data.

Inferring from Personality Measurement: The Study of Values. We can also infer traits from personality tests. Allport did some of this *nomothetic* type research. Crediting the influence of German philosophers, especially Spranger (Allport, 1937b, pp. 227–228), Allport said that among the most important characteristics that distinguish people from one another are their values, that is, those things toward which they are striving. With colleagues, he developed the Allport-Vernon-Lindzey Study of Values to measure values (Allport & Vernon, 1931). (See Table 7.1.)

This self-report instrument consists of 60 questions. Scores are compared with normative data to determine which values are relatively high for an individual. The original norms are dated, since they are based on data collected in 1960 and do not reflect changes since then (Coffield & Buckalew, 1984). Allport reported that college students who entered different occupations had different value scores. For example, those who entered business scored higher on Economic values (Allport, 1966b). In a study reported by Huntley and Davis (1983), scores on the Study of Values taken during col-

TABLE 7.1 The Allport-Vernon-Lindzey Study of Values

Scale	*Description of Value*	*Typical Occupation*
Social	helping people	social work
Theoretical	search for truth	college professor
Economic	pragmatic, applied	business
Aesthetic	artistic values	artist
Political	power and influence	politics
Religious	religion, harmony	clergy

lege were associated with occupations of male students 25 years later (see Figure 7.2).

Baird (1990) reported a 20-year longitudinal study indicating that Religious scale scores declined during the four years of college, with little change thereafter, although graduates in this sample who moved away from their conservative college regions did become more liberal. Religious values measured by this instrument were associated with a learning task that required subjects to learn to respond differentially to words related to religion and a nonreligious topic (transportation). This result supports a theoretical interpretation that values interact with aspects of the environment to influence behavior (Staats & Burns, 1982). (See Figure 7.3.)

Allowing for Inconsistency in Making Trait Inferences. There is not a one-to-one correspondence between traits and behavior. *Phenotypical* appearances or behaviors do not always correspond to underlying motives or traits, which are called *genotypical* (Allport, 1937b, p. 325). As Allport observed, "Perfect consistency will never be found and must not be expected" (1937b, p. 330).

There are several reasons for this. For one thing, more than one trait influences any particular behavior, and people often possess traits that are themselves contradictory. Consider a person who possesses the traits of "domineering" and "respectful." Such traits could cause the person to be submissive toward authority figures, but domineering over others.

Also, behavior is influenced by several traits at a time, even if the traits aren't contradictory. Any given trait may not always be active. For example, a usually generous person might not give to someone in need when he or she is in a hurry. In this example, traits of goal achievement are in "a state of ac-

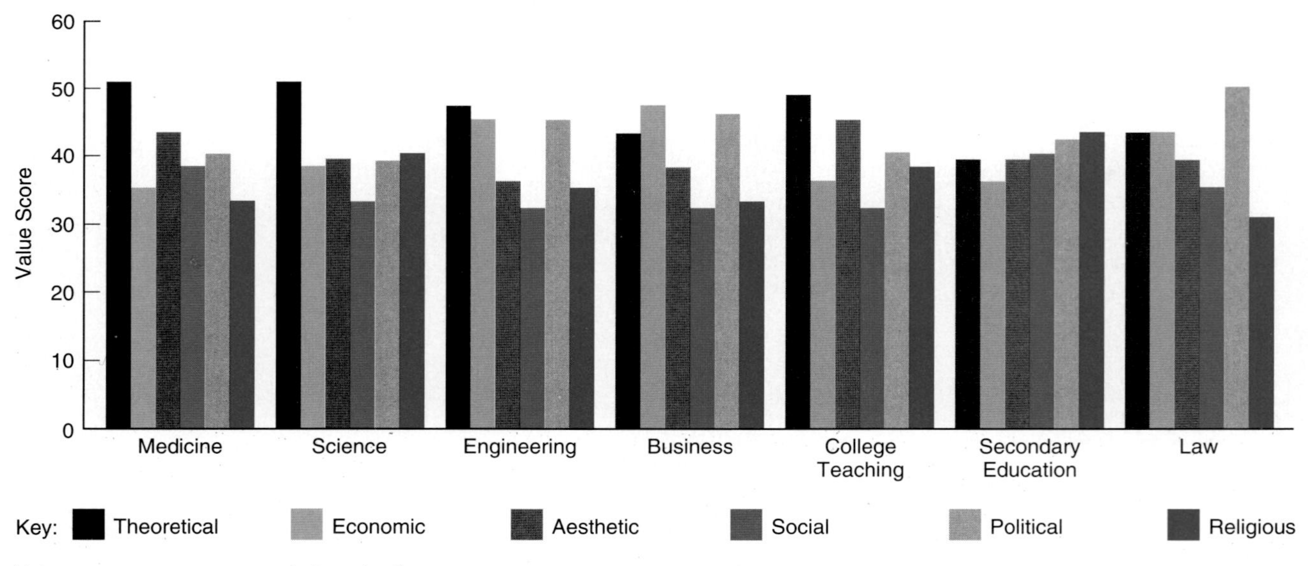

FIGURE 7.2 Values Scores Associated with Occupations 25 Years Later

(From C. W. Huntley & F. Davis (1983). Undergraduate study of value scores as predictors of occupation 25 years later. *Journal of Personality and Social Psychology*, 45, 1148–1155. Copyright 1983 by the American Psychological Association. Adapted by permission.)

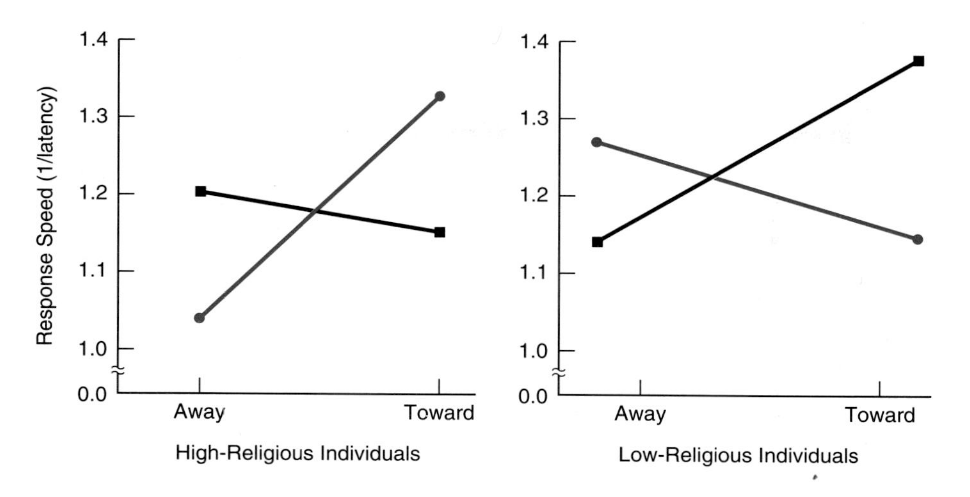

Key: Religious words Transportation words

Speed with which the religious and transportation words were approached or avoided by the high- and low-religious individuals, higher scores indicating a more rapid response.

FIGURE 7.3 Interaction of Religious Orientation and Task Demands on Performance on an Experimental Task

(From A. W. Staats & G. L. Burns (1982). Emotional personality repertoire as cause of behavior: Specification of personality and interaction principles. *Journal of Personality and Social Psychology*, 43, 873–881. Copyright 1982 by the American Psychological Association. Reprinted by permission.)

tive tension" (Allport, 1937b, p. 330) while the trait of generosity is momentarily dormant.

Allport's Attitude Toward Methodology. Allport was not enthusiastic about computers and methodology. He acknowledged the importance of "corrective empiricism" as a contribution of psychology (1937b, p. 231). However, he distrusted complicated statistical procedures, such as factor analysis, as a way of discovering traits. Factor analysis, he argued, loses the individual in the average. He remarked that "factors often seem remote from psychological fact, and as such they risk the accusation that they are primarily mathematical artifacts" (1937b, p. 245). Allport said we need to be guided by theory and common sense. To expect truth to emerge from study after study not guided by theory and common sense is folly. It can yield quite bizarre results. Allport cited as one "example of empiricism gone wild" an empirically derived scale in which "children who give the response word 'green' to a stimulus word 'grass' receive a score of +6 for 'loyalty to the gang'" (1937b, p. 329).

Allport's objection to methodological excess is an aspect of his concern for the uniqueness of the individual, who gets lost in the nomothetic, measurement-oriented approach. Allport (1940) expressed dismay at the decline in case histories, which were giving way to increasing methodological and statistical studies. The sense of the unique, whole person is lost with the nomothetic approach. Allport saw a place for methodological concerns within psychology, but he argued that psychology should be problem-centered rather than method-centered. To overvalue methods, losing sight of the questions being asked about personality, he called "methodolatry" (R.I. Evans, 1981a, p. 88).

The Pervasiveness of Traits

How pervasive is the influence of a particular trait? It varies. For example, you may have a trait of being a "drinker of decaffeinated coffee," but that would only be noticeable occasionally, such as when you are drinking coffee or buying it. On the other hand, if you have a trait of being "self-confident," it affects many more aspects of your life: how you behave with others, what risks you choose to take, and so forth.

Allport used the word **disposition** as a synonym for "trait." He categorized traits or dispositions as "cardinal," "central," or "secondary," depending upon how extensively they influence personality. The most pervasive are "cardinal traits" (or "cardinal dispositions"). The least pervasive are "secondary traits" (or "secondary dispositions"). The usual terms we use to describe someone are at the intermediate level: "central traits" (or "central dispositions").

Central Traits. In the example above, "self-confident" would be a central trait because it has pervasive effects on many behaviors. Allport's analysis of Jenny's letters led to the inference that she had eight central traits, as we have seen above. Biographers often use adjectives to describe a person. Someone who knows you well could summarize your personality in a small number of words, perhaps 7 to 10 adjectives. These characteristics that summarize personality are termed **central traits**, or "central dispositions."

The specific traits, of course, will vary from person to person. A characteristic that is a central trait for one person might not even be relevant for another. Therefore it is not the trait of "self-confidence" that makes it central, but rather the fact that many behaviors are affected. If a person is self-confident in playing chess, but not in many other things, then for that person self-confidence in chess would not be a central trait because it is not pervasive in its influence. It would be a secondary trait.

Secondary Traits. **Secondary traits** describe ways in which a person is consistent but do not affect so much of what the person does as a central trait. Secondary traits are "less conspicuous, less generalized, less consistent, and less often called into play than central traits" (Allport, 1937b, p. 338). "Liking decaffeinated coffee" in the example discussed above is an instance of a secondary trait. So, too, would be most tastes and personal preferences: "John likes spinach;" "Sarah's favorite color is mauve;" "David always orders Almond Fudge ice cream." Such personal preferences do not affect many behaviors, although they are consistent. Of course, for *some* people a personal preference may be a central trait; consider Popeye's preference for spinach. In his case the trait is not secondary; it is at least "central" or perhaps even a "cardinal trait."

Cardinal Traits. A **cardinal trait** (or "cardinal disposition") is a trait that is so pervasive that it dominates just about everything that a person does. It is "the eminent trait, the ruling passion, the master-sentiment, or the radix of a life" (Allport, 1937b, p. 338). Most people do not have any such highly pervasive single trait. When they do, the trait often makes its possessor famous, a prototype for a disposition that others may resemble to a lesser extent. Allport provided examples of traits so pervasive that they dominated all of their original possessors' behavior. Each of the following originated as a cardinal trait in one person: Calvinistic, chauvinistic, Christlike, Dionysian, Faustian, Lesbian, Machiavellian, Puckish, quixotic, and sadistic (Allport, 1937b, pp. 302–303).

Only very rarely do people have a cardinal trait. Other psychologists have challenged the usefulness of this concept. Allport did not think of cardinal traits as simply extreme scores on a nomothetic trait, although that seems more meaningful to many who have thought about his concept.

Levels of Integration of Personality: Traits, Attitudes, Habits

Cardinal, central, and secondary traits are not three discrete types; actually, traits appear on a continuum of pervasiveness (Allport, 1937b, p. 338). For Allport, these various traits exist on a broader spectrum of aspects of personality, which includes much less pervasive influences (reflexes and habits) and higher-order levels of integration ("selves"). Personality is arranged in a hierarchical structure (see Figure 7.4). At the lowest level of integration are simple conditioned *reflexes.* These become associated over time to form *habits.* Yet a higher level of integration is the notion of a self or, as sociologists sometimes refer to it, a "sub-identity"—for example, one's sense of oneself as a sister, as a professional, and so on.

The fact that we can have multiple selves suggests that there can be some higher level of integration. At least in some people, an even higher level integration occurs, "a thoroughly unified system of personality at the top of the pyramid" (Allport, 1937b, p. 142).

Integration emerges in personality because of the way traits and higher-order units develop as adaptive strategies. Traits help fulfill "the organic cravings which are the sole original motive power for activity" (Allport, 1937b, p. 114). In this biological approach to motivation, Allport says:

> The vegetative nervous system, where these cravings originate, is thought to be more primitive and more essential than the central nervous system which is primarily an agency of adjustment. The vegetative system is the master, the cerebro-spinal is the servant; the former compels adjustment, the latter effects adjustment. (Allport, 1937b, p. 115)

FIGURE 7.4 Levels of Integration in Personality

Despite Allport's criticisms of psychoanalysis, this description sounds remarkably like Freud's model of a personality in which the ego serves the id. His concept of a hierarchically organized personality is quite different from the structural concept of Freud, however, whose id, ego, and superego remain forever in conflict. It is in many ways similar to Cattell's concept of a "dynamic lattice" (see Chapter 8), and anticipates a later formal theoretical statement (Carver & Scheier, 1981).

Allport noted that many disagreements among psychologists occur because they focus on different units, aiming at different purposes (1937b, pp. 237–238). Many of the units employed by other psychological theories, including habits and factors, seemed inappropriate to Allport for the specific field of personality, which must focus on individual differences in adaptation.

Personality Development

In his description of personality development, Allport emphasized the later, more developed, stages (unlike psychoanalysis, which emphasized earlier development).

Functional Autonomy

Although traits begin as adaptive strategies to satisfy needs, ultimately the traits lose their close connection with their origins, whether these origins are in physical drives per se, or in some later developments, such as identification with parents. Thus motivation becomes fully *contemporaneous* (Allport, 1937c).

To understand the significance of this approach, recall the psychoanalytic view that regards motivation as determined by fixation in early childhood. For psychoanalysts, even adult motivation is understood in terms of its developmental origins. A highly gullible adult, for example, is still described as "orally fixated," rather than being given some contemporaneous description (such as "gullible" or "naive"). To Allport, and many others, this approach unnecessarily emphasizes the past.

In reaction to this preoccupation with the past, Allport proposed an alternative theoretical concept: **functional autonomy** of motivation (Allport, 1937c, 1950b). Whatever the original cause for developing a motive or trait, at some point it begins to function independently of its origins. For example, consider a female who, as a child, really wanted to be like her mother and admired her. As she grew up, she continued to dress like her Mom and to imitate her, and as an adult styled her hair like her mother did, entered her mother's profession, and aimed to marry someone just like her own father. One interpretation of that behavior is that the woman is doing what she is doing because her motivation is stuck in a childhood identification with her mother. Allport argued that, for the adult, the motivation is no longer to "be like mother." The particular interests and values have been internalized. They are now her own. They are, Allport would say, "functionally autonomous" from their origins.

Allport cited "workmanship" as another example of a trait that has become functionally autonomous of its origins. Though one learns to do a job well because it brings praise or security, later the work itself is satisfying (Allport, 1937b, p. 196). Similarly, hobbies and artistic or intellectual interests of people show functional autonomy (1937b, p. 207).

Allport stated, "Theoretically all adult purposes can be traced back to these seed-forms in infancy. But as the individual matures the bond is broken. The tie is historical, not functional" (1937b, p. 194). In this, Allport disagrees with Freud, in particular. The type of theory of normal personality Allport envisioned "must be a psychology of post-instinctive behavior. . . . Whatever the original drives or 'irritabilities' of the infant are, they become completely transformed in the course of growth into contemporaneous systems of motives" (1937b, pp. 194–195).

Allport criticized psychology for its preoccupation with the past. "People, it seems, are busy leading their lives into the future, whereas psychology, for the most part, is busy tracing them into the past" (1955, p. 51). The psychoanalytic preoccupation with fixation from the past does not allow understanding the integrated, forward-directed functioning of healthy persons. Allport thought the principle of functional autonomy was so important that he referred to it as "a declaration of independence for the psychology of personality" (1937b, p. 207), allowing us to study individual differences from a contemporaneous perspective.

Qualities of a Normal, Mature Adult

Allport listed several characteristics of a mature (that is, healthy) personality (1937b, 1961).

Extension of the Sense of Self. The developed person "has a variety of autonomous interests: that is, he can lose himself in work, in contemplation, in recreation, and in loyalty to others" (Allport, 1937b, p. 213). In explaining this capacity of a healthy adult for self-extension, Allport remarked that "the sign of cultivation in a man is his ability to talk for half a day without betraying [giving away] his occupation" (1937b, p. 218). Such an individual is not egocentric, but rather is involved in goals that are "extensions of the self."

Warm Human Interaction. The healthy person has a capacity for warm human interaction. Social interactions are sincere and friendly, rather than prescribed by rigid roles and expectations.

Emotional Security (Self-acceptance). Healthy individuals are emotionally secure and accept themselves, having high self-esteem.

Realistic Perception, Skills, and Assignments. The healthy person realistically perceives the world. Both unrealistic optimism, such as the conviction that this lottery ticket is going to be a winner, and unrealistic pessimism, such as the expectation of failing at everything, are avoided.

Self-objectification: Insight and Humor. Mature individuals are capable of "self-objectification," seeing themselves accurately from an objective perspective, with insight, and often with a sense of humor.

Unifying Philosophy of Life. Finally, the mature person has a "unifying philosophy of life" (Allport, 1937b, p. 214). For many people this is a religious philosophy of life, but it need not be.

Helson and Wink (1987) used Allport's criteria as a theoretical framework to examine maturity in a longitudinal study of women ages 21 to 43. Most of Allport's criteria were correlated significantly with two alternate measures of maturity, one stressing adaptation to society ("competence") and the other stressing intrapsychic development ("ego level"). Emotional security (measured by the Minnesota Multiphasic Personality Inventory, the MMPI), however, correlated only with competence (Allport's "realistic perception" and "self-objectification"), and not with ego level. Ego level was related to individuality of personality integration (Allport's "unifying philosophy of life"). These findings suggest that Allport's criteria of healthy maturity do not take into account the distress that may result from conflict between individual development and the demands of society.

Unity of Personality

With maturity comes integration or unification of personality. Integration occurs through "master-sentiments" (Allport, 1937b, p. 191). These may be religious philosophies of life. A master-sentiment may also be a nonreligious philosophy of life that constitutes a person's core consistency. Allport offered the example of Leo Tolstoy, who approached everything from his master-sentiment, the simplification of life (Allport, 1937b, pp. 190–191).

To bring about this unification, earlier motives are transformed. With maturity, the individual becomes more purposive, less pushed from the past (Allport, 1950b). Allport criticized theories that fail to recognize the transformation of motives, particularly "*Freudian psychology* [which] never regards an adult as truly adult" (1937b, p. 216; italics in original). Marsh and Colangelo (1983) criticized Allport for ambiguity about just how this unification is achieved and for not realizing that unification is not always a sign of maturity. The person's goals matter. Unity of personality toward some goals is not mature, they argued.

Unitas Multiplex. In referring to the unity of personality, Allport used the Latin term ***unitas multiplex***, the "unity of multiples." In the healthy person, there is integration of diverse elements: interests, traits, biological predispositions, and so forth. Allport urged psychologists to consider people as a whole, rather than analyzing them into isolated parts: habits, conflicts, and so forth. He stressed that the various parts are somehow directed by the person to work together toward some adaptive purpose.

The Proprium. To emphasize this unity, Allport suggested a theoretical concept, the **proprium**, which "includes all aspects of the personality that make for unity" (1955, p. 40) The proprium serves the functions that other theorists describe as belonging to the ego or the self. It is the striving part of our being, which gives us our intentionality and direction.

Stages of Development

The proprium develops gradually through a lifetime. According to Allport, "The newborn infant *lacks* personality, for he has not yet encountered the world in which he must live, and has not developed the distinctive modes of adjustment and mastery that will later comprise his personality. He is almost altogether a creature of heredity" (1937b, p. 107). The most important hereditary bases of personality, observable in infancy, are *activity level* ("motility") and *emotionality* ("temperament") (Allport, 1937b, p. 129). Upon this inherited basis, personality develops through interaction with the environment.

Allport suggested a list of stages of development, but he warned that any stages identified by a theory are somewhat arbitrary. "For the single *person* there is only *one* consecutive, uninterrupted course of life" (1937b, p. 131). We should realize that Allport did not do any developmental research to test whether his hypothesized stages really exist and whether they represent the order in which personality develops.

1. Bodily Sense. The proprium begins developing in infancy with the sense of the bodily self. An infant discovers, for example, that putting his or her own hand in the mouth feels quite different from mouthing a toy. This experience contributes to the development of a sense of "the bodily me."

2. Self-Identity. The second achievement of propriate development begins in the second year of life, from age 1 to 2, and continues until about age 4 or 5. During these years, the child develops a sense of *self-identity*, a sense of his or her existence as a separate person. This is the stage when children begin to recognize themselves by name, signifying recognition of continuing individuality.

3. Ego-Enhancement. From age 2 to 3, the child begins working on self-esteem. The capacity for pride through achievement starts to develop, but also does the capacity for humiliation and selfishness.

4. Ego-Extension. Next, perhaps beginning as early as age 3 to 4, the child begins to identify with his or her **ego-extensions**, such as personal possessions. "That is *my* bike." Of course, this process continues into adulthood, especially in a consumer-oriented culture such as ours. Besides possessions, the maturing individual identifies with "loved objects, and later, . . . [with] ideal causes and loyalties" (Allport, 1955, p. 45).

5. Self-Image. The self-image includes both evaluation of our present "abilities, status, and roles" and our aspirations for the future (Allport, 1955, p. 47). Children between ages 4 and 6, Allport suggested, begin to become capable of formulating future goals and are aware of being good and bad.

6. Rational Agent. During the middle childhood years (age 6 to 12) the child may be thought of as a **rational coper**. The child is busy solving problems and planning ways of doing things, skills that are practiced at school. In his description of these ego skills, Allport contrasted his attention to the adaptive functions of the ego with Freud's emphasis on ego defenses.

7. Propriate Striving. The seventh stage of development is labeled **propriate striving**, derived from Allport's term "proprium." Propriate striving, which begins in adolescence, is "ego-involved" motivation that has "directedness or intentionality," to use Allport's phrasing. At this time some defining object becomes the "cement" holding a life together, as the person becomes capable of genuine ideology and career planning.

8. The Knower. In adulthood, Allport described the development of the **self as knower**. The adult cognitively integrates the previous seven aspects of the self into a unified whole.

Allport stated that most people have little personality change after age 30. In this he agreed with the well-known psychologists of his day, including John Watson and William James (Allport, 1937b, p. 143). However, other theorists (e.g., Erikson and Jung) describe more personality change in adulthood.

Unlike some approaches (e.g., Freud), Allport did not claim that the earlier stages of development were necessarily the most important. Optimally, earlier stages are transformed into a new integration of personality; but sometimes earlier stages remain relatively unchanged, in isolated "archaic" (Freud would say "fixated") components (Allport, 1955, p. 28).

Though Allport sketched out a description of personality development, he felt that we are very far from being able to predict outcomes. Children growing up in the same family, for example, may turn out quite differently from one another and from their parents. We know too little about the way heredity, learning, and social factors work to predict personality accurately.

Influence of Personality on Social Phenomena

Allport viewed humans as social beings. For him the causes of behavior were always within the individual, rather than in the social environment. Thus his contributions to the understanding of prejudice, religion, and rumor transmission emphasize the importance of personality, rather than social causation.

Prejudice

Allport authored a classic text on prejudice, *The Nature of Prejudice* (1954). In that comprehensive work, he examined factors such as in-group and out-group influences, ego defenses, cognitive processes, the role of language, stereotypes in culture, scapegoating, and the learning of prejudice in childhood. In addition to his academic analysis, Allport offered practical strategies for the reduction of prejudice. He felt, for example, that when different races worked together for the common good in the war effort (World War II), this cooperation would reduce prejudice.

Religion and Prejudice

Allport criticized psychologists for ignoring the role of religion in personality (1950a). He was particularly interested in how religion relates to racial prejudice. He suggested that brotherhood and bigotry are intertwined in religion (Allport, 1966a) and tried to understand when each would prevail. He reported research showing that people who attend church were, on the average, more prejudiced that those who do not attend. When Allport distinguished various kinds of religious orientation, he found that prejudiced churchgoers were those for whom religion served a selfish purpose—for example, raising their status in the community (Allport & Ross, 1967). Such individuals had an **extrinsic religious orientation** toward religion and were likely to agree, on the Religious Orientation Survey, with such self-report statements as this: "One reason for my being a church member is that such membership helps to establish a person in the community" (Allport & Ross, 1967). Other aspects of Allport's description of intrinsic and extrinsic religiousness are presented in Table 7.2.

The finding that extrinsically religious individuals are more racially prejudiced has been confirmed by other researchers (Herek, 1987). In contrast, individuals with an **intrinsic religious orientation** have internalized their religious faith. Such people agree with self-report statements such as: "My religious beliefs are what really lie behind my whole approach to life" (Allport & Ross, 1967). Intrinsically religious people are racially tolerant,

TABLE 7.2 Concepts Associated with Intrinsic and Extrinsic Religiousness in Allport's Writings

Intrinsic	*Extrinsic*
Relates to all of life (a, b, c, d, f, g, h, j)	Compartmentalized (a, c, d, h)
Unprejudiced; tolerance (a, b, c, h, i)	Prejudiced; exclusionary (a, b, c, d, e, h)
Mature (a, d)	Immature; dependent; comfort; security (a, b, d, f, g, h, i, j)
Integrative; unifying; meaning-endowed (a, c, d, f, g, h, i)	Instrumental; utilitarian; self-serving (a, c, d, e, f, g, h, i, j)
Regular church attendance (e, g, h)	Irregular church attendance (e, g, h, i)
Makes for mental health (f, g)	Defense or escape mechanism (d, f, g)

Note: Letters in parentheses refer to the following references: (a) Allport (1950a), (b) Allport (1954), (c) Allport (1959), (d) Allport (1961), (e) Allport (1962), (f) Allport (1963), (g) Allport (1964), (h) Allport (1966a), (i) Allport (1966b), (j) Allport & Ross (1967).

(From M. J. Donahue (1985). Intrinsic and extrinsic religiousness: Review and meta-analysis. *Journal of Personality and Social Psychology*, 48, 400–419.)

rather than prejudiced. Because of the large numbers of extrinsically religious people, if churchgoers are all lumped together, they are, on average, more prejudiced than those who do not go to church. Averages are misleading, though, since they mask the tolerance of the intrinsically religious.

Intrinsic religious orientation has been found to be associated with empathy (P. J. Watson, Hood, Morris, & Hall, 1984), which may be a factor leading to greater tolerance. Allport's description of the tolerance of intrinsically religious people has, however, been challenged by the finding of increased prejudice against homosexuals (lesbians and gay men) in this group (Herek, 1987). (See Table 7.3.) Since this group of intrinsically religious people was more tolerant of racial minorities, Herek interpreted the increased prejudice against homosexuals as a direct result of intolerant religious teachings about homosexuality. In another study, however, intrinsics were *less* likely to devalue a rape victim (Joe, McGee, & Dazey, 1977). The association of religious orientation with prejudice seems to depend, in part, on the target of the potential prejudice.

Considering only prejudice in the form of antiblack attitudes, Donahue (1985) reported, based on a meta-analysis of several studies, that Allport's prediction was not confirmed overall. While extrinsic orientation was associated with greater prejudice, as Allport predicted, the association was not strong ($r = .28$), and intrinsic orientation was not correlated with tolerance ($r = -.09$ with prejudice). Why could this be? Perhaps the religious orientations Allport described were not accurate. Perhaps the measurement of religious orientation is flawed. Perhaps other factors obscure the association.

Other research also casts doubt on Allport's suggestion that intrinsically religious people are wholeheartedly, unselfishly helpful to others. Correlations between the Religious Orientation Survey and other personality mea-

TABLE 7.3 Intrinsic and Extrinsic Religious Orientation and Prejudice Against Racial Minorities and Homosexuals

		Intrinsic (mean scores)	
		Low	High
Extrinsic (mean scores)	*Low*	[Nonreligious] Race = 5.11 ATG = 46.29 ATL = 35.63 RIS = 27.22	[Intrinsic] Race = 4.29 ATG = 53.45 ATL = 41.42 RIS = 39.45
	High	[Extrinsic] Race = 8.52 ATG = 47.28 ATL = 38.00 RIS = 28.40	[Indiscriminate] Race = 13.61 ATG = 53.50 ATL = 39.80 RIS = 39.79

Note: Higher scores on "Race" indicate more prejudice against racial minorities. Higher scores on the ATL (Attitudes Toward Lesbians) and ATG (Attitudes Toward Gay Men) indicate greater prejudice against these groups. Higher scores on the RIS (Religious Ideology Scale) indicate a more fundamentalist ideology.

(From Herek, 1987, p. 39.)

sures suggest that intrinsically religious people are motivated by conscious impression management and unconscious self-deception (Leak & Fish, 1989). From his experimental study of helping, Batson (1990) argued that intrinsically religious subjects were motivated primarily by the desire to enhance their own esteem, rather than by pure altruism.

Furthermore, Allport's Religious Orientation Survey has psychometric difficulties. Though the most widely used, it is not the best measure of religious orientation available (Van Wicklin, 1990). In addition, most research on religious orientation is conducted with primarily Christian samples (Van Wicklin, 1990), which limits the conclusions that can be reached.

Rumor Transmission

Motivated by concerns about controlling the spread of rumors during World War II, Allport and Postman studied rumors in the laboratory and offered advice to the government. Their book, *The Psychology of Rumor* (1947), illustrates the interplay between history and psychological work, beginning with a classification of the rumors that circulated following the Japanese attack on Pearl Harbor in 1941. This research interweaves experimental laboratory studies of basic processes with socially relevant descriptions of real rumors and strategies in an effort to prevent them from undermining the national interest. It is an early example of applied social psychological research.

One set of concepts Allport and Postman investigated concerned the cognitive processes of "leveling" and "sharpening," which cause information to change, becoming more general or more specific, as rumors are repeated. In a classic study, they found that information which begins with an eyewitness and then is passed on by word of mouth can change considerably. One subject viewed a slide in which a white man holding a knife was apparently arguing with a black man in a subway car. The subject, while looking at the slide, described it to another subject, who could not see it. Based on this description, the second subject described it to a third subject, and so on, until, like the child's game of "telephone," the "rumor" had been passed on to several subjects. In over half the replications, the black man was erroneously reported as holding the knife at some point in the rumor transmission (Allport & Postman, 1947). This study has become a classic one supporting the idea that stereotypes lead to erroneous eyewitness reporting. Ironically, the original study is often distorted in making this point (Treadway & McCloskey, 1987). Furthermore, the actual eyewitness distortions attributable to prejudice are less striking than commonly reported (Boon & Davis, 1987).

Eclecticism

Allport believed that psychology, especially the psychology of personality, should gain truth from many areas. He called his approach "eclectic." According to Allport, who drew his distinction from the German poet Goethe, we can distinguish "jackdaw" eclecticism from systematic eclecticism. A jackdaw is a bird that, like a pack rat, collects everything. **Jackdaw eclecticism** is not selective. *Systematic eclecticism*, in contrast, is selective and tries to make one unified whole out of all that is taken. Since most psychologists consider themselves eclectic with respect to personality theory, we should take Allport's advice to heart and consider how it is that we make our selection of what to keep and what to discard from each theory.

Allport accepted insights from various theories. He accepted Freud's assertion that sexual conflict is of particular importance in the formation of personality (Allport, 1937b, p. 116), although this was a passing remark that he did not often restate. He included many psychoanalytic mechanisms in his eclectic approach (listed by Allport as including "*rationalization, projection, fantasy, infantilism, regression, dissociation, trauma,* the *complex,* and the *ego-ideal*", 1937b, p. 183). He also included Adler's concept of "inferiority" within his eclectic theory. He even investigated the frequency of various types of "inferiority complexes" in college students. He reported that 48 percent of men and 55 percent of women suffer from persistent feelings of inferiority about physical matters; 58 percent of men and 65 percent of women feel inferior about social matters; 29 percent of men but 64 percent of women feel inferior about intellectual matters; and only 17 percent of men and 18 percent of women feel inferior about moral matters (Allport, 1937b, p. 174).

Summary

Gordon Allport influenced the development of academic psychology with his emphasis on major themes: personality consistency, social influence, the concept of self, and the interaction of personality with social influence in determining behavior. Allport defined personality as "the dynamic organization within the individual of those psychophysical systems that determine his unique adjustments to the environment." The primary unit of

TABLE 7.4 Contributions of Allport's Theory to Various Topics

Biological	All behavior is influenced, in some part, by heredity; but the mechanisms are not specified.
Child Development	The proprium (ego or self) develops through stages that are outlined, but not researched in detail.
Adult Development	Adult development consists of integrating earlier developments.
Mental Health	Psychology errs if it looks too much for illness. Allport listed several characteristics of a healthy personality.
Society	Adaptation to society is of central importance. Allport made important contributions to our understanding of prejudice, rumor, and religion.
Cognitive Processes	People's self-statements can generally be taken at face value.
Individual Differences	Individuals differ in the traits that predominate in their personalities. Some traits are common; others are unique.

personality is the *trait.* Traits can be studied idiographically (individual traits) or nomothetically (common traits). The idiographic approach more adequately describes individuals (see Table 7.4).

Evidence of traits comes from many sources: from language, from behavior, from documents (such as letters), and from questionnaires, such as the Study of Values. Allport emphasized that the subject matter should take precedence over methodological issues.

Traits vary in pervasiveness. *Cardinal traits* have extremely pervasive influences, but only occur in a few people. *Central traits* have broad influences, and occur in everyone. In addition, people have *secondary traits* that influence only a few behaviors. Traits are in the middle of a spectrum of aspects of personality, ranging from very narrow reflexes through highly integrated selves.

As personality develops, traits become *functionally autonomous* from their developmental origins. Thus the study of personality should focus on contemporaneous issues. Allport listed several characteristics of a mature, healthy adult: extension of the sense of self, warm human interactions, emotional security (self-acceptance), realistic perceptions, self-objectification, and a unifying philosophy of life. The healthy personality is unified, combining various elements into a *unitas multiplex.* Personality development, the development of the unifying *proprium,* proceeds through stages: bodily sense, self-identity, ego-enhancement, ego-extensions, self-image, rational agent, propriate striving, and the self as knower. Allport studied prejudice, which he said was more frequent among *extrinsically religious* individuals and less frequent among *intrinsically religious* individuals. Overall, Allport's approach was *eclectic.*

ILLUSTRATIVE BIOGRAPHIES: Concluding Remarks

A personality analysis using Allport's theory may well begin with identification of the *central traits* of a person. It should not dwell on developmental issues, since the traits are presumed to have become *functionally autonomous* from their childhood origins. Additionally, Allport offered criteria of mental health. Using these Allportian concepts, how can we understand the personalities of Jerry Falwell and Beverly Sills?

Jerry Falwell

For Jerry Falwell, a list of central traits would include the traits *dedicated to God* and *evangelistic*. He made his life work the development of his ministry. He would also be characterized as *hard-working.* As a young preacher, he aimed to visit a hundred neighborhood houses each day and generally succeeded. He could be described as *dedicated to family.* For example, he cancelled a speaking engagement, at great financial cost and professional embarrassment, so that he could keep a family tradition to have a special day together on his son's birthday. His *leadership* was evidenced throughout his life, in childhood as an instigator of pranks and in adulthood in his professional position. As a youth, his *mischievous* side was demonstrated in pranks such as stealing his teacher's trousers. (His serious role as a preacher has, of course, mitigated the full expression of this trait.) He is *intelligent*; he skipped a grade in elementary school and graduated valedictorian of his college class. There may be other "central" traits as well. Allport did not provide an objective procedure for identifying them, but relied on the judgments of observers. Some variation might be expected from other observers, particularly if they have access to different information about the person.

Allport's greatest contrast with the psychoanalytic theorists he criticized was his concept of *functional autonomy.* Traits become independent of their developmental origins. Jerry Falwell clearly acknowledged the role his personal history has played in his development. He noted that his mother's religious example set the stage for his own conversion and that his father's alcoholism inspired him to develop programs to treat alcoholics through his ministry. Nonetheless, after both parents had died, Falwell still continued his commitment to these causes. It seems fair to conclude that these developments had become internalized, that is, *functionally autonomous.*

Falwell's personality, as described in his autobiography (Falwell, 1987), resembles Allport's description of a mature, healthy adult. Falwell's religion provided him with a *unifying philosophy of life*, giving him a framework for his efforts and for difficult decision making. His church work functioned as an *extension of his sense of self.* He described *warm relationships to others,* friends and family. He portrayed the warmth of his wife's family as a model to emulate. His autobiography conveys a sense of *emotional security* (self-acceptance), rooted in the love of family and the security of a relationship with a loving God. Overall, Jerry Falwell's achievement of his evangelistic goals and his successful efforts to gain political influence can be interpreted as evidence of *realistic perceptions.* (Those who claim that "the Moral Majority is neither moral nor a majority" might disagree that his perceptions were realistic. It seems, to this writer, most objective to accept the reality of Falwell's political influence as evidence of realism, rather than to require agreement with a particular set of values.) Of course, any judgments about mental maturity that are based on autobiographical (or even biographical) reports risk distortion owing to self-presentational biases. Nonetheless, these interpretations are consistent with Allport's strategy of taking self-reports at face value.

Allport was concerned not only with the social world but also with individual personality. On some of Falwell's most conspicuous values, Allport is silent: namely political conservatism and opposition to abortion. On the other hand, two of Allport's major social concerns, religion and racial attitudes, are conspicuous in Falwell's autobiography. Allport distinguished "intrinsic" from "extrinsic" religious attitudes. In favor of the conclusion that Falwell was genuinely intrinsic in his religion, note that he lost prestige when he decided to attend a religious institution, Baptist Bible College, rather than a more competitive secular school. His critics accused Falwell of seeking personal gain in taking over the PTL ("Praise The Lord") ministry, but he denied that. Certainly there were no reports of financial exploitation and extravagant living in the Falwell ministry, unlike the Bakker scandal.

On race relations, Falwell discussed segregation and integration in the context of history. Growing up in the segregated South, he took separation of the races for granted, and at first his own church excluded blacks. However, this troubled him. He came to believe that the Christian Church was to blame for not doing its job and that the civil rights movement would not have been necessary had Christianity practiced the brotherly love it preached. Allport would have discerned here the racial tolerance that stems from an intrinsic religious attitude. Quietly, Falwell opened a church summer camp to both races, without legal pressure and at the cost of losing some white support. When liberal Harvard students accused him of racism, he was delighted to point out that his Liberty Bible College was more racially integrated, in both the faculty and student body, than was Harvard University.

Allport's eclectic theory attempted to understand non-neurotic persons, and to a large extent Allport took self-descriptions at face value. It is consistent with Allport's approach, then, not to dig too deeply below the surface, looking for unconscious determinants of Falwell's religious and political commitments. From the perspective of Allport's theory, Jerry Falwell seems to exemplify a mature, healthy adult, unified by a religious philosophy of life that directs his *propriate striving*.

Beverly Sills

A list of Beverly Sills's central traits would necessarily include *musical* for this most talented and committed singer. She was *intelligent* in the conventional sense, with an IQ score of 155 in childhood and a reputation for learning opera parts very quickly. Her trait of *hard-working* developed in childhood when her parents expected only grades above 95 on her report card. Consistent with Allport's concept of *functional autonomy*, this hard work became a part of Beverly's adult personality. She reported, for example, working 15 hours a day as general director of the New York City Opera. Undoubtedly she was *ambitious,* aiming for opera stardom for herself and for financial stability for the opera company, both seemingly impossible tasks. She could be called *self-confident,* or perhaps "egotistical" or "temperamental" when this trait was manifested in the prima donna role. She reported little stage fright, and in her autobiography she professed high levels of confidence at succeeding in her demanding roles. As she said, "I always knew what I was capable of doing. If that sounds egotistical, try to understand that when you're in the performing arts you need a certain amount of ego, a certain self-assurance, or else you'd never have the guts to face an audience" (Sills & Linderman, 1987, p. 126).

Beverly Sills had a *sense of humor,* which she used to deal with tensions. For example, she wore a Groucho Marx nose, glasses, and moustache for at least five minutes at a dress rehearsal before the conductor noticed, and with this joke she cured his unfortunate habit of avoiding eye contact with the singers (Sills & Linderman, 1987, p. 259). Sills also could turn her sense of humor against herself, avoiding taking herself too seriously. In her autobiography, for example, she recounted the story of a Nebraska newspaper that mixed up photo captions on her early tour. As a result, her front-page picture was captioned, "Stinking Smut Hits Nebraska," while "Beverly Sills to Sing at High School" appeared with a picture of a dead cow! She may have temperamentally cut a costume in half at La Scala to emphasize a disagreement with the wardrobe mistress, but she was apparently able to laugh at herself.

Thus Beverly Sills demonstrates some of Allport's criteria of mental maturity: emotional security (self-acceptance) and self-objectification (insight and humor). One might have questioned whether her perceptions were realistic (another criterion in Allport's list), since she took on seemingly impossible tasks; but because she succeeded, this criticism is moot. Her investment in work and family constitutes self-extension. She worked on behalf of the March of Dimes to combat birth defects, thus extending her personal concern (based on family tragedy) to the larger society. While capable of warm relationships with others within her family and among close friends, Sills reported interpersonal conflicts as well, some sparked by her managerial responsibilities at the City Opera and some resulting from anti-Semitic attitudes directed against her. She frankly admitted carrying a grudge about discrimination, especially the hostility she encountered in Cleveland when she married a gentile.

The greatest discrepancy between Sills's experience and Allport's criteria of mental health concerns the integration of personality under a unifying philosophy of life. Beverly Sills did not consider herself traditionally religious, although this attitude is not essential in Allport's theory. Beyond that, however, she wrote frankly of the distress caused by the tragic birth defects of her children, especially of her son, who was institutionalized. She reported a serious depression after learning of the diagnoses of both children within a six-week period. Work, after these events, took on an escapist meaning. It provided an opportunity to forget her private tragedies while in the particular opera role she was performing. She maintained an outwardly cheery face, but inwardly felt distressed. This disunity into separate "selves" does not fulfill Allport's criterion of unity.

Is it fair to conclude from this evidence that her personality was less developed than those who present a less conflicted image? One wonders how much one person, even a maturely developed person, can bear without sacrificing honesty under a gloss of coping. Is it fair to conclude that Sills is really less unified than many others, or did she simply report the inevitable fragmentation of the human condition more honestly? This is a question that Allport does not pose; he takes people's statements rather at face value, assuming that emotional distress indicates less maturity, a questionable assumption, perhaps especially for women (Helson & Wink, 1987). Other psychologists, in contrast, have found that people who are highly developed on measures of ego development may express high levels of conflict, rather than low conflict, perhaps because they have the courage to acknowledge the distress (Bursik, 1991; Loevinger, 1976).

GLOSSARY

cardinal trait a pervasive personality trait that dominates nearly everything a person does

central trait one of the half dozen or so traits that best describe a particular person

common trait a trait characterizing many people (that is, a trait considered from the nomothetic point of view)

disposition another term for "trait"

ego-extensions objects or people that help to define a person's identity or sense of self

expressive traits traits concerned with the style or tempo of a person's behavior

extrinsic religious orientation attitude in which religion is seen as a means to a person's other goals (such as status or security)

functional autonomy a trait's independence of its developmental origins

individual trait a trait that characterizes only the one person who has it (that is, a trait considered from the idiographic point of view)

intrinsic religious orientation attitude in which religion is accepted for its own sake, rather than as a means to an end

jackdaw eclecticism considering concepts from diverse theories, without making careful selection from and evaluation of these concepts

personality for Gordon Allport, "the dynamic organization within the individual of those psychophysical systems that determine his unique adjustment to the environment"

propriate striving effort based on a sense of selfhood or identity

proprium all aspects of a person that make for unity; a person's sense of self or ego

rational coper a stage in middle childhood in which problem-solving ability is important to one's sense of self

secondary trait a trait that influences a limited range of behaviors

self as knower a stage in adulthood in which a person integrates the self into a unified whole

temperament innate emotional aspects of personality

trait a characteristic of a person that makes a person unique, with a unique style of adapting to stimuli in the world

unifying philosophy of life an attitude or set of values, often religious, that gives coherence and meaning to life

unique trait a trait that only one person has (also called "individual trait")

unitas multiplex the Latin phrase indicating that a person makes a unified whole out of many diverse aspects of personality

STUDY QUESTIONS

1. List and briefly describe some of the ways Allport influenced the study of personality.
2. How did Allport define personality? Explain the significance of this definition.

3. Discuss Allport's concept of a *trait.* Explain the difference between an individual trait and a common trait.
4. What sources provide evidence about traits? Discuss, in particular, Allport's *Letters from Jenny* and his *Study of Values.*
5. Explain how cardinal traits, central traits, and secondary traits differ in the pervasiveness of their influence.
6. Discuss Allport's concept of *functional autonomy.*
7. List and explain characteristics of a mature, healthy adult.
8. List stages in the development of the *proprium.*
9. Explain what Allport meant by *intrinsic* and *extrinsic* religious orientation.
10. Discuss the relationship between religious orientation and prejudice.
11. Summarize Allport's advice about *eclecticism.*

CHAPTER

Cattell: Factor Analytic Trait Theory

BIOGRAPHY OF RAYMOND B. CATTELL

Raymond B. Cattell

Raymond B. Cattell was born in 1905 in Staffordshire, England, the son and grandson of engineers. He had two brothers and was a bright student. As a boy, he witnessed the carnage and casualties of World War I.

In college, Cattell studied science. Shortly before graduation from the University of London, he decided, to the dismay of friends, that psychology was the field he really wished to pursue. He attended the University of London (King's College), completing his doctoral degree in 1929 at the age of 23. There he learned Spearman's factor analysis, a mathematical procedure that was developed to study intelligence but which Cattell would later apply to personality research.

Prospects for a professorship in psychology in England were slight, as his friends had warned him when they learned of his plans to study this field. Cattell reported in his autobiography that there were only six faculty positions in the country, and they were all held by men who were healthy and showed no signs of vacating them. So Cattell accepted an applied position, moving to Leicester to set up a school psychological service. Of these five years of clinical work, he later said, "though . . . I felt a charlatan it gave me many leads for personality research" (1984, p. 123). In 1930, he married Monica Rogers. They had one child.

Besides long hours of administrative work, Cattell did research in those years. He studied the relationship of intelligence to family size and social status (a research question that offended liberal critics). He developed a projective test at the same time as did Henry Murray, who is generally credited for developing this testing strategy. Cattell commented that, to his best knowledge, he himself may be the one who first used the term "projective test." These years were difficult, owing to overwork and a low salary. Cattell developed physical difficulties (stomach problems), and his first wife, Monica, left him.

In 1937, Cattell accepted an invitation from E. L. Thorndike to work in social psychology in New York for a year. Abraham Maslow was also an associate of Thorndike at that time. The proposed one year in the United States became, in fact, a permanent immigration. After the year with Thorndike, Cattell accepted a professorship at Clark University, where he worked on culture-fair intelligence tests.

A year later Cattell accepted a lectureship at Harvard University. There he was a colleague to many other famous psychologists, including the personality theorists Gordon Allport and Henry Murray. His office was next door to Allport's (Cattell, 1984, p. 141), and he remarked that "in personality theory, Allport and I spoke a different language, which . . . was tough on students" (1974, p. 71). These were bachelor years for Cattell. He worked long days and holidays, practically living in his office. During World War II, he reluctantly interrupted his basic research to do some of the applied work expected of professionals during the crisis. He labored on developing objective personality tests for officer selection, but the research was interrupted by the end of the war.

Cattell's next move, in 1945, was to the University of Illinois, where he was appointed to a research position. He married Karen Schuettler, a mathematician whom he had met at Harvard, and they raised four children. Freed from teaching responsibilities, and with access to a new and (for the times) powerful computer (which they fondly dubbed the "Sacred Illiac"), these were very productive years for Cattell. He continued to work hard, remarking that "For many years I rarely left the laboratory before 11 P.M., and then was generally so deep in thought or discussion that I could find my car only because it was the last still in the parking lot!" (1974, p. 75).

To facilitate distribution of his many new psychological tests, Cattell set up a private organization, the Institute for Personality and Ability Testing (IPAT) in 1949. The institute remains the place from which interested researchers can purchase Cattell's tests and manuals. Cattell also founded the Society for Multivariate Experimental Psychology, in 1960, to foster the kind of research he felt was necessary for the scientific advance of personality theory.

Cattell eventually left academia and retired to Hawaii where he continues to advocate statistical approaches to theory development (Cattell, 1990a) and, as this text goes to press, responds promptly and in his own handwriting to requests to include some of his classic figures in texts such as this.

ILLUSTRATIVE BIOGRAPHIES

Cattell's theory is seldom systematically applied to psychobiography. One exception is an intriguing analysis of four leaders of the Protestant Reformation (W.J. Wright, 1985). Cattell occasionally mentioned a famous person as an example of one of his theoretical concepts—for example, John Stuart Mill as an example of a trait Cattell called "Asthenia" (Cattell, Vaughan, Schuerger, & Rao, 1982, p. 375; see also Cattell & Butcher, 1968).

Cattell's theory of personality aims to describe the fundamental dimensions of individual differences. As such, it is a broadly applicable theory that has concepts that can be applied to a great diversity of individuals. It is fitting that one of those we should examine is the physicist who strived to understand the fundamental laws of the physical universe. In this encounter, two quite different sciences meet, sharing the common language of mathematics.

Albert Einstein

Without question, Albert Einstein is the best-known theoretical physicist of our century. His theory of relativity is a cultural symbol for the highest achievements of human intelligence.

Albert Einstein was born in Ulm, Germany, in 1879. He had a younger sister. He worried his parents by being very slow to start talking and did poorly in school subjects that required rote memorization. Despite these apparent weaknesses, he showed a talent for mathematics and a high level of general intelligence from an early age. He is reported to have taught himself calculus by the age of 16 and was reading Kant at 13.

His family moved from Germany to Italy. After some delay because of his schooling, Albert followed at the age of 15, finishing his studies in Italy. He graduated from the University of Zurich (Switzerland) in 1900 but was unable to find a teaching job in physics. Finally, he accepted a position in the Swiss Patent Office evaluating new inventions. He worked after hours (and during work hours, when no one was looking) on theoretical physics. He began publishing a series of papers in physics journals while in this nonacademic position.

As the world knows, these theoretical developments culminated in the Theory of Relativity, which

states that matter and energy are interrelated, and which questions the fundamental concepts of space and time that had been taken for granted by Newtonian physics. Einstein was awarded the Nobel Prize in physics in 1921, but not for his work on relativity. His prominent role in physics in the twentieth century placed him in the middle of political turmoil. He had returned to Germany because of the physics laboratory provided to him in Berlin, but emigrated to the United States after Hitler took power in Germany. He was one of several prominent physicists who warned President Roosevelt that the Germans might develop an atomic bomb. He urged the United States to do so first, in that age, not so very long ago, when the nuclear threat still existed only in one's imagination. Because of his Jewish heritage, Einstein was also recruited to support the new nation of Israel.

In his personal life, Einstein had a younger sister with whom he had lifelong close relationship. He had two wives (the first divorced him) and a schizophrenic child. He loved music, and he played the violin in the breaks between his calculations.

This genius of science, whose public positions are so interwoven with the history of our century, died in 1955. The impact of his work lives on. But what of the man? How can we understand the personality of Albert Einstein? Raymond Cattell claims to have developed a comprehensive overview of personality dimensions. Is his theory broad enough to understand even the Father of Relativity?

Florence Nightingale

Florence Nightingale's name evokes images of caring and concern, of nursing at its best. Born in an era when women of her privileged class stayed home, she forged ahead to build her own career. In so doing, she transformed nursing into a respectable profession and made significant improvements in hospital practice.

Florence Nightingale was born May 12, 1820, in Florence, Italy, while her family was traveling for an extended period (as was the custom among affluent English people). She was named after the city of her birth. Only after she became famous did "Florence" become a popular name for girls, in her honor.

Miss Nightingale was raised in Derbyshire, in rural England. Because she was a girl, she did not attend school. She received, however, a good education at home. She and her sister, Parthe, studied mathematics, Greek, and Latin (which were not usually taught to females), as well as French, German, Italian, history, religion, music, and sewing. Florence resisted the pressures of her time and her family to define her identity through domesticity. Although she was "graceful, witty, [and] vividly good-looking" (Woodham-Smith, 1951, p. 23) and was very popular, she did not accept the path to which she seemed destined. She rejected a marriage proposal, though the gentleman was a fine man who had waited nine years for an answer. She felt called to a different path, describing this as a mystical vision, a religious calling.

In that day, nursing was unthinkable for a gentlewoman. There were, aside from Catholic nuns, no schools of nursing. Hospital patients were attended only by women of the lower class, who were often prostitutes and inclined toward alcohol. When she learned of a group of nuns in Kaiserswerth, Germany, who were establishing a school for hospital nurses, Florence convinced her family to allow her to study there. She continued to educate herself about hospital nursing, making opportunities where schools did not exist, and paying for her own chaperone when that was necessary in order to make her presence in hospitals respectable. Ultimately, Florence Nightingale became the country's expert on hospital nursing, and so was called to government service during the Crimean War (1853–1856).

Newspapers had publicized the abysmal conditions at English military hospitals in the Crimea and had criticized the lack of nursing care. The press pointed out that French soldiers were cared for by the Sisters of Charity. Why was there no nursing care for English soldiers? The British government appointed Florence Nightingale to head a small group of 38 nurses to serve in English military hospitals in Turkey. Florence Nightingale is best remembered as "the Lady with the lamp" who attended to dying soldiers in the Crimean War. She believed that no man should die alone.

Her most lasting contribution was, however, not direct patient care, but rather her effective administrative work. The military establishment had no tradition of nurses, and bureaucratic battles had to be fought before the nurses were allowed to serve. Finally, these nurses brought about a tremendous improvement in hospital conditions. Unsanitary sewage and water supplies were remedied, supplies of food and clothing were improved, and the death rate dropped from 420 to 22 per thousand (Seymer, 1951, p. 61).

Upon her return to England, Miss Nightingale continued to foster nursing as a profession. She established the Nightingale Training School to educate nurses and closely supervised its graduates. She influenced hospital design in England and, through extensive correspondence, also in India. In the interim, she turned down another marriage proposal.

Florence Nightingale was popular in England and abroad and was recognized by many honors. In her later years, she was an invalid and blind, having suffered ill health since her Crimean service. She died in 1910 at the age of 90.

How are we to understand this woman, unique in her century? Why did she refuse to adjust to the expected domestic life, yet eschew the movement for woman suffrage? And how could the leader of one of women's most caring professions be criticized by family and friends for her lack of caring? Could her contributions have been predicted?

FACTOR ANALYTIC TRAIT THEORY

Personality: Prediction of Behavior

Raymond Cattell claimed that the study of personality passed through two earlier phases before reaching its current scientific status. "From biblical times until the early nineteenth century," he wrote, "it was a matter for intuitive insights expressed in the realm of literature" (Cattell, 1979, p. 6), marked by such giants as Plutarch, Bacon, and Goethe. Then came a century of clinically oriented scientific studies, including giants in the history of psychopathology (Bleuler, Janet, and Kretschmer) and primarily clinically oriented personality theorists (Freud, Adler, and Jung), with some experimental work (Jung and McDougall). Ever since World War I, the study of personality has been in the third, "experimental and quantitative" phase. Cattell saw his work as building on the valuable insights of earlier theories "but subjecting them to independent judgment on the basis of modern methods" (1979, p. 8). The most important modern method was the statistical technique of factor analysis, "a research tool as important to psychology as the microscope was to biology" (Cattell, 1957, p. 4).

Definition of Personality

Cattell's definition of personality neatly summarizes his entire theoretical and empirical approach:

> Personality is that which permits a prediction of what a person will do in a given situation. (1950, p. 2)

This definition is entirely nonspecific regarding the *content* of personality, but is clearly committed to the scientific process of prediction. Cattell emphasized the methodological issues that Allport regarded as relatively less important. Cattell's background in science, contrasting with Allport's background in social ethics, explains the contrasting emphasis.

Traits

Cattell regarded **traits** as the units of personality that had predictive value. Cattell defined a trait as "that which defines what a person will do when faced with a defined situation" (1979, p. 14). Unlike Allport, he did not feel it was necessary to define traits in psychophysical terms. For Cattell, traits were abstract concepts, conceptual tools useful for predictive purposes but not necessarily corresponding to anything within a person; traits had no specific physical reality.

Cattell's contribution to personality is his systematic *description* of personality. He argued that such description, a taxonomy of individual differences, is essential before investigation of the causes of personality can be sensibly begun. He believed, though, that personality traits were not purely statistical phenomena. Although his method was correlational rather than experimental, the sophistication of the studies and the patterns emerging from so many studies led him to believe that "traits *exist* as determiners of behavior" (1979, p. 98).

Measurement

Personality Tests

Cattell was the author or co-author of dozens of personality tests.

Normal Personality: The 16PF

Cattell's best-known and most widely used test is the 16 Personality Factor Questionnaire (16PF). "PF" stands for "personality factors," a term used prominently in his theory to refer to important traits. This test will be described more fully later in this chapter.

Clinical Scales

The 16PF is often used in clinical populations as well as with normal subjects. In addition, several tests have been specifically devised for clinical use, including the Neuroticism Scale Questionnaire, the Clinical Analysis Questionnaire, and the Marriage Counseling Report.

Intelligence Tests

Cattell developed various kinds of intelligence tests. The Culture-Fair Intelligence Test is intended to measure a person's innate capacity to learn. (In contrast, most intelligence tests are influenced by education.) He also developed a Comprehensive Ability Battery containing performance tests relevant for vocational placement.

Emotions

Cattell studied moods with his Eight State Questionnaire. Some of his other tests measure anxiety and depression.

These are only a sampling of the many tests devised and validated by Cattell. The catalogue of his Institute for Personality and Ability Testing (IPAT) contains many others and is an impressive testament to the practical applications of Cattell's work in clinical, vocational, educational, and research settings. Cattell's contribution to personality measurement is unmatched by any of the other theorists described in this book.

We can think of Cattell as a man who, through his research, gave us a new set of instruments to replace inadequate ones. One old technique he discarded was the *interview,* which he described as "an anachronism in psychology, for the preservation of which, *as an assessment device,* there are many excuses but few justifications" (1957, p. 761). Science is fostered by new tools, new measurement devices. For example, studying cells is improved by a higher-power microscope, and studying astronomy is fostered by a better telescope. In the same way, understanding personality is greatly enhanced by improved measurement.

Three Sources of Data: Q-Data, T-Data, and L-Data

Cattell obtained data from three major types of observations.

Q-Data

Questionnaire data, which Cattell called **Q-data**, consist of responses to pencil and paper self-report tests. His 16PF test, like any multiple-choice personality test, is an example.

T-Data

A second type of data is **T-data** or objective test data. Unlike questionnaire data, T-data involve a measuring instrument that is indirect; the purpose of the test is hidden. This type of test can't be faked because the subject doesn't know how answers will be interpreted. Projective measures, such as inkblot tests, fall into this category. So do objective behavioral measures observed in the laboratory, such as finger tapping and reaction time, and physiological tests, such as blood pressure and urinalysis.

L-Data

A third type of data is objective information about the life history of the individual. Cattell called this **L-data** or Life Record Data. School records, grade point average, driving history, ratings by supervisors about job performance, letters of recommendation, records of books checked out of the library—all of these data can be obtained without necessarily requiring subjects to answer a questionnaire or respond to a test in a standard setting.

Cattell looked for patterns of personality that could be independently confirmed in the three types of data. For example, a person with low emotional stability has distinctive responses in all three kinds of data. In Q-data, low emotional stability is reflected in scores on Factor C of the 16PF, called "Ego Strength." In T-data, low emotional stability is associated with objective test Factor U.I.26, called "Self-Sentiment Control," which involves components such as verbal explicitness and performance skill. In L-data, low emotional stability is reflected in "low occupational stability, high automobile accident rate, and many clinical visits" (Cattell, 1957, p. 54). Confirmation across these three very different types of data increases certainty that meaningful personality traits are being measured.

Multivariate Approach: A Mathematical Model

Cattell pioneered **multivariate** research methods. This research strategy works with several variables at one time to predict behavior. Cattell recommended against the oversimplification of predicting from one variable at a time; for example, predicting how well a person will do in school knowing only the person's intelligence but nothing about motivation, educational background, health, and so forth. Life, of course, is multivariate. Any theorist will agree that people are affected by many things at one time, yet very few theories have taken this into account in a formal sense. Much personality research considers only one or two predictors at a time. Cattell, to his credit, developed a methodology for examining multiple determinants simultaneously.

Multivariate prediction would never have been possible before modern computers because of the many computations involved in this type of prediction. With computers to do the tedious computations, it is possible to specify formally, in a *mathematical model,* the ways that many variables are related to one another. The theory can be tested for internal consistency and for its fit to data observed (Cattell, 1979). Before such mathematical sophistication was possible, only intuition and human judgment (including clinical insight) could process multiple sources of information.

Cattell's multivariate strategy requires immense amounts of data to be collected from each subject. In a study of objective test data, for example, he required 5 to 10 hours of testing per subject (1979, p. 97)!

Factor Analysis

Factor analysis is a statistical procedure that is based upon the concept of *correlation.* A **correlation coefficient** measures the relationship between two sets of numbers. There is a *positive correlation* if high numbers in one set are associated with high numbers in the other set, while low numbers in each set are associated with each other. If low numbers in one set go with high numbers in the other there is a *negative correlation* (see Figure 8.1).

A correlation coefficient may range from −1 to +1, indicating the direction and strength of the association between two variables. Several correlation coefficients are computed during the course of a factor analysis. The correlations among all pairs of variables are computed; these form a **correlation matrix**. Patterns of correlations often disclose redundant information, which may be systematically described. Factor analysis then provides a way of more simply describing large numbers of variables by identifying a smaller number of dimensions (factors), which avoids the need to repeat redundant information.

The procedure involves complicated mathematics, but the idea is simple. We do a similar sort of thinking, though less systematically, whenever we intuitively combine lots of detailed information about people into more general trait statements. For example, rather than saying "Dave is great at football, wonderful at tennis, and a great runner, but average in math, average in English, and mediocre in history," we would say "Dave is a great athlete and an average academic student." We have combined six pieces of information (variables) into two more general dimensions (factors).

Before Cattell, factor analysis was used to study intelligence. If you test people for various abilities, some scores are highly related. Tests of mathematical abilities are positively correlated, including geometry, algebra, spatial relations, and so forth. Tests of verbal abilities correlate highly together (for example, vocabulary, grammar, and spelling), but they have lower correlations with tests of mathematical abilities. Factor analysis of these variables reveals two factors, mathematical ability and verbal ability.

LIMITATIONS TO FACTOR ANALYSIS

Although factor analysis enables us to discover patterns of relationship not readily apparent without such a statistical examination, it has limitations. For one thing, an underlying dimension cannot be discovered unless it has been represented in the data. The computer simplifies existing data, but it does not fill in the gaps or read between the lines. If aspects of personality are not included in the measures that Cattell put into the computer, he could not find those factors. So we see that, empirical as this method is, if common sense or previous theory hasn't already suggested, at least roughly, the personality trait domain, there is a limit to what can be "discovered" by the computer analysis.

Methodological ambiguities exist in factor analysis. This may come as a surprise for students who have studied statistics at the beginning level only, and who feel that if one can only understand the symbols and the computational formulas, then there is only one right answer to a statistical problem. That is true for many basic statistics; if you have a set of data and a formula for

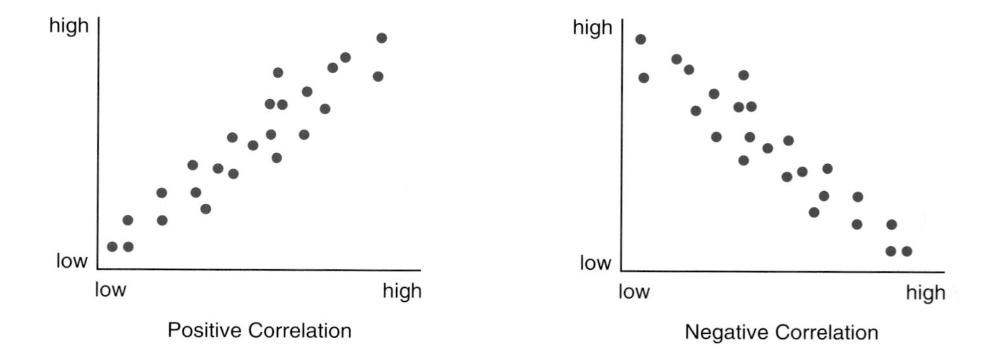

FIGURE 8.1 Scatterplots Illustrating Positive and Negative Correlations

a Pearson product-moment correlation coefficient, there is only one correlation coefficient that is correct. That is not true for factor analysis. From the same set of data many different factor analysis solutions are possible, depending upon what assumptions are made. For example, must the factors be uncorrelated ("orthogonal"), or are they allowed to be correlated with one another ("oblique")? If they are correlated (as Cattell permitted), how close can they be to each other to still be called separate factors? Another problem is how to make sense of the mathematical solution. The factors that emerge have to be interpreted, and this interpretation is reflected in how they are named.

Factor analysis combines variables in a linear equation, only adding or subtracting the effect of each variable. In principle, it would be possible to use other mathematical relationships, such as multiplying variables. (Recall that Allport suggested that "heredity" and "environment" should be multiplied.) These mathematical options would profoundly affect the results. The possibilities become extremely complex, and Cattell argued that researchers should work with the *linear model* until they reached its limits.

Factor analysis is not a magical procedure, nor is it automatic. Cattell claimed that many researchers compute factor analyses incorrectly, and so come up with misleading results (1957, p. 46). Still, it is a sophisticated mathematical tool for identifying patterns of related observations, and Cattell used this tool brilliantly to identify what he claimed were the fundamental personality traits of people.

Surface Traits and Source Traits

Cattell used factor analysis to describe the more or less readily apparent traits of people, which he called *surface traits*. He also looked deeper for hidden patterns, which he felt were the underlying determinants of personality, and which he called *source traits*.

Cattell acknowledged the truth of Allport's observation that traits are reflected in language. He believed there was merit to the Allport and Odbert (1936) study of trait names in the English-language dictionary. Allport recognized the redundancy in trait names and tried to cluster traits together on the basis of their similar meanings. Cattell's approach, substituting a computer search for correlations in place of human judgments, made it possible for him to find, empirically, underlying dimensions that a person, with perhaps a wrong implicit theory of personality, would overlook.

Surface Traits

The term "trait" roughly means patterns of observations that go together. If we make these observations systematically and represent them by numbers, then we may compute correlations, as discussed above. Sets of variables that are positively correlated are called "correlation clusters," or, to a clinician who makes these observations more intuitively, they would be called a "syndrome" (Cattell, 1957, pp. 14–15). Cattell called these patterns of intercorrelated variables **surface traits**. The term "surface" indicates that, though they appear "on the surface" to be a trait, there is no evidence that they are really a trait in any enduring sense. The pattern of correlations might not reappear under different situations—for example, in a different population, under different testing conditions, or at a different time.

Source Traits

Through many studies, Cattell identified some correlation clusters that are quite "robust," which reappear over and over again. They emerge despite differences in population, in testing situations, and so forth. Cattell argued that such a robust pattern must have only a single source of variance. It must correspond to one "cause" within personality, a fundamental trait of personality. He searched for such robust traits using factor analysis, and he called them **source traits**. In the technical language of factor analysis, Cattell described source traits as "uniquely rotated to simple structure" (1979, pp. 23–24).

Measurement of Source Traits

Cattell then went a step further and developed questionnaires to measure the source traits as directly as possible. He realized that many existing tests of personality were influenced by multiple factors. (That is, a surface trait may be affected by many source traits.) For example, one personality test might be influenced by self-esteem, achievement motivation, and warmth. Interpreting associations of such a test with behavior is ambiguous because it is multifactorial. The ideal personality test taps only one factor, one *source trait*, of personality.

The 16PF

Cattell's most well-known personality test, the **16PF**, has 16 subscales, each purely loaded on one underlying source trait of normal personality. The 16PF questionnaire represents the culmination of many factor-analytic studies. Factors found reliably in cross-validation studies with various groups of subjects are measured in a lengthy multiple-choice questionnaire. Scores are computed for each subject on the 16 personality factors, which are the fundamental source traits of personality (Cattell, Eber, & Tatsuoka, 1970).

Summary descriptions of each personality factor are contained in Table 8.1. Each factor is identified with a letter indicating the order in which it emerged from the factor analysis. Earlier letters (A, B, C, and so on) indicate factors that "explain more of the common variance," in statistical language. In everyday language, this means that they are the more important personality differences. Therefore, though there are 16 source traits in this inventory, the first half dozen or so are the most important in describing individual differences.

The set of scores on all factors is the **profile** of an individual. It can be diagrammed on a graph (see Figure 8.2). The researcher or clinician interprets the profile to make statements about the individual's personality. This interpretation can even be done by computer (Karson & O'Dell, 1975).

It is apparent, looking at the list of personality factors in Table 8.1, that some letters are missing (D, J, and K, for example). The factors corresponding to these letters did not replicate adequately in enough studies, so Cattell did not include them in this inventory. Factor D (excitability), however, is included in tests designed for younger people (The High School Personality Questionnaire and the Children's Personality Questionnaire), where this dimension is more salient than in adults (Cattell & Cattell, 1975; Cattell & Porter, 1975).

TABLE 8.1 Cattell's 16 Personality Factors (16PF)

	Factor	*Description*
A	AFFECTIA (high score)	outgoing, warm, sociable
	SIZIA (low score)	detached, cool, aloof
B	INTELLIGENCE (high score)	high general intellectual ability
	low INTELLIGENCE	low general intellectual ability
C	EGO STRENGTH (high score)	emotionally stable
	low EGO STRENGTH	emotionally unstable
E	DOMINANCE (high score)	assertive, competitive
	SUBMISSIVENESS (low score)	humble, accommodating
F	SURGENCY (high score)	enthusiastic, practical joker
	DESURGENCY (low score)	serious, quiet
G	SUPEREGO STRENGTH (high score)	conscientious, moral
	low SUPEREGO STRENGTH	expedient, law-breaking
H	PARMIA (high score)	shy, timid, easily threatened
	THRECTIA (low score)	bold, adventurous
I	PREMSIA (high score)	sensitive, tender-minded
	HARRIA (low score)	self-reliant, tough, realistic
L	PROTENSION (high score)	suspicious, paranoid
	ALAXIA (low score)	trusting
M	AUTIA (high score)	imaginative, absent-minded
	PRAXERNIA (low score)	practical, conventional
N	SHREWDNESS (high score)	socially aware, astute
	ARTLESS (low score)	forthright, socially clumsy, naive
O	GUILT PRONENESS (high score)	apprehensive, self-reproaching
	UNTROUBLED ADEQUACY (low score)	self-assured, secure
Q_1	RADICALISM (high score)	liberal, free-thinking
	CONSERVATISM (low score)	conservative, traditional
Q_2	SELF-SUFFICIENCY (high score)	resourceful, self-reliant
	GROUP ADHERENCE (low score)	follower, dependent on group
Q_3	SELF-SENTIMENT INTEGRATION (high score)	controlled, compulsive
	low SELF-SENTIMENT	impulsive
Q_4	ERGIC TENSION (high score)	tense, frustrated, driven
	low ERGIC TENSION	relaxed

Factor I, *Harria-Premsia,* illustrates the arbitrariness of naming factors in factor analysis. The high factor score, *Premsia,* is derived from the phrase "*pr*otected *em*otional *s*ensitivity," Cattell's phrase for the sense he made out of the patterns of answers that contributed to this score. Cattell made up new words for factors (e.g., "Schizothymia," "Sizia," "Parmia," and "Threctia") when he felt that they were sufficiently different from existing psychological concepts so that the old terms would be misleading.

Cattell's research has found that this tender-minded sensitive characteristic, Premsia, is related to attitude measurements, specifically opposition to capital punishment and compulsory vaccination. Cattell described the principle of this connection between source traits and specific attitudes more formally in his concept of *subsidiation,* which will be explained later.

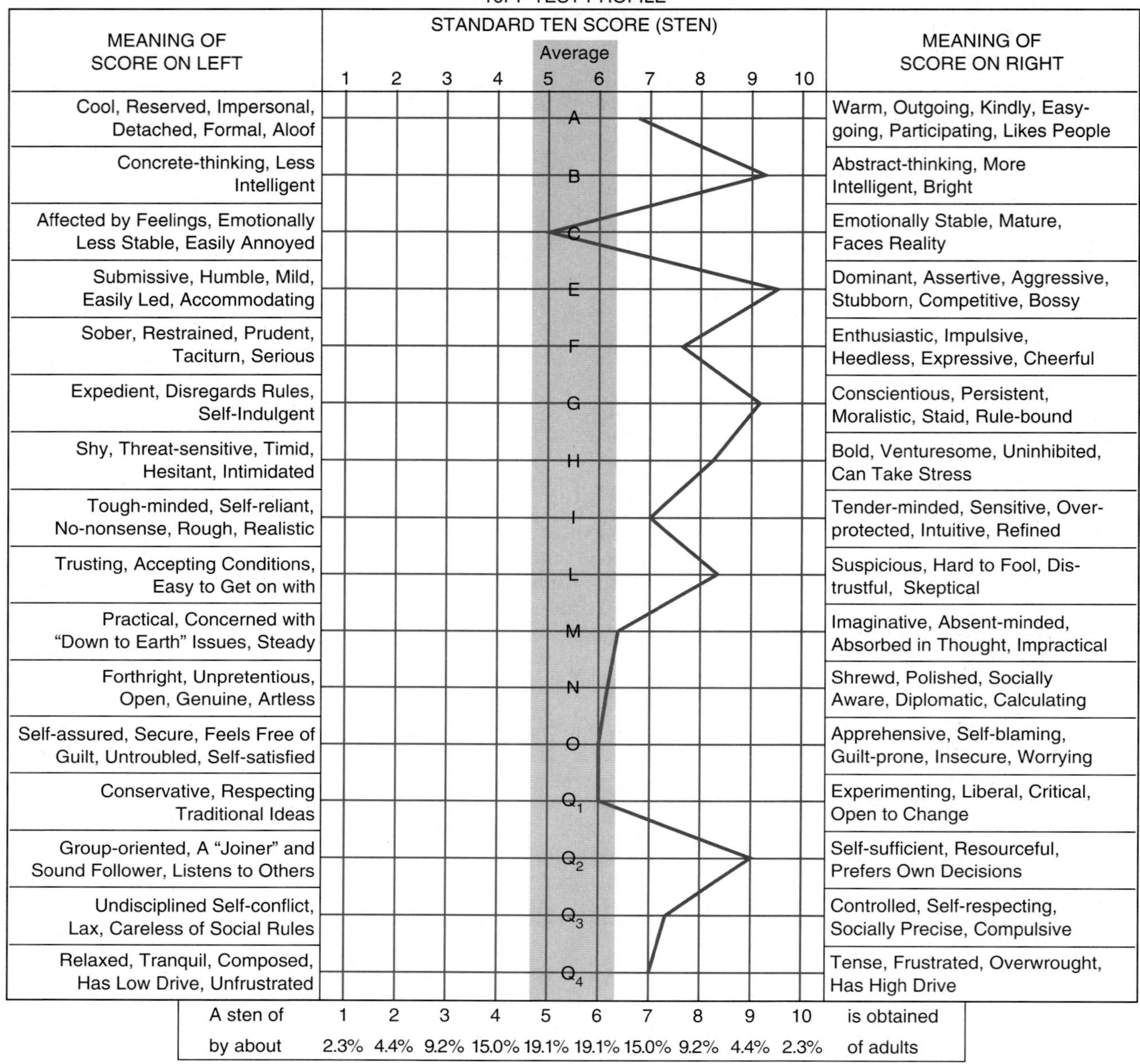

FIGURE 8.2 Profile Indicating Scores on Cattell's 16PF

These scores depict the personality of Martin Luther, as interpreted by W.J. Wright (1985, p. 20). The profile form is from the Institute for Personality and Ability Testing, Inc. (IPAT). (Reproduced by permission. Copyright © 1956, 1973, 1982 by the Institute for Personality and Ability Testing, Inc., P.O. Box 188, Champaign, Illinois, U.S.A. 61820. All rights reserved. Printed in U.S.A.)

Research indicates that occupational groups vary in their typical scores on the 16 personality factors. For example, Olympic champions score high on Factor E; they are dominant, confident, boastful, aggressive, and forceful. High scores on Factor A, indicating the outgoing, warmhearted characteristics that Cattell called "Affectia," are typical of salespersons, social workers, successful psychotherapists, teachers, sociopaths, and females. Low factor scores, which characterize reserved, detached, critical, and aloof people (called "Sizia" by Cattell), are characteristic of scientists, writers, electricians, engineers, attempted suicides, paranoids, and males.

There are sex differences on several factors (see Figure 8.3). Females are more tender-minded (Factor I) than males. Females are more submissive, while males are more dominant (Factor E). Females are more conservative, and males more radical (Factor Q_1). Males are more practical and down-to-earth (Factor M) and more secure and self-assured (Factor O), whereas females are more prone to feel guilty (Factor O). Males have weaker superegos, and females stronger superegos (Factor G). (That finding is, incidentally, just the opposite of what Freud said. Perhaps what Freud meant by superego was not the same as what Cattell meant.)

Second-Order Factor Analysis

The 16 personality factors are not totally independent of one another. That is, there are correlations among the factors. It is possible to reduce further the number of factors, therefore, by factor-analyzing scores on the 16 personality factors themselves. This is a **second-order factor analysis**, since the data analyzed are themselves factor scores. Fewer fundamental dimensions, *second-order factors* (or, to use the terminology Cattell preferred, *second-stratum factors*), result from this second-order factor analysis, since it involves even more simplification of the data. It is also possible to factor-analyze the secondaries into "tertiaries," but these results are too abstract to report here, and they are less useful for personality measurement than are the primary factors.

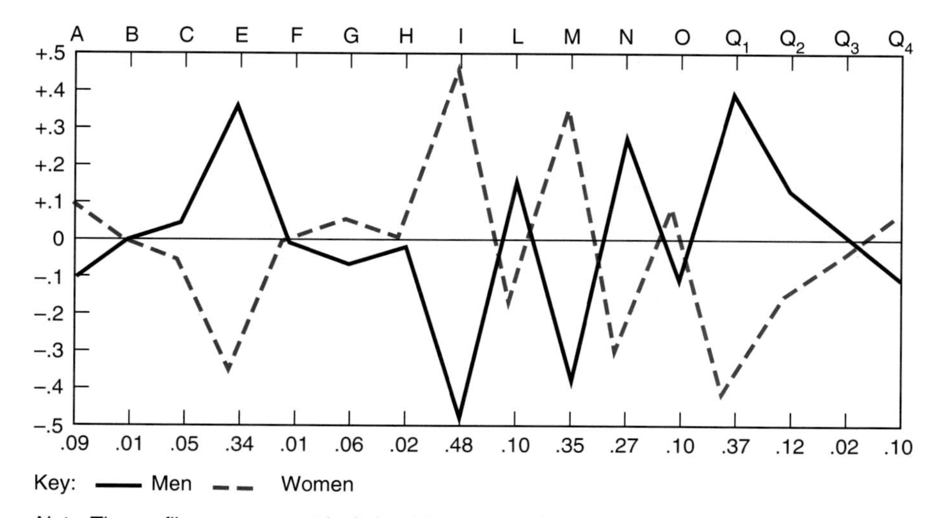

Note: The profiles are symmetrical about the average because men and women jointly *make* the average.

FIGURE 8.3 Sex Differences on Cattell's 16PF
(From Cattell, 1965, p. 260.)

Most research agrees upon five second-order factors: Exvia-Invia (commonly called "extroversion-introversion"), Anxiety, Corteria, Independence, and Discreteness (Cattell, 1978, p. 548; Reuter, Schuerger, & Wallbrown, 1985), even in a foreign population (Argentero, 1989). The results of the second-order factor analysis include two particularly interesting dimensions of personality, Exvia-Invia (extroversion) and Anxiety.

EXVIA-INVIA

Commonly called *extroversion,* this second-order factor is characterized by high loadings on Factor A (Affectia, or liking for people), Factor F (Surgency, or talkativeness and optimism), and Factor H (Parmia, or adventurous boldness). Extroversion scores are increased if subjects are told to answer the questionnaire with a "good personality," whatever that is.

Cattell (1957) suggested that there is a genetic basis for this factor. Specifically, people who inherit a tendency to react more strongly to ideas than to external stimuli tend to develop into introverts. It is as though introverts march to a different (i.e., internal) drummer, compared to extroverts, who respond more to stimuli in the external world.

This second-order factor in questionnaire data corresponds to a similar *first-*order factor in objective test data. Cattell noted that first-order factors in T-data tend to correspond to second-order factors in Q-data and L-data (e.g., 1979, pp. 116–117). His objective tests may tap more directly into underlying causes, getting around the situational and verbal influences that affect L-data and Q-data.

A quick measurement of extroversion-introversion can be made with the 40-item Contact Personality Factor (CPF) Test, in about five minutes (Cattell, 1957, pp. 771–772).

ANXIETY

The second-order factor of *anxiety* loads most strongly on Factor C (ego weakness), Factor O (guilt proneness), Factor L (paranoid tendency), Factor Q_3 (low self-sentiment), and Factor Q_4 (high drive tension) (Cattell, 1965, p. 118). Cattell devised a 40-item test to measure anxiety alone, the IPAT Anxiety Scale, which is available in both a children's and adult version (Cattell, 1965, p. 119).

It is tempting to focus on second-order factors, since there are fewer of them, and, therefore, it seems easier to comprehend Cattell's research at this level. But Cattell cautioned against the error of "thinking that higher-strata factors are higher in importance" (Cattell, 1978, p. 225). In fact, they predict behavior less well than do the primary factors. They are, however, theoretically suggestive. For example, second-order factors may indicate biological or cultural influences, which affect many diverse primary factors.

Neurosis and Psychosis

Neurosis

Neurotics differ from the general population on several traits. Neurotic persons have low Ego Strength, low Emotional Stability, high Autia and Premsia, low Surgency, and low Dominance. Of particular interest are the "controlling triumvirate" of personality, three factors involved in impulse control and emotional adjustment: Factors C (Ego Strength), G (Superego Strength), and Q_3 (Self-Sentiment Integration). Anxiety, too, is high among neurotics. Partly this is because of the way their families treat them. Their families are marked by conflict. Discipline is inconsistent; sometimes the child gets away with something and sometimes not. There is not enough affection and love, and parents may demand living up to standards that are set too high for the child at that stage of development. Heredity, however, also plays a significant role in the development of personality characteristics related to neurosis, as Cattell's research (described later in this chapter) reveals.

Psychosis

There are several different types of psychoses, although clinicians do not always agree on the diagnosis of a particular individual. In his tests, Cattell found different patterns of traits for various diagnoses. Schizophrenics have low ego strength, low drive tension, and high introversion. Manic-depressives have low intelligence (unlike schizophrenics, whose intelligence is as high as normals), conservative temperament, and high superego (that is, an inclination to feel guilty).

Cattell developed clinical scales similar to the 16PF, but focusing specifically on measuring differences among diagnostic groups. He was highly critical of clinicians for not supplementing their unreliable clinical diagnoses with empirically validated scales. Increased use of such testing could improve the reliability of diagnosis (Cattell, 1979, p. 110). This would contribute not only to the treatment of individual patients but also to research on the origins of mental illness. Cattell even offered a computer program for diagnosis (1979, p. 14).

Psychosis, like neurosis, also has a significant genetic component. Both manic-depressive psychosis and schizophrenia are highly inheritable. Family background varies too; families of manic-depressives are warmer and more overprotective than are families of schizophrenics.

Although both psychosis and neurosis are influenced by heredity, it is not the only factor influencing the diseases. It would be truer to Cattell's meaning to say that we inherit predispositions, such as a tendency toward anxiety or toward calmness, that influence the likelihood that we will develop neurotic or psychotic conflict. Cattell accepted the notion that neurosis and psychosis are due to unresolved conflict within the person. Heredity gives a predisposition to emotionality, which makes it more likely that the vulnerable person will not be able to resolve the conflict. What is inherited is a predisposition, rather than a disease.

Three Types of Traits

It is customary in personality theory to distinguish various types of traits, including dynamic traits (motives), temperament, and ability. Cattell adopted these concepts as well.

Ability Traits

Ability traits define various types of intelligence. Ability traits determine how effectively a person works toward a desired goal. In Cattell's 16PF, the second factor, Factor B, is intelligence, but intelligence is better measured through specific tests designed for that purpose.

Cattell was concerned that existing intelligence tests did not measure simply a person's innate ability to learn, but also included effects of experience. Most intelligence tests are biased in favor of those with a good education, so that a person who is innately brilliant but not well educated does not do well on such tests.

Cattell distinguished two types of intelligence. One, which he called **fluid intelligence**, is the innate ability to learn. It is "fluid" because it can be expressed in different kinds of learning, depending on the educational opportunities of an individual. In contrast, **crystallized intelligence** is simply the effects of education: what has been learned. Cattell set out to measure fluid intelligence without the confounding effects of education (Boyle, 1988; Carroll, 1984; Cattell, 1971). Not everyone agrees, however, that these two components correspond to the effects of heredity and environment (Horn, 1984).

Culture Fair Intelligence Test

In keeping with his aim to devise new and purer tests, Cattell devised the **Culture Fair Intelligence Test** to measure only fluid intelligence. It provides a better assessment of the intelligence of people who may be educationally deprived, for example, the poor.

Heredity and Intelligence

Cattell concluded that about 80 percent of the variation in people's intelligence is determined by heredity (in other words, is "fluid") and only 20 percent by experience (in other words, is "crystallized"). Based on his belief that intelligence was largely hereditary, he supported the eugenics movement, fearing that there would be a general decline in the intelligence of the British population because of the greater birth rate of less intelligent people (Cattell, 1937; Horn, 1984). This controversial position unfortunately was consistent with Nazi beliefs in the superiority of Aryan races (Horn, 1984). Subsequent research evidence has not supported his ideas (Loehlin, 1984); intelligence among British children was found to be rising, rather than falling, although evidence is inconsistent about whether this change is due to an increase in crystallized intelligence (Cattell, 1957, p. 623) or fluid intelligence (Lynn, Hampson, & Mullineux, 1987). Historical and cultural factors, in addition to genetics, influence measured intelligence.

Research on the inheritance of intelligence has been criticized because the percentage of any characteristic attributable to heredity or environment can vary drastically, depending upon the sample being studied. In a sample of subjects who all have had similar educational opportunities, the variation from one person to another is primarily due to genetics, because in fact there hasn't been very much environmental variation. Thus mandatory schooling produces a decrease in the apparent environmental component of intelligence. On the other hand, if environments vary drastically, the calculated percent of environmental variation is increased. Hence, critics argue that it is impossible to make any general statements about what percent of variation is due to heredity and what to environment. Those percentages apply only to a particular sample and do not reflect the potential of intelligence to be raised by an even richer environment than is experienced by the sample.

AGE CHANGES IN INTELLIGENCE

Fluid intelligence usually rises to about age 15 or 16 and then levels off or decreases slightly thereafter. Crystallized intelligence increases longer, up to age 25 or 30, during the time that people are still attending school.

Temperament Traits

Temperament traits are largely constitutional (inherited) source traits that determine the "general style and tempo with which [a person] carries out whatever he [or she] does" (Cattell, 1965, p. 165). Cattell gave as examples "high-strungness, speed, energy, and emotional reactivity" (1950, p. 35).

Dynamic Traits

Dynamic traits are motivational; they are traits that provide the energy and direction to action. Like many other theorists, Cattell recognized that some motivations were innate, while others were learned. He called these types of dynamic trait *ergs* and *metaergs.*

ERGS

Cattell accepted the concept from many previous psychologists that people have some innate motivational traits, or, in his language, *constitutional dynamic source traits.* He called these **ergs**. (The term comes from a Greek word meaning "energy.") They are comparable to animal instincts and involve "an innate reactivity toward a goal, though stimuli and means are learned" (Cattell, 1957, p. 893).

Cattell listed several human ergs. Each is associated with a particular goal, which Cattell identified to explain the particular erg or motivation (Cattell, 1979, p. 143). (See Table 8.2.)

Individual differences occur in various ways. For one thing, the level of an ergic trait may vary in different individuals because of genetics. Even Freud speculated that some people have a stronger libido than others. In ad-

TABLE 8.2 Human Ergs

Erg	*Goal*
Anger	pugnacity
Curiosity	exploration
Fear	escape to security
Greed	acquisitiveness
Hunger	food-seeking
Loneliness	gregariousness
Pity	parental
Pride	self-assertion
Sensuousness	narcissistic sex
Sex	mating

(Adapted from *Personality and Learning Theory,* Vol. 1, by R.B. Cattell. Copyright 1979 by Springer Publishing Company, Inc., New York 10012. Used by permission.)

dition, the ways in which ergs are channeled into complex behaviors vary widely from person to person. For example, one person seeks security through brute force, another through financial planning.

METAERGS

Ergs, with their energy, are channeled into learned patterns, called **metaergs**. Metaergs are *environmental-mold dynamic source traits.* These learned motivations can range from the very general, like *love of country* and *valuing education,* to the very specific, such as *opposition to a particular political candidate.* Cattell called the more general metaergs *sentiments.* He referred to the more specific responses to particular stimulus situations as *attitudes.*

Sentiments. Sentiments are deep underlying dynamic structures in personality that are formed early and are generally enduring. They include sentiments toward home, family, and religion, among others (see Table 8.3).

The most important sentiment is the *self-sentiment,* which Cattell referred to as a **master motive**. Self-sentiment integrates the various sentiments, attitudes, and interests of the person. (Here, Cattell, the methodologist, made a statement corresponding to Allport's description of the integrating function of the proprium.) Research showing greater attention to self-relevant information (e.g., M.W. Warren, Hughes, & Tobias, 1985) seems to confirm the centrality of the self-sentiment.

Attitudes. Attitudes are the more specific expressions of sentiments. Cattell defined an attitude as "an interest in a course of action, in a given situation" (1965, p. 175). An example would be "liking to spend Thanksgiving with the family." Because attitudes are so specific, no broad list is feasible. As we shall see below, the concept is important in considering how broader dimensions of personality—the sentiments and ergs—are actually expressed.

TABLE 8.3 Human Sentiments

alcohol	pets
business, economic	philosophical, historical
clerical interests	home decoration
clothes, self-adornment	profession
education, school attachment	religion
esthetic expressions	scientific interests
esthetic, literary appreciation	sedentary, social games
hobbies (other)	self-sentiment
household-cooking	sports and fitness
mechanical interests	superego
news, communication	theoretical, logical
outdoor, manual	travel, geography
parental family, home	wife, sweetheart
patriotic, political	

(Adapted from *Personality and Learning Theory,* Vol. 1, by R.B. Cattell. Copyright 1979 by Springer Publishing Company, Inc., New York 10012. Used by permission.)

Ergs and metaergs are dynamic traits, that is, motivational traits. They help people select goals; they afford them the energy to pursue goals. They stimulate emotional responses to certain objects: hope, fear, expectation, and so forth. These motivational traits also cause people to perceive selective opportunities for satisfying goals. When the hunger erg is aroused, one notices restaurants on a street where one may never have noticed them before, and even a rock seems like a pillow if one is tired enough.

Subsidiation

Through a process of learning, basic drives (ergs) are satisfied by multistep sequences of purposive activities. The environment demands this kind of learning. Instrumental acts must be completed before basic goals can be met. Cattell noted, as an example, that we must work in order to eat (Cattell, 1950, p. 156). Working serves (or, to use Cattell's jargon, is "subsidiary to") the motivation to eat. In general, metaergs are subsidiary to ergs. Attitudes are subsidiary to sentiments, because attitudes are more particular, more remote from the basic ergic motives. The instrumental goals along the way may be called "subsidiary goals" or "means-end activities" (Cattell, 1950, p. 156).

This idea, that the fundamental motivations are constitutional, and that learning channels them into specific forms of expression, is found in many personality theories. Freud, of course, made this assumption in his assertion that all energy flows from the id, and that the ego channels this energy. Murray named the concept **subsidiation**, and it was from Murray that Cattell borrowed the idea. Even learning theory makes such assumptions with the concept of primary reinforcement. Hence the concept of subsidiation, though not always so named, is an idea that crosses theoretical boundaries.

The Dynamic Lattice

Cattell diagrammed these subsidiation relationships in the **dynamic lattice** (see Figure 8.4). Attitudes (on the left) are subsidiary to sentiments (in the middle), which are subsidiary to ergs (on the right). The channels show the connections among these dynamic (motivational) levels. Cattell explained how to interpret this diagram:

> The man's attitude . . . to his bank account has the direction that he wants to increase it. The lines of subsidiation . . . indicate that he wants to do so in order to protect his wife . . . , to satisfy self-assertion . . . , to assuage his fear of insecurity . . . , and to satisfy hunger. . . . This attitude or sentiment to his bank account is served by an attitude of annoyance toward higher taxation . . . , by an intention to keep company with his business friend . . . , and by an attitude of avoidance to New York, where he spends too much money. . . . (Cattell, 1950, p. 188)

Metaergs (attitudes and sentiments) are learned. Their connections with each other and with the ergs are affected by learning. Sentiments may be connected to many ergs and through development these connections change. Ergs are seldom satisfied directly. Rather, they are satisfied indirectly, through metaergs. This indirect satisfaction of ergs is called *long-*

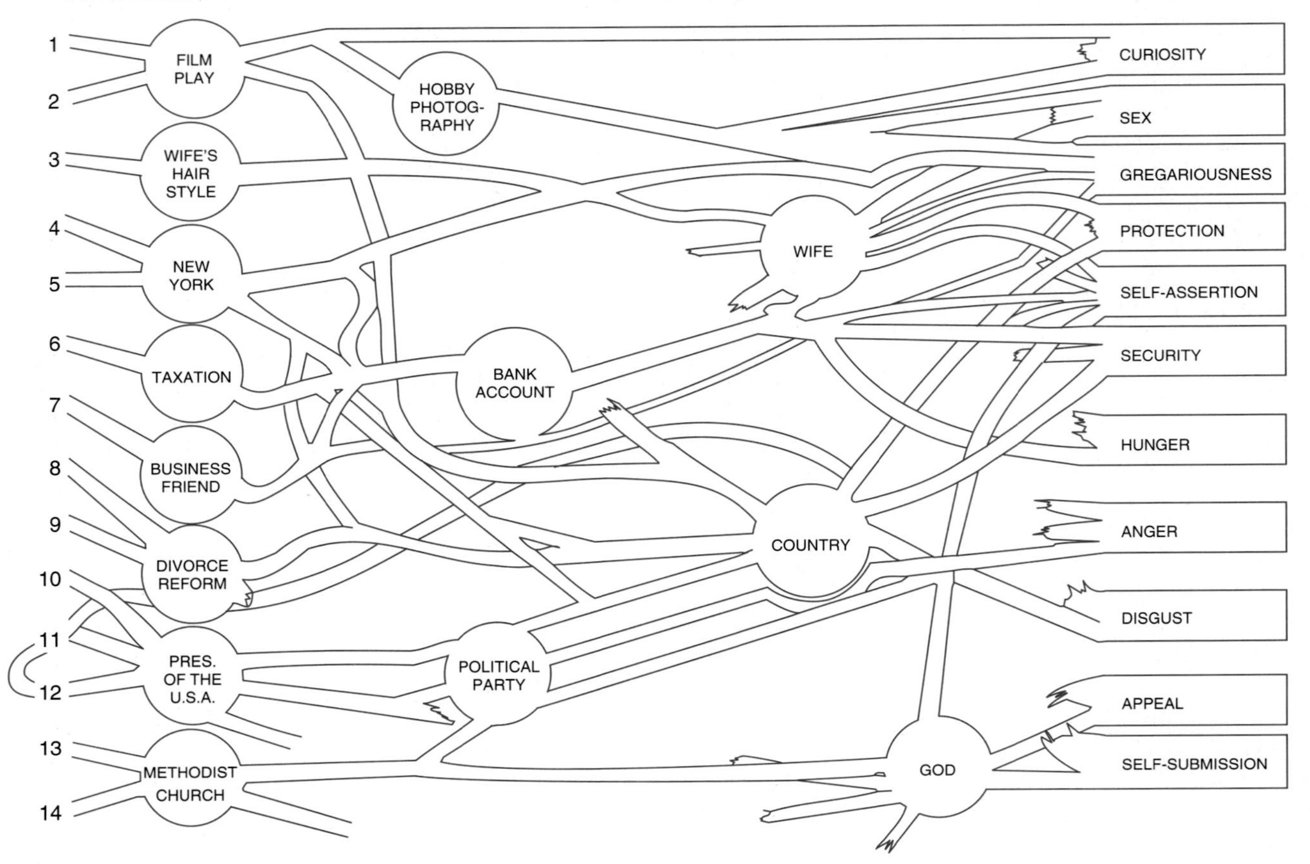

FIGURE 8.4 The Dynamic Lattice
(From Cattell, 1964, p. 187.)

circuiting. (In contrast, artificial stimulation of the pleasure centers of the brain through electrical stimulation in the laboratory, or drug use on the street, could be thought of as "short-circuiting.")

Certain types of learning involve reorganization or coordination of various traits. We may learn certain behaviors that can satisfy many motivations (many metaergs and ergs) at the same time. This is called **confluence learning**. For example, learning to ski might satisfy various social and physical motivations.

Predicting Behavior

Recall that Cattell defined personality as that which permits the prediction of behavior. Let us examine his model for making predictions.

The Specification Equation

Various traits are combined in a predictive mathematical equation, called the **specification equation**. In principle, all behavior can be predicted from such equations. The specific terms, of course, would vary from person to person, from time to time, and from situation to situation.

Source traits are entered into the predictive equation if they are relevant for predicting the particular behavior. These may include ability traits, temperament traits, ergic tensions, and metaergs (sentiments and attitudes). Situational and temporary factors may also be added to the equation if they help predict the particular behavior. *Situational factors* include factors such as the roles called for in the situation. *Temporary factors* include states such as fatigue and anxiety. The full specification equation is:

$$P_{ij} = S_{1j}T_{1i} + S_{2j}T_{2i} + \ldots + S_{Nj}T_{Ni} + S_jT_{ji}$$

The behavior being predicted, the performance of the individual i in situation j, is referred to as P_{ij}. For example, if a person is running a race, P might represent the time to run the course. It is assumed that the performance to be predicted can be expressed mathematically on some continuous scale.

Each predictive trait is referred to as a T in the specification equation. Subscripts identify the particular trait and the particular individual. Thus "T_{2i}" refers to the second trait, and the ith individual. Individual differences in the strength of each trait are reflected in different T's for each person.

The letter S refers to a *situational index*, that is, the extent to which the trait T is relevant in predicting the performance P in this situation. These situational indices are the same in the equation for each person whose behavior is being predicted.

Consider a simple example: trying to predict how fast a person runs a race, based on knowledge of the person's athletic ability and motivation. As there are only two predictive traits, we could use a short specification equation:

$$P_{ij} = S_{1j}T_{1i} + S_{2j}T_{2i}$$

In this case, P_{ij} is the running speed of the ith individual in this situation (j). T_{1i} is the first trait, athletic ability. It is weighted by its situational index, S_{1j}, which would be the same constant for each subject. To indicate that it is quite important as a predictor, let us say that S_{1j} equals 0.8 (on a scale that has 1 as a maximum). The second predictive trait, T_{2i}, is the motivation of each subject, i. It is weighted by its situational index, S_{2j}. It is less important than athletic ability as a predictor, so let us say it is 0.2. To predict running speed, then, we would multiply a person's athletic ability by 0.8 and add that to the person's motivation multiplied by 0.2.

Ability and motivation are not equal contributors to running speed. The near Olympian running with moderate effort is going to beat the klutz, however motivated. An average runner would have to be very, very motivated to surpass a veteran runner; or the veteran runner would have to be very unmotivated. The more important predictor (ability) gets a higher situational index (0.8) than the less important predictor (motivation, 0.2).

Research determines which predictors are necessary and what is the appropriate weight of each predictor. This is the sort of prediction that colleges sometimes employ to predict the potential success of each applicant using high school grades, SAT scores, letters of recommendation, and so forth. Cattell simply extended the concept of prediction to many more nonacademic behaviors.

To summarize, the outcome we are trying to predict, the *P* or performance in the situation, is the sum of several terms, each of which is a trait or characteristic of the person, weighted by its appropriate situational index reflecting how relevant that trait is to predict the performance. Each situation, of course, would require a different equation, with an appropriate selection of traits and weights (situational indices) to predict that performance. It is a theoretician's delight, but a practical impossibility, to predict all behavior. In some applications, however, clinicians and occupational psychologists have particular specification equations for diagnosis and selection (Cattell, 1990b).

Nomothetic and Idiographic Approaches: R-Technique and P-Technique

Most of Cattell's research involved the nomothetic method or, to use Cattell's terminology, the *R-technique.* In this R-technique, many subjects are analyzed together; their scores are compared with one another.

Cattell also demonstrated that factor analysis can be adapted to the intensive investigation of a single subject. Thus, in theory, it can discover unique individual traits. This variation of factor analysis, called *P-technique*, analyzes scores taken from a single person, comparing scores across time. (Allport was skeptical that Cattell's approach corresponded to his own concept of unique traits.)

This type of research requires multiple measurements on the same individual across time (rather than on hundreds of individuals). It involved so much time in data collection that, at the outset, researchers could only get their spouses to serve as subjects. Cattell's wife, Karen, served as his subject in the first P-technique experiment, published in 1947 (Cattell, 1984, p. 141). The in-house joke was that only married students could study the single subject!

Cattell reported one case of the P-technique in some detail (see Figure 8.5). Each line reflects a particular trait as it rises and falls each day. This case illustrates the general principle that "ergic tension levels do alter considerably with time and circumstances" (Cattell, 1979, p. 159).

For the most part, Cattell reported that the same factors emerge in both P-technique and R-technique, though there is some individual variation. Thus it seems that common traits have broad explanatory value. Unique traits can be discovered through the P-technique. Cattell suggested one promising application of the P-technique: the investigation of psychosomatic conditions in individuals (1957, p. 643).

Changes with Age

Although Cattell's work was not primarily developmental, it has implications for developmental psychology (Nesselroade, 1984). Cattell investigated age changes in personality using both longitudinal and cross-sectional research designs. **Longitudinal research** examines a group of people at several different times in their lives, whereas **cross-sectional research** studies subjects only once, but compares subjects of various ages.

Cattell confirmed that adolescence is a difficult period. He found a decrease in superego during ages 9 to 15, an increase in guilt and "undis-

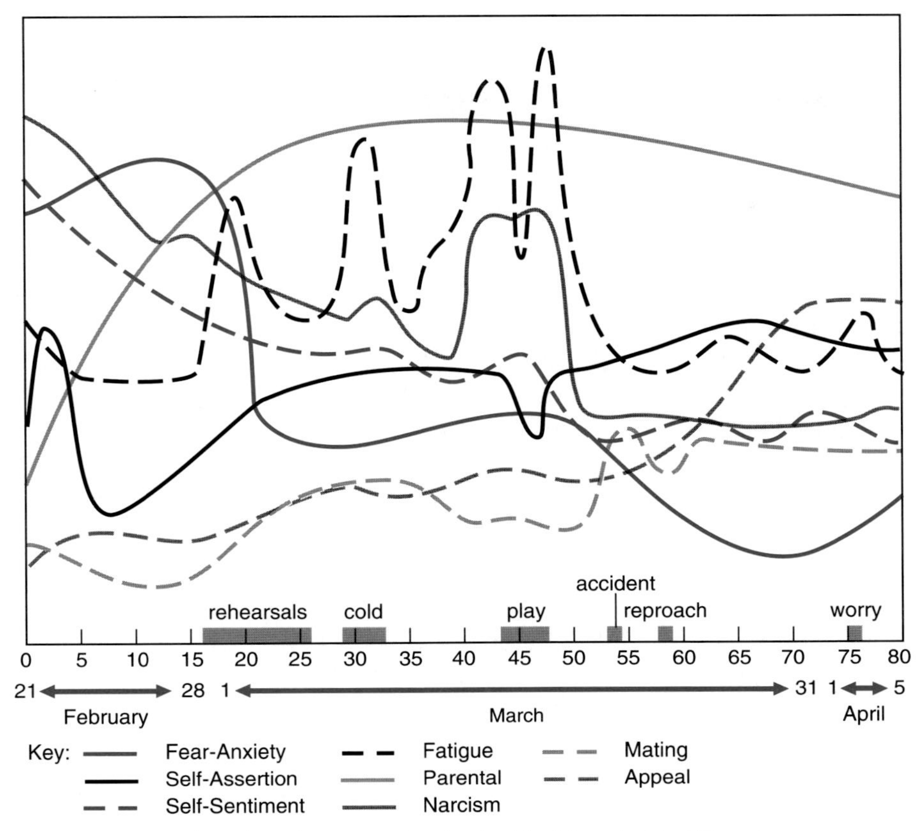

Ergic tension (and sentiment) response to stimulus (S), internal state (P), and goal satisfaction (G).

FIGURE 8.5 Illustration of P-Technique
(From Cattell, 1965, p. 229.)

charged drive tension" (an increase in sexuality), and an effort to get economic and social recognition. Emotionality increases in the early twenties, usually because a person is making major adjustments in marriage, in social tasks, and in occupational endeavors. The emotionality of housewives increases as they approach middle age, with the transitions that come with the "empty nest" syndrome. Another peak of emotionality occurs at age 60 and up for both sexes, reflecting the anxieties of the decade of retirement.

These various changes throughout life make it clear that personality can, and does, change across the life span. Still, there is much stability in personality over a 20-year period, with retest reliabilities about .70 (Cattell, 1957, pp. 626–631).

Syntality

People are, of course, influenced by the groups to which they belong. Cattell studied group differences. To parallel the individual differences described by the term "personality," Cattell offered a term to describe group differences: **syntality**. He described statistical procedures for grouping nations into those that are similar to one another (Cattell & Brennan, 1984).

Cattell reported that Americans are more extroverted, more emotionally sensitive, more radical, and have a higher superego, compared with the British. The British have higher ego strength, less anxiety, and are more conservative than the Americans. These data are based upon undergraduate samples (Cattell & Warburton, 1961).

Cattell also studied differences in emotionality among nations. He reported that Americans are less emotional or, as any world traveler will tell you, more "laid back" than many other nationalities. Empirically, on his measures, Americans have an anxiety score of only 7.1 on the average, compared to others; Italians average 13.5, and Indians, 15.1. Emotionality scores for French and Asiatics are about twice as high, and British, Japanese, and Italians are between French and Americans (Cattell, 1965). People in countries that are on the border between capitalism and communism have higher emotionality scores. Obviously these are not genetic contributions, but are "environmental-mold traits," affected by the social pressures where people live.

Other researchers, too, have reported differences in personality characteristics among nations. For example, Canadians are more extroverted and neurotic than are British and American subjects (Skinner & Peters, 1984). Differences such as these make it clear that we must be cautious when interpreting the personalities of individuals from other cultures. Unless we know what the "typical" personality of that culture is like, we are likely to try to make individual interpretations of traits that seem unusual, but which in fact may be quite typical for the other culture. To some extent, this caution also applies when we extend our ideas about the "normal" personality to other populations besides those we know well. To the extent that the white, middle-class, male personality is regarded as the norm by researchers, their understanding of the nonwhite, lower-class, and female population is likely to be erroneous.

Determinants of Personality: Heredity and Environment

Where do these traits, so useful for prediction, originate? Cattell distinguishes between **constitutional traits** and **environmental-mold** traits. Some traits originate in biological causes, especially genetics; these are constitutional traits. Others are the result of learning and social experience; these are environmental-mold traits.

Cattell investigated the nature–nurture question by using a statistical technique he developed, the **Multiple Abstract Variance Analysis**, or **MAVA** (Cattell, 1960). This technique analyzes the effects of heredity and environment based on data from relatives and nonrelatives. It examines the similarity of relatives (identical twins, fraternal twins, siblings, and unrelated children) raised together. As a control, this variation is compared with the variation occurring when relatives are raised apart, and with the variation in the general population. (The specific relatives studied vary from one research study to another.) From the data, "abstract variance" components are estimated: the variance due to heredity and the variance due to environment. To the extent that genetics determines a trait, relatives will be more similar than nonrelatives. (The MAVA is an extension of the more restricted twin method of studying heredity, which examines twins reared together and apart, but not other relatives.) Cattell obtained some of his early data for these analyses from Cyril Burt, known (and controversial) for his work on the genetics of intelligence (Cattell & Molteno, 1940).

On the basis of these studies, Cattell estimated the **heritability** *(H)* of various traits. Heritability is "the fraction of the total measured variance of the trait **X** in the population that is due to hereditary differences in individual makeup" (1973, p. 145). The highest heritability among the primary source traits in Q-data is for Intelligence, with *H* of about 0.75. Other factors with heritabilities of 0.50 or higher are Surgency (Factor F), Affectia (Factor A), Premsia-Harria (Factor I), and Protension (Factor L). (For a complete list of heritabilities, see Cattell, 1973, p. 147.)

Considering factors of particular interest to clinicians, Cattell reported a high level of heritability for aspects of personality related to neurosis: Factor C (ego strength) and, contrary to his earlier work, Factor Q_3 (self-sentiment strength). He found minor heritability for Factor G (superego strength) (Cattell & Schuerger, 1985; Cattell, Schuerger, & Klein, 1982). Objective tests, not based on self-report measures, confirm a hereditary pattern for anxiety and capacity to mobilize against regression (Cattell, Vaughan, Schuerger, & Rao, 1982). Because neurotic tendencies are generally regarded as learned ("environmental-mold"), Cattell's heritability findings are thought-provoking. He suggested that environmental influences, including therapy, can reduce anxiety and other indicators of difficulty (Cattell and others, 1966), but he recommended that people who are highly prone to anxiety because of their genetic endowment "should be treated with particular care in family and school situations" (Cattell, Vaughan, Schuerger, & Rao, 1982).

Research on introversion and extroversion also shows a strong genetic component. A tendency to be either outgoing and the life of the party, or quiet and withdrawn, is largely genetically determined. People who are "thin-skinned" inherit a tendency to be physiologically very reactive to stimuli. They tend, therefore, to seek less stimulating environments, and in this process they become introverts. On the other hand, people who inherit a tendency to not become aroused to stimuli may be thought of as "thick-skinned." Because they tolerate high levels of stimulation, they tend to become extroverted.

This is an important insight for people who may wish that they were different on introversion-extroversion. If we are limited by our genetics, then it simply isn't possible for a quiet person to become an extrovert. Such individuals can become more socially skilled, but they are not likely to become the life of the party.

Cattell was interested in heredity throughout his career, sometimes putting him at odds with the prevailing values of Americans, suspicious of the eugenics movement (e.g., Cattell, 1984, p. 137).

The Role of Theory in Cattell's Empirical Approach

Cattell has been accused of being "atheoretical": of doing empirical work blindly and predicting without a guiding theory. He disputed this (1979), saying that his mathematical models *are* theory. Critics argue that the models can cover any outcome, even random data, since the specific personality factors are not predicted in advance. Cattell asserted that this criticism was untrue, and could only be believed by people lacking adequate mathematical training. The mathematical details of Cattell's theory are so complex that most psychologists cannot fully understand them, and some suspect that apparent findings could be simply statistical artifacts.

Cattell aimed to be not simply a methodologist but also a psychologist who used statistical methodology to address substantive questions. He acknowledged the groundwork laid down by earlier, less systematic personality theories, and he used their ideas to interpret his factors. He urged students to have a background in personality theory, including Freudian and Jungian theory, before studying his own theory (1979, p. xxii). Cattell offered examples of the ways that his research revised and extended existing ideas in personality theory:

> the refinement of the Jungian notion of extroversion into exvia; the separation of anxiety, stress, and neuroticism; . . . and the confirmation and new preciseness of such clinical concepts as ego strength, superego strength, and ergic tension (undischarged "id"). (1979, p. 49)

He noted convergence of his results with the psychoanalytic concepts of the conscious and unconscious, although he felt the terms "integrated" and "unintegrated" were more accurate descriptions (Cattell, 1979, p. 137). Others have also noted the apparent convergence of factors derived from Cattell's measures with such psychoanalytic concepts as superego, ego strength, and anxiety (J.F. Campbell, 1988).

Though Cattell denied being atheoretical, he remarked, "I have always felt justifiably suspicious of theory built much ahead of data" (Cattell, 1984, p. 158). Wiggins (1984) pointed out that, for Cattell, theory was closely integrated with research and with assessment, which he (Wiggins) considered a desirable advance over many of the other theories. Cattell's metatheoretical assumptions, which emphasize holism, motivation, and functionalism, are close to the "mainstream theories," including Allport and Murray, according to Wiggins (1984).

Cattell's Work and Current Empirical Issues

Cattell's work triggered an enormous amount of research. He participated in the important controversies in personality research, and some of his earlier suggestions are still timely. He suggested that we need to do time-sampling in the personality sphere, rather than limiting our observations to brief and possibly unrepresentative samples of people's changing responses. He called for more descriptions of situations to be developed (a taxonomy of the environment), since situations combine with personality factors to predict behavior (Cattell, 1979, p. 273). Cattell was critical of some of the simplistic "personality versus situation" controversy (1979). His model had always included situational predictors and situational modulators, as well as personality traits.

Researchers debate how many traits are necessary to describe personality. Some contend that fewer than Cattell's 16 traits are sufficient

(Boyle, 1989; Eysenck & Eysenck, 1985; Matthews, 1989; J.M. Meyer, Heath, Eaves, Mosteller, & Schieken, 1988; Noller, Law, & Comrey, 1987). Currently there is much enthusiasm for a 5-factor model (e.g., Dachowski, 1987; Digman, 1989; McCrae & Costa, 1986, 1987), although others believe the enthusiasm is premature (e.g., Waller & Ben-Porath, 1987). Several studies have examined relationships among various sets of factors, hoping that they will converge (Costa & McCrae, 1988; Digman & Inouye, 1986; Noller, Law, & Comrey, 1987; Strack & Lorr, 1990; Trapnell & Wiggins, 1990; Zuckerman, Kuhlman, & Camac, 1988). Cattell defended his conclusion that no fewer than 16 traits will suffice; fewer would reduce prediction of behavior (Cattell, 1986; Cattell & Krug, 1986; Mershon & Gorsuch, 1988). Though his second-order factor analyses produced fewer factors, these do not correspond completely to the current "Big Five" factors (Eysenck, 1991).

Cattell's approach, because it is comprehensive in describing variations in personality, offers a broad perspective within which to plan systematic personality research. He criticized the haphazard way that personality researchers have decided what to study:

> The choice of "significant" variables for analysis has largely been dominated by the fads and fashions of each decade. . . . Sometimes this research has even deserved the label "magpie research," because the researcher has been fixated by the twinkle of some experimental gadget or fine-sounding scholarly term. (1979, p. 27)

Cattell claimed that his multivariate approach, which systematically examines the entire sphere of personality, resulted in many more discoveries in a briefer time than alternative approaches guided by current theory (Cattell, 1957, p. 50). Reports that personality measures that were developed outside his theory correspond to Cattellian measures (e.g., Cooper & McConville, 1989) suggest that some inefficiency of research efforts exists, with different researchers investigating comparable personality characteristics by different names.

Cattell's findings are so rich that they may be easily overlooked when searching the *Psychological Abstracts.* He stated that the number of key traits that should be indexed for a multivariate study is not reflected in the actual abstracting process (Cattell, 1958). For example, a study using the 16PF should, ideally, be abstracted on each factor. Because this is not done, many researchers overlook the literature's wealth of studies in which multivariate approaches have data relevant to particular trait issues.

Summary

Cattell defined personality simply as "that which permits a prediction of what a person will do in a given situation." He developed a great number of personality tests. His research obtained data from three sources: self-report questionnaires (Q-data), objective tests, including projective tests and behavioral measures (T-data), and life history information (L-data). He sought convergences across these sources of data (see Table 8.4).

TABLE 8.4 Contributions of Cattell's Theory to Various Topics

Biological	Heredity affects many personality traits, which Cattell named. He devised a strategy for analyzing the effects of heredity (MAVA).
Child Development	Some traits are influenced by early experience.
Adult Development	Some traits change in adulthood.
Mental Health	Neurosis and psychosis can be described as combinations of traits, can be measured by valid new tests, and are influenced by heredity.
Society	Differences among groups and nations (syntality) exist and can be measured.
Cognitive Processes	Mental abilities can be measured objectively; culture-free intelligence can be measured. Self-report measures are valid.
Individual Differences	Individuals differ in their traits, which Cattell measured with great care. In normal personalities, 16 traits account for most individual differences.

Cattell used multivariate research methods, particularly factor analysis. He described the *surface traits* of people and, through more intensive statistical analysis, sought the underlying *source traits* that determine personality. His *16PF* personality test builds on this research and measures the 16 major source traits of personality. These scores can be presented in a profile for each individual. A second-order factor analysis of these scores results in five more general factors, including extroversion (Exvia) and anxiety.

Cattell distinguished various types of traits: dynamic, temperament, and ability. He differentiated fluid intelligence (innate potential) from crystallized intelligence (influenced by experience), and developed ways to measure fluid intelligence. He concluded that about 80 percent of the variation in intelligence is due to heredity.

Cattell's *dynamic lattice* presents the relationship among *ergs* (constitutional dynamic source traits), and *metaergs* (*environmental-mold* dynamic source traits), which include sentiments and attitudes. These are related according to the principle of *subsidiation.*

In principle, behavior can be predicted by the *specification equation,* which includes traits, situational factors, and temporary factors. While most of his research was nomothetic (*R-technique*), Cattell also explored a *P-technique* for idiographic research. He described personality change across time and offered the concept of *syntality* to describe group differences, such as national character. He developed the *MAVA* technique to investigate the impact of heredity on personality. The 16 personality factors vary in how much they are influenced by heredity. Cattell found that neurosis and psychosis have some genetic basis, although experience also influences their onset.

While his approach has been criticized for being atheoretical, Cattell drew upon other theorists' concepts in interpreting his results, and he argued that extensive empirical work such as his had much to contribute to theoretical advances in personality.

ILLUSTRATIVE BIOGRAPHIES: Concluding Remarks

Albert Einstein

Cattell's list of 16 personal factors provides an inventory for assessing any personality. Ideally, we would have inventory scores for a proper assessment. As that is impossible, let us venture a rough profile based on inferences from biographical information. Einstein's most noteworthy trait was, of course, Intelligence (a high score on Factor B). He would also score as Artless, rather than shrewd (a low score on Factor N). His biographer said that "Einstein despised the careful cultivation of men or women for particular ends, the balancing of interest against interest, . . . and the ability to judge the right moment for dropping the right hint into the right ear" (R.W. Clark, 1971/1984, p. 379). His independent-mindedness and preference, from childhood, for solitary pleasures would warrant a high score on Factor Q_2, Self-sufficiency. His famous absent-mindedness, his sloppiness of dress and failure to wear socks, and his carelessness with money constitute evidence for a high score on Factor M, Autia.

At the level of Cattell's metaergs, Einstein clearly had a *sentiment* against power issues in interpersonal relationships. He disliked dealing with people of power, according to Robert Oppenheimer (R.W. Clark, 1971/1984, p. 719). At the level of the *attitude,* Einstein clearly opposed the arms race in public statements after his reluctant endorsement of such a race during the crisis of World War II (Cuny, 1965).

The fact that people belong to groups with different national characters, which Cattell investigated in his concept of *syntality,* was a pervasive theme in Einstein's life. Abba Eban, former Israeli ambassador to the United States, claimed that Einstein was one example of "the Hebrew mind [which] has been obsessed for centuries by a concept of order and harmony in the universal design. The search for laws hitherto unknown which govern cosmic forces . . ." (R.W. Clark, 1971/1984, p. 36) was the guiding vision of Einstein's quest for a unifying theory of physics. (Eban's description of "the Hebrew mind" corresponds to Cattell's general concept of syntality. Whether this is, as Eban claimed, a typical Jewish trait would require further data.) Einstein viewed German character dimly, and he gladly renounced his German citizenship.

Cattell's theory addresses the determinants, as well as the description, of personality. Undoubtedly, heredity dealt Einstein a generous hand. Intelligence is the most highly heritable personality factor, according to Cattell. Factor M (Autia) has heritability estimates of about 0.40 (Cattell, 1973, p. 147). Factors N (Artlessness) and Q_2 (Self-sufficiency) are more environmental-mold traits, with heritabilities estimated only about 0.25.

Despite the apparent scientific status of these categories, however, we do not have either the kind of intensive normative assessment or the P-technique data that Cattell would require for a proper analysis. Beyond that methodological limitation, one is tempted to agree with Einstein's second wife, who cautioned, "You cannot analyze him, otherwise you will misjudge him" (Clark, 1971/1984, p. 645).

Florence Nightingale

Even without psychological measures, we can infer several of Cattell's personality factors from the biographical evidence about Florence Nightingale. Together with concepts from the dynamic lattice, these traits help us understand the life she lived.

Like Einstein, Florence Nightingale was highly intelligent (Factor B), considering both fluid (genetic) and crystallized (educational) forms of intelligence. Also like Einstein, she was especially interested in mathematics. She overcame her mother's resistance to obtain permission to study this field, unusual for a female of her time.

Unlike Einstein, she used mathematics for applied rather than theoretical purposes. Her actions were practical and down-to-earth, suggesting a low score on Factor M, Praxernia. For example, she devised a revolutionary system for piping hot water into various hospital areas in order to save work (Woodham-Smith, 1951, p. 74). Her booklet *Notes on Nursing* contains practical advice for ordinary women taking care of the health of loved ones and children. In the Crimea, she kept detailed records about numbers and causes of deaths, which helped to identify particular health problems for reform. Later in England she improved hospital record-keeping practices. She loved records and statistics and is credited with inventing the pie diagram to represent data visually, thus enhancing its impact on an audience.

Her biographer finds this practical orientation to be contradictory to another quality of Florence Nightingale's personality. "She was also emotional, prone to exaggeration, and abnormally sensitive" (Woodham-Smith, 1951, p. 10). She suffered repeated episodes of emotional breakdown involving trance-like states, guilt, and even suicidal impulses and the fear that she was going insane (Seymer, 1951, pp. 75–76; Woodham-Smith, 1951, pp. 46–47, 51). She was often concerned with issues of guilt. She interpreted the obstacles that delayed her plan to study nursing as God's reaction to her sinfulness, to her love of opera and dancing and of the pleasures of social life. These qualities suggest a low score on Factor C, indicating Neuroticism, a high score on Factor I, Premsia, and a high score on Factor O, Guilt Proneness. What might appear contradictory, given the biographer's implicit type theory (which says that practical minded people are not sensitive, guilty, or neurotic), is quite possible in Cattell's model, which permits any combination of factor scores.

Florence Nightingale reported in her personal diary in 1843 that she often entered "trance-like" states, even when other people were present (Woodham-Smith, 1951, p. 32). As a child, she "escaped into dreams" (Woodham-Smith, 1951, p. 6). Four times in her adult life she reported that "voices" spoke to her about her mission. The first occasion was a "call from God" on February 7, 1837, which directed her toward her vocation rather than a traditional married life. In 1844, at the age of 24, she said that her calling was to care for the sick in hospitals. While there is no single Cattellian factor that produces such mystical experiences, they may be produced by Florence Nightingale's pattern of scores.

In Cattell's model, the impact of personality factors on behavior depends upon the situation. Had Florence Nightingale been born into a Catholic family of that era, she could have comfortably found her vocation as a nun, which would have legitimized her choice to remain unmarried and to become a hospital nurse. However, her family was Protestant. She considered converting to Catholicism, but was not admitted because her attitude was not sufficiently submissive (Woodham-Smith, 1951, p. 65). This independence of mind implies a high score on Factor Q_2, Self-sufficiency.

According to her biographer, "Beneath the fascination, the sense of fun, the gentle hesitating manner, the demure wit, there was the hard coldness of steel" (Woodham-Smith, 1951, p. 80). Although she could be very caring, as she was with the soldiers in the Crimea and for her mother in her old age, Florence Nightingale could be rejecting as well, suggesting a low score on Factor A, Sizia. A friend of the family, Mrs. Gaskell, said that Florence loved the human race but could be very cold-hearted toward individuals (Woodham-Smith, 1951, p. 81). She was critical of her sister and unsympathetic about her sister's illness (Woodham-Smith, 1951, p. 326). Late in life, Florence was quite unsympathetic about the health problems of a dear friend, Sidney Herbert, which limited his efforts on behalf of the hospital reform movement. Her sense of mission precluded making allowances for human frailties.

With people, Miss Nightingale was sufficiently astute to thrive in the complex political atmosphere that her actions created. She did, after all, depend upon the goodwill of politicians to permit her to serve in the Crimea and later in England, and she attained support from the public and from Queen Victoria. These political skills suggest that her score on Factor N, Shrewdness, would be above average.

The intensity of her energy and drive is striking. Cattell's Factor Q_4, Ergic Tension, reflects this tense, driven quality. It was particularly apparent in the period before Nightingale journeyed to Kaiserswerth, Germany, to begin her nursing career. At this time, she wrote a passionate indictment of the frustrated energies of an affluent but vacuous woman in a work she entitled *Cassandra* (Woodham-Smith, 1951, p. 63). After her Crimean services, her devoted Aunt Mai noticed that Florence had become very calm (Woodham-Smith, 1951, p. 169). Her level of ergic tension was high when her career was blocked, and diminished when her work had been consummated, which is consistent with Cattell's assertion that ergic tension can result from impediments to one's efforts.

Cattell's *dynamic lattice* is a useful concept for understanding this flow of energy. An adequate lattice must develop to permit the ergic energy to be expressed in attitudes and sentiments. Obviously Miss Nightingale had an important *sentiment toward public service* to alleviate suffering. In 1842 she wrote, "My mind is absorbed with the idea of the sufferings of man, it besets me behind and before . . . all that poets sing of the glories of this world seem to me untrue. All the people I see are eaten up with care or poverty or disease" (Woodham-Smith, 1951, p. 31). Sentiments are environmental-mold characteristics, and Miss Nightingale had models of service in her family. Her maternal grandfather, Samuel Smith, was a member of the House of Commons for 46 years, "fighting for the weak, the unpopular, and the oppressed" (Woodham-Smith, 1951, p. 2). The specific *attitudes* through which Miss Nightingale expressed her public-service sentiment included hospital reform and the professionalization of nursing. She did not, however, favor women's rights. When Florence Nightingale considered the lives of dissatisfied affluent women, she criticized their selfish laziness, rather than sensing their oppression. She refused to be identified with the woman's suffrage movement and she criticized women who wished to become doctors, rather than nurses. Had her efforts to promote nursing as a profession been prompted by a different sentiment, perhaps a sense of female oppression, her attitude toward the feminist movement of her day might have been more supportive.

Florence Nightingale was, indeed, a complex personality. Though pioneering a new profession for women, she opposed the concept of equal rights for women. Though serious of purpose, she loved the pleasures of music and dancing. Cattell's theory offers a rich set of personality traits to understand Florence Nightingale's complexity and encourages us to identify the sentiments and attitudes she developed to express these traits during her lifetime. Like Miss Nightingale poring over new data, we may enjoy this exercise and hope that something useful may come of it. Nonetheless, one is left with the sense that the spirit of the "Lady with the lamp" is only partially contained within these formulae, and that no set of mathematical scores can convey the dedication of this unique woman as she lived in her particular time and place.

GLOSSARY

confluence learning learning behaviors that satisfy more than one motivation

constitutional trait a trait influenced by heredity

correlation coefficient a measure of the association between two variables, in which 0 indicates no association, and +1 or −1 a strong association (positive or negative)

correlation matrix a chart of the correlations between all pairs of a set of variables

cross-sectional research research that studies a variety of people at one point in time and makes comparisons among them

crystallized intelligence intelligence influenced by education, so that it measures what has been learned

Culture Fair Intelligence Test a test designed to measure fluid intelligence only

dynamic lattice Cattell's diagram to show motivational dynamics

environmental-mold trait a trait influenced by learning

erg a constitutional dynamic source trait

factor analysis statistical procedure for determining a smaller number of dimensions in a data set with a large number of variables

fluid intelligence that part of intelligence which is the innate ability to learn, without including the effects of specific learning

heritability the extent to which a trait is influenced by genetics

L-data objective information about the life history of the individual

longitudinal research research that follows the same people over time

master motive the self

Multiple Abstract Variance Analysis (MAVA) statistical technique for assessing how much of a trait is determined by heredity and how much by environment

metaerg environmental-mold dynamic source traits; includes sentiments and attitudes

multivariate a research strategy that includes many variables

profile the pattern of a person's scores on several parts of a personality test

Q-data data from self-report tests or questionnaires

second-order factor analysis factor analysis in which the data are factor scores (rather than raw data); produces more general personality factors

16PF Cattell's questionnaire designed to measure the major source traits of normal personality

source traits basic, underlying personality traits

specification equation mathematical expression that shows how personality and situational variables combine to predict a specific behavior

subsidiation the pattern of interrelationships among ergs, metaergs, and sentiments (as diagrammed in the dynamic lattice)

surface traits traits as defined simply at the level of observable behavior

syntality group (e.g., national) differences in personality

T-data data collected from objective tests, such as reaction times

trait that which defines what a person will do in a particular situation

STUDY QUESTIONS

1. How did Cattell define *personality*?
2. Describe Cattell's contributions to personality testing.
3. List and explain the three sources of data that Cattell included in his research.
4. Explain what is meant by *multivariate research*.
5. Distinguish between *surface traits* and *source traits*.
6. Describe Cattell's 16PF. Why is it said to measure source traits, rather than surface traits?
7. What is *factor analysis*? What is *second-order* factor analysis?
8. Describe Cattell's concepts of *fluid intelligence* and *crystallized intelligence*.
9. Explain the principle of *subsidiation* in Cattell's *dynamic lattice*. Give an example.
10. What is the purpose of the *specification equation*? What terms are included in it?
11. Explain *P-technique*. How is it different from the more common *R-technique*?
12. Explain *syntality*.
13. What is the purpose of the MAVA technique of data analysis? What findings have resulted from this technique?
14. Discuss the accusation that Cattell's work is atheoretical.

PART IV

The Humanistic Perspective

The humanistic perspective in personality theory represents a "third force" (Maslow, 1968b), established to combat the deterministic and fragmenting tendencies of psychoanalysis and of behaviorism. It began as an informal network of psychologists who, organized by Abraham Maslow, exchanged mimeographed papers representing ideas not welcome in the established psychology journals (DeCarvalho, 1990a). Several of these humanists held their first meeting in 1957 and formally organized in 1961, founding the organization now known as the Association of Humanistic Psychology (Moustakas, 1986). Among the first members were Gordon Allport, Erich Fromm, George Kelly, Abraham Maslow, Rollo May, Henry Murray, and Carl Rogers (DeCarvalho, 1990a; Wertheimer, 1978). Gordon Allport's association with humanistic psychology has largely been forgotten, although he is probably the first one to have used the term "humanistic psychology," and though he was closely involved with the movement until his death (DeCarvalho, 1990b, 1990c).

The early self-proclaimed humanistic psychologists had a close affinity with Adlerians. Before their separate organization was founded, they had been invited to express their ideas within the Adlerian journal, the *American Journal of Individual Psychology,* under the editorship of Heinz

Ansbacher (DeCarvalho, 1990a). Maslow and Rogers had both studied with Adler. Rogers was taught by Adler during his internship at the Institute for Child Guidance in New York City in 1927–28, and Maslow regularly attended Adler's informal seminars in his home in New York in 1935 (Ansbacher, 1990). Both humanists acknowledged Adler's influence on their ideas. It was Adler's emphasis on holism, choice, and the intentions and subjective experience of the individual that most influenced the humanists. Other significant influences included Karen Horney and Kurt Goldstein (who found that brain-injured patients can best be understood as striving whole organisms, rather than as collections of part brain-processes).

The major distinguishing characteristics of the humanistic perspective derive from its commitment to the value of personal growth. First, the humanistic perspective focuses on "higher," more developed, and healthy aspects of human experience and their development. Among these are creativity and tolerance. Second, the humanistic perspective values the subjective experience of the individual. This is sometimes called a *phenomenological* approach. Third, the perspective emphasizes the present, rather than the past or the future. Fourth, humanists stress that each individual is responsible for his or her own life outcomes. No past conditions predetermine the present. Finally, the humanistic perspective seeks to apply its findings to the betterment of the human condition by changing the environment in which people develop. It assumes that, given appropriate conditions, individuals will develop in a desirable direction.

Humanists describe a "true self" that contains the potential for optimal growth. Alienation from this true self results from unhealthy socialization, when other people define what one should do. The view of humanism that one should be guided by one's true self or "daimon" is an old idea, with roots in eudaemonistic philosophy as old as Aristotle (Waterman, 1990). Humanistic psychology has served as an ideology, rather than science, for many (Geller, 1982; M. B. Smith, 1990). It has been compared with religious traditions (H. Smith, 1985), including Hinduism and Buddhism, though these Eastern approaches describe self-actualization as requiring considerably more effort than does humanism (Das, 1989). Closer to home, humanism is compatible with the individualism and optimism of American culture (Fuller, 1982). It served as an ideology for many in the counterculture of the 1960s, who were attracted to the emphasis on experience and self-disclosure (M. B. Smith, 1990).

Humanists have been criticized for underestimating the evil in humankind. In explaining evil, humanists cite environmental causes (Das, 1989), although they attribute "good" to the intrinsic nature of human beings. Some have criticized self-actualization as fostering selfishness or narcissism, rather than promoting what Adler called "social interest" (Geller, 1982; Wallach & Wallach, 1983). Rogers (1982b) expressed dismay at this indictment.

Humanistic psychologists are more interested in process and change than in measuring individual differences. In clinical settings, the humanistic orientation prefers not to make a diagnosis if possible (e.g., Munter, 1975a). By emphasizing the goals of behavior rather than the mechanisms by which behavior occurs, humanists are *teleological* as opposed to deterministic. Teleology searches for the overall design or purpose toward which things are developing. In contrast, the predominant philosophy of science, logical positivism, insists upon determinism, that is, explanation in terms of past or present, not future, "causes." The challenge to humanism is to be able to be rigorously, scientifically teleological (Rychlak, 1977).

CHAPTER 9

Rogers: Person-Centered Theory

BIOGRAPHY OF CARL ROGERS

Carl Rogers

Carl R. Rogers was born in Oak Park, Illinois (near Chicago), on January 8, 1902. He was the fourth of six children. His father was part owner of a successful contracting and civil engineering business. The family atmosphere valued hard work and fundamentalist Christianity, adhering to strict rules of behavior. "We did not dance, play cards, attend movies, smoke, drink, or show any sexual interest" (Rogers, 1967, p. 344). The family moved to a farm so that the children would not encounter the temptations of close contact with others in the city or suburbs. This "gently suppressive family atmosphere" (p. 352), however, took its toll. Rogers and two siblings developed ulcers.

Rogers always enjoyed reading. He read at a fourth-grade level when he first entered school, and he loved to be alone and to read when he was growing up and even later. As one might expect, his grades were always high. Chores on the family farm led to his interest in scientific farming. He enrolled in the agriculture program at the University of Wisconsin. He was active in a church-related student volunteer movement and spent more than six months in China on a YMCA program for young people. This was a very important transition experience for Rogers, since for the first time he was distant from family members and their influence. Letters at that time moved by ship, so communication took months. Rogers grew increasingly tolerant of different customs that his parents could not challenge.

Rogers graduated from college in 1924 with a bachelor's degree in history (having lost interest in agriculture). Ironically, he had taken only one psychology course as an undergraduate. That summer he married his fiancée of nearly two years, Helen, a commercial artist, although his family objected that it would be better to wait until his postgraduate studies were over. Helen gave up her work as a commercial artist, and they went to New York City, where they both entered graduate school. Rogers studied at Union Theological Seminary, continuing the religious interest that had been a major theme in his life. He also took courses at Teachers College at Columbia University, and decided to do graduate work there in psychology. For his doctoral dissertation, Rogers developed a test to measure children's personality adjustment. Researchers used this test for many years thereafter (Cain, 1987).

For several years after completing his graduate studies in 1928, Rogers worked with children. His first position was at the Rochester (N.Y.) Society for the Prevention of Cruelty to Children, where he worked with delinquent and underprivileged youngsters. He headed the Rochester Guidance Center when it first opened in 1938, although traditionally a psychiatrist would fill such a position. He struggled for many years over the status of psychologists within the mental health care establishment (Rogers, 1974a). He reported feeling alienated from the mainstream of psychology, which emphasized animal laboratory studies. Rogers felt more akin to social workers and participated actively in their professional organizations. Not constrained by disciplinary loyalty, he freely moved from one academic field to another.

In 1940, after 12 years at Rochester, Rogers and his wife and two children, David and Natalie, moved to Ohio, where he took his first academic appointment: full professor at Ohio State University. It is highly unusual for a faculty member to begin at the top academic rank, but Rogers had just published an influential book, *Clinical Treatment of the Problem Child.* In his lectures, he came to realize that his ideas about therapy were new, and he developed these ideas in a book, *Counseling and Psychotherapy,* which was published in 1942 (Rogers, 1942a). It contained the first published verbatim transcript of a therapy case, opening this private process for study (see also Rogers, 1942b). The text has become a classic. Opening therapy sessions to the scrutiny of research required persistence, since the therapeutic community objected, but the practice has now become accepted (Gendlin, 1988). His students learned not only in the classroom but also through practicum experience. This was revolutionary, "the first instance in which supervised therapy was carried on in a university setting. . . . [N]either Freud nor any other therapist had ever managed to make supervised experience in the therapeutic relationship a part of academic experience" (Rogers, 1967, p. 362).

In 1945, Rogers went to the University of Chicago to establish a new counseling center. An active and collegial atmosphere developed there, and during this time Rogers wrote another of his classic books, *Client-Centered Therapy* (1951).

In 1957, the University of Wisconsin offered Rogers a joint appointment in psychology and psychiatry. He accepted. At Wisconsin, Rogers found a competitive and unsupportive atmosphere. Only one out of seven students who began the doctoral program in psychology remained to complete the degree requirements. This conflicted with his own humanistic convictions. He protested in 1963 by resigning his appointment in the Department of Psychology. (He retained his position in Psychiatry.) He published his criticisms of the competitive environment, suggesting a more humanistic approach (1969).

His next move was away from university life. For the third time in his career he gave up a tenured appointment to begin a new phase of his professional development. In 1964 he went to the Western Behavioral Sciences Institute in La Jolla, California. With others, he formed, in 1968, the Center for the Studies of the Person. In these years, he explored encounter groups and sensitivity training. Some of his projects aimed to achieve international peace in such areas of conflict as Central America, South Africa, and Northern Ireland.

Rogers was a leader in professional organizations throughout his career. He served as president of the American Association for Applied Psychology (1944–45) and of the American Psychological Association (1946–47). He received two prestigious awards from the American Psychological Association: the Distinguished Scientific Contribution Award in 1956 (American Psychological Association, 1957) and the first Distinguished Professional Contribution Award in 1972 (American Psychological Association, 1973). He was the first (and, as of 1987, only) psychologist to receive both honors (Cain, 1987).

Rogers died in 1987, at age 85, of a heart attack.

ILLUSTRATIVE BIOGRAPHIES

The theories advanced by Carl Rogers have not prompted extensive psychobiographical analyses. He reported his analysis of a woman, Ellen West, based upon her diaries and letters as well as the psychiatric analyses of this case by others (Rogers, 1961a). Besides this case history, when he was a student, Rogers wrote a term paper entitled "The Source of Authority in Martin Luther" (Fuller, 1982), which suggests that Rogers was interested in psychobiography or psychohistory. Undoubtedly his therapeutic work could have provided biographical case histories if he had chosen to report them. His emphasis on subjective experience offers important potential insights for psychobiography.

David Suzuki

David Suzuki was born in Canada, a third-generation Japanese whose grandparents had emigrated from Japan in search of a better fortune. He has described the impact of his ethnicity in his autobiography (Suzuki, 1988). Suzuki is best known as the host of the Canadian Broadcasting program "The Nature of Things," which considers environmental matters, and which is aired in many countries, including the United States.

Suzuki was born on March 24, 1936, in Marpole, near Vancouver. He has a twin sister, Marcia, and two younger sisters. In 1942, in the aftermath of the Japanese attack on Pearl Harbor, David Suzuki and his family joined many fellow Japanese-Canadians who were placed in internment camps for the duration of the war. (Similar camps were set up in the United States.) After the war, forbidden from returning to the West Coast, the family moved to Ontario, having had most of their material possessions confiscated by the Canadian government. David learned fishing and appreciation for nature from the time spent with his father in childhood, in the camp, and thereafter.

Suzuki describes his adolescence as a time of self-consciousness, compounded by the stigma of his minority status and by his intelligence in a school that valued athletic ability.

He went to college in the United States, at Amherst, in Massachusetts, where he majored in biology. In 1961 he completed his doctorate in genetics at the University of Chicago. After that, he did basic research in genetics at a laboratory in Oak Ridge, Tennessee, and then returned to Canada to a faculty position at the University of Alberta in Edmonton. He had better career opportunities in the United States, but he describes his motivation to escape American racism for what at the time seemed greater acceptance in Canada. After a year in Edmonton, he moved to the University of British Columbia in Vancouver (from which his family had been evacuated during the war). There he taught and conducted research on temperature-sensitive genetic mutations in fruit flies. The laboratory expanded, and his administrative responsibilities increased.

Immediately after graduating from college, Suzuki married a Japanese-Canadian, Joane, whom he had met in high school. They had three children, a daughter, Tamiko, a son, Troy, and another daughter, Laura. The marriage ended in divorce. Suzuki attributes this to extreme involvement in his work. After seven years, he remarried. His second wife, Tara, was Caucasian. They have two children, and he describes himself as much less chauvinistic, more involved in childrearing in this modern, dual-career marriage than in his first, more traditional union.

His career changed drastically, as well. He had already broadcast a minor science program, "Suzuki on Science," for two years. Beginning in 1974, he moved full-time to broadcasting, starring in the television shows "Science Magazine" and "The Nature of Things" and in the radio program "Quirks and Quarks." He also writes for newspapers.

Maya Angelou

Maya Angelou is a writer of prose and poetry who has published several autobiographical works (1969, 1974, 1976, 1981, 1986). Her vivid descriptions of her own experience make it rather easy for the reader to understand life from her point of view, as Rogers urges for those who would truly understand another person.

When Maya Angelou was 3, she and her 4-year-old brother, Bailey, were sent to live with their grandmother, Annie Henderson, in Stamps, Arkansas, when their parents (in Long Beach, California) divorced. They grew up in the black section of this poor community, helping their grandmother in her grocery store. From her they learned pride and discipline. Though poor, they were relatively better off than the other blacks, who picked cotton. For a time, they lived with their other grandmother, and then with their mother and her boyfriend, Mr. Freeman, in St. Louis. Maya describes being raped by him when she was 8 years old (Angelou, 1969). For this, Mr. Freeman was convicted and sentenced to jail, but he was lynched before serving time. After this, Maya developed psychogenic mutism, and after a time she and Bailey were sent back to Stamps.

During her adolescence and young adulthood, Maya lived in various places: in Stamps with her grandmother, in Los Angeles with her father, and in San Francisco with her mother (a prostitute). For a while she lived in an abandoned car in a junkyard. At 16 she had a son. She held a variety of jobs: waitress, cook, dancer, singer, prostitute, music store clerk. She married a Greek, Tosh Angelos, but the marriage ended after a year. She worked for a time for Martin Luther King, Jr.'s, Southern Christian Leadership Conference (SCLC). Later, she lived with an African freedom fighter, a relationship that, like her earlier marriage, restricted her with its sexism, but that taught her about her African heritage. She continued living in Ghana, Africa, for a time after the dissolution of this relationship. When she returned to the United States, her son remained in Ghana to finish college.

Maya Angelou had studied dance since the age of 14. Her singing and dancing career took off when she was offered a part in the modern opera *Porgy and Bess,* which toured Europe. Her primary career, however, is writing: autobiographical books and poetry.

PERSON-CENTERED THEORY

Carl Rogers is probably the best-known spokesperson for humanistic psychology. He was one of the first members of the Association of Humanistic Psychology. He believed that all human beings are motivated fundamentally by a growth-directed process, which he called the *actualizing tendency* (Rogers, 1963). Rogers tackled the problem of providing empirical evidence for humanistic psychology through research.

The Actualizing Tendency

Rogers theorized that all motivation is subsumed under a fundamental process, the **actualizing tendency**. He described this as

> the directional trend which is evident in all organic and human life—the urge to expand, extend, develop, mature—the tendency to express and activate all the capacities of the organism, or the self. (Rogers, 1961b, p. 351)

The general tendency toward development in nature, broadly, he called the *formative tendency.* He contrasted it with a tendency toward randomness (entropy), and suggested that the tendency to move from simpler to more complex forms is just as powerful in nature (Rogers, 1979). The specific human aspect of the formative tendency is the actualizing tendency. This tendency describes humans and all other organisms, animals, and even plants. Biological motivations, such as hunger and thirst, are part of this actualizing tendency. So are the "higher" human motivations.

We do not behave irrationally, as psychoanalysis assumed. Rather, "our behavior is exquisitely rational, moving with subtle and ordered complexity toward the goals the organism is endeavoring to achieve" (Rogers, 1983, p. 292). The actualizing tendency leads to differentiation (complexity), independence, and social responsibility. For Rogers, the motivation intrinsic to each person is basically good and healthy. More negative views of human motivation prevail in psychoanalysis, Christianity, and educational institutions. In contrast, Rogers's optimism "is profoundly radical" (Rogers, 1986a, p. 127).

Rogers has been criticized as being too optimistic about human nature, not recognizing the extent of the human capacity for evil (Friedman, 1982; May, 1982; Rogers, 1982b). May (1982) points out that the issue is not simply philosophical. It has also led to an inability of client-centered therapists to deal adequately with negative emotions, including anger and hostility, in their clients. Bakan (1982) suggests a resolution of at least the philosophical side of the issue: to distinguish between the level of the individual and the collective level. Behavior that is "good" at an individual level (e.g., responsibly doing one's job) may be "evil" considered collectively (e.g., the Nazis exterminating masses of Jews in concentration camps).

The Organismic Valuing Process

A self-actualizing person is in touch with the inner experience that is inherently growth producing. Rogers names this process the **organismic valuing process**. It is a subconscious guide that evaluates experience for its growth potential. It draws the person toward experiences that are growth producing, and away from those that would inhibit growth. Even activities that might seem fun or profitable to conscious experience will be avoided if they feel wrong to this inner guide. Thus internal experience, rather than external rules, directs choices. This inner valuing process is natural in the infant, who values food and security. With development, people unfortunately substitute external rules for inner experience, as they learn values from society that interfere with psychological development (Rogers, 1964).

What about people who are emotionally disturbed, or criminals? Many people do not seem to be healthy and mature. How can this happen if the actualizing tendency motivates all people? Rogers blamed social forces that cause a person to lose touch with inner growth processes. People distrust their inner feelings because they repeatedly hear that these feelings are bad. Such messages come from parents, from schools, and even from psychoanalysts. It is people's fear and defensiveness, rather than innate evil forces, that cause them to become destructive.

The Fully Functioning Person

A person who pays attention to the organismic valuing process is "self-actualizing" or **fully functioning**. Such a person does not lose the use of some human functions through adverse socialization messages. A potentially creative person may lose touch with that capacity by being taught that idle drawing is a "waste of time." Similarly, a potentially empathic person may lose touch with that capacity by being taught that showing feelings is a "sign of weakness."

The person who is fully functioning, who is most healthy, has several characteristics, which Rogers lists. These characteristics can be interpreted to be signs of mental health.

1. Openness to Experience. The fully functioning person is open to experience, receptive to the subjective and objective happenings of life. Others may "censor" experience through defenses (for example, not recognizing an insult, or the anger that it provokes). In contrast, the fully functioning person accurately perceives such events. In this sense, one might describe such a person as having an expanded consciousness. This openness includes the ability to tolerate ambiguity in experience. A situation that appears one way at one moment may seem different another time.

2. Existential Living. A person open to experience shows "an increasing tendency to live fully in each moment" (Rogers, 1961b, p. 188). Experience changes, and each moment allows the self to emerge, possibly changed by the new experience. Part of the person is participating in each moment, but part is an observer of the process. This "means . . . a maximum of adaptability, . . . a flowing, changing organization of self and personality" (Rogers, 1983, p. 288). The self is experienced as a fluid process, rather than a fixed entity. Experience is not rigid and structured.

3. Organismic Trusting. Such a person trusts inner experience at each moment to guide behavior. This experience is accurate. The person perceives inner needs and emotions and various aspects of the social situation without distortion. The individual integrates all these facets of experience and comes to an inner sense of what is right for him or her. This sense is trustworthy; it is not necessary to depend on outside authorities to say what is right.

4. Experiential Freedom. Such a person experiences freedom, in each moment, to choose. Such freedom is subjective, and does not deny that there is determinism in the world. Viktor Frankl described concentration camp prisoners, each free to choose at least an attitude toward the experiences of life. In most circumstances, there is considerable behavioral freedom as well.

5. Creativity. The fully functioning person lives creatively. He or she finds new ways of living at each moment, instead of being locked into past, rigid patterns no longer adaptive. Rogers described fully functioning humans as the best able to adapt to new conditions, the "vanguard of human evolution" (1961b, p. 194).

Valuing Subjective Experience

In his later writing, Rogers went further in his emphasis on subjectivity. Participants in his workshops sometimes described the experience in terms of spirituality. This suggests a transpersonal dimension to human experience. Experiences of altered states of consciousness and mysticism are something like self-actualization. Rogers suggested that he might have underestimated the "mystical, spiritual dimension" of experience (1979). He cited Capra's (1975) comparison of modern physics with Eastern mysticism (cf. Bozarth, 1985). This validated Rogers's belief that subjective experience could be compatible with science. He wrote sympathetically about mysticism (1979, 1980). He reported paranormal phenomena about which he had read (1973) and suggested that paranormal phenomena should be further explored in empirical research (1980). This encouraged those who believe in extrasensory perception (ESP) and other parapsychological phenomena. D.S. Cartwright (1989) reported research on a measure of Transcendental Mental Powers, a scale developed from Rogers's theory. He found that it correlated as predicted with other self-report measures. Rogers's approach challenges us to consider the role of subjectivity within a scientific framework.

Cartwright and Mori (1988) have developed the Feelings, Reactions, and Beliefs Survey (FRBS) to assess aspects of personality described by Rogers. These aspects comprise nine scales (named here according to the revised titles reported in Cartwright, DeBruin, & Berg, 1991):

Focusing Conscious Attention
Open to Feelings in Relationships
Fully Functioning Person
Feeling Uncomfortable with People
Feeling Ambivalent in Relationships
Struggling with Feelings of Inferiority
Trust in Self as an Organism
Openness to Transcendent Experiences
Religio-spiritual Beliefs

Cartwright and Mori (1988) found that the scales of this survey are correlated with other personality measures and with self-reported autobiographical information among college freshmen. For example, the Fully Functioning scale correlated positively ($r = +.55$) with the Time-Competence scale of the Personal Orientation Inventory, a measure of self-actualization based on Maslow's theory (E.L. Shostrom, 1974). Scales correlate also with self-reported biographical information. For example, students who scored high on the Focusing Conscious Attention scale reported doing better in school, and a group of religious devotees scored higher on the Religio-spiritual Beliefs scale (Cartwright, DeBruin, & Berg, 1991). These studies support the validity of the scales.

Values are explicitly important in Rogers's theory (DeCarvalho, 1989). He argued that values emerge for each individual, and for humankind as a whole, from the process of experiencing (Rogers, 1964). This position offends those who hold that science should be value-free. It also has offended those who regard it as an invitation to selfishness, in which no one is held to an external standard of right and wrong. How ironic that Rogers, who disagreed with psychoanalysis, should be criticized along with Freud, who challenged religious values (cf. Fuller, 1982).

The Self

Much of personality growth, including that which occurs in therapy, involves changes in the *self.* Rogers hesitated to introduce this term into his theory, but clients said things to him, such as, "I'm not sure I'm being my real self." At first reluctantly, Rogers accepted the necessity of including the concept "self" in his theory. He was amazed that the concept became so popular in psychology.

We are familiar with the terms *ideal self* and *real self* from psychoanalytic theory (especially Karen Horney's theory). Rogers used these terms too. He observed that many people experience a discrepancy between the two. They wish to be like the **ideal self**; perhaps they even pretend to be like it. The **real self** is different; it contains a person's true or real qualities, including the actualizing tendency. The organismic valuing process leads to health; the ideal self leads to disturbance.

Rogers used the term *incongruence* to describe the experience of conflict between the real self and the ideal self. When a person is incongruent, the person experiences the real self as threatening. To prevent this, defense mechanisms distort and deny experience. "Me? Angry? Never!" "Lie? Never, not me!" "Tired? No—I always have energy to help a friend!" and so on. The real self may be suppressed.

Most people use the term "self-actualization" loosely to refer to the healthy actualizing process. Rogers himself did not distinguish between the two in his early work (1951). In his later work, however, Rogers described self-actualization as a "sub-aspect" of the actualization process. If the person has forsaken the real self, then actualization and "self-actualization" are in conflict. A phony self-actualization impedes the healthy actualization process. Self-actualization in the more precise sense of the term is an unhealthy tendency when a person is in a state of incongruence, because the "self" that is being actualized is defined by society, not by the individual. Actualization, the more general tendency, is always healthy (Ford & Maas, 1989; Rogers 1959). This is a complicated distinction. A clearer formulation has been offered by DeCarvalho (1990a), who suggests that everyone is "becoming," but only for some does this growth become a truly individual, self-chosen process.

Development

To understand why incongruence occurs, consider how the self-concept develops. Adults tell children to "be good." Rogers described such pressures in his own childhood: be hard-working, be respectful to adults, and so forth.

"Bad" behavior leads to punishment, or is simply ignored. Rogers called this kind of socialization *conditional positive regard.* That is, parents will love ("regard positively") children only to the extent that the children live up to their **conditions of worth**.

As a result of this socialization, children come to think of themselves as only having the "good" qualities; they disown the "bad" qualities. Despite the good intentions of parents, this socialization does not work out for the best. Unfortunately, some of the "bad" qualities parents discourage are really healthy potentials.

Consider the case of a child who has learned not to challenge the parents' authority. The ideal self is obedient and respectful. The real self would question and rebel; but it has been suppressed and is no longer experienced. As the person grows up, it is very difficult to become aware of feelings of rebellion or questioning of authority. These feelings, when they begin to surface, feel dangerous, so the person does not allow them to surface. What the young child learned in order to be "good" becomes a rigid, maladaptive trait in the adult. Such an adult relies on authority figures for direction and does not think independently.

The problem, as Rogers envisioned it, is that only those aspects of potential selfhood that are compatible with these conditions of worth develop. A better alternative would be to impose no conditions of worth. That is, give the child **unconditional positive regard**, which means loving the child regardless of his or her behavior. This allows the child to explore all his or her potentials. Since Rogers viewed human beings as essentially good, the outcome is the development of a fully functioning person.

Critics argue that such advice is impractical and neglectful. Surely Rogers did not advocate abdicating parental responsibilities to direct and teach their children, yet he contended that feeling loved, fully and unconditionally, is essential to healthy development. This is the most important experience that parents can provide for their children.

Early research suggested to Rogers that inner resources of the child were more important than external influences in determining healthy outcomes. He reported research on delinquent children in which inner influences were far more predictive of later behavior than were outer influences, including the family environment, health, economic background, intelligence, and heredity. More important than any of these was a measure that tapped various inner influences, "the degree of the child's self-understanding, self-insight; the realistic acceptance of self and the realistic appraisal of the situation in which he found himself; and the acceptance of responsibility for oneself" (Rogers, 1989, p. 204).

Development of Creativity

Rogers considered what sort of environment encourages creativity (Rogers, 1954). Creativity requires three psychological qualities: "openness to experience, an internal locus of evaluation, and the ability to toy with elements and concepts" (Harrington, Block, & Block, 1987). Harrington and colleagues (1987) studied 106 children and their parents from preschool through adolescence. Results confirmed predictions based on Rogers's ideas. Preschool parent–child interactions correlated with creative potential in early adolescence, about a decade later. Parents of preschool children who later became creative agreed with statements such as these:

"I respect my child's opinions and encourage him to express them."

"I encourage my child to be curious, to explore and question things."

They disagreed with statements such as these:

"I do not allow my child to get angry with me."

"I feel my child is a bit of a disappointment to me."

The parents taught tasks to their preschoolers in the research laboratory. Creativity-facilitating parents were more likely to offer encouragement and praise. Parents of children who became less creative were more critical and controlled or structured the tasks instead of allowing the child to work independently. Because the study was correlational, we cannot be certain whether the parents *caused* their children to become creative or not. For example, the youngsters may have already been different, causing the parents to behave differently, rather than vice versa. Nonetheless, the results offer support for Rogers's conceptualization of creativity.

Therapy

Client-Centered Therapy

Rogers developed his therapeutic technique over many years in a practical setting, away from academia. He thus was guided by "what works," rather than by considerations of theory. He described, for example, an early therapeutic encounter when he was still guided by his early training in psychoanalytic theory. He helped a pyromaniac boy discover that his motivations for setting fires stemmed from sexual desire, only to be crushed when this insight did not prevent recurrence of the fire-setting. Psychoanalysis taught that insight brought a cure. Clinical experience taught otherwise.

Rogers came to be convinced that theoretical preconceptions interfered with therapeutic progress. He learned to drop theoretical formulae, such as the "sexual drive leads to pyromania" formulation, which had failed him in the above example, and instead to listen to what his clients were telling him. Their experience, he found, provided worthwhile directions for growth. Because of this emphasis on the client's experience and direction, Rogers called his technique **client-centered therapy**.

Drawing on his therapeutic experience, Rogers listed six conditions he felt led to therapeutic progress (Rogers, 1957a). (See Table 9.1.) Foremost among these conditions were *unconditional positive regard*, *congruence*, and *empathic understanding*, conditions he regarded as necessary and sufficient for therapeutic progress.

Unconditional Positive Regard

Rogers found that clients are most likely to make progress when they feel that they are accepted by the therapist. Obviously the therapist cannot approve of the maladaptive behaviors that lead to the need for therapy. Yet it is possible to convey a feeling of **unconditional positive regard** to the cli-

TABLE 9.1 Necessary and Sufficient Conditions for Therapeutic Process

1. Two persons are in psychological contact.
2. The first, whom we shall term the client, is in a state of incongruence, being vulnerable or anxious.
3. The second person, whom we shall term the therapist, is congruent or integrated in the relationship.
4. The therapist experiences unconditional positive regard for the client.
5. The therapist experiences an empathic understanding of the client's internal frame of reference and endeavors to communicate this experience to the client.
6. The communication to the client of the therapist's empathic understanding and unconditional positive regard is to a minimal degree achieved.

(From Rogers, 1957a.)

ent, offering acceptance that is not contingent on particular behaviors. Rogers expressed his **prizing** (another term for unconditional positive regard) of a patient, Gloria, in a training film when he said to her, "You look to me like a pretty nice daughter" (Shostrom, 1965). Feeling positively valued by the therapist, the client becomes more accepting of herself or himself. Aspects of the real self become available, which were previously repressed due to childhood conditions of worth. The client begins to trust personal experience, the inner organismic valuing process. Therapeutic progress results from this prizing of the client.

Sometimes, unfortunately, a therapist simply does not like a client. An effective therapist will seldom encounter such situations. When they do occur, Rogers recommended that the therapist acknowledge feelings of anger or even dislike of the client, rather than pretending acceptance. That sort of dishonesty would violate the second condition of effective psychotherapy.

Congruence

A second condition for successful psychotherapy is that the therapist behave with **congruence** in the interaction. That is, the therapist's behavior should match his or her inner experience. The therapist should be *genuine,* and should be to a large extent *transparent,* so that the client can, as it were, see inside his or her experience, rather than see only a façade or mask that does not allow the real person of the therapist to be known to the client. How can one expect the client to become a person open to experience if the therapist is not?

Empathic Understanding

A third condition for successful psychotherapy, **empathic understanding**, is that the therapist should be able to understand the experience of the client. This, said Rogers, is easier to teach than the other two therapeutic requirements. It often involves restating the client's communications in a way that has been the brunt of anti-therapy humor. (*Client*: "I am sad." *Therapist*: "You say you are sad.")

Empathic understanding involves more than mechanical restatement. When it occurs, the therapist understands so fully the client's situation that he or she may be able to verbalize feelings that the client has been not able to express, or even fully experience. Thus, hidden, unacknowledged feelings (anger, rejection, and so forth) can be named or, as Rogers would say, "symbolized." Hence, these parts of the real self are no longer unknown.

Though research has been reported that confirms these three core conditions for therapeutic progress, it is based upon correlational designs. D. Cramer (1990c) urges that true experimental research, which can test for cause-effect relationships, be conducted.

Other psychoanalysts, including Freud and Kohut, include empathy as an important psychotherapeutic technique (Emery, 1987; Kahn, 1985, 1987; Tobin, 1991). However, for psychoanalysts, empathy is an intellectual tool aimed to increase insight about the patient's psychodynamics. For Kohut (and also for Freud), empathy is "cold" and "impersonal" (Rogers, 1986a), a tool for identifying aspects of pathology. In contrast, for Rogers empathy occurs in a context of unconditional positive regard. Though the therapist does not necessarily agree with the client's experience, no judgment is pronounced, and the client is valued (Bohart, 1988).

Empathy as a counseling technique may need to be augmented when the counselor and client come from different cultural backgrounds. White counselors are often uninformed or misinformed about the cultural context in which minority clients live. Emotional empathy must then be supplemented by "cognitive empathy" techniques, including explicitly asking clients about their culture, in order for the counselor to understand accurately the experience of the client (Scott & Borodovsky, 1990).

Research on Therapy

Rogers was committed to empirical research. No theory, he asserted, was without error when first formulated (Rogers, 1959). Research leads to revision of a theory toward greater validity and accuracy. Rogers took care to formulate his theoretical constructs in ways that could be operationally defined. He took pride in his scientific research and expressed dissatisfaction with therapists who did not turn to empirical research to test the validity of their theories (Rogers, 1968, 1986a). Rogers was challenged in particular by B. F. Skinner, who claimed that many of the concepts used by Rogers were not scientific; "freedom" and "self-actualization" are surely difficult concepts to define operationally in scientific terms.

Rogers explained behavior in terms of factors currently present. In contrast, many clinical approaches (especially psychoanalysis) focus on the distant past, leading to theories "that are of necessity speculative and untestable" (Rogers, 1986a, p. 137). Rogers especially objected to interpretations of the therapeutic relationship in terms of "transference" (Bohart, 1991; Rogers, 1986c; Weinrach, 1991). The concept of transference denies the real and present relationship between the client and the therapist, instead making the current situation simply a blank projective screen for past experience.

Early research was supportive of Rogers's "necessary and sufficient conditions" for therapeutic progress. Rogers asserted that if these conditions were present, regardless of the theoretical orientation of the therapist, progress would occur. This early enthusiasm was tempered somewhat by later findings. Unconditional positive regard, congruence, and empathy now are regarded as facilitating improvement, but are not a magic trio that, alone, are necessary and sufficient for progress to occur (W.H. Lockhart, 1984).

Studies of psychotherapy have included detailed analyses of instructional films in which Rogers modeled his therapeutic technique. These analyses indicate that Rogers was distinctively different from other therapists in what he said to clients (Essig & Russell, 1990; D.Y. Lee & Uhlemann, 1984; Mahrer, Nadler, Stalikas, Schachter, & Sterner, 1988). Rogers frequently reflected or restated what the client said, and he often offered encouragement, approval, and reassurance (D.Y. Lee & Uhlemann, 1984). Weinrach (1990) reported that Rogers offered considerable interpretation, perhaps too much to be consistent with his espoused theory. Bohart (1991) disagreed; his analysis of the same data indicated many reflections and few interpretations.

A detailed study (Wiseman & Rice, 1989) of what clients and therapists say demonstrates the impact of therapists' statements on clients. By what they say, therapists can get clients to focus on the internal subjective experiences that are critical to growth.

Outcomes of Psychotherapy

When a therapeutic climate is created that has the characteristics described above, a positive therapeutic outcome will result. In such a case, the client will develop more of the healthy characteristics of self-actualizing people, including openness to experience, self-acceptance, and trust of organismic experience (Rogers, 1961b).

Rogers reported empirical studies demonstrating the effectiveness of psychotherapy. In one such study, self-concept was measured using a Q-technique. Subjects sorted 100 self-perception statements into nine piles, indicating how well the statements described them. Examples of such statements are: "I often feel resentful"; "I feel relaxed and nothing really bothers me." These sortings were done for the actual self (as perceived by the subject) and for the ideal self (how the subject would like to be). The Q-sort procedure was repeated again after psychotherapy.

Before therapy, the real self and the ideal self were quite different. They correlated $r = -.47$, indicating that clients before therapy saw themselves as unlike their ideal selves. After therapy, the real self and the ideal self were much more similar ($r = .59$). Thus therapy produced changes in the direction of greater self-acceptance (Butler & Haigh, 1954). This heightened self-acceptance sprang from changes in both the actual self, which came to have more desirable qualities, and the ideal self, which came to include previously unappreciated positive qualities that the person already possessed.

Stages of Process

Personality change in psychotherapy occurs gradually. Rogers devised a way of measuring the types of changes that occur in psychotherapy. He called this the **Process Scale**. It constitutes a 7-stage description of the process of change (see Table 9.2).

Rogers said that therapy is generally involved in stages 3 to 6 on this continuum (Table 9.2). Before stage 3, individuals are generally unwilling to

TABLE 9.2 Seven Stages of Process

Stage	*Characteristic Behaviors*
1	communicates about externals, rather than self
	feelings not recognized or owned
	rigid perceptions ("constructs")
	fear of close relationships
	no desire to change
2	problems seen as external to self
	no sense of responsibility about problems
	some feelings described in past or belonging to others
	unaware of contradictions
3	much talk about self and past feelings
	present feelings not accepted
	recognition of contradictions; constructs less rigid
	choices seen as ineffective
4	present feelings acknowledged and expressed, but feared and only partly accepted
	more open constructs about experience
	recognition of incongruence between experience and self
	the self is acknowledged as responsible for problems
5	feelings expressed freely in the present
	feelings are surprising and frightening
	discovery of new personal constructs
	desire to be the "real me," even if imperfect
6	immediate experience of previously "stuck" feeling
	rich immediacy of experience, and acceptance of it
	self experienced as existentially living in the moment; not as an object
	physiological "loosening" (tears, sighs, muscle relaxation)
	subjective experience replaces defined "problems"
7	new feelings experienced richly and immediately
	experience is new and present, not related to past structures
	self is the awareness of experiencing, not an object
	constructs are tentative and loosely held, to be tested
	feelings match ideation
	rich experience of choice

(Adapted from Rogers, 1961b, pp. 132–155).

participate in therapy, not perceiving problems in themselves. The transition from stage 6 to stage 7 (when it occurs) involves continuing growth, often after the termination of successful therapy.

At the outset of therapy, the client generally experiences problems in the past, and external to the self. As therapy progresses, the client comes to experience a greater immediacy and ownership of experience. These changes are carried over to life outside the consulting room, so that the client lives increasingly according to the organismic valuing process, rather than according to rigid ideas that may not correspond well to subjective experience.

Encounter Groups

Therapeutic change may be brought about in groups, as well as in individual psychotherapy. Rogers reported that the first such groups were developed by Kurt Lewin in the 1940s. The group movement has continued. The National Training Laboratories (NTL) offers training sessions to business organizations in order to enhance the performance of managers and executives (Rogers, 1970). Groups often serve as growth-enhancing experiences for healthy people, rather than as a means of treatment for those with emotional problems.

Rogers labeled his groups **encounter groups**. They provide experiences intended to produce personal growth and to improve interpersonal functioning. The groups have a **facilitator** who directs participants. Rogers felt that a relatively unstructured format was best. He opened his groups with very little structure, often something as simple as the statement, "Here we are. We can make of this group experience exactly what we wish" (1970, pp. 46–47). Too much structure through highly programmed group exercises, according to Rogers, is essentially a power play by the group leader. It keeps the locus of responsibility for the group with the leader, rather than sharing it with the members. Groups should be member-centered, just as therapy is client-centered.

Meador (in Rogers, 1970) reported a study of an encounter group that met for 16 hours over an intensive weekend experience. There were eight participants and two group facilitators. Each participant was filmed in ten 2-minute segments, two during each of the five group sessions. These segments were rated by judges on Rogers's Process Scale (described above). As Figure 9.1 shows, there was clear evidence of change. On the average, participants moved up one and a half stages on the Process Scale during this weekend experience. Of course, these data do not address the question of whether such change influenced behavior when participants returned to their everyday lives.

Rogers attributed interest in encounter groups, at least in part, to the increasing loneliness of our mobile and affluent culture. Personal relationships are more transient and superficial than they were in the past, and some

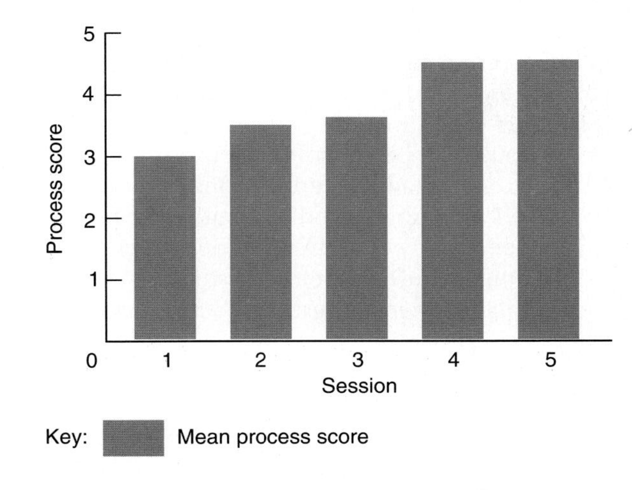

FIGURE 9.1 Changes in Process During Group Encounter

(Adapted from Rogers, 1970, p. 124.)

people turn to group experiences to alleviate the loneliness produced by this modern condition.

Treatment groups have become accepted modes of intervention for a variety of personal problems, including drug and alcohol abuse. Just as acceptance by a therapist facilitates change in individual psychotherapy, acceptance by group members promotes healing. Acceptance by other group members can help alcoholics acknowledge their drinking problem, an important first step toward change (Rugel & Barry, 1990).

Other Applications

Rogers commented, "I find a deep satisfaction in discovering that some of my basic learnings in psychotherapy apply to other areas of life" (1986a, p. 138). Let us examine some of these other areas.

Humanistic Education

Rogers wrote at length about the implications of his person-centered approach for education (DeCarvalho, 1991; Rogers, 1957b, 1969, 1974b, 1974c) . (Outside of therapy the term **person-centered** is more appropriate than "client-centered.") Traditional education focuses on the authority of the teacher, rather than on the needs and experience of the learner. Thus, it violates the fundamental value advocated by Rogers, namely making each person the evaluator and guide to his or her own experience.

The current system assumes that only the teacher can be trusted to decide what should be learned. Students are treated as though they would do nothing productive if not motivated by external demands and threats of poor grades. Hence, students are afraid: of failure, of embarrassment, of punishment. Such an atmosphere can undermine the motivation of even competent, creative scholars such as Albert Einstein (Rogers, 1969).

Rogers believed that an educational system based on trust of students would be more beneficial (1969). Ideally, students would develop their own programs of learning, either in cooperation with other students or alone. The student would have the freedom to err in choosing the direction of learning. The aim is to foster students' creativity, in which intrinsic interest in learning provides motivation, rather than the external rewards and punishments of grades and requirements.

In the ideal classroom, the authority of the teacher would be reduced. A better term for that new role would be *facilitator of education.* Such a person would provide resources to students based upon student interests. Such resources could include books, community experiences (since the classroom would not be so isolated from life as it is now), and personal experience. In a humanistic educational environment, the teacher would be perceived as an integrated and authentic person, would freely express and accept feelings, would treat students with unconditional positive regard, would empathically understand students' experiences, and would communicate his or her congruence, acceptance, and empathy to students (DeCarvalho, 1991).

Traditional education addresses only the intellect, ignoring feelings and distrusting "experiential learning" (Rogers, 1973, 1987). Rogers argued that feelings are part of the whole person, and to educate only the mind is unnecessarily limiting. B.F. Skinner (see Chapter 11), who excluded feelings and other internal states from his behavioral theory, had very different suggestions for improving education (Rogers & Skinner, 1956). Humanistically oriented educators have attempted to transform classrooms to be more consistent with Rogers's principles (e.g., Bell & Schniedewind, 1989; D.A. Read & Simon, 1975; Shapiro, 1985; Thomas, 1988). It has even been claimed that "the *real* purpose of higher education [is to develop] self-actualizing personalities" (Cangemi, 1984, p. 151).

Marriage and Relationships

Rogers's humanistic approach also has implications for marriage. He noted that modern marriage occurs in a new context, compared to past generations. Contraception makes limitation of family size possible, which changes the roles of the marriage partners. The lengthening life span makes marriages last many decades longer now, which means that the implications of psychological development (or its absence) are felt more keenly. Other factors necessitating changes in our thinking about marriage are the social acceptability of divorce, family mobility, wives who have jobs and careers, and sexual freedom (Rogers, 1977).

Rogers described a person-centered relationship as involving more mutual trust, tolerance of separate as well as shared interests, and focus on the uniqueness of each partner rather than on impersonal expectations about roles. Greater mutuality and equality result, and communication between partners is more honest.

Humanistic openness may produce more mature interaction, but there are risks (as in any change). Partners may form **satellite relationships**, significant secondary relationships that may sometimes involve extramarital sexual intimacy. While these seem, to the individuals who choose them, to meet significant growth needs, they obviously challenge trust and risk jealousy. A theory placing the locus of evaluation of experience within the individual makes choices such as these satellite relationships more frequent, and may seem to endorse them.

D. Cramer, in several studies (1985, 1986, 1990a, 1990b), has examined both romantic relationships and friendship. These studies support the growth-producing qualities of relationships identified by Rogers. Cramer (1990a) reported that high school and college students had higher self-esteem if their romantic partners possessed the characteristics identified as facilitative of growth by Rogers (unconditional acceptance, empathy, and congruence). Facilitative qualities of friends were also associated with higher self-esteem, but not so strongly as were those of romantic partners. The specific aspects of the relationships that predict later self-esteem need to be identified with later, longitudinal research. Unconditional acceptance seems to be a major influence (Cramer, 1990b). Friends appear able to be relatively directive, that is, to give advice, while still having growth-facilitating qualities. This contrasts with the nondirective mode advocated by person-centered therapists (Cramer, 1986).

Young adult females who reported having a friendship characterized by understanding, congruence, and unconditional acceptance scored higher on measures of psychological adjustment and self-esteem than did those without such friendships. Results with males did not confirm this pattern, though, perhaps because of an inadequate sample size (Cramer, 1985). Of course, in correlational studies, the direction of causality is debatable. Perhaps psychological adjustment produces better friendships, rather than the other way around.

Administration Relationships between administration and staff, like those between therapist and client, parent and child, and teacher and student, will be growth promoting if the three characteristics of genuineness (congruence), acceptance (prizing), and empathic understanding are present (Rogers, 1979). Organizations, including industrial enterprises, are traditionally based upon patterns of authority that would change under Rogers's humanistic vision of human relationships. He described an industrial experiment in sharing power and decision making with workers that was so successful it boosted the profit margin substantially, so much so that it was regarded as a "trade secret" (1977, pp. 101–102). This application sounds much like the current successes of Japanese management techniques.

Political Conflict, War, and Peace In the political realm, Rogers (1982a) suggested ways of dealing with various conflicts. He used his expertise in encounter groups to facilitate discussions between the National Health Council, composed of representatives of medical professions, and poor people concerned with their access to health care. This exchange of ideas led to real social change. Similarly, he led encounter groups in Northern Ireland between the Protestant and Catholic sides in their long-standing conflict, and reported that, at least in a small way, tensions were reduced among participants. He commended the peace talks at Camp David between Anwar Sadat of Egypt and Menachem Begin of Israel, convened in 1978 by President Jimmy Carter. Rogers felt these talks used many of the strategies he had found successful. (Rogers was not involved in these negotiations, however.) In 1985, the Center for the Studies of the Person co-sponsored the Rust Workshop, a meeting in Austria of 50 participants including government officials, academicians, and others from 17 countries (Rogers, 1986b). They met in small groups, aiming to reduce political tensions through face-to-face encounters. Rogers suggested that psychological principles, including those discovered in his encounter groups, could even help avert the threat of nuclear annihilation (Rogers & Ryback, 1984).

Summary

Carl Rogers has been a major spokesperson for the humanistic viewpoint within psychology. He offered a theory in which the person actively seeks higher development, motivated by the *actualizing tendency,* rather than being passively determined by external forces. Rogers explored the implications of this model for diverse areas, including therapy, group experiences, education, marriage, and relationships. His *client-centered therapy* emphasized three factors which contribute to therapeutic success: *unconditional positive regard, congruence,* and *empathic understanding.* He specified his theoretical constructs in ways that could be measured, so that the theory could be empirically verified. Furthermore, he conducted groundbreaking research on the therapeutic process (see Table 9.3).

Rogers acknowledged that he had focused far more on personality change than on the development or structure of personality (Rogers,

TABLE 9.3 Contributions of Rogers's Theory to Various Topics

Biological	Rogers did not consider biological factors, though his actualizing process is based on a biological metaphor.
Child Development	Children become alienated from the growth forces within them if they are raised with conditions of worth. Parents should raise their children with unconditional positive regard.
Adult Development	People can change in adulthood, becoming freer.
Mental Health	Rogers describes in detail a new, client-centered therapeutic technique. Individual therapy and group therapy, including encounter groups, lead to progress through stages of functioning, leading to greater openness to feelings, the present, and choice.
Society	The person-centered approach has implications for the improvement of society, including education, marriage, work roles, and group conflict (including conflict among nations).
Cognitive Processes	Thought and feeling may be impeded by accepting others' messages about what we should be.
Individual Differences	Rogers did not focus on stable individual differences, although individuals can be said to differ in their level of development and in the conditions they perceive must be met to be approved by others.

1986a). Rogers elaborated the change process in therapy, groups, education, and so on. However, he did not offer a general scheme for understanding personality differences.

Despite these limitations, as one of the founders of the Division of Humanistic Psychology, Rogers, together with Abraham Maslow and others, provided a forum for psychologists who believe that concepts such as "free will" and "the meaning of life" should not be ruled out of the discipline that aims to study human nature.

ILLUSTRATIVE BIOGRAPHIES: Concluding Remarks

To be true to the spirit of Rogers's approach, it is necessary, insofar as the materials permit, to allow each person to define his or her own important issues. In his therapy, for example, his eschewal of diagnosis and his insistence on listening to each person resulted in quite individualized sessions. One black client, for example, might spend an entire session talking about race, while another would feel relieved to be able to ignore it (Gendlin, 1988). To understand David Suzuki and Maya Angelou, we must understand what life felt like for them.

David Suzuki

Like Carl Rogers, David Suzuki adopted a biological metaphor in describing the process of personality development. He titled his autobiography *Metamorphosis: Stages in a Life* to emphasize the dramatic changes that occur during development. Fruit flies, which he studied assiduously as a biology student, have dramatically different forms at various life stages: egg, larva, and adult fly (Suzuki, 1988, p. 7). So too is it with human personality.

Suzuki points out that "saving face" is particularly important in traditional Japanese culture (1989, p. 24). Rogers's concept of *conditional positive regard* thus has particular significance. Canadian culture was in many ways more conducive to an individual's attending to the *organismic valuing process.* As Suzuki describes his family, it is clear that some of the acculturation his parents and grandparents experienced involved moving from a life in which conduct was determined by others to a life in which one's own experience mattered. His parents, for example, were the first in the family to have married because they "fell in love," rather than because their parents had arranged a marriage. Such parents fostered organismic trusting in their children, which contributed to David Suzuki's positive development. When David was in his late teens, his father "came to me and said I was old enough to be a man. From then on, he told me, I should make my own decisions and he would not interfere" (Suzuki, 1988, p. 43). Rogers would have applauded Suzuki's characterization of his father: "Though he was tough and demanding, his love and support served to reinforce my sense that I was worthwhile" (1988, p. 116). His parents emphasized the importance of feeling fulfilled through one's work, rather than earning a great deal of money (1988, p. 122). Suzuki echoed his parents' trust in the organismic valuing process when he advised others. "In advising youngsters today, I always tell them to go where their hearts pull them and not to try to figure out the best thing for income or long-term security" (Suzuki, 1988, p. 83).

As a teacher, Suzuki was informal. He dressed informally, particularly after a year at the University of California at Berkeley, and encouraged students to call him by his first name, contrary to the practice of his colleagues. Some of this difference was undoubtedly due to his exposure to the more informal models of professors in the United States, but it also reflected his empathic concern for the lives of his students.

When he made the transition to a broadcasting career, Suzuki described the potential of television to contribute to the solution of social problems. "Nuclear war, environmental degradation, social manipulation and control—these became matters of great concern that I could discuss through the media and hope to make an impact on people" (Suzuki, 1988, p. 219). Rogers was interested in similar issues, although his theory does not explain why Suzuki developed these interests while others do not.

Incidentally, Suzuki described an event in his mother's life that illustrates the paranormal phenomena mentioned by Rogers. He tells how his mother, in southern Ontario, woke up crying, knowing that her own mother had died. It was a month before a letter from Japan confirmed the woman's death. The respect, even awe, with which he described this event is but one striking example of the trust of feelings that is a pervasive theme in his book.

Maya Angelou

Maya Angelou also described her feelings. In the earlier decades of her life, the feelings were often of fear and need for love. Angelou sought acceptance throughout her youth, handicapped by the blatant racism of her society and by the sense of abandonment produced by her parents' divorce. She described one incident in childhood when a neighbor woman, probably at her grandmother's suggestion, invited her in for cookies and lent her books. It illustrates the acceptance Rogers described as so important:

> I was liked, and what a difference it made. I was respected not as Mrs. Henderson's grandchild or Bailey's sister but just for being Marguerite Johnson. (Angelou, 1969, p. 85)

The search for love made Maya vulnerable. She became a prostitute out of a mistaken belief that the rich man who served as her pimp was in love with her and would marry her, needing only a month's worth of prostitution money to clear up some gambling debts. More positively, when she met some whites who treated her as an equal, she found that "the old habits of withdrawing into righteous indignation or lashing out furiously against insults were not applicable in this circumstance" (1976, p. 75). Positive regard, as Rogers would say, can be transformational.

Throughout, her grandmother provided a loving and stable environment. She loved her granddaughter with few "conditions of regard." She did insist that Maya act courteously toward whites, even when she felt angry. While such incongruence is troubling from a humanist's perspective, it was adaptive under the social conditions of racial prejudice in which she grew up. When life became too frightening in California, Maya returned to Stamps, Arkansas, as a young adult with her son, seeking again the bulwark her loving grandmother provided.

Angelou's autobiography provides abundant evidence of her organismic valuing process. She felt the injustice of racism and was angry that her grandmother (who was keenly aware that protest in the South could lead to death by lynching) insisted upon polite and controlled behavior in the face of racist insults. When angry, Angelou walked away from situations: from prostitutes who had violated the rules that she (as their employer) had made, and from a babysitter who had briefly kidnapped her son. While her anger was not tempered by the self-control of her grandmother, it did keep her in touch with her self-actualization process. At other times, her organismic valuing process was reflected in a strong appetite for sex. It also made her a nonconformist, which sometimes saved her from mishap. When the singers in the cast of *Porgy and Bess* had their hair straightened in Italy, Maya insisted that the chemicals, which burned intensely, be washed out of her hair; she was the only one who didn't have her hair fall out as a consequence of this overly harsh chemical treatment.

Angelou did not always follow her organismic valuing process. It conflicted with her need to be loved. She decided to marry Thomas Allen, a bail bondsman, despite misgivings about his presumption that he could make all the important decisions. "I ignored the twinge which tried to warn me that I should stop and do some serious thinking" (Angelou, 1981, p. 103). Soon, though, another man won her heart and prevented the practical but subjectively troublesome marriage from taking place. Another relationship, too, conflicted with her inner sense, when her African lover, Sheikhali, demanded that she become less impatient, more submissive, more traditionally female (Angelou, 1986).

In Africa, Angelou (1986) learned to accept being black with pride. This came from the models of proud black tribal leaders. To a lesser extent, she had felt acceptance in Europe. The power of her feelings attests to the importance of the acceptance of other people as nourishment for self-actualization.

Angelou describes a time of great anguish when she sought help from a therapist. Though she very much needed help, she quickly concluded that the wealth and social class of this man would make it impossible for him to understand her, and turned instead to a friend (Angelou, 1976). Later she felt such a healing sense of being understood when she talked about her son to Martin Luther King, Jr. (Angelou, 1981). To what extent is the *empathic understanding,* which Rogers described as so important for therapists, possible when the client comes from a different social background? Therapists are now attending to this problem.

GLOSSARY

actualizing tendency the force for growth and development that is innate in all organisms

client-centered therapy therapy based upon the belief that the person seeking help is the best judge of the direction that will lead to growth

conditions of worth the expectations a person must live up to before receiving respect and love

congruence a feeling of consistency between the real self and the ideal self

empathic understanding the ability of the therapist to understand the subjective experience of the client

encounter group growth-enhancing technique in which a group of people openly and honestly express their feelings and opinions

facilitator the leader of an encounter group

fully functioning Rogers's term for a mentally healthy person

ideal self what a person feels he or she ought to be like

organismic valuing process inner sense within a person, which guides him or her in the directions of growth and health

person-centered Rogers's orientation to therapy and education, which focuses on the experience of the client or student rather than the therapist or teacher

prizing characteristic of a good therapist, which involves positively valuing the client; also called "unconditional positive regard"

Process Scale measuring instrument to assess how far along an individual is to the goal of becoming a fully functioning person

real self the self that contains the actualizing tendency

satellite relationships side relationships, which supplement a person's primary committed relationship

unconditional positive regard accepting and valuing a person without requiring particular behaviors as a prerequisite

STUDY QUESTIONS

1. Explain what Rogers meant by the *actualizing tendency.*
2. Discuss Rogers's idea that people are basically good, and the criticism this optimism has elicited.
3. List and explain the characteristics of a *fully functioning person.*
4. Discuss Rogers's attitude toward subjective experience.
5. Explain how Rogers used the concept of "self" in understanding personal growth.

6. Explain Rogers's concept of *congruence* and *incongruence.* What are the implications for psychological well-being?
7. What sort of environment encourages the development of creativity?
8. Why is Rogers's theory called *client-centered*?
9. List and explain the three major conditions necessary for therapeutic progress.
10. Describe research testing the effectiveness of client-centered therapy.
11. Describe some of the important changes measured by the Process Scale.
12. Describe an encounter-group experience. List some of the uses of such groups.
13. Describe Rogers's approach to education.
14. How did Rogers's humanistic approach influence his beliefs about marriage and relationships?
15. Describe the implications of Rogers's approach for business.
16. Describe Rogers's work on international tensions.

CHAPTER 10

Maslow: Humanistic Psychology and the Hierarchy of Needs

BIOGRAPHY OF ABRAHAM MASLOW

Abraham Maslow

Abraham Maslow was born April 1, 1908, in Brooklyn, New York. His parents were Russian immigrants, poor and uneducated, but hoping for something better for their son. His father was a cooper (a barrel-maker). Abraham grew up, the oldest of seven children, in the only Jewish family in the neighborhood, and he "was not always sure where his next meal was coming from" (Maddi & Costa, 1972, p. 159). He described the experience as lonely: "I grew up in libraries and among books, without friends" (A.H. Maslow, 1968a, p. 37).

Maslow was intellectually gifted. His IQ was measured at an astonishing 195! (Maslow, 1954/1987, p. xxxvi). In college, Maslow at first studied law, as his father wished. However, this did not appeal to him and he abandoned it after two weeks. He turned to a broader course of studies at Cornell, and then transferred to the University of Wisconsin in 1928 to study psychology. While still in college, he married his high school sweetheart (and cousin), Bertha, when she was 19 and he 20. His wife was an artist, and undoubtedly fostered Maslow's ongoing respect for more global and integrative approaches to knowledge.

Ironically, given the later direction of his theorizing, Maslow was at first very excited about the behaviorism he was studying at the University of Wisconsin. His doctoral work was supervised by Harry Harlow in the primate laboratory at Wisconsin. (Harlow is famous for the "cloth mother" studies that established the importance of contact comfort for monkeys.) Maslow's dissertation was an observational study of sexual behavior in monkeys. He reported that sexual behavior was influenced by dominance. Furthermore, in establishing dominance hierarchies, monkeys communicate primarily by visual cues, rather than by fighting. Harlow evaluated Maslow's work very highly (Lowry, 1973, p. 1).

Behaviorism and animal psychology did not continue to hold Maslow's interest. He read psychoanalysis and Gestalt psychology and philosophy, and these paved the way for an experiential conversion.

> Then when my baby was born that was the thunderclap that settled things. I looked at this tiny, mysterious thing and felt so stupid. I was stunned by the mystery and by the sense of not really being in control. I felt small and weak and feeble before all this. I'd say that anyone who had a baby couldn't be a behaviorist. (Maslow, 1968a, p. 56)

Maslow and his wife had two daughters. (He reported that his wife warned him not to experiment on them!)

Following successful completion of his dissertation, Maslow remained at the University of Wisconsin as Assistant Instructor and Teaching Fellow (1930–35) before going to Columbia University as a Carnegie Fellow (1935–37). While at Columbia, he interviewed female college students about their sex lives (Maslow, 1942), extending to humans his earlier observations of monkeys. This research caused some controversy and may have inspired the Kinsey studies of sexuality that began several years later. Maslow was Associate Professor at Brooklyn College (1937–51), where he was especially popular among the many students who came from immigrant families. He met many eminent psychologists who came to America to escape Nazism, including Alfred Adler, Karen Horney, and Kurt Goldstein. Besides his academic career, Maslow also was plant manager in a family company from 1947 to 1949 (Maddi & Costa, 1972). He became Professor and Chairman of the Psychology Department at the new Brandeis University (1951–69). He experienced a difficult period in about 1965, which he described as "a long spell of insomnia and . . . a writing block" (Maslow, 1966, p. xix) that responded to a brief period of psychotherapy. While on a leave of absence, working on the implications of humanistic psychology for broader social values, Maslow died of a heart attack in 1970, at age 62.

Abraham Maslow was a member and officer in several professional organizations, including the Society for the Psychological Study of Social Issues, the New York Academy of Sciences, the American Psychological Association, and, of course, the Association for Humanistic Psychology (of which he was one of the founding members, with Rollo May, Carl Rogers, and others, in 1962).

Maslow supported the **human potential movement**, in particular at the Esalen Institute in Big Sur, California, "the world's first growth center" (Maslow, 1987, p. xi). He gave workshops at Esalen, but was not comfortable with the much more emotional expression of Fritz Perls, who disrupted Maslow's first talk at Esalen by crawling toward an attractive woman saying, "You are my mother; I want my mother" (Maslow, 1987, p. xi).

Maslow's work was directed toward society at large, which he hoped to improve, more than to academic audiences, whose methodological rigidity and lack of vision he criticized. His later books have been described as "both humanistic and Messianic" (Maddi & Costa, 1972, p. 150).

ILLUSTRATIVE BIOGRAPHIES

Maslow's theory outlines a process of growth from basic needs, including the physiological needs that we share with animals, to the highest motivations that develop when humans achieve their full potential. Not everyone, however, achieves this highest level.

HUMANISTIC PSYCHOLOGY AND THE HIERARCHY OF NEEDS

Maslow's Vision of Psychology

Abraham Maslow believed that the method of mainstream psychology prevented full knowledge of human nature (Maslow, 1966). Psychological theory and research are not focused on the most important areas of human nature—that is, the higher functions that raise us above the animals. Like animals, we eat, we reproduce, we learn. However, people are capable of developing beyond these primitive processes. A theory limited to these levels cannot explain a healthy person, any more than a theory of color vision can explain what we see in a Picasso masterpiece. In addition, Maslow criticized theories based upon clinical experience with neurotic individuals who have not achieved full human potential.

Maslow believed psychology could learn from *existentialism* because of its emphasis on (1) the concept of *identity,* so important to human experience, and (2) its emphasis on **experiential knowledge.** In fact, he went so far as to claim that existentialism could "supply psychology with the underlying philosophy which it now lacks" (Maslow, 1968b, p. 10). It would replace logical positivism, which, Maslow felt, had failed to direct psychology toward the uniquely human experiences that personality theorists and clinicians face. For psychology to understand the profound meaningfulness of life, the "ultimate aloneness of the individual" (Maslow, 1968b, p. 14), and the real uncertainty of the future, it must go beyond the more limited deterministic theories available in behaviorism and in psychoanalysis. A **third force** psychology, much influenced by existentialism, was being developed. Maslow is widely acclaimed as "the spiritual father of American humanism," this new third force.

Traditional scientific methodology is **method-centered**. Human experiences that cannot be investigated in the traditional fashion are ruled

Miles Davis

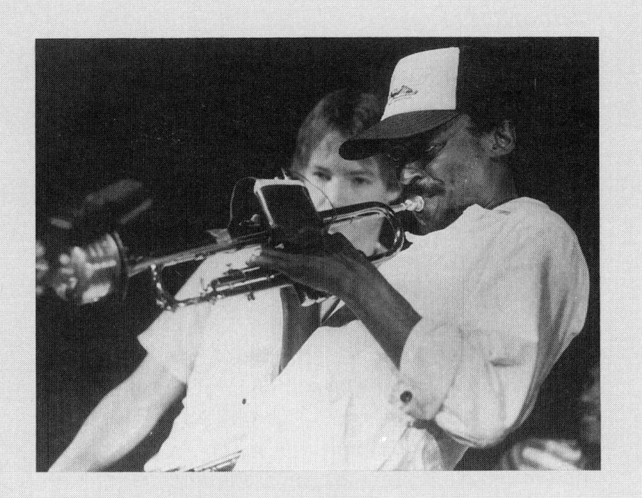

Miles Davis, born May 26, 1926, in Alton, Illinois, was an internationally acclaimed jazz musician, trumpet player, and composer who is credited with creating the "fusion movement" in music. Like many jazz musicians, he suffered repeated problems with heavy drug use, especially heroin and cocaine. For more than four years, he dropped out of public visibility and did not touch his horn. Some believed that drugs had ended his career, but in 1980 he returned to performing, renewing his career until his death in 1991.

How are we to understand this complex personality, a musical genius, a sometime drug addict, a promiscuous lover with two ex-wives, whose relationships with his children were troubled? Is his musical creativity evidence of self-actualization? Or was he, like the vast majority of people, not self-actualized?

Mary Crow Dog

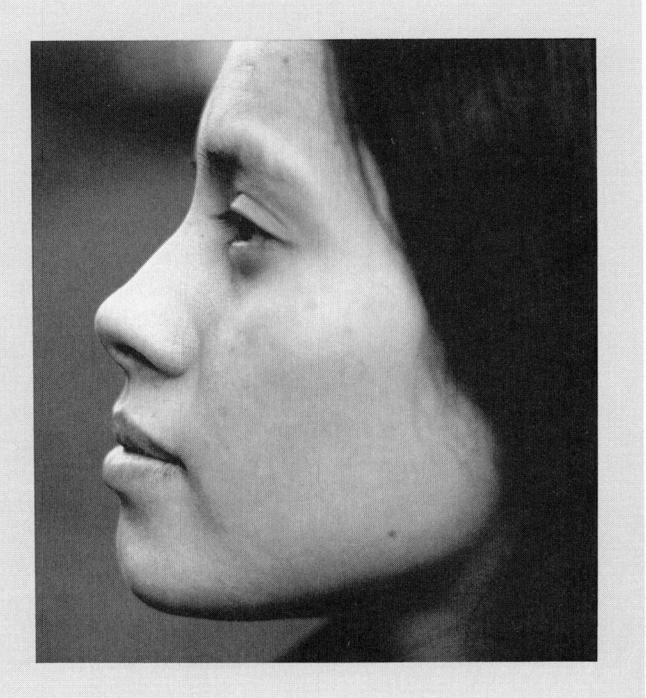

Mary Crow Dog is a Sioux woman who grew up on the Rosebud Reservation in South Dakota. She describes an early life that can be characterized as impoverished and delinquent. As an adult, she has been active in the political movement for Indian rights. She is married to a traditional Sioux medicine man, struggling to preserve a way of life.

Mary Crow Dog was fathered by a part Indian, mostly white man who left her mother before she was born (in 1953). She was the youngest of five brothers and sisters; a younger boy was also adopted after her. Her mother was trained as a nurse and worked some distance away, leaving Mary and her siblings in the care of their grandparents. Mary reports that her mother remarried "when I was nine or ten" (Crow Dog & Erdoes, 1990, p. 15). Like so many of her people, she grew up surrounded by alcoholism and violence. Their home was an unheated shack with no plumbing or electricity.

Cultures clashed in Mary's life. Her mother and grandmother encouraged her to give up traditional native ways. The Catholic religion and the English language seemed keys to a better life. This was the policy of the federal government as well. Mary attended a Catholic boarding school. She rebelled, once hitting a new teacher, a priest, giving him a bloody nose.

Her life after finishing high school included drinking, smoking pot, and shoplifting. She had been drinking heavily throughout adolescence. "At age twelve I could drink a quart of the hard stuff and not show it. . . . I came close to being an out-and-out alcoholic—very close" (Crow Dog & Erdoes, 1990, p. 44). She credits her recovery to discovering a purpose in life—aiding the Indian movement.

Mary Crow Dog participated in the political activities of the American Indian Movement (AIM), including protests in Washington in 1972, in which the group took over the Bureau of Indian Affairs for several days. She was a heroine at the protest at Wounded Knee in 1973. The Indians had declared Wounded Knee a sovereign territory, claiming old treaty rights. Under siege for 71 days, the Indians were surrounded by federal troops, and were fired upon. There Mary gave birth to her first child, Pedro. She was young and unmarried.

After this, she married a medicine man, Leonard Crow Dog (12 years her senior), who had been the spiritual leader at Wounded Knee. He led traditional Sioux ceremonies, including the Sun Dance, the Ghost Dance, the sweat lodge, and the quest for visions, aided by peyote. Traditional Indian ceremonies had been banned by law for several decades, and Crow Dog was helping to revive them, now that they were again legal. Mary describes the difficulty of adjusting to his family and of meeting the strenuous demands of his household. His active involvement in the movement for Indian rights brought frequent visitors who needed to be fed and housed. Her husband was sent to jail for over a year for his political activities. One time she left him, feeling overwhelmed, but he retrieved her. They have three children, in addition to her son.

Mary Crow Dog's life is a story that begins in great need and poverty and moves to a spotlight of political activities. Though active in political protests, Mary says that she does not consider herself a radical or revolutionary, but simply, like her people, yearning to be left alone to live the life they choose. How can her individual story be understood from the perspective of Maslow's theory of needs?

"nonscientific." Maslow recommended, instead, a **problem-centered** approach in which the issues to be investigated would be given higher priority than would the methods. Other humanists, such as Carl Rogers, shared this view. Gordon Allport, although generally classified as a "trait theorist," also argued for a problem-centered emphasis. Maslow expressed his rejection of a method-centered approach by suggesting that "what isn't worth doing, isn't worth doing well" (Maslow, 1966, p. 14).

Maslow did not want to throw out traditional scientific methods, however. Rather, he wanted to supplement them with a more honest acknowledgment of the experiential basis of the problems being investigated. Maslow argued that research should begin with phenomenology, which would provide the experiential base, defining the problem to be investigated. Then upon this experiential knowledge, the empirical methods of hypothesis testing should be built. Either emphasis alone is inadequate: methodology without "soul," or experiential knowledge without the cross-validation of the scientific method. The two approaches are less antagonistic, in Maslow's vision, than is commonly supposed. "Emotion is not always an enemy of truth and objectivity," he observed (1966, p. 140).

To understand normal personality, innovative methods must be devised, since traditional methodology is inadequate. Maslow struggled to define such a new approach. He described his vision as "Taoist Science," which he contrasted with "Controlling Science" (1966, p. 95). Taoist Science would be more subjective and experiential, rather than objective and abstract. It would honor and even love the subject matter, rather than being coolly indifferent. It would be interpersonal (in the spirit of Buber's "I-Thou" approach), truly engaged in a meaningful interaction with the object of study. It would not insist upon a false separation of the observer and the subject. Rather, it could be described as "fusion-knowledge." Furthermore, it would be explicitly concerned with values. All of these notions violate traditional assumptions of scientific methods that, Maslow argued, cannot adequately study healthy personalities.

One obstacle to the development of such a science is the limited development of scientists as human beings. Traditional science sometimes functions as a defense mechanism, offering safety and predictability. When studying the highest human potentials, scientists are likely to experience resistance against the truth, because this subject matter challenges them personally, whereas nonhuman or clinical topics do not (Maslow, 1966).

Hierarchy of Needs

Maslow postulated that people begin development with basic motives that are not noticeably different from animal motivation. As they mature, and as their lower-order needs are satisfied, people develop more uniquely human motivations. Thus, motivation changes as we progress upward through a **hierarchy of needs**, or motives. This hierarchy consists of five levels: four levels of **deficiency motivation**, and a final, highly developed level called **being motivation**, or self-actualization.

Deficiency Motivation

The first four levels of the need hierarchy can be understood as motivation to overcome the feeling of a deficiency. A **basic need**, if unmet, leads to a feeling of craving, and it directs action to get the need fulfilled. This fulfillment brings pleasure. Subjective experiences of "craving" and "pleasure" would, of course, not be possible to measure operationally in the animal studies that were the basic research approach of behaviorists under whom Maslow studied. Humans, though, can be asked to report their experience; and they should be asked to do so, according to Maslow.

What are these basic needs? Maslow listed four of them and asserted that they emerge in a particular order (see Figure 10.1). Each need must be met, more or less adequately, before the individual is free to move on to a "higher" need.

Physiological Needs

At the lowest level of the need hierarchy are physiological needs, the needs for food, water, sleep, and sex. These needs are essential to human and animal survival. If unmet, they dominate motivation, regardless whether other, higher-order needs are also unmet. "For the man who is extremely and dangerously hungry, no other interests exist but food," Maslow asserted (Maslow, 1943, in Lowry, 1973, p. 156).

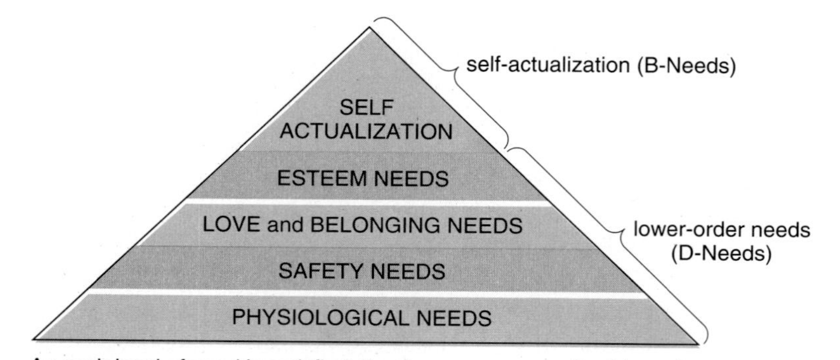

FIGURE 10.1 Maslow's Hierarchy of Needs

Lower animals may always live at this level, but humans, under normal conditions, have their physiological needs predictably met. If these needs are met adequately (though not necessarily leading to complete satisfaction), the next need level becomes salient. If, after moving on, the person encounters a situation where the physiological needs are no longer met, these needs will once again become the predominate motivation. In Maslow's terminology, needs that are dominant at a particular time are called **prepotent**.

Maslow suggested that a person's history of need satisfaction is important, not only the current level of need satisfaction. He hypothesized that "it is precisely those individuals in whom a certain need has always been satisfied who are best equipped to tolerate deprivation of that need in the future, and . . . those who have been deprived in the past will react differently to current satisfactions than the one who has never been deprived" (1943, in Lowry, 1973, p. 157). Recent research on the effects of dieting on food metabolism offers support for his claim at the physiological level.

Safety Needs

At the next level, the person's predominant motivation is to ensure a safe situation. Familiarity is perceived as safe, so the young child feels threatened when new situations occur (loud noises, strange animals, parental quarrels or divorce, and so forth). Physical violence, of course, also threatens safety for both children and adults. For the most part, the safety needs of adults are met in an ordered society, but safety is threatened by emergency situations, such as "war, disease, natural catastrophes, crime waves, societal disorganization, neurosis, brain injury, [and a] chronically bad situation" (Maslow, 1943, in Lowry, 1973, p. 160).

Maslow interpreted some neuroses as attempts to ensure a feeling of safety. Compulsive and obsessive neurotics, especially, try to keep life quite predictable, although it impedes their higher-level functioning. Russell Sage, whose financial dealings brought him great wealth but little love, exemplifies a person continuing to strive for a feeling of safety through compulsive financial dealings.

Belongingness and Love Needs

If safety and physiological needs are adequately met, the next level to become "prepotent" is the need for love and belongingness. At this level, the person seeks love and friendship. Maslow included the need to give love, as well as to receive it. He described these needs as a frequent source of maladjustment in our society.

Sex is an issue at this level to the extent that it is an expression of affection; but sex can also function at a purely physiological level (that is, the first level of the hierarchy). Maslow was interested in human sexuality, in particular, extending his doctoral studies in which he observed sexuality in animals. His work predated the rise of sexology, and it was less statistical than the later work of Kinsey. He felt that sexual dissatisfaction was an important "deficiency need," and dreamed, "If I could discover a way to improve the sexual life of even one percent, then I could improve the whole species" (Maslow, 1968a, p. 54). He interviewed 120 women about their sexuality, in the context of a greater understanding of their individual personalities. He also planned to study prostitutes, but did not complete that research. Late in his life, he said, "If I were beginning all over again, I'd study homosexuality . . . as a means to a profound understanding of humanity" (1968a, p. 54).

Esteem Needs

The next need to emerge in the hierarchy is the need for self-respect and the esteem of others. We need esteem to be "stable [and] firmly based," by which Maslow meant that it should result from our actual abilities and achievements. Reputation based upon false premises would not, therefore, meet this need.

We can interpret achievement strivings as manifestations of the esteem needs. Donald Trump, for example, whose physiological, safety, and love needs were met by his financially secure and loving family, was highly motivated for career success. Maslow's hierarchical conception also suggests that people who feel unloved, perhaps sensing parental rejection, will continue to function at the third level of the hierarchy and will not be motivated by esteem needs. Perhaps the tragic life story of Marilyn Monroe can be understood in this way.

When these needs are not met, we feel inferior. Maslow noted that Adler, who wrote so much about feelings of inferiority, paid more attention to the esteem needs than did Freud. If the needs are met, we feel "self-confidence, worth, strength, capability and adequacy of being useful and necessary in the world" (Maslow, 1943, in Lowry, 1973, p. 162). Research supports this idea; undergraduates who scored high on a measure of self-actualization (the Personal Orientation Inventory, described later) also scored higher on a measure of Physical Self-Presentation Confidence than those less self-actualized (Ryckman, Robbins, Thornton, Gold, & Kuehnel, 1985).

Being Motivation

Once the deficiency needs are more or less adequately met, the person functions at a higher level, which Maslow called *being motivation*, as opposed to *deficiency motivation*.

The Need for Self-Actualization

At this highest stage, the person is no longer motivated by deficiencies, but rather by the need to "actualize" or fulfill his or her potential. "A musician must make music, an artist must paint, a poet must write, if he [or she] is to be ultimately happy. What a man [or woman] *can* be, he [or she] *must* be. This need we may call self-actualization" (Maslow, 1943, in Lowry, 1973, p. 162). It is the desire "to become everything that one is capable of becoming" (1943, in Lowry, 1973, p. 163). Subjectively, the person feels bored if lower-order needs are met, and this boredom motivates and is relieved by self-actualization striving.

Because humans have different potentials (compared to their similar physiological needs), the particular behaviors motivated by self-actualization needs vary from person to person. For Maslow, "self-actualization is idiosyncratic since every person is different" (1968b, p. 33).

Differences Between D-motivation and B-motivation

Lower-order needs occur earlier in the development of the individual and lower in the phylogenetic chart (which compares species). Because they are necessary for survival, lower-order needs cannot be postponed as easily as can higher-order needs. Lower-order needs feel more urgent than do higher-order needs when unmet. Maslow cited an example: "Respect is a dispensable luxury when compared with food or safety" (1954/1987, p. 57). Luxury or not, living at the level of higher-order needs brings better physical health and greater subjective happiness and serenity.

At the level of self-actualization, in order to stress the difference from deficiency motivation, Maslow described people as **metamotivated**. At this level they are motivated by "metaneeds" or "B-values" ("B" for "becoming") such as beauty, truth, and justice. They are not "motivated" in the traditional sense of the term, that is, seeking to reduce a need so as to restore homeostasis. At this highest level, there is less determinism (based upon environmental availability of need satisfaction) and more psychological freedom (Maslow, 1955). Perception is no longer focused, looking for objects to satisfy needs; it can be more passive and receptive. This is *B-motivation*, in contrast to *D-motivation* (deficiency motivation).

Interpersonal relationships take on a very different quality at the level of B-motivation. Maslow described **B-love** as nonpossessive and enjoyable. In contrast, **D-love** is often contaminated by jealousy and anxiety. B-love permits the partners more independence and autonomy and it facilitates the growth of each person (Maslow, 1955).

It would be tempting to interpret Maslow's hierarchy in a simple way: that each need prevails until it is met, and then disappears. That interpretation would mean that self-actualization does not appear as a need until the top of the hierarchy. This interpretation, though, is oversimplified (Maslow, 1968b, p. 26). The difficulty is that elements of self-actualization appear even at the earlier levels of the hierarchy. Curiosity and creative tendencies and talents are examples of such early manifestations of self-actualization. Thus, self-actualization tendencies motivate us, more or less, throughout life. We do not, however, become dominated by them unless and until we reach the highest level of the need hierarchy.

Research Testing the Need Hierarchy

A fundamental postulate of Maslow's theory is that the five needs emerge in the sequence he described. W.M. Fox (1982) argued that the theory is inconsistent with both empirical research (reviewed by Wahba & Bridwell, 1976) and observations of the real world, and should therefore be abandoned. He cited several phenomena that are inexplicable within the framework of the need hierarchy theory, including suicide, refusal to cannibalize humans or to eat sacred cows when starving, and soldiers' acceptance of death for patriotic reasons. Great creative art is not always produced when other needs are satisfied. On the contrary, "many great artists and composers created their masterpieces during extended period of time in which they were subjected to grinding deprivation and critical rejection, if not outright ridicule" (W.M. Fox, 1982, p. 30). Nazi concentration camps, for all their atrocities, did not cause all prisoners to regress to the lowest levels of human functioning, as Maslow's hierarchical theory would predict. Coles (e.g., 1971a, 1971b) has observed people in dire economic conditions who, in apparent contradiction to the concept of a need hierarchy, seem to function at higher levels of human potential.

Nonetheless, some research supports the postulate of a need hierarchy. Graham and Balloun (1973) surveyed a cross section of people in a community. The higher needs in the hierarchy were judged less satisfied than were the lower needs, and needs perceived as less satisfied were judged more desirable to satisfy. Graham and Balloun interpreted these findings as evidence for the hierarchical model. Evidence from cross-cultural anthropological records also is consistent with the model; people attend to their physiological needs before their safety needs (Davis-Sharts, 1986). An examination of Chinese history and literature is consistent with Maslow's concept of a need hierarchy; periods of peace, which provide more safety, a good life, and freedom to writers, have been associated with greater literary genius for over 2,000 years (Kuo, 1987).

Other researchers have measured the satisfaction of some or all of the five need levels in Maslow's hierarchy (Haymes & Green, 1982; Lester, 1990b; Lester, Hvezda, Sullivan, & Plourde, 1983; Pierson, Archambault, & Iwanicki, 1985; Poole & Evans, 1989; Strong & Fiebert, 1987; Williams & Page, 1989). This strategy has resulted in some evidence that the needs are sequentially important in different age groups as Maslow's hierarchical theory suggests; physiological needs are more important in childhood, whereas belongingness is more important in adolescence and adulthood (Haymes & Green, 1982). Self-actualization has been reported to increase with age (Hyman, 1988). Some inconsistencies in age sequencing are reported, however. Among the very old (ages 68–84), self-actualization scores on some subscales are reported to be lower than among those less old (ages 56–67) in one study (Plouffe & Gravelle, 1989).

Undergraduates who report that their needs are satisfied score lower on neuroticism (Lester, 1990b) and higher on belief in internal locus of control than do those who report less need satisfaction (Lester and others, 1983). The Maslowian Assessment Survey (MAS) distinguishes various theoretically distinct aspects of needs (need gratification, need importance, need salience, and self-concept) and has been reported to have good preliminary validity evidence. Among other results, need gratification was positively related to self-esteem and negatively related to neuroticism and depression (Williams & Page, 1989).

Based on questionnaire data from students, Mathes (1981) suggested that a better model would be only three need levels: physiological, belongingness, and self-actualization. The other two needs, esteem and security, did not fall into Maslow's predicted order when students made paired comparisons about which of two need-related satisfiers they would rather do without. The method, however, may not be valid, or college-age subjects may not have found the particular examples equally potent. Other studies provide better confirmation of the five needs (Roberts, 1982).

Self-Actualization

Maslow preferred the term **self-actualization** to terms such as "psychological health" (or illness). His term refers to the full development of human potential, based upon our biological nature. It connotes the full potential of being human. Unlike the term "adjustment," it does not mean adjusting to a particular cultural situation. Maslow suggested that, instead of referring to "illness," we should speak of "human diminution or stunting," at least in psychology generally. He did acknowledge that psychotherapy may need more specific terminology (1968b, p. vii). From his perspective, illness comes if the person denies his or her inner potential, going against one's own nature. Karen Horney made a similar point in describing the alienation from the "real self" in neurosis, and Maslow credited her as a theorist whose ideas were in the direction he advocated for psychology.

When a person's basic needs (the first four levels of the need hierarchy) have been met, motivation is directed toward *self-actualization*, which Maslow defined as

> ongoing actualization of potentials, capacities and talents, as fulfillment of mission (or call, fate, destiny, or vocation), as a fuller knowledge of, and acceptance of, the person's own intrinsic nature, as an unceasing trend toward unity, integration or synergy within the person (1968b, p. 25).

Maslow was convinced that it was necessary for psychology to study its healthiest, most developed persons if it was to learn about human potential. He remarked that

> healthy people are so different from average ones, not only in degree but in kind as well, that they generate two very different kinds of psychology. It becomes more and more clear that the study of crippled, stunted, immature, and unhealthy specimens can yield only a cripple psychology and a cripple philosophy. The study of self-actualizing people must be the basis for a more universal science of psychology. (Maslow, 1954, 1987, p. 149)

Maslow reported a study of self-actualized people, selected from his personal acquaintances and friends and from public figures, both current and historical. In a survey of some 3,000 college students, he found only one subject who met his criterion for being considered self-actualized. This is not surprising, for few people become self-actualized, and a young college sample would not likely have many who have yet achieved that level of personal growth. Maslow (1968b) estimated that fewer than 1 percent of people are self-actualized.

His decision about whether or not a person was self-actualized was, of course, subjective. He included Rorschach tests when practical (obviously not for historical figures). Early in his observations, he found that "Possible subjects, when informed of the purpose of the research, became self-conscious, froze up, laughed off the whole effort, or broke off the relationship. As a result, since this early experience, all older subjects have been studied indirectly, indeed almost surreptitiously" (1954/1987, p. 127).

Among the public figures, Maslow included Abraham Lincoln and Thomas Jefferson, both "fairly sure" to have been self-actualized, and seven others whom he said were "probably" self-actualized: Albert Einstein, Eleanor Roosevelt, Jane Addams, William James, Albert Schweitzer, Aldous Huxley, and Benedict de Spinoza. Nominating individuals as exemplars of mental health is instructive for readers of the theory, since prototypes are easier to consider than abstract concepts. It is, however, a risky strategy. Shostrom (1972), writing for a popular audience, named Richard Nixon, then at the height of his prestige as president, as an example of a self-actualized person, only to have the later scandal of Watergate discredit this assessment (Anderson, 1975; Shostrom, 1975). The concept of self-actualization is difficult to define precisely. Psychologists may erroneously label successful people as self-actualized. In fact, many successful people do not meet Maslow's criteria of self-actualization.

Characteristics of Self-Actualized People

Based upon his observations, Maslow identified a number of characteristics of self-actualized people.

Efficient Perception of Reality

Self-actualized people have "an unusual ability to detect the spurious, the fake, and the dishonest in personality, and in general to judge people correctly and efficiently" (Maslow, 1954/1987, p. 128). They are less likely than others to be misled by their own defense mechanisms, wishes, expectations, or stereotypes. Rather, like the boy in the fairy tale, they are likely to see that the emperor has no clothes if, in fact, he has none. This accuracy perhaps comes because they are not threatened by the unknown, and because their focus is not narrowed by unfilled needs (Maslow, 1955).

Acceptance

Maslow's self-actualized subjects were more accepting of themselves, of others, and of nature, than the average person. This includes acceptance of their "animal level;" they eat well, sleep well, and enjoy sex. They accept both the bad and the good, and are thus tolerant. Research suggests that self-actualized people (measured by low discrepancies between the self and the ideal self) have less fear of death (R.A. Neimeyer, 1985a).

Spontaneity

Self-actualized people behave spontaneously, simply, and naturally. They are not generally outwardly unconventional, however. This spontaneity derives from being in close touch with their inner impulses and subjective experience. They do not hide behind a social mask. Research finds that, in older women, self-actualization (measured by the Personal Orientation Inventory) and impulsiveness are positively correlated, but this is not so among men (Plouffe & Gravelle, 1989).

Problem-Centered

Self-actualized people focus on problems outside themselves. They are *problem-centered*, not self-centered. The tasks may come from a sense of social obligation.

Need for Privacy (Solitude)

More than most people, self-actualized individuals like privacy. Maslow hypothesized that they would endure sensory deprivation experiences (which have been conducted by experimental psychologists) more easily than others. They are capable of high levels of concentration, and they make up their own minds rather than letting others make decisions for them.

Independence of Culture and Environment (Autonomy)

Self-actualized people do not depend on other people or the world for need satisfaction. They are "self-contained" and resilient in the face of difficulties. Because the self-actualized person is motivated by internal needs, rather than responding to the external world, such a person feels more "psychological freedom" (Maslow, 1968b, p. 35).

Freshness of Appreciation

The sense of awe and wonder at life remains always fresh with self-actualized individuals. This may come from aesthetic experiences, social encounters, or other sources. For many of Maslow's subjects, sexual pleasure provided a "kind of basic strengthening and revivifying that some people derive from music or nature" (Maslow, 1954/1987, p. 137).

Peak Experiences

Probably the best-known of the characteristics that Maslow described is the capacity for mystical experiences, which he called **peak experiences**. Maslow described these as

> feelings of limitless horizons opening up to the vision, the feeling of being simultaneously more powerful and also more helpless than one ever was before, the feeling of great ecstasy and wonder and awe, the loss of placing in time and space with, finally, the conviction that something extremely important and valuable has happened, so that the subject is to some extent transformed and strengthened even in daily life by such experiences. (Maslow, 1954/1987, p. 137)

A variety of events may trigger such experiences. Sometimes they occur in response to nature; sometimes they are religious experiences; sometimes they are even sexual encounters. Not all self-actualized people are "peakers," however. "Peakers" are more poetic, musical, philosophical, and religious. "Nonpeakers" are more practical, working in the social world through reform, politics, and other real-world arenas. Maslow seemed to have more admiration for peakers, whom he called "transcending," than for nonpeakers, whom he called "merely healthy" (1954/1987, p. 138).

People often do not report their peak experiences to others, since they are very personal (J. Davis, Lockwood, & Wright, 1991). Privette (1983, 1985, 1986) reports that people's reports of "peak experience" convey distinctive characteristics: "joy, fulfillment, and lasting significance, . . . and for some, spiritual; . . . clarity of process marked by absorption, intention, sense of self, freedom, and spontaneity" (Privette, 1986, p. 241). College students and artists, despite differences in age and in triggering events, report peak experiences in similar terms (Yeagle, Privette, & Dunham, 1989). Are these peak experiences simply doing something very well? They are not. Subjects' descriptions of peak experiences are different from their descriptions of "peak performances," in which they perform excellently (Privette & Bundrick, 1987). Gordon (1985) has also reported subjects' experiences of peak experiences, focusing on interpersonal communication experiences. These attempts to quantify subjective experience are commendable, but it is not clear that Maslow's peak experiences, which he regarded as characteristic of self-actualization, exactly coincide with these. A different pattern of experience, corresponding more closely to Maslow's description of peak experience, can be found among residents of a yoga ashram (S.R. Wilson & Spencer, 1990).

Maslow's claim of the rarity of peak experiences and their status as a mark of high development needs further empirical evidence. He did not claim peak experiences occur only among the self-actualized, but he did assert that these experiences are more frequent among such individuals (Daniels, 1982; Maslow, 1968b, 1969). Stamatelos (1984) claimed that peak experiences can occur even among the developmentally delayed. Perhaps such episodes would be among the exceptions that Maslow noted when he remarked that not all peak experiences are truly "Being-cognition," that is, evidence of self-actualization (Maslow, 1968b, p. 100).

Self-reported peak experiences are correlated with hypnotic susceptibility and romantic love (Mathes, 1982). Additional research on altered states of consciousness in relationship to mental health might answer unresolved issues. While it seems reasonable that some people stuck at lower levels of development would be too rigid to allow themselves to experience the altered states Maslow described as peak experiences, it is by no means demonstrated that such experiences occur exclusively among the self-actualized.

Human Kinship

Self-actualizing people identify with human beings in general, feeling a sense of kinship with the human race.

Humility and Respect

Self-actualizing people are humble, feeling that they can learn from many different people, even those of a different class or race. They are democratic, rather than authoritarian, and do not insist upon maintaining their status over others.

Interpersonal Relationships

Self-actualized people are capable of "more fusion, greater love, more perfect identification, more obliteration of the ego boundaries than other people would consider possible" (Maslow, 1954/1987, p. 140). They are discriminating, however, seeking out other self-actualized people, so that they have deep relationships with a few people, rather than many more superficial relationships. They do, also, tend to attract admirers, who may be quite devoted, even becoming disciples. Self-actualized people do not, though, encourage this reverence.

Ethics and Values

Self-actualized people have strong ethical standards, although their standards are often not conventional standards of right and wrong. They are not concerned with what Maslow regarded as trivial ethical issues, such as "card playing, dancing, wearing short dresses, exposing the head (in some churches) or *not* exposing the head (in others), drinking wine, or eating some meats and not others, or eating them on some days but not on others" (Maslow, 1954/1987, p. 147). Their values emerge from acceptance of human nature and of their own nature, including their unique potentials.

Discrimination Between Means and Ends

Maslow's subjects were clearly focused on the ends or goals of their efforts and subordinated the "means to the end." Nonetheless, they could appreciate the pleasure of the "means."

Sense of Humor

Self-actualizers have a nonhostile sense of humor, not laughing at other people's expense. Their sense of humor is more philosophical than that of most people, laughing at the human condition. Overall, though, Maslow's subjects were more serious than humorous.

Creativity

Creativity is the one characteristic Maslow claimed was present in *all* of his self-actualized subjects, without exception. He did not mean creativity in the sense that we often use it. This creativity does not necessarily involve any creative product such as a work of art or music, which Maslow calls "special talent creativeness," as contrasted with "self-actualizing creativeness" (1954/1987, p. 160). "There can be creative shoemakers or carpenters or clerks. . . . One can even *see* creatively as the child does" (1954/1987, p. 143). The creativity of a self-actualized person emerges naturally out of the other characteristics: spontaneity, resistance to enculturation, efficiency of perception, and so forth. It is a capacity in all children, but is lost by many, as both neurosis and what psychoanalysts call *secondary process* displace earlier creativity (Maslow, 1958).

Research confirms Maslow's prediction by showing correlations between measures of self-actualization and creativity, specifically judged creativity of written and art projects (Buckmaster & Davis, 1985). Maslow would, of course, insist on a broader operational definition of creativity.

Resistance to Enculturation

By this, Maslow meant that self-actualized people do not "adjust" to society at the expense of their own character, but rather "maintain a certain inner detachment from the culture in which they are immersed" (1954/1987, p. 143). They are conventional when it is easier or less disruptive to be so, but this is a superficial adaptation that readily gives way to their *autonomous* nature.

Self-actualized people should be less affected than other people by social influence pressures. Research has found that undergraduates who scored low on a measure of self-actualization were more influenced, in their performance on a reasoning test, by statements leading them to believe whether they would do well or poorly. Those scoring higher on self-actualization were less influenced by this social expectation (Bordages, 1989).

Resolution of Dichotomies

Self-actualized people do not see in "either-or" terms, as less healthy people often do. Maslow offered several examples of dichotomies that, to self-actualized people, no longer seem opposite. Among these are reason versus emotion, selfish versus unselfish, serious versus humorous, active versus passive, and masculine versus feminine (Maslow, 1954/1987, p. 149). Rather than seeing conflict between what is good for the individual and what serves others, the two operate together, with "synergy" (Maslow, 1964). This fusion of self-interest and social-interest can occur at a cultural level, too, leading to a better society, a "Utopia" or, to use the term Maslow preferred, **Eupsychia** (Maslow, 1964).

Maslow noted that his subjects were not perfect.

> They too are equipped with silly, wasteful, or thoughtless habits. They can be boring, stubborn, irritating. They are by no means free from a rather superficial vanity, pride, partiality to their own productions, family, friends, and children. Temper outbursts are not rare. (Maslow, 1954/1987, p. 146)

And, because of their autonomy, they "are occasionally capable of an extraordinary and unexpected ruthlessness," for example, when terminating a friendship or a marriage, or when recovering quickly (too quickly, most people would say) from the death of a loved one (Maslow, 1954/1987, p. 146).

Maslow's list of characteristics of self-actualized people has served, for his followers, as a description of mental health, of what people become if they develop their full potential. Mittelman (1991) interpreted these characteristics as consequences of an "open" personality, in the sense of taking in information and experience nondefensively. Mittelman suggested that this reinterpretation shows the inherent interconnectedness of the characteristics of self-actualized people listed by Maslow.

In its focus on the goal of development, Maslow's theory neglects some important areas. It stresses the end product of self-actualization, but pays little attention to the developmental process by which that end is attained

(Olds, 1955). As a theory, Maslow's model adopts a biological metaphor that has limitations. He tends, with this model, to de-emphasize the importance of the social self, as though the only real self were that which emerged biologically (Daniels, 1988; Geller, 1982; S.R. Wilson, 1988).

Measurement and Research on Self-Actualization

Maslow did not devote much effort to the development of measuring instruments, preferring for the most part to observe people more holistically, in keeping with his concept of a receptive or Taoist scientific method. He did, however, collaborate with his wife to devise the Maslow Art Test "to test for holistic perception and intuition by testing the ability to detect the style of an artist" (Maslow, 1966, p. 62). This ability, which may perhaps be described as an intuitive cognitive style, does not necessarily improve with art training, and may even sometimes be impaired by such training. Maslow valued the receptive ability measured by the test and felt that it, combined with an ability to think in the abstract, nomothetic terms of traditional science, could enable psychologists to develop the new approach he envisioned.

Maslow realized that his ideas were in the early stages of scientific validation. He acknowledged that his work "is full of affirmations which are based on pilot researches, bits of evidence, on personal observation, on theoretical deduction and on sheer hunch. . . . [T]hey are hypotheses, i.e., presented for testing rather than for final belief" (1968b, p. ix).

The key concept in Maslow's theory is self-actualization. While Maslow explored this construct through observation, rather than formal measurement, others have attempted to assess self-actualization by means of a questionnaire.

Personal Orientation Inventory

The **Personal Orientation Inventory** (POI) (Shostrom, 1964) is a 150-item multiple-choice inventory that requires subjects to choose one of a pair of responses on each item. Experts, including Maslow himself, have agreed that the content seems consistent with the theory of self-actualization (Maslow, 1976; Ryckman and others, 1985; Shostrom, 1964). The measure provides two primary scores derived from Maslow's theory. The **Inner Directed Supports** scale measures the degree to which the subject provides his or her own support (as opposed to turning to others). The **Time Competence** scale measures the degree to which the subject lives in the present. In addition, there are subscales to measure self-actualizing values, existentiality, feeling reactivity, spontaneity, self-regard, self-acceptance, the nature of people, synergy, acceptance of aggression, and capacity for intimate contact. The scales, though distinct, are correlated, in part because some items are counted in more than one scale (Tosi & Lindamood, 1975). The measure is generally interpreted as a global score, rather than as subscores (Thauberger, Cleland, & Nicholson, 1982). While its reliability is comparable to that of most personality measures (Tosi & Lindamood, 1975), a higher reliability would be desirable (Hattie, 1986; Ray, 1984). Subjects, unless they are psychologically trained, cannot fake good scores (Tosi & Lindamood, 1975).

Shostrom (1964) reported that his inventory distinguished between groups nominated by clinicians to be self-actualized or not self-actualized, and that meaningful changes in scores occurred during the course of psychotherapy. Several studies have reported validation of the POI through criterion group studies; that is, groups thought to be more self-actualized score higher than those assumed to be less self-actualized. For example, medical patients score higher than do alcoholics, who score higher than schizophrenics (Murphy, DeWolfe, & Mozdzierz, 1984). Hattie and Cooksey (1984) synthesized data from many studies of various groups, and their meta-analysis confirms the prediction that groups considered more self-actualized will vary as expected on the POI. Groups that had been trained (counselors) or that had experienced encounter groups generally scored higher than unselected adults, and disturbed groups generally scored lower. The validity of the POI has been challenged, however; some argue that the discrimination among criterion groups is less convincing than POI supporters claim (Ray, 1984, 1986; A.S. Weiss, 1987).

Researchers have often used the Personal Orientation Inventory as a criterion measure of mental health. Scores increase as a result of various therapeutic interventions, including client-centered training groups for counseling students (Elizabeth, 1983); studying Gestalt therapy for a regular term, as opposed to a concentrated summer term, which was less beneficial (Peterson-Cooney, 1987); training in neurolinguistic programming (Duncan, Konefal, & Spechler, 1990); meditation (Delmonte, 1984); reading psychological self-help books (Forest, 1987); and exercise (Gondola & Tuckman, 1985). Hypothesized increases are sometimes not found (Giltinan, 1990). In addition, the POI correlates positively with other measures of mental health, including the Hardiness Test (J.M. Campbell, Amerikaner, Swank, & Vincent, 1989).

The Personal Orientation Inventory is related to other measures in ways that confirm its validity. People scoring high on the POI have more complex conceptual structures on several measures (Hageseth & Schmidt, 1982), which is expected if they have more elaborated ego skills (to use psychoanalytic language) or greater cognitive complexity (as Kelly's school would phrase it). They are more creative (Yonge, 1975) and more assertive (Ramanaiah, Heerboth, & Jinkerson, 1985). High scorers among married couples also report greater sexual enjoyment (J.T. McCann & Biaggio, 1989). Sex differences are minimal (Tosi & Lindamood, 1975), though some studies (J.T. McCann & Biaggio, 1989; Plouffe & Gravelle, 1989) report sex differences in the correlates of self-actualization. This suggests that more attention should be paid to self-actualization in the context of gender (and other) roles (cf. also Hyman, 1988; Poole & Evans, 1989).

Other Measures

A short form of the Personal Orientation Inventory, consisting of only 15 items, has been developed (A. Jones & Crandall, 1986). Other measures of self-actualization have also been developed (e.g., Buckmaster & Davis, 1985), although none are so widely used as the POI.

Obstacles to Self-Actualization

If self-actualization is an innate potential, why is it not universally developed?

Human beings repeatedly confront situations where they must choose between growth and safety. Safety choices are appealing, but only growth choices move us toward self-actualization. If we think of the positive attractions rather than the dangers of growth, and of the dangers rather than the attractions of what appears the "safe" choice, our choices will move us more often toward self-actualization. To encourage such choices in children, parents are wise to avoid both overprotection (which orients the child toward safety) and excessive approval (which focuses the child on others' opinions, rather than the youngster's own experience). When all goes well, the child experiences the growth choice as offering delight, and the safety choice as leading to boredom. Under less ideal circumstances, the growth choice seems dangerous and the safety choice offers approval (see Figure 10.2).

Besides this intrapsychic pull against self-actualization, there are other reasons why self-actualization is not more frequent. Higher-order needs only emerge if favorable external conditions (such as adequate food and housing) allow satisfaction of the earlier needs. An inadequate social environment impedes self-actualization. Also, higher-order needs are weaker than lower-order needs; hence, they must compete with them.

External forces can more readily obscure our inner motivations than is the case for animals.

> Humans no longer have instincts in the animal sense, powerful, unmistakable inner voices which tell them unequivocally what to do, when, where, how and with whom. All that we have left are instinct-remnants. And furthermore, these are weak, subtle and delicate, very easily drowned out by learning, by cultural expectations, by fear, by disapproval. (Maslow, 1968b, p. 191)

To indicate the weakness of human instincts, Maslow added the diminutive ending *-oid,* calling them **instinctoid** (Maslow, 1955, 1965). The weakness of higher instinctoid impulses means they are sometimes inadequate to lead us fully to self-actualization.

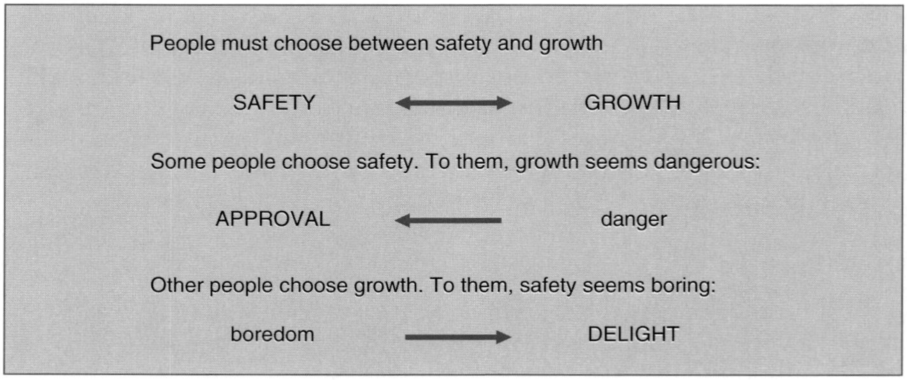

People must choose between safety and growth

SAFETY ⟷ GROWTH

Some people choose safety. To them, growth seems dangerous:

APPROVAL ⟵ danger

Other people choose growth. To them, safety seems boring:

boredom ⟶ DELIGHT

When people feel threatened, they choose safety instead of growth. Under more favorable conditions, safety seems boring, so growth is chosen instead.

FIGURE 10.2 Choice Between Safety and Growth

(Adapted from Maslow, 1962, p. 44.)

In addition, people sometimes experience a **Jonah complex**. When this happens, the person is convinced that it is impossible to do anything very important, and so avoids developing to his or her full potential. Maslow chided his students for not aspiring to make important contributions in their field. He asked them, "If not you, then who else?" (1976, p. 35). He warned them that failure to aspire to their highest potential, to self-actualization, would leave them profoundly unhappy.

Applications and Implications of Maslow's Theory

Because Maslow's aim was to improve the human condition through his theorizing, it is appropriate that his ideas have been applied to diverse areas.

Therapy

Within psychology, Maslow's theory has implications for psychotherapy. Many people, according to Maslow, turn to psychotherapy because their love and belongingness needs are unfulfilled. Therapeutic progress requires that these needs be met. Maslow believed that the therapeutic approach should be tailored to the particular patient. For seriously disturbed neurotics, a traditional Freudian approach might be appropriate. For more healthy individuals, group therapy and encounter groups would be more suitable.

Growth Centers

Growth centers, devoted to the development of human potential, have been founded using Maslow's ideas. The most well known of these centers is the Esalen Institute in Big Sur, California. At such centers, group experiences as well as lifestyle changes, often involving communal living, enhance human potential.

Work

Maslow found that many business people were similar to his self-actualizers. In 1962, he was a visiting fellow at a high-tech corporation in California, called Non-Linear Systems. Among self-actualized managers, he found positive, supportive interpersonal relationships with subordinates and more productive and creative work. Maslow's ideas have been widely explored in the business world, especially in MacGregor's concept of Theory X and Theory Y managers, and in the work of Chris Argyris. Workers are more effective when they function at the level of the higher needs. Conversely, work is a major area for the development toward self-actualization.

Religion

Maslow thought at length about religion, considering how the values emerging from his theory compared with religious traditions. He was strongly opposed to dogmatic views in religion (as in other fields). He interpreted the experiences of prophets in many of the world's religions as "peak experiences." Such moments bring important insights, useful to mankind in general and not simply to the individual. It is the task of religion to communicate these insights to their members. Unfortunately, however, it often happens that institutionalized religions are filled with "nonpeakers" who cannot communicate these prophetic experiences, and who substitute dogmatic rigidity for vision (Maslow, 1970). Some of this failure is inevitable, because it is difficult to translate right-brain mediated transcendental experience into language, which is a left-brain function (Frank, 1977).

Though he did not support traditional institutionalized religion, Maslow lamented the **desacralization** of human experience by professionals (including psychologists and physicians) as well as others. Removing a sense of the sacred, of the awesome highest human values, and treating humans as animal-like or robot-like, was a profound loss. He hoped that psychology would contribute to the "resacralization" of human experience, even if it meant experimenting with new forms, such as publishing poetry and personal testimonials in scientific journals.

Education

Maslow described the goal of education to be "the 'self-actualization' of a person, the becoming fully human, the development of the fullest height that the human species can stand up to or that the particular individual can come to" (1976, p. 162). This is surely a different aim from merely the acquisition of technical skills. Maslow realized that his theory implied drastic changes in educational practice, similar to the changes proposed by Carl Rogers. Humanistic education should foster, rather than sedate, the natural curiosity of children. In most classrooms, children learn to behave in ways that please the teacher, rather than being encouraged to think creatively.

The ideal college would have much more self-directed learning. Students would follow their own inner directions in meaningful and honest dialogue with faculty. "There would be no credits, no degrees, and no required courses" (Maslow, 1976, p. 175). For such a system to succeed, of course, students and faculty would need to be self-actualizing so that their choices would indeed be in the direction of growth.

Gender

Maslow favored the full development of women, as of men, and encouraged women to live up to their full potential. He described self-actualized people as not constrained by rigid sex roles. Both men and women could be both active and passive, in lovemaking and in life (1954/1987, p. 153). Nonetheless, Maslow believed that there are inherent, biologically based sex differences. (It seems unlikely that a psychologist whose doctoral work was based upon observation of sexual behavior in monkeys would give up this concept of biological sex differences.) Maslow envisioned men and women as achieving self-actualization along different routes or paths, a concept accepted by some feminist psychologists (e.g., Gilligan, 1982), but not all.

Values and Science in Maslow's Theory

Maslow has been accused of allowing his own values, rather than scientific observations, to dictate his description of the concept of self-actualization. That is, his list of characteristics of self-actualized persons may simply be a list of qualities that Maslow admires in a person (cf. McClelland, 1955). For example, his emphasis on mystical, nonrational experience, rather than reason, may reflect personal bias more than objective reality (Daniels, 1988; M.B. Smith, 1973). It has been suggested that the values represented in the need hierarchy are not universal, but rather are Western values. An alternate hierarchy has been proposed to reflect Chinese values, in which the highest level is "self-actualization in the service of society," rather than individual self-actualization (Nevis, 1983).

Maslow's concept of self-actualization clearly has meaning that extends beyond its status as an academic personality theory. It has been criticized for its limitations in supporting some people's political agendas (Sipe, 1987), and has been critically evaluated as a myth to foster individual development and social change (Daniels, 1988). Daniels finds fault, as a myth, with many aspects of Maslow's theory, but describes the concept of self-actualization favorably, as "one of the most optimistic and life-affirming [concepts] ever proposed within psychology" (1988, p. 19). The mythic function, however, goes beyond the standards by which scientific personality theory is evaluated.

Maslow, of course, was aware of the criticism accusing him of not following traditional methodology, not providing statistics to support his assertions, and allowing values to influence his work so blatantly. He claimed it didn't bother him:

> I have a secret. I talk over the heads of the people in front of me to my own private audience. I talk to people I love and respect. To Socrates and Aristotle and Spinoza and Thomas Jefferson and Abraham Lincoln. And when I write, I write for them. This cuts out a lot of crap. (1968a, p. 56)

Contrary to the aim of a valid scientific theory to make predictions, Maslow expected, paradoxically, that his approach would make people *less* predictable. Maslow felt that humanistic science would increase people's ability to make choices and to express their spontaneity. This would reduce the predictability of behavior by outsiders.

Surely Maslow was aware of the powers of science to persuade. In his preface to *Toward a Psychology of Being,* he remarked, "Science is the only way we have of shoving truth down the reluctant throat" (1968b, p. viii). He felt that his beliefs about human nature, if true, "promise a scientific ethics, a natural value system, a court of ultimate appeal for the determination of good and bad, of right and wrong" (1968b, p. 4). That is, a new ethics would emerge from his new view of human nature (Maslow, 1955; McClelland, 1955). He hoped that his theory would give us new models to emulate.

Regarding values, we may note that Maslow's vision went beyond his "third force" psychology with its emphasis on human values.

> I . . . consider Humanistic, Third Force Psychology to be transitional, a preparation for a still "higher" Fourth Psychology, transpersonal, transhuman, centered in the cosmos rather than in human needs and interest. (1968b, pp. iii–iv)

In the present day, with its awareness of global planetary issues and the conflict between human desires and the limits of the planet to restore itself, Maslow's vision of a Fourth Psychology seems prophetic. Yet he has not persuaded mainstream psychology that it should abandon the traditional scientific method for his more Taoist-receptive, intuitive model of experiential knowledge. As a sketch of the direction that psychological science should move, it needs to be supplemented by clear operational definitions (McClelland, 1955; Rychlak, 1988) if it is not only to inspire individuals, but also to transform the science of psychology.

Summary

Maslow proposed a *third force* humanistic psychology that was less deterministic and more focused on values than psychoanalysis or behaviorism (see Table 10.1). He proposed that people develop through five levels of a need hierarchy: physiological, safety, love and belongingness, esteem, and self-actualization. At the four lower stages, a person is motivated by deficiencies. At the highest stage, self-actualization, the person is motivated by *being motivation,* and has distinctive characteristics, foremost of which is creativity. *Peak experiences* are mystical states of consciousness that are particularly common among self-actualized people.

Maslow's theory has implications for many fields, and is closely associated with the *human potential movement.* He urged religion to be less dogmatic and more concerned with growth. In addition to psychotherapy, his work prompted the development of growth centers, such as Esalen, where people could live in a community that promoted self-actualization. He urged employers to be more concerned with the growth needs of their employees, and educators to encourage personal growth and creativity among students.

Maslow urged psychology to be more concerned with human values. He criticized mainstream psychology for being method-centered rather than problem-centered, and he argued that scientific investigation of the highest human potentials required development of new models of science.

TABLE 10.1 Contributions of Maslow's Theory to Various Topics

Biological	Biological motivations are the foundation of personality, but once satisfied, they become unimportant. Sex differences are influenced by biology.
Child Development	Children's physiological, safety, love, and esteem needs should be met. Changes in schools could facilitate growth.
Adult Development	Few adults develop to their full potential. Transformations in the workplace and elsewhere could change this.
Mental Health	Only a few people reach the highest developmental stage, self-actualization. Maslow describes these individuals in detail.
Society	A better society can be imagined (Eupsychia). Changes in schools, work settings, and religious institutions should be made. Growth centers can be established to foster development.
Cognitive Processes	Self-actualized people perceive the world accurately and are creative.
Individual Differences	Individuals can be said to differ in their position in the need hierarchy, that is, their level of development toward self-actualization. Self-actualized people develop their unique potentials.

ILLUSTRATIVE BIOGRAPHIES: Concluding Remarks

People, despite differences in culture and gender, are motivated by innate forces for growth. Yet these forces are weak, "instinctoid," and cannot always prevail over obstacles to self-actualization. How far did Miles Davis and Mary Crow Dog progress in this quest toward developing their full human potential? What obstacles did they confront?

Miles Davis

Maslow's theory is particularly pertinent to understanding Miles Davis because Maslow discussed creativity as a universal characteristic of self-actualized persons. However, Maslow distinguished creativity in the self-actualized sense from inherited special talent, such as in art or music, which does not necessarily constitute evidence of self-actualization. There can be no doubt that Miles Davis inherited musical talent to an extraordinary degree. He was admitted to the highly prestigious Juilliard School of Music in New York, and when he turned from that classical training to playing jazz, he performed with the great jazz musicians of the time, including Dizzy Gillespie and Charlie ("Bird") Parker.

Talent, even great talent, is not sufficient evidence of the kind of "creativity" that Maslow regarded as characteristic of self-actualization. In addition, we must consider the innovations that Miles Davis offered to the world of jazz, and for which he was frequently honored. Davis aimed for an improvisational spontaneity in his playing and demanded it of members of his band. He wrote partial scores and gave general guidelines for playing, changing somewhat with each performance, guided but not bound by technical rules. When performing a score that was, like traditional classical music, fully written, he urged his fellow musicians to *not* play exactly what was on the score. This improvisational style is strong evidence of the trait of *spontaneity*, which Maslow said is characteristic of self-actualized persons.

There also can be no doubt that Davis *resisted enculturation*. In his autobiography (M. Davis, 1989) he frequently complained about the expectation that blacks behave in certain ways, which avoided threatening the white establishment: smiling and acting submissive. He criticized many black musicians, even the great Louis Armstrong, for always smiling to white audiences, denying the anger and pain of being black. Miles refused to do so, and as a result was labeled as having an "attitude problem." He was outspoken against racist assumptions by whites. For example, when a white woman commented that Miles's "Mammy" would be proud that he was invited to dinner at the White House, Davis responded by criticizing her use of the term "Mammy" and pointing out that his mother was more cultured than she was, and that his father was a doctor.

Davis's background in a well-to-do family provided satisfaction of his physiological and safety needs, the first two stages of Maslow's hierarchy of needs. His description of the loving, supportive atmosphere in his family suggests that, to a large extent, his needs for love and belongingness were met. His father repeatedly sent him money when he needed it and welcomed him home, even going to New York to retrieve him when his drug addiction became severe.

What of Miles Davis's esteem needs? Clearly he won repeated honors and recognition in the musical world. Despite this, his autobiography revealed frequent feelings of lack of satisfaction of esteem needs. A recurrent theme in his life story was the passing over of black musicians, in favor of white imitators, for good pay, for contracts, and for awards. Davis clearly felt dissatisfied in obtaining recognition for his music, and it is the *feeling* of need satisfaction, rather than any "objective" assessment, that either allows or impedes progress to the next level of Maslow's hierarchy of needs. Davis did not doubt his own ability. His self-esteem needs were met, at least in the musical area. (He was not satisfied with his drug addiction.) Yet, largely as a consequence of racially motivated discrimination, his need for the esteem of others was not adequately met. This unmet esteem need would, in Maslow's theory, have precluded full self-actualization.

Mary Crow Dog

The poverty and violence of Mary Crow Dog's early life seemed to start her clearly at the bottom of Maslow's hierarchy of needs. Adults squandered food money on alcohol. Beatings, rape, and drunken brawls threatened her personal safety. Corporal punishment was frequent at school.

In an atmosphere of social disruption, love and belongingness needs are difficult to fulfill. Fortunately for Mary Crow Dog, she was permitted to stay with her grandparents, rather than being sent to a foster home, as happened to so many Indian children. Yet when she was a bit older, she was sent to Catholic boarding school and seldom saw her family.

The disruption of native culture threatened a sense of "belongingness" in a way that goes beyond the sort of personal or familial rejection we usually consider. How does one belong to a culture when one's mother and grandmother urge forgetting of the traditional language and practices? Yet to belong to mainstream American culture was impossible. Local toughs shot at Indians without provocation, and the Church and teachers also made their prejudices clear, according to Mary Crow Dog's description of her life.

Mary Crow Dog credits the American Indian Movement (AIM) for restoring her sense of meaning and for giving her a reason to give up alcohol. In Maslow's language, we can interpret that she felt loved and had found a tradition to which she belonged. The movement also cultivated development at the next stage of the hierarchy: esteem needs. Traditional native ceremonies and knowledge of the heroes of Sioux history fostered a sense of self-esteem. More personally, when Mary Crow Dog gave birth to her son, under fire from federal troops at Wounded Knee, she was praised as a heroine in the Indian struggle for survival.

Mary Crow Dog published her autobiography at the age of 37. Her determination suggests that she will continue developing toward self-actualization. Already she has shown evidence of some of the characteristics of self-actualized people. Her rebellion against the conformity pressures of her schooling illustrates *resistance to enculturation.* Other areas do not fit Maslow's list. Her description of native versus mainstream conflict has not transcended a "we-they" conflict, though perhaps to do so would conflict with another of Maslow's requirements, an efficient perception of reality. Her life story is so closely intertwined with the story of her people that Maslow's individualistic model of personality seems inadequate to describe her personality.

Maslow described *peak experiences* as characteristic of self-actualized people. Native American religious practices use peyote, a hallucinogenic plant, to produce altered states of consciousness that are interpreted to have religious significance. Mary Crow Dog valued peyote and credited it with helping her to give up alcohol. But are drug-induced altered states to be considered as peak experiences?

For the traditional Sioux, the sacred is everywhere. Mary Crow Dog described life with her husband's people this way:

> For the people among whom I lived, every part of daily life had a religious meaning. Eating, drinking, the sight or cry of an animal, the weather, a beaded or quilled design, the finding of certain plants or certain rocks, had spiritual significance. (Crow Dog & Erdoes, 1990, p. 251)

Contrast this with the *desacralization* of our culture criticized by Maslow.

GLOSSARY

B-love nonpossessive love, characteristic of a self-actualized person

basic need a fundamental deficiency need

being motivation higher-level motivation in which the need for self-actualization predominates

D-love selfish love, characteristic of a person who is not self-actualized

deficiency motivation motivation at lower levels of development

desacralization loss of a sense of the sacred or spiritual

experiential knowledge that which we know because we have experienced it for ourselves

Eupsychia a utopian society in which individual and societal needs are both met, and where society supports individual development

growth centers places where people come together for experiences to develop their full potential (e.g., Esalen)

hierarchy of needs ordered progression of motives, from basic physical needs upward to motives of the most developed human beings

human potential movement social trend to foster the full development of individuals, reflected in the development of growth centers and in transformation of social institutions

Inner Directed Supports scale of the Personal Orientation Inventory measuring a person's tendency to obtain support from himself or herself, rather than from other people

instinctoid weakly instinctive motives characteristic of humans

Jonah complex avoiding developing one's full potential because of a belief that it is impossible to do anything very important

metamotivated motivated by needs at the top of the hierarchy of needs

method-centered an approach to science that emphasizes procedure over content

peak experiences mystical states of consciousness, characteristic of many but not all self-actualized people

Personal Orientation Inventory the most popular measure of self-actualization

prepotent currently most powerful; said of a need that, because it is unmet, is most powerful at the moment

problem-centered an approach to science that emphasizes subject matter over procedure

self-actualization development of a person's full potential

third force Maslow's term for his theory, emphasizing its opposition to psychoanalysis and behaviorism

Time Competence a scale of the Personal Orientation Inventory that measures a person's concern with the present, rather than the past or future

STUDY QUESTIONS

1. Contrast Maslow's view of psychology with that of mainstream psychology.
2. List and explain the levels of Maslow's hierarchy of needs. What is implied by having these needs arranged in a hierarchy?
3. Contrast *deficiency motivation* with *being motivation*. Include the differences between *D-love* and *B-love*.
4. Discuss research testing the concept of a hierarchy of needs.
5. List and explain characteristics of a person who is self-actualized.
6. What are *peak experiences*? Discuss the types of people who experience them.
7. From the perspective of his theory, discuss Maslow's attitude toward both religion and ethics.
8. Explain what Maslow meant by *creativity* as a characteristic of a self-actualized person.
9. How is self-actualization measured?
10. Discuss research evidence testing Maslow's concept of self-actualization.
11. How common is self-actualization? Why is it not more common?
12. What did Maslow mean to convey by describing human instincts as *instinctoid*?
13. What is a *Jonah complex*?
14. Discuss implications of Maslow's theory for therapy.
15. Describe a *growth center*.
16. Discuss implications of Maslow's theory for work.
17. Explain what Maslow meant by *desacralization* and what he suggested be done about it.
18. Discuss implications of Maslow's theory for education.
19. Discuss implications of Maslow's theory for gender roles and sex differences.
20. Discuss the role of values in Maslow's theory.

PART V

The Learning Perspective

Behaviorism has been one of the major perspectives in modern psychology. *Radical behaviorism* insists that only observable behaviors should be included in a scientific theory. B.F. Skinner is the most famous radical behaviorist of our time. Early in this century, J.B. Watson proposed that personality was determined by the environment. He made an often-quoted claim:

> Give me a dozen healthy infants, well-formed, and my own specified world to bring them up in and I'll guarantee to take any one at random and train him to become any type of specialist I might select—doctor, lawyer, artist, merchant-chief and, yes, even beggar-man and thief, regardless of his talents, penchants, tendencies, abilities, vocations, and race of his ancestors. (Watson, 1924/1970, p. 104)

The "talents, penchants, tendencies, [and] abilities" that Watson said could be overcome by environment are what most people mean by personality. Watson, though, defined personality in terms of behavior. Habitual behaviors constitute personality. They are modified and expanded throughout life. Personality change comes about through learning, which is more rapid early in life, when habit patterns are forming, according to Watson. Watson believed that studying personality required extensive observation of individuals. What should be observed? Watson listed several factors: education, achievements, psychological tests, recreational activities, emotions in daily life (J.B. Watson, 1924/1970, p. 279).

The behavioral perspective has distinctive assumptions about personality. First, personality is defined in terms of behavior. What a person does constitutes his or her personality (Richards, 1986; J.B. Watson, 1924/1970). Second, behavior (and therefore personality) is determined by external factors in the environment, specifically reinforcements and discriminative stimuli. Third, behaviorism claims that it is possible to influence people for the better by changing environmental conditions, including social changes. Fourth, behaviorism asserts that change can occur throughout a person's life. Fifth, behaviorism studies the individual person, not presuming that the factors influencing one person will necessarily have similar influences on someone else.

The behavioral approach has little difficulty explaining individual differences. Each person experiences a somewhat different environment, with different conditions of learning. Inevitably, different behaviors are learned. Personality consists, for a behaviorist, of behaviors (cf. Lundin, 1969). Unlike trait and psychoanalytic approaches, behavioral approaches are not concerned with the *structure* of personality; instead, they are concerned with the "functional nature of behavior," that is, how behavior interacts with the environment (Keehn, 1980).

Behaviorists reinterpret the phenomena that psychoanalysis described, using behavioral terms. *Repression,* for example, consists of a decrease in behavior because of punishment. *Displacement* occurs because responses generalize from one stimulus to another (similar) one. *Fixation* occurs because a response has been particularly strongly conditioned (Lundin, 1969, pp. 335–336).

Learning theories vary in their specific understandings of the nature of reinforcement. Dollard and Miller adopted a theory of reinforcement proposed by Hull. In this theory, behavior is reinforced, and therefore becomes more frequent, if it reduces the drives of the organism. Skinner, on the other hand, did not make any a priori theoretical assumptions about what would be reinforcing, preferring to determine empirically what constituted reinforcement by observing the effects of potential reinforcers on the behavior of the individual being studied.

Behaviorism assumes that people's actions are determined by external factors, not by forces within the person. This assumption of determinism has led to a long-standing debate between behaviorists, particularly B.F. Skinner, and humanists, who claim that people are free to choose their actions. Skinner claimed that behaviorism represented a scientific revolution against earlier conceptions, which sought the causes of behavior within the person, yet behaviorism itself is not free of the influences on thought that derive from outside of science. Behaviorism contains themes that are part of modern thought more generally: Problems can be solved through technology, reason prevails over emotion, morality is relative rather than absolute, and the world can be improved (Woolfolk & Richardson, 1984).

B.F. Skinner: Radical Behaviorism

BIOGRAPHY OF B.F. SKINNER

B.F. Skinner

Burrhus Frederic Skinner was born March 20, 1904, in the railroad town of Susquehanna, Pennsylvania. He was named "Burrhus" after his mother's maiden name. She and her husband, William, an attorney, raised Burrhus and a younger son, Ebbe. Skinner's brother died suddenly of an acute illness (probably a massive cerebral hemorrhage) while Fred Skinner, as he was generally called, was visiting his hometown (at that time, Scranton) during his freshman year at college.

Childhood had been happy for Fred Skinner. He explored the countryside around Susquehanna, evidencing an inventive interest through various devices. These included a flotation contraption to separate ripe elderberries from green ones, a perpetual motion machine, and a device to remind himself to hang up his pajamas (Skinner, 1967, 1976).

Besides inventing things, Skinner was interested in writing. He wrote poetry and prose at Hamilton College in upstate New York, where he majored in English. He sent three short stories to Robert Frost, who had invited this when he visited the campus. Frost's response was encouraging, and Skinner was serious enough (and, thanks to his father's hard work, affluent enough) to take a year off after graduation to try to write a novel. The project failed, as his parents had anticipated. Later he concluded, "I had failed as a writer because I had had nothing important to say" (1967, p. 395). At the time, though, he felt that the fault was not his, but rather the limitations of the "literary method" for understanding human behavior.

A better method, he decided, was psychology, though he had not taken a single course in psychology as an undergraduate. Much to the relief of his parents, Skinner decided to return to school. He began studying psychology in graduate school at Harvard in 1928. He read extensively, making up for lack of prior courses. He devoured many primary sources in psychology, physiology, and philosophy in their original languages (French and German). At Harvard, Skinner encountered important personality theorists. He enrolled in Henry Murray's course in "The Psychology of the Individual" and reported that they became great friends. Gordon Allport joined the faculty in time to hear Skinner defend his dissertation, but too late for Skinner to take any courses with him.

Skinner's first experimental animal was, strangely enough, a squirrel. He soon turned to laboratory rats. He investigated learning in the new apparatus he invented (later named, by Hull, the "Skinner box"). It was a device intended to isolate particular aspects of learning, which were confounded in the mazes that dominated learning studies at the time. Already Skinner was working on a new theory of conditioning, in contrast to that of Pavlov.

Skinner received his doctorate from Harvard University in 1931. His studies at Harvard were extended by postdoctoral fellowships from the National Research Council (1931–33) and the Harvard Society of Fellows (1933–36) in the midst of the Great Depression. He married Yvonne Blue just before beginning his first teaching job at the University of Minnesota (1936–45). They had two daughters, and raised the younger in her early years in a modified crib he called an "Air Crib," designed to provide an environmentally controlled environment (Skinner, 1945a). (See Figure 11.1.) Several hundred such Air Cribs were marketed, although critics felt it was inhumane to place a human in a modified Skinner box.

One of the most unusual of Skinner's efforts was "Project Pigeon." During World War II, he trained pigeons to guide missiles toward their targets, which were enemy warships on the ocean. Though an unusual technology, preliminary work showed it effective. The government abandoned the project, however, before it was implemented. Efforts were instead channeled into the development of the atom bomb (D. Cohen, 1977).

Though Skinner's primary interest remained conditioning, evidence of his earlier interests is found in his course titled "The Psychology of Literature." Besides his scientific writing, he wrote a novel, *Walden Two* (1948b), and made extensive notes in a journal that he kept for many years (Skinner, 1958a). In 1945 Skinner accepted a position as chairman

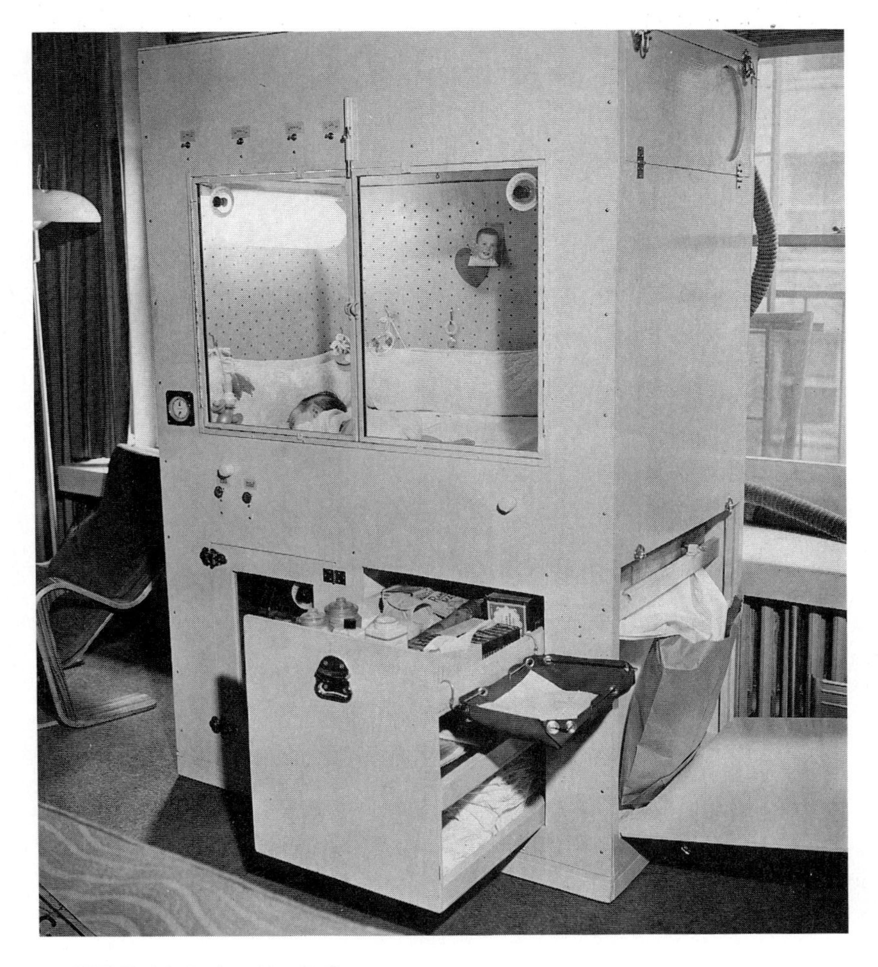

FIGURE 11.1 An Air Crib
(Culver Pictures)

of the Department of Psychology at Indiana University. He was enticed back to Harvard in 1948 with the offer of a full professorship and laboratory support and remained there, continuing his research, theory-building, and teaching, until his death in August 1990 at age 86.

Skinner was one of the most influential psychologists of the twentieth century, according to surveys of psychologists (e.g., Heyduk & Fenigstein, 1984). He received many professional awards, including the American Psychological Association's Distinguished Scientific Contribution Award (American Psychological Association, 1958) and an unprecedented honor, the Citation for Outstanding Lifetime Contribution to Psychology, awarded by the American Psychological Association just before Skinner's death (American Psychological Association, 1990).

ILLUSTRATIVE BIOGRAPHIES

Skinner's radical behavioral theory explains personality as a consequence of the conditions to which people are exposed. A captive, Patricia Hearst, and a free citizen in a new democracy, Benjamin Franklin, experienced environments that were very different. Their life stories raise issues about human freedom, issues central to Skinner's view of humanity.

Patricia Hearst

Patricia Hearst was a household name in 1974 when she was sought first as the victim of a kidnapping and later as a bank robber. Her case focused public and judicial attention on some of the fundamental issues Skinner considered. What determines a person's actions? Are we actors or pawns in this game of life?

Patricia Hearst was born in 1954 into a wealthy family in a suburb south of San Francisco. Her father, Randolf A. Hearst, was publisher of the San Francisco *Examiner.* Patricia grew up in great wealth, and she described her parents as providing both love and discipline in good balance to their five daughters.

At age 19, Patricia Hearst was a freshman at the University of California at Berkeley. Members of a small radical group, which called itself the Symbionese Liberation Army (SLA), kidnapped her from the apartment where she was living with her fiancé, Steven Weed. While the police and FBI searched futilely, she was kept bound and blindfolded in a closet for 57 days. Though the captors claimed to be observing the Geneva Convention rules for prisoners of war (considering themselves to be a revolutionary liberating army for the poor and oppressed), they provided her with inadequate food and no privacy and subjected her to psychological and physical abuse (including sexual abuse). Radical political rhetoric dominated their communications.

Her captors demanded that the Hearst family provide millions of dollars worth of food for the poor of California. The particular demands varied over time, and the SLA ultimately aimed to secure the release of two of their members from prison. Much food was distributed, but no agreement was negotiated. Soon tape recordings broadcast by local radio stations proclaimed that Patricia Hearst had joined the SLA.

After a period of no communication, the public heard of Miss Hearst through her participation in the robbery of a San Francisco bank. Pictures taken by bank cameras left no doubt about her identity. For several months, the FBI continued its hunt for her, not as a kidnapping victim but as a criminal. She and the SLA kept moving from one "safe house" to another in the San Francisco Bay Area, in Los Angeles, to the East Coast, and back again to California.

Finally, six of the SLA members were killed in an FBI raid, leaving only Patricia Hearst and two others, Bill and Emily Harris. Ultimately they, too, were apprehended. In the trial that ensued, Miss Hearst was charged with bank robbery. Her defense lawyer, F. Lee Bailey, argued that she had been coerced to participate, and that her public statements claiming that she had voluntarily joined the SLA were the result of "coercive persuasion," commonly called "brainwashing." Despite this defense, Patty Hearst was convicted and sentenced to 25 years in prison for bank robbery, plus 10 years for using a firearm in a felony. Her appeal was denied. She was released by presidential pardon after serving nearly 2 years in confinement.

The trial demanded the jurors to judge whether she had acted freely, or whether her behavior was due instead to a coercive situation. This is a central concern about all behavior in the theory of B.F. Skinner. Are we, and was Patricia Hearst, a pawn, moved by forces beyond our control? Or are we free, and therefore fully responsible for our behavior?

Benjamin Franklin

Unlike Patricia Hearst, Benjamin Franklin is regarded as a hero. He was an active participant in the American Revolution and in the development of a new society in the colonies, especially in Philadelphia. He felt constrained by lack of money and apprenticeship, but broke away to become an affluent self-made man.

Benjamin Franklin was born in Boston in 1706. Though intelligent, he had to leave school when he was 12 for economic reasons, and he became an apprentice in his brother's printing shop. Besides the printing trade, Ben Franklin excelled as a writer. He published several articles in his brother's newspaper. Finally, however, tired of being mistreated, he ran away to Philadelphia in 1723, where he worked for another printer and later opened his own printing shop. He worked hard and eventually became successful and wealthy.

Benjamin Franklin's philosophy of hard work was expressed in his popular *Poor Richard's Almanack,* from which we have inherited such proverbs as "Early to Bed, and early to rise, makes a Man healthy, wealthy and wise" (Franklin, 1961, p. 190). As a politician, Franklin is remembered as a delegate to the Second Continental Congress, a member of the committee that drafted the Declaration of Independence, and one of its signers, and a representative to France. As a citizen, Franklin started the first volunteer fire department and the first lending library in America.

Benjamin Franklin was also a scientific experimenter. What school child has not heard of his famous kite-flying experiment in which he demonstrated that lightning is electricity? Many practical uses followed from his practical applications of known scientific principles. He devised the lighting rod, the Franklin stove, and bifocals. He refused to patent his Franklin stove, since he felt its fuel-conserving effect should be made widely available.

In his later years, Franklin spent time in England (where he had a common-law second wife) and in France (where he furthered the political interests of the new American nation and enjoyed the pleasures of an admiring French citizenry, and, particularly, French women).

Clearly Benjamin Franklin enjoyed a productive, successful life. He seems to have made his own destiny. Can such a personality be understood within the deterministic model of behaviorism?

RADICAL BEHAVIORISM

B.F. Skinner proposed a theory of behavior based upon principles he called ***operant conditioning***. This theory describes how behavior is influenced by its effects, popularly referred to as "reward" and "punishment." Though most of his work was done with animals, particularly rats, Skinner wrote extensively about the implications of behaviorism for humans. His animal model of learning is widely respected, but the implications he has drawn for humans are highly controversial.

Unlike the theorists considered so far in this book, Skinner did not propose causes of behavior within the personality of the individual (Skinner, 1945b). In fact, Skinner dismissed personality as a discipline that had not become fully scientific, but was still contaminated with prescientific philosophical assumptions. The idea that behavior is caused by forces within a person (traits, thoughts, needs, and so forth) should be abandoned, according to Skinner, in favor of more scientific explanations outside the person. Thus his theory does not present a concept of personality in the usual sense, but rather a challenge to the idea that a theory of personality can be part of science.

This approach focuses on predicting and controlling overt, observable behavior. Such behavior can be reliably observed by independent observers, who can count or otherwise measure the behavior. In addition, it argues that the *causes* of behavior are external to the individual. In contrast, personality theory has traditionally looked for causes within people: traits, needs, and the like. Skinner argued that it is illogical to consider personality traits (such as extroversion) or inner motives (such as self-actualization and anxiety) to be the causes of behavior. Inner causes involve circular reasoning. Traits are inferred from behavior, whether from anecdotal observation or more formal analysis. Traits are therefore simply summary descriptions of behaviors. To say that (a) "John is aggressive because he hits people" (an inference), and (b) "John hits people because he is aggressive" (an explanation), is circular reasoning, and logically indefensible.

Skinner argued that moving from internal explanations, such as traits, to external explanations, such as reinforcements and stimuli, was a scientific step forward. External variables are convenient for science. They can be manipulated by the researcher, so that their status as *causes* of behavior is not in doubt. Skinner's behaviorism is more thoroughly external than other behavioral approaches. It is called *radical behaviorism* to distinguish it from learning theories that include some internal causes of behavior, such as drives (Dollard and Miller) and cognitive variables (Mischel and Bandura).

Common sense tells us that thoughts can cause behavior. "I thought about my friend, so I phoned." Intention is also often offered as an explanation: a person *intends* to do something, and the intention is regarded as the "cause" of the action. Why would Skinner rule out thoughts, intentions, and other inner states as causes in his theory? First, mental states are not available for observation by others. They are private experiences and can only be inferred from behavior, such as self-reports. An empirical science should be based on direct observations. Second, the individual does not know his or her inner states very accurately. Self-reports are often flawed.

Skinner (e.g., 1963, 1975, 1990) argued that scientific progress in psychology required abandoning **mentalism**, which explains behavior in terms of internal mental states. In psychoanalysis, "anxiety" is frequently invoked as the mental state responsible for various defensive behaviors. Modern cognitive science, which is currently quite popular, was also dismissed by Skinner (1985) for accepting the traditional view that the causes of behavior reside within the organism (Hayes & Brownstein, 1985; Landwehr, 1983; Wessells, 1981, 1983).

For Skinner, the inner life of feelings and thoughts should not be regarded as causing observable behavior. Rather, inner thoughts and feelings are simply "collateral products" (e.g., Skinner, 1975, p. 44) of the environmental factors causing overt behavior. In the earlier example, it may be that seeing an advertisement for a movie that you saw with the friend caused both (1) thinking of the friend, and (2) phoning the friend. The real cause is external (the advertisement), not internal (the thought). Private events—thoughts and feelings—are simply epiphenomena, though they are real in a physical sense (Allen, 1980; Creel, 1980; Natsoulas, 1983; Skinner, 1974). In everyday life, awareness of feelings can help provide clues to the causes of behavior, which are in the environment; but the language of feelings is suitable to everyday life, to literature, and to philosophy, not to science (Skinner, 1985).

Besides focusing on observable behavior and external causes, Skinner emphasized the importance of *control* over behavior. If science can provide ways of controlling behavior, we can be sure that it has identified the causes of behavior. Explanations of behavior in terms of traits and other inner determinants allow prediction and explanation of behavior, but not control, and so are inconsistent with Skinner's behaviorist orientation (Zuriff, 1985).

Skinner's theory influenced psychology more than perhaps any other modern theory. Even for those who do not accept his radical behavioral theory, its influence has focused attention on situational factors determining behavior. Skinner challenged ideas about the importance of inner determinants of behavior, which are widely accepted, not only in much of psychology, but in Western culture (Day, 1983). Skinner's conditioning model has been the focus of active intellectual debate over the human condition. Are we free agents, or pawns in the universe? It has caused a revolutionary reassessment of human nature as momentous as that proposed by Freud.

The Evolutionary Context of Operant Behavior

Humans are adaptable. They learn to adjust to their environments. Unlike lower animals, who respond to environments largely with fixed instincts, humans can learn to respond in different ways, depending upon what is effective in a given situation. The ability to adjust to the environment, to learn, is adaptive.

Evolution is a process by which adaptive physical characteristics are selected in response to the environment. Behavior, too, can be selected. Sociobiologists describe an evolutionary selection process for some behaviors (Barash, 1982; E.O. Wilson, 1975). Evolution, though, is a slow process that takes generations. Skinner argued that adaptive behavior can also be selected within the experience of one individual. In fact, the human capacity to adapt to the environment may be its most salient species characteristic. The capacity to adapt has been selected by the evolutionary process. Specific adaptations of an individual are described by Skinner's behavioral theory.

Adaptive behavior is a major concern of personality theory. Psychoanalysts praise the adaptive function of the ego, in contrast to less adaptive, unconscious forces within personality. Humanists describe the more fully functioning, self-actualized potential of humankind. Skinner aimed for a more precise and scientific description of adaptive behavior. How is it that an individual comes to behave in ways that are adaptive in a given environment?

The basic idea is that behavior is determined by the environmental outcomes *contingent* on the behavior, that is, which follow regularly from the behavior. Skinner described this as the *selection* of behavior through its consequences. He compared this selection to the evolutionary principle of natural selection, which selects organisms on the basis of their fitness for a particular environment. The behavioral selection, however, takes place more rapidly, and it does not involve genetic mechanisms. It is, in effect, the capacity to learn from experience.

Adaptive behavior requires flexibility. Although Skinner's theory is called a "learning theory," it is quite different from other learning theories in which behaviors are not changed but are simply connected with new stimuli. Pavlov's dogs, for example, may have learned to salivate to a bell rather than only to meat powder (which he presented as a controlled unconditioned stimulus), but the response of salivation was not new. Skinner did not consider himself to be an "S-R" psychologist, the popular term for learning approaches in his time (R.I. Evans, 1981b, p. 20). He moved away from the concept of a stimulus-response (S-R) "reflex," to which he referred in early writings, to a conceptualization of behavior as *selected by* the environment. Skinner introduced the terms "classical conditioning" and "operant conditioning" to differentiate Pavlov's reflex learning model (classical conditioning) from his own (Skinner, 1953a). Classical conditioning describes reflex behaviors. The behaviors Ivan Pavlov investigated had to be actively elicited by the researcher through the introduction of some eliciting stimulus. In contrast, Skinner's theory describes *operant* behaviors. **Operant responses** are freely *emitted* by an organism. That is, they occur in a particular environment without the experimenter having to do anything in particular to *elicit* them.

Not all behaviors are governed by the rules of operant conditioning. A tap to the knee, for example, will lead to a knee jerk by reflex action. It is unaffected by consequences. In contrast, an *operant behavior* is one freely emitted by the organism. For example, a rat in a cage may raise its paw, scratch its ear, or twitch its tail; these are operant behaviors. A college student in a class may ask a question, write in a notebook, or whisper to a classmate; these are also operant behaviors. Which behaviors will become more frequent, and which less? That will depend upon the consequences that follow the behaviors.

The Rate of Responding

To analyze the learning process into small steps, Skinner realized that it was necessary to select a dependent measure carefully. Earlier work, such as Thorndike's puzzle boxes, confounded several processes so that it was difficult to know just what changes were occurring as learning progressed. On the other hand, Skinner was interested in the actions of the whole organism, so he did not want to choose a mere physiological component, such as a "muscle twitch," or the neurological reflexes to which theorists in the Pavlovian tradition referred.

Skinner argued that the best operant behaviors for research purposes are those that occur distinctly and repeatedly, so that they can be clearly observed and counted. Learning is then measured by changes (increases or decreases) in the *rate* (or frequency) of such operant responses over time (Skinner, 1950, 1953b). Some researchers have criticized Skinner for ignoring other measures of learning, such as choice and latency (e.g., Marr, 1987; Nevin, 1979, Pribram, 1973).

Experimental investigation requires control of extraneous influences. Lower animals, whose behavior is largely reflexive, offer more opportunity for controlling their less predominant adaptive behaviors than is possible if humans are studied. (Presumably, basic learning processes studied in animals can be applied to humans.) In addition, placing the experimental animal in a controlled environment allows further controls. Skinner invented a new apparatus, which has come to be known as a **Skinner box**, to provide an environment in which operant responses could be readily observed and automatically recorded. He devised the apparatus as a graduate student through a series of rather drastic modifications of the mazes popular in learning studies of the period. Over time, the apparatus became more sophisticated, incorporating automatic recording and reinforcing devices.

Each time the experimental animal makes a **response** (a rat presses a lever, or a pigeon pecks a disk), the response is automatically recorded. Responses are displayed on a **cumulative record**. Machines to print out such records evolved over Skinner's early career as he tinkered with devices to simplify his task. A cumulative record presents (or graphs) responses as a function of time. As time passes (displayed on the horizontal axis), each response moves the recording pen a notch higher on the vertical axis. The *slope* of the cumulative record at any moment indicates the *rate of responding*: Higher response rates produce steeper slopes; lower response rates produce lower slopes. If an animal is not responding at all, the slope is flat. If the pen comes to the top edge of the paper, it is simply flipped back to the bottom and recording continues. This method of recording made it possible for Skinner to see at a glance the results of an experimental session without waiting for a statistical analysis. (He seldom used statistics.) Because the apparatus recorded automatically, it was not even necessary for the researcher to be present during an experimental session.

Learning Principles

In contrast to the one-way influence of the environment on reflexive behavior, operant behavior involves mutual responsiveness of the person (or other organism) and the environment. The person's behavior leads to a contingent change in the environment. In turn, the person's behavior changes. Thousands of hours of observation resulted in the description of fundamental principles of this adaptive behavior.

Fundamentally, there are two ways to *increase* the frequency of a response: positive reinforcement (usually called simply "reinforcement") and negative reinforcement. There are two ways to *decrease* the frequency of a response: punishment and extinction. In simple language, a person adapts by doing more frequently those things that increase good outcomes (positive reinforcement) or decrease bad outcomes (negative reinforcement). And a person does less frequently those things that bring bad outcomes (punishment) or that stop good things from happening (extinction).

Reinforcement

Behavior that is adaptive in a given environment is strengthened. Skinner's research indicates, though, that it is the immediate, short-term consequences of behavior that are influential, rather than any long-term vision of "adaptive" behavior.

Reinforcement corresponds to what we would commonly label "reward." Skinner did not use the term "reward" because it had connotations, such as pleasure, which were not directly observable. He preferred to define reinforcement in terms of behavior. A **positive reinforcer** is "any stimulus the presentation of which strengthens the behavior upon which it is made contingent" (Skinner, 1953a, p. 185). That is, there is an increase in the rate of responding compared to the **base rate** (the rate of responding before any reinforcement). Some reinforcers, such as food, are innate; these are called **primary reinforcers**. Other reinforcers, such as money and praise, only become effective reinforcers after their value is learned; these learned rewards are called **secondary reinforcers**. There is no guarantee that either kind of reinforcer will be beneficial in the long run in an individual case. Some people eat lots of junk food, reinforced by its taste, but suffer ill health in the long run. (Alcohol and other drugs also bring only short-term reinforcement.) Other people, reinforced by money or praise, work themselves to an early death. Despite individual exceptions, reinforcement is the principle through which adaptive behavior occurs.

People do not all respond in the same way to a specific environmental consequence of their action. If a teacher praises a student for asking a question, and if the frequency of asking questions increases, then praise has served as a reinforcement for the response of asking questions. The same praise, however, would not be called a reinforcer if it did not increase the frequency of the behavior. (Some students may prefer that the teacher not focus attention on them.) There is nothing inherent about any consequence that makes it always a reinforcer. Only by observing the effects of a contingent stimulus outcome on the rate of behavior can we determine whether that contingent outcome is a reinforcer in a particular situation, for a particular individual. Skinner's focus on studying the individual organism corresponds to the *idiographic* approach to personality.

For clarity, reinforcers such as these, the *onset* of which increases the frequency of responding, are termed *positive reinforcers* to distinguish them from another kind of reinforcer, more unusual and often confusing.

Negative Reinforcement

Besides seeking rewards, adaptation requires escaping painful or aversive stimuli. To put it in terms suggested by Skinner's evolutionary metaphor, the cave man had to find food (positive reinforcer) and come in out of the cold (negative reinforcer). A **negative reinforcer** is "any stimulus the *withdrawal* of which strengthens behavior" (Skinner, 1953a, p. 185). If cold is an aversive stimulus, and if coming indoors is followed by an end to the cold, then coming indoors becomes more frequent; it is negatively reinforced.

Negative reinforcement is often confused with punishment. Both are aversive, but they have different effects on behavior. All forms of reinforcement, positive and negative, *increase* the frequency of responding. In contrast, punishment *reduces* its frequency. Sitting on a concrete floor is followed by an increase in the aversive cold, which is punishing. Sitting on the concrete floor becomes less frequent.

Punishment

Punishment is a stimulus that, when presented contingently after a response, reduces the rate of that response. It occurs when a positive reinforcer is withdrawn or a negative reinforcer is presented (Skinner, 1953a, p. 185). For example, parents reduce the frequency of misbehavior in their children by withholding television and by scolding. Examples of punishment abound, since punishment is "the commonest technique of control in modern life" (Skinner, 1953a, p. 182). It is used by parents, educators, governments, and even religion, which threatens aversive consequences in the afterlife.

The immediate effect of punishment is, as a matter of definition, to reduce the frequency of an operant behavior. Animals in Skinner boxes learn quickly to stop doing whatever brings electric shock. Unfortunately, punishment also has unintended adverse effects that, Skinner argued, make it a generally undesirable technique for controlling behavior. First, punishment produces emotional reactions, including fear and anxiety, which remain even after the undesirable behavior has ceased. These emotions often generalize to other situations. For example, children punished for sexual exploration may experience anxiety later, even under circumstances when sexual behavior would be appropriate. Negative emotions that are learned from punishment constitute aversive states. Behaviors that end these states are thereby negatively reinforced, and thus become more frequent. Guilt-motivated defense mechanisms described by psychoanalysts can be explained in this way. Second, the punished behavior often returns later, when the environment has changed. Punishment is often successful in the short run in reducing behavior, but unless the controlling agent is able to stay to administer continuing punishments as a "reminder," in the long run the behavior often returns.

Skinner was very critical of punishment and urged society to find more effective and more humane ways of controlling behavior. One alternative is to substitute desired behaviors. By reinforcing alternative behaviors, which are incompatible with the undesired behavior, the behavior can be eliminated without punishment (R.S. Jones & Baker, 1990; Matson & Kazdin, 1981). For example, children may be rewarded for playing cooperative games, rather than punished for fighting. In some circumstances, however, Skinner felt that punishment was justified. For example, it can prevent some autistic children from injuring themselves, when other methods are ineffective (Griffin, Paisey, Stark, & Emerson, 1988).

Extinction

When the reinforcement that has been maintaining an operant behavior ends, the behavior eventually becomes less and less frequent. For example, a child may tease (operant behavior) a playmate, reinforced by the playmate's signs of embarrassment. If the playmate stops reacting, eventually the child will stop teasing. This reduction of responding when reinforcement ceases is called **extinction**. Skinner's first investigation of experimental extinction began with an accident, when the food-dispensing apparatus on his Skinner box jammed (Skinner, 1979, p. 95). (Serendipity is sometimes a fortuitous teacher!) It should be noted, however, that a behavior which has undergone extinction may later return spontaneously (S.J. Rachman, 1989). Perhaps this is the organism's way of testing whether the environment has changed back to its earlier, reinforcing mode.

Shaping

The techniques considered above can increase (reinforcement and negative reinforcement) or decrease (punishment and extinction) the frequency of a person's existing behavior. What about new behavior? To increase the frequency of a response that has a base rate of zero in the laboratory, special procedures are necessary. After all, it is impossible to reinforce a response that does not occur. Skinner presumed that these techniques also suggested why people do new things in the real world. Like new physical features in evolution, new behaviors in a person's life are not wholly new but are built up gradually from earlier components, in response to environmental selection pressures.

In training laboratory animals, Skinner developed a method called **shaping**, which involves reinforcing *successive approximations* of the desired response. At first, a response that is only roughly similar to the ultimate desired response occurs. It might be a slight raising of a paw by a rat who will be taught to press a bar, or a marginally courteous statement by a child who is to be taught to speak respectfully to adults. This response is reinforced, and therefore it increases in frequency. Gradually, the experimenter or parent who is controlling reinforcement requires responses that are increasingly similar to the desired criterion behavior. Thus, by a method of successive approximations, a response with a base rate of zero can be made to occur more frequently. Outside of the laboratory, this is how children are gradually taught courteous behavior, how some people become increasingly assertive, and others more and more shy. Different environmental consequences of behavior shape different behaviors. If the environments to which organisms adapt change gradually, shaping would occur naturally, though it does seem artificial in a Skinner box.

Discrimination

The behaving organism, whether pigeon or person, learns to behave in ways appropriate to a changing situation. If pecking, or pleading, sometimes leads to desirable outcomes and sometimes not, the organism learns to take advantage of stimuli in the environment that signal whether the behavior will "pay off" this time. These environmental signals are called *discriminative stimuli.*

Skinner demonstrated **discrimination learning** in pigeons by reinforcing them with food when a signal light was on, but not when the light was off. The pigeons learned to peck only when the discriminative stimulus (the light) was present. Such behavior is said to be "under stimulus control." The discriminative stimulus is abbreviated S^D. Behavior can be understood in terms of this model:

$$S^D \longrightarrow R \longrightarrow S^R$$

In words, the *discriminative stimulus* leads to the *response* which leads to the *reinforcing stimulus.*

Discrimination occurs frequently in human behavior. Motorists drive more slowly when they see a police car nearby than when they do not. Shoppers buy more when "sale" signs are present. Socially mature adults know when to speak, and when to keep silent. Responding to discriminative stimuli is an essential aspect of adaptive behavior. Much of what other theorists describe as "ego skills" or coping with the environment would, from a learning theory point of view, be described as discrimination learning.

Generalization

Responding is not entirely restricted to the discriminative stimuli present during training. Stimuli similar to the discriminative stimulus also produce responses. A dog trained to bark when his master says "Speak" will probably also bark when his master says "Spit." This process is called *stimulus generalization* or, more simply, **generalization**. The more closely the stimulus resembles the discriminative stimulus that was present during conditioning, the more likely the behavior is to occur. It is sensible that generalization would occur. Even a stimulus that is objectively the "same" varies from one presentation to the next, depending upon such conditions as the surrounding light, the angle from which it is seen, and so forth. Without generalization, it would be impossible for an organism to identify stimuli as the same from one presentation to another.

The concepts of stimulus discrimination and generalization help to explain personality consistency and change. Environmental stability leads to behavioral stability, since similarity of situations produces generalization. On the other hand, when situations change, stimulus discrimination allows the person to recognize new contingencies of behavior. People can behave quite differently as they move back and forth among various situations (home, work, social situations, and so forth).

Superstitious Behavior

In laboratory studies, reinforcement is determined by an experimenter. Reinforcement contingencies are carefully controlled. Humans live in far less controlled situations; thus it is reasonable to ask whether reinforcements that are not systematic have any impact on behavior.

Skinner's studies of what he called **superstitious behavior** (Morse & Skinner, 1957; Skinner, 1948a) make it clear that the principles of behaviorism apply even in the absence of a planning, controlling experimenter. Skinner placed eight pigeons in Skinner boxes programmed to deliver reinforcements at random times, not contingent on the organism's behavior. Reinforcements delivered in this way did influence behavior, though in ways that varied from one pigeon to the next. Six of the pigeons developed odd but consistent "superstitions." One turned repeatedly in circles. One kept swinging its head. Another repeatedly pecked. According to Skinner, whatever each individual pigeon was doing when reinforcement happened to occur became more frequent.

Not all researchers have found the diversity of individual responses reported by Skinner. In some replications of the superstitious learning study, pigeons increased only their pecking behavior (Staddon & Simmelhag, 1971) or activity at the feeding hopper (Timberlake & Lucas, 1985). These researchers suggested that random reinforcement increased responses that were meaningfully connected to the reinforcer (food), rather than any arbitrary response. Other researchers, however, have found individual differences from one pigeon to another (wing flapping, pecking, turning in circles, and so forth), as Skinner originally reported (Justice & Looney, 1990).

It is a large step from pigeon learning to human behavior. In principle, though, Skinner's work suggests that even random reinforcements could produce personality differences. His extensive work on schedules of reinforcements offers further suggestions.

Schedules of Reinforcement

In adapting to the environment, the organism is exquisitely modifying its behavior in response to the frequency and timing of reinforcements. The term **schedule of reinforcement** refers to the specific contingency between a response and a reinforcement. Is every response reinforced? Are only some reinforced? If only some, which? Skinner (e.g., 1953a) explored this question in detail. In fact, Ferster and Skinner's (1957) book on schedules of reinforcement reports "on 70,000 hours of continuously recorded behavior composed of about one quarter of a *billion* responses" (Skinner, 1972, p. 167).

Continuous Reinforcement (CR)

Responses that always produce reinforcement are said to be on a **continuous reinforcement** schedule. This occurs if a rat receives food every time the bar is pressed, or if a customer receives a can of soda every time money is deposited in the machine. Continuous reinforcement schedules produce quick learning, provided that reinforcement follows the response immediately. If there is a delay between the response and the reinforcement, learning will be slower. If the delay is too long, learning will not occur. Although learning is fast under continuous reinforcement, extinction is also rapid. Strategies that have always worked in the past are quickly abandoned when they fail. How many college freshmen who had an easy time succeeding in high school have given up quickly when studying no longer brought the reward of good grades? Skinner's work suggests that a few failures earlier would produce greater persistence.

Partial Reinforcement Schedules

Partial reinforcement schedules occur when only some of the responses are followed by reinforcement. Though they produce slower learning, partial reinforcement schedules bring about greater resistance to extinction than continuous reinforcement schedules. To combine the advantages of both schedules, those who apply behavioral techniques may produce quick learning using a continuous schedule of reinforcement and then "thin out" the schedule, reinforcing fewer and fewer responses so as to make the behavior resistant to extinction. Skinner described a variety of partial reinforcement schedules.

Fixed Ratio Reinforcement (FR)

Fixed ratio schedules reinforce depending upon the number of responses that have been emitted. In a FR-15 schedule, for example, the organism is reinforced after every 15th response (i.e., after response 15, after response 30, after response 45, and so forth). By responding quickly, it is possible to "earn" more reinforcements. That is what a hungry pigeon does, pecking for food pellets. Skinner (1972, p. 134) reported that one bird responded nonstop for two months! Employees who are paid on a "piece-work" basis also work at a very high rate, which makes for difficult working conditions. Rather than explaining such behavior as due to an inner trait of "persistence" or an inner "drive," Skinner's theory explains it in terms of the external history of reinforcements.

Variable Ratio Reinforcement (VR)

Under a **variable ratio schedule**, reinforcements are given according to the number of responses the organism has made, but the exact number of responses that must be made for each reinforcement varies randomly around a predetermined average. Under a VR-15 schedule, the organism will, in the long run, receive one reinforcement for each 15 responses. Sometimes, however, a reinforcement will follow the previous one by only 5 responses, or 6, or 7; and sometimes 20 or 30 or more responses must be made between responses. Like a fixed ratio schedule, a variable ratio schedule produces a high rate of responding. It is more resistant to extinction than is a fixed ratio schedule. We might explain this as a result of the organism's decreased awareness of the change from reinforcement to extinction, although Skinner would not have used such "mentalistic" terms.

Fixed Interval Reinforcement (FI)

Fixed interval schedules reinforce responses based upon the passage of time. An FI-10 schedule, for example, will reinforce the organism at the end of each 10-second interval, as long as at least one response has occurred during that interval. No extra reinforcements can be obtained by responding more than once during the interval. Hence, lower rates of responding occur, compared with ratio schedules. Fixed interval schedules produce a distinctive "scalloped" record. Few responses are made at the beginning of each interval. Response rates increase dramatically toward the end of each interval. A pigeon reinforced every 10 seconds will find other things to do during the first several seconds, but pecks rapidly at the end of each interval (see Figure 11.2). A college student in a class with weekly quizzes on Friday will typically study very little early in the week, but will really "cram" on Thursday. Just as there are some students who study throughout the week, though, the "scalloped" curve has not been found consistently in studies of humans, probably due to the modifying effects of language (Michael, 1984). Even when the alternating high response rates and lower response rates that constitute scalloping occur in humans, they may be explained by factors other than the effects of a fixed interval schedule. Such factors include instructions from the experimenter, instructions that subjects give themselves, and observation of the response (Poppen, 1982). Generalizing from animal studies to humans is complex.

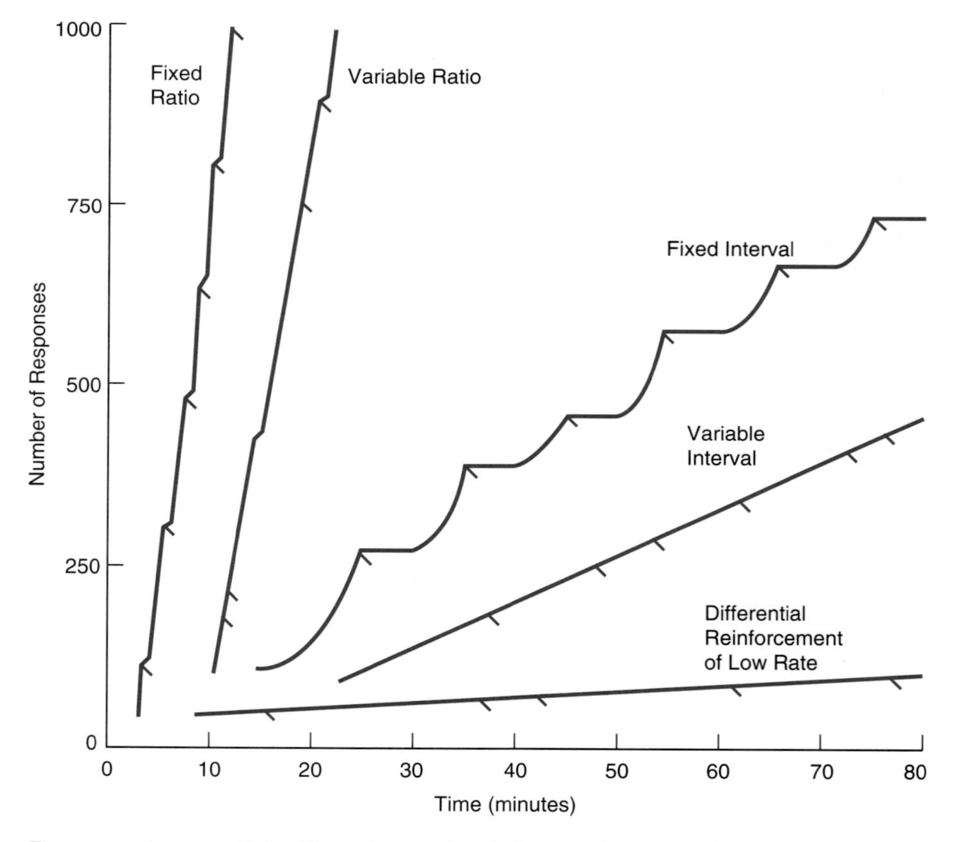

These records were obtained from pigeons, but similar cumulative records are obtained with various other organisms, including humans.

FIGURE 11.2 Effects of Various Schedules of Reinforcement on Responding

(From B.F. Skinner, "Teaching machines."

Variable Interval Reinforcement (VI)

A **variable interval schedule** reinforces according to time intervals that change from reinforcement to reinforcement. Sometimes reinforcements follow one another rapidly (as long as at least one response has been made in the interval). At other times long intervals pass between reinforcements. Without a constant interval, the scalloping of the FI schedule is smoothed.

Multiple Schedules

Life, of course, is not a Skinner box. We behave in complex ways, making diverse responses according to many schedules. Skinner therefore investigated multiple schedules of reinforcement in his animal research.

Some experimental animals were exposed to alternating schedules of reinforcement. A fixed interval schedule might be followed by a variable ratio schedule, and then a different variable interval schedule, and so forth. Skinner found that the rate of responding changed to adjust to each schedule. He also demonstrated that animals could simultaneously give two different kinds of responses to two different schedules, producing response rates for each response that were similar to those produced if that were the only response occurring. Skinner's early work on this topic was interrupted, though, and he argued that the topic required further exploration "if we are ever to give a plausible account of behavior in the world at large" (Skinner, 1986b, p. 234). Other researchers have found that animals behaving according to more than one schedule simultaneously do not keep the schedules totally independent. The multiple behaviors can influence one another (McSweeney, Melville, Buck, & Whipple, 1983). In addition, reinforcements are sometimes available without making the response that is usually required. When this happens, the response rate is influenced in complex ways, sometimes increasing, sometimes decreasing (Burgess & Wearden, 1986). Extinction of one response can also produce changes in other behavior. Previously reinforced behavior can return when a recently reinforced behavior no longer produces reinforcement, a phenomenon called "extinction-induced resurgence" (R. Epstein, 1985). Sometimes aggressive behavior increases in such circumstances (Looney & Cohen, 1982).

While Skinner claimed that the behavioral principles he was investigating apply to real life, the phenomena are extraordinarily complex, even in principle. Many behaviors occur, and they are reinforced by many different schedules, which are themselves subject to change. Critics are skeptical that reinforcement principles can be applied to humans except in special, highly controlled situations. To think that everyday life could be explained in behavioral terms alone, without some higher-order theoretical concepts, seems to many to be reductionistic.

Applications of Behavioral Techniques

Despite the concerns of skeptics, Skinner's behavioral techniques have a variety of applications, particularly in therapy and in education.

Therapy

It should not be surprising that Skinner viewed therapy as relearning. Problematic behavior, he argued, is due to troublesome contingencies of reinforcement (Skinner, 1988). It can be changed by changing reinforcement contingencies, though this is not always easy. Many of the problems that people bring to psychotherapists result from unfortunate learning histories. They may have learned ways of avoiding punishment, whether external or internal (in the form of self-punishing statements or emotions), which have not been satisfactory. Skinner thought of Freudian defense mechanisms as such avoidant behaviors. Unlike Freudian therapy, in which the symptom is considered to be merely an indicator of an underlying disorder, for Skinner the symptom *is* the disorder. When insight-oriented psychotherapy (such as psychoanalysis) changes behavior, radical behaviorists explain the change through behavioral mechanisms. Verbal behaviors can be changed in the reinforcing environment of therapy, and words can serve as discriminative cues for later behavior outside therapy (S.A. Hamilton, 1988).

The therapist is a "nonpunishing audience" (Skinner, 1953a, p. 370). Without punishment, behaviors suppressed because of punishment at first become more frequent. These behaviors include aggression, illogical thought, and other previously punished behaviors. As the therapist continues to be nonpunishing, these behaviors will eventually undergo extinction. In addition, the client can learn new and more desirable behaviors, and can learn to discriminate stimuli that signal when various behaviors should occur.

Behavior modification is the therapeutic approach that systematically applies learning principles. It has been developed considerably in recent decades (Kazdin & Hersen, 1980). First the therapist makes a *functional analysis* of the behavior to be changed. That is, the stimuli and reinforcements influencing behavior are identified carefully. Intervention is then planned. The particular schedule of reinforcements is carefully individualized. For example, a child who cries at bedtime might be placed on an extinction schedule. Parents are instructed to not provide attention that has been reinforcing the undesired bedtime tears. Behaviors to be increased are reinforced, either using *primary reinforcements* such as food, or *secondary reinforcements* such as tokens (e.g., points or gold stars), which can later be exchanged for desired rewards. **Token economies**, which systematically reward behavior with tokens in a group setting, have been used to treat many populations, from children in school to psychiatric inpatients (Kazdin, 1982). Despite their effectiveness, there is a danger. People may learn to work only for the tokens, losing intrinsic interest in the behavior itself, and thus not behaving as desired when the tokens are removed (Levine & Fasnacht, 1974).

Behavior modification techniques have been applied to an astonishing range of behaviors, including oral hygiene (Blount, Santilli, & Stokes, 1989); social skills training (R.R. Davies & Rogers, 1985; McConnell, 1987); weight control (Fox, Switzky, Rotatori, & Vitkus, 1982; Wolf, Cohen, & Rosenfeld, 1985); classroom management and teaching (Albion, 1983; Fisch & White, 1982; Jenson, 1978; Merrett & Wheldall, 1984); organizational management (Crowell & Anderson, 1982); pain control (Fordyce, 1982), and even creativity (Winston & Baker, 1985).

Behavior modification interventions have been developed for many special populations, including children suffering from a variety of disorders (J.S. Phillips & Ray, 1980); deviant children (Forehand, 1986); delinquents (Blakely & Davidson, 1984); hyperactive children (Friman & Christophersen, 1983; Prout, 1977); the retarded or developmentally disabled (D.B.

Lennox, Miltenberger, Spengler, & Erfanian, 1988; Martin & Hrydowy, 1989; Matson & Taras, 1989; Reichle, Lindamood, & Sigafoos, 1986; Scruggs, Mastropieri, Forness, & Kavale, 1988; Singh & Winton, 1983; Starin & Fuqua, 1987); hearing-impaired people (T.W. Jones, 1984); stutterers (Nittrouer & Cheney, 1984) and those who elect to be mute (Labbe & Williamson, 1984); those who suffer from asthma (Knapp & Wells, 1978), epileptic seizures (McRae & Cuvo, 1980), and insomnia (Knapp, Downs, & Alperson, 1976); patients with neurological injuries (J.V. Fox, 1983; Incagnoli & Newman, 1985); psychiatric patients (Acosta, 1990; Brady, 1984); substance abusers (Childress, McLellan, & O'Brien, 1985; Grabowski & O'Brien, 1981), and the elderly (Baltes & Barton, 1979).

Behavioral therapy is an effective mode of treatment for many patients. It is practical for clients whose verbal functioning is inadequate for traditional psychotherapy, including developmentally disabled (formerly called "mentally retarded"), autistic, and overtly psychotic people. It requires less time and money than many alternative therapies, including psychoanalysis, and it provides an objective behavioral record of success (Lundin, 1969).

Education

Skinner advocated his behavioral technology to improve education (Skinner, 1954). He developed and popularized the *teaching machine*, improving on educational devices that had been patented in the nineteenth century (Benjamin, 1988). The teaching machine enhances learning by presenting material in small increments and by providing frequent reinforcement for learning (Skinner, 1958b, 1968). The early machines were based on a crude mechanical apparatus. The principle of *programmed* instruction, as his method was called, can be more easily implemented using modern computers, which can individualize the pacing of a student's work (Chandler, 1984). There have been developments in this area, but not to the extent Skinner envisioned, much to his disappointment (Skinner, 1984, 1989b).

Skinner recommended programmed instruction to facilitate learning and behavior modification to prevent classes from being disrupted by unruly, bored students. Many educators discipline students using explicitly behavioral methods (Render, Padilla, & Krank, 1989). Modern elementary schools often include aspects of this approach. Disruptive students are placed in **time out rooms**, where they will not be reinforced for misbehavior (i.e., they will have a "time out from reinforcement"). Such behaviors then extinguish. This, Skinner felt, was far more humane than punishment. Skinner debated these ideas about education (and the more general concepts about human nature on which they were based) with the humanist Carl Rogers (Rogers & Skinner, 1956). Skinner claimed that behaviorism had been more effective than humanism in improving education (R.I. Evans, 1981b, pp. 24–25).

Radical Behaviorism and Personality Theory: Some Challenges

Skinner's work focused on animals. Although he argued that the fundamental principles of behavior are the same in rats and humans, some have questioned whether his model adequately addresses the issues that personality theory should consider.

Species-Specificity

Critics claim that Skinner's theory neglects the unique capacities of the human organism. Though he investigated primarily the behavior of rats, Skinner always intended his theory to apply to humans. As he stated: "The importance of a science of behavior derives largely from the possibility of an eventual extension to human affairs" (Skinner, 1938, p. 441). Skinner defended his attempts to understand humans based on a model derived from animal research.

> Traditional theories of autonomous man have exaggerated species differences. Some of the complex contingencies of reinforcement now under investigation generate behavior in lower organisms which, if the subjects were human, would traditionally be said to involve higher mental processes. (Skinner, 1971, p. 192)

Behaviorists agree with Skinner that much generality from animals to humans exists (Higgins & Morris, 1984; H. Weiner, 1983). Even creative behavior can be explained by this model, according to behaviorists (R. Epstein, 1991). Others disagree.

Genetic Factors Influencing Personality

Some critics say Skinner overestimated the potential of any behavior to be learned. Genetic contributions to personality (such as inherited temperament and intellect) are not described in his theory. While his theory does not formally include such factors, Skinner acknowledged that genetic factors in animals and in humans do exist and do influence behavior. In his own research, he controlled the impact of genetics through the use of genetically homogeneous strains of animals. Skinner did not adopt the extreme environmentalist position of the earlier behaviorist John B. Watson (T.L. Smith, 1983), who claimed that genetics had no influence on human personality and that "there is no such thing as an inheritance of capacity, talent, temperament, mental constitution and characteristics" (Watson, 1924/1970, p. 94). Nonetheless, Skinner felt that the influence of genetics was often overstated and that even genetically less favorably endowed persons, who might have low intelligence or high tendency to mental disturbance, could achieve an improved condition through the application of his principles of behavior.

The Complexity of the Human World

In theory, behavioral principles can be extended to complex settings. Social relationships, from a behaviorist viewpoint, can be understood by considering the mutual reinforcements each person provides for the other (Schmitt, 1984).

Behavioral research with humans has, consistent with behavioral theory, involved populations and settings in which a high degree of environmental control is possible. Institutionalized populations (psychotics, developmentally disabled people, and prisoners) have been studied in controlled environments. Language has been conditioned by simply having people say a series of words, with no phrases or sentences permitted (Greenspoon, 1955).

Further development of a behavioral theory of personality, however, will require work in less controlled settings. Navarick, Bernstein, and Fantino

(1990) note that "Human behavior often must be studied under conditions that cannot be perfectly controlled and with populations that cannot be manipulated exclusively at the discretion of our research agendas. Recognition of this change will be critical to the continued development of interesting and creative lines of human operant research" (p. 162). There is no question that operant principles describe the behavior of animals, and even humans, in controlled environments, yet it requires more to demonstrate that this approach is productive for understanding personality in natural settings. Even in a Skinner box, the effects of multiple schedules are still being explored.

To what extent, in natural settings, do the consequences of behavior actually change behavior? T.L. Smith (1983) notes that there has been very little research on this question. Some preliminary observations of early language development have been made (Michael, 1984; T.L. Smith, 1983), but there has not yet been enough study of environmental factors in language development to know how important they may be, in contrast with innate factors (Wessells, 1982). Until more evidence is collected, it is impossible to say how much human behavior in real-world environments can be explained by Skinner's theory.

Freedom and Dignity

Probably the greatest objection to Skinner's theory is that it describes people as not free (Garrett, 1985). The belief that individuals are free and responsible for their own behavior leads many to reject Skinner's deterministic assumptions, sometimes on religious grounds (e.g., Hillstrom, 1984).

Skinner (e.g., 1953a, 1986c) criticized cultural practices that are less effective than they could be in producing the good life. An accurate theory of human behavior should permit a scientist to change society for the better. Societies should be designed, argued Skinner, in such a way that reinforcements cause people to behave in desirable ways. In this way, little coercion would be necessary. Effective reinforcement schedules are more helpful than simply giving people what they need, whether the people are mental patients, prisoners, or the poor (Skinner, 1978).

Skinner (1948b) explored the question of how a culture should be designed in his utopian novel ***Walden Two***. In this fictional description of an ideal planned community, Skinner, through the character of Mr. Frazier (who has designed the community called "Walden Two") poses the question, "What would you do if you found yourself in possession of an effective science of behavior?" (Skinner, 1948b, p. 255). The philosopher in the novel, Mr. Castle, begs the question by claiming that individuals would retain much control (i.e., they would be "free"). But Frazier persists. Just for the sake of argument, grant the premise that behavior is determined. Under that circumstance, what would a Utopia look like?

Skinner's imaginary utopian community consists of about a thousand men, women, and children of all ages living on a large communal farm in the United States. Through a system of labor credits, which offer higher incentives for less desirable work, people choose their occupation without ordinarily making a commitment to a particular type of labor for a long period of time. The necessary tasks of the community are thus completed through an average of only 4 hours' work per person per day. This leaves much time for leisure activities, including the arts and music. Planners modify the work-credit reinforcement schedules periodically so as to change peoples' choices as community needs change. Above all, it is a society in which the choices of individuals are naturally good. It is a society based upon reward, rather than punishment or coercion.

The novel prompted much criticism and it raises value questions (McGray, 1984; Waller, 1982). Who will plan the society? Is this not a dictatorship, a totalitarian state? Does it not dehumanize the individual (e.g., Carpenter, 1974; Krutch, 1954)? Skinner rebutted that no freedom is really lost, since determinism is a fact, not an ideal. His characters were not governed by coercion; they made choices as much as any person in any setting can. Within his theory, freedom is an illusion. The only issue is whether we will be influenced by unplanned, accidental forces or planned ones. In writing *Walden Two,* Skinner moved from a role of scientist to become an advocate for broad social application of his principles, a change with important personal meanings for him (Elms, 1981).

Skinner recognized that behavioral technology is not without risk. Though the technology itself "is ethically neutral" (Skinner, 1971, p. 143), it can be used to malevolent ends. He said, "I think a science of behavior is just as dangerous as the atom bomb. It has the potential of being horribly misused" (R.I. Evans, 1981b, p. 54). Nonetheless, one can no more repeal behavioral laws than natural laws. Free choice, in Skinner's theory, is an illusion.

Skinner challenged traditional concepts claiming that people were autonomous and free, but that failed to provide effective means of self-control and social control. He objected to humanism as a force impeding scientific understanding of behavior (1971), and he later included cognitive psychology as well as psychotherapy as impediments to scientific psychology (Skinner, 1987; Wessells, 1982). According to Skinner, we presume that people are free to behave as they choose, thus earning dignity by their freely chosen behaviors. Though this claim that dignity must be earned has been challenged (Harcum & Rosen, 1990a, 1990b; Harcum, Rosen, & Burijon, 1989), concepts of free choice are well established in our culture. The law punishes based on the presumption of free choice, yet people may still be raised in environments that *cause* them to become criminals. Is this humane? Skinner remarked, "There remains . . . a great discrepancy between legal and scientific conceptions of human behavior" (1953a, p. 341). Critics, however, fault Skinner for confusing his role as a "good engineer" with science (Pribram, 1973). In arguing against the language of "freedom and dignity," they contend that Skinner unnecessarily refuses to allow two levels of discourse, "freedom and dignity" on the one hand and science on the other, to coexist (Rosen, 1973). Furthermore, beliefs that one has personal control contribute to psychological well-being, and even to life itself (Lefcourt, 1973; see also the chapter on Bandura and Mischel in this text).

Critics argue that Skinner's model, with its fully deterministic assumptions, dehumanizes people. If humanism represents a desirable value system, Skinner passes muster, in Evans's estimation:

> Readers who are concerned with his ostensibly mechanistic conceptions of man may be surprised to learn that Dr. Skinner appears to me to be essentially a humanist in the most straightforward connotation of this term. This is evi-

> denced by his concern with eliminating aversive control in society, his optimism concerning man's capability for dealing with his most difficult problems, and his staunch belief in the basic potential of all men for a "good life" regardless of their deficits in so-called measured intelligence and their so-called emotional limitations. (R.I. Evans, 1981b, pp. 120–121)

Garrett (1985) argued that freedom can be reconciled with a behavioral approach. Language is a key to this.

> Studies of reinforcement with children show that up until a certain mastery of language, children (like non-human organisms) respond in uniform ways to the same schedules of reinforcement, but that after a certain level of linguistic competence they respond in quite individual ways to the same schedules. . . . [Language] make[s] reasoning possible and with reasoning arise problem-solving strategies that are free of the immediate, external environment. (Garrett, 1985, p. 27)

Language may, indeed, be the key to further extension of Skinner's theory.

Thought and Language

Critics charge that Skinner's attempts to explain human language and thought are overly simplified and reductionistic. The controversy is important. It is not only about Skinner's analysis of language per se. Rather, language is the mechanism by which complex human behavior, including social behavior, can be considered within the behavioral model (V.L. Lee, 1984).

Skinner (1986a) suggested that language may have evolved from nonverbal behaviors, such as signaling. He described a hypothetical situation in which two of our remote ancestors fished, one in a position to haul up the net, and the other able to see whether fish were in it. Before language evolved, the net-controlling ancestor could have observed signals, such as the expressions of excitement by the observer. Over time, these expressions could have evolved into language.

For 23 years (Skinner, 1967), Skinner labored over his book, *Verbal Behavior* (1957). There and in other writings, he argued that human language and thought could be analyzed into component operant behaviors that could be understood using the principles emerging from his animal studies. While some agree (e.g., Stemmer, 1990), many do not, arguing that language cannot be understood without cognitive mental concepts (e.g., Chomsky, 1959). Research on language development does not support the idea that it is learned by reinforcement. Instead, innate factors are regarded as important.

Skinner offered behavioral definitions for common forms of verbal behavior. Most popular of his ideas are *tacts* and *mands*. A tact is verbal behavior that occurs as a response to a nonverbal stimulus, for example, saying "hot" when touched by a hot object. A mand is verbal behavior that occurs following a prior state of deprivation, for example, asking for food when hungry. More complex relationships among verbal elements occur with the development of grammar. These *autoclitic processes* are not so directly related to environmental events as tacts and mands. One example is the word "not" in the sentence "It is *not* raining" (Skinner, 1986a, p. 120). For Skinner, even such grammatical complexities are learned behaviors. In turn, verbal behaviors can serve as discriminative stimuli over subsequent behavior. A toddler learning the word "no" exemplifies this **verbal control**. The child, having been reinforced in the past for imitating the parent, learns to say "no" when near the stove, where the parent has said "no." This "no" then serves as a discriminative stimulus for the behavior of staying away from the stove, which has been reinforced by the parent when the parent said "no." For Skinner, speech is simply verbal behavior, and thought is simply covert speech.

Skinner argued that mental states are not even known directly by the individual. While we often assume that we have direct and accurate knowledge of our feelings, intentions, and other mental states, that is erroneous. Thought develops from experience in a social setting in which other people provide words to label stimuli they observe. English-speaking parents call a cat "a cat," and the child learns to say the word. Without this learning experience, there is no private thought about "a cat." In the same way, parents observe their child crying and a knee bleeding, and they say "It hurts." From this parental behavior, the child learns to label the experience of "hurt." If parents do not provide correct labels, the child's use of words, both in observable speech and in unobservable thought (which is nothing more than covert speech), will be adversely affected. Thought is, from this point of view, simply talking to oneself (Skinner, 1957).

Humans are capable of complex verbal behaviors. Parallels in animal behavior have been explored (e.g., R. Epstein, Lanza, & Skinner, 1980; Savage-Rumbaugh, 1984). Some verbal behaviors, such as the use of the past tense, may at least in theory be capable of expression through the simple responses pigeons can make. Other verbal behaviors, such as Skinner's challenging sentence "No black scorpion is falling upon this table" (Skinner, 1957, p. 457), seem impossible to express in behaviors that pigeons could emit (Catania, 1980).

Skinner's behavioral interpretation of thought is not universally accepted (Paniagua, 1987). Noam Chomsky (1959), the famous linguist, wrote an unfavorable criticism of Skinner's book *Verbal Behavior.* Chomsky argued that language cannot be explained simply as learned behavior. Chomsky called attention to the creative aspects of language; people are able to generate new statements that they have never heard before, following the rules of grammar, which he interprets as evidence for an innate capacity for language. Linguists favor the interpretation of language as an innate capacity, while behaviorists favor the learning interpretation. Hackenberg (1988) claimed that Chomsky seriously misunderstood Skinner's theory. Though Skinner attempted for decades to extend his theory to include language and thought, most psychologists feel that these phenomena require other, more cognitive, theories (e.g., Hocutt, 1985; Killeen, 1984; Kleinginna & Kleinginna, 1988; L. Miller, 1988; Wessells, 1981, 1982). Skinner (1967) ignored his critics, claiming that he did not read Chomsky's review until many years later, and then read only a small part of it. In one of his last papers, Skinner mustered support for his analysis of thought as a derivative of behavior from etymology, showing that words now referring to mental states originally referred to actions (Skinner, 1989a).

Motivation

What reinforcements motivate people? Skinner did not specify in advance what would be reinforcing. He adopted a strictly empirical approach, assessing the effect of each behavioral consequence by observing the individual carefully. For one child, being told "no" by a parent may constitute punishment, reducing the behavior that results in the scolding. For another child, the same parental "no" could be a reinforcement, increasing the behavior (perhaps because of the attention or sense of power it brought). In some therapeutic applications, motivation is considered. For example, the capacity of some substances, such as nicotine, to be inherently reinforcing must be recognized in designing interventions such as quitting smoking (Clarke, 1987; Dougherty, Miller, Todd, & Kostenbauder, 1981; Goldberg & Henningfield, 1988). In general, though, Skinner's approach does not address a basic question in personality: What is the nature of human motivation?

The intensity and persistence of behavior, which are often explained as due to high levels of motivation, are interpreted by Skinner as a consequence of schedules of reinforcement. Partial reinforcement schedules can produce high levels of responding. Emotions are also often taken as evidence of motivation, but Skinner understood these, too, as produced by the learning of adaptive responses. Animals, and people, are calm when in environments where they know what to do to obtain reinforcements. When they do not know what to do—for example, when on an extinction schedule or when being punished—emotionality may occur as a side effect. It is not the primary issue, however, for a behaviorist. A student who fails exams and blames the failure on test anxiety suffers, from a behavioral perspective, from a lack of behaviors that effectively produce the rewards of good grades. The anxiety is a side effect. It may be instructive, and may signal the recognition that available behaviors will not produce the desired result. The solution, though, is learning those behaviors, not focusing on reducing the anxiety alone.

Stages of Development

Humans undergo dramatic changes from infancy to adulthood. These stages of life were not considered by Skinner, whose model described change as continuous. Without acknowledgment of cognitive variables, the increasing adaptive capacities of the human from infancy through childhood and beyond are not adequately considered.

Is Skinner's Theory a Theory of Personality?

Skinner (1950) questioned the value of theoretical concepts, advocating instead that researchers carefully describe actual behavior, discovering its orderliness through extensive observations (Zuriff, 1985). Some have therefore called Skinner's work "atheoretical," but this is an overstatement. It does include hypothetical constructs, as described in Chapter 1 (Williams, 1986). These constructs, however, are not about what is inside the person, but rather about the impact of the environment. This approach accounts for individual behavior without resorting to traditional personality concepts: traits, unconscious motivations, conscious motivations, self-actualization, and so forth.

It is a "contextual" rather than an "organocentric" theory (Schnaitter, 1987). It focuses on the environment, rather than on the organism (Zuriff,

1985). This contextual emphasis is useful for applied work, but not necessarily for "understanding" (Pierce & Epling, 1984). If we require that a personality theory describe the *internal* characteristics of the person, clearly Skinner's theory is not a personality theory. On the other hand, his emphasis on the environment challenges personality theory to consider the situational context, which it has often ignored.

Of particular value for personality psychology, Skinner always emphasized the importance of observing individuals, rather than groups. From the outset of his research, Skinner presented data from individual organisms (albeit usually rats and pigeons). He opposed averaging subjects together, since averaged results hide individual differences and may present an orderly, smooth behavioral record, even when each individual organism may act much more sporadically. Group data obscure the understanding of the individual. Skinnerians carefully conduct a functional analysis for *each* person in order to discover the reinforcements that work for that individual. Many personality theories merely pay lip service to the concept of the uniqueness of each individual, but Skinner offered a truly idiographic approach.

The fact that individuals differ in their characteristic behaviors or traits, a fundamental phenomenon for personality theory, can be explained by a behavioral analysis. Each individual has been exposed to a somewhat different learning history, which has strengthened certain behaviors more than others. Some differences in reinforcement may have been planned; for example, when families and schools encourage some talents above others. Others are rather arbitrary, perhaps as randomly determined as Skinner's superstitious learning model, but with important implications for individual differences. Skinner did not describe genetic differences, but his theory can readily accommodate factors such as genetic differences that cause various individuals to respond differently to stimuli in the environment. Though behaviorists have traditionally emphasized experimental manipulations, human subjects vary widely in their responses to reinforcement contingencies, and behavioral methods are easily applicable to the study of individual differences (Harzem, 1984).

Skinner's influence is not restricted to, and not even primarily concerned with, personality, yet his work poses a challenge to fundamental assumptions of personality. If the behavior of individuals can be fully explained as a consequence of the environment, is personality theory necessary? Richard I. Evans says of Skinner that "he can [not] in any sense be called a 'personality psychologist,' but . . . he represents historically the most important alternative to a personality psychology" (1981b, p. 123).

Summary

B.F. Skinner proposed a radical behavioral theory of individual behavior in terms of environmental determinants, without referring to unobservable internal characteristics such as traits. He described *operant behavior* as behavior selected by the environment. This provides a mechanism for adaptation in the life of an individual, parallel to evolutionary selection that occurs over generations. His theory of *operant conditioning* describes the acquisition of behaviors through *reinforcement* and their elimination through *ex-*

tinction and *punishment.* Various *schedules of reinforcement* produce characteristic effects. *Variable ratio schedules* produce a high rate of responding. *Fixed interval schedules* produce a scalloped effect (alternating high and low rates of responding). New behaviors can be produced through *shaping. Discrimination* learning brings behavior under the control of environmental stimuli, and *generalization* produces similar responding in various environments (see Table 11.1).

Skinner applied behavioral principles broadly, not only to the rats and pigeons of his laboratory but also to humans. His model suggested interventions in the treatment of the mentally disturbed and developmentally disabled, as well as educational interventions for normal children. He argued that society could be improved by planned application of behavioral principles. According to Skinner, modern behavioral science could fulfill Utopian visions that "old-fashioned" political and religious principles had only dreamed possible. Critics, however, have argued that many uniquely human phenomena cannot be understood in terms of Skinner's model, which is overly reductionistic and deterministic. It is criticized for ignoring important differences between humans and other species, particularly human language capacities and the complexity of the social world.

TABLE 11.1 Contributions of Skinner's Theory to Various Topics

Biological	Species differences influence response capabilities and the effectiveness of various reinforcements.
Child Development	Children learn which behaviors will lead to positive reinforcement and which to punishment, and they respond accordingly. Stimulus control and schedules of reinforcement influence this learning.
Adult Development	Adult development is explained according to the same principles as child development.
Mental Health	Rather than considering "health" or "illness," it is more profitable to specify which behaviors should be eliminated and which increased, and to change them through behavior modification.
Society	Society provides the conditions of learning, and therefore shapes personality. Behavioral principles suggest that some aspects of society should be improved (e.g., education).
Cognitive Processes	Mental processes are difficult to study because the scientist does not have access to them. In principle, mental processes can be explained in behavioral terms. In practice, it probably is not worth the trouble; instead, the focus should be on observable behavior.
Individual Differences	Individuals differ in their behaviors owing to differences in reinforcement histories.

ILLUSTRATIVE BIOGRAPHIES: Concluding Remarks

Skinner's theory claims that each person's unique behavior can be understood as a result of a particular history of conditioning, rather than in terms of inner personality differences. Can this environmental approach explain why a wealthy young woman would rob a bank, and a poor printer become an honored member of society?

Patricia Hearst

Behavior, according to Skinner, is determined by its consequences. As the environmental contingencies for behavior change, behavior itself will change. This principle applies well to the responses of Patricia Hearst to the changing environments in her life. Before her kidnapping, radical political rhetoric, such as she later expressed, was not part of her behavioral repertoire. She did not carry a gun, rob banks, or hide from authorities. Instead, she studied, set up an apartment with her fiancé, and behaved much as any well-to-do 19-year-old would behave.

Many aspects of Patricia Hearst's captivity are comparable to the experimental conditioning environments devised by Skinner. Miss Hearst, like Skinner's laboratory rats and pigeons, was hungry. She found the minimal rations provided to be distasteful, and she states that she lost 15 pounds, so that she weighed only 90 pounds and was found medically to be malnourished at the end of her captivity. Furthermore, many of the human needs that cannot be compared directly with animal models were also not met.

She was subjected to punishment: criticism for her bourgeois background, for her manner of speech, for the ideas she expressed. She learned to avoid expressing any opinions that differed from those of her captors so as to avoid punishment, which ranged from mockery and criticism to rape. Her attempts to avoid angering her captors can be compared to the avoidance behaviors of a laboratory animal trying to prevent electric shock. It was safer to agree with SLA rhetoric. Such agreement was first reinforced by her being let out of the closet where she had been confined for 57 days, and being allowed to remove her blindfold. She learned that freely emitting SLA ideas, expressing them in her own words, won praise and respite from fear, so she did this more and more often. Saying "I want to fight for the people" was a verbal response that was positively reinforced. In fact, she perceived that convincing her captors to believe the sincerity of her conversion to the revolution was the only hope for saving her life.

While Skinner as an experimentalist was cautious to avoid basing his theory on unobservables such as thought processes, as a theorist he recognized that thinking can be regarded as covert responses, subject to the same sorts of environmental contingencies as overt responses. Patricia Hearst's SLA captors targeted thoughts, as well as actions, in their influence attempts. Cinque, the SLA leader, warned Patricia against "negative thoughts [which were] products of my past life, my bourgeois upbringing" (Hearst, 1982, p. 194).

Any behavior that might lead to her escape, such as contacting her family or the FBI, was discouraged by the SLA through threats of punishment. Not only would the SLA punish, but members convinced Miss Hearst that the FBI would also kill her, given the opportunity. She thus developed a "conditioned fear" of the FBI. She became afraid to talk to anyone not in the radical underground. As Skinner's experiments demonstrate, behavior that is punished is suppressed, so it is consistent with these behavioral principles that Miss Hearst did not attempt to escape. She abandoned all hope of escape; even thinking about escape was extinguished.

At her trial, both the public and the jury were confronted with evidence that Patricia Hearst expressed apparently genuine agreement with SLA ideas even after she was captured by the FBI, and therefore safe from SLA threats. How can this be? Prosecution lawyers argued that this was evidence that her participation in the activities of the SLA was voluntary. Why else would she raise her hand in a gesture of protest when captured? Why else would she have fired a gun to allow her two SLA confederates to escape when they were captured by store detectives for shoplifting, instead of taking the opportunity to escape herself?

Such behavior is easily explained within the framework of a behaviorist model. There are many instances in which behavior produced by one set of contingencies endures even when the contingencies have been changed. That is the phenomenon of "resistance to extinction." It takes time for well-learned behaviors to disappear. During her many months of captivity, Miss Hearst was repeatedly drilled in "combat readiness," as the SLA leader, Cinque, construed it. Weeks and months of practice made the use of a gun and the expression of SLA slogans well-learned habits, and they would not disappear immediately. Even thinking about free acts had been "extinguished" by the coercive experience of captivity.

Her identity, too, was subjected to conditioning. We might ordinarily think human identity to be outside of a behavioral analysis. But Patricia Hearst was drilled repeatedly by her captors. When asked "Who are you?" she learned to reply instantaneously: "I'm a soldier in the Symbionese Liberation Army" (Hearst, 1982, p. 154).

According to Patricia Hearst, "I had gone along with their combat drills for so long and for so intensive a period that I had, in fact, learned, as a soldier learns, to act and to react instinctively—like Pavlov's salivating dog" (Hearst, 1982, p. 225). Her particular theory of learning is incorrect. The indoctrination was based upon operant (Skinnerian) principles rather than classical (Pavlovian) conditioning. But the outcome was, nonetheless, automatic. Effective conditioning did occur. Her behavior was determined by its conditioning. While we might expect that freedom would hit at an instant, that is not the case under circumstances of confinement that are as controlling as those described by Miss Hearst. Her trial attorneys brought in expert witnesses who testified to brainwashing. Military experience with brainwashing clearly indicates that under circumstances of highly controlled captivity, apparent conversions to the enemy position can occur rapidly, and recovery can take some time. The defense lawyer, aware of this, claimed that if this were a military trial, a finding of innocence would be guaranteed.

Just as there are ways to prepare soldiers for the possibility of capture, so that they can better resist brainwashing attempts, it is possible to imagine circumstances that could have prepared Miss Hearst to resist the influence attempts of her captors, despite their power. But for this 19-year-old woman under the circumstances of her captivity, the environmental contingencies were, indeed, the crucial determinants of behavior.

Benjamin Franklin

Unlike the circumstances in captivity that constrained Patricia Hearst, Benjamin Franklin lived in circumstances that permitted many behavioral options. It was, therefore, possible for him to determine his own destiny in many of the ways recommended by B.F. Skinner. Indeed, if he had not lived two centuries earlier, we might suspect him of having heeded some of Skinner's advice.

Franklin wrote his autobiography in later life. In it, he described, for the benefit of his descendants, many of the strategies for living that he had found successful in the task he set for himself, namely "arriving at moral perfection" (Franklin, 1961, p. 94). He hoped that others would be encouraged to follow his example.

Using very behavioral language, Franklin urged the formation of good habits. "I concluded at length that the mere speculative conviction that it was our interest to be completely virtuous was not sufficient to prevent slipping, and that the contrary habits must be broken and good ones acquired and established before we can have any dependence on a steady, uniform rectitude of conduct" (Franklin, 1961, p. 94). Skinner, too, emphasized "habits."

Franklin's strategy for improving these habits would undoubtedly have pleased Skinner. He kept a list of behaviors he wished to improve. There were 13 of them: temperance, silence, order, resolution, frugality, industry, sincerity, justice, moderation, cleanliness, tranquility, chastity, and humility (Franklin, 1961, p. 95). Every day he recorded the frequency of lapses in each category. Each week one particular category was the focus of particular effort, which enabled Franklin to run through the entire list four times each year. He repeated this for several years. Although, unfortunately for the curious, Franklin does not provide us with a cumulative record of this effort (having frugally erased previous years' records in order to reuse the chart), it is clear that he was using a self-reinforcement process based upon his own self-reinforcement for success and self-reprimand for failure (cf. Mountjoy & Sundberg, 1981).

In his *Poor Richard's Almanack*, Franklin offered proverbs to posterity in a Skinnerian mode. Skinner regarded proverbs as verbal statements that allow people to profit from the prior experiences of others in their culture, especially in areas in which there is a considerable delay between the behavior and the consequences. Such conditions make it more difficult for the individual to learn from his or her own experience (Skinner, 1974, pp. 121–122, 202).

As a footnote, it is interesting that B.F. Skinner was elected as a member of the American Philosophical Society, which had been founded by Ben Franklin (Skinner, 1979, p. 341).

GLOSSARY

base rate the rate of responding before conditioning

behavior modification the application of learning principles to therapy

continuous reinforcement a reinforcement schedule in which every response is reinforced

cumulative record record of all the responses of the organism throughout a conditioning study

discrimination learning learning to respond differentially, depending upon environmental stimuli

extinction reduction in the rate of responding when reinforcement ends

fixed interval schedule a reinforcement schedule in which a reinforcement follows every *N* units of time (e.g., in FI-15, one reinforcement is given every 15 seconds if a response has occurred at least once)

fixed ratio schedule a reinforcement schedule in which a reinforcement follows every *N*th response (e.g., in FR-15, every 15th response is reinforced)

generalization responding to stimuli that were not present during learning as though they were the discriminative stimuli present during learning

mentalism the traditional view, opposed by Skinner, in which inner mental concepts (such as thoughts and intentions) are regarded as the causes of behavior

negative reinforcer an outcome stimulus that ends when a response occurs; it has the effect of increasing the rate of responding

operant responses behaviors freely emitted by an organism

partial reinforcement schedule a reinforcement schedule in which only some responses are reinforced

positive reinforcer an outcome stimulus that is presented contingent upon a response and that has the effect of increasing the rate of responding

primary reinforcer a reinforcer that is unlearned, or innate

punishment a stimulus contingent upon a response and that has the effect of decreasing the rate of responding

response a discrete behavior by an organism

schedule of reinforcement the specific contingency between a response and a reinforcement

secondary reinforcer a reinforcer that is learned

shaping reinforcement of successive approximations of a response so as to increase the frequency of a response that originally has a zero base rate

Skinner box a device that provides a controlled environment for measuring learning

superstitious behavior consistent behavior resulting from a random reinforcement schedule

time out room an environment in which no reinforcements are given so as to extinguish unwanted behavior

token economy setting in which reinforcement of behavior is systematically applied in a group setting through the use of tokens which can be exchanged for rewards or privileges later

variable interval schedule a reinforcement schedule in which a reinforcement follows, on the average, every *N* units of time, (e.g., in VI-15, one reinforcement is given every 15 seconds on the average if a response has occurred at least once, but sometimes the time span is under 15 seconds between reinforcements, and sometimes more)

variable ratio schedule a reinforcement schedule in which a reinforcement follows, on the average, every *N*th response, (e.g., in VR-15, one reinforcement is given for every 15 responses, but sometimes fewer than 15 responses occur between reinforcements, and sometimes more)

verbal control the impact of verbal behavior on overt behavior by serving as discriminative stimuli for behavior

Walden Two Skinner's imagined utopian community, based on learning principles

STUDY QUESTIONS

1. Explain what is meant by the term *radical behaviorism*. Why does this theory not consider a personality *trait* to be an acceptable theoretical construct? How does radical behaviorism explain individual differences?
2. Summarize the basic principles of operant conditioning, that is, how do reinforcement, punishment, and extinction influence the rate of responding?
3. Explain the difference among a positive reinforcer, a negative reinforcer, and punishment.
4. Describe how *shaping* builds new behaviors.
5. Explain *discrimination learning*. Devise an example to demonstrate how this type of learning could help a person cope in a particular environment.
6. Explain *generalization*. How might this concept explain the defense mechanism of *displacement*?
7. Explain *superstitious behavior*. Provide an example to demonstrate how this type of learning could help understand individual differences (or "personality traits").
8. List and explain continuous reinforcement and the four partial schedules of reinforcement. What are the typical effects of each on behavior?
9. Discuss applications of operant conditioning in therapy.
10. Discuss applications of Skinner's ideas as they apply to education.
11. Discuss Skinner's novel *Walden Two*. What issues does it raise for human society?
12. Discuss the free will versus determinism controversy. Explain Skinner's position.
13. Explain Skinner's objection to mentalistic ideas such as intention.
14. Summarize the objections to Skinner's ideas as a theory of human personality. What are the strengths of this theory as a theory of human personality?

CHAPTER 

Dollard and Miller: Psychoanalytic Learning Theory

BIOGRAPHIES OF JOHN DOLLARD AND NEAL MILLER

John Dollard

John Dollard was born in Menasha, Wisconsin, in 1900. He did his undergraduate work at the University of Wisconsin and graduate work in sociology at the University of Chicago, where he was awarded a doctorate in 1931. He also studied psychoanalysis at the Berlin Institute.

Dollard taught anthropology at Yale University for a year and then joined the new Institute of Human Relations, which was interdisciplinary in focus. Besides anthropology, he also taught psychology and sociology, and for many years was appointed as a research associate. He retired from Yale in 1969, becoming professor emeritus.

Neal Miller

Neal E. Miller was born in Milwaukee, Wisconsin, on August 3, 1909. The family moved to Bellingham, Washington, so his father, an educational psychologist, could teach at Western Washington State

College. Neal Miller received a B.S. degree in psychology from the University of Washington in 1931. He did graduate work at Stanford University (from which he received a master's degree in 1932) and Yale University (where he earned his PhD in 1935). At Yale, he studied learning theory from Clark Hull, whose concepts of drive reduction influenced Miller's later theorizing. Miller married Marion Edwards in 1948, and they have two children, York and Sara.

Like Dollard, Miller also studied psychoanalysis. He went to Vienna in 1936, funded by the Social Science Research Council. He was analyzed for eight months by Heinz Hartmann, an eminent Freudian, in Vienna. He couldn't afford the higher fees ($20 an hour) required to be analyzed by Freud himself (Moritz, 1974). Returning to the United States, Miller joined the faculty at the Institute of Human Relations at Yale University (1936–41), where he collaborated with Dollard on the books *Frustration and Aggression* (1939) and *Social Learning and Imitation* (1941). These works explored a learning theory reconceptualization of psychoanalytic insights. In 1950, they jointly published a more mature and comprehensive version of their theoretical work: *Personality and Psychotherapy: An Analysis in Terms of Learning, Thinking and Culture.* In addition, they explored anxiety among soldiers in World War II.

In 1966, Miller founded the Laboratory of Physiological Psychology at Rockefeller University in New York, where he conducted basic research on animals. He has been a longtime supporter of animal research, defending against criticisms from animal rights advocates who charge scientists with unnecessary cruelty to animals (Coile & Miller, 1984; N.E. Miller, 1985, 1991).

Besides their joint work, Dollard and Miller had individual research interests. Dollard researched the sociological issues of race relations and social class. He also explored biographical analyses, suggesting what should be included in biographical materials to permit sound psychological studies. Miller performed extensive research on physiological mechanisms of motivation, using rats and other animals. In 1969 he began applying the work to humans (Moritz, 1974). This work contributed to the development of biofeedback (N.E. Miller & Dworkin, 1977) by showing that autonomic nervous system functions such as heart rate, gastric vascular responses, and blood pressure could be influenced by operant learning (e.g., Carmona, Miller, & Demierre, 1974; DiCara & Miller, 1968; N.E. Miller, 1963, 1969; N.E. Miller & Banuazizi, 1968). This concept contradicted the prevailing assumption that operant learning could only occur for responses that were under voluntary control, and that the autonomic nervous system involved only classical conditioning. Later research by Miller and others has not been able to reliably reproduce these effects (Dworkin & Miller, 1986; R.I. Evans, 1976). Nonetheless, biofeedback remains an accepted and effective treatment technique, and Miller continues his research on the learning of autonomic nervous system responses (Grasing & Miller, 1989). He supports basic research (as opposed to applied research), much of it using animals, and is particularly interested in the workings of the brain (D. Cohen, 1977).

This chapter will not attempt to discuss all the work that Miller and Dollard have done, but rather will focus on the collaborative effort of the two theorists, which is the learning theory reinterpretation of psychoanalytic theory.

ILLUSTRATIVE BIOGRAPHIES

Dollard and Miller have proposed a learning theory that emphasizes the social context in which behavior occurs. We may well expect the social context to be important in understanding a famous rock singer such as Jim Morrison. Can the social context that shapes a career leave personality untouched? This theory explicitly considers aggressive behavior, and so promises to be pertinent to the life of a convicted murderer, Jean Harris.

Jean Harris

Jean Harris is the (in)famous convicted killer of the inventor of the Scarsdale diet, Dr. Herman ("Hy") Tarnower. In her autobiography (Harris, 1986), Jean Harris described an affluent, respectable childhood in which there was great concern with "Society." She was quiet, with no indication of an "aggressive personality," no hint that she would be convicted of premeditated murder of her longtime lover.

Jean Harris was married to a childhood sweetheart immediately after finishing college. After 19 years of a storybook marriage in Grosse Pointe, Michigan, she chose to end the marriage, feeling dissatisfied although there were no major conflicts. She had taught school for many years, but after her divorce in 1965, she took a more lucrative job as a school administrator in Philadelphia. She met Dr. Herman Tarnower and began a love affair. They were engaged but never married. Dr. Tarnower was wealthy and much sought after by many women, but he had never married. Their relationship lasted for years and he was generous, but he did not entirely give up other women.

On March 10, 1980, Jean Harris went to the upstate New York home of Dr. Tarnower and, in his bedroom where he had been sleeping alone, shot him. She was accused of premeditated murder, motivated perhaps by jealousy of another woman whom he supposedly had been seeing. She claimed that she had brought a gun to kill herself, and had wanted to speak with him first. She said the shooting was an accident. On February 28, 1981, Jean Harris was convicted of murdering Dr. Tarnower and sentenced to prison for 15 years to life. Her legal appeals were unsuccessful. While in prison, she has written two books (Harris, 1986, 1988) and has worked with the children of women prisoners.

Her aggressive action, seemingly so out of character, poses a challenge for personality theory. Dollard and Miller's theory considers aggression explicitly. Can it help us understand Jean Harris?

Jim Morrison

As lead singer for the rock group The Doors until his death in 1971 at age 27, Jim Morrison wrote and performed many songs, including "Break on Through (to the Other Side)" and "Light My Fire." His concerts were attended by fans attracted to the anti-authority counterculture The Doors celebrated. This sentiment was expressed not only in lyrics but also in the notorious behavior of Jim Morrison onstage and off. Drugs, alcohol, promiscuity: These were Morrison's way of life. In 1969, he was arrested and convicted in Florida for indecent exposure during a performance, a felony.

Morrison died in Paris in 1971, apparently as a result of drugs. Some of his fans claim his death was a hoax, staged to allow him to escape from his rock star identity and to establish the privacy needed to nurture his development as a poet. He had published poetry (Morrison, 1971) and was torn between this creative outlet and that of his singing (Hopkins & Sugerman, 1980). Conflict is a central issue in Dollard and Miller's theory.

PSYCHOANALYTIC LEARNING THEORY

Dollard and Miller took on an ambitious challenge: to translate Freud's theory into the concepts of learning theory, which they regarded as more scientific, and then to test this new theory in the laboratory. Such an approach is based upon the belief that Freud had some worthwhile clinical insights, but that his theory was phrased in largely untestable terms. By more clearly defining his theory, and then actually manipulating the causes of behavior in an animal laboratory, Dollard and Miller hoped to refine and validate the fundamental ideas of psychoanalytic theory. Other models have been offered that describe psychoanalytic conflicts and defenses in mathematical language (e.g., Ainslie, 1982; Blum, 1961, 1989) and in terms of learning principles (e.g., Eysenck, 1979; Mowrer, 1950; Watson & Rayner, 1920;

Wolpe, 1982), but none has been so historically important to personality theory as that proposed by Dollard and Miller.

Dollard and Miller drew upon various theories of learning, including those of Pavlov, Thorndike, Hull, and Skinner. From these theorists, they borrowed the basic principles of conditioning: stimulus, response, reward, generalization, discrimination, and extinction.

In addition to psychoanalysis and learning theory, a third theoretical orientation influenced Dollard and Miller: "modern social science . . . [which] describes the social conditions under which human beings learn" (1950, p. 3). This tradition influenced the two researchers to consider sociological variables, such as social class, which influenced the particular learning experiences of people. While learning theory could suggest the *principles* of learning, a sociological perspective was necessary to describe the *conditions* of learning for particular people. Sarason (1989) credits John Dollard (1937/1957, 1949) for this vision. Dollard recognized the necessity of considering actual human social conditions, and not simply abstract psychological principles that could be studied in a context-impoverished laboratory setting.

John Dollard (1949) criticized case histories that had been presented by well-known psychologists, including Freud and Adler, for their failure to consider the social context of personality appropriately. Adler, for example, presented a theory that reflected cultural bias by stressing competition, a major concern in Western cultures, but not universally. Dollard urged psychologists always to consider the culture when analyzing an individual personality. According to Dollard much can be predicted without knowing anything about the individual, simply from a knowledge of the culture into which the person is born. Many statements from research should have the phrase "in our culture" appended to them (Dollard, 1949, p. 17). Biological factors, such as drives and instincts, must be specified in terms of their social relevance. It is a mistake to ignore either the biological or the cultural factors. Theories must deal with childhood as well as adulthood. The situation may be defined differently by the individual from how it is defined by others. Both definitions need to be understood. Raw material provided by the individual does not "speak for itself." Not all information can be taken at face value.

Four Fundamental Concepts about Learning

Miller and Dollard summed up the primary concepts of learning theory by suggesting that "in order to learn one must want something, notice something, do something, and get something" (1941, p. 2). These conditions correspond to the learning theory concepts of drive ("want something"), cue ("notice something"), response ("do something"), and reward ("get something").

Drive

Freudian theory regarded *libido* as the driving force behind all action. Dollard and Miller, however, preferred the concept of **drive** from Hullian learning theory to refer to the motivating force. In his later work, however, N.E. Miller (1963) moved away from the concept of "drive," investigating learning based on instrumental learning principles instead.

In common language, a drive is a "need," such as hunger, thirst, need to sleep, need for money or recognition, and so on. More formally, Miller and Dollard defined a drive as "a strong stimulus which impels action" (1941, p. 18). (This behavioral language avoids the logical problems of whether we truly "need" something or simply believe that we do.) These drive stimuli may be of various kinds: not only external environmental stimuli, but also internal physical stimuli, or even thought processes.

Physical needs serve as *primary* drives. Hunger, thirst, fatigue, loud noises, cold, and pain are examples of such primary drives. Drives can also be learned. For example, rats who originally show no preference for a black or white experimental chamber will acquire a drive of anxiety if they are shocked in the white chamber, and will learn to press a bar to escape to the now-preferred black chamber (N.E. Miller, 1941a). Many human drives are learned or *acquired* drives. Among the most important of these are anxiety, the need for money, the need for approval, ambition, anger, and gregariousness. Different acquired needs are developed in different learning circumstances. For example, ambition is fostered more in the middle class than in the lower class.

Any "strong stimulus" has drive characteristics, and so stimuli such as loud noises, which impel us to cover our ears or act startled, are drives. It is probably clearer to think of these as "stimuli that have drive properties." There is no inherent restriction limiting certain stimuli to function as drives. "Any stimulus can become a drive if it is made strong enough" (Miller & Dollard, 1941, p. 18).

Stimuli that have drive properties may have other properties as well; they may also have "cue" characteristics. Drives impel a person to action. Cues "determine when he will respond, where he will respond, and which response he will make" (Miller & Dollard, 1941, p. 21).

Cue

Cues are discriminative stimuli. They are what a person notices at the time of behavior. Distinctive sights, sounds, smells, and so forth may serve as cues. Hidden intrapsychic stimuli, such as thoughts, are also important cues.

People can learn to respond to patterns of stimuli, as well as to isolated stimuli. For example, a child will respond differently when mother is calling (cue_1) and he or she remembers leaving his or her bike on the driveway (cue_2) than when mother is calling (cue_1) and he or she is hungry (cue_3).

Learning consists of strengthening of the cue-response connection, so that a person's tendency to respond in a particular way in the presence of certain cues or stimuli is increased.

Response

Responses are aspects of the person's behavior. Any behavior that can be changed by learning can be considered a response. These include not only overt, readily observable behaviors, such as shouting or fainting, but also covert, hidden behaviors, such as thinking.

In any situation, some responses occur more frequently than others. For example, a 2-year-old hearing "It is bedtime" is more likely to cry than to go quietly to bed. A list of all the responses that may occur in a given situation, arranged in order from the highest probability to the lowest probability, is termed a **response hierarchy**. In this example, the response hierarchy might include the following responses:

R_1 (most likely) = cry
R_2 = grab teddy bear
R_3 = hide
R_4 = demand Daddy
R_5 = go quietly to bed

The most likely response in the hierarchy is called the **dominant response**. In this example, crying is the dominant response. The dominant response will occur, unless circumstances prevent it. (For example, the parent might threaten the child or bribe the child in order to prevent crying on a particular occasion.) In this case, the second response in the hierarchy will occur. If it is blocked, the third response will occur, and so forth.

With learning, these responses change their positions in the response hierarchy. By the time a child is 8 or 10, given successful discipline, R_5 should be the most likely response. It is **reward** that makes responses move higher in the response hierarchy. *Punishment* and *extinction* make responses move lower in the hierarchy. The new hierarchy, revised by learning, is termed the **resultant hierarchy**.

Reward

Unlike Skinner's theory, which did not make any a priori assumptions about what would be reinforcing, Miller and Dollard preferred the Hullian assumption: that drive reduction is reinforcing. They asserted that "reward is impossible in the absence of drive" (1941, p. 29). This assumption, that drive reduction is reinforcing, provided a ready link with psychoanalysis, which discussed fundamental human drives, such as hunger and sex. Dollard and Miller were not, however, dogmatic about this reinforcement concept, and they realized that other assumptions about reinforcement might be suggested by further evidence, leading to revisions in their theory.

Rewards may be either innate or learned. **Primary rewards**, like food, are innately determined. **Secondary rewards**, like approval, are learned. Once we learn to value approval, money, power, and so forth, these secondary rewards can influence behavior and learning.

The Learning Process

If drives are satisfied by the dominant response, no learning will occur. If, however, the dominant response does not bring about drive reduction, then a **learning dilemma** exists: a situation in which the existing responses are not rewarded. This produces change.

Learning new responses can only occur if there is a drive, and if the desired response occurs and is rewarded (that is, leads to reduction of the drive). So it is important to arrange the situation so that the desired response will occur. This may involve simplifying the situation (to reduce cues for competing responses), or coaxing the desired response, or providing models to be imitated, or any of a variety of strategies used by parents, teachers, and therapists.

Punishment Undesirable responses can be eliminated by immediate punishment. Then another response from the response hierarchy will occur, and if it is reinforced it will move up in the hierarchy. However, punishment may not work as intended, since the person may resume the punished response when the situation changes. A child, for example, can learn to avoid teasing a sibling when the parents, who punish, are present. The absence of the parents provides a cue that indicates that no punishment will be given; and so the child may learn to tease only when the parents are absent.

Extinction In the example above, if the sibling didn't react, there would be no joy in the teasing, and it would soon be abandoned. When a response is not rewarded, it becomes less frequent and gradually stops occurring. This is **extinction**. For well-learned responses (that have been rewarded in the past), extinction may be a very slow process. Thus, if the parents of the 2-year-old described above have frequently rewarded crying at bedtime, it will take quite a while before the child gives up this response (see Figure 12.1).

While behaviors seem to extinguish completely, fear does not. Fear and anxiety may diminish with extinction but never be completely eliminated. This is consistent with clinical evidence of the enduring problems created by traumatic experiences. If the traumas can be recalled and expressed in language, extinction is more likely to occur.

Spontaneous Recovery Even after a response has extinguished, it will occasionally reoccur (**spontaneous recovery**). A child who has not cried at bedtime for many weeks may, once in a while, do so again. Learning principles do not require that an explanation be given for the return of the extinguished response on that particular occasion. Based on empirical research with animals, it is simply a characteristic of extinguished responses that they do, occasionally, return. If

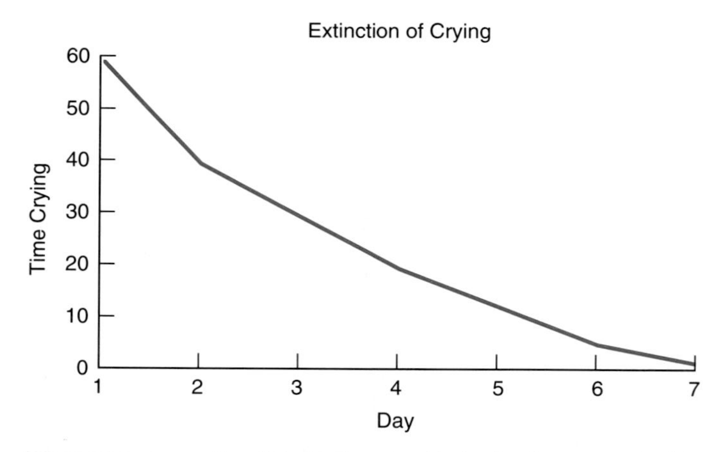

When reinforcement is withheld, the rate of behavior decreases. In this example, if parents ignore a child who cries at bedtime, the child will cry less and less as time goes on.

FIGURE 12.1 Extinction

not rewarded, these responses disappear again quickly. Former responses that have disappeared because of punishment are less likely to return spontaneously than are those that have disappeared because of extinction (Miller & Dollard, 1941, p. 43).

Generalization

Although responses have been learned in one stimulus situation, they also occur in other situations that provide cues which are more or less similar to those present when learning occurred. This phenomenon is called **stimulus generalization**. For example, a child who has learned to be afraid of one dog, who bit her, will also be afraid of other dogs. The fear "generalizes" to other dogs. The response (fear, in this example) will be more likely or stronger to cues that are quite similar to the cues present at learning, and less likely or weaker to less similar cues. If bitten by a large dog, the child will be more afraid of other large dogs than of small dogs. Generalization contributes to other behaviors as well. The tendency to follow leaders is based upon stimulus generalization; childhood tendencies to obey parents generalize so that leaders provide cues for obedience.

Discrimination

Discrimination means responding only to particular cues, and not others. The more a response generalizes, the less discrimination is present. If repeated learning experiences occur in which responses are only rewarded to highly specific cues, and not to other similar ones, then the learner will *discriminate* these stimulus cues. For example, if only one cat in the household purrs when petted, the child will learn to pet only that one, and not the others.

Gradient in the Effects of Reward

When should a reward be given? Obviously, if the cat begins purring immediately, the response of petting will be strengthened more than if the cat waits until several minutes later to purr. The concept of the **gradient of reward** states that the more closely the response is followed by reward, the more it is strengthened. Similarly, the more immediately punishment follows misbehavior, the more effective it is in reducing the strength of the tendency to misbehave.

For human beings, the capacity to think and to use language makes it possible to create greater closeness between the response and the reward (or punishment), even if time has passed. By talking about a child's misbehavior before a punishment, the parent causes the child to think about the misbehavior, and this response of thinking about the behavior is thus brought to greater immediacy with the punishment. This makes the punishment more effective. Next time the child is in a situation like the one that led to the misbehavior, he or she is less likely to think about the misdeed, because of the punishment. This will generally eliminate the misbehavior. (It is, unfortunately, also possible that the child will learn to misbehave without thinking, if the act and the thinking are not closely connected.)

Similarly, talking about a praised behavior can effectively bring these behaviors into a higher position on the gradient, strengthening laudable behaviors that a parent may not have praised at the moment of their occurrence. It is important, to make this effective, to evoke as many thoughts about the act as possible. Thus a parent who simply praises a child for getting an "A" will be less effective than one who talks about the studying, the place where studying occurred, the books read, the rewriting and proofreading, and so forth, before praising.

Anticipatory Response

Responses that precede reward are strengthened, and as they are strengthened they tend to occur earlier and earlier as the behavioral sequence is repeated. That is, they become **anticipatory responses**. A comedian who has been rewarded by laughter for telling a particular joke must struggle against the tendency to tell the punch line too soon, and a lecturer who has been rewarded upon ending past performances (with applause or, perhaps, simply the end of the hour) must similarly fight against the tendency to condense the material too much. This tendency of responses to become anticipatory often is adaptive; we learn to pull the hand away from a hot stove faster and faster so that eventually we don't even touch it. Behavior becomes more efficient.

Learning by Imitation

Dollard and Miller advanced learning theory by suggesting that learning can occur by **imitation.** They were attempting to phrase in terms of learning theory the insights of psychoanalysis, with its concept of identification. Children learn much from other children and from adults. Dollard and Miller described some specific learning processes that could be distinguished, since learning theory requires that the stimuli and responses be precisely specified.

Same Behavior

For a child to emit the *same behavior* as the person being imitated, it is necessary not only for the behavior to be the same but also for the controlling cues to be the same. Miller and Dollard (1941, p. 92) cited the example of two people who take the same bus (response), each having independently read the schedule (cue).

Copying

Often, however, what is learned by imitation is not precisely the same as what the model has learned. In **copying**, the learner's behavior is not controlled by the same cue as the model. Instead, the learner is aware of the discrepancy between his or her behavior and that of the model, and is trying to reduce that discrepancy. Often there has been past reward for similarity. While the model's behavior may be reproduced, it is not controlled by the same cues, so it is not the "same behavior." Social conformity is produced by such copying (Miller & Dollard, 1941, p. 163).

Matched Dependent Behavior

In **matched dependent behavior**, the learner produces a response that matches the model. The controlling cue, however, is different. The learner depends upon the model to provide a cue for the behavior. Dollard and Miller provided the example of an older brother (model) who runs (response) to greet his father upon hearing his father's footsteps (cue). His younger brother runs just like the model (matched response), but has not yet learned to recognize his father's footsteps as an appropriate cue for the behavior. Instead, his response is cued by seeing his brother running (dependent cue).

Matched dependent behavior is different from copying because there is a different reinforcement. In copying, recognition of response similarity is the reinforcement. In matched dependent behavior, the imitator is reinforced by some other reward. In the case of the two brothers just described, the younger brother is rewarded by candy given by his father. He hasn't learned to know when to run to the door to greet Dad home from work without depending on his brother to provide the cue; if he had learned this, he would emit the "same behavior." Also, he doesn't particularly care that his behavior is like his brother's behavior; therefore, it isn't "copying."

These distinctions indicate the conceptual clarity with which Dollard and Miller approached their task. Obviously, not all behaviors that we might loosely call "imitation" or "identification" stem from the same intrapsychic processes.

The Four Critical Training Periods of Childhood

The development of personality in childhood can be understood in terms of these learning principles. Dollard and Miller credited Freud with pointing out the importance of childhood and its conflicts. They described the three psychosexual conflicts that Freud enunciated, translated into the language of learning theory. They also added a fourth important childhood conflict, focusing on anger.

Feeding

Because eating reduces the hunger drive, it is rewarding. The responses an infant has made just before being fed are therefore strengthened. The presence of the mother, who is repeatedly on hand at these times, becomes a secondary reward. It is fundamentally important to personality to receive this reward under circumstances that reinforce desirable responses.

A child who is left to cry when hungry, and who is not consistently fed when hungry, learns not to cry for food; crying as a response is extinguished. General character traits of apathy and apprehensiveness develop. A child fed appropriately (when hungry, and in a warm interpersonal context) develops love for the mother, and by generalization a sociable personality.

Cleanliness Training

This period, corresponding to Freud's "anal stage," is a time of learning that may produce conflict between the individual and society's demands. The young child has learned to connect the internal physical cues of a full bladder and bowel with the responses of urinating and having a bowel movement. However, cleanliness training demands that these cue-response connections be weakened so that more complex behavior (going to the bathroom, undressing, sitting on the potty) may take place. These new complex behaviors, then, provide new cues (seeing the bathroom, feeling the toilet seat on one's thighs) that must be connected with the voiding responses (Dollard & Miller, 1950, p. 137).

If this stage is rushed, excessive conformity and guilt may be learned. Additionally, the child may learn to avoid the parents in order to avoid punishment. Dollard and Miller suggest that the anxiety and guilt of this stage correspond to the early development of what Freud called the "superego" (Dollard & Miller, 1950, p. 141). The complex learning of this stage is easier if toilet training is delayed until language develops sufficiently to provide mediating cues. In this way the task is learned more easily, and high levels of anxiety and anger can be avoided.

Early Sex Training

Early sex training often consists of punishment for masturbation. This results in conflict; sexual impulses remain tempting, but also arouse anxiety. By generalization, a child may develop a "bed phobia," since masturbation frequently occurs and is punished in bed. Dollard and Miller describe a child whose masturbation was discovered and punished, and who subsequently tried to avoid his bed by protesting bedtime and by sleeping in the hallway, finally even putting on two pairs of pajamas to limit access to the forbidden pleasure. Dollard and Miller favor a more permissive attitude, since punishment simply "set[s] up in the child the same sex-anxiety conflict which the adults have" (1950, p. 142).

Dollard and Miller regard their learning analysis as consistent with Freud's ideas about Oedipal rivalry and castration fear. Besides developing conflict over sexual impulses, a child at this stage may learn a fear of authority figures, generalized from experience with the punishing parents (especially the father).

Anger-Anxiety Conflicts

Childhood produces many frustrations, including those that come from childhood dependency, mental limitations, and sibling rivalry, and so children must learn to deal with anger. When children express their anger overtly, perhaps through hitting or throwing things, they are punished. In this way, they learn to be anxious about anger. To some extent this is a necessary and desirable result because it helps the child to learn self-control. It can be overdone, though, eliminating even appropriately assertive behavior.

Anger becomes a learned drive that motivates behavior. If it is unacknowledged and unlabeled, it is likely to lead to undifferentiated responses, like repression. Angry feelings can be mislabeled; a child who has been punished for angry outbursts may come to label anger as "bad feelings" rather than "angry feelings." Guilt, rather than assertion, will follow. If anger is properly labeled, it can provide discriminative cues for behaviors appropriate in the real world.

Conflict

The same situation may provide cues for more than one response. If both responses can occur, there is no **conflict**. For example, busy professionals find that eating lunch and conducting business negotiations are *compatible responses.* If a situation provides cues for two *incompatible responses* (that is, responses which cannot both occur), then there is conflict.

These conflicts assume many forms. We sometimes must choose between two desirable responses; which favorite meal shall we order at a restaurant? At other times the choices are unpleasant; would you rather die by firing squad or lethal injection? Or the same situation may cue both positive and negative responses; Charlie Brown wants to flirt with the little redheaded girl, but his fear of rejection makes him want to run away. In all of these cases, a choice between incompatible responses must be made. These are situations of conflict.

Gradients of Approach and Avoidance Responses

The concept of *gradients*, reflecting the strength of tendency to make a response depending upon distance from the goal, provided Dollard and Miller with a powerful conceptual tool for understanding conflicts, including the intrapsychic conflicts central to psychoanalytic theory. By considering the gradients for two (or more) possible responses to the same cue, it was possible to illustrate how people could face difficult conflicts.

Dollard and Miller postulated four basic assumptions about approach and avoidance tendencies:

1. The tendency to approach a goal is stronger the nearer the subject is to it. This . . . [is] called the **gradient of approach**.
2. The tendency to avoid a feared stimulus is stronger the nearer the subject is to it. This . . . [is] called the **gradient of avoidance**.
3. . . . The gradient of avoidance is *steeper* than that of approach.
4. . . . An increase in drive raises the *height* of the entire gradient. (Dollard & Miller, 1950, pp. 352–353)

These principles are illustrated in Figure 12.2. They have been verified in animal studies in which the strength of the motivational tendency was measured by the speed with which rats ran and even the pressure with which they pulled harnesses.

A variety of human conflict situations can be analyzed by applying these principles. It is necessary to consider the whole gradients, rather than sim-

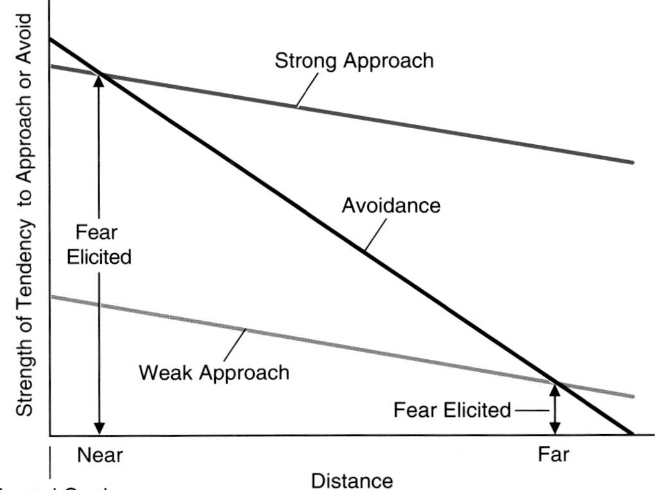

FIGURE 12.2 Gradients of Approach and Avoidance Tendencies

(From J. Dollard & N.E. Miller (1950). PERSONALITY AND PSYCHOTHERAPY: AN ANALYSIS IN TERMS OF LEARNING, THINKING, AND CULTURE. New York: McGraw-Hill. Copyright 1950. Reproduced by permission of McGraw-Hill, Inc.)

ply a single point, because as a person moves nearer to or farther from the goal, the strengths of the tendencies change. Choices that once seemed clear can now trigger conflict.

Four Types of Conflict

APPROACH-AVOIDANCE CONFLICT

In an **approach-avoidance conflict** situation, a person has tendencies to both approach and to avoid the same goal. This happens if the same course of action will lead to both reward and punishment. For example, Bill is considering signing up for a vacation trip to an exotic location that promises great enjoyment (approach) but also a big bill (avoidance). What decision will prevail?

It depends. If the approach tendency is higher, Bill will sign up. If the avoidance tendency is higher, he will not. In some cases, there is a clear answer, because one tendency is higher than the other throughout the gradients (see Figure 12.3). In either of these two cases, little anxiety is experienced, either because positive tendencies outweigh negative ones at all points, or because avoidance tendencies are so great that they always are stronger than approach tendencies.

Because the avoidance gradient is steeper than the approach gradient, the two may cross (see Figure 12.4). In this case, the approach tendency will be higher farther from the goal; when the trip is several weeks away, Bill signs up. But the avoidance tendency is higher near the goal; as the departure date nears, Bill backs out. If another trip, far in the future, is possible, Bill may sign up for that, since then he is again far from the goal, and approach tendencies outweigh avoidance tendencies. People can behave quite inconsistently in approach-avoidance conflict situations.

When the gradients cross like this, anxiety is acutely experienced at the crossover point. Reducing a very high anxiety gradient, perhaps through re-

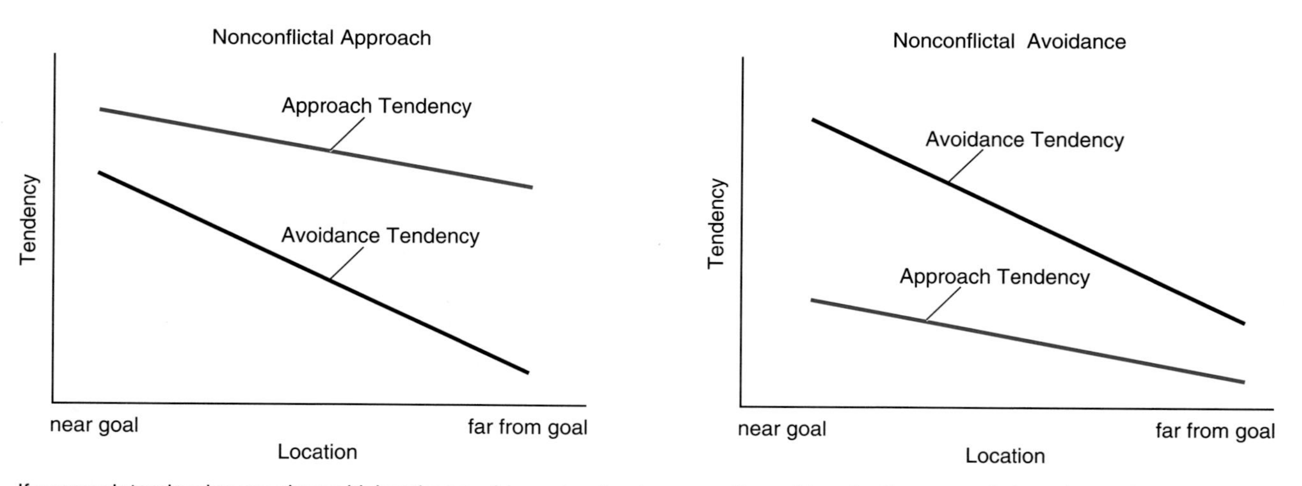

If approach tendencies are always higher than avoidance tendencies, regardless of how far the person is from the goal, the person will approach the goal without conflict. If avoidance tendencies are always higher than approach tendencies, there will also be no conflict; the person will simply stay away.

FIGURE 12.3 Nonconflict Situations

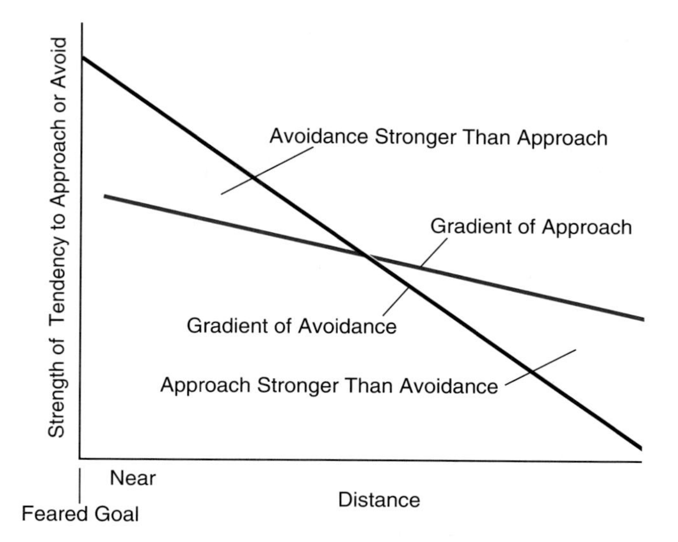

FIGURE 12.4 Approach-Avoidance Conflict

(From J. Dollard and N.E. Miller (1950). PERSONALITY AND PSYCHOTHERAPY: AN ANALYSIS IN TERMS OF LEARNING, THINKING, AND CULTURE. New York: McGraw-Hill. Copyright 1950. Reproduced by permission of McGraw-Hill, Inc.)

laxation training or tranquilizing drugs, can paradoxically *increase* the experience of anxiety if it permits the gradients to cross (that is, brings the person to confront situations previously avoided). This increase in anxiety is temporary. Further anxiety reduction, through continued therapy, will allow approach tendencies to prevail.

Avoidance-Avoidance Conflict

In an **avoidance-avoidance conflict**, the person must choose between two goals, both of which are undesirable. Given the opportunity, the person will avoid both, "leaving the field." If constrained to stay in the situation, and if no approach tendencies modify it, the person will become immobilized part-way between the two goals, where the two avoidance gradients cross. Movement in either direction would increase anxiety (see Figure 12.5).

A punitive approach to controlling the behavior of children (or employees, or students, or anyone) will often produce such immobilizing conflict situations. The only way to produce a response may be to increase one of the avoidance tendencies by escalating the threat of punishment. Since this makes "leaving the field" even more appealing, constraints must also be increased.

Approach-Approach Conflict

If the two goals are both associated with approach tendencies, there is very little conflict (**approach-approach conflict**). At the midway point, a brief equilibrium exists. This is an unstable equilibrium, though. Any movement, however minimal, toward either goal tips the balance by making that tendency stronger, drawing the person toward that goal. Since even brief thoughts serve as such "movement," choice is easy (see Figure 12.6). As

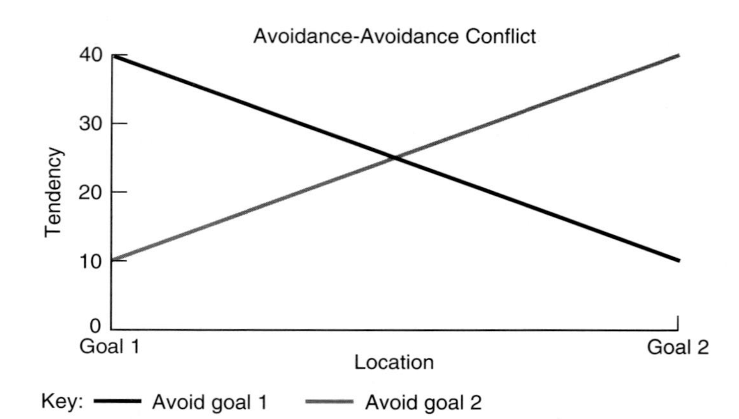

FIGURE 12.5 Avoidance-Avoidance Conflict

(From J. Dollard and N.E. Miller (1950). PERSONALITY AND PSYCHOTHERAPY: AN ANALYSIS IN TERMS OF LEARNING, THINKING, AND CULTURE. New York: McGraw-Hill. Copyright 1950. Reproduced by permission of McGraw-Hill, Inc.)

Dollard and Miller put it, "Donkeys do not starve midway between two equally desirable stacks of hay" (1950, p. 366). When people seem to be unable to choose between two positive choices, their hesitation is due to other aspects of these choices, which arouse avoidance.

DOUBLE APPROACH-AVOIDANCE CONFLICT

Indecisiveness is a sign that there is an avoidance aspect to what seems, on the surface, to be a choice between positive goals. Sometimes this avoidance

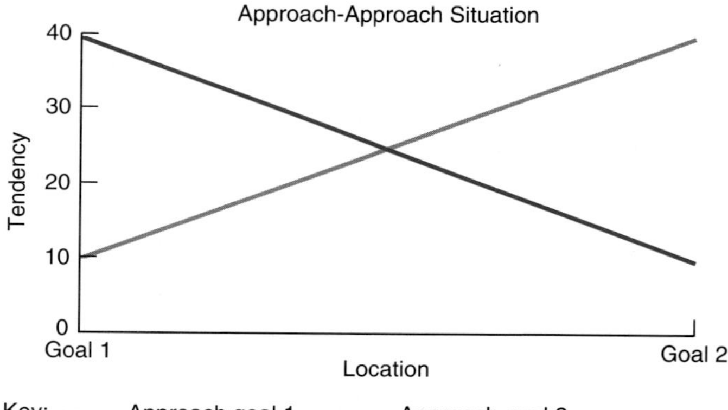

FIGURE 12.6 Approach-Approach Conflict

(From J. Dollard and N.E. Miller (1950). PERSONALITY AND PSYCHOTHERAPY: AN ANALYSIS IN TERMS OF LEARNING, THINKING, AND CULTURE. New York: McGraw-Hill. Copyright 1950. Reproduced by permission of McGraw-Hill, Inc.)

may be understood simply as "the need to renounce the other goal" (Dollard & Miller, 1950, p. 366). When a person must choose between two options, each of which has both desirable and undesirable aspects, the situation is called a **double approach-avoidance conflict**. The strength of each avoidance tendency increases more steeply than the approach tendency as the person comes nearer the goal. Thus when the person is far from either goal, little conflict is experienced, and the positive hopes of approach prevail. After the choice is made and the person moves toward a goal, avoidance tendencies increase. If they become strong enough, the approach and avoidance gradients cross (see Figure 12.7), and the person stops, hesitantly and anxiously, no longer moving toward the goal.

Reducing Conflict

Because conflict exists only if avoidance tendencies are present, a person who stays far from situations that cue avoidance will not experience conflict. This is often impractical, however, since the same situations that cue avoidance are often essential to fulfilling our approach tendencies (that is, satisfying our drives). An actor may be nervous about a stage performance, but avoiding the situation would preclude any applause.

If the avoidance tendency can be reduced enough so that it no longer crosses the approach tendency, the person will be able to continue approaching the goal. Therapy may do this. Tranquilizing drugs prescribed by a physician may similarly allow approach by reducing the avoidance tendency. For that matter, alcohol also has this effect; in animal studies, hungry rats who normally avoid a feeding area where they have been shocked will dare to approach it if they have been injected with alcohol, and frightened

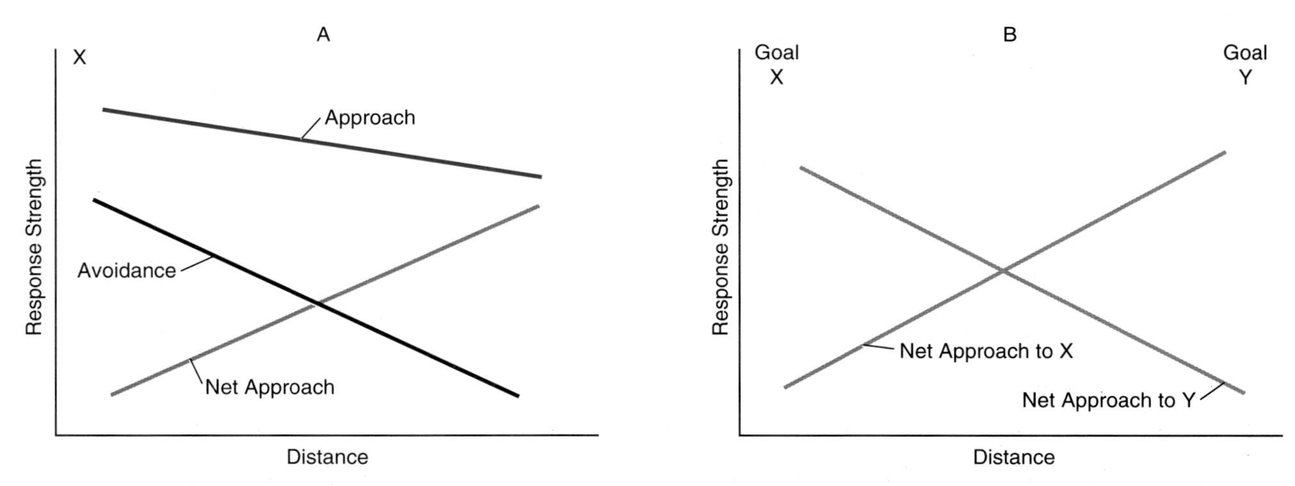

In A is represented a single approach-avoidance situation with avoidance weaker than approach at the goal, so that the subject should go completely up to the goal. Subtracting the strength of the avoidance from that of the approach results in a net approach tendency, which becomes weaker near the goal. In B the two net tendencies are represented in a double approach-avoidance situation. As the individual moves toward either of the two goals, X or Y, the net tendency to approach that goal becomes weaker and to approach the other, stronger. This should produce conflict.

FIGURE 12.7 Double Approach-Avoidance Conflict

(From J. Dollard and N.E. Miller (1950). PERSONALITY AND PSYCHOTHERAPY: AN ANALYSIS IN TERMS OF LEARNING, THINKING, AND CULTURE. New York: McGraw-Hill. Copyright 1950. Reproduced by permission of McGraw-Hill, Inc.)

cats prefer a little alcohol in their milk (Dollard & Miller, 1950, pp. 185–186).

Drugs are nonspecific, reducing avoidance tendencies generally. Thus they may have undesirable effects in other aspects of life. They may even *increase* conflict in those situations where the person has weak approach tendencies and has been avoiding the situation. When strong avoidance tendencies are reduced, such a person comes closer to the point of maximum conflict, where the approach and avoidance gradients cross. Psychotherapy, in contrast to drugs, can teach fear reduction that is specific to the problematic choice; but it is slower.

Frustration and Aggression

Dollard and Miller's hypothesis relating frustration and aggression is probably their most often cited idea. They acknowledged Freud's influence on this hypothesis. (Recall Freud's concepts of *Thanatos* and of the conflict between libidinal impulses and the restraining forces of civilization.)

The Frustration-Aggression Hypothesis

Dollard and Miller began with the assumption that "aggression is always a consequence of frustration" and, in addition, "the existence of frustration always leads to some form of aggression" (Dollard, Miller, Doob, Mowrer, & Sears, 1939, p. 1). The theorists defined *frustration* as occurring when obstacles interfere with the organism's ability to make a goal response, that is, to achieve drive reduction. *Aggression* is defined as behavior intended to injure the person toward whom it is directed. Aggression is more likely when the blocked drive is strong, when the interference is more complete, and when the frustration is repeated.

The hypothesized cause-effect relationship between frustration and aggression (**frustration-aggression hypothesis**) was a simple relationship with many implications for individual and social behavior. It implied, for example, that adolescent aggression could be understood as caused by the increased frustrations of that stage of life (due at least in part to the resurgence of sexual energies). Poverty brings many frustrations, and therefore crime rates are higher in poor neighborhoods. Economic deprivations contribute to authoritarian attitudes and prejudice and aggression against minority groups in society (Doty, Peterson, & Winter, 1991; Grossarth-Maticek, Eysenck, & Vetter, 1989; Sales, 1973).

While the simple cause-effect relationship stated above was a fruitful working hypothesis to begin research, Dollard and Miller soon revised it. Their revised theory acknowledged that aggression is only one possible response to frustration, and that its position in the response hierarchy varies depending upon past experience (N.E. Miller, 1941b). Aggression is frequently rewarded, and so it often becomes a dominant response to frustration. However, this is a learned, rather than an innate or inevitable, connection. Nonaggressive responses may be learned instead. Under some circumstances, aggression can be displaced, directed toward another target besides the source of the frustration (N.E. Miller, 1948). Such learning influences the expression of aggression against women rather than men (Donnerstein & Berkowitz, 1981).

Some theorists (Feshbach, 1964) have distinguished another type of aggression in addition to the *hostile aggression* described by Dollard and Miller, where the primary goal is to injure someone. In contrast, in *instrumental aggression,* aggression is primarily intended as a means toward some other goal. A mugger, for example, may injure someone in order to steal the person's money. Determinants of the two types of aggression may be different. Dollard and Miller's theory explains hostile aggression, but not instrumental aggression (Berkowitz, 1989).

Berkowitz (1983) agreed that frustration instigates aggressive tendencies but argued that many other factors need to be considered that can influence whether aggressive behavior occurs. Berkowitz's approach emphasizes situational factors, rather than simply the aggressive drive Dollard and Miller proposed. Berkowitz (1965) suggested that cues in the environment are necessary for aggressive tendencies to be expressed in behavior. Several studies show that subjects who are exposed to aggressive cues behave more aggressively (e.g., Gustafson, 1986a). For an angry person, aggressive cues trigger aggression. At times, the cues can even be so strong that they elicit aggression in a person who is not angry (Berkowitz, 1965, 1969). Situational factors can enhance or decrease the impact of observed violence (Berkowitz, 1986).

Dollard and Miller's model of aggression postulated a general drive that could be released by direct aggression against the source of the aggression or, indirectly, through displacement. Intercorrelations among diverse experimental measures of aggression are positive, confirming the model of a *general* aggressive drive (M. Carlson, Marcus-Newhall, & Miller, 1989). This general drive can be compared to Freud's libido, in the sense that both can be released directly or indirectly. An alternative view, presented by Berkowitz, is that aggressive drives have a specific relationship to the perceived source of the aggression. That is, aggressive drives would not be fully reduced until aggression *against the source of the aggression* occurred. This alternative view questions the theoretical validity of the concept of a *general* aggressive drive.

Research on Frustration and Aggression

Several studies have exposed subjects to frustration and then provided an opportunity for them to express aggression. Frustration often takes the form of failure or blockage in meeting a desired goal, such as earning money in an experiment (see below). Aggression is often operationally defined in research studies by having subjects administer electric shocks to another subject under the pretext that it is punishment being delivered in a learning experiment. By manipulating other variables, it is possible to investigate under what circumstances frustration leads to aggression, and when it does not.

Frustration alone, without other factors, does not necessarily lead to aggression. Aggressive tendencies can be inhibited by social rules, fear of punishment, ego strength, and a person's understanding of the situation, among other factors (Berkowitz, 1989). Mitigating circumstances can also reduce the manifestation of aggression; knowing that someone who angers us has just received a bad grade on an important exam results in less aggression toward that person than if no mitigating information is presented (Johnson &

Rule, 1986). Frustration that is unexpected is more likely to produce aggression than expected frustration (Ahmed & Mapletoft, 1989).

According to Berkowitz, unsuccessful aggressive attempts directed toward the source of the frustration constitute additional frustration and thus intensify aggression. Until aggression is successfully completed, the aggressive drive remains active. Gustafson (1989a) has tested this *completion hypothesis*. Male undergraduates were frustrated by losing a chance at earning a large sum of money through the supposed lack of concentration of a fellow subject (actually a confederate of the experimenter) in a visual scan test. The study allegedly investigated the relationship between stress and performance. The subject could administer electric shock to the ostensibly inattentive confederate as a consequence of wrong answers, thereby hoping to improve alertness. (The shock was not actually delivered, although subjects did not know this at the time of the study.) For some subjects (manipulated by experimental control), this strategy was unsuccessful, and the money was lost. These subjects continued to administer intense shock, while subjects whose earlier shock was successful in reaching the goal necessary to earn the money reduced their shock. Gustafson interpreted this result as support for Berkowitz's completion hypothesis: Successful aggression reduced aggressive tendencies.

Can aggressive tendencies be reduced through competitive games? Berkowitz (1962, 1989) concluded that competition is more likely to increase aggression than to reduce it, contrary to the concept of "catharsis." However, evidence is mixed. Playing a violent video game (boxing), for example, was found not to increase aggression (measured by projective testing) of elementary school children. If anything, it made them assertive, compared to playing nonviolent video games (Graybill, Kirsch, & Esselman, 1985).

According to Berkowitz (1962), frustration does not directly lead to aggression. Rather, frustration produces anger, which in turn leads to aggression. According to a revised model of the frustration-aggression hypothesis (Berkowitz, 1989), frustrations lead to aggression to the extent that frustrations produce various types of negative affect (emotions such as anger, sadness, and disappointment). When frustration produces this negative affect, it leads to aggression, but this is a specific instance of the more general phenomenon that negative affect leads to aggression. In the absence of negative emotions, frustration does not produce aggression (Berkowitz, 1978, 1988, 1989). Other sources of negative affect that lead to aggression have been found, including threats to identity, depression, and physical pain. Threats to identity that occur when subjects are led to believe that they are doing worse than others on tasks requiring creativity lead to aggression (Melburg & Tedeschi, 1989). Depression, too, can arouse aggression, though psychoanalytic theory regards depression as a consequence, rather than a cause, of aggression (Berkowitz, 1983, 1989).

The relationship between negative affect and aggression is not always simple, however. Berkowitz and Embree (1987) exposed subjects to either a very aversive situation, in which they kept a hand in water that was 6°C, or a mildly aversive situation, in which the water was 18°C. Meanwhile, they administered rewards and punishments (electric shock) to an experimental confederate who was ostensibly a fellow subject performing a simple concept-learning task. (As is standard in this type of research, the shock was not actually given, though subjects thought it was at the time of the study.) Some subjects were given permission to remove their hands if they wished. Others were not. Those free to end the cold stressor reported that they were less bothered by the cold water, apparently because they felt free to leave it. However, they gave more electric shocks to the learner than did those who were constrained to keep their hands in the water. Why? Perhaps they were expressing their distress by being aggressive to the learner, rather than by removing their hands; perhaps they felt constrained to keep their hands in the water even though they were given permission to remove them. Various interpretations of the result are possible. One thing is clear: The relationship between negative emotion and aggression is not simple.

The relationship between alcohol consumption and aggression has also been investigated. Under some circumstances, alcohol increases aggression, especially when subjects are frustrated and when situational cues encourage aggression (Gustafson, 1986b).

INDIVIDUAL DIFFERENCES IN AGGRESSIVE RESPONSES

Individuals differ in their aggressive behavior, even in standard experimental settings, perhaps reflecting individual differences in underlying hostility (Gustafson, 1989b). Longitudinal research that followed over 600 third-grade children as they grew up showed stability of individual differences in aggression from age 8 to 30 (Eron, 1987). (See Figure 12.8.)

Some research indicates that the situations that precipitate aggression in some people affect others differently. Josephson (1987) studied boys in

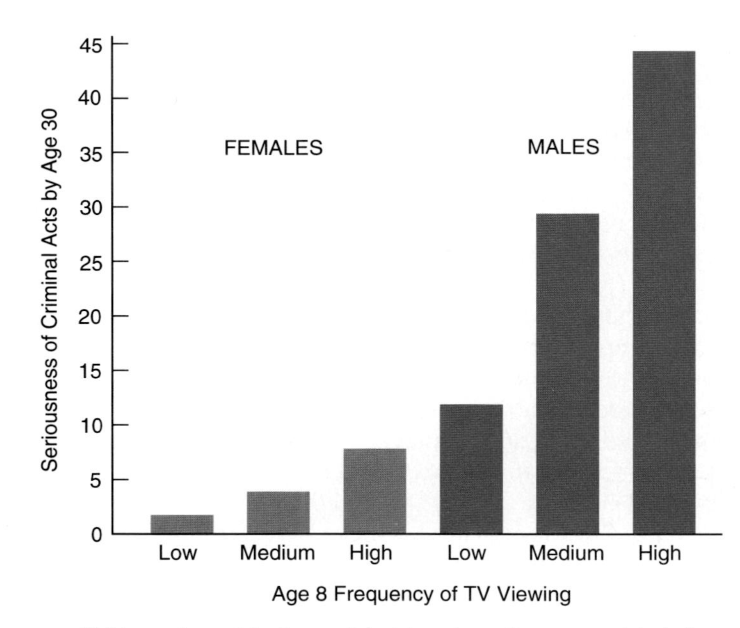

Children who watched more television at age 8 were convicted of more serious crimes in the next 22 years. This finding holds for both males and females, though the crime rate among males was higher.

FIGURE 12.8 Seriousness of Criminal Acts by Age 30 as a Function of Frequency of TV Viewing at Age 8

(From L.D. Eron (1987). The development of aggressive behavior from the perspective of a developing behaviorism. *American Psychologist*, 42, 435–442. Copyright 1987 by the American Psychological Association. Reprinted by permission.)

grades two and three who were frustrated by having an expected television cartoon become garbled. Some boys also saw a violent TV segment. Others saw a nonviolent program. The boys were later observed playing floor hockey in groups to determine which ones behaved aggressively and which did not. The violent program led to increased violence in groups that included boys who had previously been rated by their teachers as aggressive. In contrast, boys who had been rated as low in aggression responded to the violent program with decreased aggression (compared to the control nonviolent program), unless they were in groups containing highly aggressive boys. These results suggest that frustration leads to aggression in some boys, but not all, and that observing violence on television contributes to this aggression, but again only for some boys.

College students who have a history of being abused as children respond to frustration with more aggression, on projective tests, than do those without a history of abuse (Graybill, Mackie, & House, 1985). One possible interpretation of this finding is that they are influenced by the aggressive models of their childhood.

Sex roles also influence the manifestation of aggression. Among females, those who score low in masculinity on the Bem Sex-Role Inventory were more likely to turn aggression inward on the Defense Mechanisms Inventory, compared to those high in masculinity, who were more likely to express hostility outward, toward the objects of their frustration (R.G. Evans, 1982). Males who read a hypothetical situation in which they were frustrated in trying to achieve a good score on a masculine task (bodybuilding) indicated that they would behave more aggressively than did females. There were no sex differences on dance, a feminine task (Towson & Zanna, 1982). Other studies suggest that frustration may produce aggression more in some people than in others: in emotionally susceptible males (Caprara, 1982) and in those with an external locus of control (Romi & Itskowitz, 1990; Storms & Spector, 1987).

Much research on aggression has been conducted, and it indicates that frustration often produces aggression, but that this relationship is not invariant. It is influenced by situational variables, such as stimuli associated with aggression, and by individual differences in personality. Clearly we learn how to respond to life's frustrations.

Language

Language is of central importance in this learning theory. Language provides important discriminative cues that are the basis for learning how to deal with various situations. Behavior that Freud understood as ego-controlled is, for the most part, under the control of verbal cues. In contrast, the Freudian id and primary process describe experience not under verbal control—for example, the visual imagery of dreams (Dollard & Miller, 1950, pp. 122–123).

Early experiences are less accessible to consciousness because they have not been verbally labeled. The unconscious consists not only of repressed experiences but also of those that have never been verbally labeled. Some of these unlabeled experiences occurred early in development, before language skills were developed. Others simply were not given appropriate verbal labels. Often such unlabeled, and therefore unconscious, experiences are emotional (M. Rendon, 1988).

People can learn through trial and error, but this is a slow process. Language can mediate much faster learning. This is what happens when *insight* occurs. Also, language-mediated learning facilitates generalization to new situations. Other situations to which the same verbal label can be applied may thus come to elicit similar thoughts and behaviors. For example, learning to label the situations that arouse the impulses to cheat, to yell, and to exploit others as "tests of character" facilitates generalization of responses of self-control across all such situations. Self-control, once learned in one situation, does not have to be tediously relearned in each new situation. Because of the power of language to allow such generalization, humans can learn behaviors in socializing environments that are very different from the later situations where these behaviors will be needed. Responses learned on the sports field, in a Scout troop, and in school can be applied later in quite different situations, if language connects the two.

Language also facilitates problem-solving skills. People can reason and plan their activities. They can mentally imagine a trial-and-error process of solving a problem, thus avoiding the necessity of going through a tedious trial-and-error process in actual behavior. (A student may do this, for example, when considering where to find a quiet place to study for an exam. Would studying in the dorm work? No, too noisy. How about the library? No, too likely to see Jan, and have to talk about our personal difficulties. A vacant classroom, perhaps?) These symbolic trial-and-error techniques allow for faster problem solving.

In addition, symbolic problem solving can, in effect, reverse time. Problem solvers can focus on the goal and "work backwards," rather than beginning at the present and working forward toward the goal. This may allow the discovery of new ways of approaching the goal. Dollard and Miller proffered the example of a driver, stuck in traffic, who is in a long line of vehicles waiting to turn left (1950, pp. 111–113). By imagining the intersection where the turn must be made, it occurs to the driver that a right-hand turn there, from the other direction, would be easy. Aha! The problem is solved: Change lanes, go past the intersection, make a U-turn, and then come back and turn right! This creative and effective solution to the problem was made possible by symbolic processes.

Conscious, verbally cued behavior is quite different from prelanguage responses. The latter are, like Freud's unconscious, less discriminating, less future-oriented, timeless, and illogical (cf. Dollard and Miller, 1950, p. 220). The way learning implements Freud's recommendation, "Where there was id, there shall be ego," is by providing words that correctly label experience.

Neurosis

Many types of maladaptive learning can produce neurotic symptoms. Dollard and Miller developed a flowchart illustrating the factors involved in neurosis (see Figure 12.9). Fear, conflict, and repression play major roles in this process. Because repression interferes with higher mental processes, problems are not adequately solved and high drive remains undischarged. Thus, neurosis can be called a *stupidity-misery* syndrome.

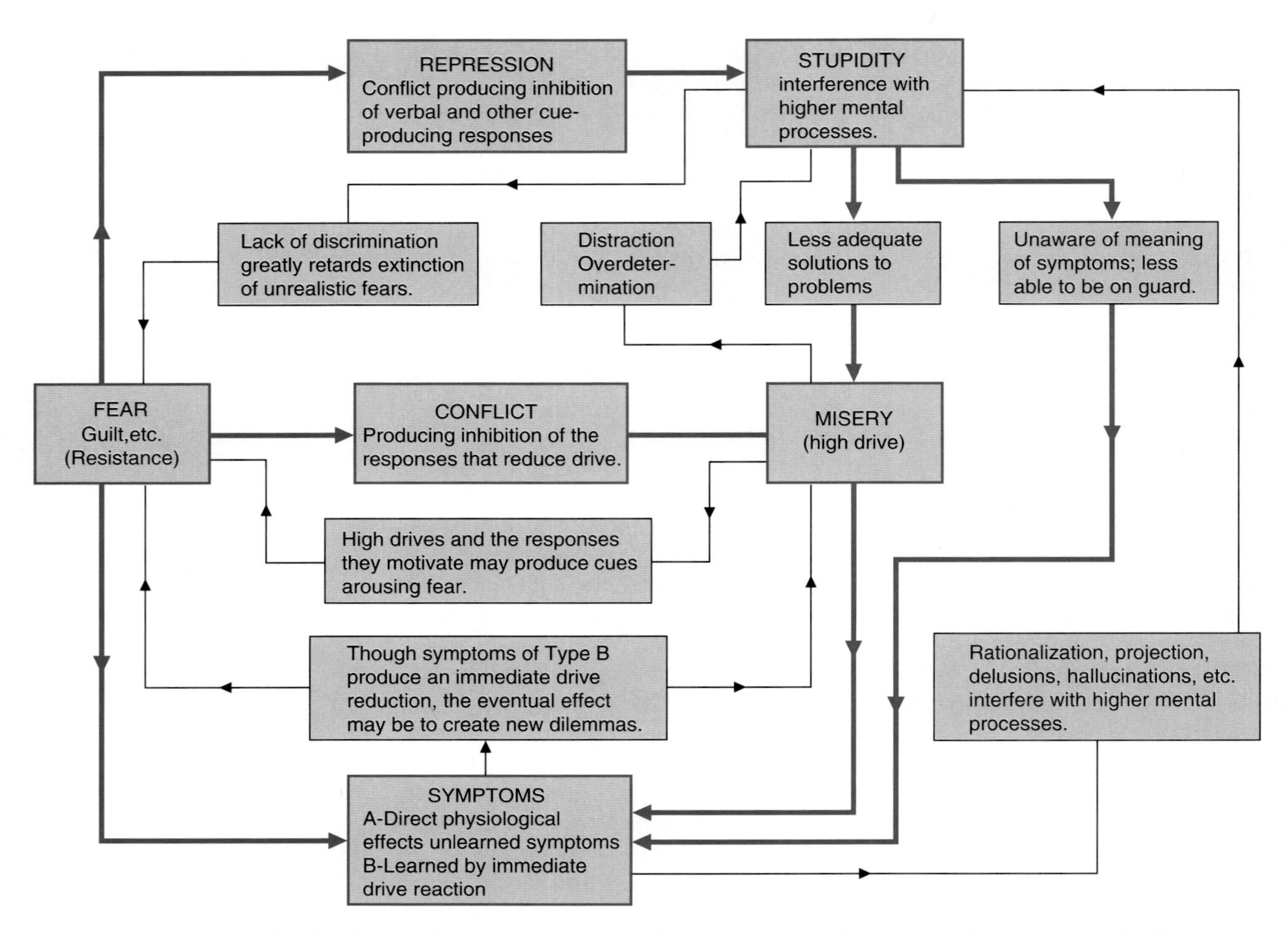

FIGURE 12.9 Schematic Diagram of Some Basic Factors Involved in Neuroses

(From J. Dollard and N.E. Miller (1950). PERSONALITY AND PSYCHOTHERAPY: AN ANALYSIS IN TERMS OF LEARNING, THINKING, AND CULTURE. New York: McGraw-Hill. Copyright 1950. Reproduced by permission of McGraw-Hill, Inc.)

Dollard and Miller stressed the role of *fear* in neurosis (Wachtel, 1978). Many neuroses can be understood as learned ways of avoiding anxiety. *Phobias* are "irrational fears" in which a fear-producing experience generalizes to produce fear to similar situations. For example, a fighter pilot, after combat, became afraid of everything connected with airplanes (Dollard & Miller, 1950, p. 158). He shunned all contact with aircraft to avoid anxiety. *Compulsive behaviors* also are interpreted as anxiety-motivated. Compulsive hand-washing may be a way of avoiding anxiety about contamination. *Alcoholism* results from the anxiety-reducing physiological effect of drinking.

The concept of *response hierarchies,* described above, also helps to explain neuroses. Whenever the dominant response in a situation is blocked or is punished, the next response in the hierarchy is tried. This next response is often behavior from an earlier period in development, in which case the result may be called *regression*. For example, a child who has learned to behave properly may, if the parents are distracted by the demands of a new baby, fail to be reinforced for good behavior; hence, the next response down in the hierarchy, having a temper outburst or wetting the bed, may occur.

Displacement is also understandable in learning terms. Behavior is directed toward a substitute target owing to *generalization* based on similarity. For example, children seek and receive the love of their parents. When they are older, a romantic partner "just like" Mom or Dad is often chosen. While this displacement may be the basis of a normal and happy outcome, it may also lead to maladaptive choices—for example, if the parent was alcoholic or abusive. Displaced avoidance behavior can also occur (E.J. Murray & Berkun, 1955).

Dollard and Miller explain *hallucinations* (false perceptions, such as seeing people who are not there) as incorrect perceptual responses resulting from extremely high levels of drive (1950, pp. 178–181). We know that drives do influence perception. Hungry people, for example, are more likely to perceive ambiguous cues in terms of food (Atkinson & McClelland, 1948). Under extremely high drive, such as the intense fears of emotionally disturbed patients, the cues that trigger such drive-motivated perceptions are so dissimilar to the perception that a normal person sees nothing in reality corresponding to the psychotic's hallucinated perception.

Dollard and Miller consider other symptoms and diagnoses as well. In all cases they interpret symptoms as responses that have been learned because they were reinforced, often by anxiety reduction. New learning can bring about a cure.

Psychotherapy

The problems that cause people to seek therapy are learned. "Neurotic conflicts are taught by parents and learned by children" (Dollard & Miller, 1950, p. 126). Therapeutic learning experiences can correct them. Psychotherapy is a relearning experience. Like all learning, it requires drive reduction. For that reason, it helps to have a patient who is "miserable" at the beginning of therapy; a contented client would have little incentive to change. One of the things therapists do is to encourage patients to stay in conflictful situations, rather than to avoid them. This permits extinction of fear to occur (Wachtel, 1978).

Dollard and Miller describe the therapist as using approval strategically to reward specific aspects of the patient's behavior. "The therapist . . . makes the patient work for approval" (1950, p. 395). The therapist is also, at times, "permissive," allowing the patient to express feared material without reprimand. This allows fears to undergo extinction. Both approval and permissiveness are dispensed according to learning principles, to increase or decrease tendencies the patient has just been exhibiting. Direction of change is clearly prescribed by the therapist, and the timing of approval and permissive acceptance is quite important. This requires considerable control by the therapist, and Dollard and Miller comment that most therapists are not disciplined enough to be maximally effective.

For the patient the extinction of fear that occurs during therapy can open up new creativity (cf. Dollard & Miller, 1950, p. 252). By eliminating maladaptive dominant responses, the person becomes free to try a greater variety of behaviors, including new ways of thinking. Psychotherapy uses the powerful discriminations possible with language, teaching the patient more adaptive ways to label situations and inner emotional states. Saying "You seem angry" provides cues for a new set of behaviors. Repressed experiences are made available to conscious control through free association and new labeling.

The patient must also learn to control thinking so as to act in the real world. **Suppression** is willful control of thinking, purposely putting thoughts out of consciousness. Dollard and Miller recommended that therapists should pay more attention to teaching this skill. Research on suppression has been conducted. While people can learn to suppress unwanted thoughts, often a rebound effect occurs later, in which the unwanted thoughts return with greater frequency. This rebound effect can be reduced by changing the context, which has potential implications for therapy (Wegner, Schneider, Knutson, & McMahon, 1991).

In all of this, the specific situation of the patient in the real world is important. Dollard and Miller criticized psychologists for not being sufficiently aware of the impact of social conditions on people, including the different conditions associated with social class. Behaviors appropriate among the middle class may not be adaptive among lower-class individuals. Therapists can be of only limited effectiveness if they are unaware of the sociological facts of life. Ultimately, the success of therapy must also be measured in the real world. The goal of therapy is to enable "real-world action which alone can reduce misery" (Dollard & Miller, 1950, p. 459). The *talking phase* of therapy must be followed by a *performance phase* in which real-world behavior is changed.

Summary

Dollard and Miller proposed a learning theory that could explain the clinical phenomena observed by psychoanalysts. Four learning concepts are fundamental: *drive, cue, response,* and *reward.* At any given time, various responses are possible in a given stimulus situation. These can be arranged in order of probability, with the *dominant response* at the top of this *response hierarchy.* Learning occurs when the response hierarchy is changed. Both primary (innate) and secondary (learned) rewards can produce learning. Learning only occurs if the dominant response does not produce drive reduction, a situation termed a *learning dilemma* (see Table 12.1).

Behaviors are increased in frequency by reward, and reduced in frequency by extinction and punishment. Behaviors that have been eliminated can return without being again rewarded, a phenomenon called *spontaneous recovery.* Reward and punishment have their greatest effects on behavior near the goal, producing *approach and avoidance tendencies.* The avoidance gradient is steeper than the approach gradient.

Dollard and Miller reinterpreted several psychoanalytic concepts in terms of their learning theory. Identification was reinterpreted in terms of imitation. Freud's first three psychosexual stages were reinterpreted as learning concerned with feeding, cleanliness training, and early sex train-

TABLE 12.1 Contributions of Dollard and Miller's Theory to Various Topics

Biological	Biological drive satisfaction is the basis of early personality development. Miller did much later work on biological mechanisms of motivation.
Child Development	Freud's stages of early child development are reconceptualized in terms of learning theory, and involve conflict.
Adult Development	Learning occurs throughout life, though adult development is less important than childhood development.
Mental Health	Neurosis is reconceptualized as learned conflict. Learning principles suggest therapy techniques, such as discrimination learning.
Society	Personality development occurs in a social context. Social applications are explored, including aggression and racism.
Cognitive Processes	Much motivation is unconscious because of inadequate labeling. Suppression of thought can sometimes be a valuable skill.
Individual Differences	Individuals differ in behaviors and in conscious and unconscious processes due to learning.

ing. A fourth stage, concerned with anger-anxiety conflicts, was added. Intrapsychic conflict was reinterpreted as conflict among incompatible responses. Various types of *conflict* were identified: approach-approach, approach-avoidance, avoidance-avoidance, and double approach-avoidance. Their *frustration-aggression hypothesis* replaced Freud's concept of Thanatos. Research has suggested several revisions in the model of aggressive behavior. *Language* is an important species-specific human behavior. Language offers cues for behavior, and presents a learning theory interpretation of Freud's concept of levels of consciousness. Various defense mechanisms can be understood from a learning perspective (for example, displacement as a consequence of generalization). Psychotherapy should take into account principles of learning theory; it should attempt to understand and modify the cues that produce various responses, and it should teach new behaviors.

ILLUSTRATIVE BIOGRAPHIES: Concluding Remarks

Jean Harris

Aggression, in Dollard and Miller's theory, occurs as a consequence of frustration. A buildup of aggressive drive, unless released in some other fashion, will be expressed as aggression. Other theorists add to this simple model a consideration of the learning of alternate responses to frustration and a consideration of specific environmental stimuli that elicit aggression.

Many aspects of Jean Harris's relationship with Herman Tarnower were frustrating. She had hoped to marry him, but he would not. She had hoped for a close relationship, but she found him instead engrossed in the fame that his best-selling diet book had brought.

Others who knew Jean Harris had remarked on her anger, which was expressed at work as well as in her personal life (Alexander, 1983). Harris's own descriptions of life in prison continue the theme of anger, with resentful accounts of the stupidity and insensitivity of both guards and fellow prisoners. She experienced depression in the months before the murder, which psychoanalysts interpret as aggression turned against the self. Toward Dr. Tarnower, however, her written statements were more guarded. Dollard and Miller might interpret a conflict over two incompatible responses: the manifestation of aggression, because of the frustration she experienced in desiring a more satisfying relationship with Dr. Tarnower, and the expression of love. Conflict between these two tendencies constitutes an approach-avoidance conflict. Any drastic change in the level of one of the components would eliminate the conflict. If approach were drastically reduced—for example, if continuation of the relationship were impossible—then the aggressive tendency would be expressed, no longer held in check by the ambivalence produced by the positive tendency. Could this have led to murder? Such a possibility is consistent with Dollard and Miller's theory.

However, there is something oversimplified about such an account. Relationships end all too frequently, yet murders are rare. Why did Jean Harris express her aggression so directly, while others do not? Her life story evidences difficulty dealing with anger, so that alternate, less drastic ways of expressing anger were not available to reduce the aggressive drive. Direct expression of anger in her childhood was discouraged. In addition, though there is limited consideration of biological factors in Dollard and Miller's classic theory, physical effects of drugs ("speed," which she alleges she was given by Dr. Tarnower), and evidence of an abnormal brain wave pattern hint at possible physiological contributors to her aggressive act. Perhaps the physiological research that Neal Miller and his colleagues have undertaken will ultimately address this aspect of the question.

Jim Morrison

Two themes from Dollard and Miller's theory help understand Jim Morrison. Like Jean Harris, Morrison is known for his *aggressive* behavior. He threatened others during drunken episodes and treated his parents and his girlfriend harshly. In addition, the *conflict* he experienced between his rock star identity and his more intellectual ambition to write visionary poetry can be analyzed from the perspective of Dollard and Miller's theory.

Before his musical career, Jim Morrison was a bright student who impressed teachers with how much he had read. He was particularly drawn to the beatnik poets of the San Francisco area where his family lived during his adolescence: Jack Kerouac, Lawrence Ferlinghetti, and Allen Ginsberg. He kept a journal and wrote poetry, exploring the rebellious ideas stimulated by his reading.

Morrison behaved aggressively, threatening his girlfriend with a knife and including vulgar language in many of his lyrics. He threw things, destroyed property, and threatened people when he drank, and that was often. He told the public that his parents were dead, and he did not communicate with his family for years, or even tell them where he was. In fact, it was only when his brother recognized Jim's picture on an album cover that his family learned about Morrison's recording success. Yet Jim rejected his mother's attempts to contact him, and he publicly insulted her.

What sort of frustration could be the drive behind this aggression? Much of it seems to have originated in Jim Morrison's relationship with his father, a Navy admiral whose strict demands frustrated Morrison's desire for long hair and the permissive way of life which that represented. Strict discipline interferes intentionally with a child's impulses to act on feelings. Morrison told of a childhood incident in which his family passed a fatal car accident. Though he saw people dying and was distressed by it, his father told him it was "only a dream" (Hopkins & Sugarman, 1980, p. 6). This was only one of many instances in which Jim's feelings pulled him in one direction, but his father's approval required a different behavior.

Morrison craved recognition, competing in childhood with his younger brother and sister for attention. As a military family, they moved frequently, so that lasting friendships were impossible. Throughout childhood and adolescence, Jim Morrison is reported to have gained attention through pranks. As a performer, he wanted to have an impact on his audience. This may be interpreted as a generalization from a child's receiving attention. He studied "crowd psychology" and calculated how to cause fans to riot (Hopkins & Sugarman,1980). He claimed to want more than simply an emotional impact. He wanted to show his audience how to see the world in a new, more profound way. He named his group The Doors after Aldous Huxley's book *The Doors of Perception,* and he aspired to show his audience a new reality, aided by the altered perceptions produced by drugs. Drugs were not enough, though. Poetry and lyrics were also important. When his audience missed the deeper levels of meaning he aimed to inspire, he grew contemptuous of them, spitting at them and appearing drunk on stage.

We may interpret an approach-avoidance conflict about getting the audience to respond: It was Morrison's much-desired goal, but it disappointed him as well. Ambivalence and escape result from approach-avoidance conflicts. Alcohol may have provided some escape from the conflict, as it does in animal studies. Ambivalence and escape also characterize Morrison's late appearances and missed flights on the way to performances. He threatened to quit performing, but was dissuaded from doing so. Perhaps even his flight to Paris was an expression of this conflict, although his legal difficulties in Florida, his pending jail sentence for indecent exposure, and several pending paternity suits were more immediate reasons for escape.

Dollard and Miller discussed identification, or learning through modeling. Morrison adopted the beat poets as his own models. His excessive use of drugs and alcohol was also modeled after many other musicians and the hippie movement of the 1960s. Dollard and Miller claimed that personality must be understood within its culture, which provides the conditions for learning. This is certainly true of Jim Morrison. The rock music culture provided a role for his rebellious behavior and his craving for attention. Intellectually, even Freud contributed to Morrison's behavior, providing the idea of an Oedipus conflict reflected in the lyrics to one of Morrison's songs ("Father . . . I want to kill you. Mother . . . I want to f— you") (Hopkins & Sugerman, 1980, p. 96).

GLOSSARY

anticipatory response tendency of responses that precede reward to occur earlier and earlier in the behavioral sequence

approach-approach conflict conflict in which an organism simultaneously wishes to approach two incompatible goals

approach-avoidance conflict conflict in which an organism simultaneously wishes to approach and to avoid the same goal

avoidance-avoidance conflict conflict in which an organism must choose between two goals, both of which it finds undesirable, but is constrained from "leaving the field" (abandoning the situation)

conflict a situation in which cues for two incompatible responses are provided

copying learning to behave in the same way as a model, but not necessarily in response to the same cues as the model

cue what a person notices, which provides a discriminative stimulus for learning

discrimination responding only to particular cues

dominant response a person's most likely response in a given situation

double approach-avoidance conflict conflict in which an organism must choose between two options, both of which have positive and negative aspects

drive what a person wants, which motivates learning

extinction reduction in the frequency of a nonrewarded response

frustration-aggression hypothesis the hypothesis that frustration always leads to aggression, and aggression is always caused by frustration

gradient of approach the greater tendency to approach a goal, the closer one is to it

gradient of avoidance the greater tendency to avoid a goal, the closer one is to it

gradient of reward the greater strengthening of responses that are immediately followed by reward

imitation learning by observing the actions of others

learning dilemma a situation in which existing responses are not rewarded, which leads to change

matched dependent behavior learning to make the same response as a model, in response to a cue from the model

primary reward a reward that is innate, such as food

responses what a person does, which can be learned

response hierarchy list of all the responses a person could make in a given situation, arranged from most likely to least likely

resultant hierarchy a response hierarchy after it has been modified by learning

reward what a person gets as a result of a response in the learning sequence

secondary reward a reward that is learned, such as approval or money

spontaneous recovery return of a response that was previously extinguished

stimulus generalization occurrence of a response to a stimulus other than the one that was a cue during learning

suppression willfully putting thoughts out of consciousness

STUDY QUESTIONS

1. Describe the relationship between Dollard and Miller's theory and psychoanalysis.
2. Discuss some advice Dollard offered for writing a life history.
3. List and explain the four fundamental concepts about learning.
4. Explain what is meant by *response hierarchy.* Give an example.
5. Explain the difference between a *primary reward* and a *secondary reward.*
6. What is a *learning dilemma?* Give an example.
7. Discuss how behaviors may be eliminated. Consider extinction, punishment, and spontaneous recovery.
8. Explain what is meant by *gradient of reward* and *gradient of punishment.*
9. Discuss Dollard and Miller's concept of imitation as a learning model for identification.
10. List the four critical training periods of childhood. Explain what is learned in each stage.
11. Discuss Dollard and Miller's learning model of conflict. Describe various types of conflict. Contrast this model with Freud's concept of intrapsychic conflict.
12. Using a learning model, discuss various strategies for reducing conflict. Give examples.
13. Discuss Dollard and Miller's frustration-aggression model. Contrast this with Freud's *Thanatos.*
14. Discuss research on aggression. What changes in the frustration-aggression hypothesis seem justified on the basis of this research?
15. What role does language play in Dollard and Miller's model of personality development and neurosis?
16. List some neurotic defense mechanisms that can be interpreted from a learning theory perspective. Explain how they can be interpreted.
17. What suggestions do Dollard and Miller offer for psychotherapy?

PART 

Cognitive Social Learning Perspective

According to the cognitive social learning perspective, to describe people's overt behaviors without paying attention to what people are thinking cannot provide an adequate model of personality. Behaviorism that does not involve extended consideration of cognitive variables risks neglecting much that is human (Staats, 1981). To study only the physiological aspects of emotion, for example, without considering what people are thinking when they are frightened or angry or otherwise emotionally aroused, cannot lead to a full understanding of human personality (Staats & Eifert, 1990).

Cognitive psychology studies mental processes and their effects on behavior. Cognition has been highlighted in recent years as a major concern in psychological theorizing. A "cognitive challenge" has been posed to behaviorism. Zettle summarizes the cognitive challenge as "the proposition that cognitive psychology, with its appeal to mental processes, offers a more complete and adequate account of human behavior than that provided by behavior analysis" (1990, p. 41). Many behaviorists have responded to this challenge by including cognitive aspects within learning theory (Ladouceur & Mercier, 1984; Stuart, 1989). Although a cognitive emphasis is often regarded as new, it has been part of learning theory for decades, with the exception of some radical behaviorists, especially Skinner (Spence, 1981).

Traditional behaviorists object to the inclusion of cognitive variables in behavioral theories. They argue that cognitive variables are not directly observable and cannot be unambiguously produced by experimental manipulations. Thus cognitive variables are not appropriate constructs to explain the causes of behavior (C. Lee, 1989, 1990; Skinner, 1977, 1987). Further, they question whether the addition of cognitive variables to behavior modification leads to any improvement in therapeutic effectiveness (Ledwidge, 1978). Radical behaviorists have responded to the cognitive challenge by interpreting cognitive control in behavioral terms (Zettle, 1990). Is this radical behavioral interpretation of cognitive functioning successful? Zettle (1990) concludes that "the jury is still out."

Theorists in the cognitive behavioral perspective share several characteristic assumptions. First, like the behaviorists considered in the last section, theorists who advocate a cognitive social learning theory perspective maintain that personality is formed through interaction with the environment. Second, they agree with behaviorists that what people do is, to a large extent, environmentally determined and situation-specific. Third, they include in their theories much more elaborate descriptions of the mental processes within people than did theorists discussed in the previous section. Fourth, these theorists assume that people differ from one another in the ways they think about themselves and the people around them, and that these cognitions are key variables to understand personality differences. These theorists attempt to measure cognitions in a systematic way. Fifth, these theorists assert that cognitive change is the key to personality change.

Besides their purely theoretical interest, cognitive approaches have led to new strategies of therapy (e.g., Försterling, 1985). They differ from the behaviorists in the research methods they use to study therapy (O'Donohue & Houts, 1985). Behavioral approaches employ primarily single-subject research designs, and thus are idiographic. Cognitive approaches use primarily group designs, and thus are nomothetic. Yet this approach avoids global, trait-like constructs. Instead, recognizing that situations have important influences, questions are asked specific to situations or domains of behavior and thought (Bandura, 1989a). In addition, theorists in this perspective emphasize modeling as a planned method of influencing behavior (Decker & Nathan, 1985).

This perspective offers more potential for understanding uniquely human experiences. Higher cognitive processes cannot be studied in the animal models so central to earlier behaviorism. M. Brewster Smith (1990), writing from a humanistic perspective, suggests that theoretical developments within the cognitive social learning perspective can be reconciled with the concerns of humanistic psychology:

> Albert Bandura has stretched his social learning theory to accommodate central humanistic concerns in developing a theory of reciprocal determinism in

> which he manages to take into account self-control and personal initiative in constituting one's environment. (M.B. Smith, 1990, p. 15)

Others, however, feel that cognitive behaviorism is still too deterministic to meet the needs of personality theory (Rychlak, 1984a, 1988). Whatever the case, it is one of the most active areas of theory and research within current personality theory.

Chapter 13

Mischel and Bandura: Cognitive Social Learning Theory

BIOGRAPHIES OF WALTER MISCHEL AND ALBERT BANDURA

Walter Mischel

Walter Mischel was born in 1930 in Vienna, Austria. His family fled Europe to avoid the Nazi persecutions at the beginning of World War II, when he was a young boy. Like many Europeans, they immigrated to New York City, where Mischel later studied at the City College of New York. He became a social worker, focusing on juvenile delinquents.

Mischel's graduate work at Ohio State University in the 1950s had an effect on his developing cognitive emphasis. In particular, he was influenced by the work of his mentors George Kelly and Julian Rotter (Mischel, 1984b). He used the concept of "personal construct," an idea developed by George Kelly, in his own theory. After several brief faculty positions, Mischel moved to Stanford University, where he taught and did research from 1962 to 1983. Since 1983, he has been on the faculty of Columbia University.

Albert Bandura

Albert Bandura was born December 4, 1925, in northern Alberta, Canada. Elementary and high school were combined in one school in the small town of Mundare. Bandura worked on the Alaska Highway before beginning college at the University of British Columbia, graduating in three years. He did his graduate work at the University of Iowa, finishing his doctorate in clinical psychology in 1952. There he met his future wife, Virginia Varns, who taught in the School of Nursing.

Bandura did a postdoctoral internship at the Wichita Guidance Center. Then he went to Stanford University in California, where he began as instructor. Bandura has been on the faculty of Stanford his entire career, becoming a full professor in 1964 and becoming holder of an endowed chair in 1974. He headed the Department of Psychology in 1976–77.

His interests have been broad, including not only the therapeutic concerns that might have been anticipated from his clinical training, but also broad issues in child development and social problems. He was president of the American Psychological Association in 1974, and has received many professional honors for his scholarly work, including the American Psychological Association's Award for Distinguished Scientific Contributions in 1980 (American Psychological Association, 1981).

Bandura has two daughters. In addition to research, he enjoys hiking in the mountains and attending the opera.

ILLUSTRATIVE BIOGRAPHIES

A few psychobiographical analyses have been published from the cognitive social learning perspective. Griffith (1984) analyzed the life of Elizabeth Cady Stanton, a nineteenth-century advocate of women's rights, emphasizing concepts such as "role model." Mischel (1968b, pp. 262–272) interpreted a case study of Pearson Brack, an American bombardier in World War II, which had been previously reported (Grinker & Spiegel, 1945; R.W. White, 1964). Brack had been injured during a flight, and he subsequently experienced debilitating anxiety when flying above 10,000 feet. Psychoanalytic interpretations sought character flaws deep in the unconscious. Mischel, in contrast, interpreted the altitude as a conditioned stimulus that triggered the fear because of its association with the trauma of the flight on which he was injured. This case illustrates a fundamental strategy of this perspective. The actual situation in which behavior occurs is important. The remote past is far less important. In addition, cognitive variables are central to personality interpretation in this perspective.

Leonard Bernstein

Leonard Bernstein is one of the best-known American composers and orchestra conductors of the twentieth century. He was born August 25, 1918, to Russian Jewish immigrants in Mattapan, a suburb of Boston. Best known for composing the popular opera *West Side Story* (with Stephen Sondheim as lyricist), Bernstein explored a variety of musical forms and influences.

It was as a conductor, however, that Bernstein achieved his most consistent success. He was conductor of the New York Philharmonic (1958–69). He recorded many performances for Deutsche Grammophon, ensuring a wider audience and increased financial profit from his work.

Bernstein's life aroused public controversy as well as fame. He offended some when, though Jewish, he signed contracts with the German company Deutsche Grammophon for performances and recordings. In addition, his fondness for performing in Vienna, reputed to be a highly anti-Semitic city (Peyser, 1987), was puzzling. Some of his compositions were offensive because of their treatment of religious and political themes. And although married and a father, he maintained homosexual relationships.

Bernstein without music would not have been Bernstein. How did music come to be so central to his life? Can we understand why he succeeded so phenomenally?

COGNITIVE SOCIAL LEARNING THEORY

Albert Bandura and Walter Mischel offer the most current theoretical analysis of personality in the tradition of learning theory. They have focused particularly on *cognitive* variables, because the human capacity to think is central to the phenomena that constitute personality. Thus their theory is uniquely relevant to the human species, and cannot be faulted for too close a tie to an animal model (as were Skinner's and Dollard and Miller's theories). Like those theories, though, it considers situational variables.

While Bandura and Mischel have similar theoretical orientations, have cited one another's work, and have collaborated (Bandura & Mischel, 1965), most of their formal theoretical developments and research have been published independently. In this chapter, specific theoretical terms are attributed to the theorist who proposed them. It would generally be accurate, however, to expect that both Bandura and Mischel would agree with one another's theoretical statements.

Emily Dickinson

Emily Dickinson is one of the best-known American poets. Many schoolchildren have memorized her poem that begins, "I heard a fly buzz—when I died." She is, however, probably best known as a recluse. She withdrew from public life in adulthood. She is surely an apt nominee for a prototypical introverted personality, yet cognitive social learning theory is not content with trait labels as explanations of personality. It insists upon knowing the behavior and the environmental context in which it occurred.

Emily Dickinson was born December 10, 1830, the middle of three children, with an older brother, Austin, and a younger sister, Lavinia. Her grandfather had risked, and lost, his fortune establishing Amherst College (Massachusetts). Her father, Edward Dickinson, was less committed to the church-affiliated college and more sensible financially. Emily's parents provided a stable but passionless home.

Emily, like her younger sister, never married. Her life was in many ways shaped by the traditional expectations for women. She assisted her mother in keeping house, taking over when her mother was out of town caring for her own sick mother. She received a fine secondary education but was not allowed to attend college because of her sex. Her father, who encouraged her older brother's literary efforts, thought it undesirable for a woman to be a poet.

For most of her adult years, Emily Dickinson lived the life of a recluse. She was seldom seen by people other than her family. While Emily did publish several poems during her lifetime, her family was surprised to find hundreds of poems, many undated and on scraps of paper, after she died. Her sister arduously prepared them for publication. Emily Dickinson, then, led a reclusive yet conventional life of a spinster in nineteenth-century New England. Why did she withdraw so much from the world? How can we understand her great dedication to poetry? The theories presented by Bandura and Mischel suggest examining the environment in which she lived and the ways she thought about that environment and herself.

WALTER MISCHEL

The Trait Controversy: Mischel's Challenge

Traditional personality theories, including trait and psychodynamic approaches, assume that individual differences consist of *global* characteristics affecting a wide variety of behaviors (Mischel, 1973). Mischel startled the field by questioning this fundamental assumption. He stated, after examining the research literature, that "With the possible exception of intelligence, highly generalized behavioral consistencies have not been demonstrated, and the concept of personality traits as broad predispositions is thus untenable" (Mischel, 1968b, p. 140). Mischel reported that the average relationship between self-report personality measures and behavior was only $r = .30$, which he termed the *personality coefficient.* It is low, accounting for less than 10 percent of the variability in behavior. His challenge to traditional assumptions of trait and psychodynamic theories contributed to a "paradigm crisis" in personality theory (Epstein & O'Brien, 1985; Mischel, 1973, p. 254).

Personality psychologists commonly believe that "people are characterized by broad dispositions resulting in extensive cross-situational consistency, [but] the research in the area has persistently failed to support that intuition" (Mischel, 1984a, p. 357). In a much-cited study, Mischel and Peake (1982) examined the consistency of college students on two characteristics, conscientiousness and friendliness. While common sense would seem to predict that each student would behave consistently across situations, depending upon their traits of friendliness or unfriendliness and conscientiousness or unconscientiousness, the results indicated inconsistency. There was virtually no tendency for inter-situational consistency ($r = .13$). Critics (Bem, 1983; Conley, 1984b; S. Epstein, 1983b; Epstein & O'Brien, 1985; M.W. Eysenck & H.J. Eysenck, 1980; Funder, 1983; Houts, Cook, & Shadish, 1986; Olweus, 1980) objected that this result could be due to methodological faults, such as inappropriate items, unreliable measurement, failure to aggregate across situations, failure to assess subjects idiographically, and inadequate sampling of behavior over time and over situations. Mischel, however, believed the lack of consistency across situations was real.

Personality consistency can be considered from two perspectives. *Situational consistency,* that is, similar behavior across various situations, is the focus of Mischel's criticism, and he has demonstrated that there is much less consistency than had been thought. *Temporal consistency* refers to consistency across time. Evidence for temporal consistency is much stronger than for situational consistency (Mischel, 1968b).

The Consistency Paradox

This discrepancy between intuition and empirical findings is a **consistency paradox**. We perceive people as consistent, yet research data indicate low cross-situational consistency. People who are honest in the classroom may cheat on taxes; children who wait patiently in the presence of a parent may act impulsively when the situation changes. People actually change more from one situation to another than one would expect if their behavior were determined by general personality traits. That is, behavior is situation-specific.

A social learning approach does not necessarily expect behavior to be consistent across situations. Behavior depends upon the consequences (rewards and punishments) it produces. If different situations produce different consequences, adaptive responses will vary from situation to situation. Consistency is expected only when the same behavior is reinforced in a variety of situations, or if a person is unable to discriminate situations. For example, a child who is rewarded by friends, teachers, and parents for speaking will learn to speak in a great variety of situations. A child who cannot tell when speaking will result in punishment, and when it will not, may learn to be quiet all the time. When such consistency is found, social learning theory can explain it as a consequence of a particular learning history, without resorting to a concept of "trait" such as extroversion or introversion that explains the behavior.

Mischel pointed out that laypeople have always made trait attributions and undoubtedly will continue to do so. Traits are convenient ways for individuals to talk about other people (cf. Hoffman, Mischel, & Baer, 1984). Traits constitute summaries of multiple behavioral observations and may have some descriptive usefulness for salient characteristics (Mischel, 1973). The average person overlooks inconsistencies in behavior, explaining behavior in terms of consistent traits despite the evidence (Hayden & Mischel, 1976). This usage is, however, too vague and too error-prone for the types of predictions that science attempts. For Mischel, traits are not *causes,* but merely summary labels. They describe, but do not explain, personality.

Mischel's challenge to an overgeneralized conceptualization of traits was not intended to displace traits entirely from personality theory. Rather, he asserted that it was time for theorists to replace *overgeneralized* trait concepts with more refined analyses, and to understand when people behave consistently and when they discriminate among situations (Mischel, 1983a, 1984b; Mischel & Peake, 1983; Peake & Mischel, 1984). This is a "pressing challenge" in the field (Endler & Edwards, 1986).

The Situational Context of Behavior

Wright and Mischel (1987) suggested a refined model of the relationship between traits and behavior (see Figure 13.1). This model suggests that a given trait, such as aggressiveness, influences behavior only under certain conditions. These conditions ought to be specified theoretically. For example, the trait of aggressiveness will influence behavior (hitting, yelling, and so forth) only under certain conditions: when a person feels angry or frustrated, and when people threaten or criticize the person. Under appropriate instigating conditions, people with a trait of aggressiveness will behave noticeably differently from others. Under other conditions, however, no effect of trait on behavior will be observed. This was confirmed in Wright and Mischel's (1987) observations of children experiencing social adjustment problems at a treatment camp.

This situational context for behavior is consistent with people's everyday descriptions. When individuals describe other people's behavior, Wright and Mischel (1988) have shown that they "hedge" their statements with pronouncements about the conditions under which traits will be manifested. For example, they may say that "Johnny will hit back [aggressive behavior] when he is teased [conditional modifier or 'hedge']." Conditional statements about the expression of dispositionally relevant behaviors take the form, "Person does *x* when *y*." Children are less adept at this statement of conditions, but they still report that other children only sometimes exhibit certain behaviors, thus showing awareness that behavior does not invariably follow from dispositions (Wright & Mischel, 1988). Thus, when people de-

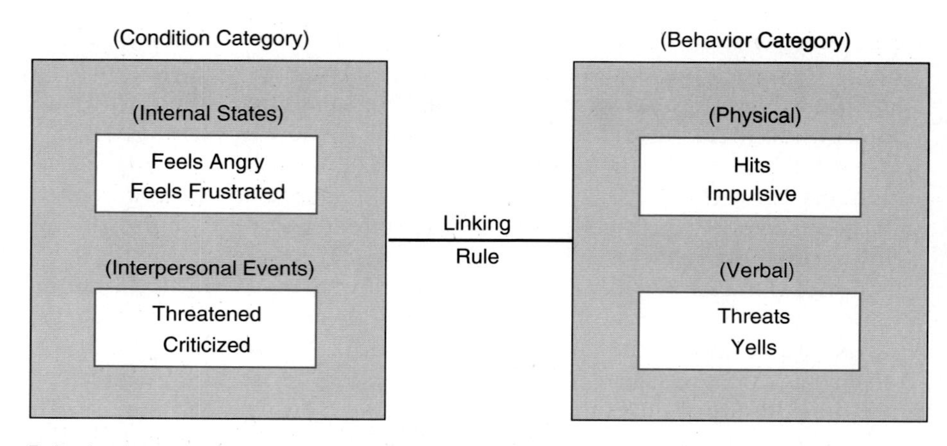

Behavioral results from a set of conditions, rather than from a trait alone. Only under certain conditions does a trait of "aggressiveness" influence behavior.

FIGURE 13.1 Illustration of a Dispositional Construct (Aggressive) as an If–Then Linkage Between a Category of Conditions and a Category of Behaviors

(From J.C. Wright & W. Mischel (1987). A conditional approach to dispositional constructs: The local predictability of social behavior. *Journal of Personality and Social Psychology,* 53, 1159–1177. Copyright 1987 by the American Psychological Association. Reprinted by permission.)

scribe behavior, they do not use trait terms (e.g., "aggressive") in a global, overly simplified manner that ignores situations.

When the naturally occurring conditionality of behavior is artificially changed in information presented to judges, their judgments are influenced. Accurate situational descriptions of children's behavior (e.g., "child hits when provoked") were perceived meaningfully. Descriptions that distorted the situational context of behavior in unnatural ways (e.g., "child hits when praised") yielded descriptions of children as odd, withdrawn, or psychotic (Shoda, Mischel, & Wright, 1989). This finding confirms Mischel's argument that trait perceptions are based upon knowledge of the situation in which behavior occurs.

Situational variation should not be considered a problem for personality theory. In fact, the ability to discriminate among situations is characteristic of people who are well adapted. Failure to differentiate among situations, responding with consistent behavior to unlike situations, may be maladaptive (Mischel, 1968b, 1973, 1984a). As Mischel puts it,

> Personologists have long searched for behavioral consistencies from situation to situation as if such consistency were the essence of personality. Perhaps that form of consistency will prove to be more characteristic of rigid, maladaptive, incompetent social functioning than of the integrated individual. (Mischel, 1984a, p. 360)

Cognitive Person Variables

Instead of global traits, which label behavioral tendencies but do not really explain them, Mischel (1973) proposes that personality psychologists consider several psychological processes within a person that enable adaptation to the environment. He calls these concepts *cognitive social learning person variables* since they were derived from cognition and from social learning. More briefly, we may call them **cognitive person variables**. These concepts include consideration of traits and the way people use trait labels to describe themselves and others. They also go beyond this, providing a broad list of the cognitive person variables constituting personality: encoding strategies and personal constructs, competencies, expectancies, subjective stimulus values, and self-regulatory systems and plans.

Encoding Strategies and Personal Constructs

Trait terms, which people use to describe themselves and other people, are called *personal constructs.* They are "personal" both in the sense that they describe individuals and in the sense that they vary from one person to another. Personal constructs that people use to describe themselves may be termed a "self-system." They are unique to each person (as Allport and Kelly also thought). Scientific personality theory must understand how people use these trait terms, although the theory itself should not adopt these trait terms.

Mischel cited a study by Bem and Allen (1974) showing that people can accurately identify traits on which they themselves are consistent, and others on which they change from situation to situation. This finding confirms Mischel's general belief that "each person knows his or her own behavior best" (1977a, p. 336). This emphasis on self-knowledge emerged in one of Mischel's early studies, conducted from the point of view of the old paradigm, which emphasized global personality traits. Mischel (1965) found that the success of Peace Corps volunteers assigned as teachers in Nigeria could be predicted better from self-report measures (F-Scale, Ego Strength, and Manifest Anxiety scales) than from ratings by staff. Overall, however, prediction of success was not very good. As Mischel came to articulate later (e.g., 1984a), more specific aspects of subjects' cognitions about the situation would improve prediction.

Besides personal constructs, people also have other kinds of **encoding strategies**, including concepts for describing situations and events. Because of their widely different and idiosyncratic learning histories, the meaning of situations varies from person to person. Behavior is influenced by environmental stimuli, but it is a person's unique interpretation of these stimuli, rather than objective environmental aspects, which matters. Mischel suggests, "Assessing the acquired meaning of stimuli [for the individual] is the core of social behavior assessment" (1968b, p. 190). For this purpose, it is necessary to rely on subjects' reports, since only they have access to their cognitions (1973).

PROTOTYPES

The concepts people use to describe themselves and others are different, in important ways, from the "traits" of personality researchers. Understanding this difference helps explain the *consistency paradox* described above. Rather than judging personality consistency based on similar behavior across many situations (as a researcher might), the average person looks for consistency across time in a small number of behaviors that are seen as particularly characteristic ("prototypical") of a given trait (Mischel, 1984b).

In formal logic and in the simplified environment of a Skinner box, events either do or do not belong to a particular category. Logical reasoning demands that we be able to say that something either is "A" or "not A," and it seems the two choices cover all options. In a Skinner box, a discriminative stimulus may consist of a signal light, which is either "on" or "off." But what if the light is flickering? What if the thing we are judging as "A" or "not A" is an ostrich, and "A" is the category "bird"? Suddenly things are not so easy, and we must turn from logical categories to *prototypes.*

A **prototype** is a typical example of a category. For example, a robin is a prototypical bird. Other objects are judged to be members of the class (in this case, "birds") depending upon their similarity to the prototypical example. A canary is a bird; it is quite similar to a robin. An ostrich, which shares fewer features with the robin, may still be a bird, but it is nearer the boundaries of this "fuzzy" category. Closer to the interests of personality theory, we also have "personality prototypes—abstract representations of particular personality types" (Cantor & Mischel, 1979b, p. 188)—such as "introverts" and "extroverts." We judge whether a particular individual is an introvert or an extrovert based on similarity to the prototype. Some people are difficult to classify, just as the ostrich was difficult to categorize as a bird or not a bird (Cantor & Mischel, 1979a).

Prototypes can be arranged in a hierarchy, ranging from very broad categories (e.g., "extrovert") to narrow ones (e.g., "door-to-door salesman"). Broader categories are distinctive, with little overlap among categories. They correspond to broad personality "types" (cf. Chapter 1). Narrower categories are more vivid and concrete, conjuring up clearer visual images and trait descriptions (Cantor & Mischel, 1979a). It is more difficult to recall information about people who don't consistently fit a prototype (Cantor & Mischel, 1979b). Prototypes include social stereotypes, such as "redneck," and "do-gooder," though researchers generally use more value-neutral labels, such as "comedian type" or "pet-owner type" (Andersen & Klatzky, 1987).

Competencies

What can a person do? What can a person think? These are the person's cognitive and behavioral construction **competencies**. These competencies "to construct (generate) diverse behaviors under appropriate conditions" (Mischel, 1973, p. 265) vary widely from person to person, "as becomes obvious from even casual comparison of the different competencies, for example, of a professional weight lifter, a distinguished chemist, a retardate, an opera star, or a convicted forger" (Mischel, 1977a, p. 342). For example, leaders of neighborhood block organizations have higher construction competencies for skills relevant to leadership. Such competencies include being able to talk in front of a group and being able to get others to follow one's ideas (Florin, Mednick, & Wandersman, 1986).

The concept of construction competencies is a broad one, encompassing many learned behaviors and concepts (see Table 13.1). It refers to what a person knows or is *able* to do (not what the person actually does). Therefore, assessing competencies requires providing incentives for the performance of the behavior. Competencies have better stability across time and situations than do many of the personality traits that Mischel criticizes

TABLE 13.1 Examples of Cognitive and Behavioral Construction Competencies

Sexual gender identity
Knowing the structure of the physical world
Social rules and conventions
Personal constructs about self and others
Rehearsal strategies for learning

(Adapted from Mischel, 1973, p. 266.)

(1973, p. 267). That is because they are free of the variable factors that determine whether a person will do what he or she can do. Such factors include various *expectancies* about the situation.

Expectancies

Whether or not people will behave in a particular way depends not only upon whether they know how (their competencies), but also upon their **expectancies**. Mischel said that internal, subjective expectancies of the person determine performance. This emphasis on thought distinguishes the cognitive learning approach from a more external behavioral theory, such as that of Skinner. Several kinds of expectancies can be distinguished.

BEHAVIOR-OUTCOME EXPECTANCIES

Will racing to the corner in 11 seconds result in catching the bus, or will the driver ignore me and not stop? Will getting an *A* on a math test result in approval, or embarrassment? A *behavior-outcome expectancy* is an expectation about what will happen if a person behaves in a particular way. Such expectancies are already evident in preschool children, who have ideas about their control over the positive and negative events that happen to them (Hegland & Galejs, 1983; Mischel, Zeiss, & Zeiss, 1974).

STIMULUS-OUTCOME EXPECTANCIES

People also develop expectancies about how events will develop in the world, aside from their own actions. These are termed *stimulus-outcome expectancies.* "If the Number 10 bus has just left, the Number 23 must be coming soon." "If Jerry is shouting, he may soon hit." Although not always directly connected with immediate behavior, these expectancies are important in maintaining a person's ongoing awareness of the environment. Sometimes they may motivate a person to change environments.

SELF-EFFICACY EXPECTANCIES

"Can I even make it to the bus stop in 11 seconds, or will I fall flat on my face trying?" Expectancies about whether one actually can do the behavior are termed *self-efficacy expectancies.* They are different from behavior-outcome expectancies, as any student knows who believes that 12 hours of straight study would result in an *A* on an exam (high behavior-outcome expectancy), but who also believes that such a feat would not be possible to perform (low self-efficacy expectancy). Bandura has developed the concept of self-efficacy most fully, but Mischel (e.g., 1981b, p. 349) also uses this idea.

These various types of expectancies develop from experience in situations. When a person is in a new situation, expectancies are derived from past experience in similar situations (Mischel & Staub, 1965). Such generalized expectancies are replaced by specific situational expectancies when experience permits. A child may expect that a new babysitter will ignore obscene language, if past babysitters have done so, but with experience will learn that such utterances can be expected to result in punishment. Performance expectancies and other cognitive person variables may also be influenced by emotional states (Wright & Mischel, 1982), though the evidence is mixed (Stanley & Maddux, 1986).

Subjective Stimulus Values

People do not all value the same outcomes. The term **subjective stimulus value** refers to the extent to which a person regards an outcome as desirable or undesirable. In learning terms, it is the value of the reward. Mischel (1981a) offers the example of teacher's praise. This outcome may have high subjective stimulus value for a student trying to get good grades, but would have quite a different value for a rebellious adolescent who rejects school.

Self-Regulatory Systems and Plans

Among the most important, though complicated, cognitive person variables are **self-regulatory systems and plans**. These are internal mechanisms that have powerful implications for behavior. People set performance goals for themselves (whether it is running a 4-minute mile, or skiing an advanced slope, or finishing a term paper before it is due). They reward themselves. They criticize themselves. They pass by immediate pleasure for long-term goals (delay of gratification). All these are self-regulatory systems "through which we can influence our environment substantially, overcoming 'stimulus control' (the power of the situation)" (Mischel, 1981b, p. 350). Self-regulatory mechanisms are a more refined description of what Freud called "the transition from primary to secondary process" (Mischel, 1974, p. 263). Much of Mischel's research effort was devoted to the investigation of one such self-regulatory system, the ability to delay gratification.

Delay of Gratification

Delay of gratification, or the ability to defer present gratification for larger future goals, is an important adaptational skill that develops in childhood. Mischel and his colleagues explored this self-regulatory system in several studies (e.g., Mischel, 1966, 1974). They gave young children the choice of receiving a small reward (for example, one marshmallow) immediately or a larger reward (two marshmallows) later. Some children were tested with pretzels instead of marshmallows. By manipulating aspects of the situation, and by teaching the children strategies for waiting, Mischel and his colleagues learned what facilitates delay of gratification, and what prevents it.

Delay is more difficult if the rewards are visible (Mischel & Ebbesen, 1970) and if the child is thinking about how wonderful the marshmallow will taste (Mischel & Baker, 1975). If the marshmallows are out of sight (Mischel & Ebbesen, 1970), and if the child is thinking about something else (Mischel, Ebbesen, & Zeiss, 1972), delay of gratification is easier. Paying attention to symbolically presented rewards (that is, pictures of the rewards) instead of the actual rewards increases delay of gratification (Mischel & Moore, 1973). Strangely enough, even television commercials depicting toys (Crayolas) and food (Sugar Pops or Froot Loops cereal) can distract kindergarten children enough to enable them to delay gratification for the cereal (Dawson, Jeffrey, Peterson, Sommers, & Wilson, 1985). By age 5, children develop effective strategies that enable them to wait for rewards: covering the rewards (marshmallows) and thinking about something else (H. Mischel & W. Mischel, 1983). Children can be taught to think about other things, which improves their ability to delay gratification (Mischel, Ebbesen, & Zeiss, 1972). The ability to delay gratification can also be improved by exposure to models who delay their own gratification (Bandura & Mischel, 1965; Mischel & Liebert, 1966).

The delay of gratification research seems to be tapping a core "ego strength" (as it would be called in psychoanalytic language). Preference for delayed gratification is associated with greater resistance to the temptation to cheat on a game in order to get more points (Mischel & Gilligan, 1964). When children learn to delay gratification, they are mastering a skill with important consequences in their future. Children's ability to delay gratification was quite stable over time. Preschool youngsters who waited longer for marshmallows or pretzels were rated higher by parents on cognitive and social competence years later, when they were juniors and seniors in high school (Mischel, 1983b, 1984a; Mischel, Shoda, & Peake, 1988; Mischel, Shoda, & Rodriguez, 1989). (See Table 13.2.) Preschoolers who delayed gratification longer were, in high school, likely to have higher SAT verbal and math scores. They were described by their parents as better able to concentrate and to cope with frustration and stress (Shoda, Mischel, & Peake, 1990).

Personality is adaptational, and the important personality characteristics proposed by Mischel prepare the individual to cope with situations. The findings of Mischel's program of research offer suggestions for intervention programs for children who do not develop normal abilities to delay gratification, such as those who are aggressive or hyperactive (Mischel, Shoda, & Rodriguez, 1989; Rodriguez, Mischel, & Shoda, 1989).

TABLE 13.2 Examples of High School Behavior Ratings Predicted from Preschool Delay of Gratification

Is attentive and able to concentrate.
Is verbally fluent, can express ideas well.
Uses and responds to reason.
Tends to go to pieces under stress, becomes rattled. **(disagree)**
Reverts to more immature behavior under stress. **(disagree)**

(From W. Mischel (1984). Convergences and challenges in the search for consistency. *American Psychologist*, 39, 351–364. Copyright 1984 by the American Psychological Association. Adapted by permission.)

Mischel emphasizes *cognitive* competencies that enable children to delay gratification. In contrast, Funder and Block (1989) suggest that *motivational* considerations are more important in the types of situations confronted in real life, where gratifications more tempting than marshmallows and pretzels are immediately available. In the research conducted by Funder and Block, 14-year-old girls and boys were paid relatively well for participating in research. Those who increased their earnings "with interest" by delaying payment until the end of a series of six experimental sessions, conducted over several weeks, were more intelligent (higher IQ) and more ego-controlled and ego-resilient (on the Q-sort) than were those who chose immediate payment. Funder and Block argue that ego control, and not simply cognitive ability, is essential for delay of gratification when the rewards immediately available are truly tempting. Yet it is clear that although Mischel's theory is "cognitive" in name, it encompasses far more than what ordinarily is labeled cognitive.

Interaction Between Personality and Situation

Personality may be thought of as a distinctive way of adapting to situations. Rather than saying that situations determine behavior (which ignores individual differences in reactions) or that personality determines behavior (which is misleading because of the low cross-situational consistency of behavior), we should phrase it differently. *Personality interacts with situations* in determining behavior. **Interactionism** is the approach to personality that examines these personality-by-situation interactions (e.g., Endler & Magnusson, 1976; Magnusson & Endler, 1977).

The interaction between personality and situations is illustrated in a study by Mischel, Ebbesen, and Zeiss (1973). College students were given supposed intellectual tests. Then, while they waited for the rest of the study, they could examine information about their assets and liabilities related to the task, if they chose. The personality trait of repression-sensitization was measured (Byrne, 1961). This trait refers to the tendency of people to pay attention to (sensitizers) or to avoid thinking about (repressors) conflictful information concerning oneself. Repressors spent less time examining information about their liabilities than did sensitizers, regardless of whether they thought this was the end of the study (No Expectancy Condition) or whether they expected to take another test (Expectancy Condition).

However, another dependent variable showed an interaction between personality and situation. Repressors and sensitizers both spent about the same amount of time on their assets when they expected to take another test; but when they thought this was the end of the study, repressors spent more time on their assets than did sensitizers. That is, personality *interacts with* situation in determining behavior. Such interactions generally account for more of behavior than does personality or situation alone (Mischel, 1973).

As Mischel emphasized in his 1968 challenge to the field, situations are powerful influences on behavior, and should not be ignored by personality psychologists. We now know more than at that time about when to expect personality to influence behavior. Some situations are so powerful that they affect everyone (or at least nearly everyone) similarly, making individual differences unimportant as predictors of behavior. These are called *strong situations*. For example, when the telephone rings, nearly everyone answers it. Other situations have less uniform effects on people. These are *weak situations.* For example, when a sales pitch is delivered on the phone, some people listen politely, while others hang up. Personality traits predict how individuals will differ in their response to such weak situations, but have no predictive value for strong situations. Situations that are ambiguous about expected behaviors are especially likely to show the effects of personality (cf. Dollinger & Taub, 1977).

Mischel challenged the traditional concept of global, cross-situational traits. He did not attempt to replace personality with situationalism, as some of his critics charged (see Mischel, 1973, 1979), but rather urged greater attention to the impact of situations, greater clarity in the conceptualization of personality, and a sensitivity to the interaction between the two. Consistency of personality may be demonstrable only when theorists abandon their search for distinctive nomothetic traits and instead look for more idiographic patterns of person-environment interactions (cf. Cantor & Mischel, 1979a, p. 43). Mischel's focus on competencies and other cognitive person variables emphasizes the adaptational function of personality. His research on the delay of gratification shows how individual children learn to overcome the power of situations to gain self-control (e.g., Mischel, 1984a, p. 353). Mischel has offered an exciting and practical theory, rich with implications for research and intervention.

ALBERT BANDURA

Albert Bandura agrees with Mischel's emphasis on personality concepts that recognize the importance of the social context. He is probably best known, especially in social psychology, for his classic work on the modeling of aggression. His more recent research and theorizing have focused on describing processes of self-regulated behavior and understanding how these are developed through learning.

Observational Learning and Modeling

We are so aware today of the importance of "good models" for children that it is easy to overlook the theoretical advance that occurred when modeling was introduced to the learning theory paradigm within personality. Radical learning theory, in the Skinnerian tradition, required that responses must occur and be reinforced in order to be strengthened. Even Miller and Dollard (1941), for all their theoretical innovation, assumed that responses must be reinforced to be learned. Laboratory rats and pigeons in Skinner boxes were subjected to exhausting shaping interventions to bring about these necessary conditions for learning. If elaborate procedures such as these were necessary to trigger relatively simple motor responses, how could learning theory possibly explain the much more extensive developments that occur in human personality formation?

Humans learn by observing. This is the simple answer that Bandura proposed. Intuitively, it is obvious. However, observational learning violates a traditional assumption of learning theory—that learning can only occur if there is reinforcement. Bandura asserted that learning and performance could be distinguished. Reinforcement provides incentives necessary for performance, but it is not necessary for learning.

Behavioral changes that result from exposure to models are variously called imitative learning, observational learning, or vicarious learning (Bandura, 1965c, p. 3). These terms are interchangeable in Bandura's usage. He defines **vicarious learning** as learning in which

> new responses are acquired or the characteristics of existing response repertoires are modified as a function of observing the behavior of others and its reinforcing consequences, without the modeled responses being overtly performed by the viewer during the exposure period. (1965c, p. 3)

In everyday experience, a child may see a friend grab a ball away from a classmate and learn to grab as a result. Or a TV viewer may see a mass murder on television and later imitate the crime. More positively, exposure to competent and socialized adults teaches children desirable behaviors. Bandura does not question that traditional learning by reinforcement occurs. There is more, though.

> Our theories have been incredibly slow in acknowledging that man can learn by observation as well as by direct experience. This is another example of how steadfast adherence to orthodox paradigms makes it difficult to transcend the confines of conceptual commitment. . . . The rudimentary form of learning based on direct experience has been exhaustively studied, whereas the more pervasive and powerful mode of learning by observation is largely ignored. A shift of emphasis is needed. (Bandura, 1974, p. 863)

Modeling in Child Development

Bandura has explored the role of modeling in child development through laboratory investigation of a variety of behaviors. He reports that exposure to adult models can lead to diverse effects, including elevating the level of moral reasoning (Bandura, 1969; Bandura & McDonald, 1963) or, conversely, increasing aggressive behavior. Let us examine some of these experiments.

IDENTIFICATION

Bandura's interest in modeling had roots in other theoretical traditions. Psychoanalytic approaches stress *identification* with parents as the basis for much personality development. Bandura translated this concept into the learning concept of **modeling** in order to explore the determinants of the process in the laboratory. Basing their understanding of identification on psychoanalytic and other theories, previous researchers reasoned that children may identify with parents because of their *power* (as controllers of rewards) or because of their *status* (as recipients of rewards). Bandura designed a laboratory experiment to test these proposed causes of identification. Preschool children observed various kinds of models, some powerful, called Controller Models (because they controlled access to highly desirable toys) and some high status, called Consumer Models (because they received rewards). The children observed the models engaging in playful behavior with several distinctive components, such as putting on a hat backward or walking and saying "Left, right, left, right."

Then the children were observed playing with the same toys, and the number of responses patterned after each model was counted. Children modeled their behavior more after the Controller Models, rather than the Consumer Models. In a "traditional" family, with a working father and a homemaker mother, this would produce greater identification with the father, as much psychoanalytically derived research has suggested. Other family power structures are also possible, of course, and were explored in this study. Whether the Controller Model was male or female, and whether the subjects were boys or girls, the Controller Model was imitated more than the Consumer Model. This would suggest that "househusbands" would suffer the same sort of oversight as "housewives" have long endured. (Since there is no discussion in this 1963 article of changing family patterns, it seems that these experimental manipulations were motivated more by theoretical considerations than social considerations. The implications are nonetheless relevant.)

A complicated interaction effect in the study does suggest that the subjects were influenced by sex roles, however. When the Non-Controller Model was ignored, left out of the games and snacks supplied by the Controller Model, the children responded differently, depending upon the sex of the Ignored Model. If a Female Controller Model ignored a male, the Ignored Male Model received more sympathy and was imitated more than a Female Ignored Model. Apparently the belief that males do, and should, control resources influenced the children, especially the boys. Overall, the research indicates that power leads to identification and suggests that "social learning variables, such as the distribution of rewarding power within the family constellation, may be highly influential in the formation of inverted sex role behavior" (Bandura, Ross, & Ross, 1963a). Other research has confirmed that models that dispense rewards to children have more effect on children's learning than do nonrewarding models (Grusec & Mischel, 1966).

Standards for Behavior

Models also can influence children's development of standards for behavior (cf. Mischel, 1966). How good does a performance have to be before self-congratulations are deserved? Bandura and Whalen (1966) exposed 8- to 11-year-olds to models who rewarded themselves for their scores on a bowling task, giving themselves praise and candy according to a performance criterion that varied for different groups of subjects. Some children observed models reward themselves only for superior performance; others saw models who demanded of themselves moderately good performance; and other youngsters saw lenient models who rewarded themselves for all but the very worst scores. The children later played the bowling game themselves. Their self-reward standards were influenced by the models they had seen. Youngsters demanded very high performance before rewarding themselves only if their models had set high standards for self-reward. Even the most permissive models, however, produced self-reward standards higher than a control group of children who had not observed any model (see Figure 13.2).

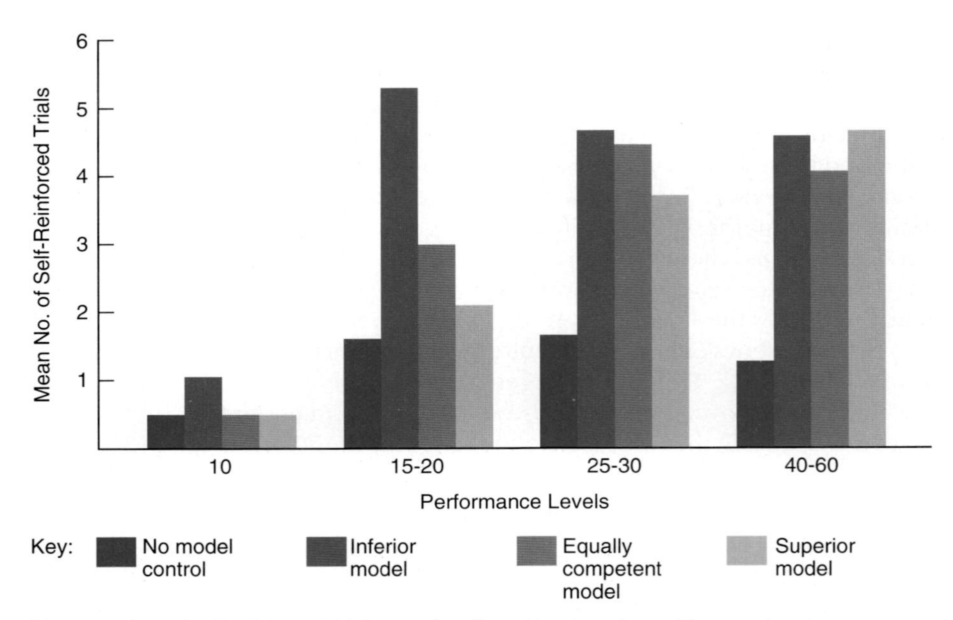

Mean number of self-reinforced trials as a function of treatment conditions and performance level by subjects in the success condition.

FIGURE 13.2 Modeling of Self-Reinforcement

(From A. Bandura & C.K. Whalen (1966). The influence of antecendent reinforcement and divergent modeling cues on patterns of self-reward. *Journal of Personality and Social Psychology,* 3, 373–382. Copyright 1966 by the American Psychological Association. Reprinted by permission.)

Later research (Bandura, Grusec, & Menlove, 1967a) found that children were influenced by peer models, as well as adult models; either could increase standards for self-reward. Further, models were more effective if they were seen being reinforced for their high standards. These findings make it clear that a social context that conveys positive values for high standards leads to the internalization of such standards in children.

To their surprise, the researchers found that adult models who were low in nurturance were imitated more than those who were highly nurturant to the subjects (Bandura, Grusec, & Menlove, 1967a). Writers in the psychoanalytic tradition have long distinguished various forms of identification, and for them nurturant ("anaclitic") identification has not been associated with achievement standards (cf. Bandura, Ross, & Ross, 1963a). Yet psychoanalytic concepts are not specified with sufficient precision to allow experimental tests of the sort Bandura and his colleagues have undertaken. This research suggests that power, more than love, produces imitation.

Modeling of Aggression

In his much-cited experimental investigations, Bandura (1965a, 1965b, 1973) studied the processes by which children learn aggressive responses by watching adult models. The subjects were boys and girls, aged 3 to 5, attending the Stanford University Nursery School. They watched a film in which adults played with a variety of toys, including a large inflated Bobo doll. (To the children, this film appeared to be a television show. Through clever preparation of the apparatus, the researchers produced what a VCR would achieve more easily today. They went to this trouble because of their awareness that children closely watch television shows; thus the mode of presentation ensured exposure to the models presented.)

The adult models engaged in distinctive aggressive behaviors that the children would not have seen before so as to provide an opportunity for the learning of new responses.

> First, the model laid the Bobo doll on its side, sat on it, and punched it in the nose while remarking, "Pow, right in the nose, boom, boom." The model then raised the doll and pommeled it on the head with a mallet. Each response was accompanied by the verbalization, "Sockeroo . . . stay down." Following the mallet aggression, the model kicked the doll about the room, and these responses were interspersed with the comment, "Fly away." Finally, the model threw rubber balls at the Bobo doll, each strike punctuated with "Bang." This sequence of physically and verbally aggressive behavior was repeated twice. (Bandura, 1965b, pp. 590–591)

For some children, this was the end of the film (No Consequences Condition). Other children saw the film continue, ending with the model being punished by another adult for his aggression (Model Punished Condition) or with another adult praising the aggressive model for being a "strong champion" and rewarding him with food (Model Rewarded Condition).

To test for modeling, the youngsters were brought to a playroom similar to that which they had seen on the film. Observers counted the number of aggressive responses the children imitated from the film. As predicted, there was less imitation in the Model Punished Condition than in the other two conditions. There was no difference between the Model Rewarded Condition and the No Consequences Condition. These modeling effects were similar for boys and for girls, although the girls behaved less aggressively overall (see Figure 13.3).

It is tempting to conclude that aggressive television is no danger, as long as the villain is punished in the end. While observing a model who is punished can sometimes inhibit aggression (Bandura, Ross, & Ross, 1963b), such a conclusion is not always warranted. Bandura included another feature in this study, which discredits this erroneous conclusion. He reasoned that some behaviors that are learned may not be carried out. That is, he distinguished between *learning* and *performance*. To determine whether subjects might have learned more aggression than the above data indicate, for some subjects in each condition Bandura offered the children incentives (stickers and juice) if they could behave like the model they had seen. These children showed high levels of learning of the aggressive behaviors in all conditions. Thus, punishing the villain may temporarily suppress the performance of imitative aggression, but the behaviors have been learned and may emerge later when incentive conditions change.

Modeling as a strategy for producing change clearly can have powerful effects on behavior. The exact processes are harder to isolate. Bandura (1971) suggests several possible effects of vicarious reinforcement: the informative function of observed outcomes, discrimination learning, incentive motivational effects, vicarious conditioning and extinction of arousal (Bandura, Grusec, & Menlove, 1967b; Bandura & Rosenthal, 1966), and modification

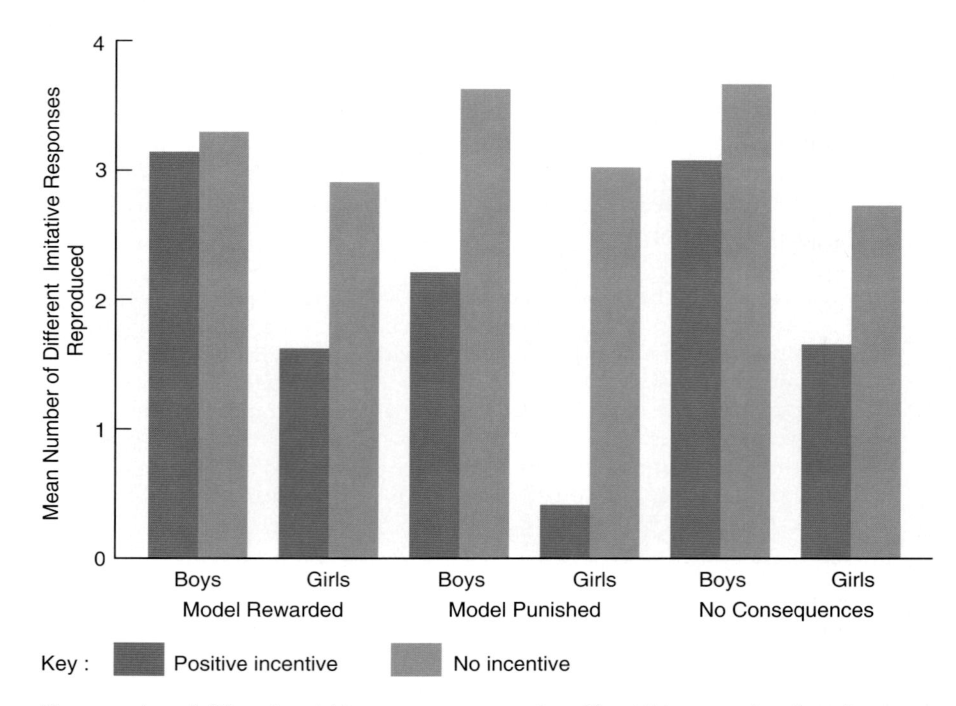

FIGURE 13.3 Modeling of Aggression

(From A. Bandura (1965). Influences of models' reinforcement contingencies on the acquisition of imitative responses. *Journal of Personality and Social Psychology,* 1, 589–595. Copyright 1965 by the American Psychological Association. Reprinted by permission.)

of model status. There may also be other effects. Hayes, Rincover, and Volosin (1980) found that children who imitated models punching a Bandura-type Bobo doll continued this aggression longer if the doll moved as they had seen in the film, but stopped sooner if the doll moved less. Thus while modeling can produce imitative aggression, the "sensory reinforcement" of seeing the consequences of actions maintains aggressive behavior.

Ever since Bandura's early research, hundreds of studies using a variety of research methods have examined the relationship between television violence and behavior. The overwhelming finding is that in the real world as well as the laboratory, models do teach aggression (Geen & Thomas, 1986; Huesmann & Malamuth, 1986; Turner, Hesse, & Peterson-Lewis, 1986). Violent rock videos contribute to men's violent attitudes toward women (Peterson & Pfost, 1989). Bandura suggests (1973, p. 323) that it could be possible to reduce aggression by changing society.

Modeling in Adulthood

Modeling is not limited to childhood. Industrial psychologists use principles of learning through modeling to train workers (Decker & Nathan, 1985). In a field experiment, female college students who were in a car were more likely to use a seat belt if the driver did so, which shows the influence of modeling (Howell, Owen, & Nocks, 1990).

Modeling is obviously a powerful determinant of the sorts of behaviors that have traditionally been of interest to personality theorists. Clear theoretical specification of the processes involved in modeling and other forms of learning makes a precise, verifiable theory. Bandura provides that.

Processes Influencing Learning

Much more happens in learning than an automatic "stamping in" of preceding responses, based upon reinforcement. Bandura offers a new set of theoretical concepts for understanding the complex events within people that must occur for observed models to produce changes in performance. Briefly, the learner must observe the behavior, remember it, be able to do it, and be motivated to do it. Let us examine these processes in more detail (see Table 13.3).

Attentional Processes

Nothing will be learned that is not observed. People who have difficulty remembering names, for example, are often people who simply don't pay attention to them in the first place. Several characteristics of the model and of the observer influence modeling (see Table 13.3). Models catch our attention more when they look distinctive because of clothes or other aspects of

TABLE 13.3 Processes in Observational Learning

1. ATTENTIONAL PROCESSES: Noticing the Model's Behavior.		
	The Model:	Distinctive
		Affective Valence
		Complexity
		Prevalence
		Functional Value
	The Observer:	Sensory Capacities
		Arousal Level
		Motivation
		Perceptual Set
		Past Reinforcement
2. RETENTION PROCESSES: Putting the Behavior into Memory.		
		Symbolic Coding
		Cognitive Organization
		Symbolic Rehearsal
		Motor Rehearsal
3. MOTOR REPRODUCTION PROCESSES: Being Able to Do It.		
		Physical Capabilities
		Availability of Component Responses
		Self-Observation of Reproductions
		Accuracy Feedback
4. MOTIVATIONAL PROCESSES: Deciding It Is Worth Doing.		
		External Reinforcement
		Vicarious Reinforcement
		Self-Reinforcement

(Albert Bandura, SOCIAL FOUNDATIONS OF THOUGHT & ACTION: A Social Cognitive Theory, © 1986, p. 52. Reprinted by permission of Prentice Hall, Englewood Cliffs, New Jersey.)

physical appearance, when they are liked or disliked, and when they are seen repeatedly, as advertisers well know. Television models of aggression are vivid and dramatic, nearly guaranteeing that they will be observed. On the other hand, prosocial models who are less glamorous may be easily overlooked. All these are examples of **attentional processes**.

Characteristics of the observer, too, influence attention, including sensory capacities, arousal level, motivation, perceptual set, and past reinforcement.

Retention Processes

As any student knows who has paid attention to a classroom lecture or film, not all that is observed is retained. Retention occurs through imaginational representations (such as images of places or people that are familiar) and through verbal coding, which can be much more efficient. Bandura suggests several factors that influence the **retention process**.

Symbolic coding facilitates retention, as cognitive psychology suggests it should. In academic settings, pedagogues teach students to work actively with material to remember it. The same advice applies in other settings as well (e.g., Bandura, Grusec, & Menlove, 1966). Additional factors influencing retention include *cognitive organization, symbolic rehearsal,* and *motor rehearsal.*

Motor Reproduction Processes

The behavior being modeled must then be reproduced based on its remembered encoding (**motor reproduction process**). No response can be emitted that is beyond the physical capacity of the individual. Complex behaviors can be reproduced by combining their component response elements, if they are known.

Feedback from our own performance can facilitate improvement. Feedback from others, such as a coach, about the accuracy of our responses can also facilitate behavior. Athletic trainers have always emphasized fine-tuning this motor reproduction phase of learning and are now expanding upon it with technological aides, such as videotaping performance to enhance feedback.

Motivational Processes

Coaches also give pep talks, recognizing the importance of **motivational processes** to learning. Bandura clearly distinguishes between learning and performance. Unless motivated, the person will not produce learned behavior. This motivation can come from external reinforcement, such as the experimenter's promise of reward in some of Bandura's studies, or the bribe of a parent. Or it can come from vicarious reinforcement, based upon the observation that models are rewarded. People are capable of internalizing motivational processes, becoming self-regulating and providing self-reinforcement for much of their behavior. The person and the environment are intertwined in a complex causal network.

Although Bandura generally described model status in terms of its influence on attentional processes, high-status models can also affect performance through motivation. For example, girls aged 11 to 14 performed better on a motor performance task when they thought it was demonstrated by a high-status cheerleader than by a low-status model (McCullagh, 1986).

Besides his theoretical description of how personality is learned, Bandura has also analyzed the way personality influences behavior in a social context: his model of *reciprocal determinism.*

Reciprocal Determinism

Many psychological approaches deal with only some aspects of the complex network of interacting causes. Trait theories describe the impact of the person on behavior. For example, people who are achievement-motivated are successful in business. Traditional learning theories describe the impact of the environment on behavior. For example, reinforcements can produce changes in verbal behavior. Social-action-oriented approaches describe the impact of behavior on the environment. For instance, political action may reduce pollution. None of these approaches can accommodate all such causal patterns, however.

To improve upon these overly simplified approaches, Bandura (1978; 1984b) proposed a concept of **reciprocal determinism**. This concept recognizes that the person, the environment, and behavior all influence each other. All directions of causal connections are possible, as illustrated in Figure 13.4.

The concept of reciprocal determinism recognizes that the environment influences behavior, as behaviorism has always suggested. (Libraries are conducive to studying; the student lounge is not.) It recognizes that characteristics within a person influence behavior, as trait approaches have traditionally emphasized. (Achievement-motivated students study; affiliation-motivated students spend time with friends.) Reciprocal determinism goes beyond these approaches, pointing out that behavior also causes changes in the environment (studying instead of spending time with friends reduces social pressures or invitations to go out) and in the person (studying increases academic self-confidence). The environment is not only a cause of behavior but also an effect of behavior. One way in which personality influences situations is that people choose situations differently, depending on their personalities (Emmons, Diener, & Larsen, 1985). (Achievement-motivated students go to the library. To return to the start of the paragraph, in the library they are in an environment conducive to studying, and so on.) In this case, these mutual influences produce consistency of behavior. A

Undirectional

$B = f(P,E)$

Partially Bidirectional

$B = f(P \rightleftarrows E)$

Reciprocal

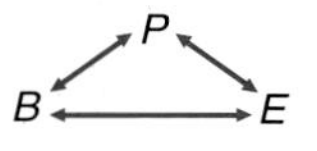

Schematic representation of three alternative conceptions of interaction. *B* signifies behavior, *P* the cognitive and other internal events that can affect perceptions and actions, and *E* the external enviroment.

FIGURE 13.4 Reciprocal Determinism

(From A. Bandura (1978). The self system in reciprocal determinism. *American Psychologist*, 33, 344–358. Copyright 1978 by the American Psychological Association. Reprinted by permission.)

complete understanding of personality requires recognizing all of these mutual influences among personality, the situation, and behavior.

Perhaps what is most new about this model is that behavior can be a cause, and not simply an effect. Sometimes behaviors themselves predict other behaviors better than does personality or the situation (Zautra, Finch, Reich, & Guarnaccia, 1991). Personality psychologists must pay more attention than they have in the past to what a person *does.*

Self-Regulation of Behavior: The Self-System

Understanding the role of the person in this reciprocal determinism model involves a description of cognitive processes that occur within the individual. "A **self-system** within the framework of social learning theory comprises cognitive structures and subfunctions for perceiving, evaluating, and regulating behavior, not a psychic agent that controls action" (Bandura, 1978, p. 344; emphasis added). These cognitive processes are outlined in Figure 13.5.

Notice that self-regulation is not simply a matter of giving yourself reinforcements. That strategy for self-improvement has not been found to work very well in controlled experiments (Sohn & Lamal, 1982). Perhaps simple self-reinforcement fails because it is too structured. Setting subgoals generally enhances performance, but strategies of planning for longer-term goals work better if they leave some flexibility about immediate tasks (Kirschenbaum, 1985).

Bandura's self-regulating processes describe intrapsychic dynamics within a person. Consider the example of an insurance salesperson. Such an

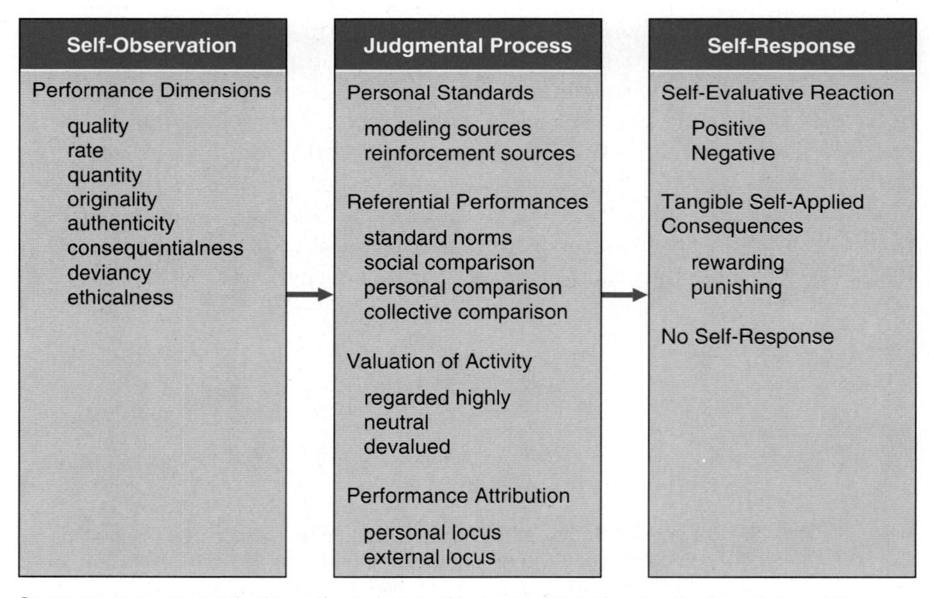

Component processes in the self-regulation of behavior by self-prescribed contingencies.

FIGURE 13.5 Self-Regulation Processes

(From A. Bandura (1978). The self system in reciprocal determinism. *American Psychologist,* 33, 344–358. Copyright 1978 by the American Psychological Association. Reprinted by permission.)

individual observes his (or her) sales performance. "How many prospective clients have I contacted? Have I presented all relevant aspects of the policies, and has the presentation been ethical?" He (or she) judges this behavior. "If I've been somewhat one-sided in favor of the policy with the biggest commission, is that what is generally accepted by people in this field? Did I do a good job?" And finally, the salesperson may or may not respond to his or her own performance. "That was great; I'll reward myself by taking the rest of the afternoon off." Such self-regulation enhances performance (Bandura, 1991b). Successful novelists, who have little external structure to provide discipline, monitor their progress in terms of number of pages written or hours worked each day, and they make rewards contingent on meeting these goals (I. Wallace, 1977).

Bandura (1990b, 1991b) warns that individuals often fail to regulate their own behavior in ways that live up to high moral standards. They exploit others, commit aggressive acts, pollute the atmosphere, and engage in many other behaviors that violate moral standards. This is a problem of *moral disengagement* (Bandura, 1978; R.I. Evans, 1989). He argues that societies must exert social control to supplement individuals' undependable moral self-control.

Therapy

Bandura criticizes therapy based only on talking. Instead, psychotherapy should more completely apply known learning principles (Bandura, 1961). He has demonstrated the effectiveness of therapeutic interventions based on social learning principles for the treatment of phobias in adults (Bandura, Adams, & Beyer, 1977; Bandura & Barab, 1973; Bandura, Blanchard, & Ritter, 1969; Bandura, Jeffery, & Wright, 1974) and in children (Bandura, Grusec, & Menlove, 1967b; Bandura & Menlove, 1968). Improvement occurred when patients observed live or filmed models who displayed no fear of snakes (Bandura, Blanchard, & Ritter, 1969). Systematic desensitization (a therapy technique involving relaxation training and imagined images of snakes) was also effective on some outcome measures, though to a lesser extent, compared to a control condition, in which untreated subjects did not improve. Improvements produced by therapy continued in the real world, enabling subjects to do things they hadn't been able to do before, such as hiking outdoors in areas where snakes might be encountered.

Other studies confirm that therapies based on learning principles are effective for various phobias, including agoraphobia, a fear of public places (Bandura, Adams, Hardy, & Howells, 1980). These findings contradict the prediction of psychoanalytic theory that only resolution of deep-seated unconscious conflicts could bring about a cure. Bandura (1961) argues that psychotherapy should be regarded as a learning process. More systematic application of learning principles (including reward, extinction, and discrimination learning, among others) can improve therapeutic outcomes.

Self-Efficacy

Bandura has proposed **self-efficacy** as a theoretical concept that can explain the effectiveness of various types of therapies for fears and avoidant behavior (Bandura, 1977, 1984a; Bandura, Adams, Hardy, & Howells, 1980). Self-efficacy means believing "that one can organize and execute given courses of action required to deal with prospective situations" (Bandura, 1980). A person who has a high self-efficacy expectation in a particular situation is confident of mastery. For example, a tennis player who believes his or her serve is reliably excellent has a high self-efficacy expectation. A person who doubts that he or she can do the required behavior has a low self-efficacy expectation. A stage-frightened performer, who believes the first lines will be spoken with a squeaky voice, suffers from low self-efficacy. High perceived self-efficacy leads to effort and persistence at a task, whereas low self-efficacy produces discouragement and giving up (Bandura, 1989b).

Therapy will succeed if it increases self-efficacy. Bandura stated that "treatments that are most effective are built on an empowerment model. If you really want to help people, you provide them with the competencies, build a strong self-belief, and create opportunities for them to exercise those competencies" (R.I. Evans, 1989, p. 16). Although therapies based on behavior models are most effective in treating phobias, other therapies, including psychoanalysis, have some benefits compared to no treatment at all. Bandura suggests that various therapies are effective for a common reason: They change dysfunctional expectancies. People avoid actions that they don't expect they are able to do. This low expectancy produces avoidance, including phobia (Bandura, 1986a, 1989a, 1991a).

Self-efficacy enhances the effectiveness of treatments for weight loss (Weinberg, Hughes, Critelli, England, & Jackson, 1984) and pain reduction (Dolce, 1987; Kores, Murphy, Rosenthal, Elias, & North, 1990). People high in self-efficacy are more likely to adhere to exercise programs (Desharnais, Bouillon, & Godin, 1986; Dzewaltowski, 1989) and to succeed if they try to quit smoking (Garcia, Schmitz, & Doerfler, 1990; Wojcik, 1988). Self-defense programs for women increase their self-efficacy, which leads participants to feel safer so that their mobility is no longer unreasonably restricted by fear (E.M. Ozer & Bandura, 1990). Programs to increase clients' ability to avoid relapse after giving up alcohol have been devised, using social learning principles to individualize treatment for each alcoholic's high-risk situations (Annis, 1990). Efficacy is also relevant to health-related prevention programs, including adolescents' resistance to using alcohol and other drugs (Hays & Ellickson, 1990). Bandura (1990a) recommends developing AIDS-prevention programs that recognize the importance of self-efficacy, which is particularly low among runaway teens (Kaliski, Rubinson, Lawrance, & Levy, 1990).

Students who have higher self-efficacy beliefs are more persistent in their academic work and achieve higher levels of academic performance (Multon, Brown, & Lent, 1991). Students with low self-efficacy are especially likely to perform better if they are instructed to set goals for each day's work (Tuckman, 1990). Cognitive-behavioral skills training can increase the self-efficacy expectancies of test-anxious college students, and higher academic performance follows (R.E. Smith, 1989).

Bandura measures self-efficacy specifically for a particular domain of behavior. A person may have high self-efficacy for one behavior (e.g., hitting home runs) and low for another (e.g., playing the piano well). Scales to measure self-efficacy in particular areas of behavior have been developed (Wells-Parker, Miller, & Topping, 1990). A public health survey confirms that health self-efficacy consists of several specific dimensions (nutrition, medical care, and exercise), as Bandura predicted, rather than one global dimension (Hofstetter, Sallis, & Hovell, 1990). Other researchers have suggested measuring general self-efficacy, a broad trait applicable to a variety of behaviors (Shelton, 1990; Sherer & Adams, 1983; Sherer, Maddux, Mercandante and others, 1982), although this is contrary to Bandura's model. As Bandura's model suggests, measures of efficacy that refer to a particular situation predict better than do global measures (Wollman & Stouder, 1991). Some areas of research on locus of control (Marshall, 1991b) or "hope" (Snyder and others, 1991) combine efficacy with expectations about the outcomes of behavior; here, too, measuring expectations in specific areas rather than globally leads to improved prediction.

Bandura distinguishes between *self-efficacy* (the belief that one has the ability to perform the behavior) and **outcome expectations** (see Figure 13.6). The latter refers to the belief that if the behavior is successfully done, it will lead to desirable outcomes. If I am confident that I can put my coins in a soda machine, but doubt that the machine will deliver my chosen soda, then I have low outcome expectations, despite high efficacy expectations. Obviously, both types of expectations must be high for a person to attempt behavior. Bandura suggests that phobias result from low efficacy expectations. A person with a fear of flying may be convinced that, if only it were possible to get on the plane, life would be improved by desirable recreational and business outcomes (high outcome expectation). As long as it seems impossible to board the plane and sit calmly in a seat during a flight (low efficacy expectation), the person will not be able to fly. Critics have questioned whether it is possible to consider self-efficacy expectations independently from outcome expectations (Eastman & Marzillier, 1984; Marzillier & Eastman, 1984), a criticism that Bandura (1984a, 1991a) rejects.

Behavioral therapies, according to Bandura, are the most efficient and effective ways of raising efficacy expectations and therefore are the treatment of choice for phobias. Other techniques may be effective, but only to the extent that efficacy expectations are raised. Even depth psychoanalysis can change dysfunctional expectancies, but slowly. After many months or years, a patient may come to expect that adult life will be improved, since problems are seen as stemming from childhood conflicts that are considered resolved. Some of the therapeutic alternatives for increasing efficacy expectations are listed in Figure 13.7.

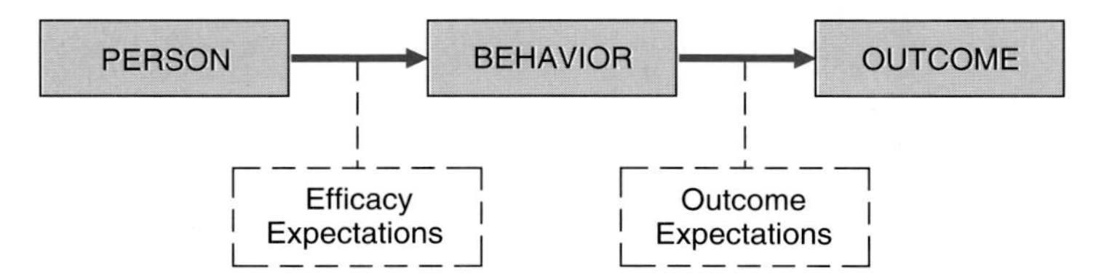

FIGURE 13.6 Diagrammatic Representation of the Difference Between Efficacy Expectations and Outcome Expectations

(From A. Bandura (1977). Self-efficacy: Toward a unifying theory of behavioral change. *Psychological Review*, 84, 191–215. Copyright 1977 by the American Psychological Association. Reprinted by permission.)

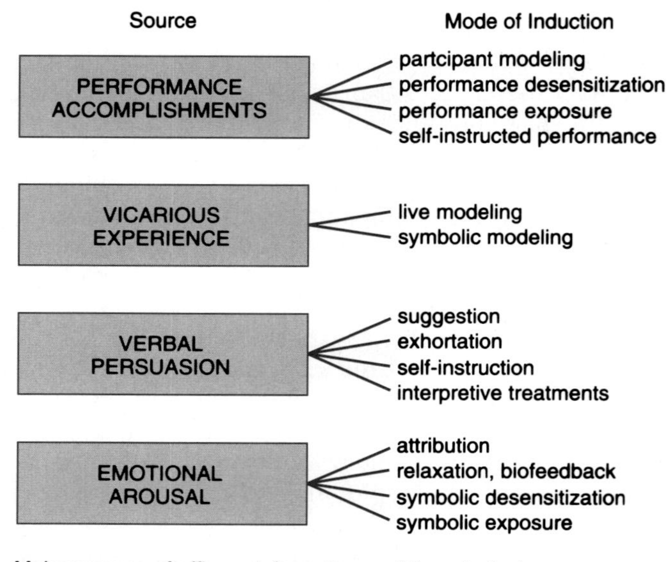

FIGURE 13.7 Changing Efficacy Expectations Through Therapy

(From A. Bandura (1977). Self-efficacy: Toward a unifying theory of behavioral change. *Psychological Review*, 84, 191–215. Copyright 1977 by the American Pscyhological Association. Reprinted by permission.)

Most studies of therapeutic outcomes simply relate exposure to the therapy with an outcome measure, and thus leave the specific processes of psychological change rather ambiguous. By detailed assessment of changes during therapy, Bandura demonstrated that self-efficacy was, in fact, the best predictor of improvement, even more predictive than past performance (Bandura, 1977) or autonomic responses indicating emotion. Examining the processes that are proposed to explain behavioral change in great detail is a *microanalysis* of the process, as opposed to a *macroanalysis,* which would look at only gross changes. Bandura's microanalysis allows more precise understanding of the processes that produce therapeutic outcomes. By showing that patients who increased self-efficacy also reduced their fear, Bandura provided a more exacting test of his theory than is usual (Bandura, Adams, & Beyer, 1977). Bandura's microanalysis has been criticized on statistical grounds (Kirsch, 1980); but Bandura (1980) has rebutted the criticism.

Other Research Related to Efficacy

The concept of efficacy has been applied to many areas of life. Low perceived self-efficacy is associated with negative emotions, including depression (Bandura, 1989a; Bandura, Adams, Hardy, & Howells, 1980; Davis-Berman, 1990). Efficacy—along with other social learning variables, reinforcement expectations and outcome expectations—is an important factor preventing job burnout (Meier, 1983). People with high efficacy expectations about computers are more likely to use them (Hill, Smith, & Mann, 1987). Politically active citizens score higher on a measure of political efficacy (Zimmerman, 1989). Mothers who are higher in self-efficacy for specific problems in caring for their infants were rated higher in maternal competence by observers who watched them interact with their children (Teti & Gelfand, 1991). A sense of efficacy can come not only from therapy, but also from the social support of others, as was demonstrated in a study of women's adjustment to abortion (Major, Cozzarelli, Sciacchitano and others, 1990).

Efficacy and Striving Toward Goals

Self-efficacy promotes striving toward goals. Occupational choice is influenced by efficacy. In a study of high school equivalency students, those who had a broader generality of self-efficacy considered a wider possible range of occupations; they also had a greater range of interests (Bores-Rangel, Church, Szendre, & Reeves, 1990). Athletes who are more confident perform better, and elite coaches use a variety of techniques to build such a sense of efficacy, including enhancing performance through instruction-drilling, modeling of confidence, and encouraging positive talk (Gould, Hodge, Peterson, & Giannini, 1989).

Bandura and Cervone (1986) studied self-efficacy and other self-reactive influences (self-evaluation and self-set goals) when subjects were confronted with manipulated feedback about their performance on a task. Subjects worked out for 5-minute periods on an ergometer, a type of exercise machine. They were given a goal of improving their effort by 50 percent. Manipulated performance scores indicated how they had done: considerably below the target, moderately below the target, slightly below the target, or slightly above the target. As one might expect, subjects rated their self-efficacy higher when they had been told their performance was better. There were, however, striking individual differences. While most subjects who were told that they had exceeded the target reported feeling efficacious, a small subgroup did not, and these subjects doubted they could repeat their good performance. Informed that they had fallen slightly short of the goal, some subjects were highly confident that they could reach it next time, while others doubted that they could. Thus, self-efficacy is influenced by performance feedback, but not all people respond in the same way.

Self-efficacy also promoted good performance among graduate students in business in simulated managerial decision making (Bandura & Wood, 1989; Wood, Bandura, & Bailey, 1990). The subjects were especially likely to develop high self-efficacy if they were led to believe that they could influence the simulated organization, and if the goals set for them were relatively easy to attain (Bandura & Wood, 1989). Their higher self-efficacy led them to use more effective analytic strategies to figure out how to make sound managerial decisions (supervising employees in such a way as to lead them to perform well). Ultimately, the performance of the organization was improved.

A sense of self-efficacy leads to persistence in the face of setbacks. Persistence, in turn, ultimately leads to greater success (Wood & Bandura, 1989b). Leading subjects in the managerial task to believe that performance is a skill that can be learned, rather than a stable ability trait, makes them more persistent, so that early failures do not lead to giving up (Wood & Bandura, 1989a) (see Figure 13.8). Efficacy is increased if subjects experience progressive mastery of a task, gradually improving their performance.

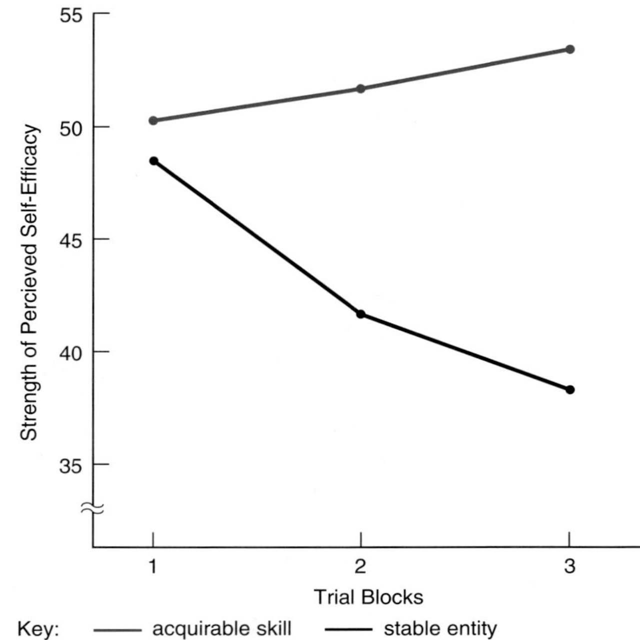

FIGURE 13.8 Changes in Strength of Perceived Managerial Self-Efficacy Across Trial Blocks under Acquirable Skill and Entity Conceptions of Ability

(From R. Wood & A. Bandura (1989). Impact of conceptions of ability on self-regulatory mechanisms and complex decision making. *Journal of Personality and Social Psychology*, 56, 407–415.)

This efficacy in turn improves later decision making (Bandura & Jourden, 1991).

At least under some circumstances, breaking a large task into smaller subgoals has beneficial effects on performance because it increases a sense of efficacy. Stock and Cervone (1990) found that subjects who worked toward proximal subgoals on complex problems had increased self-efficacy and persisted longer than those who worked only toward more remote goals. To understand the exact processes by which self-efficacy beliefs influence behavior, research should follow subjects over time. Sexton and Tuckman (1991) studied female college students on a series of mathematics tasks. Based on changes over time, they proposed that self-efficacy beliefs are especially important at the beginning of a task. Thereafter, the behaviors themselves become more important than cognitive variables.

Sex Differences and Race Differences in Efficacy

While most of the research conducted by Mischel and Bandura has sought to understand the *processes* of personality, their efforts have also uncovered interesting findings about group differences. Several studies report sex differences in self-perceptions of efficacy. Generally, males report higher self-efficacy than do females in a variety of areas. Poole and Evans (1989) found that male adolescents rated themselves higher in "coping with stressful situations, academic ability, health, success, and outgoing behavior," whereas females rated themselves higher only on "considerateness." Females tended to underestimate their own competence (Poole & Evans, 1989, p. 159). Among working women, those who scored high on the masculinity dimension of the Bem Sex Role Inventory had higher levels of self-efficacy than did those who scored lower on masculinity; they also reported less strain and anxiety and more problem-focused and preventive coping (Long, 1989). Female undergraduates with higher efficacy report greater willingness to engage in activities exploring nontraditional careers for women (Nevill & Schlecker, 1988). Long (1989) suggests that masculinity (as measured by the Bem Sex Role Inventory) and self-efficacy may not be independent concepts.

Black Americans, according to national survey data collected in 1980, have a lower sense of personal efficacy than do whites, although their self-esteem is not lower (Hughes & Demo, 1989). The researchers suggest this lower efficacy is due to institutionalized racial discrimination. Blacks are not given equal opportunities to experience success, which leads to a lower sense of efficacy. Nursing students who speak languages other than English as a native language were found to have lower self-efficacy on a subscale measuring Tendency to Avoid/Give Up, although they were not different from native English speakers on a Tendency to Persist scale (Keane & Morgan, 1991).

These studies provide evidence that a sense of efficacy is more prevalent among some social groups than among others (cf. Gecas, 1989), and it seems reasonable to conclude that different experiences in society have produced these differences in efficacy. In addition to individual efficacy, Bandura suggests that a sense of **collective efficacy** occurs when groups believe they, as a group, can do what needs to be done (R.I. Evans, 1989). Bandura's model of reciprocal determinism suggests that personal and collective efficacy will, in turn, have further effects on behavior and the situation.

Efficacy in Childhood and Across the Life Span

How does self-efficacy develop over the life span? Developmentalists ask this question (Berry, 1989). Ellen Skinner (1985) theorizes that activity, particularly in childhood, leads to a sense of control by providing information about how one's actions influence outcomes. In a series of studies, Chapman, Skinner, and colleagues investigated the development of several aspects of perceived control: control beliefs, means-ends beliefs, and agency beliefs. Their concept of *agency* corresponds to Bandura's concept of *efficacy* (E.A. Skinner, Chapman, & Baltes, 1988). By age 9 to 12 (grades 3 through 5), children differ in agency beliefs. These beliefs predict how engaged they are in school work (as rated by teachers), which in turn influences their grades and achievement scores (E.A. Skinner, Wellborn, & Connell, 1990). In second grade, agency beliefs are unrelated to cognitive performance, but the relationship increases through fourth and sixth grade (Chapman & Skinner, 1989; Chapman, Skinner, & Baltes, 1990). Beliefs about the reasons for other children's outcomes develop separately, with less emphasis on internal causes (E.A. Skinner, Schindler, & Tschechne, 1990). This finding is consistent with Bandura's concept of *self*-efficacy rather than generalized efficacy. A meta-analytic review of the literature confirms that the relationship between self-efficacy and behavior is significant in 26 studies of children under age 16, and that the relationship is stronger when brief periods (less than a day) intervene between the efficacy assessment and the behavior (Holden, Moncher, Schinke, & Barker, 1990).

Physiological Correlates of Efficacy

When a person has a low self-efficacy belief, the body as well as the mind responds. The autonomic nervous system is aroused (Bandura, Reese, & Adams, 1982). In one study, women phobic of spiders confronted spiders in the laboratory. Sometimes the task was one that subjects felt they had high efficacy to accomplish (e.g., seeing a spider at a distance); other tasks were more difficult. The women's level of efficacy predicted changes in plasma catecholamine secretion (epinephrine, norepinephrine, and dopac). When therapy increased their efficacy expectations, the physiological indicators also changed (Bandura, Taylor, Williams, Mefford, & Barchas, 1985).

Recently, Bandura and his colleagues investigated the relationship between perceived self-efficacy and the immune system. Stress can impair immune functioning, but when subjects who had snake phobias perceived that they had self-efficacy to control phobic stressors (due to an experimental manipulation), immune functioning was enhanced (Wiedenfeld, O'Leary, Bandura and others, 1990). Stressors can enhance or suppress immune functioning. In another study, when subjects in a laboratory had low self-efficacy about performing the tasks they were given, their endogenous opioid systems were activated (Bandura, Cioffi, Taylor, & Brouillard, 1988; Bandura, O'Leary, Taylor, Gauthier, & Gossard, 1987). Although these physiological changes produce resistance to pain, they also interfere with the immune system (Bandura, Cioffi, Taylor, & Brouillard, 1988).

The Promise of Cognitive Behaviorism as a Model of Humans

Mischel and Bandura have provided an important corrective to the field of personality, which had overemphasized individual differences and minimized the importance of the social context of behavior. They expanded learning theory by including cognitive variables. Bandura had published early work on performance standards for self-reinforcement in animals (Bandura, 1976; Bandura & Mahoney, 1974; Bandura, Mahoney, & Dirks, 1976; Mahoney & Bandura, 1972), but abandoned the animal model and moved to a cognitive theory. Radical behaviorists remain unconvinced that cognitive explanations are necessary. An unusual series of studies with pigeons is reported by Grosch and Neuringer (1981). Using carefully devised stimuli and reinforcement conditions designed to replicate Mischel's studies on delay of gratification, Grosch and Neuringer concluded that pigeon behavior is comparable to that of human children. Most psychologists, though, feel that cognitive social learning theory does describe real and uniquely human phenomena. This expansion makes behaviorism more convincing as a theoretical approach to humans.

Opposition to behavioral approaches derives from many people who find environmental determinism offensive to the concept of human freedom and choice. Bandura's concept of reciprocal determinism, however, provides a role for self-determination within a behaviorist model. Self-efficacy as a concept is consistent with philosophical concerns about free will and human agency (Gecas, 1989). Cognitive control and planning enable people to have some influence over their outcomes (e.g., Bandura, 1989a). Thought prevents humans from being pawns of environmental determinism. Instead, people are free to be "proactive, aspiring organisms" (Bandura, 1991a, p. 158). Bandura argues thus:

> It is within the framework of reciprocal determinism that the concept of freedom assumes meaning. . . . Because people's conceptions, their behavior, and their environments are reciprocal determinants of each other, individuals are neither powerless objects controlled by environmental forces nor entirely free agents who can do whatever they choose. (Bandura, 1978, pp. 356–357)

Freedom is defined as having options or choices (Bandura, 1974, 1986b). It is influenced at the personal level by such factors as an increase in competencies, and at the societal level by behavioral options and outcomes. Recognition of the importance of the social environment brings with it a mandate for psychology to apply its knowledge to what Bandura refers to as "human betterment" (1974, p. 867). Social forces can foster or impede individual development and can encourage or discourage desirable actions. Some of the social applications Bandura (e.g., 1986b) has addressed are media modeling of aggression, pornography, improvement of therapy techniques, smoking, and pollution. His theory has implications for a variety of vulnerable populations whose perception of control is threatened, including the ill, the elderly, children, and those who work at lower-level jobs (Thompson & Spacapan, 1991). A theory that has applied value in such diverse areas is surely worthy of the great respect it has received among psychologists today.

Summary

Mischel and Bandura, leading theorists in the cognitive social learning perspective, have expanded our understanding of cognition as an important variable in human personality. Mischel challenged the assumption of global personality traits that led to consistent behavior across many situations, finding inconsistency instead. Behavior is much more situationally variable than trait theory had assumed. Instead of traits, Mischel proposed *cognitive person variables,* including competencies, encoding strategies, and personal constructs (see Table 13.4).

TABLE 13.4 Contributions of Bandura and Mischel's Theory to Various Topics

Biological	Bandura found that self-efficacy improves immune functioning among phobic subjects.
Child Development	Children learn much through modeling processes, as demonstrated in research using children as subjects.
Adult Development	Learning can occur throughout life.
Mental Health	New therapies using modeling and other techniques have been found effective. Techniques increasing self-efficacy are effective.
Society	Modeling has major implications for society, especially TV violence.
Cognitive Processes	Cognitive processes (including expectancies and self-efficacy) are central to personality.
Individual Differences	Individuals differ in behaviors and in cognitive processes because of learning.

Mischel has investigated children's development of a capacity to delay gratification. Cognitive variables are important in this development. Children learn strategies such as thinking about something else in order to avoid impulsive behavior.

Bandura demonstrated that children are influenced by models of desirable and undesirable behavior. They can learn to delay gratification or to be aggressive by watching adults in real life and on television. Bandura has analyzed learning into four processes, allowing more precise prediction of when learning will occur. These four processes are: attentional processes, retention processes, motor reproduction processes, and motivational processes. Bandura's concept of *reciprocal determinism* describes the mutual influences among the person, the environment, and behavior.

Self-efficacy refers to the belief that one can perform a particular behavior. Extensive research shows that efficacy beliefs influence the choice and persistence of behavior. Efficacy beliefs can be increased in therapy, and this is the mechanism by which therapy is effective, according to Bandura.

ILLUSTRATIVE BIOGRAPHIES: Concluding Remarks

According to the cognitive social learning perspective, consistent characteristics of a personality are explained in terms of cognitive variables, such as competencies and expectancies, rather than traits. Self-efficacy is a particularly important concept for Bandura. He notes that many creative artists, including Gertrude Stein, Vincent Van Gogh, Frank Lloyd Wright, and Fred Astaire, encountered considerable rejection. Not all of these people achieved success in their own lifetimes. Self-efficacy afforded them the persistence to continue in the face of rejection (Bandura, 1989a). How does this concept, along with other social learning concepts, enlighten our understanding of Leonard Bernstein and Emily Dickinson?

Leonard Bernstein

Leonard Bernstein's attitude toward his conducting exudes confidence. He offended Rodzinski, for whom he was assistant conductor, by claiming credit for perhaps more than he was entitled (Peyser, 1987, p. 89), and was criticized in a newspaper review, by composer Virgil Thomson for his "career of sheer vainglory" (Peyser, 1987, p. 133). This confident attitude on the part of Bernstein, whatever it may be called colloquially (perhaps "egotism" or "chutzpah") exemplifies the psychological concept of *efficacy.* Learning theory predicts some situational specificity in behavior, and Bernstein's egotism, though broad, was not uniform across all manifestations. He tolerated no criticism of his conducting, but was less confident of his composition (Peyser, 1987, p. 312).

Where did Bernstein's sense of efficacy originate? Surely it did not come from echoing what he had been told by his father, who thought Lenny should join the business he had started. (His father had made money in the beauty supply business franchising a permanent wave machine.) Bernstein's father, in fact, questioned whether a musical career was a practical choice that would allow his son to earn a living. He did, though, provide financial support for music lessons, and even paid for his son to play the piano on the radio in 1934. A behavioral analysis, were adequate data available, could well find efficacy-enhancing communications even from an apparently discouraging father. Surely Leonard's mother supported his musicianship from childhood on, proclaiming her son's great talent. The role of innate talent and intelligence in contributing to this sense of efficacy is also clear, since in school and in his later musical career, Bernstein quickly learned difficult material.

Despite his choice of a career not approved by his father, Leonard Bernstein did achieve tremendous financial success, which his father had always regarded as important. Father and son both took pride in Leonard's financial success, suggesting a shared evaluation of money as having a high *subjective stimulus value*. Such "ends" are, in social learning theory, separable from the "means" (expectancies) over which they disagreed. Another, even more important reward for Leonard Bernstein was being visible, the center of attention, for which his appetite seemed insatiable (Peyser, 1987).

The musical style that Bernstein developed can also be traced to his experiences. Role models (Reiner, Koussevitzky, and Mitropoulos) influenced Bernstein's style. Peyser suggests that Bernstein's investment in particularly American musical forms, especially the influence of jazz, could be traced to his family's lack of involvement in music. Unlike musicians raised with the usual veneration of European musical influence, Bernstein "had begun so late and his family tie to European culture was so fragile that he never totally annihilated jazz from his creative life" (Peyser, 1987, p. 32). Though he could produce outstanding popular music, Bernstein did not wish to be known simply as the composer of *West Side Story*. He longed for the highest professional recognition, and felt this required that he compose serious music, not simply musical theater (see Peyser, 1987, p. 352). In social learning terms, such expectations about the consequences of behavior are termed *behavior-outcome expectancies*.

Music is, of course, a profession in which success is difficult to foresee. Bernstein developed *expectancies* early in his career that shaped the way he sought success. An early break came "not . . . through disciplined study, an audition, or a competition" (Peyser, 1987, p. 87), but rather from a favor of one well-placed musician (Rodzinski) for another (Koussevitzky) who asked that Bernstein be given a job. The "support of an influential person" (Peyser, 1987, p. 87) thus became associated with the expectancy of a better chance. Another situational factor that came to be associated with a high expectancy of success was media exposure. Early in his career he substituted for Bruno Walter, who was ill. This performance of the New York Philharmonic, broadcast over the radio, catapulted Bernstein to fame. Of course, had he conducted poorly, the event would have been disastrous. The quality of his achievement, though, is relevant to *efficacy expectancies*; the impact of the media, to *outcome expectancies*. Such an outcome expectancy contributed to Bernstein's insistence, later in his career, that many of his performances be recorded. Recognizing the importance of the media, he sought it. This behavior was consistent with his tendency, since childhood, to seek visibility (Peyser, 1987, pp. 346–347).

Bernstein expressed the expectation that making demands (for example, that two harps be provided, rather than only one, regardless of the extra expense) would be rewarded. "Don't worry. They respect you more when you make such demands," he is quoted as saying (Peyser, 1987, p. 344).

Bernstein may have married in order to improve his chances of acceptance in the music world, which then discriminated against homosexuals (Peyser, 1987, p. 176). Interpretation of Bernstein's open homosexuality in social learning terms is complex. Furthermore, since research into the roles of genetics and experience as determinants of homosexuality is still ongoing, it remains unclear how much a social learning interpretation needs to be supplemented by other, constitutional factors. Still, even if genetics plays a role in determining sexual orientation, there can be no doubt that learning influences the manner in which sexuality is socially expressed. Other conductors modeled homosexuality. Most were careful to avoid publicity about their homosexuality. One important exception, Mitropoulos, who was an early influence on Bernstein's conducting career and much admired by him, lived an openly homosexual lifestyle. Bernstein felt guilt over his homosexuality (Peyser, 1987, pp. 168–169) and attempted to abandon his homosexuality when he married. However, he returned to it and did not attempt to conceal his affairs, thus embarrassing his wife. Peyser suggests (1987, p. 421) that the rise of gay liberation as a movement supporting open homosexuality may have given Bernstein the courage finally to separate from his wife, ending his pretense of heterosexuality.

Clearly, then, modeling influenced the expression of Bernstein's sexual orientation. What of its origin? Here, biographical data are inadequate for an indisputable interpretation. One childhood incident is reported (Peyser, 1987, p. 432) in which Bernstein's mother discovered him and his sister engaged in sex play; she reacted punitively. This incident did not, however, end sexual expressiveness between the two, who remained close throughout life, so it seems doubtful that it could have produced a flight to homosexuality. It is plausible, but by no means certain, that forbidden partners (his sister and men) were themselves more attractive because of the attention they could produce in others. That would explain why Bernstein was not more discreet. His rebelliousness behavior in nonsexual matters is consistent with this interpretation. Bernstein produced indignation among strict Jews with his *Kaddish* (a composition including Hebrew prayers in a popularized rendition), among Christians with his *Mass,* and among patriots with *1600 Pennsylvania Avenue.* While some homosexuals may, then, choose their sexual orientation in spite of its social stigma, this interpretation suggests that others, perhaps including Leonard Bernstein, may find the social disapproval to be in itself rewarding.

Emily Dickinson

Like Leonard Bernstein, Emily Dickinson was drawn to effort in areas where she had a sense of efficacy. Mischel and Bandura ask, "What can a person do? What does the person believe he or she can do?" Talent in writing seemed to run in her family. She had always done well in school. She knew influential authors of her day and was encouraged by them in her writing. The more traditional areas for women left Emily Dickinson feeling far less than efficacious. Like many women, she nursed family members when they were ill, yet all around her she witnessed people dying despite such dedicated feminine care.

Mischel suggests several categories of *cognitive person variables* as an alternative to simply offering trait labels. Among *competencies,* we must clearly list Emily Dickinson's literary talents and her awareness of them. Her school years provided success sufficient to make her confident of her talent.

Emily Dickinson's reclusion is often attributed to a trait of introversion. Yet from a cognitive perspective, the interpretation is not so simple. Given that she knew she had a gift for writing and cared to develop it, what *prototypes* of this career were available to her? Male poets did not need to run households and care for sick relatives. Male poets were not expected to subordinate their writing to the needs of a spouse, if they married. She rejected marriage, according to her biographer (C.G. Wolff, 1988) to further her writing. Perhaps the prototype (if it is one) of a recluse seemed the best choice for a serious female poet of that era.

What would Emily have expected had she married (*behavior outcome expectancies*)? Common outcomes for women at that time included exhausting work running households and the dangers of pregnancy, in an age when infants and sometimes their mothers frequently died in childbirth or soon thereafter.

Some of Emily Dickinson's behavior may have been modeled after her own mother, who was also disinclined to be sociable. In such a household, surely Emily would not have been expected to develop extroverted social behaviors so much as she might with a different maternal model. (Social learning theory does not, however, consider possible constitutional bases for such behavior.)

Bandura's concept of *reciprocal determinism* requires that we consider the person, the environment, and behavior as all mutually influencing one another. The poet's behavior of writing, of withdrawing from society and family simply to write, influenced her personality, and did not simply follow from it. Just as Leonard Bernstein's successes in conducting shaped his confidence and his motivations, so did Emily Dickinson's more private experiences of success, when she recognized (as she must have) the beauty of her verse, shape her sense of self, leading to self-confidence and increased commitment to her vocation.

GLOSSARY

attentional processes noticing the model's behavior (a prerequisite for learning by modeling)

consistency paradox the mismatch between intuition, which says that people are consistent, and research findings, which say they are not

cognitive person variables cognitive factors within a person, less global than traits, which influence how an individual adapts to the environment

collective efficacy the sense that a group can do what is to be done

competencies person variables concerned with what a person is able to do

delay of gratification the ability to give up immediate gratifications for larger, more distant rewards

encoding strategies person variables concerned with how a person construes reality

expectancies subjective beliefs about what will happen in a particular situation (including behavior outcomes, stimulus outcomes, and self-efficacies)

interactionism the approach to personality that stresses the combined effects of personality and situations in determining behavior

modeling learning by observing others; also called "vicarious learning"

motivational processes deciding whether it is worthwhile to behave as a model has behaved

motor reproduction processes being able to do what one has seen a model do

outcome expectations the belief about what desirable or undesirable things will happen if a behavior is successfully performed

prototype a typical example of an object or type of person; a "fuzzy concept" typical of the categories people use in perceiving others

reciprocal determinism the interacting mutual influences of the person, the environment, and the behavior

retention processes remembering what a model has done

self-efficacy subjective beliefs about what a person will be able to do

self-regulatory systems and plans ways that a person works on complicated behavior (e.g., by setting goals and by self-criticism)

self-system cognitive structures and subfunctions for perceiving, evaluating, and regulating behavior (not a psychic agent that controls action)

subjective stimulus value how much an outcome is valued by an individual

vicarious learning learning by observing others, without being directly rewarded oneself

STUDY QUESTIONS

1. Explain the term *cognitive* in *cognitive social learning theory.* What does this theory include that other learning theories (such as Skinner's) do not?
2. Summarize the trait controversy and Mischel's role in it.
3. Explain what Mischel meant by *cognitive person variables.* Give examples.
4. Define *self-efficacy.* Why are self-efficacy expectancies important?
5. Summarize research on delay of gratification.
6. Explain the concept of *interactionism.*
7. Summarize Bandura's research on modeling. Explain the relevance of this research for personality development.
8. List and explain the four processes that influence learning, as described by Bandura. Give an example of each.
9. Diagram and explain Bandura's concept of *reciprocal determinism.* Discuss how this concept is different from Skinner's concept of environmental determinism.
10. What has cognitive social learning theory contributed to psychotherapy?
11. Explain why cognitive social learning theory is more readily accepted by many people as a model of human personality than is Skinnerian behaviorism.

CHAPTER 14

George Kelly: The Psychology of Personal Constructs

BIOGRAPHY OF GEORGE KELLY

George Kelly

George A. Kelly was born in 1905 on a farm in Perth, Kansas, the only child in a family headed by a Presbyterian minister.

Kelly first studied engineering, but changed to education, completing his degree at the University of Edinburgh, Scotland, in 1930. In graduate school he turned his attention "to learn[ing] something about sociology and labor relations" (Kelly, 1963a, p. 47). While a graduate student, he taught in many nonpsychological fields, including oratory, public speaking, dramatics, and government. Kelly's first reading of Freud led to "the mounting feeling of incredulity that anyone could write such nonsense, much less publish it. It was not the pan-sexualism that makes Freud objectionable to some new readers, but the elastic meanings and arbitrary syntax that disturbed me" (1963a, p. 47). Kelly reported spending only nine months studying psychology before completing his doctorate at the University of Iowa. This left him free to develop a theory that was quite original, not closely tied to that of any earlier theorist.

For 12 years, Kelly taught at a small college in western Kansas. Although his training was in education rather than clinical psychology, he saw many students in a free counseling clinic that he set up, and which became the laboratory for his emerging theory. He served as a traveling psychologist for many rural Kansas schools during this time, and so should be recognized as a school psychologist, though this is usually overlooked (Guydish, Jackson, Markley, & Zelhart, 1985). Also often forgotten is his early use of bipolar adjective ratings, which did not become popular until many years later (J.T. Jackson, Markley, Zelhart, & Guydish, 1988). He reports that he never, even later, charged for his consultations. Kelly was aware of the impact of the Great Depression on his students, but he felt that psychology had an important role, "to generate the imagination needed to envision . . . possibilities" of overcoming the limitations of circumstances (1963a, p. 50). Thus, despite his scientific background as an engineer, the dramatist's imagination played an important role in his sense of what psychology should be, and he integrated this approach with science. As he alternated between seeing clients and supervising graduate students, Kelly came to view both as doing similar cognitive work. "Man-the-scientist" became his metaphor for therapeutic work.

After a year at the University of Maryland, Kelly moved to Ohio State University, where he took Carl Rogers's former position heading the clinical training program. It was there he wrote his two-volume work, *The Psychology of Personal Constructs* (1955), explaining his theory and its clinical implications.

Kelly influenced the training of clinicians not only in Ohio and Kansas, but nationwide. He was president of the American Board of Examiners for Professional Psychologists from 1951 to 1953, a member of the Special Advisory Group for the Veterans Administration from 1955 to 1960, and a member of the Training Committee of the National Institute for Mental Health and the National Institutes of Health from 1958 to 1967. In the final year of his life, he accepted the invitation of Abraham Maslow to accept a position at Brandeis University. Kelly died on March 6, 1967.

ILLUSTRATIVE BIOGRAPHIES

Kelly's approach is well suited to a narrative understanding of people's lives, to telling the stories of lives (Harvey, 1989; G.S. Howard, 1988; Mair, 1988). His personal construct theory has been applied to the understanding of political debates in South Africa (duPreez, 1975). The concept of cognitive complexity, which derives from Kelly's theory, has been applied to political debate in Israel (Maoz, 1987; Maoz & Shayer, 1987; S.G. Walker, 1987). Allport's classic case study, *Letters from Jenny,* has been reinterpreted from a personal construct perspective by Feixas and Villegas (1991), who have outlined a method for analyzing autobiographical texts such as this in terms of personal construct theory.

Richard Nixon

Richard Milhous Nixon, born in 1913, was elected the 37th president of the United States (1969–1974). His administration was widely praised for increasing contact with Communist China, but most Americans remember him for the disgrace that ended his presidency. He resigned under the threat of impeachment for the Watergate scandal, a bungled act of political espionage that he tried to cover up.

Richard Nixon was the second child of five boys. His older brother, Arthur, died of meningitis in 1925, and a younger brother, Harold, died of tuberculosis in 1933. Nixon was raised (after age 9) in Whittier, California, where he worked in the family store. His mother's family was Quaker, and this background influenced his upbringing by emphasizing emotional control, modesty, and hard work. His father (not a Quaker) was more emotional and punitive, and Nixon became interested in politics because of his influence (Ambrose, 1987). At times, Nixon avoided his father when the atmosphere became too tense, often going off somewhere alone to read.

Nixon enjoyed debate. His first formal debate was in seventh grade (Ambrose, 1987, p. 39). He continued with this interest at Whittier College. (Though he had been admitted to Harvard University and awarded a scholarship there, he could not afford to attend. His brother's bout with tuberculosis had been costly.) After college, Nixon attended Duke University Law School on a scholarship; he was an excellent student. He later became an attorney in California. During World War II, Nixon volunteered for the Navy, though as a Quaker he would have qualified for conscientious objector status. He was popular in this structured environment. He was also very good at poker, winning enough to start a political campaign for Congress when the war ended.

Elected to public office, Nixon became nationally known for his role in the House Committee on Un-American Activities, where he forcefully investigated Alger Hiss, who had served in the State Department, for his secret Communist associations and espionage activities. Nixon served in the House and then in the Senate before becoming vice-president under Dwight Eisenhower (1953–1961). He had a reputation for dirty campaign tactics and was disliked by many because of his personality, seeming to be insincere and calculating (Ambrose, 1987). In 1960, Nixon lost a close election for the presidency to John F. Kennedy, and two years later he lost a bid to become governor of California. He seemed to have retired from politics. However, he garnered the Republican presidential nomination in 1968 and won the general election that November.

As president, Richard Nixon grappled with the Vietnam War, but like his predecessor, Lyndon Johnson, he could not easily end it. He opened diplomatic relations with Communist China and signed an historic Strategic Arms Limitation Treaty with the Soviet Union. Despite these bold initiatives in foreign policy, most Americans remember Nixon primarily for the Watergate scandal. It began as a fumbled political espionage caper, with burglars hired by the Committee to Reelect the President breaking into the Washington, D.C., headquarters of the Democratic National Committee at the Watergate apartment-office complex. As the case developed, the break-in became less salient than Nixon's involvement in a coverup of the operation. Ultimately, threatened with impeachment, Richard Nixon resigned from office on August 9, 1974 (Woodward & Bernstein, 1976).

Many psychological analyses of Richard Nixon have been published, and various theories have been explored to understand him (Renshon, 1975), including psychoanalysis (e.g., Brown, 1978; J.W. Hamilton, 1977; Mazlish, 1972), Jungian theory (Greene, 1976), and a motivational approach derived from Murray's theory (Winter & Carlson, 1988). Kelly's theory differs from these by focusing on the cognitions of the person being studied. What did Nixon think? His personality cannot be understood, according to Kelly's approach, without grappling with this question.

THE PSYCHOLOGY OF PERSONAL CONSTRUCTS

George Kelly proposed a theory of personality that emphasized cognition. When it was proposed, it was outside the mainstream of psychology. Despite the fact that a cognitive revolution has taken place within psychology, Kelly's theory is still relatively isolated from other theories, perhaps because of its idiographic emphasis and its teleological orientation (Howard, 1988). Some argue that it is not even a cognitive theory (W.G. Warren, 1990a, 1990b), and Kelly (1955) agreed. He argued for a holistic, even humanistic (Kelly, 1969) integration of "cognition" with other processes, usually separately considered as "emotional" and "motivational."

George Kelly proposed what he called a **jackass theory** of personality. By this, he meant that the theory concerns the "nature of the animal," rather than the environmental forces that push ("pitchfork theories") or pull the individual ("carrot theories") (Kelly, 1958).

Drawing upon his experiences as both a clinician and a faculty member in a research discipline, Kelly developed a metaphor of personality that described a human being as a scientist. Just as a scientist uses theories to plan observations, a human uses **personal constructs** to predict what will happen in life. Like a scientist seeking a theory with maximum predictive ability, the person tries to develop concepts that will make personal life, especially in the realm of interpersonal relationships, most predictable. Accurate predictions permit control. The person, like the scientist, finds that predictions are not always confirmed by experience, and so must sometimes revise these personal concepts. This, then, is Kelly's metaphor of **man-the-scientist** (1955, p. 4).

Broadly speaking, Kelly's view is similar to that of Alfred Adler. In fact, he published some of his work in the Adlerian journal, *Individual Psychology* (Kelly, 1963b, 1964) and, like Adler, cited the philosopher Hans Vaihinger (Kelly, 1964). People are not pawns in the face of reality. They make their own destiny. They do this by how they interpret events.

Carol Burnett

The famous comedienne Carol Burnett was raised by her mother and her grandmother, to whom she was especially close. Her family was poor. Her parents were separated. She had fond memories of her father, though he was alcoholic and only occasionally visited. (For a time he was treated in a sanatorium for tuberculosis.) Carol grew up in a crowded one-room apartment in Hollywood with her mother and younger sister; her grandmother had another apartment in the building.

As a child, Carol Burnett acted as part of her playing. She loved to imitate radio broadcasts. Once she fooled a neighbor for hours by pretending to be her own (fictional) twin sister. At Hollywood High School, she wrote for the school paper about famous actors who had attended the school. She attended the University of California at Los Angeles (UCLA), majoring in Theater Arts and winning great acclaim for comic roles in Music Department performances. After a few semesters, an anonymous benefactor provided a loan to enable her to try to launch her career in New York. She went East, struggled, and made her own break by organizing other beginning actresses to put on their own show in order to be seen by agents. Within five years she was able to repay her benefactor's loan. Performances on Gary Moore's television show made Carol Burnett nationally known.

How is it that a poor child with two alcoholic parents, separated, supported by welfare, rose to stardom? Kelly's theory suggests that the way a person thinks about her or his interpersonal world is a key to the answer.

Constructive Alternativism

Kelly makes the philosophical position behind his theory explicit: "We assume that all of our present interpretations of the universe are subject to revision or replacement" (1955, p. 15). He calls this assumption **constructive alternativism**.

Rather than being *determined,* as stimulus-response theories and psychoanalytic theory assume, people are free, to the extent that they are able to construct alternate "interpretations of the universe." Kelly's theory suggests some alternatives, helping people revise their construct systems, and thus their personalities, in order to become more adaptive.

The theory is stated clearly and explicitly in 12 succinct statements. (Kelly wrote at a time in American psychology when formal theoretical statements were in vogue.) These dozen statements consist of one *Fundamental Postulate* and eleven *corollaries.*

The Fundamental Postulate

Kelly's **Fundamental Postulate** states:

> A person's processes are psychologically channelized by the ways in which he anticipates events. (Kelly, 1955, p. 46)

If events occur as they are anticipated, then **validation** has occurred. If not, there has been *invalidation* (Landfield, 1988). This cycle of construing events and having the construction confirmed or not is repeated, sometimes with revision of the construct system (see Figure 14.1).

Kelly pointed out that, in this starting point for his theory, he did not find it necessary to postulate some motivation or force to get a person moving. That is, no motivational theory was necessary: no concept akin to Freud's "libido" or learning theorists' "reward." The person is already active, and the direction of this activity is determined by "the ways in which he anticipates events." Thus the person is actively adapting in a future-oriented way. To continue with his "man-the-scientist" metaphor, the person is hypothesizing future events as best he or she can.

This omission of motivation from Kelly's theory has been criticized (Henry & Maze, 1989). It did, however, focus attention on the phenomenological experience of the individual, rather than on abstract and unobservable theoretical constructs (cf. B.M. Walker, 1990).

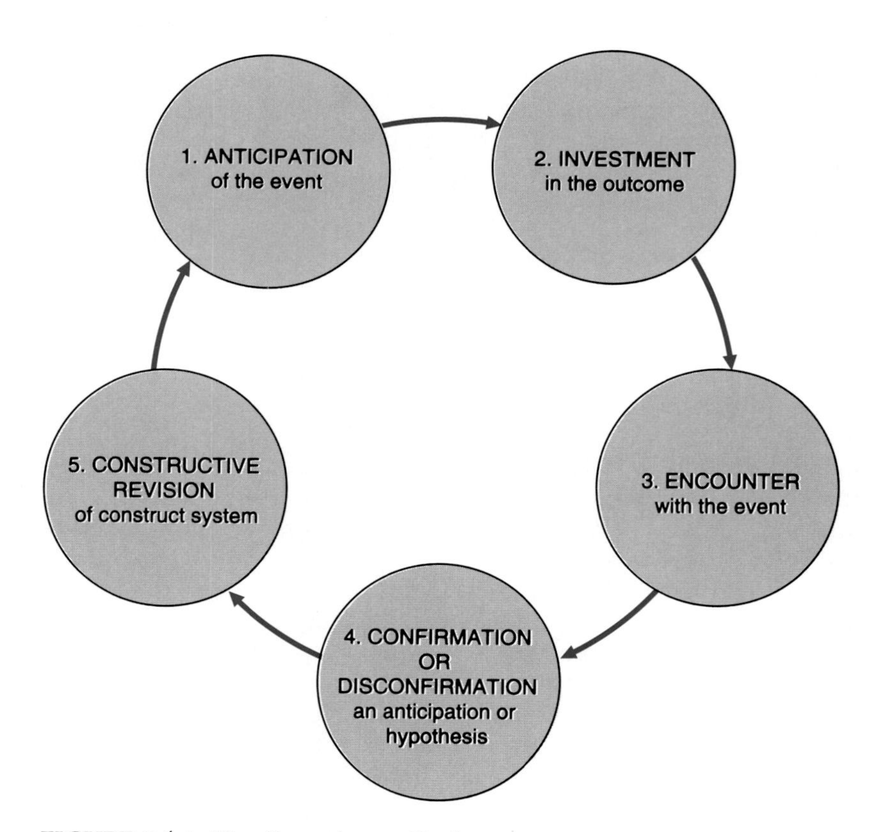

FIGURE 14.1 The Experience Cycle
(From R.A. Neimeyer, 1985b.)

The Process of Construing

Four of Kelly's corollaries explain the process of construing (R.A. Neimeyer, 1987).

The Construction Corollary

According to the **Construction Corollary**:

> A person anticipates events by construing their replications. (Kelly, 1955, p. 50)

Events, more or less similar, happen repeatedly, and we plan for the future based upon the lessons of the past. Of course, there is always some difference. Events do not repeat themselves exactly. Nonetheless, adaptation would be impossible if we did not identify sufficient similarity among events to allow prediction of the future. We accomplish this by applying *constructs* to various "events."

"Events" is a broad, inclusive term. It can be applied to "events" in the usual sense of the term. For example, saying "New Year's Eve is a time for celebration" exemplifies applying the construct "a time for celebration" to the event "New Year's Eve." Most often, though, Kelly's concept of "events" is used to refer to people. Thus if we say that "Hitler was disturbed" we are applying the construct "disturbed" to the event (in this case a person) "Hitler."

The language of "constructs" and "prediction" sounds quite cognitive and has been criticized as being overly intellectualized, ignoring the emotional side of human experience (Bruner, 1956; Rogers, 1956). Kelly intended these processes to be understood more broadly (cf. J. Adams-Webber, 1990). Unverbalized and unconscious anticipations are also included. Kelly refers to a **preverbal construct** as "one which continues to be used even though it has no consistent word symbol" (1955, p. 459). Constructs may be experienced as emotions (Landfield & Epting, 1987, p. 15). If a person becomes tense every time his or her father is present, that is evidence for a construct relating to the father, even if the individual is unaware of any ideas about it and cannot verbalize a construct. While such unverbalized constructs are more difficult to uncover, even for a Kellian therapist, they are important personality influences. Many psychosomatic disorders result from unverbalized constructs; the body expresses constructs in its own language.

The Experience Corollary

The **Experience Corollary** is Kelly's statement of a developmental principle. It says:

> A person's construction system varies as he successively construes the replications of events. (Kelly, 1955, p. 72)

Briefly, people change with experience. The directions of this change vary individually and can be understood from the other corollaries. They may include such changes as elaboration of constructs, constriction, and slot movement. Though the directions of change vary widely from person to person, Kelly asserted that the person is not static. Change occurs. Personality is not unchanging.

Perhaps Kelly's theory is as interesting for what he does *not* say about change. Some theorists have proposed universal stages of development (e.g., Freud and Erikson); Kelly does not. Nor does he emphasize the role of the environment in producing change.

The Choice Corollary

Kelly's **Choice Corollary** states:

> A person chooses for himself that alternative in a dichotomized construct through which he anticipates the greater possibility for extension and definition of his system. (Kelly, 1955, p. 64)

The person, in Kelly's terminology, always makes "the **elaborative choice**" (1955, p. 65). Sometimes the elaborative choice involves *extension* of the construct system. In the absence of threat we may explore and experiment, developing new constructs in the process. The opposite, *constriction,* may happen under threat, when existing constructs no longer predict accurately. The ultimate constriction is suicide.

It is not easy to predict what choice an individual will make. The elaborative choice may take various forms, as Kelly notes:

> One may anticipate events by trying to become more and more certain about fewer and fewer things or by trying to become vaguely aware of more and more things on the misty horizon. (Kelly, 1955, p. 67)

With a detailed understanding of a particular individual's constructs, the therapist can make an educated guess of the direction a person will move when currently operating choices cease being validated. This may offer an advance warning of dangerous change. On the positive side, a therapist armed with such information can use planned invalidation of currently operative constructs to trigger change in a client, when it is judged that such change would be in a safe and desirable direction.

The Modulation Corollary

How extensively can a person's constructs be applied to new experiences? That is the question addressed by Kelly's **Modulation Corollary**:

> The variation in a person's construction system is limited by the permeability of the constructs within whose ranges of convenience the variants lie. (Kelly, 1955, p. 77)

A construct that can be applied to new elements is called a **permeable construct**:

> A construct is permeable if it will admit to its range of convenience new elements which are not yet construed within its framework. (Kelly, 1955, p. 79)

For example, assume a person thinks of many people as "trustworthy versus not trustworthy." Several family members and friends are construed as trustworthy; a few family members and some acquaintances are construed as not trustworthy. Now the person meets someone new. Will he or she be able to think of this person as either trustworthy or not trustworthy? If so, the construct is permeable.

Permeable constructs are useful for dealing with new experiences. This is especially true of *superordinate constructs.* If experience does not confirm existing constructs, permeable superordinate constructs permit adaptation. For a religious person, "God's will" is such a permeable superordinate construct, covering everything from birth and success to death and war.

The opposite of a permeable construct is a **concrete construct**. It is not open to new elements. For example, most people regard the "age of miracles" as past, even those who accept that miracles once occurred (Kelly, 1955, p. 1076). Kellian therapists may deal with problematic constructs (or poles) by working with a client to make these more concrete, impermeable, so that they, with their devastating effects, will not be applied to new experiences.

The Structure of Construct Systems

Four of Kelly's corollaries explain the structure of construct systems (R.A. Neimeyer, 1987).

The Dichotomy Corollary

Constructs are always bipolar. Kelly's **Dichotomy Corollary** states:

> A person's construction system is composed of a finite number of dichotomous constructs. (Kelly, 1955, p. 59)

"Good-bad," "popular-unpopular," "intelligent-stupid," and so on are examples of dichotomous constructs. The poles are referred to as the *likeness* end and the *contrast* end because of the way they are measured in the REP test (discussed later in the chapter). The likeness end is generally most used, and describes how several people are seen to be alike. The contrast end tells how other people are seen as different.

Either one pole or the other may be applied to an event (person). It is also possible for the construct itself to be deemed irrelevant to the person (see the Range Corollary below), and neither pole applicable to a particular event. The nature of an individual's dichotomies may come as a surprise to the individual. It is generally the contrast end that is less available, or *submerged.*

When people change, especially in response to stress, the dichotomous nature of constructs has important predictive implications for Kellian therapists. Under stress, people often change from one pole to the opposite pole of a dichotomous construct. Kelly offers the example of a client who changes from "kindly" to "hostile" (1955, p. 938). Such changes from one pole to another are called **slot movement**. Kellian therapists are especially attentive to the client's often unstated opposites, since these are directions in which change may occur, especially when stress (either in therapy or in the world) makes current patterns inadequate. According to Landfield and Epting, the "elevation of contrast to a paramount position in theory could become one of Kelly's most profound contributions to science" (1987, p. 17).

Both poles of the construct must be understood from the individual's point of view. Often dichotomies are not strictly "logical." The opposite of "ambitious," for example, may be "happy." Dichotomies also vary from one person to another. Landfield (1982) cites the example of two people with quite different contrasts to "liveliness". For one, the contrast was "exhaustion"; for the other, "suicide." The implications of these different dichotomous constructs hardly need elaboration.

The Organization Corollary

Having many constructs, a person must have some way of selecting the relevant one or ones to anticipate various events. As an effective mechanic keeps his (or her) tools well-organized, so a person keeps his or her constructs organized. (The comparison is apt, since constructs are, after all, tools for psychological adaptation to the world.)

According to the **Organization Corollary**,

> Each person characteristically evolves, for his convenience in anticipating events, a construction system embracing ordinal relationships between constructs. (Kelly, 1955, p. 56)

Some constructs are **superordinate** and apply, broadly, to several lower-order constructs. Superordinate constructs are more abstract. The superordinate concept "vegetables" encompasses several lower-order concepts: carrots, beans, corn, and so on. If some things are true of all vegetables (for example, they provide vitamins and little fat), it is more convenient to have a superordinate concept than to have only more limited constructs.

Well-chosen constructs help prevent incorrect anticipations. Consider the case of the poisonous mushroom. Developing subcategories of "edible mushrooms" and "poisonous mushrooms" is adaptive, and potentially lifesaving. Similarly, constructs about people may need to be elaborated in such a hierarchical arrangement to improve adaptation. For example, we distinguish between trustworthy people and con artists.

The term **core constructs** refers to constructs central to a person's identity and existence (Kelly, 1955, p. 482). They are the stabilizing elements within personality, and they are slower to change than less comprehensive **peripheral constructs**.

Developing more superordinate, abstract concepts helps a person to transcend contradictions. These higher-order constructs vary from person to person. "One man may resolve the conflicts between his anticipations by means of an ethical system. Another may resolve them in terms of self-preservation" (Kelly, 1955, p. 56). If these core constructs are not adaptive, it may be possible for therapy to change them. This is not true of education, which deals with peripheral constructs (Kelly, 1955, p. 483).

The Fragmentation Corollary

Kelly's **Fragmentation Corollary** helps us to understand inconsistency:

> A person may successively employ a variety of construction subsystems which are inferentially incompatible with each other. (Kelly, 1955, p. 83)

Not all of a person's constructs are operative at the same moment. Like serial monogamists, our fidelity does not span time. This potential for fragmentation suggests that observers may err if they infer personality from a limited sample of behavior.

The Range Corollary

Any construct has only limited usefulness. Kelly's **Range Corollary** states:

> A construct is convenient for the anticipation of a finite range of events only. (Kelly, 1955, p. 68)

The **range of convenience** of a construct refers to the events to which it applies. If either pole of a dichotomous construct describes the event (or person), then that event is within the range of convenience of the construct. Apples, bananas, yogurt, and Cholesterol Clusters are all within the range of convenience of the dichotomous construct "nutritious food versus junk food"; but "cement" is outside of the range of convenience of this construct. Examples with personal constructs are more problematic, because each of us has somewhat different constructs. Most people, probably, would agree that Saddam Hussein, Hitler, and Mother Teresa are within the range of convenience of the construct "villain versus saint." They might disagree whether other individuals (Magic Johnson? Charlie Brown?) fall within the scope of this construct.

The Social Embeddedness of Construing Efforts

Finally, three corollaries place the construing process in its social context (R.A. Neimeyer, 1987).

The Individuality Corollary

Kelly's **Individuality Corollary** states:

> Persons differ from each other in their constructions of events. (Kelly, 1955, p. 55)

It is in these constructions that individual differences, so important for any personality theory, are to be found. They are not to be found in different environments or different histories. Only through the construction processes of individuals do such external events have an effect.

The Commonality Corollary

While each person is unique, there are some similarities from person to person. Kelly's **Commonality Corollary** suggests where we should look for them.

> To the extent that one person employs a construction of experience which is similar to that employed by another, his psychological processes are similar to those of the other person. (Kelly, 1955, p. 90)

In contrast to what one might infer from other theories, similarity between persons is not a necessary consequence of similar experiences. It is the sense that has been made of that experience that is critical. (In this, Kelly sounds Adlerian.)

The Sociality Corollary

Kelly's theory emphasizes interpersonal relationships. This last corollary addresses such relationships and provides the key for Kellian therapists to enable them to establish a therapeutic relationship with their clients. The **Sociality Corollary** states:

> To the extent that one person construes the construction processes of another, he may play a role in a social process involving the other person. (Kelly, 1955, p. 95)

Note that psychological similarity, addressed in the preceding Commonality Corollary, is not necessary for a social interaction to occur. Understanding, rather than similarity, is necessary. This understanding may be mutual, as between two friends. Or it may be unilateral, as between a parent and child, or a therapist and client. If, however, neither person can "construe the construction processes" of the other, a social process is not possible. This mutual construction failure may occur, for example, between a psychotic and a "normal" person, or between two people from vastly differing backgrounds.

Kelly defines *role* as "a psychological process based upon the role player's construction of aspects of the construction systems of those with whom he attempts to join in a social enterprise" (1955, p. 97).

The Role Construct Repertory (REP) Test

Kelly devised a measuring instrument to assess a person's constructs. This **Role Construct Repertory Test**, referred to as the **REP test**, is easily adapted to particular clients. It has been widely used in research as well as in clinical and applied settings.

The REP test identifies the constructs a person uses to understand others. The first step in the REP test is to list several particular people with whom the client (or subject) is acquainted. (See Table 14.1 for an example of such a list.) The subject is sometimes, but not always, included on this list.

Next, three of the persons identified are selected by the researcher. The subject is instructed to identify one way in which two of these individuals are the same, and different from the third. The word or phrase used by the subject to identify how two individuals are the same is termed the *construct.* The word or phrase used to describe how the third person is different is termed the *contrast.* In keeping with Kelly's theory, these do not need to be logical opposites, and often they are not. Additional constructs are elicited by repeating the preceding step for several different triads of persons. Some subjects repeat constructs, exactly or approximately. Examples of constructs elicited by one subject, a therapy client, are presented in Figure 14.2.

After several constructs have been elicited (which may include duplicates), the subject is instructed to consider each person for every construct-contrast, and to indicate whether or not the construct applies to the person. This creates a grid, rating each person on every construct.

Even without further analysis, the grid and list of constructs may offer insights. A great deal of thought goes into the identification of constructs, and even the subject (or client) may be surprised to learn what constructs come to mind through this technique. A clinician may use these results to identify material for further exploration in psychotherapy sessions.

TABLE 14.1 Role Specifications for One Version of the REP Test

1. Mother
2. Father
3. Brother
4. Sister
5. Spouse (or girlfriend/boyfriend)
6. Same-sex friend
7. Work partner who disliked you
8. Person you feel uncomfortable with
9. Someone you would like to know better
10. Teacher whose viewpoint you accepted
11. Teacher whose viewpoint was objectionable
12. Unsuccessful person
13. Successful person
14. Happy person
15. Unhappy person

(Adapted from Landfield & Epting, 1987, p. 33, who give more detailed descriptions of these roles.)

The grid, however, practically begs for mathematical analysis. A variety of scoring methods have been devised (J.R. Adams-Webber, 1970; Bannister & Fransella, 1966; Bannister, Fransella & Agnew, 1971; Fransella & Bannister, 1977; Jankowicz & Thomas, 1982–1983; Leitner & Cado, 1982; Slater, 1977). Naturally, measurement issues have been debated (e.g., Soldz & Soldz, 1989). The derived scores may sometimes be mathematical artifacts rather than psychologically meaningful measures (Chambers, Grice, & Fourman, 1987), and so must be empirically validated—for example, by comparing grid analyses with clinical judgments (e.g., Chambers, Olson, Carlock, & Olson, 1986).

Constructs are judged to be similar or different not simply from the verbal labels but also from the way they are applied to the persons being rated. For example, a person may propose two constructs, "rich–poor" and "happy–unhappy." The words alone do not reliably disclose whether these are entirely different constructs. If all (or nearly all) of the individuals rated as "rich" are also rated as "happy," while all or nearly all of those rated as "poor" are also rated as "unhappy," then these are essentially the same construct, though with more than one way of referring to them in words. On the other hand, little overlap may occur in the use of the constructs. There may be many "happy, rich" persons, many "unhappy, rich" persons, and similarly a large number of both happy and unhappy poor persons. In this case, clearly two constructs have been elicited.

The more that different constructs are elicited, the more cognitively complex the individual. The **cognitive complexity** of a person is reflected by the number of different constructs elicited (Bieri, 1955). Many measures of cognitive complexity based on the REP test have been proposed, and they do not necessarily correlate with one another (W.H. Crockett, 1982). In addition, some researchers have studied cognitive complexity using measures not derived from the REP test or from Kelly's theory (e.g., J.D. Campbell, Chew, & Scratchley, 1991; Lennon & Davis, 1987; Pratt, Pancer, Hunsberger,

Response Sheet

#	Column 1	Mother	Father	Happy Person	Successful Person	Andy (self)	Brian (son)	Mike (son)	Sharon (wife)	Beth (lover)	Therapist	Column 2	#
1	Someone I love	1	**1**	1	1	2	**1**	1	1	1	**1**	Someone I hate	1
2	Lack sensitivity	**1**	2	**1**	2	2	**2**	2	2	2	2	Sensitive	2
3	Committed to family	1	1	1	1	**1**	1	2	**2**	**2**	2	Independent	3
4	Understanding	**2**	1	1	**1**	1	2	1	2	1	**1**	Impatient	4
5	Bright	1	**1**	1	**1**	2	1	**1**	1	1	1	Just average	5
6	Very inward	1	1	**2**	1	1	1	**1**	2	2	1	Very outspoken	6
7	Childlike inside	2	1	2	**1**	1	**1**	1	2	**1**	2	Get what you see	7
8	Have real communication	**2**	**2**	2	2	**2**	2	1	1	1	1	Aloof	8
9	Easy going	2	1	1	1	1	1	**1**	**2**	1	**1**	Emotional	9
10	Unaffectionate	2	2	**1**	1	2	2	2	**1**	**2**	0	Likes to touch	10

FIGURE 14.2 Example of One Client's Personal Constructs
(From R. A. Neimeyer, 1992.)

& Manchester, 1990; Suedfeld & Tetlock, 1977; Tanaka, Panter, & Winborne, 1988). Cognitively complex people are able to view social behavior from several different dimensions, and thus have greater flexibility. As one might expect of such an adaptive characteristic, cognitive complexity increases with age (Signell, 1966; Vacc & Greenleaf, 1975).

In addition to developing cognitive complexity, healthy development requires that people learn to integrate their various constructs. Complexity without integration is an unhealthy sign (e.g., Landfield & Epting, 1987).

Personality Change

Personal constructs can change. Kelly considered in some detail the possible types of change. These concepts were of particular interest to him because they suggested both possibilities and dangers in psychotherapy. The same principles of change operate outside therapy, in life itself.

Emotions Related to Change

Personality change leads to strong emotions. **Threat** is "the awareness of imminent comprehensive change in one's core structures" (Kelly, 1955, p. 489). Once we have become dislodged from our core role structures, we experience *guilt* (Kelly, 1955, 1962).

Threat may be caused by major life changes, including the anticipation of death (Moore & Neimeyer, 1991; R.A. Neimeyer, Moore, & Bagley, 1988). Threat has been studied among music students performing for evaluation in front of faculty (Tobacyk & Downs, 1986) and among counselors in training conducting sessions for evaluation by faculty (Froehle, 1989). In both cases, threat produced anxiety, and the most threatened subjects experienced the greatest anxiety. Experiences in therapy that lead to changes in core constructs also arouse threat. Since people have different core structures, they will find different situations threatening. For example, the possibility of becoming a homosexual is more threatening to some people than to others (Leitner & Cado, 1982). Threat is not always triggered by negative events. Personality developments in psychotherapy are (presumably) desired, yet still threatening. Kelly supplies an example: "a prisoner of twenty years, while eager, is nevertheless threatened on the last day by the imminence of his release" (1955, p. 490). Researchers since Kelly have documented adverse effects of life change, even when the changes themselves are desirable (Dohrenwend & Dohrenwend, 1974); this is consistent with Kelly's thinking.

When core constructs are changed by new incidental (rather than comprehensive) constructs, *fear* is experienced (rather than threat). The less we think about a matter, the more likely we are to experience *fear*; the more we think about it, the more likely we are to experience *threat.* A car crash that seems caused by incidental reasons about which we have thought little, like a hole in the road that seemed to come from nowhere, causes fear. But a car crash that seems caused by reasons about which we have comprehensive constructs, such as one caused by intoxication, elaborated by our concepts about social drinking, responsibility, and so forth, would cause threat instead. In either case, core constructs change: Death or disability can result in either case.

Anxiety occurs when we recognize that we are confronted by events outside the range of convenience of our construct system. Our constructs are not adequate to deal with events, and we know it. This definition of anxiety is quite different from the psychoanalytic concept of the lifting of repression. We may try to avoid anxiety by changing constructs. Since anticipation of events is the function of constructs, anxiety is a sign of construct failure and the need for change.

People do not change their constructs easily. Sometimes they continue to try to make constructs work, rather than changing them. Kelly defined **hostility** as "the continued effort to extort validational evidence in favor of a type of social prediction which has already proved itself a failure" (1955, p. 510). He distinguished it from aggressiveness, which is simply "the active elaboration of one's perceptual field" (Kelly, 1955, p. 509), and which may occur in behavior that is not hostile (Kelly, 1957, 1964). (This sense is similar to Adler's use of the term "aggressive.")

Various theorists have built upon Kelly's work, expanding a personal construct approach to emotions (e.g., D.D. Fisher, 1990; Katz, 1984; McCoy, 1977; Miall, 1989).

Effective Action: The C-P-C Cycle

A person who is making a decision about how to act typically engages in a three-step process called the **C-P-C Cycle**. In the first stage, **circumspection**, the person "employs a series of propositional constructs in dealing with the elements at hand" (Kelly, 1955, p. 515). That is, he or she tries out several available constructs tentatively to see how they might fit in the situation. (For example, is a new teacher a slave driver, a mentor, or what?)

The second phase, **preemption**, involves selecting which of the constructs to actually use. The person selects which construct to apply to the situation. (After the first exam, some students decide "slave driver" applies.)

The third phase, **control**, involves action. (The student may study harder, or drop the course.) Kelly emphasized, though, that action or behavior was not simply an outcome, a "dependent variable" in the scientific metaphor. Instead, he argued, "Behavior is man's independent variable in the experiment of creating his own existence" (1966, p. 36). He cautioned that psychologists must "appreciate the creative role of behavior in the affairs of man" (1966, p. 45). Behavior, after all, produces consequences that permit hypothesis-testing, and therefore confirmation or revision of a person's constructs.

Each step contributes to effective action. Some people are less effective because they do not devote enough attention to the circumspection phase, instead impulsively deciding to act. Others continue considering alternatives long after the time for decision has arrived. A therapist can help a client act more effectively by noticing which stages are inadequate and working on those.

Loosening and Tightening Constructs: The Creativity Cycle

Although the C-P-C Cycle enables us to select constructs for action, it does not involve change in those constructs. The **Creativity Cycle**, on the other hand, involves the development of constructs. It is involved in therapy, which Kelly calls "a creative process" (1955, p. 529), though not exclusively there.

The first stage of the Creativity Cycle involves loosened construction (**loosening**). Constructs are applied in ways that may seem to make little sense. Brainstorming sessions illustrate this. Kelly remarked that "creativity always arises out of preposterous thinking" (1955, p. 529). In therapy, techniques to loosen constructs include free association, fantasy, dream reporting, and silence (Kelly, 1955, p. 484). The constructs involved are often preverbal.

In the next phase, one variation of the construct is selected, tightened, and applied in action. Without validation in action, the cycle is not complete, and the person is left with loose constructs that are no doubt too unclear to be adaptive.

Therapy

Kelly's therapy requires the therapist "to understand the client in the client's own terms" (Landfield & Epting, 1987, p. 275). This does not mean that the therapist will agree with the client. Instead, the therapist should have a construct system (largely developed from Kelly's theory) that will allow him or her to subsume the client's construct system under the therapist's own construct system. If the therapist cannot understand the client then it will not be possible to enter into a role, even a therapeutic role, with the client (cf. the Sociality Corollary above).

Kelly recommended a spirit of cooperative problem-solving techniques between client and therapist, stressing the importance of the therapist's acceptance of the client. The therapist is not seen as someone with all the answers. Both therapist and client focus on understanding, testing, and improving the client's constructs. This task-centered focus prevents the client from developing an overly dependent relationship with the therapist. In fact, Kelly discouraged clients who consulted him in his clinic from disclosing too much personal material early in the therapy, until they came to understand what his mode of therapy was all about.

This is a very individualized approach. Traditional clinical diagnosis is too remote from the original observations to be helpful in either theory-building (Kelly, 1968) or in therapy and treatment. The REP test is used early in therapy to explore the client's construct system. Knowing the client's constructs enables the therapist to establish a relationship with the client (according to the Sociality Corollary). Later, when constructs are being revised, several techniques can be used.

One of the most important of these therapeutic techniques is **fixed-role therapy**. In this technique, the client experiments with new constructs by role-playing a fictitious personality specifically devised by the therapist. For example, Viney (1981) described a case study in which a bright and attractive female client, Susan, aged 24, sought counseling for anxiety that focused on her limited social life. Her therapist devised the following fixed role for Susan, using constructs that had been elicited from the client in her REP test, so that they had much personal meaning for her. As Kelly recommended, this fictitious personality was given a different name ("Mary Jones"), so that Susan could experiment with this role without losing her own identity or committing herself to change before she was ready.

> Mary Jones is a *friendly* young woman who is *open and frank* with the people she meets. She enjoys *giving* to these people and the feelings of *companionship* she has with them. She sees herself as *united* with her fellows, as *part of the world* with them.
>
> Mary is a *down-to-earth* kind of person, and most of the time she is *calm and relaxed*. She is able to be *patient* with the people she knows and is *not very critical* of them.
>
> Mary is also *searching and inquisitive* about her world. She can be *forceful* when the occasion demands it and *lively* too.
>
> Mary is the kind of person people like to know. (Viney, 1981, pp. 274–275)

As therapy progressed, the client changed in the direction of this role, as was evident on the REP test and, though more subjectively, in life.

Therapy generally involves the discovery of new constructs, and not merely the realignment of the individual in relation to existing constructs. Development of the fixed role is a significant collaborative effort between client and therapist. The new role in fixed therapy is enacted in an exploratory way. Kelly thought that the protection of "make-believe . . . is probably man's oldest protective screen for reaching out into the unknown" (1955, p. 373). Role-play in therapy also gives the client an opportunity to learn how the other person in the interaction views a situation. Sometimes the roles are reversed, so that the client plays the other person, while the therapist plays the role of the client. Besides teaching the client to view the situation from the other's viewpoint, this allows the therapist to model the new role.

Therapeutic techniques to tighten constructs include *time binding* and *word binding* (Kelly, 1955, pp. 484, 1074–1076). Constructs elicited can be made less harmful in the present by learning to say such things as, "That happened long ago, and does not happen any more," or "That is really exploitation, not love." Some of the client's constructs may need to be changed because they are immature constructs from childhood, when traumatic events were understood as well as the child could understand them (Morrison & Cometa, 1982). Children tend to use the extreme ends of poles, and (like psychopaths) generally use only one pole of a dichotomous construct (Hayden, 1982). Children also have less hierarchical organization than do adults; their thought is less complex.

Kelly's therapy typically was brief, ranging from six sessions completed within two weeks to as long as three months. Of course, he was working in a college counseling context, so that his clients were already functioning reasonably well, compared with other clinical populations. He claimed, however, that the method itself is more efficient.

> [Fixed-role therapy is] a method of substituting whole new prefabricated constructions . . . rather than "analyzing away" old rickety structures [as in psychoanalysis]—thus it takes less time. (1955, p. 682)

The client must continue to use constructs, and this requires greater cognitive activity than traditional psychoanalysis recognizes. Kelly takes another gibe at psychoanalysis by noting that "*Insight* is what you are left with after you have been stripped of your imagination" (1960, p. 347). Fixed-role therapy creates in clients the belief that they can change. The attitude of experimentation facilitates self-directed change after the end of formal therapy.

Several therapists practice *personal construct therapy* based upon Kelly's foundation (Bannister, 1975; Epting, 1984; R.A. Neimeyer & G.J. Neimeyer, 1987). This method has been used with diverse populations. In treating schizophrenics, who have serious thought disorders, Bannister and his colleagues begin by identifying whatever weak constructs exist, and systematically confirming these through a process of "serial validation" in an effort to reverse the thought disorder (Bannister, Adams-Webber, Penn, & Radley, 1975). Among neurotic clients at a university, therapeutic improvement has been associated with increased integrative complexity of construct systems (Raz-Duvshani, 1986). Personal construct therapy is reported to be effective in reducing anxiety and depression in the elderly (Viney, Benjamin, & Preston, 1989).

Research Findings

Kelly's theory has generated a great deal of research in a variety of settings. It has the potential for expanded theoretical connections with other areas within personality and in other fields (Mancuso & Adams-Webber, 1982).

Clinical Populations

Researchers have explored the personal constructs of various clinical populations. Different kinds of faulty constructs are characteristic of schizophrenia and paranoia (Lorenzini, Sassaroli, & Rocchi, 1989). Schizophrenics have thought disorders (Bannister, 1960, 1962, 1963, 1965; Bannister & Fransella, 1966), with particular impairment for constructs about people and psychological phenomena, more than about objects and the physical world (Bannister & Salmon, 1966; McPherson, Barden, & Buckley, 1970; McPherson & Buckley, 1970). Schizophrenics show impaired perception of themselves as well as of others (Gara, Rosenberg, & Mueller, 1989). Among nonpsychotics, constructs have been studied in relationship to anxiety (McPherson & Gray, 1976), phobias (Huber & Altmaier, 1983), and eating disorders (G.J. Neimeyer & Knouzam, 1985). Many other cognitive approaches to clinical issues, while not referring to Kelly or to personal construct theory, use similar concepts, such as "conceptual complexity" (e.g., N.S. Johnson & Holloway, 1988) and "cognitive simplicity" (e.g., Ortega & Weinstein, 1988).

Business Applications and Vocational Choice

Kelly's theory is popular in many business fields—for example, with industrial-organizational psychologists, management development specialists, and occupational counselors (Jankowicz, 1987; Stewart & Stewart, 1982). Grid analyses can be used to analyze job requirements (M. Smith, 1980; Tyson, 1979). They can reveal how experienced managers (Eden & Sims, 1981; Jankowicz, 1987; Jankowicz & Hisrich, 1987) and school psychologists (Salmon & Lehrer, 1989) make decisions, so that their expertise can be taught to less experienced personnel.

Research on vocational development is an extension of the more general theory that Kelly offered (G.J. Neimeyer, 1988; G.J. Neimeyer & Metzler, 1987a). Several studies suggest that cognitive complexity is associated with more appropriate vocational choice (Bodden, 1970; Harren, Kass, Tinsley, & Moreland, 1979; G.J. Neimeyer, 1988). Measures derived from repertory grids have been developed for vocational guidance (R. Davies, 1985; Edmonds, 1979; Jankowicz & Cooper, 1982; G.J. Neimeyer, 1989; M. Smith, Hartley, & Stewart, 1978). Sex differences in occupational constructs have also been reported (G.J. Neimeyer & Metzler, 1987b).

Social Interaction and Groups

Early research with Bieri's measure of cognitive complexity explored its value for understanding social interaction. People with higher cognitive complexity perceive others more accurately (Bieri, 1955; Mayo & Crockett, 1964) and have higher social intelligence (Sechrest & Jackson, 1961). Others may have more difficulty understanding complex subjects, though, at least at the beginning of a relationship (R.A. Neimeyer, G.J. Neimeyer, & Landfield, 1983).

S.L. Kline (1990) had subjects complete repertory test ratings in specific contexts—for example, "when the figure is talking to another person at a large social gathering" (p. 331). Ratings were different from those obtained under the usual context-free instructions, which suggests that the impact of social context on constructs is an area worthy of further research. Sex differences deserve further exploration as well (Pratt, Pancer, Hunsberger, & Manchester, 1990). Research on social interaction can also be derived from Landfield's (1988) proposal that particular other people serve as "validating agents" for our personal constructs.

Kelly's personal construct theory has been applied to sensitivity training roups (Beck, 1980, 1987, 1988a, 1988b, 1988c; Kuypers, Davies, & Van der Vegt, 1987). Such groups produce changes in emotions and personal constructs. Results are interesting, though not always as predicted. For example,

Beck (1988c) reports that feeling accepted is associated with increased dilation of constructs (which facilitates change) and tends to reduce feelings of threat.

Other Research Personal construct theory has been extended to other topics as well, including biofeedback therapy (Zolten, 1989) and hypnosis (Burr & Butt, 1989). Researchers have explored the relationship between personal constructs and measures of identity (Berzonsky, 1989; Berzonsky & Neimeyer, 1988; Berzonsky, Rice, & Neimeyer, 1990; Côté & Reker, 1979). A new measure of sex roles, the Sex-Rep, measures individuals' concepts of sex roles (Baldwin, Critelli, Stevens, & Russell, 1986). In addition, values and beliefs, important constructs in much of social science, have been interpreted as corresponding to core and peripheral constructs (Horley, 1991). In summary, Kelly's theory has implications for a variety of applied and theoretical issues.

Summary

Kelly proposed a theory of personal constructs based on the fundamental postulate of *constructive alternativism,* which says that people can interpret any event in a variety of ways. His metaphor for personality was *man-the-scientist.* He elaborated this model in a formal theory, which consisted of a Fundamental Postulate and 11 corollaries. The *Fundamental Postulate* states that "a person's processes are psychologically channelized by the ways in which he anticipates events." The process of construing is described in four corollaries (the *Construction Corollary,* the *Experience Corollary,* the *Choice Corollary,* and the *Modulation Corollary*). These statements describe how constructs are formed and chosen to apply to a particular situation. People choose a particular way of construing events that offers the best possibility for extending the construct system (see Table 14.2).

Four corollaries describe the structure of construct systems: the *Dichotomy Corollary,* the *Organization Corollary,* the *Fragmentation Corollary,* and the *Range Corollary.* Dichotomous constructs vary in their centrality and organization within the construct system. With development, constructs become elaborated into hierarchical arrangements. Incompatible constructs may be applied in succession. Each construct has only a limited range of convenience.

Finally, the social context of construing is described by the *Individuality Corollary,* the *Commonality Corollary,* and the *Sociality Corollary.* People have different construct systems, and personalities are judged to be similar if they use similar construct systems. Interpersonal relationships depend upon at least one of the parties understanding the constructs used by the other.

Personality change produces a variety of emotions, including anxiety and threat. The *C-P-C Cycle* describes the process by which a person selects a construct to apply in a particular instance. The *Creativity Cycle* describes the progressive loosening and tightening of constructs that occurs during change, including during therapy.

TABLE 14.2 Contributions of Kelly's Theory to Various Topics

Biological	Kelly does not consider biological factors.
Child Development	Children develop constructs for making sense of their experience, especially their experience with people.
Adult Development	Adults continue to use the personal constructs developed earlier, changing them when they do not predict accurately.
Mental Health	Constructs that can predict a broad variety of experience accurately are more adaptive than constructs that predict only limited experience. Mental health is improved by changing constructs. Fixed-role therapy is a strategy for change.
Society	Social relationships require that one person can understand the other's personal constructs. Kelly does not consider broader social institutions.
Cognitive Processes	Cognition is central to personality. Cognitive processes are elaborately described in Kelly's theory. Behaviors and emotions follow from cognitions.
Individual Differences	Individuals differ in the personal constructs (cognitions) they apply to experience. Other differences (emotions, behavior) follow from this.

Kelly developed a *Role Construct Repertory* (REP) test to measure personal constructs. Cognitive complexity, which is considered adaptive, can be measured from the REP test. The REP test has been used to measure change due to therapy, and has been modified for applications in industry. In therapy, Kelly used *fixed-role therapy* to produce change through the development and practice of new constructs. Besides its applications to therapy, Kelly's theory has stimulated research in business, group processes, social perception, and other areas.

ILLUSTRATIVE BIOGRAPHIES: Concluding Remarks

Richard Nixon and Carol Burnett are both public figures who have written autobiographies, as well as having been analyzed by others. According to Kelly's theory, the concepts they use to understand the world are the keys to their personalities.

Richard Nixon

Richard Nixon aimed for success, working long hours on his election campaigns, and before that in law school, surviving on little sleep. Winter and Carlson (1988) concluded, from a content analysis of Nixon's first inaugural address, that he was high in achievement motivation. How did Nixon define success? It was not in financial terms; he regularly returned speaking fees to charity (Ambrose, 1987). Nixon considered himself to have outgrown concern with his ego (Ambrose, 1989, p. 509) and wrote of the importance of having goals larger than the individual (Nixon, 1962, 1990). He considered success to be achievable by hard work. Some of Nixon's important personal constructs, then, concerned "hard work." Perhaps his expression of this work ethic was a factor in his political success among middle-class and working-class voters.

Ambrose describes the divisiveness of Nixon's campaign speeches. "He wanted to divide the community into 'us' and 'them,' and he succeeded" (Ambrose, 1987, p. 614). The construct of "us" versus "them" applied to domestic politics (Republicans versus the opposition) and to international relations (the United States versus the Communists). Nixon's dogged investigations of Communists when he was a member of the House Committee on Un-American Activities similarly reflects the "us" (patriotic Americans) versus "them" (Communist sympathizers) construct. In his successful 1968 campaign for the presidency, Nixon defined "us" as "the Silent Majority, Middle America, the white, comfortable, patriotic, hawkish 'forgotten Americans'" (Ambrose, 1989, p. 222). "Them" included long-haired antiwar protesters and the elite who attended Ivy League schools. At other times, the press was the enemy (Ambrose, 1989, p. 250). Nixon's reputed vindictiveness also stems from an "us versus them" construct system. Ambrose described Nixon as "a vindictive man, with a long memory and a deep capacity to hate" (1989, p. 172; cf. also p. 267). He maintained an "Enemies List" of political opponents. Secretary of Defense Elliot Richardson suggested that Nixon was unable to move away from thinking of others as enemies, which impeded his effectiveness as Chief Executive (T.H. White, 1975, p. 180). "We-they" may work as a construct in political campaigns (and Nixon was a dedicated campaigner), but it is a divisive construct for a sitting president.

Nonetheless, Ambrose points out that Nixon "refused to use race, class, or religion as his issues" (1987, p. 614). To understand a construct, it is necessary to consider how it is elaborated; not all "us" versus "them" constructs are the same. Furthermore, once in office, Nixon sought relaxation of tensions with America's foes, namely the Soviet Union and Communist China.

Nixon's interpersonal manner was cold toward others, including his wife, at least in public. For Nixon, loneliness was inevitable for a politician. As he said, "Politics is not a team sport" (Nixon, 1990, p. 32). Yet Ambrose (1987, p. 618) argues that other politicians, including Dwight Eisenhower, were in fact gregarious. Kelly's theory provides theoretical tools for describing this discrepancy. For Nixon, the construct of "politician" included, on the positive pole, loneliness; close interpersonal relationships belonged to the contrast pole, which for Nixon would also include the dimension of insecurity, given the death of two of his brothers and the absence of his mother during significant periods of his youth (Levey, 1986). The constructs of "politician" by others did not include this loneliness component. It is noteworthy that, in other conditions, where he was not vulnerable, Nixon showed a friendly, considerate side of himself (Winter & Carlson, 1988). For example, he was especially considerate to hired help at the White House. Such fragmentation is consistent with Kelly's Fragmentation Corollary.

Another aspect of Nixon's construct of "a successful politician" was *pragmatism* (Nixon, 1990, chap. 32; Ambrose, 1989, p. 171). Political realism or pragmatism could produce changes of opinion and illegal actions that others, with other construct systems, would regard as unprincipled (cf. Winter & Carlson, 1988). Nixon's construct system facilitated his bold initiatives in foreign affairs, most notably his visit to the People's Republic of China in 1972 and arms reductions negotiations with the Soviet Union.

The construct of privacy or secrecy was important for Richard Nixon. He seemed to regard secret activities as more effective, and public ones less effective, for show but not for effective action. Public behavior called for a politician to behave as an actor (Nixon, 1990). He often made executive decisions with little consultation. For example, his secretary of state learned of Nixon's plan to visit China by reading it in the newspaper (Ambrose, 1989, p. 454). Nixon preferred to negotiate in "back-channel" communications, where fewer people were involved. He often acted through his National Security Adviser, Henry Kissinger, rather than through the State Department. He is remembered for his favoring of covert operations, including wiretaps and the infamous break-in of the headquarters of the Democratic National Committee in the Watergate office complex in Washington, D.C.

Kelly's Sociality Corollary asserts that understanding another person's construct system makes possible a relationship with that person. Nixon and Kissinger understood one another. According to Ambrose, "They shared a love of eavesdropping on others (the taps and the tapes), of secrecy, of surprises, of conspiracy, of backbiting, of power plays. They were alike in their utter cynicism, and in their contempt for everyone else, including each other" (1989, pp. 490–491). Theodore White (1975, p. 163) describes the "negative synergism" between Nixon and close advisers (Ehrlichman, Haldeman, and Colson), which brought out the tough, negative side of Nixon's personality.

Nixon's greatest presidential achievements were, it is generally acknowledged, in foreign affairs. His knowledge was immense in this area. He eschewed simple tactics and criticized simplistic slogans about war and peace (Nixon, 1990, p. 346) and simplistic approaches to combatting Communism (Nixon, 1962, pp. 287–291). In Kelly's language, we may conclude that Nixon's construct system in the area of foreign affairs was cognitively complex. In this area, he functioned commendably. His constructs served to predict accurately. In domestic affairs, his constructs did not lead to accurate predictions, or there would never have been the tragedy of Watergate.

Carol Burnett

Carol Burnett loved to act and seemed to do naturally what George Kelly recommended as a therapeutic strategy: role-playing. She described an incident from high school that illustrates this. As a reporter for the school paper, she wanted to interview movie stars who had attended Hollywood High. The teacher who would have to grant permission, however, was somber. Students avoided him. Carol worked up her courage "by pretending to be Rosalind Russell" (C. Burnett, 1986, p. 147). Perhaps she preferred comic roles because they helped her to achieve a sense that life's tragedies were not overwhelming.

Role-playing permits a fragmented view of personality. It is not necessary to be a unified whole. Carol Burnett described experiences of disunity.

> Sometimes it was as if I were two different people: the one who thought things and the one who said and did things. I couldn't, for the life of me, bring the two together. I don't know what I thought might happen if I did, but whatever it was, it scared me. Scared me enough to keep a wall up.
>
> Mama called it my shade.
>
> "Carol, sometimes you don't act like you're in there. When you pull that goddamn shade down, there's just no talking to you." (C. Burnett, 1986, p. 134)

This is a dramatic example of the kind of disunity Kelly recognized in his Fragmentation Corollary. With time, it became apparent that a new personality was forming behind the shade. As Carol Burnett described it,

> Some of the things that went on in my head were 180 degrees from the way I behaved. There was another whole different person in there, and *she* had spunk, grit, sand, a personality, *courage*. But, oh, God, the outside me was a complete chicken. (C. Burnett, 1986, p. 146)

In Kelly's theory, the *contrast* of a construct is generally not clearly understood. Carol Burnett described pulling down her "shade" to keep things simple, to avoid hearing the sordid details of life that people around her were discussing. This effectively suppressed the contrast poles, at least until she had matured enough to explore these aspects of her personality.

Though she has not provided us with a repertory grid (REP test), Carol Burnett listed constructs that described her mother but not herself. She portrayed her mother as "smart and pretty and funny and sexy and all those things. All those things I wasn't" (C. Burnett, 1986, p. 109). She does not believe that she is beautiful (Latham, 1986).

Kelly's theory does not describe in detail how constructs are first developed, but it seems reasonable to suggest that some are learned as children, in the family. Constructs are developed to make predictions, according to Kelly's metaphor of "man-the-scientist." As Carol was the child of an alcoholic parent, what sorts of constructs allowed predictions? She learned to observe evidence of her father's degree of intoxication. "If his legs were wobbly, I knew Mama would be mad, and he'd catch it" (C. Burnett, 1986, p. 7).

Carol Burnett describes the conflicting messages she heard about "love" from her grandmother and her mother. Her grandmother criticized Carol's mother for pursuing relationships based on love. For her, love was unrealistic and maladaptive. It contrasted with practical consideration of financial reality. These constructs shaped Carol Burnett's description of her own love life and marriage to a fellow actor. They married in hope of both succeeding in show business. Their divorce was provoked at least in part by her greater success. The construct of "impractical love" versus "success," which she had heard throughout childhood, provided the language to describe and shape her own adult experience.

She did not, however, have a rigid set of constructs. She was open to experience. In Kelly's term, her constructs were *permeable.* Carol was aware that other views were possible, as Kelly assumed in his fundamental postulate of *Constructive Alternativism.* For example, questioning her lack of sophistication about sexuality, Carol asked, "Was I really that *simple*? Or was that the image I chose for myself? And why would I choose such an image?" (C. Burnett, 1986, p. 189). She dedicated her autobiography to her three daughters. Unlike some autobiographies, which seem designed to support one particular interpretation of one's own life experiences, Carol Burnett said that she hoped her daughters would be able to understand her better than she herself did (C. Burnett, 1986, p. 2).

GLOSSARY

Choice Corollary statement that people choose the pole of a construct which promises greater possibility of extending and defining the system of constructs

circumspection the first stage in the C-P-C Cycle, in which various constructs are tentatively explored

cognitive complexity elaborateness of a person's construct system, reflected in a large number of different constructs

Commonality Corollary statement describing similarity between people

concrete construct a construct that cannot be extended to include new elements

Construction Corollary Kelly's statement that people anticipate replications of events

constructive alternativism the assumption that people can interpret the world in a variety of ways

control the third stage in the C-P-C Cycle; the way in which the person acts

core constructs constructs central to a person's identity and existence

C-P-C Cycle the three-step process leading to effective action

Creativity Cycle the process of changing constructs by loosening and tightening them

Dichotomy Corollary statement that constructs are bipolar

elaborative choice the term for a choice that allows a construct system to be extended; the Choice Corollary says this will be selected

Experience Corollary Kelly's statement about personality development

fixed-role therapy Kelly's method of therapy, based on role-playing

Fragmentation Corollary statement describing the inconsistency of people

Fundamental Postulate Kelly's main assumption, which stresses the importance of psychological constructs

hostility continuing to try to validate constructs that have already been invalidated

Individuality Corollary Kelly's assertion that people use different constructs from other people

jackass theory Kelly's phrase to indicate that his theory is a theory of the "nature of the animal" rather than of the environment

loosening applying constructs in ways that seem not to make sense, such as in brainstorming and free association

man-the-scientist Kelly's metaphor for human personality

Modulation Corollary statement that the permeability of constructs sets limits to construction possibilities

Organization Corollary describes the hierarchical relationships among constructs

peripheral constructs constructs not central to one's identity

permeable construct a construct that can be extended to include new elements

personal construct a person's concept for predicting events

preemption the second stage in the C-P-C Cycle, in which a construct is selected

preverbal construct a construct that is not conscious

Range Corollary statement that a construct applies only to some events, not to all

range of convenience the events to which a construct applies

Role Construct Repertory (REP) Test instrument for measuring a person's constructs

slot movement abrupt change from one pole of a construct to its opposite, often precipitated by stress

Sociality Corollary statement describing understanding another person (or being understood) as a prerequisite for a social process with that person

superordinate construct a construct that applies broadly and subsumes lower-order constructs

threat awareness of imminent comprehensive change in one's core structures

validation confirmation of an anticipation by events

STUDY QUESTIONS

1. Explain Kelly's concept of *constructive alternativism.* Compare it with Adler's ideas.
2. According to Kelly, what is the main way in which individuals differ from one another?
3. What concepts from Kelly's theory would be relevant for understanding why a person makes a radical change in personality—for example, a criminal who repents and becomes a born-again Christian?
4. Why do we make the choices we do, according to Kelly's *Choice Corollary*? Give an example to illustrate this idea.
5. What concepts from Kelly are relevant to understanding personality development? Contrast this approach with theories that propose stages of development.
6. Explain concepts from Kelly's theory that help understand interpersonal relationships.
7. Describe the REP test. What scores from it have been found useful? Summarize research using this test.
8. Although Kelly's theory is "cognitive," he does consider emotion. Explain how.
9. Describe the C-P-C Cycle. Contrast it with the Creativity Cycle.
10. Describe Kelly's fixed-role therapy. In what ways is it like acting?

CHAPTER

Conclusion

Many theories have been devised to explain personality. Why so many? Do they offer competing explanations of the same phenomena? Sometimes they do. Or do they address different issues, trying to explain divergent facets of personality? Sometimes that, too, is the reason for the proliferation of theories. Possibly there are also less rational contributions to theoretical multiplicity, including lack of appreciation of the contributions that have already been made, and egotistical motivations of those who wish to have theories named for them.

If the field of personality had widespread agreement on which theoretical concepts were most useful, we could say that a dominant **paradigm** prevailed. Agreement on a common paradigm would guide personality researchers in their choice of research questions and methods. However, no such agreement prevails. Various paradigms compete: the psychoanalytic paradigm and its sociocultural variant; the learning paradigm; cognitive behaviorism; the trait paradigm; and the humanistic paradigm. No one paradigm has been able to replace the others by demonstrating its clear superiority in explaining relevant observations. Indeed, lack of agreement about which observations are relevant makes it difficult to imagine the kind of direct scientific competition that would allow a critical test among theories.

Some theories share a common language and have large areas of agreement. Freud, Jung, Horney, and other theorists in the psychoanalytic tradition can be so described. This level of agreement reflects a shared paradigm. In other cases, theories agree about observations of humans, but explain them differently (alternative paradigms). Dollard and Miller's approach, compared with psychoanalysis, illustrates this sort of different theoretical language but shared perception of clinical facts. In other cases, theories have little agreement about either theoretical concepts or factual observations. Comparing Jung with Bandura and Mischel illustrates this kind of fundamental difference of orientation.

Lacking a shared theoretical understanding, the field of personality is fragmented (Hyland, 1985; Staats, 1981). Researchers in various theoretical schools largely restrict their communications to others of their own persuasion. Journals have emerged that are devoted to developments within a particular theory, which further hinders meaningful communication among theories. This impedes theoretical cross-fertilization. For example, Cattell's findings about a genetic contribution to neuroticism are relevant to the clinical behaviors that psychoanalysts and Rogerians treat, but these theories have not been revised to include the new empirical findings. Indeed, the theories have no constructs for discussing such evidence.

Multiplicity of theory is not necessarily undesirable (Koch, 1981). Having a number of "limited range" theories, each developing concepts to understand a relatively narrow range of phenomena, may at some stages of scientific development lead to faster advances than a more comprehensive, but less precise, theory. Even the more comprehensive theories considered in this text have varied in their contributions to topics of interest.

Contributions of the Theories to Various Topics

Throughout this text the contributions of each theory to certain substantive questions have been summarized. (See the summary tables at the end of Chapters 2 to 14.) Let us now review these contributions, looking for major themes.

Biological Factors

Personality theories vary considerably in how they deal with biological factors. Some theories ignore them entirely (e.g., Rogers, Kelly). Most theories recognize the importance of biological factors at the abstract theoretical level, but do not investigate them empirically. Only a few of the theorists in this book included physiological measures in their research, and then only occasionally.

Theorists who ignore biological factors assume, implicitly, that *biological factors are outside the scope of personality theory.* This approach implies that psychological and biological phenomena are separate, at least at the current state of knowledge. Theories that integrate the two areas may come later, after each approach has been more fully developed, and after more biological and psychological discoveries are made.

Other theorists propose, as an abstract assumption, that *biological motivation underlies personality.* Psychological processes are built on a biological foundation. Freud's libido theory, Maslow's hierarchy of needs theory, Cattell's dynamic lattice, and Dollard and Miller's drive theory all propose that biological needs are shaped and channeled to form personality. Maslow argued that biological motivations are the foundation of personality, but that once satisfied they become unimportant. Dollard and Miller based their learning theory on the assumption that satisfaction of biological (and other) drives is inherently reinforcing. These theorists do not, however, focus on individual differences in biological drives. Rather, they propose an underlying universal biological mechanism for the development of personality.

In general, with the exception of Dollard and Miller's psychoanalytic learning theory, learning theorists have not paid much attention to biological mechanisms. Skinner did not investigate biological determinants of behavior, although he recognized that biological factors often determined what was reinforcing to an individual, and that species differ in their reinforcers and in the responses they can learn. The cognitive social learning theorists Bandura and Mischel did not focus on biological factors, although some recent research shows that cognitions do have impact on biological processes (see Chapter 13).

According to some theorists, *personality can be described in terms of physical phenomena.* Allport asserted that traits of personality have some physical reality, but he did not further describe the biology of personality. However, most theorists would agree with the opposite statement, that *personality cannot be described in physical terms.*

According to some theorists, *some aspects of personality can be inherited.* According to others, *heredity has little influence on personality.* Cattell's research shows that some traits are influenced by heredity, while others are not. Other theorists discussed heredity more speculatively, without conducting research. Freud speculated that heredity could influence the amount of libido a person has, and perhaps could even influence sexual orientation. Jung proposed that the contents of the collective unconscious were inherited, extending inheritance into areas that other psychoanalysts presumed were formed by experience. Adler's theory proposed that inherited organ inferiorities set the context within which personality was formed, without determining the outcome. Allport acknowledged the importance of heredity on personality, although he did not conduct empirical studies of its effect.

According to some theorists, *sex differences in personality are determined by biology.* Freud and Erikson thought so. Maslow, like the psychoanalysts, presumed that sex differences have a biological basis. According to other theorists, *sex differences in personality are produced by society, not by biology.* Horney argued that biology is far less important than orthodox psychoanalysis believes; culture, instead, was important. (See Chapter 6 for a further discussion of this issue.) Adler also stressed the impact of society on sex differences.

It is not an easy matter to determine how much heredity contributes to a particular behavior. Besides requiring careful selection of subjects, the range of environments studied influences the heritability estimate. It is also important to select the behavior carefully so as to ensure theoretical meaningfulness (Prescott, Johnson, & McArdle, 1991).

Without reducing personality to biology, most theorists would probably agree that *biology can set limits on personality,* although they do not describe such limits explicitly. While biological determinants are not central to most personality theories, it is reasonable to suggest that serious deviations from normal biological apparatus may at times cause such gross impairment of personality that they seem the overriding factor in understanding a particular person. Such factors could include medical disorders with psychological implications (e.g., brain tumors or hormonal imbalances). A comprehensive personality theory would address the question of how much maladaptive behavior is influenced by biological factors, and how much is due to aberrant psychological development alone. Perhaps biological factors also contribute to positive psychological phenomena.

Individual differences in biology, whether inherited or engendered by environmental factors (including diet, disease, and stress), can produce personality differences. These can occur directly. Inherited differences in emotionality, such as those described by Cattell, are examples of such direct influences. Recent research has considered biological influences on personality more than these classic theorists were able to do. The term *temperament* refers to constitutional differences in activity and emotionality, present from birth. Research supports the idea that personality is influenced by inherited biological factors (e.g., Gray, 1987), beginning with infant differences in temperament (Saudino & Eaton, 1991). Eysenck's model of personality (e.g., Eysenck, 1967; Eysenck & Eysenck, 1985) considers mechanisms by which inherited biological differences (e.g., in reactivity to stimuli) can produce psychological personality characteristics (e.g., introversion).

Biological factors can also influence personality indirectly, by influencing the outcome at critical points in development or in a behavioral sequence. For example, emotional reactivity may cause a person to make a bad occupational decision. Biological factors may also work indirectly by setting up a pattern of environmental influences; for example, a facial birthmark may cause social ridicule. A comprehensive theory would need to specify the mechanisms by which biology (including heredity) influences personality. This task remains to be done.

Eysenck and other theorists (e.g., Zuckerman, 1990c) have studied how various situations pose different impacts on people with different inherited levels of arousability. Biological factors are predicted to *interact with* situations in determining behavior, although these predictions are often difficult to demonstrate (Stemmler & Meinhardt, 1990; Zuckerman, 1990b). While biologically determined temperament undoubtedly influences personality, Chess (1986) cautions that temperament must be considered in its social context. The "goodness of fit" between an individual (including temperament and other aspects of personality) and "environmental opportunities, demands, and stresses" (Chess, 1986, p. 134) is a more useful model than simply temperament alone.

Child Development

Most theorists agree that *important personality development occurs in childhood.* Psychoanalysis, in particular, considers the experience of the early years to be critical to personality throughout life. (Jung, however, did not focus on early experience in his analytical psychology.) Various theorists emphasize different issues. Freud focused on three early stages in which the child develops ways of resolving conflict between unconscious needs and social demands. Adler called attention to interaction with siblings and cautioned against parental pampering and neglect. Horney emphasized love.

For some theorists, *childhood can be considered in terms of a sequence of stages in which distinct developmental tasks are accomplished.* In stage theories, developmental tasks are described for a sequence of developmental periods, which occur in an invariant order. Sometimes, but not always, each stage occurs at a time determined by the age of the individual. Several theorists in this book list stages of development. Freud's oral, anal, and phallic stages of child development are well known. Dollard and Miller offered learning theory reinterpretations of Freud's stages and added a fourth stage. Erikson described four stages of child development, each with ego skills to be mastered through the experience of psychosocial crisis. Allport proposed a stage theory to describe the development of the proprium, beginning with the sense of the body and becoming increasingly inclusive. Maslow described a hierarchy of needs, which can be regarded as a stage theory, although he did believe that age determined a person's stage.

Many theorists hold that *the family has an important influence on personality development in childhood.* Most theorists emphasize the role of parents. Freud underscored the role of the parents in their response to the child's libidinal needs, and as objects of love and identification. Horney stressed parents' love for the child. Overall, with the exception of Jung, psychoanalytic theories describe parent–infant interaction as critical to the formation of personality, shaping personality dynamics for a lifetime. Outside of psychoanalysis, Rogers emphasized the importance of fostering the inherent growth forces within children through unconditional positive regard (much like Horney).

Many theorists agree that *childhood personality development is influenced by models in the family and in society.* Such phenomena are described by the psychoanalytic concept of *identification* and the learning concept of *modeling.* Bandura's studies of modeling are exemplars of the learning approach.

For many theories, *the sense of self that develops in childhood is central to personality.* Allport's "proprium" corresponds to this self. Some theorists describe the self in terms of the ideals toward which a child aspires (Adler and Freud, for example). Some theorists, instead, propose that the ideal self interferes with a more healthy true self (Horney and Rogers). In either case, childhood is an important time for the development of a sense of self.

Other kinds of learning also occur during childhood. Kelly proposed that children, like adults, develop constructs for making sense of their experience. Many, but not all, of these constructs refer to the self. Bandura and Mischel described cognitive learning, much of which occurs in childhood. Skinner's learning approach does not differentiate children from adults. Both learn which behaviors lead to reinforcement and which ones to punishment, and both behave accordingly. A functional analysis of each person is necessary to determine the controlling conditions, and such analyses would be expected to show different reinforcers to influence children and adults. Cattell devised personality and intelligence measures for children, and he suggested that some traits are influenced by early experience.

Empirical investigation of the effect of early experience is difficult. Only rarely do we have accurate information about the circumstances of an individual's early life. In addition, such experience is difficult to interpret, since infants with different temperaments may elicit different behaviors from caregivers. In that case, is personality caused by early environment, or is personality (temperament) itself the cause of the different early experience? These ambiguities notwithstanding, longitudinal research confirms that children who, at age 5, had warm, affectionate fathers or mothers were more successful in their adult interpersonal relationships than those with less fortunate childhood experiences. They fared better in marriage, parenthood, friendship, and work, and they scored higher on a measure of psychological well-being at age 41 (Franz, McClelland, & Weinberger, 1991). Evidence thus supports the major prediction from these personality theories about early childhood: that it has important effects on adult personality.

Adult Development

Adult personality development builds on the foundation of personality developed in childhood. For many theorists, *personality is largely stable in adulthood,* the major developments having occurred earlier in life. Most psychoanalytic theories, including those of Freud, Horney, and Adler, claim that most people change very little in adulthood. Allport proposed that adult personality development consists of integrating earlier developments.

To varying degrees, theorists would agree that *significant personality change can occur in adulthood.* Jung was particularly interested in the individuation process of mid-life. Erikson continued his life-span approach to development, proposing four stages of development from adolescence to old age. Cattell investigated personality change across time, finding that some traits change in adulthood (including anxiety and some types of intelligence), while others do not. Learning approaches suggest that relearning can occur at any time.

The impetus for adult personality development can occur from external, societal sources or from within the individual. Some theorists emphasize external sources. Erikson said that adults, like children, develop by facing psychosocial crises and adjusting to the age-specific expectations of society. Learning theorists emphasize external determinants. Changes in reinforcements produce changes in behavior. Cognitive social learning theorists consider subjective variables, such as self-efficacy, as determinants of behavior; since behavior in turn leads to reinforcements, these internal person variables are indirect causes of development. Other theorists, like Jung and the humanistic theorists, describe change as motivated directly by internal forces.

It is not always easy to determine whether change or consistency should be attributed to causes in the environment or in the person. Caspi and Herbener (1990) analyzed personality development among married adults based on longitudinal data. They reported that people tended to marry spouses who were similar to them in personality (a phenomenon called **homogamy**). This similarity to the spouse contributed to consistency of personality in adulthood. As Bandura's model of reciprocal determinism suggests, mutual influences from the person and the environment occur. Change and stability in adulthood, then, occur for reasons that include both personal and environmental causes, in complex interaction.

Mental Health

Many of these theories were developed in a clinical context, including those of Freud, Jung, Adler, Horney, Erikson, Rogers, and Kelly. Others, developed outside the clinical setting, have suggested new forms of therapy;

these include the theories proposed by Skinner and Bandura. Even Cattell's empirical theory has examined neurosis and psychosis.

Personality can be evaluated along a dimension of health or adjustment. Theorists vary in the way they describe these judgments and in their statements about how many people can be considered healthy. Humanists were particularly concerned with the development of full human potential in adulthood. For Rogers, such development involves increasing freedom. According to Maslow, few adults develop to their full potential, though changes in the workplace and elsewhere could remedy this. Freud also saw a great deal of unhealthy behavior in most people.

Evaluation of healthy functioning is influenced by cultural values, as well as scientific considerations, since cultural values are implicit in personality theories. Freud's criticisms of women as inherently inferior to men are well known. In addition, it was not long ago (1979) that the American Psychiatric Association fundamentally changed its official diagnostic criteria regarding homosexuality, deciding that homosexuality should no longer be a sufficient reason to diagnose an individual. How many more personality variations are labeled healthy or unhealthy because of cultural bias?

The mental health of individuals is evaluated in a variety of ways. Theory serves various functions in the clinical assessment of individuals: It organizes observations, integrates data, clarifies gaps in the data, and permits prediction (Sugarman, 1991). Clinicians rely on theory when they interpret psychological tests (P.M. Lerner, 1990), and when they conduct therapy.

Many theories, particularly those based in therapy settings, make evaluations on the basis of clinical interviews. Cattell developed measures of neurosis and psychosis, advocating that clinicians use objective measures rather than interviews to make their diagnoses. Besides Cattell's clinical scales, self-report measures of adjustment have been developed based on other theories, including those of Maslow, Rogers, and Freud.

Learning theorists focus on behaviors. Skinner believed concepts of "health" and "illness" were not scientific. Undesirable behaviors, though, which other approaches regard as symptoms of an underlying disorder, could be eliminated through behavior modification. More desirable behaviors could be learned instead. Cognitive learning theorists have described the learning of adaptive behaviors such as the capacity to delay gratification (Mischel) and the ability to set high standards for performance (Bandura). Modeling influences both desirable and undesirable behaviors, such as aggression, according to Bandura.

Many theorists assert that *the healthy personality is characterized by integration, the unhealthy one by conflict.* Healthy functioning is generally described as integrated or unified, that is, with little conflict, and as adaptive in the social world (cf. Vinacke, 1984). Psychoanalytic theorists described intrapsychic conflict as evidence of maladjustment, and Dollard and Miller explained such conflict in learning terms. Allport also emphasized integration or unity.

Many theorists assert that *healthy personality functioning is more conscious, unhealthy functioning more unconscious.* While Freud said health results from a predominance of ego functioning, Jung argued instead for a balance between the conscious ego and the unconscious aspects of the psyche. For Jung, the unconscious has much to contribute to healthy functioning. Allport criticized the tendency to look too much for unconscious and unhealthy aspects of personality.

Many theorists note that language is a key to adaptive, healthy functioning, probably because language makes consciousness possible. Dollard and Miller emphasized the role of language in producing discriminations necessary for healthy functioning. Mischel, Bandura, and Kelly also focus on language, in the specific form of "personal constructs." Changing the concepts that people use for coping with reality can produce significant improvement in adaptation.

One common criterion of health is that *healthy personalities are more flexible in adapting to the demands of situations* than are unhealthy ones. Freud emphasized "love and work" as areas where the mentally healthy could function well. Erikson listed eight ego strengths emerging from his stages of psychosocial conflict, and he emphasized the social context in which health or illness develops. Horney also emphasized social aspects of mental health. People are healthy to the extent that they can freely move toward, against, and away from others, as is appropriate to a given situation. The psychoanalysts described many ego defense mechanisms that attempt to preserve health but which, in excess, prevent good adaptation.

This adaptability, though, has limits. The healthy person is also seen as having a core stability that is not eclipsed by situational demands. Many theorists assert that *healthy functioning occurs when the inner, "true self" of personality is expressed; unhealthy functioning occurs when this is suppressed by social forces.* Rogers and Maslow described people's basic nature as good and healthy. They blamed environmental forces for producing maladjustment. Horney and Rogers described the basic alienation from a healthy real self as a result of parents' withholding of love, or making love dependent on the child's moving in directions contrary to its true nature. Other theorists, such as learning theorists, are skeptical of the usefulness of a concept of a "true self."

Some theorists suggest that *healthy personalities contribute more to society than do less healthy personalities.* Adler emphasized the social responsibilities of people, saying that a healthy individual should show social interest, in addition to the love and work listed by Freud. Allport described intrinsically religious people as less prejudiced than those motivated by a less healthy extrinsic religious orientation.

Various therapy techniques have been developed that reflect the different theoretical interpretations of adjustment. Psychoanalysis, which emphasizes the unconscious, seeks increases in consciousness through insight. Rogers developed client-centered therapy and encounter groups to help restore the true self through unconditional acceptance by others. Learning theorists emphasize behavioral interventions through systematic reinforcement and through such techniques as discrimination learning. To the extent that adjustment is influenced by heredity, as Cattell suggested, therapeutic interventions are less obvious.

Empirical comparisons of various therapeutic methods have been made. For the treatment of phobias, behavioral methods are often reported to be preferable to psychoanalytic treatment, which is more lengthy and no more effective (Barber & Luborsky, 1991; Goisman, 1983; Norcross, 1991). Examination of the particular behaviors of therapists using different approaches confirms that they do, in fact, say different things (use different "microstrategies") in their therapy (Mahrer, Sterner, Lawson, & Dessaulles, 1986).

Society

Personality is expressed through behavior in the social world. Failure in social behavior can motivate people to seek therapy to improve their personality, and personality tests are used to select people for social roles, such as particular jobs. Not all personality theorists have focused on the social world, however. Dollard reminded theorists of the importance of considering the social environment in which personality functions, but psychoanalysts still devote more attention to intrapsychic than to societal phenomena. Allport's contributions to social psychology (prejudice, rumor, and religion) testify to his recognition of the importance of society in personality. Learning theorists consistently attend to the social environment in their explanations of personality. Cattell described differences among groups and nations, suggesting the term "syntality" to describe group differences, and he improved intelligence testing by developing tests that were relatively free of cultural influence.

Some theorists have been criticized for ignoring the implications of personality for social behavior. Jung has been criticized for ignoring important social phenomena—for example, racism. Humanists, too, have sometimes been accused of focusing too much on the individual while ignoring society.

Society influences personality development. It provides tasks and models, and it influences the way parents raise children. Dollard and Miller described the importance of the social context for personality learning, and they explored social applications, including aggression and racism. Erikson featured society throughout his life-span developmental theory. People develop by mastering psychosocial tasks, and cultural institutions continue to support ego strengths throughout life. Erikson noticed the impact of society in his therapeutic practice, finding that identity issues were particularly prevalent in America. Horney, similarly, noted that changes that had taken place in society since the time of Freud influenced the types of problems patients brought to therapy.

Some theorists have been blamed for lack of awareness of societal influences on personality. Freud, in particular, has been faulted for describing sex differences as universal when in fact they were culturally specific (e.g., Lerman, 1986a, 1986b), but other theories have not escaped criticism (Torrey, 1987). Increasingly, psychologists are recognizing the impact of historical, cultural and socioeconomic conditions on personality (e.g., Baumeister, 1987; Holt, 1984; Markus & Kitayama, 1991; J.G. Miller, Bersoff, & Harwood, 1990).

Cross-cultural personality studies show that the dimensions of personality identified as fundamental in American culture (i.e., the "Big Five" trait dimensions) are different from the personality dimensions derived from Chinese students in Taiwan, and do not correlate well with those dimensions (Yang & Bond, 1990). Given cultural diversity, exploration of personality theories from other cultures and traditions, such as Buddhism (Nitis, 1989) and other Eastern approaches (Atwood & Maltin, 1991) may help us to evaluate the extent to which the personality theories we have studied are biased by the assumptions of Western culture.

There is also great diversity within each culture: different social classes, men and women. Are our theories broad enough to apply to all groups, beyond the largely white, middle-class, college and clinical populations in relation to which they were originally formulated? Clinicians have become increasingly aware of the impact of race and ethnicity on mental health and on the process of psychotherapy (e.g., A.C. Jones, 1985; N.S.C. Jones, 1990; Sue, 1988). To the extent that personality differences exist among groups, ignoring them limits the usefulness of theories and the effectiveness of therapies (Scott & Borodovsky, 1990). However, the investigation of personality differences between the races (Zuckerman, 1990a) and sexes (Baumeister, 1988; Benbow, 1990; Eagly, 1987a; Mednick, 1989) is controversial. Prejudices may bias such research and its interpretation. Furthermore, social change can influence research findings. For example, before the 1960s, research reported lower self-concepts in Afro-American children than in whites. This difference was not found later, when the civil rights movement changed the social environment in which the children were developing (Spurlock, 1986).

If society influences personality, can this knowledge be used to make improvements? Freud was pessimistic, since he believed that conflict was inevitable and universal between the individual's libidinal drives and civilization's restrictive forces. Many theories, however, are more optimistic, and assert that *with changes, society could support improved personality functioning.* Some theorists (Skinner and Maslow) have offered explicit Utopian visions. Others have focused their suggestions on specific areas within society.

What societal changes are desirable? Changes in sex roles and the relationships between men and women are desirable, according to Horney, Adler, and Rogers. Research in recent years has been more aware of gender, testing for and reporting sex differences routinely (e.g., Haring, Stock, & Okun, 1984). Males and females have different rates of ego development, as well as physical development; adolescent females achieve higher levels of ego development earlier than do adolescent males (Cohn, 1991). Some researchers have suggested that men and women develop different ego strengths (Gilligan, 1982), while others disagree (Cohn, 1991). Archer and Waterman (1988) report, on the basis of a review of relevant research, that there are no sex differences in the relationship of psychological individualism (personal identity, self-actualization, internal locus of control, and principled moral reasoning) to measures of psychological functioning (personal well-being, competence, and social interdependence). Earlier research indicating that older women have more mental health problems, particularly depression, compared to men, has been challenged (Feinson, 1987).

Several theorists have advocated changes in schooling (including Adler, Rogers, and Skinner). Rogers called for changes in work roles and made suggestions for the resolution of group conflicts. Jung emphasized the importance of cultural myths and rituals as pathways to the unconscious, encouraging the development of new myths. Bandura and Mischel's emphasis on modeling has implications for the role of the media in society, supporting the suggestion that aggressive models be replaced with more prosocial models on television and in film.

The impact of society, however, should not be overestimated. *Social or environmental forces have different impacts on people with different personalities.* Allport was an early *interactionist,* recognizing the joint impact of personality traits and the social environment on behavior. Social behaviorists, especially Mischel and Bandura, have given modern expression to this theme.

Cognitive Processes

Recent theoretical developments in psychology generally and in personality in particular have emphasized cognitive processes. Mischel and Bandura exemplify this recent tendency. They have argued that cognitive concepts (e.g., *person variables*) are the most useful concepts for understanding personality. That is, *people differ in the ways they think about themselves and their worlds.*

Cognitive processes are not, however, a new interest to personality. *Realistic cognition is described as a criterion of mental health* by many theorists (e.g., Freud, Allport, Rogers, Maslow, and Bandura). Freud warned that conscious experience often cannot be trusted because of defense mechanisms and the distorting influence of the unconscious. Other psychoanalysts generally share this view, including Horney and Erikson. Adler was less pessimistic; he thought that conscious experience and thought are generally trustworthy.

Psychoanalysts were particularly concerned with the difference between conscious and unconscious processes. They believed that *both rational thought and irrational, symbolic thought are important to personality.* Jung's work on the collective unconscious represents an extensive consideration of symbolic thought. Maslow, too, was interested in these less rational modes of cognition, including mystical experiences.

Individual differences in what are sometimes considered "cognitive styles" have also been explored. Jung described different cognitive functions (sensation and intuition, thinking and feeling), asserting that people vary in their use of these, but that all should be fully developed for optimal functioning. Cattell's interest in intelligence resulted in improved scales for measuring mental abilities. Further, some of the scales of his 16PF reflect differences in cognitive styles.

Language is a significant concern of many theorists. It has been described as the key to making experience conscious (Dollard and Miller). Dollard and Miller emphasized the importance of the correct labeling of experience. Cognition is central to Kelly's theory, which asserts that behaviors and emotions follow from a person's "personal constructs." Mischel and Bandura further developed this idea, describing the cognitive processes of personality, including expectancies and self-efficacy.

Mental experience is problematic for Skinner's theory because it is private and impossible to observe in others. In principle, Skinner explained mental processes in behavioral terms, although his analysis of language is widely criticized as overly reductionistic.

There is disagreement about how to evaluate people's self-statements. Some theorists assert that *people's self-statements cannot be trusted,* while others claim that *people's self-statements are generally accurate.* Psychoanalysts distrust self-statements. Allport, like Adler, thought that people's self-statements can generally be taken at face value.

Individual Differences

How important are differences among people? *In some ways, individuals are unique; in other ways, they are like other people.* While trait approaches emphasize the identification of differences among people, many other theories focus on dynamics common to all people (e.g., humanistic theories). Skinner's approach focuses on the individual, rather than making comparisons across individuals.

For some theorists, *the important differences among people can be observed in their behavior.* For others, *the important differences among people are not directly observable, but must be inferred indirectly.* The two extremes of this controversy are trait approaches and radical learning approaches. Trait theorists, Allport and Cattell, proposed that the basic units of personality must be inferred from behavior. Skinner, on the other hand, proposed that only overt behavior should be considered. Some theorists have specified the types of behaviors that are most important in describing personality. Horney emphasized differences in defensive interpersonal orientations, moving toward, against, or away from people.

Individual differences are often conceptualized as traits. Considerable research effort, reported in earlier chapters, has sought to identify the fundamental traits that differentiate people. Hampson, John, and Goldberg (1986) suggest that traits can be considered in a hierarchical arrangement of varying breadth. For example, a person may be described as "musical," or, more broadly, as "artistic," or, even more broadly, as "talented." Musical people are artistic. Artistic people are talented. However, talented people are not necessarily artistic or musical. "Talented" is at the top of this particular hierarchy. Some of the differences between narrower trait approaches and broader type approaches can be understood within this framework.

An alternative approach to traits has emerged more recently; that is, to define the units of personality in terms of *social-cognitive units* (Cervone, 1991) such as self-conceptions and goals. These units emphasize the social context of personality. Cognitive theorists (Mischel, Bandura, and Kelly) stress the cognitive labels that people apply to the environment and their experience, assessing personality by measuring such cognitions.

People vary in their patterns of motivation (in the goals they seek, and their ability to tolerate obstacles to goal attainment). Adler asserted that personality differences should be understood as consequences of the different goals people are trying to achieve and the style of life by which they try to achieve the goal. Some recent researchers have investigated individual striving toward goals (e.g., Omodei & Wearing, 1990) and "life tasks" (Cantor, 1990).

Personality theorists and researchers have been interested in devising ways to measure individual differences in personality. Many of these measurement procedures have involved self-report measures. Cattell identified 16 traits of normal personality (though recent work suggests five is sufficient). Though Rogers and Maslow did not focus on individual differences, measures of individual differences in the extent of self-actualization have been derived from their theories. Jung described two attitudes (introversion and extroversion) and four functions (thinking, feeling, sensation, and intuition) that have been interpreted as a typology of individual differences. Allport argued that comparing people (the nomothetic approach) is only one strategy, and that personality should also study the unique individual (the idiographic approach).

Personality theory generally assumes consistency of differences among people, despite personality change. *Some aspects of individual differences endure over time.* Freud's classical psychoanalysis, for example, describes patterns of defensive styles as enduring from early childhood throughout life, constituting personality. Much of the controversy over traits involves the issue of personality consistency. Longitudinal studies show considerable stability of personality (N. Brody, 1991; Kenny & Campbell, 1989). Some people change more than others, in part because of their interactions with different social environments (R.M. Lerner & Tubman, 1989; Ozer & Gjerde, 1989). Ozer and Gjerde (1989), continuing a line of research begun by Block (1971), reported that most of the subjects in their longitudinal sample had consistent personality patterns from age 3 to 18. Nonetheless, individual differences appeared in the pattern of consistency. Some changed relatively little, showing similar patterns of personality as assessed by the Q-sort technique throughout the time period. Others changed a great deal. Consistency was especially characteristic of males who, in high school, were "confident, poised, and earnest," and females who were "submissive, dependent, and less troublesome" (Ozer & Gjerde, 1989, p. 505).

Some aspects of individual differences endure over situations. In Skinner's theory, differences in behavior are said to result from differences in reinforcement histories. Such differences are not necessarily stable, but can change when the situation changes. These themes also describe other learning approaches: Dollard and Miller, Mischel and Bandura, and Kelly. Since personality involves adaptation to situations, consistency over situations is necessarily limited.

Choosing or Combining Theories

How many theories of personality are needed? Should we try to select the one best theory, or devise a new single theory to guide the field? Or is it better to have several theories coexist? Various opinions have been offered.

Eclecticism

One way of dealing with the diversity of theories is to advocate **eclecticism**. To be *eclectic* is to value selected contributions from diverse theories, without accepting any theory completely. For example, we could value psychoanalytic understandings of symbolism in art, while at the same time accepting the usefulness of behavioral methods of treating phobias. Eclecticism does not, however, provide a systematic framework for understanding personality. It does not offer a rationale for deciding when to select from among the diverse models.

Unified Theory

Staats (1981, 1991) argues that the time has come for psychology to develop a **unified theory**. In his view, all sciences progress from disunity to unity. Such has happened, for example, with physics. He says that it is time for psychology to search for links among phenomena that are now explained by diverse theories. This task of developing a unified theory has received little attention. Staats dismisses attempts to unify theory by reducing all phenomena either to physiological or learning phenomena. He urges greater respect for alternative points of view to encourage the discovery of conceptual bridges.

Several attempts to integrate theories have been made. Dollard and Miller, for example, combined psychoanalysis with learning theory. Convergences have also been explored between psychoanalysis and personal construct theory (B. Warren, 1990), between Adlerian Individual Psychology and behaviorism (Pratt, 1985), and between the theories of Erikson and Kelly (G.J. Neimeyer & Rareshide, 1991).

Pluralism

Alternatively, various paradigms can coexist, each maintaining its theoretical distinctiveness. This is theoretical **pluralism**. At present, psychology is a pluralistic discipline (Walsh & Peterson, 1985), as should be apparent from this text. This may be the desirable condition, at present. Terry Smith (1983) argues that it would be undesirable to focus entirely on one theoretical approach, since we cannot be certain which approach would be most productive:

> Given our current lack of knowledge, we should not be staking everything on what, through the dark glass of our ignorance, looks to be the best available alternative; but rather we should take a more experimental approach . . . and ask what alternatives are worth trying. Presumably there will be more than one. (T.L. Smith, 1983, p. 148)

Levels of Explanation: A Basis for Multiple Theories

People simultaneously exist at several levels: as biological beings, as conscious humans, as behaving organisms, and so on. Theories vary in which of these levels of experience they try to understand. As noted above, some theories include the biological level; others do not. Some describe cognitive variables; others avoid them.

Hyland (1985) has proposed a multilevel model. He suggests that person variables can be considered from three different perspectives: physiological, mentalistic, and mechanistic. He suggests that causality should only be proposed within a given level. For example, physiological outcomes such as "illness" should only be attributed to physiological causes. If mentalistic variables such as "feeling inadequate" are suggested, they should not be theorized to cause physiological changes directly, but only through proposing intermediate theoretical concepts, such as "illness-oriented thoughts," which exist at both the mentalistic and physiological levels (see Figure 15.1). In the area of the emotion, Staats has offered a multilevel theory that includes biological, behavioral, and cognitive variables (Staats & Eifert, 1990).

One way to make sense of the diversity of theories is to recognize that they explain different phenomena, often at different levels. A theory may be more precise if it restricts consideration to only one level of explanation. This restriction, though, limits the comprehensiveness of the theory.

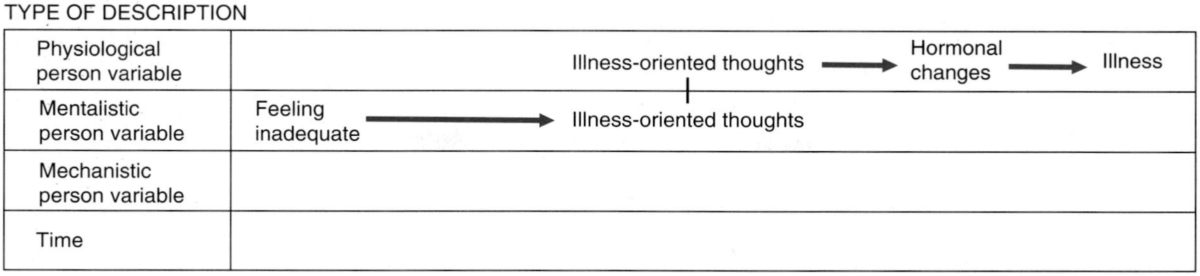

TYPE OF DESCRIPTION				
Physiological person variable		Illness-oriented thoughts →	Hormonal changes →	Illness
Mentalistic person variable	Feeling inadequate →	Illness-oriented thoughts		
Mechanistic person variable				
Time				

Note : Causal relations are indicated by horizontal lines and identity relations are indicated by vertical lines

FIGURE 15.1 A Model of Multiple Levels of Explanation: Psychosomatic Illness Explained in Terms of Mentalistic and Physiological Person Variables

(From Hyland, M.E. (1985). Do person variables exist in different ways? *American Psychologist*, 40, 1003–1010. Copyright 1985 by the American Psychological Association. Reprinted by permission.)

Criteria of a Good Theory: Revisited

Recall from Chapter 1 the criteria of a good theory: precision, verifiability, comprehensiveness, parsimony, applied value, and heuristic value. Often there are trade-offs among these criteria. Psychoanalytic and social psychoanalytic approaches attempt to explain a broad range of behaviors (comprehensiveness), but have concepts (for example, "libido") that are imprecise and not readily verified. Humanistic theory generally has been criticized as imprecise (e.g., Walsh & Peterson, 1985). Rogers's description of conditions of effective therapy, however, is phrased precisely and has stimulated considerable research. Behavioral and cognitive behavioral theories have also engendered considerable research. The reader may wish to review the various theories discussed in this text by considering how they measure up to these criteria of a sound theory.

The list of criteria is itself incomplete. For example, cognitive social learning approaches stand up well when evaluated in terms of the criteria of verifiability and applied value. Yet they have been criticized by humanistic psychologists for continuing a scientific model that objectifies humans, rather than enabling them to achieve their full potential. This criticism, based on the ideological or philosophical implications of a theory, does not correspond to any of the criteria defining a sound theory that have been presented. The model of science itself as a guide for personality theory has been questioned. Are scientific values a sufficient guide to personality theory? Science is traditionally considered objective, value-free. Some question whether such a value-free stance is desirable, or even possible, for personality theory (Kukla, 1982; Sampson, 1977, 1978).

Theoretical Paradigms as Metaphors

Theories are simply abstract systems, metaphors for understanding. The underlying metaphors are important, for they profoundly shape the types of constructs and theoretical propositions that a theory offers. Several metaphors for personality have been implicit in these theories.

The *mechanistic metaphor* presumes that personality is determined with the same external, decisive determinism that propels physical objects through space. It underlies Freudian theory and behaviorism. This metaphor has been adopted from the physical sciences (Rychlak, 1984b; Wolman, 1971), and historically has appealed to psychologists because it makes psychology seem more rigorous.

However, critics point out that psychologists continue to model their philosophy of science after eighteenth-century Newtonian physics, despite the fact that physicists themselves have dismissed this model as outdated (Atwood & Maltin, 1991; Oppenheimer, 1956; Slife, 1981). In Newton's eighteenth-century physics, the world could be understood mechanically. Objects did not move unless they were acted upon by outside forces, and then the change was continuous, in proportion to the outside force. With Einstein's formulation of the interrelationship between energy and matter (his famous $E = mc^2$ equation) and with the development of quantum theory, all that has changed. In modern physics, energies within matter can produce change without outside intervention, and change can occur in discontinuous "quantum leaps" within the atom (Einstein & Infeld, 1961). In contrast to the false dichotomy between the person and the environment (and other false dichotomies such as between free will and determinism, or mind and matter), the new physics proposes an integrated field approach (Midgley & Morris, 1988). Even the assumption that time moves in one direction has been questioned (Slife, 1981).

What about a biological metaphor? The *organic metaphor* compares personality with the growth of plants and animals. Rogers used this metaphor when he described the actualizing tendency, and it is also the underlying metaphor of Erikson's epigenetic principle. Potentials for development are located by this metaphor within the person, rather than externally. The environment is seen not as a determining force, as in the mechanistic metaphor, but rather as an environment conducive to the inherent growth of the personality or that impedes it, just as a seed may fall on good soil or poor.

The *information processing metaphor* is represented in cognitive theories, such as those of Kelly, Bandura, and Mischel. Unlike the organic metaphor, which implies only one healthy potential for a person, this metaphor recognizes multiple potentials, without focusing only on external determinants (as the mechanistic metaphor does). It recognizes developmental change, since personal constructs (like computer programs) can develop and change over time.

Many current psychological theories emphasize cognition (Pervin, 1985). Older approaches question the necessity of a separate cognitive approach, arguing that cognitive processes can be fully explained by environmental events (e.g., Skinner). Others have suggested that cognition can be explained in terms of neuronal events. The "consciousness revolution" (Sperry, 1988, 1990), in contrast, regards higher mental functioning, including subjective experience, as causal in its own right. Ziller (1988) has proposed that the concept of **orientation** provides "the cognitive link in person-situation interaction." An orientation directs a person to specific aspects of the environment. Ziller interprets concepts from diverse personality theory and research as exemplars of the orientation concept, including Jung's psychological types, Allport's Study of Values, and Maslow's hierarchy of needs. Ziller proposes "that hierarchies of orientations define personality. We are what we orient toward in our environment" (Ziller, 1988, p. 7).

Other important cognitions include those about early memories (Bruhn, 1990) and about the self (S. Epstein, 1973, 1980a, 1985). Such cognitions are of particular interest and can be considered as belonging to a separate metaphor. The metaphor of the *emergent self* suggests that a self-directed, willful personality emerges from the more deterministic and predictable forces described by the earlier metaphors. In science fiction, computers and robots are sometimes portrayed as evolving to a willful state, reflecting this image that self-will can emerge from parts that are, in less complex form, determined. This metaphor describes Adler's emphasis on choice and striving, and humanistic psychology's discussions of free will. It highlights people's purposeful behavior (cf. Sappington, 1990; Ziller, 1990).

Cognitions about the self have been a major focus of research and theory in recent years. S. Epstein (1973, 1980a, 1985) has proposed a Cognitive-Experiential Self-Theory that derives concepts from Kelly's theory of constructive alternativism, learning theory, psychoanalysis, and other approaches. He proposes that this theory is comprehensive (in the sense discussed in Chapter 1), able to address many current issues in personality research, including the person-situation debate, and the relationship between emotions and thought. Bruhn has proposed a cognitive-perceptual model of early memories. He suggests that memory processes explain diverse phenomena from other theories, including "drives (psychoanalysis), fictive final goals (Adlerian theory) [and] reinforcement (social learning theory)" (Bruhn, 1990, p. 96). This theory takes memory processes that have been investigated outside the field of personality and applies them to the study of individual personality. Autobiographical memory, that is, memory about the self and one's past, is central to personality, according to Bruhn.

Finally, a metaphor of the *transcendent self* is suggested by Jung's mysticism and by the suggestions of experience beyond individual ego that Maslow and Rogers mentioned. This metaphor, however, has few advocates within personality theory, which is still struggling to understand the experience of individuals.

Is a New Paradigm Emerging?

Theoretical work within the field of personality continues to develop, challenging old assumptions about determinism and self-direction. The recent emphasis within psychology on cognition has brought new ways of thinking about causality to a discipline that previously tried to understand causes in terms of antecedent events and physiological processes. Sperry has argued that "micro" control from neurological processes now is accompanied with "macro" control from higher levels, from emergent mental processes. This higher control can be called "emergent" determinism (Sperry, 1988).

Though it seems obvious that causes must precede effects in time, this is simply one possible assumption of a philosophy of science. It corresponds to Aristotle's concept of the **efficient cause**, which occurs across time. Aristotle's **final cause** (purpose), **formal cause** (form or organization), and **material cause** (substance) do not presume a time dimension. The *final cause* provides an alternative philosophical assumption for some of the new trends within psychology (Rychlak, 1977, 1986, 1988; Slife, 1981). Rychlak's Logical Learning Theory proposes the concept of a **telosponse**, "behavior done for the sake of a premised reason (purpose, intention, etc.)"

(Rychlak, 1984b, p. 92). He compares his approach to aspects of several of the theories included in this text: "the Freudian *wish,* the Adlerian *prototype,* the Jungian *archetype,* . . . [and] the Kellyian *construct*" (1986, p. 757), as well as the humanists Rogers and Maslow (Rychlak, 1977). Rychlak's model offers a philosophical basis for **teleology**, and he predicts that "the future is bright for the teleologist" (1986, p. 758).

Most psychologists maintain that teleology is incompatible with science, which requires the assumption of determinism. In response, Rychlak (1977, 1984b) charges that psychologists have not adequately differentiated between theory and method. Though experimentation requires a causal rather than a teleological model, theory does not. Rychlak argues that teleological ideas have been an important part of human thought throughout history, from before Aristotle up to twentieth-century physics. Psychology is unduly narrow to rule them out of its theorizing. Many factors must be considered to understand personality, and some of these factors are teleological (e.g., purpose, "free will"). To permit them adequate representation within personality theory requires a shift of paradigm, not borrowed from physics or another science, but developed explicitly to understand human personality. As we move toward such a new paradigm, it is well that researchers are paying serious attention to people's real life experiences (e.g., Baumeister, Stillwell, & Wotman, 1990) and life stories (e.g., G.S. Howard, 1991; Vitz, 1990), and to biographical analyses. Theory, after all, should not be imposed on the data, but should emerge from it.

Summary

Several theoretical perspectives toward personality have been discussed in this text. They are here considered for their contributions and assumptions on several topics of interest to the field of personality. *Biological factors* relevant to personality include temperament and biological motivations; the issue of heredity has been researched by few perspectives. Most theories assume that *child development* is important for the development of personality because it provides key learning opportunities, although only a few perspectives have conducted extensive research with children. Changes in personality during *adult development* are discussed by various theories. Many personality theories have originated in clinical contexts, and even those that have not generally make some statements about *mental health,* adjustment, or therapy. The metaphors used to describe mental health are astonishingly varied, ranging from Freud's model of libidinal energies to the learning theorist's focus on the particular behaviors. Few theories have recognized the role of *society* in shaping personality, although Horney urged consideration of cultural factors influencing neurosis and sex roles, and Dollard stressed that personality be systematically studied in relation to its cultural context. *Cognitive processes* have become increasingly important for personality theory, which from its origins recognized phenomena of varying levels of conscious awareness; dramatic theoretical and empirical developments have been reported by Bandura and Mischel in particular. Personality theorists have quite varied perspectives on *individual differences,* with some (e.g., Cattell) urging increased work on personality measurement to identify stable differences among individuals, and others concerned that trait and other labels falsely imply personality stability, thereby impeding investigation of the dynamic and changing processes of personality.

Comparison among theories is difficult because many of them are designed to explain different phenomena. Observations and measurements relevant to one theory are often irrelevant to others. Furthermore, not all theorists presented ideas in ways that could readily be empirically verified. An *eclectic* approach accepts contributions, piecemeal, from a variety of theories. A *pluralistic* approach encourages the coexistence of a variety of systematic theories. Theories may deal with different *levels of explanation* of phenomena. Ultimately a more comprehensive *unified theory* may emerge.

Finally, theoretical paradigms may be considered as *metaphors,* including the *mechanistic metaphor,* the *organic metaphor,* the *information processing metaphor,* the metaphor of the *emergent self,* and the metaphor of the *transcendent self.* Theoretical developments continue to unfold, challenging philosophical assumptions that insist upon determinism and preclude self-direction.

GLOSSARY

eclecticism combining ideas from a variety of theories

efficient cause explanation in terms of the sequence of events through time, that is, the mechanisms by which events happen

final cause explanation in terms of the goal toward which events aim

formal cause explanation in terms of the design or organization of things or events

homogamy the tendency of people to marry others who are similar to themselves

material cause explanation in terms of the underlying substance of which things are made, including genetic and physical causes

orientation a person's tendency to be directed toward specific aspects of the environment

paradigm a general framework that provides direction to a field of science, within which theoretical concepts are elaborated and empirical work is conducted

pluralism the coexistence of various theories without attempting to combine them

teleology the study of phenomena in terms of their overall purpose, design, or intent (rather than in terms of the mechanisms by which they come about)

telosponse Rychlak's term for behavior that is done for the sake of a particular purpose or intention

unified theory a theory that combines diverse aspects from various approaches, indicating how they are organized and related

STUDY QUESTIONS

1. Discuss the way personality theorists have considered *biological factors* in personality.
2. Discuss the role of *child development* in various personality theories.
3. Discuss the role of *adult development* in various personality theories.
4. Discuss the relationship of personality theory to *therapy*. Consider contributions of therapists to personality theory, and suggestions of various personality theories for therapy.
5. To what extent have personality theories reflected an awareness of *cultural* factors? What cultural factors have not been adequately considered?
6. Describe the role of *cognition*, including levels of consciousness, in personality theories.
7. How have various theories described *individual differences* in personality? Include traits and other concepts in your discussion.
8. Discuss the ways that one can deal with theoretical diversity, including eclecticism, pluralism, and the search for a unified theory.
9. Evaluate the theories covered in this course according to the criteria for a good theory.
10. What is a theoretical *paradigm*? List and explain several metaphors for personality.

References

Abelson, R. P. (1981). Psychological status of the script concept. *American Psychologist, 36*, 715–729.

Abraham, K. (1986). Ego identity differences among Anglo-American and Mexican-American adolescents. *Journal of Adolescence, 9*, 151–167.

Acklin, M. W., Bibb, J. L., Boyer, P., & Jain, V. (1991). Early memories as expressions of relationship paradigms: A preliminary investigation. *Journal of Personality Assessment, 57*, 177–192.

Acklin, M. W., Sauer, A., Alexander, G., & Dugoni, B. (1989). Predicting depression using earliest childhood memories. *Journal of Personality Assessment, 53*, 51–59.

Acosta, S. (1990). Auditory hallucinations and delusional thinking: A review and critique of outcome studies. *Behavioral Residential Treatment, 5,* 189–206.

Adams, G. R., & Fitch, S. A. (1982). Ego stage and identity status development: A cross-sequential analysis. *Journal of Personality and Social Psychology, 43*, 574–583.

Adams-Webber, J. (1990). Personal construct theory and cognitive science. *International Journal of Personal Construct Psychology, 3*, 415–421.

Adams-Webber, J. R. (1970). An analysis of the discriminant validity of several repertory grid indices. *British Journal of Psychology, 60*, 83–90.

Adler, A. (1927). *Understanding human nature.* (W. B. Wolfe, Trans.). New York: Fawcett. (Original work published 1921)

Adler, A. (1929). *The practice and theory of individual psychology.* (P. Radin, Trans.) (2nd ed.). London: Routledge & Kegan Paul. (Original work published 1923)

Adler, A. (1958). Suicide. *Journal of Individual Psychology, 14*, 57–61. (Original work published 1937)

Adler, A. (1964). *Social interest: A challenge to mankind.* New York: Capricorn. (Original work published 1936)

Adler, A. (1978). *Co-operation between the sexes: Writings on women and men, love and marriage, and sexuality.* (H. L. Ansbacher & R. R. Ansbacher, Eds. and Trans.). New York: Norton.

Adler, A. (1982a). The fundamental views of Individual Psychology. *Individual Psychology, 38*, 3–6. (Original work published 1935)

Adler, A. (1982b). The progress of mankind. *Individual Psychology, 38*, 13–17. (Original work published 1937)

Adler, A. (1988a). The child's inner life and a sense of community. *Individual Psychology, 44*, 417–423. (Original work published 1917)

Adler, A. (1988b). Problem children. *Individual Psychology, 44*, 406–416. (Original work published 1926)

Adler, A. (1988c). Personality as a self-consistent unity. *Individual Psychology, 44*, 431–440. (Original work published 1932)

Ahmed, S. M. S., & Mapletoft, S. J. (1989). A new approach to explain aggression. *Perceptual and Motor Skills, 69*, 403–408.

Ainslie, G. (1982). A behavioral economic approach to the defense mechanisms: Freud's energy theory revisited. *Social Science Information, 21*, 735–779.

Ainsworth, M. D. S. (1972). Attachment and dependency. In J. L. Gewirtz (Ed.), *Attachment and dependency* (pp. 97–137). Washington, DC: Winston.

Ainsworth, M. D. S., Blehar, M. C., Waters, E., & Wall, S. (1978). *Patterns of attachment: A psychological study of the Strange Situation.* Hillsdale, NJ: Erlbaum.

Albion, F. M. (1983). A methodological analysis of self-control in applied settings. *Behavioral Disorders, 8*, 87–102.

Alexander, I. E. (1988). Personality, psychological assessment, and psychobiography. *Journal of Personality, 56*, 265–294.

Alexander, I. E. (1990). *Personology: Method and content in personality assessment and psychobiography.* Durham, NC: Duke University Press.

Alexander, S. (1983). *Very much a lady.* New York: Dell.

Allen, H. J. (1980). P. W. Bridgman and B. F. Skinner on private experience. *Behaviorism, 8*, 15–29.

Allers, C. T., White, J., & Hornbuckle, D. (1990). Early recollections: Detecting depression in the elderly. *Individual Psychology, 46*, 61–66.

Allport, G. W. (1929). The study of personality by the intuitive method: An experiment in teaching from the locomotive god. *Journal of Abnormal and Social Psychology, 24*, 14–27.

Allport, G. W. (1931). What is a trait of personality? *Journal of Abnormal and Social Psychology, 25*, 368–371.

Allport, G. W. (1937a). The functional autonomy of motives. *American Journal of Psychology, 50*, 141–156.

Allport, G. W. (1937b). *Personality: A psychological interpretation.* New York: Henry Holt.

Allport, G. W. (1940). The psychologist's frame of reference. *Psychological Bulletin, 37*, 1–28.

Allport, G. W. (1950a). *The individual and his religion.* New York: Macmillan.

Allport, G. W. (1950b). *The nature of personality: Selected papers.* Cambridge, MA: Addison-Wesley.

Allport, G. W. (1954). *The nature of prejudice.* Cambridge, MA: Addison-Wesley.

Allport, G. W. (1955). *Becoming: Basic considerations for a psychology of personality.* New Haven, CT: Yale University Press.

Allport, G. W. (1959). Religion and prejudice. *Crane Review, 2,* 1–10.

Allport, G. W. (1961). *Pattern and growth in personality.* New York: Holt, Rinehart & Winston.

Allport, G. W. (1962). Prejudice: Is it societal or personal? *Journal of Social Issues, 18*(2), 120–134.

Allport, G. W. (1963). Behavioral science, religion, and mental health. *Journal of Religion and Health, 2,* 187–197.

Allport, G. W. (1964). Mental health: A generic attitude. *Journal of Religion and Health, 4,* 7–21.

Allport, G. W. (Ed.). (1965). *Letters from Jenny.* New York: Harcourt Brace Jovanovich.

Allport, G. W. (1966a). The religious context of prejudice. *Journal for the Scientific Study of Religion, 5,* 447–457.

Allport, G. W. (1966b). Traits revisited. *American Psychologist, 21,* 1–10.

Allport, G. W. (1967). "Gordon W. Allport." In E. G. Boring & G. Lindzey (Eds.), *A history of psychology in autobiography* (Vol. 5, pp. 3–25). Englewood Cliffs, NJ: Prentice-Hall.

Allport, G. W., & Allport, F. H. (1921). Personality traits: Their classification and measurement. *Journal of Abnormal and Social Psychology, 16,* 6–40.

Allport, G. W., Bruner, J. S., & Jandorf, E. M. (1941). Personality under social catastrophe: Ninety life-histories of the Nazi revolution. *Character and Personality, 10,* 1–21.

Allport, G. W., & Odbert, H. S. (1936). Trait-names: A psycholexical study. *Psychological Monographs, 47,* No. 211.

Allport, G. W., & Postman, L. (1947). *The psychology of rumor.* New York: Henry Holt.

Allport, G. W., & Ross, J. M. (1967). Personal religious orientation and prejudice. *Journal of Personality and Social Psychology, 5,* 432–443.

Allport, G. W., & Vernon, P. E. (1931). *A study of values.* Boston: Houghton Mifflin.

Allport, G. W., & Vernon, P. E. (1933). *Studies in expressive movement.* New York: Macmillan.

Alter-Reid, K., Gibbs, M. S., Lachenmeyer, J. R., Sigal, J., & Massoth, N. A. (1986). Sexual abuse of children: A review of the empirical findings. *Clinical Psychology Review, 6,* 249–266.

Altman, K. E., & Rule, W. R. (1980). The relationship between social interest dimensions of early recollections and selected counselor variables. *Journal of Individual Psychology, 36,* 227–234.

Ambrose, S. E. (1987). *Nixon: Vol. 1. The education of a politician, 1913–1962.* New York: Simon & Schuster.

Ambrose, S. E. (1989). *Nixon: Vol. 2. The triumph of a politician, 1962–1972.* New York: Simon & Schuster.

American Psychological Association. (1957). The American Psychological Association Distinguished Scientific Contribution Awards for 1956. *American Psychologist, 12,* 125–133.

American Psychological Association. (1958). Distinguished Scientific Contribution Awards. *American Psychologist, 13,* 729–738.

American Psychological Association. (1973). Distinguished Professional Contribution Award for 1972. *American Psychologist, 28*, 71–74.

American Psychological Association. (1981). Awards for distinguished scientific contributions: 1980. Albert Bandura. *American Psychologist, 36*, 27–34.

American Psychological Association. (1990). Citation for outstanding lifetime contribution to psychology: Presented to B.F. Skinner, August 10, 1990. *American Psychologist, 45*, 1204–1205.

Amerikaner, M., Elliot, D., & Swank, P. (1988). Social interest as a predictor of vocational satisfaction. *Individual Psychology, 44*, 316–323.

Andersen, S. M., & Klatzky, R. L. (1987). Traits and social stereotypes: Levels of categorization in person perception. *Journal of Personality and Social Psychology, 53*, 235–246.

Anderson, W. (1975). The self-actualization of Richard M. Nixon. *Journal of Humanistic Psychology, 15*(1), 27–34.

Andrews, J. D. (1989). Integrating visions of reality: Interpersonal diagnosis and the existential vision. *American Psychologist, 44*, 803–817.

Angelou, M. (1969). *I know why the caged bird sings.* New York: Bantam.

Angelou, M. (1974). *Gather together in my name.* New York: Bantam.

Angelou, M. (1976). *Singin' and swingin' and gettin' merry like Christmas.* New York: Bantam.

Angelou, M. (1981). *The heart of a woman.* New York: Bantam.

Angelou, M. (1986). *All God's children need traveling shoes.* New York: Vintage.

Annis, H. M. (1990). Relapse to substance abuse: Empirical findings within a cognitive-social learning approach. *Journal of Psychoactive Drugs, 22*, 117–124.

Ansbacher, H. L. (1982). Alfred Adler's views on the unconscious. *Individual Psychology, 38*, 32–41.

Ansbacher, H. L. (1988). Dreikurs's four goals of children's disturbing behavior and Adler's social interest–activity typology. *Individual Psychology, 44*, 282–289.

Ansbacher, H. L. (1989). Adlerian psychology: The tradition of brief psychotherapy. *Individual Psychology, 45*, 26–33.

Ansbacher, H. L. (1990). Alfred Adler's influence on the three leading cofounders of humanistic psychology. *Journal of Humanistic Psychology, 30*, 45–53.

Ansbacher, H. L., & Ansbacher, R. R. (Eds.). (1956). *The individual psychology of Alfred Adler: A systematic presentation in selections from his writings.* New York: Harper Torchbooks.

Antrobus, J. (1991). Dreaming: Cognitive processes during cortical activation and high afferent thresholds. *Psychological Review, 98*, 96–121.

Apostal, R., & Marks, C. (1990). Correlations between the Strong-Campbell and Myers-Briggs scales of introversion-extraversion and career interests. *Psychological Reports, 66*, 811–816.

Archer, S. L. (1982). The lower age boundaries of identity development. *Child Development, 53*, 1551–1556.

Archer, S. L. (1989). Gender differences in identity development: Issues of process, domain and timing. *Journal of Adolescence, 12*, 117–138.

Archer, S. L., & Waterman, A. S. (1988). Psychological individualism: Gender differences or gender neutrality? *Human Development, 31*, 65–81.

Arend, R. A., Gove, F., & Sroufe, L. A. (1979). Continuity of individual adaptation from infancy to kindergarten: A predictive study of ego-resiliency and curiosity in preschoolers. *Child Development, 50*, 950–959.

Argentero, P. (1989). Second-order factor structure of Cattell's 16 Personality Factor Questionnaire. *Perceptual and Motor Skills, 68,* 1043–1047.

Arlow, J. A. (1977). Psychoanalysis as scientific method. In M.M. Rahman (Ed.), *The Freudian paradigm: Psychoanalysis and scientific thought.* Chicago: Nelson-Hall.

Arnow, D., & Harrison, R. H. (1991). Affect in early memories of borderline patients. *Journal of Personality Assessment, 56,* 75–83.

Atkinson, R. (1991). A new myth of humanity. *Humanistic Psychologist, 19,* 354–358.

Atkinson, J. W., & McClelland, D. C. (1948). The effect of different intensities of the hunger drive on thematic apperception. *Journal of Experimental Psychology, 38,* 643–658.

Atwood, J. D., & Maltin, L. (1991). Putting Eastern philosophies into Western psychotherapies. *American Journal of Psychotherapy, 45,* 368–382.

Baird, L. L. (1990). A 24-year longitudinal study of the development of religious ideas. *Psychological Reports, 66,* 479–482.

Bakan, D. (1982). On evil as a collective phenomenon. *Journal of Humanistic Psychology, 22*(4), 91–92.

Baker, L. A., & Daniels, D. (1990). Nonshared environmental influences and personality differences in adult twins. *Journal of Personality and Social Psychology, 58,* 103–110.

Balay, J., & Shevrin, H. (1988). The subliminal psychodynamic activation method: A critical review. *American Psychologist, 43,* 161–174.

Baldwin, A. C., Critelli, J. W., Stevens, L. C., & Russell, S. (1986). Androgyny and sex role measurement: A personal construct approach. *Journal of Personality and Social Psychology, 51,* 1081–1088.

Baltes, M. M., & Barton, E. M. (1979). Behavioral analysis of aging: A review of the operant model and research. *International Journal of Behavioral Development, 2,* 297–320.

Bandura, A. (1961). Psychotherapy as a learning process. *Psychological Bulletin, 58,* 143–159.

Bandura, A. (1965a). Behavioral modifications through modeling procedures. In L. Krasner & L. Ullmann (Eds.), *Research in Behavior Modification* (pp. 310–340). New York: Holt, Rinehart & Winston.

Bandura, A. (1965b). Influences of models' reinforcement contingencies on the acquisition of imitative responses. *Journal of Personality and Social Psychology, 1,* 589–595.

Bandura, A. (1965c). Vicarious processes: A case of no-trial learning. In L. Berkowitz (Ed.), *Advances in experimental social psychology* (Vol. 2, pp. 1–55). New York: Academic Press.

Bandura, A. (1969). Social learning of moral judgments. *Journal of Personality and Social Psychology, 11,* 275–279.

Bandura, A. (1971). Analysis of modeling processes. In A. Bandura (Ed.), *Psychological modeling: Conflicting theories* (pp. 1–62). Chicago: Aldine-Atherton.

Bandura, A. (1973). *Aggression: A social learning analysis.* Englewood Cliffs, NJ: Prentice-Hall.

Bandura, A. (1974). Behavior theory and the models of man. *American Psychologist, 29,* 859–869.

Bandura, A. (1976). Self-reinforcement: Theoretical and methodological considerations. *Behaviorism, 4,* 135–155.

Bandura, A. (1977). Self-efficacy: Toward a unifying theory of behavioral change. *Psychological Review, 84,* 191–215.

Bandura, A. (1978). The self system in reciprocal determinism. *American Psychologist, 33,* 344–358.

Bandura, A. (1980). Gauging the relationship between self-efficacy judgment and action. *Cognitive Therapy and Research, 4,* 263–268.

Bandura, A. (1984a). Recycling misconceptions of perceived self-efficacy. *Cognitive Therapy and Research, 8,* 231–255.

Bandura, A. (1984b). Representing personal determinants in causal structures. *Psychological Review, 91,* 508–511.

Bandura, A. (1986a). Fearful expectations and avoidant actions as coeffects of perceived self-inefficacy. *American Psychologist, 41,* 1389–1391.

Bandura, A. (1986b). *Social foundations of thought and action: A social cognitive theory.* Englewood Cliffs, NJ: Prentice-Hall.

Bandura, A. (1989a). Human agency in social cognitive theory. *American Psychologist, 44,* 1175–1184.

Bandura, A. (1989b). Regulation of cognitive processes through perceived self-efficacy. *Developmental Psychology, 25,* 729–735.

Bandura, A. (1990a). Perceived self-efficacy in the exercise of control over AIDS infection. *Evaluation and Program Planning, 13,* 9–17.

Bandura, A. (1990b). Selective activation and disengagement of moral control. *Journal of Social Issues, 46* (1), 27–46.

Bandura, A. (1991a). Human agency: The rhetoric and the reality. *American Psychologist, 46,* 157–162.

Bandura, A. (1991b). Social cognitive theory of self-regulation. *Organizational Behavior and Human Decision Processes, 50,* 248–287.

Bandura, A., Adams, N. E., & Beyer, J. (1977). Cognitive processes mediating behavioral change. *Journal of Personality and Social Psychology, 35,* 125–139.

Bandura, A., Adams, N. E., Hardy, A. B., & Howells, G. N. (1980). Tests of the generality of self-efficacy theory. *Cognitive Therapy and Research, 4,* 39–66.

Bandura, A., & Barab, P. G. (1973). Processes governing disinhibitory effects through symbolic modeling. *Journal of Abnormal Psychology, 82,* 1–9.

Bandura, A., Blanchard, E. B., & Ritter, B. (1969). The relative efficacy of desensitization and modeling approaches for inducing behavioral, affective, and attitudinal changes. *Journal of Personality and Social Psychology, 13,* 173–199.

Bandura, A., & Cervone, D. (1986). Differential engagement of self-reactive influences in cognitive motivation. *Organizational Behavior and Human Decision Processes, 38,* 92–113.

Bandura, A., Cioffi, D., Taylor, C. B., & Brouillard, M. E. (1988). Perceived self-efficacy in coping with cognitive stressors and opioid activation. *Journal of Personality and Social Psychology, 55,* 479–488.

Bandura, A., Grusec, J. E., & Menlove, F. L. (1966). Observational learning as a function of symbolization and incentive set. *Child Development, 37,* 499–506.

Bandura, A., Grusec, J. E., & Menlove, F. L. (1967a). Some social determinants of self-monitoring reinforcement systems. *Journal of Personality and Social Psychology, 5,* 449–455.

Bandura, A., Grusec, J. E., & Menlove, F. L. (1967b). Vicarious extinction of avoidance behavior. *Journal of Personality and Social Psychology, 5,* 16–23.

Bandura, A., Jeffery, R. W., & Wright, C. L. (1974). Efficacy of participant modeling as a function of response induction aids. *Journal of Abnormal Psychology, 83,* 56–64.

Bandura, A., & Jourden, F. J. (1991). Self-regulatory mechanisms governing the impact of social comparison on complex decision making. *Journal of Personality and Social Psychology, 60,* 941–951.

Bandura, A., & Mahoney, M. J. (1974). Maintenance and transfer of self-reinforcement functions. *Behaviour Research and Therapy, 12,* 89–97.

Bandura, A., Mahoney, M. J., & Dirks, S. J. (1976). Discriminative activation and maintenance of contingent self-reinforcement. *Behaviour Research and Therapy, 14,* 1–6.

Bandura, A., & McDonald, F. J. (1963). The influence of social reinforcement and the behavior of models in shaping children's moral judgments. *Journal of Abnormal Psychology, 67,* 274–281.

Bandura, A., & Menlove, F. L. (1968). Factors determining vicarious extinction of avoidance behavior through symbolic modeling. *Journal of Personality and Social Psychology, 8,* 99–108.

Bandura, A., & Mischel, W. (1965). Modification of self-imposed delay of reward through exposure to live and symbolic models. *Journal of Personality and Social Psychology, 2,* 698–705.

Bandura, A., O'Leary, A., Taylor, C. B., Gauthier, J., & Gossard, D. (1987). Perceived self-efficacy and pain control: Opioid and nonopioid mechanisms. *Journal of Personality and Social Psychology, 53,* 563–571.

Bandura, A., Reese, L., & Adams, N. E. (1982). Microanalysis of action and fear arousal as a function of differential levels of perceived self-efficacy. *Journal of Personality and Social Psychology, 43,* 5–21.

Bandura, A., & Rosenthal, T. L. (1966). Vicarious classical conditioning as a function of arousal level. *Journal of Personality and Social Psychology, 3,* 54–62.

Bandura, A., Ross, D., & Ross, S. A. (1963a). A comparative test of the status envy, social power, and secondary reinforcement theories of identificatory learning. *Journal of Abnormal and Social Psychology, 67,* 527–534.

Bandura, A., Ross, D., & Ross, S. A. (1963b). Vicarious reinforcement and imitative learning. *Journal of Abnormal and Social Psychology, 67,* 601–607.

Bandura, A., Taylor, C. B., Williams, S. L., Mefford, I. N., & Barchas, J. D. (1985). Catecholamine secretion as a function of perceived coping self-efficacy. *Journal of Consulting and Clinical Psychology, 53,* 406–414.

Bandura, A., & Whalen, C. K. (1966). The influence of antecedent reinforcement and divergent modeling cues on patterns of self-reward. *Journal of Personality and Social Psychology, 3,* 373–382.

Bandura, A., & Wood, R. (1989). Effect of perceived controllability and performance standards on self-regulation of complex decision making. *Journal of Personality and Social Psychology, 56,* 805–814.

Banks, H. C., & Juni, S. (1991). Defense mechanisms in minority African-American and Hispanic youths: Standardization and scale reliabilities. *Journal of Personality Assessment, 56,* 327–334.

Bannister, D. (1960). Conceptual structure in thought disordered schizophrenics. *Journal of Mental Science, 106,* 1230–1249.

Bannister, D. (1962). The nature and measurement of schizophrenic thought disorder. *Journal of Mental Science, 108,* 825–842.

Bannister, D. (1963). The genesis of schizophrenic thought disorder: A serial invalidation hypothesis. *British Journal of Psychiatry, 109,* 680–686.

Bannister, D. (1965). The genesis of schizophrenic thought disorder: Re-test of the serial invalidation hypothesis. *British Journal of Psychiatry, 111,* 377–382.

Bannister, D. (1975). Personal construct theory psychotherapy. In D. Bannister

(Ed.), *Issues and approaches in the psychological therapies* (pp. 31–47). Chichester, UK: Wiley.

Bannister, D., Adams-Webber, J. R., Penn, W. L., & Radley, A. R. (1975). Reversing the process of thought-disorder: A serial validation experiment. *British Journal of Social and Clinical Psychology, 14,* 169–180.

Bannister, D., & Fransella, F. (1966). A grid test of schizophrenic thought disorder. *British Journal of Social and Clinical Psychology, 5,* 95–102.

Bannister, D., Fransella, F., & Agnew, J. (1971). Characteristics and validity of the grid test on thought disorder. *British Journal of Social and Clinical Psychology, 10,* 144–151.

Bannister, D., & Salmon, P. (1966). Schizophrenic thought disorder: Specific or diffuse? *British Journal of Medical Psychology, 39,* 215–219.

Barash, D. P. (1982). *Sociobiology and behavior* (2nd ed.). New York: Elsevier.

Barber, J. P., & Luborsky, L. (1991). A psychodynamic view of simple phobias and prescriptive matching: A commentary. *Psychotherapy, 28,* 469–472.

Baron, S. H., & Pletsch, C. (Eds.). (1985). *Introspection in biography.* Hillsdale, NJ: Erlbaum.

Baruth, L., & Eckstein, D. (1981). *Life style: Theory, practice and research* (2nd ed.). Dubuque, IA: Kendall/Hunt.

Bassoff, E. S., & Glass, G. V. (1982). The relationship between sex roles and mental health: A meta-analysis of twenty-six studies. *Counseling Psychologist, 10,* 105–112.

Batson, C. D. (1990). Good Samaritans—or priests and Levites? Using William James as a guide in the study of religious prosocial motivation. *Personality and Social Psychology Bulletin, 16,* 758–768.

Baumeister, R. F. (1987). How the self became a problem: A psychological review of historical research. *Journal of Personality and Social Psychology, 52,* 163–176.

Baumeister, R. F. (1988) Should we stop studying sex differences altogether? *American Psychologist, 43,* 1092–1095.

Baumeister, R. F. (1990). Suicide as escape from self. *Psychological Review, 97,* 90–113.

Baumeister, R. F. (1991). On the stability of variability: Retest reliability of metatraits. *Personality and Social Psychology Bulletin, 17,* 633–639.

Baumeister, R. F., Stillwell, A., & Wotman, S. R. (1990). Victim and perpetrator accounts of interpersonal conflict: Autobiographical narratives about anger. *Journal of Personality and Social Psychology, 59,* 994–1005.

Baumeister, R. F., & Tice, D. M. (1988). Metatraits. *Journal of Personality, 56,* 571–598.

Baumrind, D. (1967). Child care practices anteceding three patterns of preschool behavior. *Genetic Psychology Monographs, 75,* 43–88.

Baumrind, D. (1971). Current patterns of parental authority. *Developmental Psychology Monograph, 4*(1), part 2.

Beck, J. E. (1980). Learning from experience in sensitivity training groups: A personal construct theory model and framework for research. *Small Group Behavior, 11,* 279–296.

Beck, J. E. (1987). Participant change in sensitivity training groups: Repertory grid measures of change in participants' construct systems. *Small Group Behavior, 18,* 336–355.

Beck, J. E. (1988a). Testing a personal construct theory model of the experiential learning process: A. The impact of invalidation on the construing processes of participants in sensitivity training groups. *Small Group Behavior, 19,* 79–102.

Beck, J. E. (1988b). Testing a personal construct theory model of the experiential learning process: B. Defensive responses to invalidation and the construing processes of participants in sensitivity training groups. *Small Group Behavior, 19,* 240–258.

Beck, J. E. (1988c). Testing a personal construct theory model of the experiential learning process: C. The effect of the experience of acceptance and the construing processes of participants in sensitivity training groups. *Small Group Behavior, 19,* 342–362.

Bell, L., & Schniedewind, N. (1989). Realizing the promise of humanistic education: A reconstructed pedagogy for personal and social change. *Journal of Humanistic Psychology, 29,* 200–223.

Bem, D. J. (1983). Further déjà vu in the search for cross-situational consistency: A reply to Mischel and Peake. *Psychological Review, 90,* 390–393.

Bem, D. J., & Allen, A. (1974). On predicting some of the people some of the time: The search for cross-situational consistencies in behavior. *Psychological Review, 81,* 506–520.

Bem, D. J., & Funder, D. C. (1978). Predicting more of the people more of the time: Assessing the personality of situations. *Psychological Review, 85,* 485–501.

Bem, S. L. (1974). The measurement of psychological androgyny. *Journal of Consulting and Clinical Psychology, 42,* 155–162.

Bem, S. L. (1976). Probing the promise of androgyny. In A. G. Kaplan & J. P. Bean (Eds.), *Beyond sex-role stereotypes: Readings towards a psychology of androgyny.* Boston: Little, Brown.

Benbow, C. P. (1990). Gender differences: Searching for facts. *American Psychologist, 45,* 988.

Benjamin, L. T. (1988). A history of teaching machines. *American Psychologist, 43,* 703–712.

Berger, M. M. (1991). Introduction: Paying homage to my teacher: Karen Horney (1885–1952). *American Journal of Psychoanalysis, 51,* 191–207.

Bergman, M., Akin, S. B., & Felig, P. (1990). Understanding the diabetic patient from a psychological dimension: Implications for the patient and the provider. *American Journal of Psychoanalysis, 50,* 25–33.

Bergmann, M. S. (1973). Limitations of method in psychoanalytic biography: A historical inquiry. *Journal of the American Psychoanalytic Association, 21,* 833–850.

Berkowitz, L. (1962). *Aggression: A social psychological analysis.* New York: McGraw-Hill.

Berkowitz, L. (1965). The concept of aggressive drive: Some additional considerations. In L. Berkowitz (Ed.), *Advances in experimental social psychology* (Vol. 2). New York: Academic Press.

Berkowitz, L. (1969). The frustration-aggression hypothesis revisited. In L. Berkowitz (Ed.), *Roots of aggression.* New York: Atherton.

Berkowitz, L. (1978). Whatever happened to the frustration-aggression hypothesis? *American Behavioral Scientist, 21,* 691–707.

Berkowitz, L. (1983). Aversively stimulated aggression: Some parallels and differences in research with animals and humans. *American Psychologist, 38,* 1135–1144.

Berkowitz, L. (1986). Situational influences on reactions to observed violence. *Journal of Social Issues, 42*(3), 93–106.

Berkowitz, L. (1988). Frustrations, appraisals, and aversively stimulated aggression. *Aggressive Behavior, 14,* 3–11.

Berkowitz, L. (1989). Frustration-aggression hypothesis: Examination and reformulation. *Psychological Bulletin, 106*, 59–73.

Berkowitz, L., & Embree, M. C. (1987). The effect of escape possibility on aversively stimulated aggression. *Journal of Research in Personality, 21*, 405–416.

Bernay, T. (1982). Separation and the sense of competence-loss in women. *American Journal of Psychoanalysis, 42*, 293–305.

Berry, J. M. (1989). Cognitive efficacy across the life span: Introduction to the special series. *Developmental Psychology, 25*, 683–686.

Berzonsky, M. D. (1989). The self as a theorist: Individual differences in identity formation. *International Journal of Personal Construct Psychology, 2*, 363–376.

Berzonsky, M. D., & Neimeyer, G. J. (1988). Identity status and personal construct systems. *Journal of Adolescence, 11*, 195–204.

Berzonsky, M. D., Rice, K. G., & Neimeyer, G. J. (1990). Identity status and self-construct systems: Process X structure interactions. *Journal of Adolescence, 13*, 251–263.

Bettelheim, B. (1976). *The uses of enchantment: The meaning and importance of fairy tales.* New York: Knopf.

Bieri, J. (1955). Cognitive complexity-simplicity and predictive behavior. *Journal of Abnormal and Social Psychology, 51*, 263–268.

Blakely, C. H., & Davidson, W. S. (1984). Behavioral approaches to delinquency: A review. *Advances in Child Behavioral Analysis and Therapy, 3*, 241–272.

Blasi, A., & Milton, K. (1991). The development of the sense of self in adolescence. *Journal of Personality, 59*, 217–242.

Block, J. (1971). *Lives through time.* Berkeley, CA: Bancroft Books.

Blount, R. L., Santilli, L., & Stokes, T. F. (1989). Promoting oral hygiene in pediatric dentistry: A critical review. *Clinical Psychology Review, 9*, 737–746.

Blum, G. S. (1953). *Psychoanalytic theories ofpersonality.* New York: McGraw-Hill.

Blum, G. S. (1961). *A model of the mind.* New York: Wiley.

Blum, G. S. (1989). A computer model for unconscious spread of anxiety-linked inhibition in cognitive networks. *Behavioral Science, 34*, 16–45.

Blustein, D. L., Devenis, L. E., & Kidney, B. A. (1989). Relationship between the identity formation process and career development. *Journal of Counseling Psychology, 36*, 196–202.

Bodden, J. C. (1970). Cognitive complexity as a factor in appropriate vocational choice. *Journal of Counseling Psychology, 17*, 364–368.

Bohart, A. C. (1988). Empathy: Client centered and psychoanalytic. *American Psychologist, 43*, 667–668.

Bohart, A. C. (1991). The missing 249 words: In search of objectivity. *Psychotherapy, 28*, 497–503.

Bolen, J. S. (1984). *Goddesses in everywoman: A new psychology of women.* San Francisco: Harper & Row.

Bolger, N. (1990). Coping as a personality process: A prospective study. *Journal of Personality and Social Psychology, 59*, 525–537.

Boon, J. C., & Davis, G. M. (1987). Rumours greatly exaggerated: Allport and Postman's apocryphal study. *Canadian Journal of Behavioural Science, 19*, 430–440.

Bordages, J. W. (1989). Self-actualization and personal autonomy. *Psychological Reports, 64*, 1263–1266.

Bores-Rangel, E., Church, A. T., Szendre, D., & Reeves, C. (1990). Self-efficacy in relation to occupational consideration and academic performance in high school equivalency students. *Journal of Counseling Psychology, 37,* 407–418.

Borkenau, P. (1990). Traits as ideal-based and goal-derived social categories. *Journal of Personality and Social Psychology, 58,* 381–396.

Borkenau, P., & Ostendorf, F. (1987). Fact and fiction in implicit personality theory. *Journal of Personality, 55,* 415–443.

Bottome, P. (1947). *Alfred Adler: Apostle of freedom* (J. Linton & R. Vaughan, Trans.). London: Faber & Faber.

Bowlby, J. (1988). Developmental psychiatry comes of age. *American Journal of Psychiatry, 145,* 1–10.

Boyers, R. (Ed.). (1971). *R.D. Laing and anti-psychiatry.* New York: Harper & Row.

Boyle, G. J. (1988). Contribution of Cattellian psychometrics to the elucidation of human intellectual structure. *Multivariate Experimental Clinical Research, 8,* 267–273.

Boyle, G. J. (1989). Re-examination of the major personality-type factors in the Cattell, Comrey and Eysenck scales: Were the factor solutions by Noller et al. optimal? *Personality and Individual Differences, 10,* 1289–1299.

Bozarth, J. D. (1985). Quantum theory and the person-centered approach. *Journal of Counseling and Development, 64,* 179–182.

Brady, J. P. (1984). Social skills training for psychiatric patients: I. Concepts, methods, and clinical results. *Occupational Therapy in Mental Health, 4,* 51–68.

Brand, C. R., & Egan, V. (1989). The "Big Five" dimensions of personality? Evidence from ipsative, adjectival self-attributions. *Personality and Individual Differences, 10,* 1165–1171.

Brems, C., & Johnson, M. E. (1990). Reexamination of the Bem Sex-Role Inventory: The Interpersonal BSRI. *Journal of Personality Assessment, 55,* 484–498.

Breuer, J., & Freud, S. (1955). Studies on hysteria. In J. Strachey (Ed. and Trans.), *The standard edition of the complete psychological works of Sigmund Freud* (Vol. 2). London: Hogarth Press. (Original work published 1925)

Briggs, K. C., & Myers, I. B. (1976). *Myers-Briggs Type Indicator: Form F.* Palo Alto, CA: Consulting Psychologists Press.

Briggs, S. R., & Cheek, J. M. (1986). The role of factor analysis in the development and evaluation of personality scales. *Journal of Personality, 54,* 106–148.

Brink, T. L., & Matlock, F. E. (1982). Nightmares and birth order: An empirical study. *Individual Psychology, 38,* 47–49.

Britzman, M., & Main, F. (1990). Wellness and personality priorities. *Individual Psychology, 46,* 43–50.

Brody, N. (1991). Reflections on dispositions. *Psychological Science, 2,* 380–381.

Brody, S. (1982). Psychoanalytic theories of infant development and its disturbances: A critical evaluation. *Psychoanalytic Quarterly, 51,* 526–597.

Brogden, H. E. (1972). Some observations on two methods in psychology. *Psychological Bulletin, 77,* 431–437.

Bronson, G. W. (1959). Identity diffusion in late adolescence. *Journal of Abnormal and Social Psychology, 59,* 414–417.

Brown, S. R. (1978). Richard Nixon and the public conscience: The struggle for authenticity. *Journal of Psychohistory, 6,* 93–111.

Browne, A., & Finkelhor, D. (1986). Impact of child sexual abuse: A review of the research. *Psychological Bulletin, 99,* 66–77.

Bruhn, A. R. (1990). Cognitive-perceptual theory and the projective use of autobiographical memory. *Journal of Personality Assessment, 55,* 95–114.

Bruner, J. S. (1956). A cognitive theory of personality. *Contemporary Psychology, 1*, 355–359.

Bubenzer, D. L., Zimpfer, D. G., & Mahrle, C. L. (1990). Standardized individual appraisal in agency and private practice: A survey. *Journal of Mental Health Counseling, 12*, 51–66.

Buchanan, D. R., & Taylor, J. A. (1986). Jungian typology of professional psychodramatists: Myers-Briggs Type Indicator analysis of certified psychodramatists. *Psychological Reports, 58*, 391–400.

Buckmaster, L. R., & Davis, G. A. (1985). ROSE: A measure of self-actualization and its relationship to creativity. *Journal of Creative Behavior, 19*, 30–37.

Budd, B. E., Clance, P. C., & Simerly, D. E. (1985). Spatial configurations: Erikson reexamined. *Sex Roles, 12*, 571–577.

Burgess, I. S., & Wearden, J. H. (1986). Superimposition of response-independent reinforcement. *Journal of the Experimental Analysis of Behaviour, 45*, 75–82.

Burnett, C. (1986). *One more time.* New York: Avon.

Burnett, P. C. (1988). Evaluation of Adlerian parenting programs. *Individual Psychology, 44*, 63–76.

Burr, V., & Butt, T. W. (1989). A personal construct view of hypnosis. *British Journal of Experimental and Clinical Hypnosis, 6*, 85–90.

Bursik, K. (1991). Adaptation to divorce and ego development in adult women. *Journal of Personality and Social Psychology, 60*, 300–306.

Buss, A. H. (1989). Personality as traits. *American Psychologist, 44*, 1378–1388.

Buss, A. H., & Plomin, R. (1975). *A temperament theory of personality development.* New York: Wiley.

Buss, D. M. (1984). Evolutionary biology and personality psychology: Toward a conception of human nature and individual differences. *American Psychologist, 39*, 1135–1147.

Buss, H. M. (1990). The different voice of Canadian feminist autobiographers. *Biography, 13*, 154–167.

Butler, J. M., & Haigh, G. V. (1954). Changes in the relation between self-concepts and ideal concepts consequent upon client-centered counseling. In C. R. Rogers & R. F. Dymond (Eds.), *Psychotherapy and Personality Change* (pp. 55–75). Chicago: University of Chicago Press.

Byrne, D. (1961). The repression-sensitization scale: Rationale, reliability, and validity. *Journal of Personality, 29*, 334–349.

Cain, D. J. (1987). Carl Rogers's life in review. *Person-Centered Review, 2*, 476–506.

Caldwell, R. A., Bogat, G. A., & Cruise, K. (1989). The relationship of ego identity to social network structure and ego function in young men and women. *Journal of Adolescence, 12*, 309–313.

Campbell, J. (1949). *The hero with a thousand faces.* New York: Pantheon.

Campbell, J. (1972). *Myths to live by.* New York: Viking.

Campbell, J. B., & Heller, J. F. (1987). Correlations of extraversion, impulsivity and sociability with sensation seeking and MBTI-introversion. *Personality and Individual Differences, 8*, 133–136.

Campbell, J. D., Chew, B., & Scratchley, L. S. (1991). Cognitive and emotional reactions to daily events: The effects of self-esteem and self-complexity. *Journal of Personality, 59*, 473–505.

Campbell, J. F. (1988). The primary personality factors of younger adolescent Hawaiians. *Genetic, Social, and General Psychology Monographs, 114*, 141–171.

Campbell, J. M., Amerikaner, M., Swank, P., & Vincent, K. (1989). The relationship between the Hardiness Test and the Personal Orientation Inventory. *Journal of Research in Personality, 23,* 373–380.

Cangemi, J. P. (1984). The *real* purpose of higher education: Developing self-actualizing personalities. *Education, 105,* 151–154.

Cann, D. R., & Donderi, D. C. (1986). Jungian personality typology and the recall of everyday and archetypal dreams. *Journal of Personality and Social Psychology, 50,* 1021–1030.

Cantor, N. (1990). From thought to behavior: "Having" and "doing" in the study of personality and cognition. *American Psychologist, 45,* 735–750.

Cantor, N., & Kihlstrom, J. F. (1987). *Personality and social intelligence.* Englewood Cliffs, NJ: Prentice-Hall.

Cantor, N., & Mischel, W. (1979a). Prototypes in person perception. In L. Berkowitz (Ed.), *Advances in experimental social psychology* (Vol. 12, pp. 3–52). New York: Academic Press.

Cantor, N., & Mischel, W. (1979b). Prototypicality and personality: Effects on free recall and personality impressions. *Journal of Research in Personality, 13,* 187–205.

Caplan, P. J. (1979). Erikson's concept of inner space: A data-based reevaluation. *American Journal of Orthopsychiatry, 49,* 100–108.

Capra, F. (1975). *The Tao of physics.* Boston: Shambhala.

Caprara, G. V. (1982). A comparison of the frustration-aggression and emotional susceptibility hypotheses. *Aggressive Behavior, 8,* 234–236.

Carlson, J. G. (1985). Recent assessments of the Myers-Briggs Type Indicator. *Journal of Personality Assessment, 49,* 356–365.

Carlson, J. G. (1989a). Affirmative: In support of researching the Myers-Briggs Type Indicator. *Journal of Counseling and Development, 67,* 484–486.

Carlson, J. G. (1989b). Rebuttal: The MBTI: Not ready for routine use in counseling. A reply. *Journal of Counseling and Development, 67,* 489.

Carlson, M., Marcus-Newhall, A., & Miller, N. (1989). Evidence for a general construct of aggression. *Personality and Social Psychology Bulletin, 15,* 377–389.

Carlson, R. (1971). Where is the person in personality research? *Psychological Bulletin, 75,* 203–219.

Carlson, R. (1980). Studies of Jungian typology: II. Representations of the personal world. *Journal of Personality and Social Psychology, 38,* 801–810.

Carlson, R. (1981). Studies in script theory: I. Adult analogs of a childhood nuclear scene. *Journal of Personality and Social Psychology, 40,* 501–510.

Carlson, R. (1988). Exemplary lives: The uses of psychobiography for theory development. *Journal of Personality, 56,* 105–138.

Carlson, R., & Levy, N. (1973). Studies of Jungian typology: I. Memory, social perception, and social action. *Journal of Personality, 41,* 559–576.

Carlson, R., & Williams, J. (1984). Studies of Jungian typology: III. Personality and marriage. *Journal of Personality Assessment, 48,* 87–94.

Carmona, A., Miller, N. E., & Demierre, T. (1974). Instrumental learning of gastric vascular tonicity responses. *Psychosomatic Medicine, 36,* 156–163.

Carpenter, F. (1974). *The Skinner primer: Behind freedom and dignity.* New York: Free Press.

Carroll, J. B. (1984). Raymond B. Cattell's contribution to the theory of cognitive abilities. *Multivariate Behavioral Research, 19,* 300–306.

Cartwright, D. (1989). Concurrent validation of a measure of transcendental powers. *Journal of Parapsychology, 53,* 43–59.

Cartwright, D., DeBruin, J., & Berg, S. (1991). Some scales for assessing personality based on Carl Rogers' theory: Further evidence of validity. *Personality and Individual Differences, 12,* 151–156.

Cartwright, D., & Mori, C. (1988). Scales for assessing aspects of the person. *Person-Centered Review, 3,* 176–194.

Carver, C. S. (1989). How should multifaceted personality constructs be tested? Issues illustrated by self-monitoring, attributional style, and hardiness. *Journal of Personality and Social Psychology, 56,* 577–585.

Carver, C. S., & Scheier, M. F. (1981). *Attention and self-regulation: A control-theory approach to human behavior.* New York: Springer-Verlag.

Caspi, A. (1987). Personality in the life course. *Journal of Personality and Social Psychology, 53,* 1203–1213.

Caspi, A., & Herbener, E. S. (1990). Continuity and change: Assortative marriage and the consistency of personality in adulthood. *Journal of Personality and Social Psychology, 58,* 250–258.

Catania, A. C. (1980). Autoclitic processes and the structure of behavior. *Behaviorism, 8,* 175–186.

Cattell, R. B. (1937). *The fight for our national intelligence.* London, UK: King.

Cattell, R. B. (1943a). The description of personality: Basic traits resolved into clusters. *Journal of Abnormal and Social Psychology, 38,* 476–506.

Cattell, R. B. (1943b). The description of personality: I. Foundations of trait measurement. *Psychological Review, 50,* 559–594.

Cattell, R. B. (1946). *Description and measurement of personality.* New York: World.

Cattell, R. B. (1950). *Personality: A systematic theoretical and factual study.* New York: McGraw-Hill.

Cattell, R. B. (1957). *Personality and motivation structure and measurement.* Yonkers, NY: World.

Cattell, R. B. (1958). A need for alertness to multivariate experimental findings in integrative surveys. *Psychological Bulletin, 55,* 253–256.

Cattell, R. B. (1960). The multiple abstract variance analysis equations and solutions: For nature-nurture research on continuous variables. *Psychological Review, 67,* 353–372.

Cattell, R. B. (1964). *Personality and social psychology.* San Diego, CA: Robert R. Knapp.

Cattell, R. B. (1965). *The scientific analysis of personality.* Baltimore: Penguin.

Cattell, R. B. (1971). *Abilities: Their structure, growth and action.* Boston: Houghton Mifflin.

Cattell, R. B. (1973). *Personality and mood by questionnaire.* San Francisco: Jossey-Bass.

Cattell, R. B. (1974). Raymond B. Cattell. In G. Lindzey (Ed.), *A history of psychology in autobiography* (Vol. 6, pp. 59–100). Englewood Cliffs, NJ: Prentice-Hall.

Cattell, R. B. (1978). *The scientific use of factor analysis.* New York: Plenum.

Cattell, R. B. (1979). *Personality and learning theory: Vol. 1. The structure of personality in its environment.* New York: Springer-Verlag.

Cattell, R. B. (1984). The voyage of a laboratory, 1928–1984. *Multivariate Behavioral Research, 19,* 121–174.

Cattell, R. B. (1986). The 16PF personality structure and Dr. Eysenck. *Journal of Social Behavior and Personality, 1,* 153–160.

Cattell, R. B. (1990a). Advances in Cattellian personality theory. In L. A. Pervin (Ed.). *Handbook of personality: Theory and research* (pp. 101–110). New York: Guilford.

Cattell, R. B. (1990b). The birth of the Society of Multivariate Experimental Psychology. *Journal of the History of the Behavioral Sciences, 26*, 48–57.

Cattell, R. B., & Brennan, J. (1984). The cultural types of modern nations, by two quantitative classification methods. *Sociology and Social Research, 68*, 208–235.

Cattell, R. B., & Butcher, H. J. (1968). *The prediction of achievement and creativity* (pp. 276–277). Indianapolis: Bobbs-Merril.

Cattell, R. B., & Cattell, M. D. (1975). *Handbook for the High School Personality Questionnaire* (2nd ed.). Champaign, IL: IPAT.

Cattell, R. B., Eber, H. W., & Tatsuoka, M. M. (1970). *Handbook for the 16 Personality Factor Questionnaire.* Champaign, IL: IPAT.

Cattell, R. B., & Krug, S. E. (1986). The number of factors in the 16PF: A review of the evidence with special emphasis on methodological problems. *Educational and Psychological Measurement, 46*, 509–522.

Cattell, R. B., & Molteno, E. V. (1940). Contributions concerning mental inheritance: II. Temperament. *Journal of Genetic Psychology, 57*, 31–47.

Cattell, R. B., & Porter, R. B. (1975). *Handbook for the Children's Personality Questionnaire.* Champaign, IL: IPAT.

Cattell, R. B., Rickels, K., Wiese, O., Gray, B., Mallin, Y., Yee, R., & Aaronson, H. (1966). The effects of psychotherapy on measured anxiety and regression. *American Journal of Psychotherapy, 20*, 261–269.

Cattell, R. B., & Schuerger, J. M. (1985). Heritability in the personality control system: Ego strength (C), super ego strength (G) and the self-sentiment (Q_3); by the MAVA model, Q-data, and maximum likelihood analyses. *Social Behavior and Personality, 13*, 33–41.

Cattell, R. B., Schuerger, J. M., & Klein, T. W. (1982). Heritabilities of ego strength (Factor C), super ego strength (Factor G), and self-sentiment (Factor Q_3) by multiple abstract variance analysis. *Journal of Clinical Psychology, 38*, 769–779.

Cattell, R. B., Vaughan, D. S., Schuerger, J. M., & Rao, D. C. (1982). Heritabilities, by the multiple abstract variance analysis (MAVA) model and objective test measures, of personality traits U.I.23, capacity to mobilize, U.I.24, anxiety, U.I.26, narcistic ego, and U.I.28, asthenia, by maximum-likelihood methods. *Behavior Genetics, 12*, 361–378.

Cattell, R. B., & Warburton, F. W. (1961). A cross-cultural comparison of patterns of extraversion and anxiety. *British Journal of Psychology, 52*, 3–16.

Cella, D. F., DeWolfe, A. S., & Fitzgibbon, M. (1987). Ego identity status, identification, and decision-making style in late adolescents. *Adolescence, 22*, 849–861.

Cervone, D. (1991). The two disciplines of personality psychology. *Psychological Science, 2*, 371–377.

Chambers, W. V. (1985). A repertory grid measure of mandalas. *Psychological Reports, 57*, 923–928.

Chambers, W. V., Grice, J. W., & Fourman, T. A. (1987). The validity of Landfield's measure of personal construct ordination. *Journal of Psychology, 121*, 523–525.

Chambers, W. V., Olson, C., Carlock, J., & Olson, D. (1986). Clinical and grid predictions of inconsistencies in individuals' personal constructs. *Perceptual and Motor Skills, 62*, 649–650.

Chandler, H. N. (1984). Skinner and CAI. *Journal of Learning Disabilities, 17*, 441–442.

Chaplin, C. (1964). *My autobiography.* New York: Simon & Schuster.

Chaplin, W. F., John, O. P., & Goldberg, L. R. (1988). Conceptions of states and traits: Dimensional attributes with ideals as prototypes. *Journal of Personality and Social Psychology, 54*, 541–557.

Chapman, M., & Skinner, E. A. (1989). Children's agency beliefs, cognitive performance, and conceptions of effort and ability: Individual and developmental differences. *Child Development, 60,* 1229–1238.

Chapman, M., Skinner, E. A., & Baltes, P. B. (1990). Interpreting correlations between children's perceived control and cognitive performance: Control, agency, or means-ends beliefs? *Developmental Psychology, 26,* 246–253.

Cheek, J. (1982). Aggregation, moderator variables, and the validity of personality tests: A peer-rating study. *Journal of Personality and Social Psychology, 43,* 1254–1269.

Cheek, J. M. (1985). Toward a more inclusive integration of evolutionary biology and personality psychology. *American Psychologist, 40,* 1269–1270.

Chess, S. (1986). Early childhood development and its implications for analytic theory and practice. *American Journal of Psychoanalysis, 46,* 123–148.

Chessick, R. D. (1986). Transference and countertransference revisited. *Dynamic Psychotherapy, 4,* 14–30.

Chetwynd, T. (1982). *A dictionary of symbols.* London, UK: Paladin.

Childress, A. R., McLellan, A. T., & O'Brien, C. P. (1985). Behavioral therapies for substance abuse. *International Journal of the Addictions, 20,* 947–969.

Chodorow, N. (1978). *The reproduction of mothering.* Berkeley: University of California Press.

Chomsky, N. (1959). Review of Skinner's *Verbal Behavior. Language, 35,* 26–58.

Christopher, S. B., & Leak, G. (1982). Evolutionary logic and Adlerian social interest. *Psychological Reports, 51,* 375–378.

Ciaccio, N. (1971). A test of Erikson's theory of ego epigenesis. *Developmental Psychology, 4,* 306–311.

Ciardiello, J. A. (1985). Beethoven: Modern analytic views of the man and his music. *Psychoanalytic Review, 72,* 129–147.

Cicogna, P., Cavallero, C., & Bosinelli, M. (1991). Cognitive aspects of mental activity during sleep. *American Journal of Psychology, 104,* 413–425.

Cirlot, J. E. (1971). *A dictionary of symbols* (2nd ed.). (J. Sage, Trans.). New York: Philosophical Library.

Clark, J. M., & Paivio, A. (1989). Observational and theoretical terms in psychology: A cognitive perspective on scientific language. *American Psychologist, 44,* 500–512.

Clark, R. W. (1984). *Einstein: The life and times.* New York: Avon. (Original work published 1971)

Clarke, P. B. (1987). Nicotine and smoking: A perspective from animal studies. *Psychopharmacology, 92,* 135–143.

Clemmens, E. R. (1984). The work of Karen Horney. *American Journal of Psychoanalysis, 44,* 242–253.

Clinch, N. (1973). *The Kennedy neurosis.* New York: Grosset & Dunlap.

Coan, R. W. (1989). Dimensions of masculinity and femininity: A self-report inventory. *Journal of Personality Assessment, 53,* 816–826.

Coffield, K. E., & Buckalew, L. W. (1984). The Study of Values: Toward revised norms and changing values. *Counseling and Values, 28,* 72–75.

Cohen, D. (1977). Neal Miller. *Psychologists on psychology* (pp. 240–261). New York: Taplinger.

Cohen, J. B. (1967). An interpersonal orientation to the study of consumer behavior. *Journal of Marketing Research, 4,* 270–278.

Cohn, L. D. (1991). Sex differences in the course of personality development: A meta-analysis. *Psychological Bulletin, 109,* 252–266.

Coile, D. C., & Miller, N. E. (1984). How radical animal activists try to mislead humane people. *American Psychologist, 39,* 700–701.

Cole, N. S. (1981). Bias in testing. *American Psychologist, 36,* 1067–1077.

Coles, R. (1970). *Erik H. Erikson: The growth of his work.* Boston: Little, Brown.

Coles, R. (1971a). *Children of crisis.* Vol. 2. *Migrants, sharecroppers, mountaineers.* Boston: Atlantic–Little, Brown.

Coles, R. (1971b). *Children of crisis.* Vol. 3. *The South goes north.* Boston: Atlantic–Little, Brown.

Conley, J. J. (1984a). Longitudinal consistency of adult personality: Self-reported psychological characteristics across 45 years. *Journal of Personality and Social Psychology, 47,* 1325–1333.

Conley, J. J. (1984b). Relation of temporal stability and cross-situational consistency in personality: Comment on the Mischel-Epstein debate. *Psychological Review, 91,* 491–496.

Conrad, H. S. (1932). The validity of personality ratings of preschool children. *Journal of Educational Psychology, 23,* 671–680.

Constantinople, A. (1969). An Eriksonian measure of personality development in college students. *Developmental Psychology, 1,* 357–372.

Cooper, C., & McConville, C. (1989). The factorial equivalence of state anxiety–negative affect and state extraversion–positive affect. *Personality and Individual Differences, 10,* 919–920.

Cooper, S. H., Perry, J. C., & Arnow, D. (1988). An empirical approach to the study of defense mechanisms: I. Reliability and preliminary validity of the Rorschach defense scales. *Journal of Personality Assessment, 52,* 187–203.

Cooper, S. H., Perry, J. C., & O'Connell, M. O. (1991). The Rorschach defense scales: II. Longitudinal perspectives. *Journal of Personality Assessment, 56,* 191–201.

Corey, M. A. (1988). The psychology of channeling. *Psychology, A Journal of Human Behavior, 25,* 86–92.

Corsini, R. J. (1986). The present science of personality: Comments on Eysenck's article. *Journal of Social Behavior and Personality, 1,* 483–488.

Corsini, R. J. (1989). *Manual: Corsini 4-R System of Individual Education.* Chicago: North American Society of Adlerian Psychology.

Costa, P. T., Jr., & McCrae, R. R. (1988). From catalog to classification: Murray's needs and the five-factor model. *Journal of Personality and Social Psychology, 55,* 258–265.

Côté, J. E. (1986). Identity crisis modality: A technique for assessing the structure of the identity crisis. *Journal of Adolescence, 9,* 321–335.

Côté, J. E., & Levine, C. (1988a). A critical examination of the ego identity status paradigm. *Developmental Review, 8,* 147–184.

Côté, J. E., & Levine, C. (1988b). On critiquing the identity status paradigm: A rejoinder to Waterman. *Developmental Review, 8,* 209–218.

Côté, J. E., & Levine, C. (1988c). The relationship between ego identity status and Erikson's notions of institutionalized moratoria, value orientation stage, and ego dominance. *Journal of Youth and Adolescence, 17,* 81–99.

Côté, J. E., & Reker, G. T. (1979). Cognitive complexity and ego identity formation: A synthesis of cognitive and ego psychology. *Social Behavior and Personality, 7,* 107–112.

Cowan, D. A. (1989). An alternative to the dichotomous interpretation of Jung's psychological functions: Developing more sensitive measurement technology. *Journal of Personality Assessment, 53,* 459–471.

Coward, H. (1989). Jung's conception of the role of religion in psychological development. *Humanistic Psychologist, 17,* 265–273.

Craig-Bray, L., & Adams, G. R. (1986). Different methodologies in the assessment of identity: Congruence between self-report and interview techniques? *Journal of Youth and Adolescence, 15,* 191–204.

Craik, K. H. (1986). Personality research methods: An historical perspective. *Journal of Personality, 54,* 18–51.

Cramer, D. (1985). Psychological adjustment and the facilitative nature of close personal relationships. *British Journal of Medical Psychology, 58,* 165–168.

Cramer, D. (1986). An item factor analysis of the revised Barrett-Lennard Relationship Inventory. *British Journal of Guidance and Counselling, 14,* 314–325.

Cramer, D. (1990a). Disclosure of personal problems, self-esteem, and the facilitativeness of friends and lovers. *British Journal of Guidance and Counselling, 18,* 186–196.

Cramer, D. (1990b). Self-esteem and close relationships: A statistical refinement. *British Journal of Social Psychology, 29,* 189–191.

Cramer, D. (1990c). Towards assessing the therapeutic value of Rogers's core conditions. *Counselling Psychology Quarterly, 3,* 57–66.

Cramer, P. (1987). The development of defense mechanisms. *Journal of Personality, 55,* 597–614.

Cramer, P. (1991). Anger and the use of defense mechanisms in college students. *Journal of Personality, 59,* 39–55.

Cramer, P., & Hogan, K. (1975). Sex differences in verbal and play fantasy. *Developmental Psychology, 11,* 145–154.

Crandall, J. E. (1975). A scale for social interest. *Journal of Individual Psychology, 31,* 187–195.

Creel, R. (1980). Radical epiphenomenalism: B.F. Skinner's account of private events. *Behaviorism, 8,* 31–53.

Crockett, J. B., & Crawford, R. L. (1989). The relationship between Myers-Briggs Type Indicator (MBTI) Scale scores and advising style preferences of college freshmen. *Journal of College Student Development, 30,* 154–161.

Crockett, W. H. (1982). The organization of construct systems: The organization corollary. In J.C. Mancuso & R. Adams-Webber (Eds.), *The construing person.* New York: Praeger.

Cronbach, L. J. (1957). The two disciplines of scientific psychology. *American Psychologist, 12,* 671–684.

Cronbach, L. J. (1975). Beyond the two disciplines of scientific psychology. *American Psychologist, 30,* 116–127.

Cronbach, L. J., & Meehl, P. E. (1955). Construct validity in psychological tests. *Psychological Bulletin, 52,* 281–302.

Cross, H. J., & Allen, J. G. (1970). Ego identity status, adjustment, and academic achievement. *Journal of Consulting and Clinical Psychology, 34,* 288.

Crow Dog, M., & Erdoes, R. (1990). *Lakota woman.* New York: Harper Perennial.

Crowell, C. R., & Anderson, D. C. (1982). The scientific and methodological basis of a systematic approach to human behavior management. *Journal of Organizational Behavior Management, 4,* 1–31.

Cuny, H. (1965). *Albert Einstein: The man and his theories.* New York: Eriksson.

Dachowski, M. M. (1987). A convergence of the tender-minded and the tough-minded? *American Psychologist, 42*, 886–887.

Dalal, F. (1988). Jung: A racist. *British Journal of Psychotherapy, 4*, 263–279.

Daly, M. (1978). *Gyn/Ecology: The metaethics of radical feminism.* Boston: Beacon Press.

Daniels, M. (1982). The development of the concept of self-actualization in the writings of Abraham Maslow. *Current Psychological Reviews, 2*, 61–75.

Daniels, M. (1988). The myth of self-actualization. *Journal of Humanistic Psychology, 28*(1), 7–38.

Das, A. K. (1989). Beyond self-actualization. *International Journal for the Advancement of Counselling, 12*, 13–27.

Davidow, S., & Bruhn, A. R. (1990). Earliest memories and the dynamics of delinquency: A replication study. *Journal of Personality Assessment, 54*, 601–616.

Davidson, R. J., Ekman, P., Saron, C. D., Senulis, J. A., & Friesen, W. V. (1990). Approach-withdrawal and cerebral asymmetry: I. Emotional expression and brain physiology. *Journal of Personality and Social Psychology, 58*, 330–341.

Davies, M. F. (1985). Self-consciousness and paranormal belief. *Perceptual and Motor Skills, 60*, 484–486.

Davies, R. (1985). Using grids in vocational guidance. In N. Beail (Ed.), *Repertory grid technique and personal constructs: Applications in clinical and educational settings* (pp. 333–348). London, UK: Croom Helm.

Davies, R. R., & Rogers, E. S. (1985). Social skills training with persons who are mentally retarded. *Mental Retardation, 23*, 186–196.

Davis, D. L., Grove, S. J., & Knowles, P. A. (1990). An experimental application of personality type as an analogue for decision-making style. *Psychological Reports, 66*, 167–175.

Davis, J., Lockwood, L., & Wright, C. (1991). Reasons for not reporting peak experiences. *Journal of Humanistic Psychology, 31*(1), 86–94.

Davis, M. (with Q. Troupe) (1989). *Miles.* New York: Simon & Schuster.

Davis, T. (1986). Book reviews. *Individual Psychology, 42*, 133–142.

Davis-Berman, J. (1990). Physical self-efficacy, perceived physical status, and depressive symptomatology in older adults. *Journal of Psychology, 124*, 207–215.

Davis-Sharts, J. (1986). An empirical test of Maslow's theory of need hierarchy using hologeistic comparison by statistical sampling. *Advances in Nursing Science, 9*, 58–72.

Dawson, B., Jeffrey, D. B., Peterson, P. E., Sommers, J., & Wilson, G. (1985). Television commercials as symbolic representation of reward in the delay of gratification paradigm. *Cognitive Therapy and Research, 9*, 217–224.

Day, W. (1983). On the difference between radical and methodological behaviorism. *Behaviorism, 11*, 89–102.

DeCarvalho, R. J. (1989). Contributions to the history of psychology: LXII. Carl Rogers' naturalistic system of ethics. *Psychological Reports, 65*, 1155–1162.

DeCarvalho, R. J. (1990a). The growth hypothesis and self-actualization: An existential alternative. *Humanistic Psychologist, 18*, 252–258.

DeCarvalho, R. J. (1990b). A history of the "third force" in psychology. *Journal of Humanistic Psychology, 30*, 22–44 .

DeCarvalho, R. J. (1990c). Who coined the term "humanistic psychology"? *Humanistic Psychologist, 18*, 350–351.

DeCarvalho, R. J. (1991). The humanistic paradigm in education. *Humanistic Psychologist, 19*, 88–104.

deChesnay, M. (1985). Father-daughter incest: An overview. *Behavioral Sciences and the Law, 3*, 391–402.

DeMause, L. (1988). On writing childhood history. *Journal of Psychohistory, 16*, 135–171.

deSoto, C. B., Hamilton, M. M., & Taylor, R. B. (1985). Words, people, and implicit personality theory. *Social Cognition, 3*, 369–382.

DeWaele, J. P., & Harré, R. (1979). Autobiography as a psychological method. In G. P. Ginsburg (Ed.), *Emerging strategies in social psychological research.* New York: Wiley.

Deberry, S. T. (1989). The effect of competitive tasks on liking of self and other. *Social Behavior and Personality, 17*, 67–80.

Decker, P. J., & Nathan, B. N. (1985). *Behavior modeling training: Principles and applications.* New York: Praeger.

Della Selva, P. C., & Dusek, J. B. (1984). Sex role orientation and resolution of Eriksonian crisis during the late adolescent years. *Journal of Personality and Social Psychology, 47*, 204–212.

Delmonte, M. M. (1984). Psychometric scores and meditation practice: A literature review. *Personality and Individual Differences, 5*, 559–563.

Dembo, M. H., Sweitzer, M., & Lauritzen, P. (1985). An evaluation of group parent education: Behavioral, PET, and Adlerian programs. *Review of Educational Research, 55*, 155–200.

Desharnais, R., Bouillon, J., & Godin, G. (1986). Self-efficacy and outcome expectations as determinants of exercise adherence. *Psychological Reports, 59*, 1155–1159.

DiCara, L. V., & Miller, N. E. (1968). Changes in heart rate instrumentally learned by curarized rats as avoidance responses. *Journal of Comparative and Physiological Psychology, 65*, 8–12.

Dickson, L. (1973). *Wilderness man: The strange story of Grey Owl.* Scarborough, Ontario: Signet.

Digman, J. M. (1989). Five robust trait dimensions: Development, stability, and utility. *Journal of Personality, 57*, 195–214.

Digman, J. M. (1990). Personality structure: Emergence of the five-factor model. *Annual Review of Psychology, 41*, 417–440.

Digman, J. M., & Inouye, J. (1986). Further specification of the five robust factors of personality. *Journal of Personality and Social Psychology, 50*, 116–123.

Dignan, M. H. (1965). Ego identity and maternal identification. *Journal of Personality and Social Psychology, 1*, 476–483.

Dinkmeyer, D., & Dinkmeyer, D., Jr. (1989). Adlerian psychology. *Psychology, 26*, 26–34.

Dinkmeyer, D., & McKay, G. (1976). *Systematic training for effective parenting.* Circle Pines, MN: American Guidance Service.

Dinkmeyer, D., McKay, G., & Dinkmeyer, J. (1982). *The next step: Effective parenting through problem solving.* Circle Pines, MN: American Guidance Service.

Dinnerstein, D. (1976). *The mermaid and the minotaur: Sexual arrangements and human malaise.* New York: Harper & Row.

Dixon, P. N., & Strano, D. A. (1989). The measurement of inferiority: A review and directions for scale development. *Individual Psychology, 45*, 313–322.

Dohrenwend, B. S., & Dohrenwend, B. P. (Eds.). (1974). *Stressful life events: Their nature and effects.* New York: Wiley.

Dolce, J. J. (1987). Self-efficacy and disability beliefs in behavioral treatment of pain. *Behaviour Research and Therapy, 25*, 289–299.

Dollard, J. (1949). *Criteria for the life history: With analyses of six notable documents.* New York: Peter Smith.

Dollard, J. (1957). *Caste and class in a southern town* (3rd ed.). Garden City, NY: Doubleday Anchor. (Original work published 1937)

Dollard, J., & Miller, N. E. (1950). *Personality and psychotherapy: An analysis in terms of learning, thinking and culture.* New York: McGraw-Hill.

Dollard, J., Miller, N. E., Doob, L. W., Mowrer, O. H., & Sears, R. R. (1939). *Frustration and aggression.* New Haven, CT: Yale University Press.

Dollinger, S. J., Levin, E. L., & Robinson, A. E. (1991). The Word Association Test. *Journal of Personality Assessment, 57,* 368–380.

Dollinger, S. J., & Orf, L. A. (1991). Personality and performance in "personality": Conscientiousness and openness. *Journal of Research in Personality, 25,* 276–284.

Dollinger, S. J., & Taub, S. I. (1977). The interaction of locus of control expectancies and providing purpose on children's motivation. *Journal of Research in Personality, 11,* 118–127.

Domino, G., & Affonso, D. D. (1990). A personality measure of Erikson's life stages: The Inventory of Psychosocial Balance. *Journal of Personality Assessment, 54,* 576–588.

Domino, G., & Hannah, M. T. (1989). Measuring effective functioning in the elderly: An application of Erikson's theory. *Journal of Personality Assessment, 53,* 319–328.

Donahue, M. J. (1985). Intrinsic and extrinsic religiousness: Review and meta-analysis. *Journal of Personality and Social Psychology, 48,* 400–419.

Donnerstein, E., & Berkowitz, L. (1981). Victim reactions in aggressive erotic films as a factor in violence against women. *Journal of Personality and Social Psychology, 41,* 710–724.

Doty, R. M., Peterson, B. E., & Winter, D. G. (1991). Threat and authoritarianism in the United States, 1978–1987. *Journal of Personality and Social Psychology, 61,* 629–640.

Dougherty, J., Miller, D., Todd, G. D., & Kostenbauder, H. B. (1981). Reinforcing and other behavioral effects of nicotine. *Neuroscience and Biobehavioral Reviews, 5,* 487–495.

Douvan, E., & Adelson, J. (1966). *The adolescent experience.* New York: Wiley.

Dreger, R. M. (1986). Comment on H. J. Eysenck, "Can personality study ever be scientific?" *Journal of Social Behavior and Personality, 1,* 161–164.

Dreikurs, R. (1950). *Fundamentals of Adlerian psychology.* Chicago: Alfred Adler Institute.

Dreikurs, R. (1982). Adleriana. *Individual Psychology, 38,* 7. (Original work published 1940)

Dreikurs, R., & Soltz, V. (1964). *Children: The challenge.* New York: Hawthorn.

Duke, M. P. (1986). Personality science: A proposal. *Journal of Personality and Social Psychology, 50,* 382–385.

Dukes, W. F. (1965). N = 1. *Psychological Bulletin, 64,* 74–79.

Duncan, R. C., Konefal, J., & Spechler, M. M. (1990). Effect of neurolinguistic programming training on self-actualization as measured by the Personal Orientation Inventory. *Psychological Reports, 66,* 1323–1330.

duPreez, P. (1975). The application of Kelly's personal construct theory to the analysis of political debates. *Journal of Social Psychology, 95,* 267–270.

Dworkin, B. R., & Miller, N. E. (1986). Failure to replicate visceral learning in the acute curarized rat preparation. *Behavioral Neuroscience, 100,* 299–314.

Dzewaltowski, D. A. (1989). Toward a model of exercise motivation. *Journal of Sport and Exercise Psychology, 11*, 251–269.

Eagly, A. H. (1987a). Reporting sex differences. *American Psychologist, 42*, 756–757.

Eagly, A. H. (1987b). *Sex differences in social behavior: A social-role interpretation.* Hillsdale, NJ: Erlbaum.

Eagly, A. H., & Wood, W. (1991). Explaining sex differences in social behavior: A meta-analytic perspective. *Personality and Social Psychology Bulletin, 17*, 306–315.

Eastman, C., & Marzillier, J. S. (1984). Theoretical and methodological difficulties in Bandura's self-efficacy theory. *Cognitive Therapy and Research, 8*, 213–229.

Eckardt, M. H. (1991). Feminine psychology revisited: A historical perspective. *American Journal of Psychoanalysis, 51*, 235–243.

Edelson, M. (1985). The hermeneutic turn and the single case study in psychoanalysis. *Psychoanalysis and Contemporary Thought, 8*, 567–614.

Eden, C., & Sims, D. (1981). Computerised vicarious experience: The future for management induction? *Personnel Review, 10*, 22–25.

Edinger, E. F. (1968). An outline of analytical psychology. *Quadrant, 1*, 1–12.

Edmonds, T. (1979). Applying personal construct theory in occupational guidance. *British Journal of Guidance and Counseling, 7*, 225–233.

Ehrenwald, J. (1979). Beethoven: Hero and anti-hero, portrait of a right hemisphere genius. *Journal of the American Academy of Psychoanalysis, 7*, 45–55.

Ehrman, M., & Oxford, R. (1989). Effects of sex differences, career choice, and psychological type on adult language learning strategies. *Modern Language Journal, 73*, 1–13.

Einstein, A., & Infeld, L. (1961). *The evolution of physics: The growth of ideas from early concepts to relativity and quanta.* New York: Simon & Schuster. (Original work published 1938)

Ekman, P., Davidson, R. J., & Friesen, W. V. (1990). The Duchenne smile: II. Emotional expression and brain physiology. *Journal of Personality and Social Psychology, 58*, 342–353.

Elizabeth, P. (1983). Comparison of psychoanalytic and a client-centered group treatment model on measures of anxiety and self-actualization. *Journal of Counseling Psychology, 30*, 425–428.

Ellenberger, H. F. (1970). *The discovery of the unconscious: The history and evolution of dynamic psychiatry.* New York: Basic Books.

Ellenberger, H. F. (1972). The story of "Anna O": A critical review with new data. *Journal of the History of the Behavior Sciences, 8*, 267–279.

Elliott, D., Amerikaner, M., & Swank, P. (1987). Early recollections and the Vocational Preference Inventory as predictors of vocational choice. *Individual Psychology, 43*, 353–359.

Elms, A. C. (1981). Skinner's dark year and *Walden Two. American Psychologist, 36*, 470–479.

Elms, A. C. (1988a). Freud as Leonardo: Why the first psychobiography went wrong. *Journal of Personality, 56*, 19–40.

Elms, A. C. (1988b). *The psychologist as biographer.* Paper presented at the Henry A. Murray Award Lecture, American Psychological Association Annual Convention, Atlanta, GA (unpublished manuscript).

Emery, E. J. (1987). Empathy: Psychoanalytic and client centered. *American Psychologist, 42*, 513–515.

Emmerich, W. (1968). Personality development and concepts of structure. *Child Development, 39*, 671–690.

Emmons, R. A., (1986). Personal strivings: An approach to personality and subjective well-being. *Journal of Personality and Social Psychology, 51*, 1058–1068.

Emmons, R. A., Diener, E., & Larsen, R. J. (1985). Choice of situations and congruence models of interactionism. *Personality and Individual Differences, 6*, 693–705.

Emmons, R. A., Diener, E., & Larsen, R. J. (1986). Choice and avoidance of everyday situations and affect congruence: Two models of reciprocal interactionism. *Journal of Personality and Social Psychology, 51*, 815–826.

Endler, N. S., & Edwards, J. M. (1986). Interactionism in personality in the twentieth century. *Personality and Individual Differences, 7*, 379–384.

Endler, N. S., & Magnusson, D. (Eds.). (1976). *Interactional psychology and personality.* New York: Wiley.

Enns, C. Z. (1989). Toward teaching inclusive personality theories. *Teaching of Psychology, 16*, 111–117.

Epstein, A. W. (1987). The phylogenesis of the "ego," with remarks on the frontal lobes. *American Journal of Psychoanalysis, 47*, 161–166.

Epstein, R. (1985). Extinction-induced resurgence: Preliminary investigations and possible applications. *Psychological Record, 35*, 143–153.

Epstein, R. (1991). Skinner, creativity, and the problem of spontaneous behavior. *Psychological Science, 2*, 362–370.

Epstein, R., Lanza, R. P., & Skinner, B. F. (1980). Symbolic communication between two pigeons (*Columba livia domestica*), *Science, 207*, 543–545.

Epstein, S. (1973). The self-concept revisited, or a theory of a theory. *American Psychologist, 28*, 404–416.

Epstein, S. (1979). The stability of behavior: I. On predicting most of the people much of the time. *Journal of Personality and Social Psychology, 37*, 1097–1126.

Epstein, S. (1980a). The self-concept: A review and the proposal of an integrated theory of personality. In E. Staub (Ed.), *Personality: Basic issues and current research.* Englewood Cliffs, NJ: Prentice-Hall.

Epstein, S. (1980b). The stability of behavior: II. Implications for psychological research. *American Psychologist, 35*, 790–806.

Epstein, S. (1983a). A research paradigm for the study of personality and emotions. In M. M. Page (Ed.), *Personality—Current theory and research: 1982 Nebraska Symposium on Motivation* (pp. 91–154). Lincoln: University of Nebraska Press.

Epstein, S. (1983b). The stability of confusion: A reply to Mischel and Peake. *Psychological Review, 90*, 179–184.

Epstein, S. (1985). The implications of cognitive-experimental self-theory for research in social psychology and personality. *Journal for the Theory of Social Behavior, 15*, 283–310.

Epstein, S., & O'Brien, E. J. (1985). The person-situation debate in historical and current perspective. *Psychological Bulletin, 98*, 513–537.

Epting, F. R. (1984). *Personal construct counselling and psychotherapy.* New York: Wiley.

Ericsson, K. A., & Simon, H. A. (1980). Verbal reports as data. *Psychological Review, 87*, 215–251.

Erikson, E. H. (1950). *Childhood and society.* New York: Norton.

Erikson, E. H. (1951a). Sex differences in the play configurations of preadolescents. *American Journal of Orthopsychiatry, 21*, 667–692.

Erikson, E. H. (1951b). Statement to the committee on privilege and tenure of the University of California concerning the California loyalty oath. *Psychiatry, 14,* 243–245.

Erikson, E. H. (1958a). On the nature of clinical evidence. *Daedalus, 87,* 65–87.

Erikson, E. H. (1958b). *Young man Luther: A study in psychoanalysis and history.* New York: Norton.

Erikson, E. H. (1959). Identity and the life cycle. Selected papers. *Psychological Issues, 1* (Monograph 1). New York: International Universities Press.

Erikson, E. H. (1961). The roots of virtue. In J. Huxley (Ed.), *The humanist frame.* New York: Harper & Brothers.

Erikson, E. H. (1963). *Childhood and society* (2nd ed.). New York: Norton.

Erikson, E. H. (1964). *Insight and responsibility: Lectures on the ethical implications of psychoanalytic insight.* New York: Norton.

Erikson, E. H. (1965). Inner and outer space: Reflections on womanhood. In R. J. Lifton (Ed.), *The woman in America.* Boston: Houghton Mifflin.

Erikson, E. H. (1968a). Identity and identity diffusion. In C. Gordon & K. J. Gergen (Eds.), *The self in social interaction.* New York: Wiley.

Erikson, E. H. (1968b). *Identity: Youth and crisis.* New York: Norton.

Erikson, E. H. (1969). *Gandhi's truth: On the origins of militant nonviolence.* New York: Norton.

Erikson, E. H. (1975). *Life history and the historical moment.* New York: Norton.

Erikson, E. H. (1977). *Toys and reasons: Stages in the ritualization of experience.* New York: Norton.

Erikson, E. H. (1982). *The life cycle completed: A review.* New York: Norton.

Erikson, E. H. (1985). Pseudospeciation in the nuclear age. *Political Psychology, 6,* 213–217.

Erikson, E. H., Erikson, J. M., & Kivnick, H. Q. (1986). *Vital involvement in old age.* New York: Norton.

Erikson, J. M. (1967). Nothing to fear: Notes on the life of Eleanor Roosevelt. In R.J. Lifton (Ed.), *The woman in America.* Boston: Houghton Mifflin.

Eron, L. D. (1987). The development of aggressive behavior from the perspective of a developing behaviorism. *American Psychologist, 42,* 435–442.

Essig, T. S., & Russell, R. L. (1990). Analyzing subjectivity in therapeutic discourse: Rogers, Perls, Ellis and Gloria revisited. *Psychotherapy, 27,* 271–281.

Evans, M. G. (1991). The problem of analyzing multiplicative composites: Interactions revisited. *American Psychologist, 46,* 6–15.

Evans, R. G. (1982). Defense mechanisms in females as a function of sex-role orientation. *Journal of Clinical Psychology, 38,* 816–817.

Evans, R. I. (1976). Neal Miller. *The making of psychology: Discussions with creative contributors* (pp. 169–183). New York: Knopf.

Evans, R. I. (1981a). *Dialogue with Gordon Allport.* New York: Praeger.

Evans, R. I. (1981b). *Dialogue with B.F. Skinner.* New York: Praeger.

Evans, R. I. (1989). *Albert Bandura: The man and his ideas—a dialogue.* New York: Praeger.

Exner, J. E. (1986). *The Rorschach: A comprehensive system* (Vol. 1) (rev. ed.). New York: Wiley.

Eysenck, H. J. (1954). The science of personality: Nomothetic! *Psychological Review, 61,* 339–342.

Eysenck, H. J. (1967). *The biological basis of personality.* Springfield, IL: Chas. C Thomas.

Eysenck, H. J. (1979). The conditioning model of neurosis. *Behavioral and Brain Sciences, 2*, 155–199.

Eysenck, H. J. (1982). *Personality, genetics and behavior.* New York: Praeger.

Eysenck, H. J. (1986). Can personality study ever be scientific? *Journal of Social Behavior and Personality, 1*, 3–19.

Eysenck, H. J. (1991). Dimensions of personality: 16, 5, or 3?—Criteria for a taxonomic paradigm. *Personality and Individual Differences, 12*, 773–790.

Eysenck, H. J., & Eysenck, M. W. (1985). *Personality and individual differences: A natural science approach.* New York: Plenum.

Eysenck, M. W., & Eysenck, H. J. (1980). Mischel and the concept of personality. *British Journal of Psychology, 71*, 191–204.

Fairfield, B. (1990). Reorientation: The use of hypnosis for life-style change. *Individual Psychology, 46*, 451–458.

Fakouri, M. E., & Hafner, J. L. (1984). Early recollections of first-borns. *Journal of Clinical Psychology, 40*, 209–213.

Falk, J. L. (1956). Issues distinguishing idiographic from nomothetic approaches to personality theory. *Psychological Review, 63*, 53–62.

Falwell, J. (1987). *Strength for the Journey: An autobiography.* New York: Pocket Books.

Fanon, F. (1967). *Black skin, white masks.* New York: Grove Press.

Feinson, M. C. (1987). Mental health and aging: Are there gender differences? *Gerontologist, 27*, 703–711.

Feiring, C. (1984). Behavioral styles in infancy and adulthood: The work of Karen Horney and attachment theorists collaterally considered. *American Journal of Psychoanalysis, 44*, 197–208.

Feixas, G., & Villegas, M. (1991). Personal construct analysis of autobiographical texts: A method presentation and case illustration. *International Journal of Personal Construct Psychology, 4*, 51–83.

Feldman, C. F., & Hass, W. A. (1970). Controls, conceptualization, and the interrelation between experimental and correlational research. *American Psychologist, 25*, 633–635.

Ferster, C. B., & Skinner, B. F. (1957). *Schedules of reinforcement.* New York: Appleton-Century-Crofts.

Feshbach, S. (1964). The function of aggression and the regulation of aggressive drive. *Psychological Review, 71*, 257–272.

Fisch, M. C., & White, M. A. (1982). Verbal reinforcement and school learning. *Communication and Cognition, 15*, 69–77.

Fisher, D. D. (1990). Emotional construing: A psychobiological model. *International Journal of Personal Construct Psychology, 3*, 183–203.

Fisher, S., & Greenberg, R. P. (1977). *The scientific credibility of Freud's theories and therapy.* New York: Basic Books.

Fiske, D. W. (1973). Can a personality construct be validated empirically? *Psychological Bulletin, 80*, 89–92.

Fitzpatrick, J. J. (1976). Erik H. Erikson and psychohistory. *Bulletin of the Menninger Clinic, 40*, 295–314.

Florin, P., Mednick, M., & Wandersman, A. (1986). Cognitive social learning variables and the characteristics of leaders. *Journal of Applied Social Psychology, 16*, 808–830.

Folkman, S. (1984). Personal control, stress, and coping processes: A theoretical analysis. *Journal of Personality and Social Psychology, 46*, 839–852.

Ford, J. G., & Maas, S. (1989). On actualizing person-centered theory: A critique of textbook treatments of Rogers's motivational constructs. *Teaching of Psychology, 16*, 30–31.

Fordham, F. (1966). *An introduction to Jung's psychology.* (3rd ed.) Baltimore: Penguin.

Fordyce, W. E. (1982). A behavioural perspective on chronic pain. *British Journal of Clinical Psychology, 21*, 313–320.

Forehand, R. (1986). Parental positive reinforcement with deviant children: Does it make a difference? *Child and Family Behavior Therapy, 8*, 19–25.

Forer, L. (1976). *The birth order factor.* New York: D. McKay.

Forest, J. J. (1987). Effects on self-actualization of paperbacks about psychological self-help. *Psychological Reports, 60*, 1243–1246.

Försterling, F. (1985). Attributional retraining: A review. *Psychological Bulletin, 98*, 495–512.

Fourqurean, J. M., Meisgeier, C., & Swank, P. (1990). The link between learning style and Jungian psychological types: A finding of two bipolar preference dimensions. *Journal of Experimental Education, 58*, 225–237.

Fox, J. V. (1983). Unilateral neglect: Evaluation and treatment. *Physical and Occupational Therapy in Geriatrics, 2*, 5–15.

Fox, R., Switzky, H. N., Rotatori, A. F., & Vitkus, P. (1982). Successful weight loss techniques with mentally retarded children and youth. *Exceptional Children, 49*, 238–244.

Fox, W. M. (1982). Why we should abandon Maslow's need hierarchy theory. *Journal of Humanistic Education and Development, 21*, 29–32.

Frank, J. D. (1977). Nature and functions of belief systems: Humanism and transcendental religion. *American Psychologist, 32*, 555–559.

Franklin, B. (1961). *Benjamin Franklin: The autobiography and other writings.* (L. Jesse Lemisch, Ed.). New York: Signet.

Fransella, F., & Bannister, D. A. (1977). *A manual for repertory grid technique.* New York: Academic Press.

Franz, C. E., & White, K. M. (1985). Individuation and attachment in personality development: Extending Erikson's theory. *Journal of Personality, 53*, 224–256.

Franz, C. E., McClelland, D. C., & Weinberger, J. (1991). Childhood antecedents of conventional social accomplishment in midlife adults: A 36-year prospective study. *Journal of Personality and Social Psychology, 60*, 586–595.

Freud, A. (1935). *Psychoanalysis for teachers and parents.* (B. Low, Trans.) New York: Emerson Books.

Freud, A. (1966). *The ego and the mechanisms of defense* (rev. ed.) New York: International Universities Press. (Original work published 1936)

Freud, S. (1953). The interpretation of dreams. In J. Strachey (Ed. and Trans.), *The standard edition of the complete psychological works of Sigmund Freud* (Vols. 4 & 5). London: Hogarth Press. (Original work published 1900)

Freud, S. (1955). *Moses and monotheism* (K. Jones, Trans.). New York: Vintage Books. (Original work published 1939)

Freud, S. (1957). Leonardo da Vinci and a memory of his childhood. In J. Strachey (Ed. and Trans.), *The standard edition of the complete psychological works of Sigmund Freud* (Vol. 11, pp. 59–137). London: Hogarth Press. (Original work published 1910)

Freud, S. (1958). *On creativity and the unconscious.* New York: Harper & Row. (Original work published 1925)

Freud, S. (1962a). The aetiology of hysteria. In J. Strachey (Ed. and Trans.), *The standard edition of the complete psychological works of Sigmund Freud* (Vol. 3, pp. 187–221). London: Hogarth Press. (Original work published 1896)

Freud, S. (1962b). *The ego and the id.* (J. Riviere, Trans.; J. Strachey, Ed.). New York: Norton. (Original work published 1923)

Freud, S. (1963a). *An autobiographical study.* (J. Strachey, Trans.). New York: Norton. (Original work published 1935)

Freud, S. (1963b). *Jokes and their relation to the unconscious.* (J. Strachey, Ed. and Trans.). New York: Norton. (Original work published 1916)

Freud, S. (1966a). *The complete introductory lectures on psychoanalysis.* (J. Strachey, Ed. and Trans.). New York: Norton. (Original work published 1933)

Freud, S. (1966b). Project for a scientific psychology. In J. Strachey (Ed. and Trans.), *The standard edition of the complete psychological works of Sigmund Freud* (Vol. 1, pp. 283–397). London: Hogarth Press. (Original work published 1895)

Freud, S., & Bullitt, W. C. (1966). *Thomas Woodrow Wilson: A psychological study.* Boston: Houghton Mifflin.

Frick, R. B. (1982). The ego and the vestibulocerebellar system: Some theoretical perspectives. *Psychoanalytic Quarterly, 51,* 93–122.

Friedman, M. (1982). Comment on the Rogers-May discussion of evil. *Journal of Humanistic Psychology, 22,* 93–96.

Friedman, M., & Rosenman, R. H. (1974). *Type A behavior and your heart.* Greenwich, CT: Fawcett Crest.

Friman, P. C., & Christophersen, E. R. (1983). Behavior therapy and hyperactivity: A brief review of therapy for a big problem. *Behavior Therapist, 6,* 175–176.

Froehle, T. C. (1989). Personal construct threat as a mediator of performance anxiety in a beginning course in counseling techniques. *Journal of College Student Development, 30,* 536–540.

Fuller, R. C. (1982). Carl Rogers, religion, and the role of psychology in American culture. *Journal of Humanistic Psychology, 22,* 21–32.

Fullerton, C. S., Ursano, R. J., Wetzler, H. P., & Slusarcick, A. (1989). Birth order, psychological well-being, and social supports in young adults. *Journal of Nervous and Mental Disease, 177,* 556–559.

Funder, D. C. (1983). Three issues in predicting more of the people: A reply to Mischel and Peake. *Psychological Review, 90,* 283–289.

Funder, D. C., & Block, J. (1989). The role of ego-control, ego-resiliency, and IQ in delay of gratification in adolescence. *Journal of Personality and Social Psychology, 57,* 1041–1050.

Funder, D. C., & Colvin, C. R. (1991). Explorations in behavioral consistency: Properties of persons, situations, and behaviors. *Journal of Personality and Social Psychology, 60,* 773–794.

Furnham, A. (1990a). The development of single trait personality theories. *Personality and Individual Differences, 11,* 923–929.

Furnham, A. (1990b). The fakeability of the 16PF, Myers-Briggs and FIRO-B personality measures. *Personality and Individual Differences, 11,* 711–716.

Gandhi, M. K. (1957). *An autobiography: The story of my experiments with truth.* Boston: Beacon Press.

Gangestad, S., & Snyder, M. (1985). "To carve nature at its joints": On the existence of discrete classes in personality. *Psychological Review, 92,* 317–349.

Gara, M. A., Rosenberg, S., & Mueller, D. R. (1989). Perception of self and other in schizophrenia. *International Journal of Personal Construct Psychology, 2,* 253–270.

Garcia, M. E., Schmitz, J. M., & Doerfler, L. A. (1990). A fine-grained analysis of the role of self-efficacy in self-initiated attempts to quit smoking. *Journal of Consulting and Clinical Psychology, 58,* 317–322.

Garrett, K. R. (1985). Elbow room in a functional analysis: Freedom and dignity regained. *Behaviorism, 13,* 21–36.

Garrison, D. (1981). Karen Horney and feminism. *Signs,* 6, 672–691.

Garrow, D. J. (1986). *Bearing the cross: Martin Luther King, Jr., and the Southern Christian Leadership Conference.* New York: Vintage Books.

Gecas, V. (1989). The social psychology of self-efficacy. *Annual Review of Sociology, 15,* 291–316.

Geen, R. G., & Thomas, S. L. (1986). The immediate effects of media violence on behavior. *Journal of Social Issues, 42*(3), 7–27.

Geisler, C. (1985). Repression: A psychoanalytic perspective revisited. *Psychoanalysis and Contemporary Thought, 8,* 253–298.

Geller, L. (1982). The failure of self-actualization theory: A critique of Carl Rogers and Abraham Maslow. *Journal of Humanistic Psychology, 22*(2), 56–73.

Gendlin, E. T. (1988). Carl Rogers (1902–1987). *American Psychologist, 43,* 127–128.

Gigerenzer, G. (1991). From tools to theories: A heuristic of discovery in cognitive psychology. *Psychological Review, 98,* 254–267.

Gilligan, C. (1982). *In a different voice.* Cambridge, MA: Harvard University Press.

Giltinan, J. M. (1990). Using life review to facilitate self-actualization in elderly women. *Gerontology and Geriatrics Education, 10,* 75–83.

Glad, B. (1980). *Jimmy Carter.* New York: Norton.

Godbill, B. M. (1983). Power relations, homosexuality and the family: A review of the literature, including cross-cultural studies (homosexuality and the family in the Mohave, Chinese and Iraqi cultures). *Journal of Comparative Family Studies, 14,* 315–331.

Goebel, B. L., & Boeck, B. E. (1987). Ego integrity and fear of death: A comparison of institutionalized and independently living older adults. *Death Studies, 11,* 193–204.

Goertzel, M. G., Goertzel, V., & Goertzel, T. G. (1978). *Three hundred eminent personalities.* San Francisco: Jossey-Bass.

Goisman, R. M. (1983). Therapeutic approaches to phobia: A comparison. *American Journal of Psychotherapy, 37,* 227–234.

Goldberg, S. R., & Henningfield, J. E. (1988). Reinforcing effects of nicotine in humans and experimental animals responding under intermittent schedules of IV drug injection. *Pharmacology, Biochemistry and Behavior, 30,* 227–234.

Goldenberg, N. R. (1979). *Changing of the gods: Feminism and the end of traditional religions.* Boston: Beacon Press.

Goldwert, M. (1986). Childhood seduction and the spiritualization of psychology: The case of Jung and Rank. *Child Abuse and Neglect, 10,* 555–557.

Gondola, J. C., & Tuckman, B. W. (1985). Effects of a systematic program of exercise on selected measures of creativity. *Perceptual and Motor Skills, 60,* 53–54.

Gonzalez-Balado, J., & Playfoot, J. N. (Eds.). (1985). *My life for the poor: Mother Teresa of Calcutta.* New York: Ballantine.

Goodspeed, R. B., & DeLucia, A. G. (1990). Stress reduction at the worksite: An evaluation of two methods. *American Journal of Health Promotion, 4,* 333–337.

Gordon, R. D. (1985). Dimensions of peak communication experiences: An exploratory study. *Psychological Reports, 57,* 824–826.

Gould, D., Hodge, K., Peterson, K., & Giannini, J. (1989). An exploratory examination of strategies used by elite coaches to enhance self-efficacy in athletes. *Journal of Sport and Exercise Psychology, 11*, 128–140.

Grabowski, J., & O'Brien, C. P. (1981). Conditioning factors in opiate use. *Advances in Substance Abuse, 2*, 69–121.

Graham, W. K., & Balloun, J. (1973). An empirical test of Maslow's need hierarchy theory. *Journal of Humanistic Psychology, 13*, 97–108.

Grasing, K. W., & Miller, N. E. (1989). Self-administration of morphine contingent on heart rate in the rat. *Life Sciences, 45*, 1967–1976.

Gray, J. A. (1987). Perspectives on anxiety and impulsivity: A commentary. *Journal of Research in Personality, 21*, 493–509.

Graybill, D., Kirsch, J. R., & Esselman, E. D. (1985). Effects of playing violent versus nonviolent video games on the aggressive ideation of aggressive and nonaggressive children. *Child Study Journal, 15*, 199–205.

Graybill, D., Mackie, D. J., & House, A. E.(1985). Aggression in college students who were abused as children. *Journal of College Student Personnel, 26*, 492–495.

Greenberg, R. P., & Fisher, S. (1978, September). Testing Dr. Freud. *Human Behavior*, pp. 28–33.

Greenberg, R. P., & Fisher, S. (1983). Freud and the female reproductive process: Tests and issues. In J. Masling (Ed.), *Empirical studies of psychoanalytic theories* (Vol. 1, pp. 251–281). Hillsdale, NJ: Analytic Press.

Greene, T. A. (1976). America's loss of innocence: Bicentennial reflections. *Psychological Perspectives, 7*, 137–154.

Greeno, C. G., & Maccoby, E. E. (1986). How different is the "different voice"? *Signs, 11*, 310–316.

Greenspoon, J. (1955). The reinforcing effect of two spoken sounds on the frequency of two responses. *American Journal of Psychology, 68*, 409–416.

Greever, K. B., Tseng, M. S., & Friedland, B. U. (1973). Development of the Social Interest Index. *Journal of Consulting and Clinical Psychology, 41*, 454–458.

Griffin, J. C., Paisey, T. J., Stark, M. T., & Emerson, J. H. (1988). B.F. Skinner's position on aversive treatment. *American Journal on Mental Retardation, 93*, 104–105.

Griffith, E. (1984). *In her own right: The life of Elizabeth Cady Stanton.* New York: Oxford University Press.

Grinker, R. R., & Spiegel, J. P. (1945). *Men under stress.* Philadelphia: Blakiston.

Grosch, J., & Neuringer, A. (1981). Self-control in pigeons under the Mischel paradigm. *Journal of the Experimental Analysis of Behavior, 35*, 3–21.

Grossarth-Maticek, R., Eysenck, H. J., & Vetter, H. (1989). The causes and cures of prejudice: An empirical study of the frustration-aggression hypothesis. *Personality and Individual Differences, 10*, 547–558.

Grossman, F. K., Pollack, W. S., Golding, E. R., & Fedele, N. M. (1987). Affiliation and autonomy in the transition to parenthood. *Family Relations, 36*, 263–269.

Grotevant, H. D., & Adams, G. R. (1984). Development of an objective measure to assess ego identity in adolescence: Validation and replication. *Journal of Youth and Adolescence, 13*, 419–438.

Groth-Marnat, G., & Schumaker, J. F. (1989). The near-death experience: A review and critique. *Journal of Humanistic Psychology, 29*(1), 109–133.

Gruber, H. E. (1989). The evolving systems approach to creative work. In D. B. Wallace & H. E. Gruber (Eds.), *Creative people at work: Twelve cognitive case studies* (pp. 3–43). New York: Oxford University Press.

Grünbaum, A. (1984). *The foundations of psychoanalysis: A philosophical critique.* Berkeley: University of California Press.

Grünbaum, A. (1990). "Meaning" connections and causal connections in the human sciences: The poverty of hermeneutic philosophy. *Journal of the American Psychoanalytic Association, 38,* 559–577.

Grusec, J., & Mischel, W. (1966). Model's characteristics as determinants of social learning. *Journal of Personality and Social Psychology, 4,* 211–215.

Gustafson, R. (1986a). Alcohol, frustration, and aggression: An experiment using the balanced placebo design. *Psychological Reports, 59,* 207–218.

Gustafson, R. (1986b). Human physical aggression as a function of frustration: Role of aggressive cues. *Psychological Reports, 59,* 103–110.

Gustafson, R. (1989a). Frustration and successful vs. unsuccessful aggression: A test of Berkowitz' completion hypothesis. *Aggressive Behavior, 15,* 5–12.

Gustafson, R. (1989b). Human physical aggression as a function of magnitude of frustration: Indirect support and a possible confounding influence. *Psychological Reports, 64,* 367–374.

Guydish, J., Jackson, T. T., Markley, R. P., & Zelhart, P. F. (1985). George A. Kelly: Pioneer in rural school psychology. *Journal of School Psychology, 23,* 297–304.

Hackenberg, T. D. (1988). Operationism, mechanism, and psychological reality: The second-coming of linguistic relativity. *Psychological Record, 38,* 187–201.

Hageseth, J. A., & Schmidt, L. D. (1982). Self-actualization and conceptual structures. *Psychological Reports, 51,* 672.

Hall, C. S. (1966). *The meaning of dreams.* New York: McGraw-Hill.

Hall, C. S., & Nordby, V. J. (1973). *A primer of Jungian psychology.* New York: Mentor.

Hamachek, D. E. (1988). Evaluating self-concept and ego development within Erikson's psychosocial framework: A formulation. *Journal of Counseling and Development, 66,* 354–360.

Hamilton, J. W. (1977). Some reflections on Richard Nixon in the light of his resignation and farewell speeches. *Journal of Psychohistory, 4,* 491–511.

Hamilton, S. A. (1988). Behavioral formulations of verbal behavior in psychotherapy. *Clinical Psychology Review, 8,* 181–193.

Hamon, S. A. (1987). Some contributions of Horneyan theory to enhancement of the Type A behavior construct. *American Journal of Psychoanalysis,* 47, 105–115.

Hampson, S. E., John, O. P., & Goldberg, L. R. (1986). Category breadth and hierarchical structure in personality: Studies of asymmetries in judgments of trait implication. *Journal of Personality and Social Psychology, 51,* 37–54.

Hankoff, L. D. (1987). The earliest memories of criminals. *International Journal of Offender Therapy and Comparative Criminology, 31,* 195–201.

Harcum, E. R., & Rosen, E. F. (1990a). Perceived dignity as a function of perceived voluntary control of behaviors. *Journal of Psychology, 124,* 495–511.

Harcum, E. R., & Rosen, E. F. (1990b). The two faces of freedom and dignity: Credit or extenuation. *Psychological Reports, 66,* 1295–1298.

Harcum, E. R., Rosen, E. F., & Burijon, B. N. (1989). Popular versus Skinnerian views on the relation between human freedom and dignity. *Journal of Psychology, 123,* 257–267.

Hardaway, R. A. (1990). Subliminally activated symbiotic fantasies: Facts and artifacts. *Psychological Bulletin, 107,* 177–195.

Haring, M. J., Stock, W. A., & Okun, M. A. (1984). A research synthesis of gender and social class as correlates of subjective well-being. *Human Relations, 37,* 645–657.

Harren, V. A., Kass, R. A., Tinsley, H. E. A., & Moreland, J. R. (1979). Influence of gender, sex-role attitudes, and cognitive complexity on gender-dominant career choices. *Journal of Counseling Psychology, 26*, 227–234.

Harrington, D. M., Block, J. H., & Block, J. (1987). Testing aspects of Carl Rogers's theory of creative environments: Child-rearing antecedents of creative potential in young adolescents. *Journal of Personality and Social Psychology, 52*, 851–856.

Harris, J. (1986). *Jean Harris: Stranger in two worlds.* New York: Kensington.

Harris, J. (1988). *They always call us ladies: Stories from prison.* New York: Kensington.

Hartmann, H. (1958). *Ego psychology and the problem of adaptation* (D. Rapaport, Trans.). New York: International Universities Press. (Original work published 1939)

Harvey, J. H. (1989). People's naive understandings of their close relationships: Attributional and personal construct perspectives. *International Journal of Personal Construct Psychology, 2*, 37–48.

Harzem, P. (1984). Experimental analysis of individual differences and personality. *Journal of the Experimental Analysis of Behavior, 42*, 385–395.

Hattie, J. A. (1986). A defense of the Shostrom Personal Orientation Inventory: A rejoinder to Ray. *Personality and Individual Differences, 7*, 593–594.

Hattie, J., & Cooksey, R. W. (1984). Procedures for assessing the validities of tests using the "known-groups" method. *Applied Psychological Measurement, 8*, 295–305.

Hayden, B. C. (1982). Experience—A case for possible change: The modulation corollary. In J. C. Mancuso & J. R. Adams-Webber (Eds.), *The construing person* (pp. 170–197). New York: Praeger.

Hayden, T., & Mischel, W. (1976). Maintaining trait consistency in the resolution of behavioral inconsistency: The wolf in sheep's clothing? *Journal of Personality, 44*, 109–132.

Hayes, S. C., & Brownstein, A. J. (1985). Mentalism and the "as-yet-unexplained": A reply to Killeen. *Behaviorism, 13*, 151–154.

Hayes, S. C., Rincover, A., & Volosin, D. (1980). Variables influencing the acquisition and maintenance of aggressive behavior: Modeling versus sensory reinforcement. *Journal of Abnormal Psychology, 89*, 254–262.

Haymes, M., & Green, L. (1982). The assessment of motivation within Maslow's framework. *Journal of Research in Personality, 16*, 179–192.

Hays, R. D., & Ellickson, P. L. (1990). How generalizable are adolescents' beliefs about pro-drug pressures and resistance self-efficacy? *Journal of Applied Social Psychology, 20*, 321–340.

Healy, C. C. (1989a). Negative: The MBTI: Not ready for routine use in counseling. *Journal of Counseling and Development, 67*, 487–488.

Healy, C. C. (1989b). Rebuttal: In response to Professor Carlson. *Journal of Counseling and Development, 67*, 490.

Hearst, P. (with A. Moscow). (1982). *Patty Hearst: Her own story.* New York: Avon.

Heath, A. C., & Martin, N. G. (1990). Psychoticism as a dimension of personality: A multivariate genetic test of Eysenck and Eysenck's Psychoticism construct. *Journal of Personality and Social Psychology, 58*, 111–121.

Hegland, S. M., & Galejs, I. (1983). Developmental aspects of locus of control in preschool children. *Journal of Genetic Psychology, 143*, 229–239.

Hellinga, G. (1975). Fame as a guiding fiction. *Journal of Individual Psychology, 31*, 219–229.

Helson, R., & Picano, J. (1990). Is the traditional role bad for women? *Journal of Personality and Social Psychology, 59,* 311–320.

Helson, R., & Wink, P. (1987). Two conceptions of maturity examined in the findings of a longitudinal study. *Journal of Personality and Social Psychology, 53,* 531–541.

Henry, J. (1967). Discussion of Erikson's eight ages of man. In *Current Issues in Psychiatry* (Vol. 2). New York: Science House.

Henry, R. M., & Maze, J. R. (1989). Motivation in personal construct theory: A conceptual critique. *International Journal of Personal Construct Psychology, 2,* 169–183.

Herbert, N. (1988). How Bell proved reality cannot be local. *Psychological Perspectives, 19,* 313–319.

Herek, G. M. (1987). Religious orientation and prejudice: A comparison of racial and sexual attitudes. *Personality and Social Psychology Bulletin, 13,* 34–44.

Herman, J., & Hirschman, L. (1977). Father-daughter incest. *Signs: Journal of Women in Culture and Society, 2,* 735–756.

Hermans, H. J. (1988). On the integration of nomothetic and idiographic research methods in the study of personal meaning. *Journal of Personality, 56,* 785–812.

Hersen, M., & Barlow, D. H. (1976). *Single-case experimental design: Strategies for studying behavioral change.* New York: Pergamon Press.

Hettman, D. W., & Jenkins, E. (1990). Volunteerism and social interest. *Individual Psychology, 46,* 298–303.

Heyduk, R. G., & Fenigstein, A. (1984). Influential works and authors in psychology: A survey of eminent psychologists. *American Psychologist, 39,* 556–559.

Hicks, L. E. (1984). Conceptual and empirical analysis of some assumptions of an explicitly typological theory. *Journal of Personality and Social Psychology, 46,* 1118–1131.

Hicks, L. E. (1985). Is there a disposition to avoid the fundamental attribution error? *Journal of Research in Personality, 19,* 436–456.

Higgins, S. T., & Morris, E. K. (1984). Generality of free-operant avoidance conditioning to human behavior. *Psychological Bulletin, 96,* 247–272.

Hilgard, E. R. (1965). *Hypnotic susceptibility.* New York: Harcourt, Brace & World.

Hilgard, E. R. (1976). Neodissociation theory of multiple cognitive control systems. In G. E. Schwartz & D. Shapiro (Eds.), *Consciousness and self-regulation: Advances in research* (Vol. 1, pp. 137–171). New York: Plenum.

Hill, A. B. (1976). Methodological problems in the use of factor analysis: A critical review of the experimental evidence for the anal character. *British Journal of Medical Psychology, 49,* 145–159.

Hill, T., Smith, N. D., & Mann, M. F. (1987). Role of efficacy expectations in predicting the decision to use advanced technologies: The case of computers. *Journal of Applied Psychology, 72,* 307–313.

Hillman, J. (1980). Egalitarian typologies versus the perception of the unique. *Eranos Lectures* (Vol. 4). Dallas: Spring Publications.

Hillstrom, E. (1984). Human personality: Deterministic or merely predictable? *Journal of Psychology and Christianity, 3,* 42–48.

Hocutt, M. (1985). The truth in behaviorism: A review of G. E. Zuriff, *Behaviorism: A Conceptual Reconstruction.* In *Behaviorism, 13,* 77–82.

Hodgson, J. W., & Fischer, J. L. (1979). Sex differences in identity and intimacy development in college youth. *Journal of Youth and Adolescence, 8,* 37–50.

Hoffman, C., Mischel, W., & Baer, J. S. (1984). Language and person cognition: Effects of communicative set on trait attribution. *Journal of Personality and Social Psychology, 46,* 1029–1043.

Hoffman, C., & Tchir, M. A. (1990). Interpersonal verbs and dispositional adjectives: The psychology of causality embodied in language. *Journal of Personality and Social Psychology, 58,* 765–778.

Hoffman, L. W. (1991). The influence of the family environment on personality: Accounting for sibling differences. *Psychological Bulletin, 110,* 187–203.

Hofstetter, C. R., Sallis, J. F., & Hovell, M. F. (1990). Some health dimensions of self-efficacy: Analysis of theoretical specificity. *Social Science and Medicine, 31,* 1051–1056.

Hogan, R., & Nicholson, R. A. (1988). The meaning of personality test scores. *American Psychologist, 43,* 621–626.

Holden, G. W., Moncher, M. S., Schinke, S. P., & Barker, K. M. (1990). Self-efficacy of children and adolescents: A meta-analysis. *Psychological Reports, 66,* 1044–1046.

Holmes, D. S. (1978). Projection as a defense mechanism. *Psychological Bulletin, 85,* 677–688.

Holt, R. R. (1962). Individuality and generalization in the psychology of personality. *Journal of Personality, 30,* 377–404.

Holt, R. R. (1981). The death and transfiguration of metapsychology. *International Review of Psychoanalysis, 8* (part 2), 129–143.

Holt, R. R. (1984). Can psychology meet Einstein's challenge? *Political Psychology, 5,* 199–225.

Holzman, P. S. (1985). Psychoanalysis: Is the therapy destroying the science? *Journal of the American Psychoanalytic Association, 33,* 725–770.

Hopkins, J., & Sugerman, D. (1980). *No one here gets out alive.* New York: Warner Books.

Horley, J. (1991). Values and beliefs as personal constructs. *International Journal of Personal Construct Psychology, 4,* 1–14.

Horn, J. (1984). Genetical underpinnings. *Multivariate Behavioral Research, 19,* 307–309.

Horner, M. S. (1972). Toward an understanding of achievement-related conflicts in women. *Journal of Social Issues, 28*(2), 157–175.

Horney, K. (1937). *The neurotic personality of our time.* New York: Norton.

Horney, K. (1939). *New ways in psychoanalysis.* New York: Norton.

Horney, K. (1942). *Self-analysis.* New York: Norton.

Horney, K. (1945). *Our inner conflicts: A constructive theory of neurosis.* New York: Norton.

Horney, K. (1950). *Neurosis and human growth: The struggle toward self-realization.* New York: Norton.

Horney, K. (1967a). The flight from womanhood: The masculinity complex in women as viewed by men and by women. In H. Kelman (Ed.), *Feminine psychology* (pp. 54–70). New York: Norton. (Original work published 1926)

Horney, K. (1967b). Inhibited feminity: Psychoanalytical contribution to the problem of frigidity. In H. Kelman (Ed.), *Feminine psychology* (pp. 71–83). New York: Norton. (Original work published 1926)

Horney, K. (1967c). On the genesis of the castration complex in women. In H. Kelman (Ed.), *Feminine psychology* (pp. 37–53). New York: Norton. (Original work published 1923)

Horney, K. (1967d). The neurotic need for love. In H. Kelman (Ed.), *Feminine psychology* (pp. 245–258). New York: Norton. (Original work published 1937)

Horney, K. (1967e). The problem of feminine masochism. In H. Kelman (Ed.), *Feminine psychology* (pp. 214–233). New York: Norton. (Original work published 1935)

Houts, A. C., Cook, T. D., & Shadish, W. R. (1986). The person-situation debate: A critical multiplist perspective. *Journal of Personality, 54,* 52–105.

Howard, G. S. (1985). The role of values in the science of psychology. *American Psychologist, 40,* 255–265.

Howard, G. S. (1988). Kelly's thought at age 33: Suggestions for conceptual and methodological refinements. *International Journal of Personal Construct Psychology, 1,* 263–272.

Howard, G. S. (1991). Culture tales: A narrative approach to thinking, cross-cultural psychology, and psychotherapy. *American Psychologist, 46,* 187–197.

Howard, G. S., & Conway, C. G. (1986). Can there be an empirical science of volitional action? *American Psychologist, 41,* 1241–1251.

Howard, J. A., Blumstein, P., & Schwartz, P. (1986). Sex, power, and influence tactics in intimate relationships. *Journal of Personality and Social Psychology, 51,* 102–109.

Howarth, E., & Zumbo, B. D. (1989). An empirical investigation of Eysenck's typology. *Journal of Research in Personality, 23,* 343–353.

Howe, M. J. A. (1982). Biographical evidence and the development of outstanding individuals. *American Psychologist, 37,* 1071–1081.

Howell, R. H., Owen, P. D., & Nocks, E. C. (1990). Increasing safety belt use: Effects of modeling and trip length. *Journal of Applied Social Psychology, 20,* 254–263.

Huber, J. W., & Altmaier, E. M. (1983). An investigation of the self-statement systems of phobic and nonphobic individuals. *Cognitive Therapy and Research, 7,* 355–362.

Hudson, V. M. (1990). Birth order of world leaders: An exploratory analysis of effects on personality and behavior. *Political Psychology, 11,* 583–601.

Huesmann, L. R., & Malamuth, N. M. (1986). Media violence and antisocial behavior: An overview. *Journal of Social Issues, 42*(3), 1–6.

Huffman, J. R. (1989). Young man Johnson. *American Journal of Psychoanalysis, 49,* 251–265.

Hughes, M., & Demo, D. H. (1989). Self-perceptions of black Americans: Self-esteem and personal efficacy. *American Journal of Sociology, 95,* 132–159.

Hunter, F., & Levy, N. (1982). Relationship of problem-solving behaviors and Jungian personality types. *Psychological Reports, 51,* 379–384.

Huntley, C. W., & Davis, F. (1983). Undergraduate study of value scores as predictors of occupation 25 years later. *Journal of Personality and Social Psychology, 45,* 1148–1155.

Huot, B., Makarec, K., & Persinger, M. A. (1989). Temporal lobes signs and Jungian dimensions of personality. *Perceptual and Motor Skills, 69,* 841–842.

Hutton, P. H. (1983). The psychohistory of Erik Erikson from the perspective of collective mentalities. *Psychohistory Review, 12,* 18–25.

Hyland, M. E. (1985). Do person variables exist in different ways? *American Psychologist, 40,* 1003–1010.

Hyman, R. B. (1988). Four stages of adulthood: An exploratory study of growth patterns of inner-direction and time-competence in women. *Journal of Research in Personality, 22,* 117–127.

Incagnoli, T., & Newman, B. (1985). Cognitive and behavioral rehabilitation interventions. *International Journal of Clinical Neuropsychology, 7,* 173–182.

Ingram, D. H. (1985). Karen Horney at 100: Beyond the frontier. *American Journal of Psychoanalysis, 45,* 305–309.

Ivancevich, J. M., Matteson, M. T., & Gamble, G. O. (1987). Birth order and the Type A coronary behavior pattern. *Individual Psychology, 43,* 42–49.

Jabin, N. (1987). Attitudes toward disability: Horney's theory applied. *American Journal of Psychoanalysis, 47,* 143–153.

Jackson, D. N., Chan, D. W., & Stricker, L. J. (1979). Implicit personality theory: Is it illusory? *Journal of Personality, 47,* 1–10.

Jackson, D. N., & Paunonen, S. V. (1985). Construct validity and the predictability of behavior. *Journal of Personality and Social Psychology, 49,* 554–570.

Jackson, T. T., Markley, R. P., Zelhart, P. F., & Guydish, J. (1988). Contributions to the history of psychology: XLV. Attitude research: George A. Kelly's use of polar adjectives. *Psychological Reports, 62,* 47–52.

Jacobson, J. L., & Wille, D. E. (1986). The influence of attachment patterns on developmental changes in peer interaction from the toddler to the preschool period. *Child Development, 57,* 338–347.

Jaffe, L. S. (1990). The empirical foundations of psychoanalytic approaches to psychological testing. *Journal of Personality Assessment, 55,* 746–755.

Jankowicz, A. D. (1987). Whatever became of George Kelly? Applications and implications. *American Psychologist, 42,* 481–487.

Jankowicz, A. D., & Cooper, K. (1982). The use of focused repertory grids in counselling. *British Journal of Guidance and Counselling, 10,* 136–150.

Jankowicz, A. D., & Hisrich, R. (1987). Intuition in small-business lending decisions. *Journal of Small Business Management, 25,* 45–52.

Jankowicz, A. D., & Thomas, L. F. (1982–1983). The Focus cluster analysis algorithm in human resource development. *Personnel Review, 11,* 15–22 and erratum, *12,* 22.

Jenkins, C. D., Rosenman, R. H., & Zyzanski, S. J. (1974). Prediction of clinical coronary heart disease by a test for the coronary-prone behavior pattern. *New England Journal of Medicine, 290,* 1271–1275.

Jennings, J. L. (1986). The revival of "Dora": Advances in psychoanalytic theory and technique. *Journal of the American Psychoanalytic Association, 34,* 607–635.

Jenson, W. R. (1978). Behavior modification in secondary schools: A review. *Journal of Research and Development in Education, 11,* 53–63.

Joe, V. C., McGee, S. J., & Dazey, D. (1977). Religiousness and devaluation of a rape victim. *Journal of Clinical Psychology, 33,* 64.

John, O. P., Angleitner, A., & Ostendorf, F. (1988). The lexical approach to personality: A historical review of trait taxonomic research. *European Journal of Personality, 2,* 171–203.

Johnson, D. A., & Saunders, D. R. (1990). Confirmatory factor analysis of the Myers-Briggs Type Indicator—expanded analysis report. *Educational and Psychological Measurement, 50,* 561–571.

Johnson, N. S., & Holloway, E. L. (1988). Conceptual complexity and obsessionality in bulimic college women. *Journal of Counseling Psychology, 35,* 251–257.

Johnson, T. E., & Rule, B. G. (1986). Mitigating circumstance information, censure, and aggression. *Journal of Personality and Social Psychology, 50,* 537–542.

Jones, A., & Crandall, R. (1986). Validation of a short index of self-actualization. *Personality and Social Psychology Bulletin, 12,* 63–73.

Jones, A. C. (1985). Psychological functioning in black Americans: A conceptual guide for use in psychotherapy. *Psychotherapy, 22,* 363–369.

Jones, E. E., & Nisbett, R. E. (1972). The actor and the observer: Divergent perceptions of the causes of behavior. In E. E. Jones, D. E. Kanouse, H. H. Kelley, R. E. Nisbett, S. Valins, & B. Weiner (Eds.), *Attribution: Perceiving the causes of behavior.* Morristown, NJ: General Learning Press.

Jones, E. E., & Windholz, M. (1990). The psychoanalytic case study: Toward a method for systematic inquiry. *Journal of the American Psychoanalytic Association, 38,* 985–1015.

Jones, M. M. (1980). Conversion reaction: Anachronism or evolutionary form? A review of the neurologic, behavioral, and psychoanalytic literature. *Psychological Bulletin, 87,* 427–441.

Jones, N. S. C. (1990). Black/white issues in psychotherapy: A framework for clinical practice. *Journal of Social Behavior and Personality, 5,* 305–322.

Jones, R. M., & Streitmatter, J. L. (1987). Validity and reliability of the EOM-EIS for early adolescents. *Adolescence, 22,* 647–659.

Jones, R. S., & Baker, L. J. (1990). Differential reinforcement and challenging behaviour: A critical review of the DRI schedule. *Behavioural Psychotherapy, 18,* 35–47.

Jones, T. W. (1984). Behavior modification studies with hearing-impaired students: A review. *American Annals of the Deaf, 129,* 451–458.

Josephson, W. L.(1987). Television violence and children's aggression: Testing the priming, social script, and disinhibition predictions. *Journal of Personality and Social Psychology, 53,* 882–890.

Josselson, R. (1973). Psychodynamic aspects of identity formation in college women. *Journal of Youth and Adolescence, 2,* 3–52.

Josselson, R. (1987). *Finding herself: Pathways to identity development in women.* San Francisco: Jossey-Bass.

Judd, C. M., Jessor, R., & Donovan, J. (1986). Structural equation models and personality research. *Journal of Personality, 54,* 149–198.

Jung, C. G. (1954). Marriage as a psychological relationship. In C. G. Jung, *The development of personality* (pp. 187–201) (W. McGuire, Ed.; R. F. C. Hull, Trans.). Princeton, NJ: Princeton University Press. (Original work published 1931)

Jung, C. G. (1959). *Aion: Researches into the phenomenology of the self* (2nd ed.) (R. F. C. Hull, Trans.). Princeton, NJ: Princeton University Press.

Jung, C. G. (1960a). *The psychogenesis of mental disease* (R. F. C. Hull, Trans.). Princeton, NJ: Princeton University Press.

Jung, C. G. (1960b). *Synchronicity: An acausal connecting principle* (R. F. C. Hull, Trans.). Princeton, NJ: Princeton University Press.

Jung, C. G. (1961). *Memories, dreams, reflections* (A. Jaffe, Ed.; R. Winston and C. Winston, Trans.). New York: Random House.

Jung, C. G. (1964). *Civilization in transition* (R. F. C. Hull, Trans.). Princeton, NJ: Princeton University Press.

Jung, C. G. (1968a). *Alchemical studies* (R. F. C. Hull, Trans.). Princeton, NJ: Princeton University Press.

Jung, C. G. (1968b). *Psychology and alchemy* (2nd ed.) (R. F. C. Hull, Trans.). Princeton, NJ: Princeton University Press. (Original work published 1944)

Jung, C. G. (1969). *Four archetypes: Mother, rebirth, spirit, trickster* (R. F. C. Hull, Trans.). Princeton, NJ: Princeton University Press.

Jung, C. G. (1970). *Mysterium coniunctionis: An inquiry into the separation and synthesis of psychic opposites in alchemy* (2nd ed.) (R. F. C. Hull, Trans.). Princeton, NJ: Princeton University Press.

Jung, C. G. (1971). *Psychological types* (R. F. C. Hull and H. G. Baynes, Trans.). Princeton, NJ: Princeton University Press.

Jung, C. G. (1973). *Experimental Researches* (L. Stein & D. Riviere, Trans.). Princeton, NJ: Princeton University Press.

Jung, C. G. (1974). The practical use of dream-analysis. In C. G. Jung, *Dreams* (pp. 87–109) (W. McGuire, Ed.; R. F. C. Hull, Trans.). Princeton, NJ: Princeton University Press.

Jung, C. G. (1987). The association method: Lecture III. *American Journal of Psychology, 100,* 489–509. (Original work published 1910)

Juni, S. (1982). The composite measure of the Defense Mechanism Inventory. *Journal of Research in Personality, 16,* 193–200.

Justice, T. C., & Looney, T. A. (1990). Another look at "superstitions" in pigeons. *Bulletin of the Psychonomic Society, 28,* 64–66.

Kagan, J. (1988). The meanings of personality predicates. *American Psychologist, 43,* 614–620.

Kahn, E. (1985). Heinz Kohut and Carl Rogers: A timely comparison. *American Psychologist, 40,* 893–904.

Kahn, E. (1987). A reply to Emery's comments. *American Psychologist, 42,* 515–516.

Kaliski, E. M., Rubinson, L., Lawrance, L., & Levy, S. R. (1990). AIDS, runaways, and self-efficacy. *Family and Community Health, 13*(1), 65–72.

Kalliopuska, M. (1985). Rationales for an implicit personality theory. *Psychological Reports, 57,* 1071–1076.

Karson, S., & O'Dell, J. W. (1975). A new automated interpretation system for the 16PF. *Journal of Personality Assessment, 39,* 256–260.

Katz, J. O. (1984). Personal construct theory and the emotions: An interpretation in terms of primitive constructs. *British Journal of Psychology, 75,* 315–327.

Kazdin, A. E. (1982). The token economy: A decade later. *Journal of Applied Behavior Analysis, 15,* 431–445.

Kazdin, A. E., & Hersen, M. (1980). The current status of behavior therapy. *Behavior Modification, 4,* 283–302.

Keane, M. C., & Morgan, B. S. (1991). Perceived self-efficacy and language differences. *Psychological Reports, 69,* 291–298.

Keehn, J. D. (1980). Beyond an interactional model of personality: Transactionalism and the theory of reinforcement schedules. *Behaviorism, 8,* 55–65.

Keirsey, D., & Bates, M. (1978). *Please understand me: Character and temperament types* (3rd ed.). Del Mar, CA: Prometheus Nemesis.

Kelly, G. A. (1955). *The psychology of personal constructs* (Vols. 1 and 2). New York: Norton.

Kelly, G. A. (1957). Hostility. (Presidential Address, 1957, Clinical Division, American Psychological Association). Reprinted in B. Maher (Ed.), *Clinical psychology and personality: The selected papers of George Kelly* (1969, pp. 267–280). New York: Wiley.

Kelly, G. A. (1958). Man's construction of his alternatives. In G. Lindzey (Ed.), *The assessment of human motives* (pp. 33–64). New York: Holt, Rinehart & Winston.

Kelly, G. A. (1960). Epilogue: Don Juan. Reprinted in B. Maher (Ed.), *Clinical psychology and personality: The selected papers of George Kelly* (1969, pp. 333–351). New York: Wiley.

Kelly, G. A. (1962). *Sin and psychotherapy.* Temple University Symposium on Psychotherapy, Philadelphia, Pennsylvania, March 9, 1962. Reprinted in B. Maher

(Ed.), *Clinical psychology and personality: The selected papers of George Kelly* (1969, pp. 165–188). New York: Wiley.

Kelly, G. A. (1963a). The autobiography of a theory. Reprinted in B. Maher (Ed.), *Clinical psychology and personality: The selected papers of George Kelly* (1969, pp. 46–65). New York: Wiley.

Kelly, G. A. (1963b). Nonparametric factor analysis of personality theories. *Journal of Individual Psychology, 19*, 115–147. Reprinted in B. Maher (Ed.), *Clinical psychology and personality: The selected papers of George Kelly* (1969, pp. 301–332). New York: Wiley.

Kelly, G. A. (1964). The language of hypotheses: Man's psychological instrument. *Journal of Individual Psychology, 20*, 137–152. Reprinted in B. Maher (Ed.), *Clinical psychology and personality: The selected papers of George Kelly* (1969, pp. 147–162). New York: Wiley.

Kelly, G. A. (1966). Ontological acceleration. Reprinted in B. Maher (Ed.), *Clinical psychology and personality: The selected papers of George Kelly* (1969, pp. 7–45). New York: Wiley.

Kelly, G. A. (1968). The role of classification in personality theory. *Proceedings of the Conference on the Role and Methodology of Classification in Psychiatry and Psychopathology.* In M. Katz, J. O. Cole, & W. E. Barton (Eds.), *Classification in Psychiatry and Psychopathology.* Chevy Chase, MD: United States Public Health Service. Reprinted in B. Maher (Ed.), *Clinical psychology and personality: The selected papers of George Kelly* (1969, pp. 289–300). New York: Wiley.

Kelly, G. A. (1969). Humanistic methodology in psychological research. In B. Maher (Ed.), *Clinical psychology and personality: The selected papers of George Kelly* (pp. 133–146). New York: Wiley.

Kenny, D. A., & Campbell, D. T. (1989). On the measurement of stability in over-time data. *Journal of Personality, 57*, 445–481.

Kenrick, D. T., & Braver, S. L. (1982). Personality: Idiographic and nomothetic! A rejoinder. *Psychological Review, 89*, 182–186.

Kenrick, D. T., & Funder, D. C. (1988). Profiting from the controversy: Lessons from the person-situation debate. *American Psychologist, 43*, 23–34.

Kenrick, D. T., & Stringfield, D. O. (1980). Personality traits and the eye of the beholder: Crossing some traditional philosophical boundaries in the search for consistency in all of the people. *Psychological Review, 87*, 88–104.

Kern, R. M., & White, J. (1989). Brief therapy using the life-style scale. *Individual Psychology, 45*, 186–190.

Kernberg, O. (1975). *Borderline conditions and pathological narcissism.* New York: Jason Aronson.

Keutzer, C. S. (1984). The power of meaning: From quantum mechanics to synchronicity. *Journal of Humanistic Psychology, 24*(1), 80–94.

Kiesler, D. J. (1983). The 1982 Interpersonal Circle: A taxonomy for complementarity in human transactions. *Psychological Review, 90*, 185–214.

Killeen, P. R. (1984). Emergent behaviorism. *Behaviorism, 12*, 25–39.

Kimble, G. A. (1984). Psychology's two cultures. *American Psychologist, 39*, 833–839.

King, C. S. (1969). *My Life with Martin Luther King, Jr.* New York: Avon.

Kiracofe, N. M., & Kiracofe, H. N. (1990). Child-perceived paternal favoritism and birth order. *Individual Psychology, 46*, 74–81.

Kirsch, I. (1980). "Microanalytic" analyses of efficacy expectations as predictors of performance. *Cognitive Therapy and Research, 4*, 259–262.

Kirschenbaum, D. S. (1985). Proximity and specificity of planning: A position paper. *Cognitive Therapy and Research, 9,* 489–506.

Kiser, L. J., Heston, J., Millsap, P. A., & Pruitt, D. B. (1991). Physical and sexual abuse in childhood: Relationship with post-traumatic stress disorder. *Journal of the American Academy of Child and Adolescent Psychiatry, 30,* 776–783.

Klein, M. (1946). Notes on some schizoid mechanisms. In M. Klein, P. Heimann, S. Issacs, & J. Riviere (Eds.), *Developments in psychoanalysis.* London: Hogarth Press.

Kleinginna, P. R., Jr., & Kleinginna, A. M. (1988). Current trends toward convergence of the behavioristic, functional, and cognitive perspectives in experimental psychology. *Psychological Record, 38,* 369–392.

Kline, P. (1972). *Fact and fantasy in Freudian theory.* London: Methuen.

Kline, S. L. (1990). Situational variability in personal construing and social cognitive development. *International Journal of Personal Construct Psychology, 3,* 327–337.

Kluckhohn, C., & Murray, H. A. (1953). Personality formation: The determinants. In C. Kluckhohn, H. Murray, & D. Schneider (Eds.), *Personality in nature, society and culture* (pp. 53–67). New York: Knopf.

Knapp, T. J., Downs, D. L., & Alperson, J. R. (1976). Behavior therapy for insomnia: A review. *Behavior Therapy, 7,* 614–625.

Knapp, T. J., & Wells, L. A. (1978). Behavior therapy for asthma: A review. *Behaviour Research and Therapy, 16,* 103–115.

Kobasa, S. C. (1979). Stressful life events, personality, and health: A prospective study. *Journal of Personality and Social Psychology, 37,* 1–11.

Kobasa, S. C., Maddi, S. R., & Kahn, S. (1982). Hardiness and health: A prospective study. *Journal of Personality and Social Psychology, 42,* 168–177.

Koch, S. (1981). The nature and limits of psychological knowledge: Lessons of a century qua "science." *American Psychologist, 36,* 257–269.

Kohut, H. (1971). *The analysis of the self.* New York: International Universities Press.

Kohut, H., & Wolf, E. S. (1978). The disorders of the self and their treatment: An outline. *International Journal of Psychoanalysis, 59,* 413–425.

Kores, R. C., Murphy, W. D., Rosenthal, T. L., Elias, D. B., & North, W. C. (1990). Predicting outcome of chronic pain treatment via a modified self-efficacy scale. *Behaviour Research and Therapy, 28,* 165–169.

Kowaz, A. M., & Marcia, J. E. (1991). Development and validation of a measure of Eriksonian industry. *Journal of Personality and Social Psychology, 60,* 390–397.

Kratochwill, T. R. (Ed.). (1978). *Single subject research.* New York: Academic Press.

Kris, E. (1964). *Psychoanalytic explorations in art.* New York: Shocken. (Original work published 1952)

Kroger, J. (1986). The relative importance of identity status interview components: Replication and extension. *Journal of Adolescence, 9,* 337–354.

Kroger, J., & Haslett, S. J. (1988). Separation-individuation and ego identity status in late adolescence: A two-year longitudinal study. *Journal of Youth and Adolescence, 17,* 59–79.

Krutch, J. W. (1954). *The measure of man.* New York: Grosset & Dunlap.

Krzystofiak, F., Cardy, R. L., & Newman, J. (1988). Implicit personality and performance appraisal: The influence of trait inferences on evaluations of behavior. *Journal of Applied Psychology, 73,* 515–521.

Kuhn, T. S. (1970). *The structure of scientific revolutions* (2nd ed.). Chicago: University of Chicago Press.

Kukla, A. (1982). Logical incoherence of value-free science. *Journal of Personality and Social Psychology, 43,* 1014–1017.

Kukla, A. (1989). Nonempirical issues in psychology. *American Psychologist, 44,* 785–794.

Kull, S. (1983). Nuclear arms and the desire for world destruction. *Political Psychology, 4,* 563–591.

Kuo, Y. (1987). Environmental factors associated with the growth of Chinese literary genius: A test of Rogerian assumption. *Creative Child and Adult Quarterly, 12,* 93–102, 132.

Kuypers, B. C., Davies, D., & Van der Vegt, R. (1987). Training group development and outcomes. *Small Group Behavior, 18,* 309–335.

Labbe, E. E., & Williamson, D. A. (1984). Behavioral treatment of elective mutism: A review of the literature. *Clinical Psychology Review, 4,* 273–292.

Lacks, R. (1980). *Women and Judaism: Myth, history, and struggle.* Garden City, NY: Doubleday.

Ladouceur, R., & Mercier, P. (1984). Awareness: An understudied cognitive factor in behavior therapy. *Psychological Reports, 54,* 159–178.

Lamborn, S. D., Mounts, N. S., Steinberg, L., & Dornbusch, S. (1991). Patterns of competence and adjustment among adolescents from authoritative, authoritarian, indulgent, and neglectful families. *Child Development, 62,* 1049–1065.

Lamiell, J. T. (1981). Toward an idiothetic psychology of personality. *American Psychologist, 36,* 276–289.

Lamke, L. K., & Peyton, K. G. (1988). Adolescent sex-role orientation and ego identity. *Journal of Adolescence, 11,* 205–215.

Lampl-de Groot, J. (1982). Thoughts on psychoanalytic views of female psychology, 1927–1977. *Psychoanalytic Quarterly, 51,* 1–18.

Landfield, A. W. (1982). A construction of fragmentation and unity: The fragmentation corollary. In J. C. Mancuso & J. R. Adams-Webber (Eds.), *The construing person* (pp. 170–197). New York: Praeger.

Landfield, A. W. (1988). Personal science and the concept of validation. *International Journal of Personal Construct Psychology, 1,* 237–249.

Landfield, A. W., & Epting, F. R. (1987). *Personal construct psychology: Clinical and personality assessment.* New York: Human Sciences Press.

Landwehr, K. (1983). On taking Skinner on his own terms: Comments on Wessells' critique of Skinner's view of cognitive theories. *Behaviorism, 11,* 187–191.

Landy, F. J. (1986). Stamp collecting versus science: Validation as hypothesis testing. *American Psychologist, 41,* 1183–1192.

Langenfeld, S., & Main, F. (1983). Personality profiles: A factor analytic study. *Individual Psychology, 39,* 41–51.

Langer, W. (1972). *The mind of Adolph Hitler: The secret wartime report.* New York: Basic Books.

Lash, J. P. (1971). *Eleanor and Franklin.* New York: Norton.

Lash, J. P. (1972). *Eleanor: The years alone.* New York: Signet.

Lasko, J. K. (1954). Parent behavior toward first and second children. *Genetic Psychology Monographs, 49,* 97–137.

Latham, C. (1986). *Carol Burnett: Funny is beautiful.* New York: Signet.

Lauter, E., & Rupprecht, C. S. (Eds.). (1985). *Feminist archetypal theory: Interdisciplinary re-visions of Jungian thought.* Knoxville: University of Tennessee Press.

Lawrence, L. (1988). The covert seduction theory: Filling the gap between the seduction theory and the Oedipus complex. *American Journal of Psychoanalysis, 48,* 247–250.

Leak, G. K. (1982). Two social interest measures and social desirability response sets. *Individual Psychology, 38,* 42–46.

Leak, G. K., & Christopher, S. B. (1982). Freudian psychoanalysis and sociobiology: A synthesis. *American Psychologist, 37,* 313–322.

Leak, G. K., & Fish, S. (1989). Religious orientation, impression management, and self-deception: Toward a clarification of the link between religiosity and social desirability. *Journal for the Scientific Study of Religion, 28,* 355–359.

Leak, G. K., Millard, R. J., Perry, N. W., & Williams, D. E. (1985). An investigation of the nomological network of social interest. *Journal of Research in Personality, 19,* 197–207.

Leak, G. K., & Williams, D. E. (1989). Relationships between social interest, alienation, and psychological hardiness. *Individual Psychology, 45,* 369–375.

Leary, T. (1957). *Interpersonal diagnosis of personality: A functional theory and methodology for personality evaluation.* New York: Ronald Press.

Ledwidge, B. (1978). Cognitive behavior modification: A step in the wrong direction? *Psychological Bulletin, 85,* 353–375.

Lee, C. (1989). Theoretical weaknesses lead to practical problems: The example of self-efficacy theory. *Journal of Behavior Therapy and Experimental Psychiatry, 20,* 115–123.

Lee, C. (1990). Theoretical weaknesses: Fundamental flaws in cognitive-behavioral theories are more than a problem of probability. *Journal of Behavior Therapy and Experimental Psychiatry, 21,* 143–145.

Lee, D. Y., & Uhlemann, M. R. (1984). Comparison of verbal responses of Rogers, Shostrom, and Lazarus. *Journal of Counseling Psychology, 31,* 91–94.

Lee, V. L. (1984). Some notes on the subject matter of Skinner's *Verbal Behavior. Behaviorism, 12,* 29–40.

Lefcourt, H. M. (1973). The function of the illusions of control and freedom. *American Psychologist, 28,* 417–425.

Leifer, M., Shapiro, J. P., Martone, M. W., & Kassem, L. (1991). Rorschach assessment of psychological functioning in sexually abused girls. *Journal of Personality Assessment, 56,* 14–28.

Leitner, L. M., & Cado, S. (1982). Personal constructs and homosexual stress. *Journal of Personality and Social Psychology, 43,* 869–872.

Lennon, S. J., & Davis, L. L. (1987). Individual differences in fashion orientation and cognitive complexity. *Perceptual and Motor Skills, 64,* 327–330.

Lennox, D. B., Miltenberger, R. G., Spengler, P., & Erfanian, N. (1988). Decelerative treatment practices with persons who have mental retardation: A review of five years of the literature. *American Journal on Mental Retardation, 92,* 492–501.

Lennox, R. (1988). The problem with self-monitoring: A two-sided scale and a one-sided theory. *Journal of Personality Assessment, 52,* 58–73.

Lerman, H. (1986a). From Freud to feminist personality theory: Getting here from there. *Psychology of Women Quarterly, 10,* 1–18.

Lerman, H. (1986b). *A mote in Freud's eye: From psychoanalysis to the psychology of women.* New York: Springer-Verlag.

Lerner, J. A. (1986). Contrasting views of felt aliveness. *American Journal of Psychoanalysis, 46,* 318–326.

Lerner, P. M. (1990). The clinical inference process and the role of theory. *Journal of Personality Assessment, 55,* 426–431.

Lerner, R. M., & Tubman, J. G. (1989). Conceptual issues in studying continuity and discontinuity in personality development across life. *Journal of Personality, 57,* 343–373.

Lester, D. (1989a). Jungian dimensions of personality, subclinical depression and suicidal ideation. *Personality and Individual Differences, 10,* 1009.

Lester, D. (1989b). A neurotransmitter basis for Eysenck's theory of personality. *Psychological Reports, 64,* 189–190.

Lester, D. (1989c). A test of Jung's hypothesis of the determination of type of symptom. *Personality and Individual Differences, 10,* 473–474.

Lester, D. (1990a). Galen's four temperaments and four-factor theories of personality: A comment on "Toward a four-factor theory of temperament and/or personality." *Journal of Personality Assessment, 54,* 423–426.

Lester, D. (1990b). Maslow's hierarchy of needs and personality. *Personality and Individual Differences, 11,* 1187–1188.

Lester, D., Hvezda, J., Sullivan, S., & Plourde, R. (1983). Maslow's hierarchy of needs and psychological health. *Journal of General Psychology, 109,* 83–85.

Lester, D., Thinschmidt, J. S., & Trautman, L. A. (1987). Paranormal belief and Jungian dimensions of personality. *Psychological Reports, 61,* 182.

Levey, J. (1986). Richard Nixon as elder statesman. *Journal of Psychohistory, 13,* 427–448.

Levine, F. M., & Fasnacht, G. (1974). Token rewards may lead to token learning. *American Psychologist, 29,* 816–820.

Levit, D. B. (1991). Gender differences in ego defenses in adolescence: Sex roles as one way to understand the differences. *Journal of Personality and Social Psychology, 61,* 992–999.

Levitz-Jones, E. M., & Orlofsky, J. L. (1985). Separation-individuation and intimacy capacity in college women. *Journal of Personality and Social Psychology, 49,* 156–169.

Lewis, C. N. (1990). Personality analysis of an artist and imposter. *Journal of Personality Assessment, 54,* 656–670.

Lewis, T. D. (1983). Gordon Liddy: A life style analysis. *Individual Psychology, 39,* 259–273.

Lewis, T. T. (1985). Gordon Allport's eclectic humanism: A neglected approach to psychohistory. *Psychohistory Review, 13,* 33–41.

Lieberman, A. F. (1977). Preschoolers' competence with a peer: Relations with attachment and peer experience. *Child Development, 48,* 1277–1287.

Lisle, L. (1980). *Portrait of an artist: A biography of Georgia O'Keeffe.* New York: Seaview.

Lobel, T. E., & Gilat, I. (1987). Type A behavior pattern, ego identity, and gender. *Journal of Research in Personality, 21,* 389–394.

Lobel, T. E., & Winch, G. L. (1988). Psychosocial development, self-concept, and gender. *Journal of Genetic Psychology, 149,* 405–411.

Lockhart, R. A. (1977). Cancer in myth and dream: An exploration into the archetypal relation between dreams and disease. In J. Hillman (Ed.), *Spring: An annual of archetypal psychology and Jungian thought* (pp. 1–26). Zürich, Switzerland: Spring Publications.

Lockhart, W. H. (1984). Rogers' "necessary and sufficient conditions" revisited. *British Journal of Guidance and Counselling, 12,* 113–123.

Loehlin, J. C. (1984). R. B. Cattell and behavior genetics. *Multivariate Behavioral Research, 19,* 310–321.

Loevinger, J. (1966). The meaning and measurement of ego development. *American Psychologist, 21,* 195–206.

Loevinger, J. (1976). *Ego development: Conceptions and theories.* San Francisco: Jossey-Bass.

Loevinger, J. (1979). Construct validity of the sentence completion test of ego development. *Applied Psychological Measurement, 3,* 281–311.

Loevinger, J., Cohn, L. D., Bonneville, L. P., Redmore, C. D., Streich, D. D., & Sargent, M. (1985). Ego development in college. *Journal of Personality and Social Psychology, 48,* 947–962.

Loewenberg, P. (1988). Psychoanalytic models of history: Freud and after. In W. M. Runyan (Ed.), *Psychology and historical interpretation* (pp. 126–156). New York: Oxford University Press.

Lomranz, J. (1986). Personality theory: Position and derived teaching implications in clinical psychology. *Professional Psychology Research and Practice, 17,* 551–559.

Londerville, S., & Main, M. (1981). Security of attachment, compliance, and maternal training methods in the second year of life. *Developmental Psychology, 17,* 289–299.

Long, B. C. (1989). Sex-role orientation, coping strategies, and self-efficacy of women in traditional and nontraditional occupations. *Psychology of Women Quarterly, 13,* 307–324.

Looney, T. A., & Cohen, P. S. (1982). Aggression induced by intermittent positive reinforcement. *Neuroscience and Biobehavioral Reviews, 6,* 15–37.

Lorenzini, R., Sassaroli, S., & Rocchi, M. T. (1989). Schizophrenia and paranoia as solutions to predictive failure. *International Journal of Personal Construct Psychology, 2,* 417–432.

Lorimer, R. (1976). A reconsideration of the psychological roots of *Gandhi's Truth. Psychoanalytic Review, 63,* 191–207.

Lott, B. (1985). The potential enrichment of social/personality psychology through feminist research and vice versa. *American Psychologist, 40,* 155–164.

Lowry, R. J. (Ed.). (1973). *Dominance, self-esteem, self-actualization: Germinal papers of A. H. Maslow.* Monterey, CA: Brooks/Cole.

Lundin, R. W. (1969). *Personality: A behavioral analysis.* London: Macmillan.

Lupfer, M. B., Clark, L. F., & Hutcherson, H. W. (1990). Impact of context on spontaneous trait and situational attributions. *Journal of Personality and Social Psychology, 58,* 239–249.

Lykes, M. B. (1985). Gender and individualistic vs. collectivist bases for notions about the self. *Journal of Personality, 53,* 356–383.

Lynn, R., Hampson, S. L., & Mullineux, J. C. (1987). A long-term increase in the fluid intelligence of English children. *Nature, 328,* 797.

Lyon, D., & Greenberg, J. (1991). Evidence of codependency in women with an alcoholic parent: Helping out Mr. Wrong. *Journal of Personality and Social Psychology, 61,* 435–439.

MacLaine, S. (1970). *Don't fall off the mountain.* New York: Bantam.

MacLaine, S. (1975). *You can get there from here.* New York: Bantam.

MacLaine, S. (1983). *Out on a limb.* New York: Bantam.

MacLaine, S. (1985). *Dancing in the light.* New York: Bantam.

MacLaine, S. (1987). *It's all in the playing.* New York: Bantam.

Mack, J. E. (1971). Psychoanalysis and historical biography. *Journal of the American Psychoanalytic Association, 19,* 143–179.

Mack, J. E. (1980). Psychoanalysis and biography: Aspects of a developing affinity. *Journal of the American Psychoanalytic Association, 28,* 543–562.

Maddi, S. R., & Costa, P. T., Jr. (1972). *Humanism in personology: Allport, Maslow, and Murray.* Chicago: Aldine Atherton.

Magnusson, D., & Endler, N. S. (1977). *Personality at the crossroads: Current issues in interactional psychology.* New York: Wiley.

Mahoney, M. F. (1966). *The meaning in dreams and dreaming: The Jungian viewpoint.* Secaucus, NJ: Citadel Press.

Mahoney, M. J., & Bandura, A. (1972). Self-reinforcement in pigeons. *Learning and Motivation, 3,* 293–303.

Mahony, P. J. (1986). *Freud and the Rat Man.* New Haven, CT: Yale University Press.

Mahrer, A. R., Nadler, W. P., Stalikas, A., Schachter, H. M., & Sterner, I. (1988). Common and distinctive therapeutic change processes in client-centered, rational-emotive, and experiential psychotherapies. *Psychological Reports, 62,* 972–974.

Mahrer, A. R., Sterner, I., Lawson, K. C., & Dessaulles, A. (1986). Microstrategies: Distinctively patterned sequences of therapist statements. *Psychotherapy, 23,* 50–56.

Mair, M. (1988). Psychology as storytelling. *International Journal of Personal Construct Psychology, 1,* 125–137.

Major, B., Cozzarelli, C., Sciacchitano, A. M., Cooper, M. L., Testa, M., & Mueller, P. M. (1990). Perceived social support, self-efficacy, and adjustment to abortion. *Journal of Personality and Social Psychology, 59,* 452–463.

Mallory, M. E. (1989). Q-Sort definition of ego identity status. *Journal of Youth and Adolescence, 18,* 399–412.

Malone, M. (1977). *Psychetypes: A new way of exploring personality.* New York: Pocket Books.

Mancuso, J. C., & Adams-Webber, J. R. (Eds.). (1982). *The construing person.* New York: Praeger.

Mandrosz-Wroblewska, J. (1989). Strategies for resolving identity problems: "Self-we" and "we-they" differentiation. *Journal of Social and Clinical Psychology, 8,* 400–413.

Manicas, P. T., & Secord, P. F. (1983). Implications for psychology of the new philosophy of science. *American Psychologist, 38,* 399–413.

Manicas, P. T., & Secord, P. F. (1984). Implications for psychology: Reply to comments. *American Psychologist, 39,* 922–926.

Manuel, F. (1971). The use and abuse of psychology in history. *Daedalus, 100,* 187–213.

Maoz, Z. (1987). Revisionism or misinterpretation? A reply to Professor Walker. *Political Psychology, 8,* 623–636.

Maoz, Z., & Shayer, A. (1987). The cognitive structure of peace and war argumentation: Israeli prime ministers versus the Knesset. *Political Psychology, 8,* 575–604.

Marceil, J. C. (1977). Implicit dimensions of idiography and nomothesis: A reformulation. *American Psychologist, 32,* 1046–1055.

Marcia, J. E. (1966). Development and validation of ego-identity status. *Journal of Personality and Social Psychology, 3,* 551–558.

Marcia, J. E. (1967). Ego identity status: Relationship to change in self-esteem, "general maladjustment" and authoritarianism. *Journal of Personality, 35,* 118–133.

Marcovitz, E. (1982). Jung's three secrets: Slochower on "Freud as Yahweh in Jung's Answer to Job." *American Imago, 39,* 59–72.

Markstrom-Adams, C. (1989). Androgyny and its relation to adolescent psychosocial well-being: A review of the literature. *Sex Roles, 21,* 325–340.

Markus, H. (1977). Self-schemata and processing information about the self. *Journal of Personality and Social Psychology, 35,* 63–78.

Markus, H. R., & Kitayama, S. (1991). Culture and the self: Implications for cognition, emotion, and motivation. *Psychological Review, 98,* 224–253.

Marr, M. J. (1987). The long shadow on the lawn. Review of B.F. Skinner, Upon Further Reflection. *Contemporary Psychology, 32,* 930–932.

Marsh, C. S., & Colangelo, N. (1983). The application of Dabrowski's concept of multilevelness to Allport's concept of unity. *Counseling and Values, 27,* 213–228.

Marshall, G. N. (1991a). Levels of analysis and personality: Lessons from the person-situation debate? *Psychological Science, 2,* 427–428.

Marshall, G. N. (1991b). Multidimensional analysis of internal health locus of control beliefs: Separating the wheat from the chaff? *Journal of Personality and Social Psychology, 61,* 483–491.

Martin, E. S. (1989). The relationship among college student characteristics and their assigned importance to dimensions of course choice information. *Journal of College Student Development, 30,* 69–76.

Martin, G. L., & Hrydowy, E. R. (1989). Self-monitoring and self-managed reinforcement procedures for improving work productivity of developmentally disabled workers: A review. *Behavior Modification, 13,* 322–339.

Martinetti, R. F. (1985). Cognitive antecedents of dream recall. *Perceptual and Motor Skills, 60,* 395–401.

Marzillier, J., & Eastman, C. (1984). Continuing problems with self-efficacy theory: A reply to Bandura. *Cognitive Therapy and Research, 8,* 257–262.

Masling, J., Weiss, L., & Rothschild, B. (1968). Relationships of oral imagery to yielding behavior and birth order. *Journal of Consulting and Clinical Psychology, 32,* 89–91.

Maslow, A. H. (1942). Self-esteem (dominance-feeling) and sexuality in women. *Journal of Social Psychology, 16,* 259–294.

Maslow, A. H. (1943). A theory of human motivation. *Psychological Review, 50,* 370–396. Reprinted in R. J. Lowry, (Ed.), *Dominance, self-esteem, self-actualization: Germinal papers of A. H. Maslow* (1973). (pp. 153–173). Monterey, CA: Brooks/Cole.

Maslow, A. H. (1955). Deficiency motivation and growth motivation. In M. R. Jones (Ed.), *Nebraska Symposium on Motivation* (pp. 1–30). Lincoln: University of Nebraska Press.

Maslow, A. H. (1958). Emotional blocks to creativity. *Journal of Individual Psychology, 14,* 51–56.

Maslow, A. H. (1964). Synergy in the society and in the individual. *Journal of Individual Psychology, 20,* 153–164.

Maslow, A. H. (1965). Criteria for judging needs to be instinctoid. In M. R. Jones (Ed.), *Human motivation: A symposium* (pp. 33–47). Lincoln: University of Nebraska Press.

Maslow, A. H. (1966). *The psychology of science: A reconnaissance.* New York: Harper & Row.

Maslow, A. H. (1968a, July). A conversation with Abraham H. Maslow. *Psychology Today,* pp. 34–37, 54–57.

Maslow, A. H. (1968b). *Toward a psychology of being* (2nd ed.). New York: D. Van Nostrand.

Maslow, A. H. (1969). Theory Z. *Journal of Transpersonal Psychology, 1*, 31–47.

Maslow, A. H. (1970). *Religions, values, and peak-experiences.* New York: Viking.

Maslow, A. H. (1976). *The farther reaches of human nature* (2nd ed.). New York: Viking.

Maslow, A. H. (1987). *Motivation and personality* (3rd ed.). New York: Harper & Row. (Original work published 1954)

Masson, J. M. (1984). *The assault on truth: Freud's suppression of the seduction theory.* New York: Farrar, Straus & Giroux.

Masters, A. (1988). Freud, seduction and his father. *Journal of Psychohistory, 15*, 501–509.

Mathes, E. W. (1981). Maslow's hierarchy of needs as a guide for living. *Journal of Humanistic Psychology, 21*(4), 69–72.

Mathes, E. W. (1982). Mystical experiences, romantic love, and hypnotic susceptibility. *Psychological Reports, 50*, 701–702.

Matson, J. L., & Kazdin, A. E. (1981). Punishment in behavior modification: Pragmatic, ethical, and legal issues. *Clinical Psychology Review, 1*, 197–210.

Matson, J. L., & Taras, M. E. (1989). A 20-year review of punishment and alternative methods to treat problem behaviors in developmentally delayed persons. *Research in Developmental Disabilities, 10*, 85–104.

Matthews, G. (1989). The factor structure of the 16PF: Twelve primary and three secondary factors. *Personality and Individual Differences, 10*, 931–940.

Mattoon, M. A. (1978). *Applied dream analysis: A Jungian approach.* New York: Wiley.

May, R. (1982). The problem of evil: An open letter to Carl Rogers. *Journal of Humanistic Psychology, 22*, 10–21.

May, R. (1991). *The cry for myth.* New York: Norton.

Mayo, C. W., & Crockett, W. H. (1964). Cognitive complexity and primacy-recency effects in impression formation. *Journal of Abnormal and Social Psychology, 68*, 335–338.

Mazlish, B. (1972). *In search of Nixon.* New York: Basic Books.

McAdams, D. P. (1988). Biography, narrative, and lives: An introduction. *Journal of Personality, 56*, 1–18.

McAdams, D. P. (1990). Unity and purpose in human lives: The emergence of identity as a life story. In A. I. Rabin, R. A. Zucker, R. A. Emmons, & S. Frank (Eds.), *Studying persons and lives* (pp. 148–200). New York: Springer-Verlag.

McAdams, D. P., Ruetzel, K., & Foley, J. H. (1986). Complexity and generativity at mid-life: Relations among social motives, ego development, and adults' plans for the future. *Journal of Personality and Social Psychology, 50*, 800–807.

McCann, J. T., & Biaggio, M. K. (1989). Sexual satisfaction in marriage as a function of life meaning. *Archives of Sexual Behavior, 18*, 59–72.

McCann, S. J. H., Stewin, L. L., & Short, R. H. (1990). Frightening dream frequency and birth order. *Individual Psychology, 46*, 304–310.

McCaulley, M. H. (1990). The Myers-Briggs Type Indicator: A measure for individuals and groups. *Measurement and Evaluation in Counseling and Development, 22*, 181–195.

McClain, E. W. (1975). An Eriksonian cross-cultural study of adolescent development. *Adolescence, 10*, 527–541.

McClelland, D. C. (1955). Comments on Professor Maslow's Paper. In M. R. Jones (Ed.), *Nebraska Symposium on Motivation* (pp. 31–37). Lincoln: University of Nebraska Press.

McClelland, D. C., & Winter, D. G. (1969). *Motivating economic achievement.* New York: Free Press.

McConnell, S. R. (1987). Entrapment effects and the generalization and maintenance of social skills training for elementary school students with behavioral disorders. *Behavioral Disorders, 12,* 252–263.

McCoy, M. M. (1977). A reconstruction of emotion. In D. Bannister (Ed.), *New perspectives in personal construct theory* (pp. 93–124). London: Academic Press.

McCrae, R. R., & Costa, P. T., Jr. (1984). *Emerging lives, enduring dispositions: Personality in adulthood.* Boston: Little, Brown.

McCrae, R. R., & Costa, P. T., Jr. (1985). Updating Norman's "adequate taxonomy": Intelligence and personality dimensions in natural language and in questionnaires. *Journal of Personality and Social Psychology, 49,* 710–721.

McCrae, R. R., & Costa, P. T., Jr. (1986). Clinical assessment can benefit from recent advances in personality psychology. *American Psychologist, 41,* 1001–1003.

McCrae, R. R., & Costa, P. T., Jr. (1987). Validation of the five-factor model of personality across instruments and observers. *Journal of Personality and Social Psychology, 52,* 81–90.

McCrae, R. R., & Costa, P. T., Jr. (1991). Adding Liebe und Arbeit: The full five-factor model and well-being. *Personality and Social Psychology Bulletin, 17,* 227–232.

McCullagh, P. (1986). Model status as a determinant of observational learning and performance. *Journal of Sport Psychology, 8,* 319–331.

McGrath, J. (1986). *Freud's discovery of psychoanalysis: The politics of hysteria.* Ithaca, NY: Cornell University Press.

McGray, J. W. (1984). *Walden Two* and Skinner's ideal observer. *Behaviorism, 12,* 15–24.

McGuire, W. (Ed.). (1974). *The Freud/Jung letters: The correspondence between Sigmund Freud and C. G. Jung.* (R. Manheim & R. F. C. Hull, Trans.). Princeton, NJ: Princeton University Press.

McPherson, F. M., Barden, V., & Buckley, F. (1970). The use of "psychological" constructs by affectively flattened schizophrenics. *British Journal of Medical Psychology, 43,* 291–293.

McPherson, F. M., & Buckley, F. (1970). Thought-process disorder and personal construct subsystems. *British Journal of Social and Clinical Psychology, 9,* 380–381.

McPherson, F. M., & Gray, A. (1976). Psychological construing and psychological symptoms. *British Journal of Medical Psychology, 49,* 73–79.

McRae, S., & Cuvo, A. J. (1980). Operant control of seizure behavior: Review and evaluation of research. *Behavior Research of Severe Developmental Disabilities, 1,* 215–248.

McSweeney, F. K., Melville, C. L., Buck, M. A., & Whipple, J. E. (1983). Local rates of responding and reinforcement during concurrent schedules. *Journal of the Experimental Analysis of Behavior, 40,* 79–83.

Mednick, M. T. (1989). On the politics of psychological constructs: Stop the bandwagon, I want to get off. *American Psychologist, 44,* 1118–1123.

Meier, S. T. (1983). Toward a theory of burnout. *Human Relations, 36,* 899–910.

Meilman, P. W. (1979). Cross-sectional age changes in ego identity status during adolescence. *Developmental Psychology, 15,* 230–231.

Meisgeier, C., & Murphy, E. A. (1987). *The Murphy-Meisgeier Type Indicator for Children.* Palo Alto, CA: Consulting Psychologists Press.

Meissner, W. W. (1990). Foundations of psychoanalysis reconsidered. *Journal of the American Psychoanalytic Association, 38,* 523–557.

Melburg, V., & Tedeschi, J. T.(1989). Displaced aggression: Frustration or impression management? *European Journal of Social Psychology, 19*, 139–145.

Meloy, J. R., & Singer, J. (1991). A psychoanalytic view of the Rorschach comprehensive system "special scores." *Journal of Personality Asssessment, 56*, 202–217.

Menaker, E. (1990). Discussion: The feminine self. *American Journal of Psychoanalysis, 50,* 63–65.

Merenda, P. F. (1987). Toward a four-factor theory of temperament and/or personality. *Journal of Personality Assessment, 51*, 367–374.

Merrett, F. E., & Wheldall, K. (1984). Training teachers to use the behavioral approach to classroom management: A review. *Educational Psychology, 4*, 213–231.

Mershon, B., & Gorsuch, R. L. (1988). Number of factors in the personality sphere: Does increase in factors increase predictability of real-life criteria? *Journal of Personality and Social Psychology, 55*, 675–680.

Messer, S. B. (1986). Behavioral and psychoanalytic perspectives at therapeutic choice points. *American Psychologist, 41*, 1261–1272.

Messer, S. B., & Winokur, M. (1980). Some limits to the integration of psychoanalytic and behavior therapy. *American Psychologist, 35*, 818–827.

Meyer, B. C. (1987). Notes on the uses of psychoanalysis for biography. *Psychoanalytic Quarterly, 56*, 287–316.

Meyer, J. M., Heath, A. C., Eaves, L. J., Mosteller, M., & Schieken, R. M. (1988). The predictive power of Cattell's personality questionnaires: An eighteen-month prospective study. *Personality and Individual Differences, 9*, 203–212.

Miall, D. S. (1989). Anticipating the self: Toward a personal construct model of emotion. *International Journal of Personal Construct Psychology, 2*, 185–198.

Michael, J. (1984). Verbal behavior. *Journal of the Experimental Analysis of Behavior, 42*, 363–376.

Midgley, B. D., & Morris, E. K. (1988). The integrated field: An alternative to the behavior-analytic conceptualization of behavioral units. *Psychological Record, 38*, 483–500.

Mill, J. (1984). High and low self-monitoring individuals: Their decoding skills and empathic expression. *Journal of Personality 52*, 372–388.

Miller, G. (1969). Psychology as a means of promoting human welfare. *American Psychologist, 24*, 1063–1075.

Miller, J. B. (1976). *Toward a new psychology of women.* Boston: Beacon Press.

Miller, J. G., Bersoff, D. M., & Harwood, R. L. (1990). Perceptions of social responsibilities in India and in the United States: Moral imperatives or personal decisions? *Journal of Personality and Social Psychology, 58*, 33–47.

Miller, L. (1988). Behaviorism and the new science of cognition. *Psychological Record, 38*, 3–18.

Miller, L. (1989). On the neuropsychology of dreams. *Psychoanalytic Review, 76*, 375–401.

Miller, M. J., Smith, T. S., Wilkinson, L., & Tobacyk, J. (1987). Narcissism and social interest among counselors-in-training. *Psychological Reports, 60*, 765–766.

Miller, N. E. (1941a). An experimental investigation of acquired drives. Abstract of paper presented at the 49th Annual Meeting of the American Psychological Association, September 3–6, 1941. *Psychological Bulletin, 38*, 534–535.

Miller, N. E. (1941b). The frustration-aggression hypothesis. *Psychological Review, 48*, 337–342.

Miller, N. E. (1948). Theory and experiment relating psychoanalytic displacement to stimulus-response generalization. *Journal of Abnormal and Social Psychology, 43*, 155–178.

Miller, N. E. (1963). Some reflections on the law of effect produce a new alternative to drive reduction. In M. R. Jones (Ed.), *Nebraska symposium on motivation, 1963* (pp. 65–112). Lincoln: University of Nebraska Press.

Miller, N. E. (1969). Learning of visceral and glandular responses. *Science, 163,* 434–445.

Miller, N. E. (1985). The value of behavioral research on animals. *American Psychologist, 40,* 423–440.

Miller, N. E. (1991). Commentary on Ulrich: Need to check truthfulness of statements by opponents of animal research. *Psychological Science, 2,* 422–423.

Miller, N. E., & Banuazizi, A. (1968). Instrumental learning by curarized rats of a specific visceral response, intestinal or cardiac. *Journal of Comparative and Physiological Psychology, 65,* 1–7.

Miller, N. E., & Dollard, J. (1941). *Social learning and imitation.* New Haven, CT: Yale University Press.

Miller, N. E., & Dworkin, B. R. (1977). Effects of learning on visceral functions: Biofeedback. *New England Journal of Medicine, 296,* 1274–1278.

Minton, H. L. (1968). Contemporary concepts of power and Adler's views. *Journal of Individual Psychology, 24,* 46–55.

Mirels, H. L. (1976). Implicit personality theory and inferential illusions. *Journal of Personality, 44,* 467–487.

Mirels, H. L. (1982). The illusory nature of implicit personality theory: Logical and empirical considerations. *Journal of Personality, 50,* 203–222.

Mischel, H. N., & Mischel, W. (1983). The development of children's knowledge of self-control strategies. *Child Development, 54,* 603–619.

Mischel, W. (1965). Predicting the success of Peace Corps Volunteers in Nigeria. *Journal of Personality and Social Psychology, 1,* 510–517.

Mischel, W. (1966). Theory and research on the antecedents of self-imposed delay of reward. In B. Maher (Ed.) *Progress in experimental personality research,* (Vol. 3, pp. 85–132). New York: Academic Press.

Mischel, W. (1968a, March). *Implications of behavior theory for personality assessment.* Paper presented at the Western Psychological Association, San Diego. Reprinted in H. N. Mischel & W. Mischel (Eds.), *Readings in personality* (1973). New York: Holt, Rinehart & Winston.

Mischel, W. (1968b). *Personality and assessment.* New York: Wiley.

Mischel, W. (1973). Toward a cognitive social learning reconceptualization of personality. *Psychological Review, 80,* 252–283.

Mischel, W. (1974). Processes in delay of gratification. In L. Berkowitz (Ed.), *Advances in experimental social psychology* (Vol. 7, pp. 249–292). New York: Academic Press.

Mischel, W. (1977a). The interaction of person and situation. In D. Magnusson & N. S. Endler (Eds.), *Personality at the crossroads: Current issues in interactional psychology* (pp. 333–352). Hillsdale, NJ: Erlbaum.

Mischel, W. (1977b). On the future of personality measurement. *American Psychologist, 32,* 246–254.

Mischel, W. (1979). On the interface of cognition and personality: Beyond the person-situation debate. *American Psychologist, 34,* 740–754.

Mischel, W. (1981a). *Introduction to personality* (3rd ed.). New York: Holt, Rinehart & Winston.

Mischel, W. (1981b). Personality and cognition: Something borrowed, something new? In N. Cantor & J. F. Kihlstrom (Eds.), *Personality, cognition, and social interaction.* Hillsdale, NJ: Erlbaum.

Mischel, W. (1983a). Alternatives in the pursuit of the predictability and consistency of persons: Stable data that yield unstable interpretations. *Journal of Personality, 51*, 578–604.

Mischel, W. (1983b). Delay of gratification as process and as person variable in development. In D. Magnusson & V. P. Allen (Eds.), *Interactions in human development.* New York: Academic Press.

Mischel, W. (1984a). Convergences and challenges in the search for consistency. *American Psychologist, 39*, 351–364.

Mischel, W. (1984b). On the predictability of behavior and the structure of personality. In R. A. Zucker, J. Aronoff, & A.I. Rabin (Eds.), *Personality and the prediction of behavior* (pp. 269–305). New York: Academic Press.

Mischel, W., & Baker, N. (1975). Cognitive appraisals and transformations in delay behavior. *Journal of Personality and Social Psychology, 31*, 254–261.

Mischel, W., & Ebbesen, E. B. (1970). Attention in delay of gratification. *Journal of Personality and Social Psychology, 16*, 329–337.

Mischel, W., Ebbesen, E. B., & Zeiss, A. R. (1972). Cognitive and attentional mechanisms in delay of gratification. *Journal of Personality and Social Psychology, 21*, 204–218.

Mischel, W., Ebbesen, E. B., & Zeiss, A. R. (1973). Selective attention to the self: Situational and dispositional determinants. *Journal of Personality and Social Psychology, 27*, 129–142.

Mischel, W., & Gilligan, C. (1964). Delay of gratification, motivation for the prohibited gratification, and responses to temptation. *Journal of Abnormal and Social Psychology, 69*, 411–417.

Mischel, W., & Liebert, R. M. (1966). Effects of discrepancies between observed and imposed reward criteria on their acquisition and transmission. *Journal of Personality and Social Psychology, 3*, 45–53.

Mischel, W., & Moore, B. (1973). Effects of attention to symbolically presented rewards on self-control. *Journal of Personality and Social Psychology, 28*, 172–179.

Mischel, W., & Peake, P. K. (1982). Beyond déjà vu in the search for cross-situational consistency. *Psychological Review, 89*, 730–755.

Mischel, W., & Peake, P. K. (1983). Some facets of consistency: Replies to Epstein, Funder, and Bem. *Psychological Review, 90*, 394–402.

Mischel, W., Shoda, Y., & Peake, P. K. (1988). The nature of adolescent competencies predicted by preschool delay of gratification. *Journal of Personality and Social Psychology, 54*, 687–696.

Mischel, W., Shoda, Y., & Rodriguez, M. L. (1989). Delay of gratification in children. *Science, 244*, 933–938.

Mischel, W., & Staub, E. (1965). Effects of expectancy on working and waiting for larger rewards. *Journal of Personality and Social Psychology, 2*, 625–633.

Mischel, W., Zeiss, R., & Zeiss, A. (1974). Internal-external control and persistence: Validation and implications of the Stanford Preschool Internal-External Scale. *Journal of Personality and Social Psychology, 29*, 265–278.

Mitchell, C. E. (1989). Psychosocial redevelopment of codependents: A framework for therapeutic assistance. *Family Therapy, 16*, 161–170.

Mittelman, W. (1991). Maslow's study of self-actualization: A reinterpretation. *Journal of Humanistic Psychology, 31*(1), 114–135.

Monte, C. F. (1980). *Beneath the mask: An introduction to theories of personality.* (2nd ed). New York: Henry Holt.

Moore, M. K., & Neimeyer, R. A. (1991). A confirmatory factor analysis of the Threat Index. *Journal of Personality and Social Psychology, 60*, 122–129.

Morehouse, R. E., Farley, F. H., & Youngquist, J. V. (1990). Type T personality and the Jungian classification system. *Journal of Personality Assessment, 54,* 231–235.

Moritz, C. (Ed.). (1974). Miller, Neal E(lgar) [biography]. *Current Biography Yearbook* (pp. 276–279). New York: W.H. Wilson.

Morrison, J. (1971). *The lords and the new creatures.* Englewood Cliffs, NJ: Touchstone.

Morrison, J. K., & Cometa, M. C. (1982). Variations in developing construct systems: The experience corollary. In J.C. Mancuso & J. R. Adams-Webber (Eds.), *The construing person* (pp. 152–169). New York: Praeger.

Morse, C., Bockoven, J., & Bettesworth, A. (1988). Effects of DUSO-2 and DUSO-2-revised on children's social skills and self-esteem. *Elementary School Guidance and Counseling, 22,* 199–205.

Morse, W. H., & Skinner, B. F. (1957). A second type of superstition in the pigeon. *American Journal of Psychology, 70,* 308–311.

Moskowitz, D. S. (1982). Coherence and cross-situational generality in personality: A new analysis of old problems. *Journal of Personality and Social Psychology, 43,* 754–768.

Motley, M. T., Baars, B. J., & Camden, C. T. (1983). Polysemantic lexical access: Evidence from laboratory-induced double entendres. *Communication Monographs, 50,* 79–101.

Mountjoy, P. T., & Sundberg, M. L. (1981). Ben Franklin the protobehaviorist: I. Self-management of behavior. *Psychological Record, 31,* 13–24.

Moustakas, C. (1986). Origins of humanistic psychology. *Humanistic Psychologist, 14,* 122–123.

Mowrer, O. H. (1950). *Learning theory and personality dynamics.* New York: Ronald Press.

Mozdzierz, G. J., Greenblatt, R. L., & Murphy, T. J. (1988). Further validation of the Sulliman Scale of Social Interest and the Social Interest Scale. *Individual Psychology, 44,* 30–34.

Mullis, F. Y., Kern, R. M., & Curlette, W. L. (1987). Life-style themes and social interest: A further factor analytic study. *Individual Psychology, 43,* 339–352.

Multon, K. D., Brown, S. D., & Lent, R. W. (1991). Relation of self-efficacy beliefs to academic outcomes: A meta-analytic investigation. *Journal of Counseling Psychology, 38,* 30–38.

Munro, G., & Adams, G. R. (1977). Ego-identity formation in college students and working youth. *Developmental Psychology, 13,* 523–524.

Munson, J. M., & Spivey, W. A. (1982). The factorial validity of an inventory assessing Horney's interpersonal response traits of compliance, aggression, and detachment. *Educational and Psychological Measurement, 42,* 889–898.

Munter, P. O. (1975a). The medical model revisited: A humanistic reply. *Journal of Personality Assessment, 39,* 4.

Munter, P. O. (1975b). Psychobiographical assessment. *Journal of Personality Assessment, 39,* 424–428.

Murphy, T. J., DeWolfe, A. S., & Mozdzierz, G. J. (1984). Levels of self-actualization among process and reactive schizophrenics, alcoholics, and normals: A construct validity study of the Personal Orientation Inventory. *Educational and Psychological Measurement, 44,* 473–482.

Murray, E. J., & Berkun, M. M. (1955). Displacement as a function of conflict. *Journal of Abnormal and Social Psychology, 51,* 47–56.

Murray, H. A. (1938). *Explorations in personality.* New York: Oxford University Press.

Murray, J. B. (1990). Review of research on the Myers-Briggs Type Indicator. *Perceptual and Motor Skills, 70,* 1187–1202.

Muslin, H., & Desai, P. (1984). Ghandi [sic] and his fathers. *Psychohistory Review, 12,* 7–18.

Myers, I. B., & McCaulley, M. H. (1985). *Manual: A guide to the development and use of the Myers-Briggs Type Indicator.* Palo Alto, CA: Consulting Psychologists Press.

Naffin, N. (1985). The masculinity-femininity hypothesis: A consideration of gender-based personality theories of female crime. *British Journal of Criminology, 25,* 365–381.

Nash, M. R. (1987). What, if anything, is regressed about hypnotic age regression? A review of the empirical literature. *Psychological Bulletin, 102,* 42–52.

Nash, M. R. (1988). Hypnosis as a window on regression. *Bulletin of the Menninger Clinic, 52,* 383–403.

Natsoulas, T. (1983). Perhaps the most difficult problem faced by behaviorism. *Behaviorism, 11,* 1–26.

Navarick, D. J., Bernstein, D. J., & Fantino, E. (1990). The experimental analysis of human behavior. *Journal of the Experimental Analysis of Behavior, 54,* 159–162.

Neimeyer, G. J. (1988). Cognitive integration and differentiation in vocational behavior. *Counseling Psychologist, 16,* 440–475.

Neimeyer, G. J. (1989). Applications of repertory grid technique to vocational assessment. *Journal of Counseling and Development, 67,* 585–589.

Neimeyer, G. J., & Khouzam, N. (1985). A repertory grid study of restrained eaters. *British Journal of Medical Psychology, 58,* 365–367.

Neimeyer, G. J., & Metzler, A. E. (1987a). The development of vocational structures. *Journal of Vocational Behavior, 30,* 26–32.

Neimeyer, G. J., & Metzler, A. E. (1987b). Sex differences in vocational integration and differentiation. *Journal of Vocational Behavior, 30,* 167–174.

Neimeyer, G. J., & Rareshide, M. B. (1991). Personal memories and personal identity: The impact of ego identity on autobiographical memory recall. *Journal of Personality and Social Psychology, 60,* 562–569.

Neimeyer, R. A. (1985a). Actualization, integration, and fear of death: A test of the additive model. *Death Studies, 9,* 235–244.

Neimeyer, R. A. (1985b). Personal constructs in clinical practice. In P. C. Kendall (Ed.), *Advances in cognitive-behavioral research and therapy* (Vol. 4, pp. 275–339). New York: Academic Press.

Neimeyer, R. A. (1987). An orientation to personal construct therapy. In R. A. Neimeyer & G. J. Neimeyer (Eds.). *Personal construct therapy casebook* (pp. 3–19). New York: Springer-Verlag.

Neimeyer, R. A. (1992). Constructivist approaches to the measurement of meaning. In G. J. Neimeyer (Ed.), *Handbook of constructivist assessment.* Newbury Park, CA: Sage Publications.

Neimeyer, R. A., Moore, M. K., & Bagley, K. J. (1988). A preliminary factor structure for the threat index. *Death Studies, 12,* 217–225.

Neimeyer, R. A., Neimeyer, G. J., & Landfield, A. W. (1983). Conceptual differentiation, integration and empathic prediction. *Journal of Personality, 51,* 185–191.

Nesselroade, J. R. (1984). Concepts of intraindividual variability and change: Impressions of Cattell's influence on lifespan developmental psychology. *Multivariate Behavioral Research, 19,* 269–286.

Neumann, E. (1963). *The great mother: An analysis of the archetype* (2nd ed.). Princeton, NJ: Princeton University Press.

Nevill, D. D., & Schlecker, D. I. (1988). The relation of self-efficacy and assertiveness to willingness to engage in traditional/nontraditional career activities. *Psychology of Women Quarterly, 12,* 91–98.

Nevin, J. A. (1979). Reinforcement schedules and response strength. In M. D. Zeiler & P. Harzem (Eds.), *Reinforcement and the organization of behavior* (pp. 117–158). Chichester, UK: Wiley.

Nevis, E. C. (1983). Using an American perspective in understanding another culture: Toward a hierarchy of needs for the People's Republic of China. *Journal of Applied Behavioral Science, 19,* 249–264.

Nichtern, S. (1985). Gandhi: His adolescent conflict of mind and body. *Adolescent Psychiatry, 12,* 17–23.

Nitis, T. (1989). Ego differentiation: Eastern and Western perspectives. *American Journal of Psychoanalysis, 49,* 339–346.

Nittrouer, S., & Cheney, C. (1984). Operant techniques used in stuttering therapy: A review. *Journal of Fluency Disorders, 9,* 169–190.

Nixon, R. M. (1962). *Six crises.* Garden City, NY: Doubleday.

Nixon, R. M. (1990). *In the arena: A memoir of victory, defeat, and renewal.* New York: Simon & Schuster.

Noller, P., Law, H., & Comrey, A. L. (1987). Cattell, Comrey, and Eysenck personality factors compared: More evidence for the five robust factors? *Journal of Personality and Social Psychology, 53,* 775–782.

Norcross, J. C. (1991). Prescriptive matching in psychotherapy: An introduction. *Psychotherapy, 28,* 439–443.

Noreager, J. P. (1979). An assessment of CAD—A personality instrument developed specifically for marketing research. *Journal of Marketing Research, 16,* 53–59.

Norman, W. T. (1963). Toward an adequate taxonomy of personality attributes: Replicated factor structure in peer nomination personality ratings. *Journal of Abnormal and Social Psychology, 66,* 574–583.

Oates, S. B. (1982). *Let the trumpet sound: The life of Martin Luther King, Jr.* New York: Mentor.

Ochberg, R. L. (1988). Life stories and the psychosocial construction of careers. *Journal of Personality, 56,* 173–204.

Ochse, R., & Plug, C. (1986). Cross-cultural investigation of the validity of Erikson's theory of personality development. *Journal of Personality and Social Psychology, 50,* 1240–1252.

O'Connell, A. N. (1976). The relationship between life style and identity synthesis and resynthesis in traditional, neo-traditional, and non-traditional women. *Journal of Personality, 44,* 675–688.

O'Connell, A. N. (1980). Karen Horney: Theorist in psychoanalysis and feminine psychology. *Psychology of Women Quarterly, 5,* 81–93.

O'Connell, A. N., & Russo, N. F. (1980). Models for achievement: Eminent women in psychology. *Psychology of Women Quarterly, 5,* 6–10.

O'Connell, W. (1990). Natural high theory and practice (NHTP) as a model of Adlerian holism. *Individual Psychology, 46,* 263–269.

O'Connor, M. (1987). The cancer patient: An Adlerian perspective. *Individual Psychology, 43,* 378–389.

Odajnyk, V. W. (1976). *Jung and politics: The political and social ideas of C. G. Jung.* New York: Harper & Row.

O'Donohue, W. T., & Houts, A. C. (1985). The two disciplines of behavior therapy: Research methods and mediating variables. *Psychological Record, 35,* 155–163.

Olds, J. (1955). Comments on Professor Maslow's paper. In M. R. Jones (Ed.), *Nebraska Symposium on Motivation* (pp. 37–39). Lincoln: University of Nebraska Press.

Olson, E. E. (1990). The transcendent function in organizational change. *Journal of Applied Behavioral Science, 26,* 69–81.

Olweus, D. (1980). The consistency issue in personality psychology revisited—with special reference to aggression. *British Journal of Social and Clinical Psychology, 19,* 377–390.

Omodei, M. M., & Wearing, A. J. (1990). Need satisfaction and involvement in personal projects: Toward an integrative model of subjective well-being. *Journal of Personality and Social Psychology, 59,* 762–769.

O'Neill, R. M., & Bornstein, R. F. (1990). Oral-dependence and gender: Factors in help-seeking response set and self-reported psychopathology in psychiatric inpatients. *Journal of Personality Assessment, 55,* 28–40.

Oppenheimer, R. (1956). Analogy in science. *American Psychologist, 11,* 127–135.

Orlofsky, J. L. (1977). Sex-role orientation, identity formation and self-esteem in college men and women. *Sex Roles, 3,* 561–575.

Orlofsky, J. L. (1978a). Identity formation, achievement, and fear of success in college men and women. *Journal of Youth and Adolescence, 7,* 49–62.

Orlofsky, J. L. (1978b). The relationship between intimacy and antecedent personality components. *Adolescence, 13,* 419–441.

Orlofsky, J. L., & Frank, M. (1986). Personality structure as viewed through early memories and identity status in college men and women. *Journal of Personality and Social Psychology, 50,* 580–586.

Orlofsky, J. L., Marcia, J. E., & Lesser, I. M. (1973). Ego identity status and the intimacy versus isolation crisis of young adulthood. *Journal of Personality and Social Psychology, 27,* 211–219.

O'Roark, A. M. (1990). Comment on Cowan's interpretation of the Myers-Briggs Type Indicator and Jung's psychological functions. *Journal of Personality Assessment, 55,* 815–817.

Ortega, D. F., & Weinstein, K. (1988). Cognitive simplicity in the Type A "coronary-prone" pattern. *Cognitive Therapy and Research, 12,* 81–87.

Overton, R. K. (1958). Experimental studies of organ inferiority. *Journal of Individual Psychology, 14,* 62–63.

Ozer, D. J., & Gjerde, P. F. (1989). Patterns of personality consistency and change from childhood through adolescence. *Journal of Personality, 57,* 483–507.

Ozer, E. M., & Bandura, A. (1990). Mechanisms governing empowerment effects: A self-efficacy analysis. *Journal of Personality and Social Psychology, 58,* 472–486.

Paludi, M. A. (1984). Psychometric properties and underlying assumptions of four objective measures of fear of success. *Sex Roles, 10,* 765–781.

Paniagua, F. A. (1987). "Knowing" the world within the skin: A remark on Skinner's behavioral theory of knowledge. *Psychological Reports, 61,* 741–742.

Paris, B. J. (1989). Introduction: Interdisciplinary applications of Horney. *American Journal of Psychoanalysis, 49,* 181–188.

Parisi, T. (1987). Why Freud failed: Some implications for neurophysiology and sociobiology. *American Psychologist, 42,* 235–245.

Patai, R. (1967). *The Hebrew goddess.* New York: Avon.

Paul, H. A. (1985). Current psychoanalytic paradigm controversy: A Horneyan perspective. *American Journal of Psychoanalysis, 45,* 221–233.

Paul, R. (1985). Freud and the seduction theory: A critical examination of Masson's *The assault on truth. Journal of Psychoanalytic Anthropology, 8,* 161–187.

Paunonen, S. V. (1988). Trait relevance and the differential predictability of behavior. *Journal of Personality, 56*, 599–619.

Peabody, D. (1984). Personality dimensions through trait inferences. *Journal of Personality and Social Psychology, 46*, 384–403.

Peake, P. K., & Mischel, W. (1984). Getting lost in the search for large coefficients: Reply to Conley (1984). *Psychological Review, 91*, 497–501.

Perlman, M. (1983). Phaethon and the thermonuclear chariot. *Spring: An Annual of Archetypal Psychology and Jungian Thought* (pp. 87–108). Zürich, Switzerland: Spring Publications.

Persinger, M. A., & Valliant, P. M. (1985). Temporal lobe signs and reports of subjective paranormal experiences in a normal population: A replication. *Perceptual and Motor Skills, 60*, 903–909.

Pervin, L. A. (1985). Personality: Current controversies, issues and directions. *Annual Review of Psychology, 36*, 83–114.

Peterson, C., Seligman, M. E. P., & Vaillant, G. E. (1988). Pessimistic explanatory style is a risk factor for physical illness: A thirty-five-year longitudinal study. *Journal of Personality and Social Psychology, 55*, 23–27.

Peterson, D. L., & Pfost, K. S. (1989). Influence of rock videos on attitudes of violence against women. *Psychological Reports, 64*, 319–322.

Peterson-Cooney, L. (1987). Time-concentrated instruction as an immediate risk to self-actualization. *Psychological Reports, 61*, 183–190.

Peyser, J. (1987). *Bernstein: A biography.* New York: Ballantine.

Phillips, A. S., Long, R. G., & Bedeian, A. G. (1990). Type A status: Birth order and gender effects. *Individual Psychology, 46*, 365–373.

Phillips, J. S., & Ray, R. S. (1980). Behavioral approaches to childhood disorders. *Behavior Modification, 4*, 3–34.

Phillips, K. L. (1980). The riddle of change. In G. Epstein (Ed.), *Studies in nondeterministic psychology* (pp. 229–253). New York: Human Sciences Press.

Pichot, P. (1984). Centenary of the birth of Hermann Rorschach. *Journal of Personality Assessment, 48*, 591–596.

Piechowski, M. M., & Tyska, C. (1982). Self-actualization profile of Eleanor Roosevelt, a presumed nontranscender. *Genetic Psychology Monographs, 105*, 95–153.

Piedmont, R. L., McCrae, R. R., & Costa, P. T., Jr. (1991). Adjective checklist scales and the five-factor model. *Journal of Personality and Social Psychology, 60*, 630–637.

Pierce, W. D., & Epling, W. F. (1984). On the persistence of cognitive explanation: Implications for behavior analysis. *Behaviorism, 12*, 15–27.

Pierson, D., Archambault, F. X., & Iwanicki, E. F. (1985). A cross validation of the Porter Needs Satisfaction Questionnaire for educators. *Educational and Psychological Measurement, 45*, 683–688.

Plomin, R. (1986). Behavioral genetic methods. *Journal of Personality, 54*, 226–261.

Plouffe, L., & Gravelle, F. (1989). Age, sex, and personality correlates of self-actualization in elderly adults. *Psychological Reports, 65*, 643–647.

Podd, M. H. (1972). Ego identity status and morality: The relationship between two developmental constructs. *Developmental Psychology, 6*, 497–507.

Podd, M. H., Marcia, J. E., & Rubin, R. (1970). The effects of ego identity and partner perception on a prisoner's dilemma game. *Journal of Social Psychology, 82*, 117–126.

Pois, R. A. (1990). The case for clinical training and challenges to psychohistory. *Psychohistory Review, 18,* 169–187.

Poole, M. E., & Evans, G. T. (1989). Adolescents' self-perceptions of competence in life skill areas. *Journal of Youth and Adolescence, 18,* 147–173.

Poppen, R. (1982). The fixed-interval scallop in human affairs. *Behavior Analyst, 5,* 127–136.

Pozzuto, R. (1982). Toward an Adlerian psychohistory. *Individual Psychology, 38,* 261–270.

Pratt, A. B. (1985). Adlerian psychology as an intuitive operant system. *Behavior Analyst, 8,* 39–51.

Pratt, M. W., Pancer, M., Hunsberger, B., & Manchester, J. (1990). Reasoning about the self and relationships in maturity: An integrative complexity analysis of individual differences. *Journal of Personality and Social Psychology, 59,* 575–581.

Prerost, F. J. (1989). Humor as an intervention strategy during psychological treatment: Imagery and incongruity. *Psychology, 26,* 34–40.

Prescott, C. A., Johnson, R. C., & McArdle, J. J. (1991). Genetic contributions to television viewing. *Psychological Science, 2,* 430–431.

Pribram, K. H. (1973). Operant behaviorism: Fad, fact-ory, and fantasy? In H. Wheeler (Ed.), *Beyond the punitive society: Operant conditioning: Social and political aspects* (pp. 101–112). San Francisco: W. H. Freeman.

Privette, G. (1983). Peak experience, peak performance, and flow: A comparative analysis of positive human experiences. *Journal of Personality and Social Psychology, 45,* 1361–1368.

Privette, G. (1985). Experience as a component of personality theory. *Psychological Reports, 56,* 263–266.

Privette, G. (1986). From peak performance and peak experience to failure and misery. *Journal of Social Behavior and Personality, 1,* 233–243.

Privette, G., & Bundrick, C. M. (1987). Measurement of experience: Construct and content validity of the experience questionnaire. *Perceptual and Motor Skills, 65,* 315–332.

Progoff, I. (1975). *At a journal workshop.* New York: Dialogue House Library.

Protinsky, H. (1988). Identity formation: A comparison of problem and nonproblem adolescents. *Adolescence, 23,* 67–72.

Prout, H. T. (1977). Behavioral intervention with hyperactive children: A review. *Journal of Learning Disabilities, 10,* 141–146.

Quimby, S. L. (1989). The near-death experience as an event in consciousness. *Journal of Humanistic Psychology, 29,* 87–198.

Quinn, S. (1988). *A mind of her own: The life of Karen Horney.* Reading, MA: Addison-Wesley.

Rachman, A. W. (1989). Confusion of tongues: The Ferenczian metaphor for childhood seduction and emotional trauma. *Journal of the American Academy of Psychoanalysis, 17,* 181–205.

Rachman, S. J. (1989). The return of fear: Review and prospect. *Clinical Psychology Review, 9,* 147–168.

Ramanaiah, N. V., Heerboth, J. R., & Jinkerson, D. L. (1985). Personality and self-actualizing profiles of assertive people. *Journal of Personality Assessment, 49,* 440–443.

Rapaport, D. (1959a). Introduction: A historical survey of psychoanalytic ego psychology. In E. H. Erikson, *Identity and the life cycle. Selected papers. Psy-*

chological Issues, 1 (Monograph 1, pp. 5–17). New York: International Universities Press.

Rapaport, D. (1959b). The structure of psychoanalytic theory: A systematizing attempt. In S. Koch (Ed.), *Psychology: A study of a science* (Vol. 3, pp. 55–183). New York: McGraw-Hill.

Raskin, R., Novacek, J., & Hogan, R. (1991). Narcissistic self-esteem management. *Journal of Personality and Social Psychology, 60,* 911–918.

Rasmussen, J. E. (1964). Relationship of ego identity to psychosocial effectiveness. *Psychological Reports, 15,* 815–825.

Ray, J. J. (1984). A caution against use of the Shostrom Personal Orientation Inventory. *Personality and Individual Differences, 5,* 755.

Ray, J. J. (1986). Perils in clinical use of the Shostrom POI: A reply to Hattie. *Personality and Individual Differences, 7,* 591.

Raz-Duvshani, A. (1986). Cognitive structure changes with psychotherapy in neurosis. *British Journal of Medical Psychology, 59,* 341–350.

Read, D. A., & Simon, S. B. (Eds.). (1975). *Humanistic education sourcebook.* Englewood Cliffs, NJ: Prentice-Hall.

Read, S. J., Jones, D. K., & Miller, L. C. (1990). Traits as goal-based categories: The importance of goals in the coherence of dispositional categories. *Journal of Personality and Social Psychology, 58,* 1048–1061.

Reichle, J., Lindamood, L., & Sigafoos, J. (1986). The match between reinforcer class and response class: Its influence on communication intervention strategies. *Journal of the Association for Persons with Severe Handicaps, 11,* 131–135.

Reiser, M. F. (1985). Converging sectors of psychoanalysis and neurobiology: Mutual challenge and opportunity. *Journal of the American Psychoanalytic Association, 33,* 11–34.

Render, G. F., Padilla, J. N. M., & Krank, H. M. (1989). Assertive discipline: A critical review and analysis. *Teachers College Record, 90,* 607–630.

Rendon, D. (1987). Understanding social roles from a Horneyan perspective. *American Journal of Psychoanalysis, 47,* 131–142.

Rendon, M. (1988). A cognitive unconscious? *American Journal of Psychoanalysis, 48,* 291–293.

Renshon, S. A. (1975). Psychological analysis and presidential personality: The case of Richard Nixon. *History of Childhood Quarterly: The Journal of Psychohistory, 2,* 415–450.

Resnick, M. N., & Nunno, V. J. (1991). The Nuremberg mind redeemed: A comprehensive analysis of the Rorschachs of Nazi war criminals. *Journal of Personality Assessment, 57,* 19–29.

Reuter, E. K., Schuerger, J. M., & Wallbrown, F. H. (1985). Higher-order analysis of 16PF scores: An alternative method. *Psychological Reports, 57,* 564–566.

ReVille, S. (1989). Young adulthood to old age: Looking at intergenerational possibilities from a human development perspective. *Journal of Children in Contemporary Society, 20,* 45–53.

Reyher, J. (1962). A paradigm for determining the clinical relevance of hypnotically induced psychopathology. *Psychological Bulletin, 59,* 344–352.

Richards, N. (1986). A conception of personality. *Behaviorism, 14,* 147–157.

Rideout, C. A., & Richardson, S. A. (1989). A teambuilding model: Appreciating differences using the Myers-Briggs Type Indicator with developmental theory. *Journal of Counseling and Development, 67,* 529–533.

Roberts, T. B. (1982). Comments on Mathes's article. *Journal of Humanistic Psychology, 22*(4), 97–98.

Robinson, D. N. (1984). The new philosophy of science: A reply to Manicas and Secord. *American Psychologist, 39*, 920–921.

Robinson, R. (1989). *Georgia O'Keeffe: A life.* New York: Harper & Row.

Rodriguez, M. L., Mischel, W., & Shoda, Y. (1989). Cognitive person variables in the delay of gratification of older children at risk. *Journal of Personality and Social Psychology, 57*, 358–367.

Roemer, W. W. (1986). Leary's circle matrix: A comprehensive model for the statistical measurement of Horney's clinical concepts. *American Journal of Psychoanalysis, 46*, 249–262.

Roemer, W. W. (1987). An application of the interpersonal models developed by Karen Horney and Timothy Leary to Type A-B behavior patterns. *American Journal of Psychoanalysis, 47*, 116–130.

Rogers, C. R. (1942a). *Counseling and psychotherapy: Newer concepts in practice.* Boston: Houghton Mifflin.

Rogers, C. R. (1942b). The use of electrically recorded interviews in improving psychotherapeutic techniques. *American Journal of Orthopsychiatry, 12*, 429–434.

Rogers, C. R. (1951). *Client-centered therapy.* Boston: Houghton Mifflin.

Rogers, C. R. (1954). Towards a theory of creativity. *ETC: A Review of General Semantics, 11*, 249–260.

Rogers, C. R. (1956). Intellectualized psychotherapy. *Contemporary Psychology, 1*, 355–358.

Rogers, C. R. (1957a). The necessary and sufficient conditions of therapeutic personality change. *Journal of Consulting Psychology, 21*, 95–103.

Rogers, C. R. (1957b). Personal thoughts on teaching and learning. *Merrill-Palmer Quarterly, 3*, 241–243.

Rogers, C. R. (1959). A theory of therapy, personality, and interpersonal relationships, as developed in the client-centered framework. In S. Koch (Ed.), *Psychology: A study of a science: Vol. 3. Formulations of the person and the social context* (pp. 185–256). New York: McGraw-Hill.

Rogers, C. R. (1961a). Ellen West—and loneliness. *Review of Existential Psychology and Psychiatry, 1*, 94–101.

Rogers, C. R. (1961b). *On becoming a person: A therapist's view of psychotherapy.* Boston: Houghton Mifflin.

Rogers, C. R. (1963). The actualizing tendency in relation to "motives" and consciousness. In M. R. Jones (Ed.). *Nebraska symposium on motivation* (Vol. 11, pp. 1–24). Lincoln: University of Nebraska Press.

Rogers, C. R. (1964). Toward a modern approach to values: The valuing process in the mature person. *Journal of Abnormal and Social Psychology, 68*, 160–167.

Rogers, C. R. (1967). Carl R. Rogers. In E. G. Boring & G. Lindzey (Eds.), *A history of psychology in autobiography* (Vol. 5, pp. 341–384). New York: Appleton-Century-Crofts.

Rogers, C. R. (1968). Some thoughts regarding the current presuppositions of the behavioral sciences. In W. Coulson & C. R. Rogers (Eds.), *Man and the science of man.* Columbus, OH: Chas. E. Merrill.

Rogers, C. R. (1969). *Freedom to learn: A view of what education might become.* Columbus, OH: Chas. E. Merrill.

Rogers, C. R. (1970). *Carl Rogers on encounter groups.* New York: Harper & Row.

Rogers, C. R. (1973). Some new challenges. *American Psychologist, 28*, 379–387.

Rogers, C. R. (1974a). In retrospect: Forty-six years. *American Psychologist, 29,* 115–123.

Rogers, C. R. (1974b). The project at Immaculate Heart: An experiment in self-directed change. *Education, 95,* 172–196.

Rogers, C. R. (1974c). Can learning encompass both ideas and feelings? *Education, 95,* 103–114.

Rogers, C. R. (1977). *Carl Rogers on personal power.* New York: Delacorte.

Rogers, C. R. (1979). The foundations of the person-centered approach. *Education, 100,* 98–107.

Rogers, C. R. (1980). *A way of being.* Boston: Houghton Mifflin.

Rogers, C. R. (1982a). A psychologist looks at nuclear war: Its threat, its possible prevention. *Journal of Humanistic Psychology, 22*(4), 9–20.

Rogers, C. R. (1982b). Reply to Rollo May's letter to Carl Rogers. *Journal of Humanistic Psychology, 22*(4), 85–89.

Rogers, C. R. (1983). *Freedom to learn for the 80's.* Columbus, OH: Chas. E. Merrill.

Rogers, C. R. (1986a). Rogers, Kohut, and Erickson: A personal perspective on some similarities and differences. *Person-Centered Review, 1,* 125–140.

Rogers, C. R. (1986b). The Rust workshop. *Journal of Humanistic Psychology, 26*(3), 23–45.

Rogers, C. R. (1986c). Transference. *Person-Centered Review, 2,* 182–188.

Rogers, C. R. (1987). Comments on the issue of equality in psychotherapy. *Journal of Humanistic Psychology, 27*(1), 38–40.

Rogers, C. R. (1989). What I learned from two research studies. In H. Kirschenbaum & V. L. Henderson (Eds.), *The Carl Rogers reader* (pp. 203–211). Boston: Houghton Mifflin.

Rogers, C. R., & Ryback, D. (1984). One alternative to nuclear planetary suicide. *Counseling Psychologist, 12,* 3–12.

Rogers, C. R., & Skinner, B. F. (1956). Some issues concerning the control of human behavior. *Science, 124,* 1057–1066.

Romi, S., & Itskowitz, R. (1990). The relationship between locus of control and type of aggression in middle-class and culturally deprived children. *Personality and Individual Differences, 11,* 327–333.

Romm, S., & Slap, J. W. (1983). Sigmund Freud and Salvador Dali: Personal moments. *American Imago, 40,* 337–347.

Roosevelt, E. (1958). *The autobiography of Eleanor Roosevelt.* New York: Harper & Brothers.

Rose, G. J. (1983). Sigmund Freud and Salvador Dali: Cultural and historical processes. *American Imago, 40,* 349–353.

Rosen, R. (1973). Can any behavior be conditioned? In H. Wheeler (Ed.), *Beyond the punitive society: Operant conditioning: Social and political aspects* (pp. 135–148). San Francisco: W.H. Freeman.

Rosenberg, S., & Jones, R. (1972). A method for investigating and representing a person's implicit theory of personality: Theodore Dreiser's view of people. *Journal of Personality and Social Psychology, 22,* 372–386.

Rosenman, S. (1989). Guardians, ferrets and defilers of the treasure: The Masson-Freudians controversy. *Journal of Psychohistory, 16,* 297–321.

Rosenthal, D. R., Gurney, R. M., & Moore, S. M. (1981). From trust to intimacy: A new inventory for examining Erikson's stages of psychosocial development. *Journal of Youth and Adolescence, 10,* 525–536.

Rosenzweig, S. (1958). The place of the individual and of idiodynamics in psychology: A dialogue. *Journal of Individual Psychology, 14,* 3–21.

Rosenzweig, S. (1986a). Background to idiodynamics. *Clinical Psychologist, 39,* 83–89.

Rosenzweig, S. (1986b). Idiodynamics vis-à-vis psychology. *American Psychologist, 41,* 241–245.

Rosenzweig, S. (1988). The identity and idiodynamics of the multiple personality "Sally Beauchamp": A confirmatory supplement. *American Psychologist, 43,* 45–48.

Ross, L. (1977). The intuitive psychologist and his shortcomings: Distortions in the attribution process. In L. Berkowitz (Ed.), *Advances in experimental social psychology* (Vol. 10, pp. 173–220). New York: Academic Press.

Rotter, J. B. (1966). Generalized expectancies for internal versus external control of reinforcement. *Psychological Monographs* [80, Whole No. 609].

Rotter, J. B. (1990). Internal versus external control of reinforcement: A case history of a variable. *American Psychologist, 45,* 489–493.

Rowe, D. C. (1987). Resolving the person-situation debate: Invitation to an interdisciplinary dialogue. *American Psychologist, 42,* 218–227.

Rubinstein, B. B. (1980). The problem of confirmation in clinical psychoanalysis. *Journal of the American Psychoanalytic Association, 28,* 397–417.

Ruble, T. L., & Cosier, R. A. (1990). Effects of cognitive styles and decision setting on performance. *Organizational Behavior and Human Decision Processes, 46,* 283–295.

Ruch, W., & Hehl, F. J. (1988). Attitudes to sex, sexual behaviour and enjoyment of humour. *Personality and Individual Differences, 9,* 983–994.

Rudnytsky, P. (1987). *Freud and Oedipus.* New York: Columbia University Press.

Rugel, R. P., & Barry, D. (1990). Overcoming denial through the group: A test of acceptance theory. *Small Group Research, 21,* 45–58.

Runyan, W. M. (1981). Why did Van Gogh cut off his ear? The problem of alternative explanations in psychobiography. *Journal of Personality and Social Psychology, 40,* 1070–1077.

Runyan, W. M. (1982a). In defense of the case study method. *American Journal of Orthopsychiatry, 52,* 440–446.

Runyan, W. M. (1982b). *Life histories and psychobiography: Explorations in theory and method.* New York: Oxford University Press.

Runyan, W. M. (1982c). The psychobiography debate: An analytical review. In L. Wheeler (Ed.), *Review of personality and social psychology* (Vol. 3, pp. 225–253). Beverly Hills, CA: Sage Publications.

Runyan, W. M. (1983). Idiographic goals and methods in the study of lives. *Journal of Personality, 51,* 413–437.

Runyan, W. M. (1987). The growth of literature in psychohistory: A quantitative analysis. *Psychohistory Review, 15,* 121–135.

Runyan, W. M. (1988a). Alternatives to psychoanalytic psychobiography. In W. M. Runyan (Ed.), *Psychology and historical interpretation* (pp. 219–244). New York: Oxford University Press.

Runyan, W. M. (1988b). Progress in psychobiography. *Journal of Personality, 56,* 295–326.

Runyan, W. M. (1988c). *Psychology and historical interpretation.* New York: Oxford University Press.

Runyan, W. M. (1990). Individual lives and the structure of personality psychology.

In A. I. Rabin, R. A. Zucker, R. A. Emmons, & S. Frank (Eds.) *Studying persons and lives* (pp. 10–40). New York: Springer-Verlag.

Runyon, R. S. (1984). Freud and Adler: A conceptual analysis of their differences. *Psychoanalytic Review, 71*, 413–421.

Rushton, J. P., Jackson, D. N., & Paunonen, S. V. (1981). Personality: Nomothetic or idiographic? A response to Kenrick and Stringfield. *Psychological Review, 88*, 582–589.

Ruth, W. J., Mosatche, H. S., & Kramer, A. (1989). Freudian sexual symbolism: Theoretical considerations and an empirical test in advertising. *Psychological Reports, 64*, 1131–1139.

Ryback, D. (1983). Jedi and Jungian forces. *Psychological Perspectives, 14*, 238–244.

Rychlak, J. F. (1977). *The psychology of rigorous humanism.* New York: Wiley-Interscience.

Rychlak, J. F. (1984a). Logical learning theory: Kuhnian anomaly or medievalism revisited? *Journal of Mind and Behavior, 5*, 389–416.

Rychlak, J. F. (1984b). Newtonianism and the professional responsibility of psychologists: Who speaks for humanity? *Professional Psychology: Research and Practice, 15*, 82–95.

Rychlak, J. F. (1986). Logical learning theory: A teleological alternative in the field of personality. *Journal of Personality, 54*, 734–762.

Rychlak, J. F. (1988). *The psychology of rigorous humanism* (2nd ed). New York: New York University Press.

Ryckman, R. M., Robbins, M. A., Thornton, B., Gold, J. A., & Kuehnel, R. H. (1985). Physical self-efficacy and actualization. *Journal of Research in Personality, 19*, 288–298.

Sales, S. M. (1973). Threat as a factor in authoritarianism: An analysis of archival data. *Journal of Personality and Social Psychology, 28*, 44–57.

Salmon, D., & Lehrer, R. (1989). School consultant's implicit theories of action. *Professional School Psychology, 4*, 173–187.

Sampson, E. E. (1977). Psychology and the American ideal. *Journal of Personality and Social Psychology, 35*, 767–782.

Sampson, E. E. (1978). Scientific paradigms and social values: Wanted—A scientific revolution. *Journal of Personality and Social Psychology, 36*, 1332–1343.

Sampson, E. E. (1981). Cognitive psychology as ideology. *American Psychologist, 36*, 730–743.

Sanger, M. (1971). *Margaret Sanger: An autobiography.* New York: Dover. (Original work published 1938)

Sanitioso, R., Kunda, Z., & Fong, G. T. (1990). Motivated recruitment of autobiographical memories. *Journal of Personality and Social Psychology, 59*, 224–241.

Sappington, A. A. (1990). Recent psychological approaches to the free will versus determinism issue. *Psychological Bulletin, 108*, 19–29.

Sarason, S. B. (1989). The lack of an overarching conception in psychology. *Journal of Mind and Behavior, 10*, 263–279.

Saudino, K. J., & Eaton, W. O. (1991). Infant temperament and genetics: An objective twin study of motor activity level. *Child Development, 62*, 1167–1174.

Savage-Rumbaugh, E. S. (1984). Verbal behavior at a procedural level in the chimpanzee. *Journal of the Experimental Analysis of Behavior, 41*, 223–250.

Schachter, F. F., & Stone, R. K. (1985). Pediatricians' and psychologists' implicit personality theory: Significance of sibling differences. *Journal of Developmental and Behavioral Pediatrics, 6*, 295–297.

Schachter, S. (1963). Birth order, eminence, and higher education. *American Sociological Review, 3*, 757–767.

Schafer, R. (1954). *Psychoanalytic interpretation in Rorschach testing.* New York: Grune & Stratton.

Schepeler, E. (1990). The biographer's transference: A chapter in psychobiographical epistemology. *Biography, 13*, 111–129.

Schibuk, M., Bond, M., & Bouffard, R. (1989). The development of defenses in childhood. *Canadian Journal of Psychiatry, 34*, 581–588.

Schiedel, D. G., & Marcia, J. E. (1985). Ego identity, intimacy, sex role orientation and gender. *Developmental Psychology, 24*, 149–160.

Schmidt, F. L., & Hunter, J. E. (1974). Racial and ethnic bias in psychological tests: Divergent implications of two definitions of test bias. *American Psychologist, 29*, 1–8.

Schmitt, D. R. (1984). Interpersonal relations: Cooperation and competition. *Journal of the Experimental Analysis of Behavior, 42*, 377–383.

Schnaitter, R. (1987). Behaviorism is not cognitive and cognitivism is not behavioral. *Behaviorism, 15*, 1–11.

Schneider, D. J. (1973). Implicit personality theory, a review. *Psychological Bulletin, 79*, 294–309.

Schnell, R. L. (1980). Contributions to psychohistory: IV. Individual experience in historiography and psychoanalysis: Significance of Erik Erikson and Robert Coles. *Psychological Reports, 46*, 591–612.

Schuerger, J. M., Zarrella, K. L., & Hotz, A. S. (1989). Factors that influence the temporal stability of personality by questionnaire. *Journal of Personality and Social Psychology, 56*, 777–783.

Schurr, K. T., Ruble, V. E., Henriksen, L. W., & Alcorn, B. K. (1989). Relationships of National Teacher Examination Communication Skills and General Knowledge scores with high school and college grades, Myers-Briggs Type Indicator characteristics, and self-reported skill ratings and academic problems. *Educational and Psychological Measurement, 49*, 243–252.

Schwarz, K., & Robins, C. J. (1987). Psychological androgyny and ego development. *Sex Roles, 16*, 71–81.

Scott, N. E., & Borodovsky, L. G. (1990). Effective use of cultural role taking. *Professional Psychology: Research and Practice, 21*, 167–170.

Scruggs, T. E., Mastropieri, M. A., Forness, S. R., & Kavale, K. A. (1988). Early language intervention: A quantitative synthesis of single-subject research. *Journal of Special Education, 22,* 259–283.

Sears, D. O. (1986). College sophomores in the laboratory: Influences of a narrow data base on social psychology's view of human nature. *Journal of Personality and Social Psychology, 51*, 515–530.

Sechrest, L. (1986). Modes and methods of personality research. *Journal of Personality, 54*, 318–331.

Sechrest, L., & Jackson, D. N. (1961). Social intelligence and accuracy of interpersonal predictions. *Journal of Personality, 29*, 169–182.

Seegmiller, R. A., & Epperson, D. L. (1987). Distinguishing thinking-feeling preferences through the content analysis of natural language. *Journal of Personality Assessment, 51*, 42–52.

Semin, G. R., & Krahe, B. (1987). Lay conceptions of personality: Eliciting tiers of a scientific conception of personality. *European Journal of Social Psychology, 17*, 199–209.

Senchak, M., & Wheeler, L. (1988). Fear of success in the social domain. *Journal of Social and Clinical Psychology, 6,* 398–407.

Sexton, T. L., & Tuckman, B. W. (1991). Self-beliefs and behavior: The role of self-efficacy and outcome expectation over time. *Personality and Individual Differences, 12,* 725–736.

Seymer, L. R. (1951). *Florence Nightingale.* New York: Macmillan.

Shapiro, J. P., Leifer, M., Martone, M. W., & Kassem, L. (1990). Multimethod assessment of depression in sexually abused girls. *Journal of Personality Assessment, 55,* 234–248.

Shapiro, S. B. (1985). An empirical analysis of operating values in humanistic education. *Journal of Humanistic Psychology, 25*(1), 94–108.

Shelton, S. H. (1990). Developing the construct of general self-efficacy. *Psychological Reports, 66,* 987–994.

Sherer, M., & Adams, C. (1983). Construct validity of the self-efficacy scale. *Psychological Reports, 53,* 899–902.

Sherer, M., Maddux, J. E., Mercandante, B., Prentice-Dunn, S., Jacobs, B., & Rogers, R. W. (1982). The self-efficacy scale: Construction and validation. *Psychological Reports, 51,* 663–671.

Sherman, E. D. (1983). Geriatric profile of Eleanor Roosevelt (1884–1962). *Journal of the American Geriatrics Society, 31,* 28–33.

Sherman, R., & Dinkmeyer, D. (1987). *Systems of family therapy: An Adlerian integration.* New York: Brunner/Mazel.

Sherry, J. (1986). Jung, the Jews, and Hitler. *Spring: An Annual of Archetypal Psychology and Jungian Thought* (pp. 163–175). Zürich, Switzerland: Spring Publications.

Shiflett, S. C. (1989). Validity evidence for the Myers-Briggs Type Indicator as a measure of hemisphere dominance. *Educational and Psychological Measurement, 49,* 741–745.

Shoda, Y., Mischel, W., & Peake, P. K. (1990). Predicting adolescent cognitive and self-regulatory competencies from preschool delay of gratification: Identifying diagnostic conditions. *Developmental Psychology, 26,* 978–986.

Shoda, Y., Mischel, W., & Wright, J. C. (1989). Intuitive interactionism in person perception: Effects of situation-behavior relations on dispositional judgments. *Journal of Personality and Social Psychology, 56,* 41–53.

Shostrom, E. L. (1964). An inventory for the measurement of self-actualization. *Educational and Psychological Measurement, 24,* 207–217.

Shostrom, E. L. (Producer). (1965). *Three approaches to psychotherapy* (part 1). (Film). Orange, CA: Psychological Films.

Shostrom, E. L. (1972). *Freedom to be: Experiencing and expressing your total being.* Englewood Cliffs, NJ: Prentice-Hall.

Shostrom, E. L. (1974). *Manual for the Personal Orientation Inventory.* San Diego, CA: Educational and Industrial Testing Service.

Shostrom, E. L. (1975). Rejoinder to Anderson's article. *Journal of Humanistic Psychology, 15*(1), 35.

Shulim, J. I. (1977). The birth of Robespierre as a revolutionary: A Horneyan psychohistorical approach. *American Journal of Psychoanalysis, 37,* 343–350.

Shulman, D. G. (1990). The investigation of psychoanalytic theory by means of the experimental method. *International Journal of Psycho-Analysis, 71,* 487–498.

Shulman, D. G., & Ferguson, G. R. (1988). An experimental investigation of

Kernberg's and Kohut's theories of narcissism. *Journal of Clinical Psychology, 44,* 445–451.

Siegel, B. (1982). Penis envy: From anatomical deficiency to narcissistic disturbance. *Bulletin of the Menninger Clinic, 46,* 363–376.

Signell, K. (1966). Cognitive complexity in person perception and nation perception: A developmental approach. *Journal of Personality, 34,* 517–537.

Sills, B., & Linderman, L. (1987). *Beverly: An autobiography.* New York: Bantam.

Silverman, L. H. (1976). Psychoanalytic theory: "The reports of my death are greatly exaggerated." *American Psychologist, 31,* 621–635.

Silverman, L. H. (1983). The subliminal psychodynamic activation method: Overview and comprehensive listing of studies. In J. Masling (Ed.), *Empirical studies of psychoanalytic theories* (Vol. 1, pp. 69–100). Hillsdale, NJ: Analytic Press.

Silverman, L. H., Bronstein, A., & Mendelsohn, E. (1976). The further use of the subliminal psychodynamic activation method for the experimental study of the clinical theory of psychoanalysis: On the specificity of relationships between manifest psychopathology and unconscious conflict. *Psychotherapy: Theory, Research and Practice, 13,* 2–16.

Silverman, L. H., Frank, S. G., & Dachinger, P. (1974). A psychoanalytic reinterpretation of the effectiveness of systematic desensitization: Experimental data bearing on the role of merging fantasies. *Journal of Abnormal Psychology, 83,* 313–318.

Silverman, L. H., Kwawer, J. S., Wolitzky, C., & Coron, M. (1973). An experimental study of aspects of the psychoanalytic theory of male homosexuality. *Journal of Abnormal Psychology, 82,* 178–188.

Silverman, L. H., Martin, A., Ungaro, R., & Mendelsohn, E. (1978). Effect of subliminal stimulation of symbiotic fantasies on behavior modification treatment of obesity. *Journal of Consulting and Clinical Psychology, 46,* 432–441.

Silverman, L. H., Ross, D. L., Adler, J. M., & Lustig, D. A. (1978). Simple research paradigm for demonstrating subliminal psychodynamic activation: Effects of Oedipal stimuli on dart-throwing accuracy in college males. *Journal of Abnormal Psychology, 87,* 341–357.

Simmons, D. D. (1970). Development of an objective measure of identity achievement status. *Journal of Projective Techniques, 34,* 241–244.

Simon, B. (1991). Is the Oedipus complex still the cornerstone of psychoanalysis? Three obstacles to answering the question. *Journal of the American Psychoanalytic Association, 39,* 641–668.

Singh, N. N., & Winton, A. S. (1983). Social skills training with institutionalized severely and profoundly mentally retarded persons. *Applied Research in Mental Retardation, 4,* 383–398.

Sipe, R. B. (1987). False premises, false promises: A re-examination of the human potential movement. *Issues in Radical Therapy, 12*(4), 26–29, 49–53.

Sipps, G. J., & Alexander, R. A. (1987). The multifactorial nature of extraversion-introversion in the Myers-Briggs Type Indicator and Eysenck Personality Inventory. *Educational and Psychological Measurement, 47,* 543–552.

Sipps, G. J., & DiCaudo, J. (1988). Convergent and discriminant validity of the Myers-Briggs Type Indicator as a measure of sociability and impulsivity. *Educational and Psychological Measurement, 48,* 445–451.

Sizemore, C. C., & Huber, R. J. (1988). The twenty-two faces of Eve. *Individual Psychology, 44,* 53–62.

Skaggs, E. B. (1945). Personalistic psychology as science. *Psychological Review, 52,* 234–238.

Skinner, B. F. (1938). *The behavior of organisms.* New York: Appleton-Century.

Skinner, B. F. (1945a, October). Baby in a box. *Ladies' Home Journal,* p. 30.

Skinner, B. F. (1945b). Operational analysis of psychological terms. *Psychological Review, 52,* 270–281.

Skinner, B. F. (1948a). "Superstition" in the pigeon. *Journal of Experimental Psychology, 38,* 168–172.

Skinner, B. F. (1948b). *Walden Two.* New York: Macmillan.

Skinner, B. F. (1950). Are theories of learning necessary? *Psychological Review, 57,* 193–216.

Skinner, B. F. (1953a). *Science and human behavior.* New York: Free Press.

Skinner, B. F. (1953b). Some contributions to an experimental analysis of behavior and to psychology as a whole. *American Psychologist, 8,* 69–78.

Skinner, B. F. (1954). The science of learning and the art of teaching. *Harvard Educational Review, 24,* 86–97.

Skinner, B. F. (1957). *Verbal behavior.* New York: Appleton-Century-Crofts.

Skinner, B. F. (R. Epstein, Ed.). (1958a). *Notebooks.* Englewood Cliffs, NJ: Prentice-Hall.

Skinner, B. F. (1958b). Teaching machines. *Science, 128,* 969–977.

Skinner, B. F. (1961). Teaching machines. *Scientific American, 205*(5), 91–102.

Skinner, B. F. (1963). Behaviorism at fifty. *Science, 140,* 951–958.

Skinner, B. F. (1967). Autobiography. In E. G. Boring & G. Lindzey (Eds.), *A history of psychology in autobiography* (Vol. 5, pp. 385–413). New York: Appleton-Century-Crofts.

Skinner, B. F. (1968). *The technology of teaching.* New York: Appleton-Century-Crofts.

Skinner, B. F. (1971). *Beyond freedom and dignity.* New York: Knopf.

Skinner, B. F. (1972). *Cumulative record: A selection of papers* (3rd ed.). New York: Appleton-Century Crofts.

Skinner, B. F. (1974). *About behaviorism.* New York: Knopf.

Skinner, B. F. (1975). The steep and thorny way to a science of behavior. *American Psychologist, 30,* 42–49.

Skinner, B. F. (1976). *Particulars of my life.* New York: Knopf.

Skinner, B. F. (1977). Why I am not a cognitive psychologist. *Behaviorism, 5,* 1–10.

Skinner, B. F. (1978). *Reflections on behaviorism and society.* Englewood Cliffs, NJ: Prentice-Hall.

Skinner, B. F. (1979). *The shaping of a behaviorist.* New York: Knopf.

Skinner, B. F. (1983). Intellectual self-management in old age. *American Psychologist, 38,* 239–244.

Skinner, B. F. (1984). The shame of American education. *American Psychologist, 39,* 947–954.

Skinner, B. F. (1985). Cognitive science and behaviourism. *British Journal of Psychology, 76,* 291–301.

Skinner, B. F. (1986a). The evolution of verbal behavior. *Journal of the Experimental Analysis of Behavior, 45,* 115–122.

Skinner, B. F. (1986b). Some thoughts about the future. *Journal of the Experimental Analysis of Behavior, 45,* 229–235.

Skinner, B. F. (1986c). What is wrong with daily life in the Western world? *American Psychologist, 41,* 568–574.

Skinner, B. F. (1987). Whatever happened to psychology as the science of behavior? *American Psychologist, 42,* 780–786.

Skinner, B. F. (1988). The operant side of behavior therapy. *Journal of Behavior Therapy and Experimental Psychiatry, 19,* 171–179.

Skinner, B. F. (1989a). The origins of cognitive thought. *American Psychologist, 44,* 13–18.

Skinner, B. F. (1989b). Teaching machines. *Science, 243,* 1535.

Skinner, B. F. (1990). Can psychology be a science of mind? *American Psychologist, 45,* 1206–1210.

Skinner, E. A. (1985). Action, control judgments, and the structure of control experience. *Psychological Review, 92,* 39–58.

Skinner, E. A., Chapman, M., & Baltes, P. B. (1988). Control, means–ends, and agency beliefs: A new conceptualization and its measurement during childhood. *Journal of Personality and Social Psychology, 54,* 117–133.

Skinner, E. A., Schindler, A., & Tschechne, M. (1990). Self–other differences in children's perceptions about the causes of important events. *Journal of Personality and Social Psychology, 58,* 144–155.

Skinner, E. A., Wellborn, J. G., & Connell, J. P. (1990). What it takes to do well in school and whether I've got it: A process model of perceived control and children's engagement and achievement in school. *Journal of Educational Psychology, 82,* 22–32.

Skinner, N. F., & Peters, P. L. (1984). National personality characteristics: Comparison of Canadian, American and British samples. *Psychological Reports, 54,* 121–122.

Slater, P. (1977). *The measurement of intrapersonal space by grid technique: Vol. 2. Dimensions of intrapersonal space.* London: Wiley.

Slife, B. D. (1981). Psychology's reliance on linear time: A reformulation. *Journal of Mind and Behavior, 2,* 27–46.

Smith, H. (1985). The sacred unconscious, with footnotes on self-actualization and evil. *Journal of Humanistic Psychology, 25,* 65–80.

Smith, M. (1980). An analysis of three managerial jobs using repertory grids. *Journal of Management Studies, 17,* 205–213.

Smith, M., Hartley, J., & Stewart, B. (1978). A case study of repertory grids used in vocational guidance. *Journal of Occupational Psychology, 51,* 97–104.

Smith, M. B. (1973). On self-actualization: A transambivalent examination of a focal theme in Maslow's psychology. *Journal of Humanistic Psychology, 13*(2), 17–33.

Smith, M. B. (1990). Humanistic psychology. *Journal of Humanistic Psychology, 30*(4), 6–21.

Smith, R. E. (1989). Effects of coping skills training on generalized self-efficacy and locus of control. *Journal of Personality and Social Psychology, 56,* 228–233.

Smith, T. L. (1983). Skinner's environmentalism: The analogy with natural selection. *Behaviorism, 11,* 133–153.

Snyder, C. R., Harris, C., Anderson, J. R., Holleran, S. A., Irving, L. M., Sigmon, S. T., Yoshinobu, L., Gibb, J., Langelle, C., & Harney, P. (1991). The will and the ways: Development and validation of an individual-differences measure of hope. *Journal of Personality and Social Psychology, 60,* 570–585.

Sohier, R. (1985–1986). Homosexual mutuality: Variation on a theme by Erik Erikson. *Journal of Homosexuality, 12*(2), 25–38.

Sohn, D., & Lamal, P. A. (1982). Self-reinforcement: Its reinforcing capability and its clinical utility. *Psychological Record, 32,* 179–203.

Soldz, S., & Soldz, E. (1989). A difficulty with the functionally independent construction measure of cognitive differentiation. *International Journal of Personal Construct Psychology, 2*, 315–322.

Spence, J. T. (1981). Rogers's "Models of man": A sidelight. *Personality and Social Psychology Bulletin, 7*, 404–405.

Spence, J. T., Helmreich, R., & Stapp, J. (1975). Ratings of self and peers on sex-role attributes and their relation to self-esteem and concepts of masculinity and femininity. *Journal of Personality and Social Psychology, 32*, 29–39.

Sperling, M. B. (1987). Ego identity and desperate love. *Journal of Personality Assessment, 51*, 600–605.

Sperry, R. W. (1988). Psychology's mentalist paradigm and the religion/science tension. *American Psychologist, 43*, 607–613.

Sperry, R. W. (1990). Structure and significance of the consciousness revolution. *Person-Centered Review, 5*, 120–129.

Spurlock, J. (1986). Development of self-concept in Afro-American children. *Hospital and Community Psychiatry, 37*, 66–70.

Sroufe, L. A., Fox, N. E., & Pancake, V. R. (1983). Attachment and dependency in developmental perspective. *Child Development, 54*, 1615–1627.

Staats, A. W. (1981). Social behaviorism, unified theory, unified theory construction methods, and the Zeitgeist of separatism. *American Psychologist, 36*, 239–256.

Staats, A. W. (1991). Unified positivism and unification psychology. *American Psychologist, 46*, 899–912.

Staats, A. W., & Burns, G. L. (1982). Emotional personality repertoire as cause of behavior: Specification of personality and interaction principles. *Journal of Personality and Social Psychology, 43*, 873–881.

Staats, A. W., & Eifert, G. H. (1990). The paradigmatic behaviorism theory of emotions. *Clinical Psychology Review, 10*, 539–566.

Staddon, J. E. R., & Simmelhag, V. L. (1971). The "superstitious" experiment: A reexamination of its implications for the principles of adaptive behavior. *Psychological Review, 78*, 3–43.

Stamatelos, T. (1984). Peak and plateau experiences among persons labeled mentally retarded. *Arts in Psychotherapy, 11*, 109–115.

Stanley, M. A., & Maddux, J. E. (1986). Self-efficacy expectancy and depressed mood: An investigation of causal relationships. *Journal of Social Behavior and Personality, 1*, 575–586.

Stannard, D. E. (1980). *Shrinking history: On Freud and the failure of psychoanalysis.* New York: Oxford University Press.

Stannard, K. (1988). Archetypal images in contemporary television: The mythology of Doctor Who. *Humanistic Psychologist, 16*, 361–367.

Starin, S. P., & Fuqua, R. W. (1987). Rumination and vomiting in the developmentally disabled: A critical review. *Research in Developmental Disabilities, 8*, 575–605.

Steinem, G. (1986). *Marilyn: Norma Jeane.* New York: Signet.

Steiner, C., Wyckoff, H., Marcus, J., Larivere, P., Goldstine, D., Schwebel, R. & Members of the Radical Psychiatry Center (1975). *Readings in radical psychiatry.* New York: Grove Press.

Stemmer, N. (1990). Skinner's *Verbal behavior*, Chomsky's review, and mentalism. *Journal of the Experimental Analysis of Behavior, 54*, 307–315.

Stemmler, G., & Meinhardt, E. (1990). Personality, situation and physiological arousability. *Personality and Individual Differences, 11*, 293–308.

Sterling, C. M., & Van Horn, K. R. (1989). Identity and death anxiety. *Adolescence, 24*, 321–326.

Stern, P. J. (1976). *The haunted prophet.* New York: Delta.

Stewart, A. J., Franz, C., & Layton, L. (1988). The changing self: Using personal documents to study lives. *Journal of Personality, 56,* 41–74.

Stewart, V., & Stewart, A. (1982). *Business applications of repertory grid.* London: McGraw-Hill.

Stiles, W. B., Shapiro, D. A., & Elliott, R. (1986). "Are all psychotherapies equivalent?" *American Psychologist, 41,* 165–180.

Stillman, R. C., & Walker, J. A. (1989). The anatomy of mental unity and volition: An alternate view. *Psychiatry, 52,* 410–413.

Stock, J., & Cervone, D. (1990). Proximal goal-setting and self-regulatory processes. *Cognitive Therapy and Research, 14,* 483–498.

Stone, L. (1981). *The past and the present.* Boston: Routledge & Kegan Paul.

Stone, M. (1976). *When God was a woman.* New York: Harcourt Brace Jovanovich.

Storms, P. L., & Spector, P. E. (1987). Relationships of organizational frustration with reported behavioural reactions: The moderating effect of locus of control. *Journal of Occupational Psychology, 60,* 227–234.

Strack, S., & Lorr, M. (1990). Three approaches to interpersonal behavior and their common factors. *Journal of Personality Assessment, 54,* 782–790.

Strano, D. A., & Dixon, P. N. (1990). The Comparative Feeling of Inferiority Index. *Individual Psychology, 46,* 29–42.

Strauman, T. J. (1990). Self-guides and emotionally significant childhood memories: A study of retrieval efficiency and incidental negative emotional content. *Journal of Personality and Social Psychology, 59,* 869–880.

Strong, L. L., & Fiebert, M. S. (1987). Using paired comparisons to assess Maslow's hierarchy of needs. *Perceptual and Motor Skills, 64,* 492–494.

Stroud, W. L., Jr. (1984). Biographical explanation is low-powered science. *American Psychologist, 39,* 921–922.

Strube, M. J. (1989). Evidence for the *Type* in Type A behavior: A taxometric analysis. *Journal of Personality and Social Psychology, 56,* 972–987.

Strube, M. J., & Ota, S. (1982). Type A coronary-prone behavior pattern: Relationship to birth order and family size. *Personality and Social Psychology Bulletin, 8,* 317–323.

Stuart, R. B. (1989). Social learning theory: A vanishing or expanding presence? *Psychology, 26*(1), 35–50.

Sue, S. (1988). Psychotherapeutic services for ethnic minorities: Two decades of research findings. *American Psychologist, 43,* 301–308.

Suedfeld, P., & Tetlock, P. (1977). Integrative complexity of communications in international crises. *Journal of Conflict Resolution, 21,* 169–184.

Sugarman, A. (1991). Where's the beef? Putting personality back into personality assessment. *Journal of Personality Assessment, 56,* 130–144.

Sullivan, G. (1990). Discrimination and self-concept of homosexuals before the gay liberation movement: A biographical analysis examining social context and identity. *Biography, 13,* 203–221.

Sullivan, H. S. (1953). *The interpersonal theory of psychiatry.* New York: Norton.

Sulloway, F. J. (1979). *Freud, biologist of the mind: Beyond the psychoanalytic legend.* New York: Basic Books.

Summers, A. (1985). *Goddess: The secret lives of Marilyn Monroe.* New York: New American Library.

Sundberg, N. D. (1965). *The sixth mental measurements yearbook* (pp. 322–325). Highland Park, NJ: Gryphon Press.

Suzuki, D. (1988). *Metamorphosis: Stages in a life.* Toronto, Canada: General Paperbacks.

Sweeny, T. J., & Myers, J. E. (1986). Early recollections: An Adlerian technique with older people. *Clinical Gerontologist, 4,* 3–12.

Symonds, A. (1991). Gender issues and Horney theory. *American Journal of Psychoanalysis, 51,* 301–312.

Szasz, T. S. (1965). *The ethics of psychoanalysis.* New York: Basic Books.

Tan, A. L., Kendis, R. J., Fine, J. T., & Porac, J. (1977). A short measure of Eriksonian ego identity. *Journal of Personality Assessment, 41,* 279–284.

Tanaka, J. S., Panter, A. T., & Winborne, W. C. (1988). Dimensions of the need for cognition: Subscales and gender differences. *Multivariate Behavioral Research, 23,* 35–50.

Taylor, J. A. (1975). Early recollections as a projective technique: A review of some recent validation studies. *Journal of Individual Psychology, 31,* 213–218.

Tegano, D. W. (1990). Relationship of tolerance of ambiguity and playfulness to creativity. *Psychological Reports, 66,* 1047–1056.

Teixeira, B. (1987). Comments on ahimsa (nonviolence). *Journal of Transpersonal Psychology, 19,* 1–17.

Tennen, H., & Affleck, G. (1990). Blaming others for threatening events. *Psychological Bulletin, 108,* 209–232.

Teti, D. M., & Gelfand, D. M. (1991). Behavioral competence among mothers of infants in the first year: The mediational role of maternal self-efficacy. *Child Development, 62,* 918–929.

Thauberger, P. C., Cleland, J. F., & Nicholson, L. (1982). Existential measurement: A factor analytic study of some current psychometric instruments. *Journal of Research in Personality, 16,* 165–178.

Thomas, H. F. (1988). Keeping person-centered education alive in academic settings. *Person-Centered Review, 3,* 337–352.

Thompson, B., & Borrello, G. M. (1986). Construct validity of the Myers-Briggs Type Indicator. *Educational and Psychological Measurement, 46,* 745–752.

Thompson, S. C., & Spacapan, S. (1991). Perceptions of control in vulnerable populations. *Journal of Social Issues, 47*(4), 1–21.

Thorne, B. M., Fyfe, J. H., & Carskadon, T. G. (1987). The Myers-Briggs Type Indicator and coronary heart disease. *Journal of Personality Assessment, 51,* 545–554.

Ticho, E. A. (1982). The alternate schools and the self. *Journal of the American Psychoanalytic Association, 30,* 849–862.

Timberlake, W., & Lucas, G. A. (1985). The basis of superstitious behavior: Chance contingency, stimulus substitution, or appetitive behavior? *Journal of the Experimental Analysis of Behavior, 44,* 279–299.

Tinling, L. (1990). Perpetuation of incest by significant others: Mothers who do not want to see. *Individual Psychology, 46,* 280–297.

Tinnin, L. (1989a). The anatomy of the ego. *Psychiatry, 52,* 404–409.

Tinnin, L. (1989b). Response to Stillman and Walker. *Psychiatry, 52,* 414–415.

Tobacyk, J. J., & Downs, A. (1986). Personal construct threat and irrational beliefs as cognitive predictors of increases in musical performance anxiety. *Journal of Personality and Social Psychology, 51,* 779–782.

Tobin, S. A. (1991). A comparison of psychoanalytic self psychology and Carl Rogers's person-centered therapy. *Journal of Humanistic Psychology, 31*(1), 9–33.

Tomarken, A. J., Davidson, R. J., & Henriques, J. B. (1990). Resting frontal brain asymmetry predicts affective responses to films. *Journal of Personality and Social Psychology, 59,* 791–801.

Torres, J. (1989). *Fire & fear: The inside story of Mike Tyson.* New York: Warner Books.

Torrey, J. W. (1987). Phases of feminist re-vision in the psychology of personality. *Teaching of Psychology, 14,* 155–160.

Tosi, D. J., & Lindamood, C. A. (1975). The measurement of self-actualization: A critical review of the Personal Orientation Inventory. *Journal of Personality Assessment, 39,* 215–224.

Towson, S. M., & Zanna, M. P. (1982). Toward a situational analysis of gender differences in aggression. *Sex Roles, 8,* 903–914.

Trapnell, P. D., & Wiggins, J. S. (1990). Extension of the interpersonal adjective scales to include the Big Five dimensions of personality. *Journal of Personality and Social Psychology, 59,* 781–790.

Treadway, M., & McCloskey, M. (1987). Cite unseen: Distortions of the Allport and Postman rumor study in the eyewitness testimony literature. *Law and Behavior, 11,* 19–25.

Tresemer, D. W. (1974, March). Fear of success: Popular but unproven. *Psychology Today,* pp. 82–85.

Tresemer, D. W. (1977). *Fear of success.* New York: Plenum.

Tribich, D., & Messer, S. (1974). Psychoanalytic character type and status of authority as determiners of suggestibility. *Journal of Consulting and Clinical Psychology, 42,* 842–848.

Trump, D. J. (1987). *Trump: The art of the deal.* New York: Warner Books.

Tuccille, J. (1985). *Trump.* New York: Jove.

Tucker, R. C. (1973). *Stalin as revolutionary.* New York: Norton.

Tucker, R. C. (1985). A Stalin biographer's memoir. In S. H. Baron & C. Pletsch (Eds.), *Introspection in biography: The biographer's quest for self-awareness* (pp. 249–271). Hillsdale, NJ: Analytic Press.

Tuckman, B. W. (1990). Group versus goal-setting effects on the self-regulated performance of students differing in self-efficacy. *Journal of Experimental Education, 58,* 291–298.

Turner, C. W., Hesse, B. W., & Peterson-Lewis, S. (1986). Naturalistic studies of the long-term effects of television violence. *Journal of Social Issues, 42*(3), 51–73.

Turner, T. (1986). *I, Tina.* New York: Avon.

Tyson, S. (1979). The study of personnel management as an occupation, using repertory grid. *Personnel Review, 8,* 34–39.

Tzeng, O. C., Ware, R., & Chen, J. (1989). Measurement and utility of continuous unipolar ratings for the Myers-Briggs Type Indicator. *Journal of Personality Assessment, 53,* 727–738.

Vacc, N. A., & Greenleaf, W. (1975). Sequential development of cognitive complexity. *Perceptual and Motor Skills, 41,* 319–322.

Van De Water, D., & McAdams, D. P. (1989). Generativity and Erikson's "belief in the species." *Journal of Research in Personality, 23,* 435–449.

Van den Daele, L. (1981). The self-psychologies of Heinz Kohut and Karen Horney: A comparative examination. *American Journal of Psychoanalysis, 41,* 327–337.

Van den Daele, L. (1987). Research in Horney's psychoanalytic theory. *American Journal of Psychoanalysis, 47,* 99–104.

Van der Kloot, W. A., Kroonenberg, P. M., & Bakker, D. (1985). Implicit theories of personality: Further evidence of extreme response. *Multivariate Behavioral Research, 20,* 369–387.

Vander Mey, B. J., & Neff, R. L. (1982). Adult-child incest: A review of research and treatment. *Adolescence, 17,* 717–735.

Vane, J. R., & Guarnaccia, V. J. (1989). Personality theory and personality assessment measures: How helpful to the clinician? *Journal of Clinical Psychology, 45,* 5–19.

Van Wicklin, J. F. (1990). Conceiving and measuring ways of being religious. *Journal of Psychology and Christianity, 9,* 27–40.

Veroff, J. (1983). Contextual determinants of personality. *Personality and Social Psychology Bulletin, 9,* 331–344.

Viglione, D. J., Brager, R., & Haller, N. (1991). Psychoanalytic interpretation of the Rorschach: Do we have better hieroglyphics? *Journal of Personality Assessment, 57,* 1–9.

Vinacke, W. E. (1984). Healthy personality: Toward a unified theory. *Genetic Psychology Monographs, 109,* 279–329.

Viney, L. L. (1981). Experimenting with experience: A psychotherapeutic case study. *Psychotherapy, 18,* 271–278.

Viney, L. L., Benjamin, Y. N., & Preston, C. A. (1989). An evaluation of personal construct therapy for the elderly. *British Journal of Medical Psychology, 62,* 35–41.

Vitz, P. C. (1990). The use of stories in moral development: New psychological reasons for an old education method. *American Psychologist, 45,* 709–720.

Von Broembsen, F. (1989). Role identity in personality disorders: Validation, valuation, and agency in identity formation. *American Journal of Psychoanalysis, 49,* 115–125.

von Franz, M. L. (1964). Conclusion: Science and the unconscious. In C. G. Jung (Ed.), *Man and his symbols* (pp. 304–310). Garden City, NY: Doubleday.

Wachtel, P. L. (1978). On some complexities in the application of conflict theory to psychotherapy. *Journal of Nervous and Mental Disease, 166,* 457–471.

Wahba, M. A., & Bridwell, L. G. (1976). Maslow reconsidered: A review of research on the need hierarchy theory. *Organizational Behavior and Human Performance, 15,* 212–240.

Waite, R. G. L. (1977). *The psychopathic God: Adolf Hitler.* New York: Basic Books.

Walker, B. M. (1990). Construing George Kelly's construing of the person-in-relation. *International Journal of Personal Construct Psychology, 3,* 41–50.

Walker, S. G. (1987). Personality, situation, and cognitive complexity: A revisionist analysis of the Israeli cases. *Political Psychology, 8,* 605–621.

Wallace, E. R., IV (1989). Pitfalls of a one-sided image of science: Adolf Grünbaum's Foundations of Psychoanalysis. *Journal of the American Psychoanalytic Association, 37,* 493–529.

Wallace, I. (1977). Self-control techniques of famous novelists. *Journal of Applied Behavior Analysis, 10,* 515–525.

Wallach, M. A., & Wallach, L. (1983). *Psychology: Sanction for selfishness.* San Francisco: W.H. Freeman.

Waller, B. (1982). Skinner's two-stage value theory. *Behaviorism, 10,* 25–44.

Waller, N. G., & Ben-Porath, Y. S. (1987). Is it time for clinical psychology to embrace the five-factor model of personality? *American Psychologist, 42,* 887–889.

Wallerstein, R. S. (1989). The Psychotherapy Research Project of the Menninger Foundation: An overview. *Journal of Consulting and Clinical Psychology, 57,* 195–205.

Wallerstein, R. S., & Sampson, H. (1971). Issues in research in the psychoanalytic process. *International Journal of Psycho-Analysis, 42,* 11–50.

Wallston, B. S. (1987). Social psychology of women and gender. *Journal of Applied Social Psychology, 17*, 1025–1050.

Walsh, B. W., & Peterson, L. E. (1985). Philosophical foundations of psychological theories: The issue of synthesis. *Psychotherapy, 2*, 145–153.

Ward, R. A., & Loftus, E. F. (1985). Eyewitness performance in different psychological types. *Journal of General Psychology, 112*, 191–200.

Ware, R., Yokomoto, C., & Morris, B. B. (1985). A preliminary study to assess validity of the Personal Style Inventory. *Psychological Reports, 56*, 903–910.

Warren, B. (1990). Psychoanalysis and personal construct theory: An exploration. *Journal of Psychology, 124*, 449–463.

Warren, C. (1990). Use of hypnogogic reverie in collection of earliest recollections. *Individual Psychology, 46*, 317–323.

Warren, M. W., Hughes, A. T., & Tobias, S. B. (1985). Autobiographical elaboration and memory for adjectives. *Perceptual and Motor Skills, 60*, 55–58.

Warren, W. G. (1990a). Is personal construct psychology a cognitive psychology? *International Journal of Personal Construct Psychology, 3*, 393–414.

Warren, W. G. (1990b). Personal construct theory and the Aristotelian and Galileian modes of thought. *International Journal of Personal Construct Psychology, 3*, 263–280.

Washburn, M. (1990). Two patterns of transcendence. *Journal of Humanistic Psychology, 30*, 84–112.

Waterman, A. S. (1982). Identity development from adolescence to adulthood: An extension of theory and a review of research. *Developmental Psychology, 18*, 341–358.

Waterman, A. S. (1988). Identity status theory and Erikson's theory: Communalities and differences. *Developmental Review, 8*, 185–208.

Waterman, A. S. (1990). Personal expressiveness: Philosophical and psychological foundations. *Journal of Mind and Behavior, 11*, 47–73.

Waterman, A. S., Geary, P. S., & Waterman, C. K. (1974). Longitudinal study of changes in ego identity status from the freshman to the senior year at college. *Developmental Psychology, 10*, 387–392.

Waterman, A. S., & Waterman, C. K. (1970). The relationship between ego identity status and satisfaction in college. *Journal of Educational Research, 64*, 165–168.

Waterman, C. K., & Nevid, J. S. (1977). Sex differences in the resolution of the identity crisis. *Journal of Youth and Adolescence, 6*, 337–342.

Waters, E., Wippman, J., & Sroufe, L. A. (1979). Attachment, positive affect, and competence in the peer group: Two studies in construct validation. *Child Development, 50*, 821–829.

Watkins, C. E. (1982a). A decade of research in support of Adlerian psychological theory. *Individual Psychology, 38*, 90–99.

Watkins, C. E. (1982b). The Self-Administered Life-Style Analysis (SALSA). *Individual Psychology, 38*, 343–352.

Watkins, C. E. (1983). Some characteristics of research on Adlerian psychological theory. *Individual Psychology, 39*, 99–110.

Watkins, C. E. (1986). A research bibliography on Adlerian psychological theory. *Individual Psychology, 42*, 123–132.

Watkins, C. E., Jr., & Hector, M. (1990). A simple test of the concurrent validity of the Social Interest Index. *Journal of Personality Assessment, 55*, 812–814.

Watson, J. B. (1970). *Behaviorism*. New York: Norton. (Original work published 1924)

Watson, J. B., & Rayner, R. (1920). Conditioned emotional reactions. *Journal of Experimental Psychology, 3,* 1–14.

Watson, P. J., Hood, R. W., Morris, R. J., & Hall, J. R. (1984). Empathy, religious orientation, and social desirability. *Journal of Psychology, 117,* 211–216.

Wegner, D. M., Schneider, D. J., Knutson, B., & McMahon, S. R. (1991). Polluting the stream of consciousness: The effect of thought suppression on the mind's environment. *Cognitive Therapy and Research, 15,* 141–152.

Wehr, D. S. (1987). *Jung and feminism.* Boston: Beacon.

Wehr, G. (1987). *Jung: A biography* (D. M. Weeks, Trans.) Boston: Shambhala.

Weiland S. (1989). Aging according to biography. *Gerontologist, 29,* 191–194.

Weinberg, R. S., Hughes, H. H., Critelli, J. W., England, R., & Jackson, A. (1984). Effects of preexisting and manipulated self-efficacy on weight loss in a self-control program. *Journal of Research in Personality, 18,* 352–358.

Weiner, H. (1983). Some thoughts on discrepant human–animal performances under schedules of reinforcement. *Psychological Record, 33,* 521–532.

Weiner, I. B. (1991). Developments in research in personality assessment. *Journal of Personality Assessment, 56,* 370–372.

Weinrach, S. G. (1990). Rogers and Gloria: The controversial film and the enduring relationship. *Psychotherapy, 27,* 282–290.

Weinrach, S. G. (1991). Rogers' encounter with Gloria: What did Rogers know and when? *Psychotherapy, 28,* 504–506.

Weinstein, L., & Sackhoff, J. (1987). Adler is right. *Bulletin of the Psychonomic Society, 25,* 201.

Weiss, A. S. (1987). Shostrom's Personal Orientation Inventory: Arguments against its basic validity. *Personality and Individual Differences, 8,* 895–903.

Weiss, J. (1988). Testing hypotheses about unconscious mental functioning. *International Journal of Psycho-Analysis, 69,* 87–95.

Weiss-Rosmarin, T. (1990). Adler's psychology and the Jewish tradition. *Individual Psychology, 46,* 108–118. (Original work published 1958)

Wells-Parker, E., Miller, D. I., & Topping, J. S. (1990). Development of control-of-outcome scales and self-efficacy scales for women in four life roles. *Journal of Personality Assessment, 54,* 564–575.

Wertheimer, M. (1978). Humanistic psychology and the humane but tough-minded psychologist. *American Psychologist, 33,* 739–745.

Wessells, M. G. (1981). A critique of Skinner's views on the explanatory inadequacy of cognitive theories. *Behaviorism, 9,* 153–170.

Wessells, M. G. (1982). A critique of Skinner's views on the obstructive character of cognitive theories. *Behaviorism, 10,* 65–85.

Wessells, M. G. (1983). Unusual terminology or unusual metatheory: A reply to Professor Landwehr. *Behaviorism, 11,* 193–197.

Wessman, A. E., & Ricks, D. F. (1966). *Mood and personality.* New York: Holt, Rinehart & Winston.

West, S. G. (1986). Methodological developments in personality research: An introduction. *Journal of Personality, 54,* 1–17.

Westkott, M. (1986a). *The feminist legacy of Karen Horney.* New Haven, CT: Yale University Press.

Westkott, M. (1986b). Historical and developmental roots of female dependency. *Psychotherapy, 23,* 213–220.

Westkott, M. (1989). Female relationship and the idealized self. *American Journal of Psychoanalysis, 49,* 239–250.

Wheeler, M. S. (1989). A theoretical and empirical comparison of typologies. *Individual Psychology, 45*, 335–353.

Wheelwright, J. B., Wheelwright, J. H., & Buehler, H. A. (1964). *Jungian Type Survey: The Gray Wheelwright Test* (16th rev.). San Francisco: Society of Jungian Analysts of Northern California.

White, P. (1980). Limitations on verbal reports of internal events: A refutation of Nisbett and Wilson and of Bem. *Psychological Review, 87*, 105–112.

White, R. W. (1964). *The abnormal personality.* New York: Ronald Press.

White, T. H. (1975). *Breach of faith: The fall of Richard Nixon.* New York: Atheneum.

Whitmont, E. C. (1982). *Return of the goddess.* New York: Crossroad.

Wiebe, D. J. (1991). Hardiness and stress moderation: A test of proposed mechanisms. *Journal of Personality and Social Psychology, 60*, 89–99.

Wiedenfeld, S. A., O'Leary, A., Bandura, A., Brown, S., Levine, S., & Raska, K. (1990). Impact of perceived self-efficacy in coping with stressors on components of the immune system. *Journal of Personality and Social Psychology, 59*, 1082–1094.

Wiggins, J. S. (1984). Cattell's system from the perspective of mainstream personality theory. *Multivariate Behavioral Research, 19*, 176–190.

Wilber, K. (1990). "Two patterns of transcendence": A reply to Washburn. *Journal of Humanistic Psychology, 30*, 113–136.

Wild, C. (1965). Creativity and adaptive regression. *Journal of Personality and Social Psychology, 2*, 161–169.

Wilhelm, H. (1960). *Change: Eight lectures on the I Ching.* Princeton, NJ: Princeton University Press.

Williams, B. A. (1986). On the role of theory in behavior analysis. *Behaviorism, 14*, 111–124.

Williams, D. E., & Page, M. M. (1989). A multi-dimensional measure of Maslow's hierarchy of needs. *Journal of Research in Personality, 23*, 192–213.

Wilson, E. O. (1975). *Sociobiology: The new synthesis.* Cambridge, MA: Harvard University Press.

Wilson, S. R. (1988). The "real self" controversy: Toward an integration of humanistic and interactionist theory. *Journal of Humanistic Psychology, 28*(1), 39–65.

Wilson, S. R., & Spencer, R. C. (1990). Intense personal experiences: Subjective effects, interpretations, and after-effects. *Journal of Clinical Psychology, 46*, 565–573.

Winbush, R. A. (1977). What is good for the goose is apparently not good for the gander. *American Psychologist, 32*, 987.

Winston, A. S., & Baker, J. E. (1985). Behavior analytic studies of creativity: A critical review. *Behavior Analyst, 8*, 191–205.

Winter, D. G., & Carlson, L. A. (1988). Using motive scores in the psychobiographical study of an individual: The case of Richard Nixon. *Journal of Personality, 56*, 75–103.

Wiseman, H., & Rice, L. N. (1989). Sequential analyses of therapist-client interaction during change events: A task-focused approach. *Journal of Consulting and Clinical Psychology, 57*, 281–286.

Wittels, F. (1939). The neo-Adlerians. *American Journal of Sociology, 45*, 433–445.

Wojcik, J. V. (1988). Social learning predictors of the avoidance of smoking relapse. *Addictive Behaviors, 13*, 177–180.

Wolf, M. C., Cohen, K. R., & Rosenfeld, J. G. (1985). School-based interventions for obesity: Current approaches and future prospects. *Psychology in the Schools, 22,* 187–200.

Wolff, C. G. (1988). *Emily Dickinson.* Reading, MA: Addison-Wesley.

Wolff, P. H. (1986). Alternative theories of development and their implications for studying the ontogeny of behavior and social adaptations: Discussion of Dr. Chess' paper. *American Journal of Psychoanalysis, 46,* 153–165.

Wollman, N., & Stouder, R. (1991). Believed efficacy and political activity: A test of the specificity hypothesis. *Journal of Social Psychology, 13,* 557–566.

Wolman, B. B. (1971). Does psychology need its own philosophy of science? *American Psychologist, 26,* 877–886.

Wolpe, J. (1982). *The practice of behavior therapy* (3rd ed.). New York: Pergamon Press.

Wolpe, J., & Rachman, S. (1960). Psychoanalytic "evidence": A critique based on Freud's case of Little Hans. *Journal of Nervous and Mental Disease, 131,* 135–148.

Wood, J. V., Saltzberg, J. A., Neale, J. M., Stone, A. A., & Rachmiel, T. B. (1990). Self-focused attention, coping responses, and distressed mood in everyday life. *Journal of Personality and Social Psychology, 58,* 1027–1036.

Wood, R., & Bandura, A. (1989a). Impact of conceptions of ability on self-regulatory mechanisms and complex decision making. *Journal of Personality and Social Psychology, 56,* 407–415.

Wood, R., & Bandura, A. (1989b). Social cognitive theory of organizational management. *Academy of Management Review, 14,* 361–384.

Wood, R., Bandura, A., & Bailey, T. (1990). Mechanisms governing organizational performance in complex decision-making environments. *Organizational Behavior and Human Decision Processes, 46,* 181–201.

Woodham-Smith, C. (1951). *Florence Nightingale: 1820–1920.* New York: McGraw-Hill.

Woodward, B., & Bernstein, C. (1976). *The final days.* New York: Avon.

Woolfolk, R. L., & Richardson, F. C. (1984). Behavior therapy and the ideology of modernity. *American Psychologist, 39,* 777–786.

Worell, J. (1978). Sex roles and psychological well-being: Perspectives on methodology. *Journal of Consulting and Clinical Psychology, 46,* 777–791.

Wright, J. C., & Mischel, W. (1982). Influence of affect on cognitive social learning person variables. *Journal of Personality and Social Psychology, 43,* 901–914.

Wright, J. C., & Mischel, W. (1987). A conditional approach to dispositional constructs: The local predictability of social behavior. *Journal of Personality and Social Psychology, 53,* 1159–1177.

Wright, J. C., & Mischel, W. (1988). Conditional hedges and the intuitive psychology of traits. *Journal of Personality and Social Psychology, 55,* 454–469.

Wright, W. J. (1985). Personality profiles of four leaders of the German Lutheran Reformation. *Psychohistory Review, 14,* 12–22.

Wurgaft, L. D. (1976). Erik Erikson: From Luther to Gandhi. *Psychoanalytic Review, 63,* 209–233.

Yang, K., & Bond, M. H. (1990). Exploring implicit personality theories with indigenous or imported constructs: The Chinese case. *Journal of Personality and Social Psychology, 58,* 1087–1095.

Yeagle, E. H., Privette, G., & Dunham, F. Y. (1989). Highest happiness: An analysis of artists' peak experience. *Psychological Reports, 65,* 523–530.

Yogev, S. (1983). Judging the professional woman: Changing research, changing values. *Psychology of Women Quarterly, 7,* 219–234.

Yonge, G. D. (1975). Time experiences, self-actualizing values, and creativity. *Journal of Personality Assessment, 39,* 601–606.

Zarski, J. J., Bubenzer, D. L., & West, J. D. (1986). Social interest, stress, and the prediction of health status. *Journal of Counseling and Development, 64,* 386–389.

Zautra, A. J., Finch, J. F., Reich, J. W., & Guarnaccia, C. A. (1991). Predicting the everyday life events of older adults. *Journal of Personality, 59,* 507–538.

Zettle, R. D. (1990). Rule-governed behavior: A radical behavioral answer to the cognitive challenge. *Psychological Record, 40,* 41–49.

Ziller, R. C. (1988). Orientations: The cognitive link in person-situation interaction. *Journal of Social Behavior and Personality, 3,* 1–9.

Ziller, R. C. (1990). Environment-self behavior: A general theory of personal control. *Journal of Social Behavior and Personality, 5,* 227–242.

Zimmerman, M. A. (1989). The relationship between political efficacy and citizen participation: Construct validation studies. *Journal of Personality Assessment, 53,* 554–566.

Zirkel, S., & Cantor, N. (1990). Personal construal of life tasks: Those who struggle for independence. *Journal of Personality and Social Psychology, 58,* 172–185.

Zivkovic, M. (1982). Dream test. *Perceptual and Motor Skills, 55,* 935–938.

Zolten, A. J. (1989). Constructive integration of learning theory and phenomenological approaches to biofeedback training. *Biofeedback and Self-Regulation, 14,* 89–99.

Zuckerman, M. (1990a). Some dubious premises in research and theory on racial differences: Scientific, social, and ethical issues. *American Psychologist, 45,* 1297–1303.

Zuckerman, M. (1990b). Still another failure of arousal theory: A critique of "Personality, situation and physiological arousability" by G. Stemmler and E. Meinhardt. *Personality and Individual Differences, 11,* 309–312.

Zuckerman, M. (1990c). The psychophysiology of sensation seeking. *Journal of Personality, 58,* 313–345.

Zuckerman, M., Koestner, R., DeBoy, T., Garcia, T., Maresca, B. C., & Sartoris, J. M. (1988). To predict some of the people some of the time: A reexamination of the moderator variable approach in personality theory. *Journal of Personality and Social Psychology, 54,* 1006–1019.

Zuckerman, M., Kuhlman, D. M., & Camac, C. (1988). What lies beyond E and N? Factor analyses of scales believed to measure basic dimensions of personality. *Journal of Personality and Social Psychology, 54,* 96–107.

Zuckerman, M., & Wheeler, L. (1975). To dispel fantasies about the fantasy-based measure of fear of success. *Psychological Bulletin, 82,* 932–946.

Zuriff, G. E. (1985). *Behaviorism: A conceptual reconstruction.* New York: Columbia University Press.

Zuroff, D. C. (1986). Was Gordon Allport a trait theorist? *Journal of Personality and Social Psychology, 51,* 993–1000.

Acknowledgments

28: WHO
30: UPI/Bettmann
31: Eugene Gordon
61: The Bettmann Archive
63: Culver Pictures
64: UPI/Bettmann
95: UPI/Bettmann
98: UPI/Bettmann
99: UPI/Bettmann
121: UPI/Bettmann
124: Franklin D. Roosevelt Library
123: The Bettmann Archive
151: Culver Pictures
154: AP/Wide World
155: UPI/Bettmann
183: Historical Picture Service
186: UPI/Bettmann
187: Culver Pictures
214: Courtesy Raymond B. Cattell

216: Library of Congress
217: N.Y. Public Library Picture Collection
252: Carl Rogers Memorial Library
255: F.M. Phipps/Canadian Broadcasting Corporation
256: AP/Wide World
276: Courtesy of Brooks/Cole Publishing Co.
279: Columbia
279: Richard Erdoes
305: Courtesy Estate of B.F. Skinner
308: UPI/Bettmann
337: Yale University Library
338: Yale University Archives, Manuscripts & Archives, Yale University Library
339: UPI/Bettmann
340: UPI/Bettmann
372: Courtesy of Walter Mischel
373: Courtesy of Albert Bandura
374: UPI/Bettmann
375: N.Y. Public Library Picture Collection
409: Courtesy of Brandeis University
411: The White House
413: AP/Wide World

Name Index

This index lists pages in the text on which authors are cited.

Subject Index